THE POETICAL WORKS
OF
ROBERT BROWNING

General Editor: IAN JACK

THE POETICAL WORKS
OF
ROBERT BROWNING

Volume III

BELLS AND POMEGRANATES
I–VI

(including *Pippa Passes*
and *Dramatic Lyrics*)

EDITED BY

IAN JACK
AND
ROWENA FOWLER

CLARENDON PRESS · OXFORD
1988

This book has been printed digitally and produced in a standard design
in order to ensure its continuing availability

OXFORD
UNIVERSITY PRESS

Great Clarendon Street, Oxford OX2 6DP

Oxford University Press is a department of the University of Oxford.
It furthers the University's objective of excellence in research, scholarship,
and education by publishing worldwide in

Oxford New York

Athens Auckland Bangkok Bogotá Buenos Aires Cape Town
Chennai Dar es Salaam Delhi Florence Hong Kong Istanbul Karachi
Kolkata Kuala Lumpur Madrid Melbourne Mexico City Mumbai Nairobi
Paris São Paulo Shanghai Singapore Taipei Tokyo Toronto Warsaw
with associated companies in Berlin Ibadan

Oxford is a registered trade mark of Oxford University Press
in the UK and in certain other countries

Published in the United States
by Oxford University Press Inc., New York

© Ian Jack and Rowena Fowler 1988

ISBN 0-19-812762-6

PREFACE AND
ACKNOWLEDGEMENTS

THE General Introduction and Textual Introduction (which includes a brief account of the most important collected editions published in Browning's lifetime) may be found in Vol. I. In the present volume Ian Jack is responsible for the principal part of the introductions, the explanatory notes, and the appendices, while Rowena Fowler is responsible for the text, the textual notes, and the parts of the introductions which relate to the text and its transmission.

This is the first edition of Browning's poetry to attempt to take account of all available manuscript material: an attempt which would hardly have been possible but for the work of Philip Kelley.[1] We are indebted to many libraries, and many librarians. We wish to thank the Harry Ransom Humanities Center of the University of Texas at Austin for permission to cite variants in their important manuscript of the 'Introduction' to *Pippa Passes*. We are grateful to the Houghton Library of Harvard College for leave to use the two sets of proofs of *Dramatic Lyrics*, and to the Beinecke Library of Yale University (and in particular to Miss Marjorie G. Wynne) for permission to use their manuscript of two of the 'Cavalier Tunes' and Macready's working copy of *A Blot in the 'Scutcheon*. The authorities of the Robert H. Taylor Collection at Princeton University Library, and in particular Nancy N. Coffin, have been prompt and generous with their assistance. Professor Donald H. Reiman granted us access to the holograph of *Colombe's Birthday* in the Carl H. Pforzheimer Library (for which we thank the Carl and Lily Pforzheimer Foundation, Inc.). We have been allowed to cite corrections and revisions in the set of *Bells and Pomegranates* in the Harold N. Lee Library of Brigham Young University, and are grateful to Dr Chad J. Flake, the Curator of Special Collections. We have also been permitted to cite corrections and revisions in the set which belongs to the Humanities Research Center at Austin. We have consulted the 'Dykes Campbell' copy of *The Poetical Works*, 1888–9, in the British Library.[2] Dr Gordon N.

[1] See Kelley and Coley, in 'References and Abbreviations', below.
[2] For the corrections in volumes in Brown University Library we have relied on Philip Kelley and William S. Peterson, 'Browning's Final Revisions': *Browning Institute Studies*, i (1973), 101–8.

Ray and the Curator of the Ray Collection in the Pierpont Morgan Library kindly allowed Mr Ronald Hudson to consult the marginalia in his volumes of the 1888-9 edition, on our behalf: work which Mr Hudson executed for us promptly and with the greatest accuracy.

For permission to print versions of the poem on the Pied Piper story by Browning's father we are indebted to the authorities of the Alexander Turnbull Library in the National Library of New Zealand and to the Curator of Special Collections in Northwestern University Library, Illinois.

We also wish to thank the Librarian of Balliol College and the staff of the British Library and Cambridge University Library. We are grateful, too, to the Armstrong Browning Library at Baylor, and to the libraries of the universities of Bristol, Bath, and Keele.

Our greatest debt, first and last, has been to Dr Philip Kelley. As we go to press, four volumes of *The Brownings' Correspondence* have made their appearance, under his editorship and that of Mr Ronald Hudson. The senior editor has had the advantage of consulting most of the letters which will appear in their next two volumes, an experience which has made it evident to him how seriously earlier editors of Browning have been handicapped by the lack of a complete and authoritative edition of the letters.[1] Since all known reviews of any volume by Browning published in the relevant period are being printed in an appendix to each volume of the *Correspondence*, our own references to reviews are relatively few. Those who wish to consult selections may turn to *Browning: The Critical Heritage*, edited by Boyd Litzinger and Donald Smalley.

Help of various kinds has been provided by Mrs Margaret Smith; Professor Uberto Limentani; Dr Kevin Van Anglen; Professor William Kneale; Dr Richard McCabe; and by Professor Malcolm Lyons, Dr Rivkah Zim, and other Fellows of Pembroke College, Cambridge. Dr Robert Burchfield, busy as he is, has more than once provided a quick and authoritative answer to a question.

In the later stages of the preparation of the volume we have been assisted by discussion with Mr Michael Meredith, whose edition of the *Parleyings* and of *Asolando* will be published out of sequence, as the last volume of the Oxford English Texts Edition, as soon as it is ready. Vol. IV will include the remaining *Bells and Pomegranates* (notably *Dramatic*

---

[1] When we refer to letters yet to be included in the *Correspondence*, we use the list-numbers in the Kelley and Hudson *Checklist* (see 'References and Abbreviations', below).

Romances and Lyrics, *Christmas-Eve and Easter-Day,* and the essay on Shelley)

Lastly, we wish to thank Dr Leofranc Holford-Strevens for the expert attention which he has been kind enough to give this volume.

I. J.
R. F.

16 September 1986

CONTENTS

REFERENCES AND ABBREVIATIONS

Note: the place of publication is given if it is not London or Oxford

Berdoe   *The Browning Cyclopædia*, by Edward Berdoe, 2nd ed., 1892.

Biographie universelle   *Biographie universelle, ancienne et moderne*, 52 vols., Paris, 1811–28.

BIS   *Browning Institute Studies*

Browning and his Circle   *Studies in Browning and his Circle*, Armstrong Browning Library, Waco, Texas.

Browning Collections   *see* Kelley and Coley.

Browning and Domett   *Robert Browning and Alfred Domett*, ed. Frederick G. Kenyon, 1906.

Browning Institute Studies (an annual volume published by the Browning Institute).

Browning Newsletter   *The Browning Newsletter*, Armstrong Browning Library, Waco, Texas.

Bryan   *A Biographical and Critical Dictionary of Painters and Engravers*, by Michael Bryan, 2 vols., 1816.

BSN   *Browning Society Notes* (published by the Browning Society of London).

Checklist   *The Brownings' Correspondence: A Checklist*, compiled by Philip Kelley and Ronald Hudson, The Browning Institute and Wedgestone Press, 1978. (Supplements in later volumes of *Browning Institute Studies*.)

Collections   *see* Kelley and Coley.

Collier   *The Great Historical . . . Dictionary*, Vol. I, 2nd ed., revised by Jeremy Collier, 1701.

Correspondence   *The Brownings' Correspondence*, ed. Philip Kelley and Ronald Hudson, Wedgestone Press, Winfield, Kansas, 1984– (in progress).

DeVane   *A Browning Handbook*, by William Clyde DeVane, 2nd ed., New York, 1955 (1st ed., 1935).

Domett   *The Diary of Alfred Domett 1872–1885*, ed. E. A. Horsman, 1953.

Drew   *Robert Browning: A Collection of Critical Essays*, ed. Philip Drew, 1966.

EBB   Elizabeth Barrett Browning.

Encyclopædia Britannica   *The Encyclopædia Britannica*, 11th ed., 29 vols., 1910–11.

Enkvist   *British Letters in Scandinavian Public Collections*, by N. E. Enkvist, Åbo Akademi, Finland, 1964.

Furnivall, Frederick J., *A Bibliography of Robert Browning, from 1833 to 1881*, 2nd ed., Browning Society, 1881.

Gosse   *Robert Browning: Personalia*, by Edmund Gosse, Boston and New York, 1890. (Part of the impression was sold in London in 1891, under the imprint of T. Fisher Unwin.)

Griffin and Minchin   *The Life of Robert Browning*, by W. Hall Griffin, completed and edited by H. C. Minchin, 3rd ed., revised and enlarged, 1938 (1st ed., 1910).

Handbook   *A Handbook to the Works of Robert Browning*, by Mrs Sutherland Orr, 7th ed., 1896 (1st ed., 1885).

Harrison   'Birds in the Poetry of Browning', by Thomas P. Harrison: *Review of English Studies*, NS, vol. vii, no. 28 (October 1956), pp. 393–405.

Hood   'Browning's Ancient Classical Sources', by T. L. Hood: *Harvard Studies in Classical Philology*, xxxiii, 1922, pp. 79–180.

Hudson   *Browning to his American Friends*, ed. Gertrude Rees Hudson, 1965.

Johnson   *A Dictionary of the English Language*, by Samuel Johnson, 9th ed., 2 vols., 1806.

Kelley and Coley   *The Browning Collections: A Reconstruction with Other Memorabilia*, compiled by Philip Kelley and Betty A. Coley, Armstrong Browning Library, Baylor University, Texas, 1984

Kelley and Hudson   *see Checklist.*

Kintner   *The Letters of Robert Browning and Elizabeth Barrett Barrett 1845–1846*, ed. Elvan Kintner, 2 vols., Cambridge, Mass., 1969.

Landis   *Letters of the Brownings to George Barrett*, ed. Paul Landis, Urbana, Illinois, 1958.

Learned Lady: Letters from Robert Browning to Mrs. Thomas FitzGerald, ed. Edward C. McAleer, Cambridge, Mass., 1966.

Lemprière   *A Classical Dictionary*, by J. Lemprière, 5th ed., 1804.

Letters   *Letters of Robert Browning Collected by Thomas J. Wise*, ed. Thurman L. Hood, 1933.

Letters of EBB   *The Letters of Elizabeth Barrett Browning*, ed. Frederic G. Kenyon, 2 vols., 1898.

Life   *Life and Letters of Robert Browning*, by Mrs Sutherland Orr, new ed., rev. ... by Frederic G. Kenyon, 1908 (1st ed., 1891).

Litzinger and Smalley   *Browning: The Critical Heritage*, ed. Boyd Litzinger and Donald Smalley, 1970.

Maynard   *Browning's Youth*, by John Maynard, Cambridge, Mass., 1977.

Meredith   *More Than Friend: The Letters of Robert Browning to Katharine de Kay Bronson*, ed. Michael Meredith, Armstrong Browning Library and Wedgestone Press, 1985.

MLQ   *Modern Language Quarterly*.

More Than Friend   *see* Meredith.

New Letters   *New Letters of Robert Browning*, ed. William Clyde DeVane and Kenneth Leslie Knickerbocker, New Haven, 1951.

New Poems   *New Poems by Robert Browning and Elizabeth Barrett Browning*, ed. Sir Frederic G. Kenyon, 1914.

NQ   *Notes and Queries*.

OED   *Oxford English Dictionary*.

Ohio Edition   *The Complete works of Robert Browning*, ed. Roma A. King, Jr., and others, Vols. III and IV, Athens, Ohio, 1971, 1973.

Parleyings   *Browning's Parleyings: The Autobiography of a Mind*, by William Clyde DeVane, New Haven, 1927.

Personalia   *see* Gosse.

Pettigrew *or* Pettigrew and Collins   *Robert Browning: The Poems, Volume I*, ed. John Pettigrew, supplemented and completed by Thomas J. Collins, 1981 (Penguin English Poets: Yale University Press).

PMLA   *Publications of the Modern Language Association of America*.

Porter and Clarke   *The Complete Works of Robert Browning*, ed. Charlotte Porter and Helen A. Clarke, 12 vols., New York, 1898 (published in different formats, at different times, and under various names, e.g. as the Florentine Edition, the Camberwell Edition, etc.).

PQ   *Philological Quarterly*.

Raymond and Sullivan   *The Letters of Elizabeth Barrett Browning to Mary Russell Mitford 1836-1854*, ed. Meredith B. Raymond and Mary Rose Sullivan, Armstrong Browning Library, etc., 3 vols., 1983.

RES   *The Review of English Studies*.

SP   *Studies in Philology*.

Tilley   *A Dictionary of the Proverbs in England in the Sixteenth and Seventeenth Centuries*, by Morris Palmer Tilley, Ann Arbor, Michigan, 1950.

TLS   *The Times Literary Supplement*.

Trumpeter   *Browning's Trumpeter: The Correspondence of Robert Browning and Frederick J. Furnivall 1872-1889*, ed. William S. Peterson, Washington, DC, 1979.

UTQ   *University of Toronto Quarterly*.

VP   *Victorian Poetry*.

Wedgwood   *Robert Browning and Julia Wedgwood*, ed. Richard Curle, 1937.

Note: references to Shakespeare are to *William Shakespeare: The Complete Works* (Tudor Edition), ed. Peter Alexander, 1951.

Abbreviations and signs used in the textual notes

*	Emendation.
†	So in text (e.g. four dots appear in the text and do not indicate an omission by the editors).
....	Omission by the editors.[1]
{ }	Comment by the editors.
[ ]	Addition or substitution.
⟨ ⟩	Deletion.
BrU	Brown University list of corrections in RB's hand to vols. IV–X of *1888–9*.
DC	British Library copy of Browning's *Poetical Works* (1888–9), formerly belonging to James Dykes Campbell and corrected by Browning.
|	Division between lines.
1842P[1]	First proof of *Dramatic Lyrics*, 1842.
1842P[2]	Second proof of *Dramatic Lyrics*, 1842.
1849	*Poems by Robert Browning. In Two Volumes . . . A New Edition.*
1863	*The Poetical Works of Robert Browning . . . Third Edition*, 3 vols., 1863.
1865	*The Poetical Works of Robert Browning . . . Fourth Edition*, 3 vols., 1865.
1868	*The Poetical Works of Robert Browning*, 6 vols., 1868.
1888–9	*The Poetical Works of Robert Browning*, 16 vols., 1888–9.

[1] It should be noted that RB and EBB often used '. .' as a form of punctuation in their letters. The normal '. . .' is used in this edition to indicate an omission, except in the textual notes, where '. . . .' is used.

INTRODUCTION TO
BELLS AND POMEGRANATES

•

Mr Browning is said to have finished two plays . . . I am sorry. He appears to me capable of most dramatic effluences & passionate insights—& it w.^d be wise in him I think to spend this faculty upon poems which the sympathizing c.^d read, rather than on plays cast to the mercy of the great unwashed who cant read right.

ELIZABETH BARRETT.[1]

An advertisement at the end of *Sordello* announced as 'Nearly Ready' three 'Dramas by R. B.': *Pippa Passes*, *King Victor and King Charles*, and *Mansoor the Hierophant* (later to be called *The Return of the Druses*). On 9 March 1840, two days after the publication of the poem, Browning wrote to Eliza Flower in high spirits, telling her that he had 'a headful of projects—mean[t] to song-write, play-write forthwith'.[2] About the same time he denied Domett's belief that he was 'difficult on system', acknowledged that he had not thought enough about the audience for which he should be writing, and told him that he was 'busy on some plays (those advertised) that shall be plain enough if my pains are not thrown away'.[3] The following month, on 7 April, he wrote to a publisher, William Smith of 113 Fleet Street:

Mr Moxon has just published a long Poem of mine, 'Sordello', meant for a limited class of readers—and I am on the point of following it up by three new Dramas, written in a more popular style, and addressed to the Public at large:—a friend has called my notice to your handsome Reprints and suggested the proposal I am about to make. Would it answer your purpose to try the experiment of coming out with a *new* work as part of your series?—As in that case I will give you the 1.st Edition for nothing—for the sake of your large circulation among a body to which my works have little access at present. Of course I mean that these Dramas should form one publication, of the same size and at the same low price as your other pamphlets.[4]

Browning's excitement and sense of urgency are emphasized by his postscript: 'Be so kind as to answer at your earliest convenience'.

[1] To Miss Mitford, 4 May 1843: Raymond and Sullivan, ii. 218–19.
[2] *Correspondence*, iv. 256.   [3] *Browning and Domett*, pp. 28–9.
[4] *Correspondence*, iv. 267. 'Smith's Standard Library' is advertised in the *Athenæum* for 18 January 1840. Twenty-eight 'popular Works are now published in this Series': p. 60a.

We must assume that Smith's reply was unfavourable, since later in the year, or early in 1841, Browning called on Moxon to beg his advice 'about a work of mine I want to publish'.[1] This may well have been *Pippa Passes*. Our account of what happened then depends on the record of Edmund Gosse, talking with Browning when the latter was an old man:

One day, as the poet was discussing the matter with Mr. Edward Moxon, . . . the latter remarked that at that time he was bringing out some editions of the old Elizabethan dramatists in a comparatively cheap form, and that if Mr. Browning would consent to print his poems as pamphlets, using this cheap type, the expense would be very inconsiderable. The poet jumped at the idea, and it was agreed that each poem should form a separate brochure of just one sheet, sixteen pages, in double columns, the entire cost of which should not exceed twelve or fifteen pounds.[2]

That was a moderate expense which Browning was willing to ask his father to incur, and eight pamphlets with the general title *Bells and Pomegranates*, each 'By Robert Browning, Author of "Paracelsus"', appeared between April 1841 and April 1846, as follows:

N⁰· I.–PIPPA PASSES, 1841.
N⁰· II.–KING VICTOR AND KING CHARLES, 1842.
N⁰· III.–DRAMATIC LYRICS, 1842.
N⁰· IV.–THE RETURN OF THE DRUSES. *A Tragedy. In Five Acts*, 1843.
N⁰· V.–A BLOT IN THE 'SCUTCHEON. *A Tragedy, In Three Acts*, 1843.
N⁰· VI.–COLOMBE'S BIRTHDAY. *A Play, In Five Acts*, 1844.
No. VII. DRAMATIC ROMANCES & LYRICS, 1845.
No. VIII. AND LAST. LURIA; and A SOUL'S TRAGEDY, 1846.

The prices were 6*d.* for No. I, 1*s.* o*d.* for the next five, 2*s.* o*d.* for No. VII, and 2*s.* 6*d.* for No. VIII.[3] Only I, III, and V are of the specified sixteen pages (III having been made up by the last-minute addition of 'The Pied Piper'); II and VI have 20 pages, IV has 19, while VII and VIII have 24 and 32 pages respectively. Browning decided, after hesitating, not to include *Strafford*.[4]

The following 'Advertisement' to the series as a whole appears on the reverse of the title-page of *Pippa Passes*:

Two or three years ago I wrote a Play, about which the chief matter I much care to recollect at present is, that a Pit-full of goodnatured people applauded it:—

---

[1] Letter first published by John Maynard in the *Browning Newsletter*, Fall 1972, pp. 36–7.
[2] *Personalia*, pp. 52–3.   [3] The price of No. I was later increased to 1*s.* o*d.*
[4] For his original intention of including *Strafford* see a letter written in 1842: *Browning and Domett*, p. 38 n.

ever since, I have been desirous of doing something in the same way that should better reward their attention. What follows I mean for the first of a series of Dramatical Pieces, to come out at intervals, and I amuse myself by fancying that the cheap mode in which they appear will for once help me to a sort of Pit-audience again. Of course such a work must go on no longer than it is liked; and to provide against a certain and but too possible contingency, let me hasten to say now—what, if I were sure of success, I would try to say circumstantially enough at the close—that I dedicate my best intentions most admiringly to the Author of 'Ion'—most affectionately to Serjeant Talfourd.[1]

ROBERT BROWNING.

The title of the series was sufficient in itself to make it unlikely that Browning would reach any very considerable 'Pit-audience'. 'Mr. Browning's conundrums begin with his very title-page', complained the reviewer of *Pippa Passes* in the *Athenæum*. '"Bells and Pomegranates" is the general title given (it is reasonable to suppose Mr. Browning knows why, but certainly we have not yet found out—indeed we "give it up") to an intended "Series of Dramatical Pieces," of which this is the first.'[2] Reviewing *Dramatic Lyrics* and *The Return of the Druses* two years later, a writer in the same periodical remarked that the title 'as yet remains a mystery. Which of these poems are Bells, and which Pomegranates—or why any one of them is either—is one of those secrets which we may suppose "shall be unriddled by and bye".' The following year Elizabeth Barrett complimented Browning in her poem 'Lady Geraldine's Courtship':

> Or from Browning some 'Pomegranate,' which, if cut deep down the middle,
> Shows a heart within blood-tinctured, of a veined humanity![3]

Yet even she, writing in *A New Spirit of the Age*, confessed to being puzzled by this 'pretty and most unsatisfactory title'.

By October 1845 she was in a position to ask him what 'precisely' he meant: 'I have always understood it to refer to the Hebraic priestly garment—but Mr. Kenyon held against me the other day that your reference was different, though he had not the remotest idea how. And yesterday I forgot to ask, for not the first time. Tell me too why you should not in the new number satisfy, by a note somewhere . . . the majority . . . with a solution of this one Sphinx riddle. Is there a reason against it?'[4] 'I will make a note as you suggest', he replied,

—or, perhaps, keep it for the closing number, (the next) when it will come fitly in with two or three parting words I shall have to say. The Rabbis make Bells and

---

[1] See p. 19 n. below. [2] *Athenæum, 1841*, p. 952a; and *1843*, p. 385a.
[3] See her *Poems* (2 vols., 1844), i. 225. [4] Kintner, i. 239, 241, and 553.

Pomegranates symbolical of Pleasure and Profit, the Gay & the Grave, the Poetry & the Prose, Singing and Sermonizing—such a mixture of effects as in the original hour (that is quarter of an hour) of confidence & creation, I meant the whole should prove at last.

There was no note in No. VII, and three weeks before the publication of No. VIII Elizabeth Barrett was afraid that Browning had decided not to explain his title. 'Dearest,' she wrote on 24 March 1846,

I persist in thinking that you ought not to be too disdainful to explain your meaning in the Pomegranates. Surely you might say in a word or two that, your title having been doubted about (to your surprise, you *might* say!), you refer the doubters to the Jewish priest's robe, & the Rabbinical gloss . . for I suppose it is a gloss on the robe . . do you not think so? Consider that Mr. Kenyon & I may fairly represent the average intelligence of your readers,—& that *he* was altogether in the clouds as to your meaning . . had not the most distant notion of it,—while I, taking hold of the priest's garment, missed the Rabbins & the distinctive significance, as completely as he did.

He had referred her to Vasari, but his work 'is not the handbook of the whole world, however it may be Mrs. Jameson's'.

Here is the note which Browning printed opposite the first page of *A Soul's Tragedy*:

Here ends my first series of 'Bells and Pomegranates:' and I take the opportunity of explaining, in reply to inquiries, that I only meant by that title to indicate an endeavour towards something like an alternation, or mixture, of music with discoursing, sound with sense, poetry with thought; which looks too ambitious, thus expressed, so the symbol was preferred. It is little to the purpose, that such is actually one of the most familiar of the many Rabbinical (and Patristic) acceptations of the phrase; because I confess that, letting authority alone, I supposed the bare words, in such juxtaposition, would sufficiently convey the desired meaning. 'Faith and good works' is another fancy, for instance, and perhaps no easier to arrive at: yet Giotto placed a pomegranate fruit in the hand of Dante, and Raffaelle crowned his Theology (in the *Camera della Segnatura*) with blossoms of the same; as if the Bellari and Vasari would be sure to come after, and explain that it was merely '*simbolo delle buone opere—il qual Pomo granato fu però usato nelle vesti del Pontefice appresso gli Ebrei*'[1]

R.B.

[1] In 1841 a series of frescoes was uncovered in the Bargello or Palace of the Podestà in Florence, among them portrayals of Hell and Paradise in one of which there is a portrait of Dante. These paintings were attributed to Giotto (d. 1337). As Eleanor Cook pointed out (NQ 1970, pp. 334–5), Browning had read of the paintings by Raphael in *Descrizione delle Immagini dipinte da Raffaelle d'Urbino nel Palazzo Vaticano, e nella Farnesina alla Lungara*, by Giovanni Pietro Bellori. His copy, which is of the edition published in Rome in 1751 with

Elizabeth Barrett was amused by the note's lack of prominence: 'One of my first searches was for the note explanatory of the title,' she wrote on 13 April, '—& I looked, & looked, at the end, at the beginning, at the end again. At last I made up my mind that you had persisted in not explaining, or that the printer had dropped the manuscript. Why, what could make you thrust that note on all but the title-page of the "Soul's Tragedy"? Oh—I comprehend. Having submitted to explain, quite at the point of a bayonet, you determined at least to do it where nobody could see it done. Be frank & tell me that it was just *so*. Also the poor "Soul's Tragedy", you have repudiated *so* from the Bells & Pomegranates .. pushing it gently aside.'[1] She added that she liked the note, 'all, except the sentence about "Faith & Works," which does not apply, I think . . .'. She was too tactful to point out the misprint in 'Bellari' or the obscurity of the two names as plurals—or to suggest that a simple reference to Exod. 28: 33-4 would have been much more helpful. She may have been unaware—and Browning oblivious—of the relevance of a passage in the tenth of the 'Eleven Pious Meditations' in the *Divine Poems* of Francis Quarles:

> Upon the *skirts* (in order as they fell)
> First, a *Pomegranat* was, and then a *Bell*;
> By each *Pomegranat* did a *Bell* appear;
> Many *Pomegranates*, many *Bells* there were:
> *Pomegranats* nourish, *Bells* do make a sound;
> As *Blessings* fall, *Thanksgiving* must rebound.[2]

Browning defended himself by pleading that 'The explanatory note fills up an unseemly blank page—and does not come at the end of the "Soul's Tragedy"—prose after prose', admitted that it 'does look awkwardly', and continued: '—but then I don't consider that it excludes this last from the "Bells"—rather that it says this *is* the last, (*no, nine* if you like,—as the title says "eight *and* last"—from whence will be this advantage—that, in the

the Life of Raphael by Giorgio Vasari added, is in the Fitzwilliam Museum Library in Cambridge, and is dated 'Oct. 1. 1845'. The text (pp. 6-7, from the description of 'La Teologia') should read: 'La corona, ch'ella porta in capo, è contesta di frondi, e fiori di Pomo granato, simbolo della Carità estessa, e delle buone opere, che devono germogliare con le virtù; il qual Pomo fù però usato nelle vesti del Pontefice appresso gli Ebrei.' Browning's abbreviated version translates: 'symbol of good works—which Pomegranate was therefore used on the robes of the High Priest among the Jews'.

[1] Kintner, ii. 619.

[2] Kintner points out the relevance of this passage from Quarles, at i. 241. Browning's copy of the *Divine Poems* is A 1910 in *Collections*, while A 1911 is another copy inscribed 'Robert and Elizabeth Barrett Browning'. For Browning's deep interest in Quarles see our Vol. I, p. 157 n.

case of another edition, all the lyrics &c may go together under one common head of Lyrics & Romances—and the "Soul's Tragedy," . . . step into the place and take the style of No. 8 . . .).'[1]

Five months after the appearance of the last of the 'first series' of *Bells and Pomegranates* Browning set out for Italy with his wife. There was to be no second series, but before the end of the year he was already at work on the 'New Edition' of the best of his poems and plays which was not to appear until 1849. Letters now available make it evident how eager he was to appear before the reading public as the author of a considerable body of work.

'All success to the revision of Paracelsus & the Bells & Pomegranates', wrote Joseph Arnould from London on 6 December 1846:

I can fancy no pleasanter occupation for the six weeks of Italian winter. We [shall] all be eager here to see the results. Of course as one of the pit audience in the great literary theatre I say run the risk of all things for the sake of being clear; sacrifice the private boxes to the gallery, the coteries to the multitude, as far as is practicably consistent with the plan of revision; but, of course don't let us miss one of the characteristic features or well known hues which have long since settled so deeply into all our hearts.[2]

On 21 December EBB told H. S. Boyd that Browning was 'going to bring out a new edition of his collected poems', adding, 'and you are not to read any more, if you please, till this is done'.[3] In a reference to the edition in another letter, written to an American correspondent the following month, she mentioned that Browning was paying 'peculiar attention to the objections made against certain obscurities', while on 4 February 1847 she reported that he was '*very* busy with his new edition', and particularly concerned to render *Pippa Passes* less difficult. On 8 February, however, we hear that Moxon was dragging his feet: 'Moxon desires, . . . as some copies remain of some of Robert's works, that the issue of the new edition shd be delayed till our return to England, in order to secure, as he says, "an immediate success".'

On the 24th of the same month Browning sent Moxon an important letter:

With respect to what you recommend to me in the matter of a new edition, nothing can be more sensible—only, observe, I use the words people put into my mouth when they begin to advise me. They will have it that the form, the cheap

[1] Kintner, ii. 623.
[2] See Donald Smalley, 'Joseph Arnould and Robert Browning: New Letters (1842–50) and a Verse Epistle': PMLA 80 (1965), 95–6.
[3] *Letters of EBB* i. 315; *Checklist* 47:1, 47:7, 47:9.

way of publication, the double columns, &c., do me harm, keep reviewers from noticing what I write—retard the sale—and so on. For myself, I always liked the packed-up completeness and succinctness, and am not much disposed to care for the criticism that is refused because my books are not thick as well as heavy. But the point which decided me to wish to get printed over again was the real good I thought I could do to *Paracelsus*, *Pippa*, and some others; good, not obtained by cutting them up and reconstructing them, but by affording just the proper revision they ought to have had before they were printed at all.[1]

He added that he did not expect to be in England again for 'another year', at the least.

By 1848 Moxon had made his decision. EBB wrote indignantly to her sister Arabella describing him as 'a shabby man': 'Shameful it was, to refuse the risk of Robert's second edition, after some thirteen years publishing connection . . . Oh, I have quite been in a passion, . . a good rational passion, that is!'[2] Fortunately Chapman and Hall had published her *Poems* in two volumes in 1844, and they were selling well enough for a further edition to be envisaged (it appeared in 1850); they agreed to publish Browning in a similar format. On 15 April EBB was able to report this to Miss Mitford: 'My husband has the second edition of his collected poems in the press by this time, by grace of Chapman & Hall, who accept all risks.' At the same time she told Arabella that the edition was 'just *in* the press', so that she need not 'look out for it at present', adding, however: 'You will see how Robert's new edition, with the advantages of type & energetic advertising, will sell! Of Paracelsus, not a copy remains.'

The following month we have evidence of the eagerness of Browning's friends to help at what they clearly regarded as a critical point in his poetic career. EBB wrote to Kenyon: 'For your and Mr. Chorley's and Mr. Forster's kind dealings with Robert's poems I thank you gratefully; and as a third volume can bring up the rear quickly in the case of success, I make no wailing for my "Luria," however dear it may be.'[3] In fact *Luria* was included, but *Strafford* and *Sordello* were not. On 4 July EBB reported that the books were 'in the press now', and would 'come out in the autumn'; but on 3 December Browning wrote to Mary Boyle: 'My new edition sticks fast,—I only hear all is ready, when the minute appears lucky.' A proof copy survives with the date '1848' on the title-page.[4] The *Athenæum*

    [1] *Letters*, p. 14.
    [2] *Checklist*, 48:7; *Letters of EBB* i. 361; *Checklist*, 48:11.
    [3] *Letters of EBB* i. 364–5; *Checklist*, 48:21; Enkvist, p. 81.
    [4] This copy, given by Browning to his sister Sarianna, is now in the Armstrong Library at Baylor. Its existence was pointed out by Ian Jack in the *Browning Newsletter* for April 1969, pp. 30–1. There are slight differences in the wording of the preliminary note on the

for 2 December carried an advertisement for 'The POETICAL WORKS of Robert Browning. A New Edition. With numerous Alterations and Additions', stating that the book would be published that month.[1] By the 26th Arnould had received a copy: 'I have not yet had time to go through your new edition,' he wrote, 'but I am looking forward to it as one of the great treats of my leisure. I like much your external shape & from what I can hear & learn think it not unlikely that you may be much more widely circulated in cloth at 16 s than in the former little well-loved tracts at 2 s 6 d.'[2]

By the third week of January the Brownings themselves still had not received a copy, as we know from a letter of EBB's to Arabella;[3] but the 'New Edition' had certainly been published. Vol. I contains *Paracelsus, Pippa Passes, King Victor and King Charles*, and *Colombe's Birthday*: Vol. II contains *A Blot in the 'Scutcheon, The Return of the Druses, Luria, A Soul's Tragedy*, and *Dramatic Romances and Lyrics*—the last-named consisting of the third and seventh of the *Bells*, the poems remaining in their original order.[4] In our introductions to the individual *Bells* we indicate the nature of the 'numerous Alterations and Additions'.

The first of the three volumes of *The Poetical Works* of 1863 bears the title *Lyrics, Romances, Men, and Women*. The following note appears opposite the first page of the text: 'In this Volume are collected and redistributed the pieces first published in 1842, 1845, and 1855, respectively, under the titles of "Dramatic Lyrics," "Dramatic Romances," and "Men and Women".' Browning was attempting to classify his shorter poems. In 1842 'Lyric' had meant no more than a short poem. In 1845, realizing that many of his shorter poems were by no means lyrical, but essentially narrative in nature, he used *Dramatic Romances & Lyrics* as his title, but made no attempt to discriminate between the types. In the great collection of *Men and Women*, published in two volumes in 1855, we find lyrical poems, narrative poems—and a few others, such as 'Fra Lippo

recto of the leaf following the title-page, a period follows the word POEMS on the title-page, and the Contents page is set in different type. (Cf. *BN*, Fall, 1969, p. 40). In the same periodical for Spring 1972 John Pettigrew reported that 'A fairly extensive collation of *1848* and *1849* indicates . . . that the texts of the poems are in every way identical.'

[1] P. 1224b.

[2] Op. cit., p. 98. On 23 March he commented: 'I could not have supposed the mere difference of type & form could have made so advantageous a difference in the ease & pleasure of the reading': p. 99.

[3] *Checklist*, 49:7.

[4] Two pieces were dropped from *Dramatic Romances and Lyrics*: 'Claret and Tokay' and the second part of 'Home-Thoughts, from Abroad' ('Here's to Nelson's Memory!')

Lippi', which are neither.[1] In 1863, as well as making this attempt at classi-fication, he also changed the titles of many of the poems.

In the editions of 1865 and 1868 Browning continued to make minor alterations to the texts of the *Bells and Pomegranates*. In 1865 the ending '-ize' replaces '-ise', and many exclamation-marks are removed. In 1868 italics used for emphasis are removed, and indentations are changed so that stanzas and verse paragraphs more accurately reflect the rhyme-scheme.

Even after Browning's careful work on the text of *1888-9* a few errors, mainly in accidentals, remained.[2] Where necessary we have restored earlier readings or emended.

---

[1] On Browning's classification of his shorter poems, see Ian Jack, *Browning's Major Poetry* (1973), particularly pp. 77 ff., 96 ff., and 195 ff. In *1863* Browning does not use the word 'Dramatic', either on his title-page or in the general titles preceding the 'Lyrics', 'Romances', and 'Men, and Women' (with this comma). On p. [1] we find the footnote 'Such Poems as the majority in this volume . . .' (see p. 178 below). As in subsequent editions this is given at the foot of the first page of the 'Cavalier Tunes'. In *1868* a note on the oppo-site page reads: 'In a late edition were collected and redistributed the pieces first published in 1842, 1845 and 1855, respectively, under the titles of "Dramatic Lyrics," "Dramatic Romances," and "Men and Women." It is not worth while to disturb this arrangement': p. [74]. We conclude that Browning had forgotten that he had not used the word 'Dramatic' in *1863*.

The fact that the Dramatic Lyrics, Dramatic Romances, and Men and Women occur in different volumes of *The Poetical Works*, from *1868*, makes the placing and wording of the footnote misleading.

[2] See e.g. Thomas J. Collins, 'Browning's Text: A Question of Marks': *The Library*, 6th ser., 4 (March 1982), 70–5, which cites examples of the misplacement of question marks in relation to quotation marks.

INTRODUCTION TO *PIPPA PASSES*

MRS SUTHERLAND ORR'S account of the origin of *Pippa Passes*, which no doubt derives from Browning himself, tells how he 'was walking alone, in a wood near Dulwich, when the image flashed upon him of some one walking thus alone through life; one apparently too obscure to leave a trace of his or her passage, yet exercising a lasting though unconscious influence at every step of it; and the image shaped itself into the little silk-winder of Asolo, Felippa or Pippa'.[1]

Browning visited Asolo, the scene of the work, in the summer of 1838, on his first visit to Italy. On his return he told Fanny Haworth that he 'did not write six lines while absent (except a scene in a play, jotted down as we sailed thro' the Straits of Gibraltar)' and 'some four' lines intended for *Sordello*. It is tempting to conjecture that the 'scene in a play' may have become one of the Parts of *Pippa Passes*; but in a late letter about Asolo in which he told his correspondent that he had 'carried away a lively recollection of the general beauty' of the place, Browning added: 'but I did not write a word of "Pippa Passes"—the idea struck me when walking in an English wood,—and I made use of the Italian memories'.[2]

Unless his memory had temporarily failed him, we must conclude that Part I, at least, was written in the latter part of 1838 or before June 1839, since B. W. Procter referred to 'Sebald, led astray / By the fierce, loose, magnificent Ottima' in 'A Familiar Epistle to Robert Browning', which is headed 'St. John's Wood, June, 1839'.[3] When *Sordello* was published, on 7 March 1840, *Pippa Passes* was one of the three 'Dramas' advertised at the end as 'Nearly Ready'. It seems probable that Eliza Flower had seen it by 9 March, when Browning wrote, in a postscript to a letter to her: 'By the way, you speak of *Pippa*. Could we not make some arrangement about it? The Lyrics *want* your music—five or six in all—how say you? When these three plays are out I hope to "build" a huge Ode—but, "all goeth by God's will!"'[4] What happened to *Pippa* during the following year we do not know. In 1864 Browning told Julia Wedgwood that he remembered suffering from 'a slight touch of something unpleasant in the head which

---

[1] *Handbook*, p. 55, followed by *Correspondence*, iv. 67.   [2] Meredith, p. 94.
[3] The 'Epistle' was published in the first part of *English Songs, and Other Small Poems* (1851), the Preface stating that the poems in the first part are additions to the contents of previous editions.
[4] *Letters*, p. 4.

came on, one Good *Saturday*, as I sat reading the revise of "Pippa Passes"',[1] which points to 10 April 1841: *Pippa* was probably published during the last week of the month. On the 28th Browning sent a copy of 'the trifle' to Dr John Anster in Dublin: the following day he despatched a copy to Ripert-Monclar, describing it as 'un effort pour contenter presque tout le monde,' adding, 'et vous savez comme cela réussit ordinairement'.[2]

Two earlier projects may possibly have some bearing on *Pippa*. In at least two of the notes which he added to copies of *Pauline* Browning mentioned his ambition of writing an 'opera'[3]—and more than one critic has noticed the affinity of *Pippa* to opera, particularly in its opening. Secondly, in August 1845 he told Elizabeth Barrett that he had been looking through his portfolio and had found in it '"Only a Player-Girl" . . . and the sayings and doings of her, and the others—such others! . . . what makes me recall it. . . . is, that it was Russian, and about a fair on the Neva, and booths and droshkies and fish-pies and so forth, with the Palaces in the background.'[4]

To imagine *Pippa Passes* without its (very different) 'background' would be impossible. Asolo is a small ancient town some nineteen miles from Treviso and ten miles from Bassano. Having read of it in Verci's *Storia degli Ecelini*, as he worked on the source-material for *Sordello*, Browning visited it on his first journey to Italy in 1838, after his initial stay in Venice—so that he could later describe it as 'properly speaking . . . the first spot of Italian soil' he had set foot on.[5] In that poem he refers to 'our delicious Asolo' (iii. 683), and at the end we hear how

> . . on a heathy brown and nameless hill
> By sparkling Asolo, in mist and chill,
> Morning just up, higher and higher runs
> A child barefoot and rosy.

This singing child, near 'the castle's inner-court's low wall' at Asolo, contrasts with the scene of horror eighty lines earlier as Pippa, in her innocence, contrasts with the evil described in *Pippa Passes*.

For the rest of his life Asolo remained potent in Browning's imagination. He had a recurrent dream that he found himself in sight of it, but was unable to reach it.[6] It was appropriate that it should have provided him with the title for his last volume of all, *Asolando*.

[1] Wedgwood, p. 102.   [2] *Checklist*, 41:20.
[3] Our Vol. I, p. 4.   [4] Kintner, i. 149.
[5] *Life*, p. 394. Browning described Asolo as 'my very own of all Italian towns' (Meredith, p. 97), and 'my spot of predilection in the whole world, I think' ('Letters . . . To the Rev. J. D. Williams', ed. T. J. Collins, BIS 4 (1976), p. 56.
[6] Meredith, pp. 127–8.

It was vividly present in his memory as he wrote about Pippa, who works in one of the silk-mills. Soon we hear of Possagno church and of the turret which is important in Part III, as also of a house which 'looks over Orcana valley'. On a clear morning Ottima

> . . can see St. Mark's;
> That black streak is the belfry. Stop: Vicenza
> Should lie . . . there's Padua, plain enough, that blue!
> Look o'er my shoulder, follow my finger![1]

Part I ends with 'Foreign *Students* of painting and sculpture', who were in the habit of visiting the home of Canova at Possagno. In Part II we hear of Caterina Cornaro, the Venetian who had been forced to abdicate the crown of Cyprus in 1489, and who had spent the remainder of her life as the centre of a brilliant court in Asolo. The Austrian police, who formed a sort of army of occupation, also make their appearance. Part III is set in the ruined turret which so impressed Browning that he returned to test its echo almost forty years later: we also hear of 'The Titian at Treviso'.[2] Part IV takes us into the palace by the Duomo, and we hear of 'the Brenta', where Zanze comes from.

The conception of the silk-winder of Asolo enabled Browning to link together four Dramatic Scenes, to use the name of a minor genre of the period later exemplified in 'In a Gondola' and 'In a Balcony'. 'Barry Corn-wall' (B. W. Procter), to whom *Colombe's Birthday* was to be dedicated, had published *Dramatic Scenes, and Other Poems* in 1819 and *Marcian Colonna . . . with Three Dramatic Scenes* the following year; while Mary Russell Mitford, who discussed *Pippa Passes* with Elizabeth Barrett soon after its publication, had published *Dramatic Scenes* of her own in 1827.[3] What was more important to Browning was the fact that Landor had included two Dramatic Scenes—'Ines de Castro' and 'Ippolito di Este'—in his volume, *Gebir, Count Julian and Other Poems*, in 1831: in the dedication of five of his Dramatic Scenes in 1837, he stated that he never wrote 'more than a scene or two of the same drama, giving too short a hold for the rabble to seize and pull at'.[4] As we note below, Elizabeth Barrett was reminded of Landor when she read *Pippa Passes*.[5]

---

[1] I. 28 ff.

[2] See note to III. 4, below, and III. 163.

[3] In 1842, encouraging R. H. Horne to publish 'a volume of miscellanies', Miss Mitford commented that 'A few dramatic scenes, w.ᵈ tell nobly among them'.

[4] *The Complete Works of Walter Savage Landor*, ed. T. Earle Welby and Stephen Wheeler (16 vols., 1927–36, repr. 1969), xiii. 260.

[5] See below, I. 7 n.

Whereas Dramatic Scenes are usually isolated fragments, in Browning's work four of them are drawn together and unified by the presence and influence of Pippa. The four Parts are set at different times in the same day, each of them exemplifying a different kind of love. The work begins and ends with Pippa alone, while three quasi-choric passages, two of them in prose, link the Parts.

The only Part for which a source has been seriously suggested is the second. Following a hint by Allardyce Nicoll, F. E. Faverty[1] showed that Browning saw *The Lady of Lyons; or, Love and Pride*, by Bulwer Lytton, on 1 February 1839 (see *The Diaries of . . . Macready*, i. 494), and supported the view that the Jules–Phene episode had been influenced by the main plot of this drama of sentimental republicanism, which is dedicated to Talfourd, 'whose Genius and Example have alike contributed towards the Regeneration of The National Drama'. The proud young heroine scorns the son of a Marquis and another wealthy suitor only to be tricked into marriage with the son of a gardener. An intelligent and generous young man, he is prepared to allow her a divorce, if she wants one; but in the event he goes off to make his fortune, and returns to claim her from her parents and participate in the most conventional of happy endings. Faverty also suggests that Browning may have known Bulwer's acknowledged source, *The History of Perourou; or the Bellows-Mender*, translated from the French by Helen Maria Williams (Dublin, 1801), a play dealing with artists and their concerns in which six engravers witness the humiliation of the proud Aurora. There is no proof that Browning knew the latter, however, and a careful reading of *The Lady of Lyons* leads one to agree with the theme of Terry Otten's article, 'What Browning Never Learned from Bulwer-Lytton'.[2] The claim that the Jules–Phene episode is indebted to Diderot's *Jacques le fataliste*, in which a Marquis is tricked into marrying the daughter of a Parisian courtesan, is hardly more convincing.[3] Jules and the Marquis have little in common, while the Parisian girl, unlike Phene, is an accomplice in the scheme.

Whether or not he had any identifiable source, Browning took a familiar comedy plot—in which a man is tricked into falling in love with a woman who is less innocent than she seems—and gave it an idealistic and

---

[1] 'The Source of the Jules–Phene Episode in Pippa Passes': SP xxxviii (1941), 97-105.

[2] *Research Studies* (Washington State University), 37 (1969), 338-42.

[3] C. Wade Jennings, 'Diderot: A Suggested Source of the Jules–Phene Episode in *Pippa Passes*': *English Language Notes* (Boulder, Colo.), ii (1964-5), 32-6. Swinburne had made the suggestion in 1876: see *The Swinburne Letters*, ed. Cecil Y. Lang (6 vols., Yale 1959-62), iii (1960), 139.

romantic turn. What matters in Part II is the character and aspiration of the young artist, and the Shelleyan love which provides the episode with its conclusion.

Those who read *Pippa Passes* as it originally appeared will understand why its first readers found it obscure. 'I have read the Bells & Pomegranates!' Elizabeth Barrett wrote to Miss Mitford on 15 July 1841:

—'Pippa passes' . . comprehension, I was going to say!—Think of me living in my glass house & throwing pebbles out of the windows!! But really 'Pippa passes', I must say, M! Brownings ordinary measure of mystery . . . There are fine things in it—& the presence of genius, never to be denied!—At the same time it is hard . . to *understand* —is'nt it?—Too hard?—I think so!¹

We have given a brief account of the preparation of the two-volume *Poems . . . A New Edition*, 1849, on pp. 6–8. It began soon after the publication of the last of the *Bells and Pomegranates*. On 4 February 1847 EBB wrote to Mrs Jameson: 'Robert is *very* busy with his new edition, and has been throwing so much golden light into "Pippa", that everybody shall see her "pass" properly . . yes, and *surpass*.'² The revisions in the Introduction were so extensive that Browning wrote it out afresh. The manuscript, now in the library of the University of Texas, consists of three leaves of white paper, without a watermark. Using black ink, Browning wrote two 'pages' on the recto of each leaf, leaving the verso blank. Hardly a line of the original Introduction remains unrevised: eighty-two new lines are added, six lines (203a–f in the present edition) are omitted, and many of the short lines are expanded.

No other part of *Pippa Passes* was so extensively revised. Browning wrote out the first seven lines of Part I, with slight revisions: below these he stuck a column of printed text from p. 4 of *1841* (ll. 8–36), with autograph emendations to the punctuation and 'Hinds' for 'Herds' in l. 19. A few later passages of *Pippa* were recast, as will be evident from the textual notes. Two annotated copies are known, Browning's own (now at Brigham Young University), and Domett's (now at Texas). Both copies

¹ Raymond and Sullivan, i. 235–6. Two days later Elizabeth Barrett reported that she, who was 'used to mysteries, caught the light at my second reading—but the full glory, not until the third': ibid., 238–9. Cf. ii. 52–3. 'Those who esteem him, are of a small circle', she wrote on 22 January 1845, 'but generally esteemed themselves for their insight into imaginative poetry . . a fit audience of few': iii. 62. Domett's indignation at 'A Certain Critique of "Pippa Passes"' led him to send satirical 'Lines' to Browning on the critic: see his *Flotsam and Jetsam* (1871), and the quotation in *Life*, pp. 103–4. Later Elizabeth Barrett told Browning that she 'could find in [her] heart to covet the authorship of *Pippa Passes* more than that of any other of his works: Kintner, i. 22.

² *Checklist*, 47:7. Quotation by permission of Wellesley College.

have 'Charon's ferry' corrected to 'Charon's wherry' at II. 356, and both indicate, at III. 291, that the second and third speakers should be switched. There are ten markings in the Brigham Young copy which were not adopted, usually because Browning went on to revise more comprehensively.

In general the first edition had been accurately printed, however. *1849* corrected 'Rose-reddened' to 'Rose, reddened' in l. 11 of the Introduction, but more errors are to be found in this edition than in *1841*. A few misprints were introduced in *1865* and *1868*, but few survived in *1888*. Very occasionally we have preferred an earlier reading, as in the matter of Monsignor's 'brother's' or 'brothers'' (Introduction, 64, and IV. 87). The three alterations which Browning made to *Pippa* in the Dykes Campbell copy are incorporated here.

As well as including *Pippa* in all his collected editions, Browning included four of the seven songs in various selections from his work. The Moxon *Selection* of 1865 contains 'You'll love me yet', 'The year's at the spring', and 'Give her but a least excuse to love me': the two latter were retained in the 1872 *Selections*. The fourth song, 'A king lived long ago', which had originally appeared in the *Monthly Repository* for November 1835 as 'The King', and which was later reworked for *Pippa Passes* (see our Vol. I, pp. 530–1), is included in the *Selection* of 1865 (as 'Romance from "Pippa Passes"') in a text almost identical with that of *1868*.

PIPPA PASSES;

A DRAMA

title *1841* BELLS AND POMEGRANATES. Nᵒ· I.–PIPPA PASSES. BY ROBERT
BROWNING, Author of "Paracelsus." LONDON: EDWARD MOXON, DOVER
STREET. MDCCCXLI. *MS* Pippa Passes. A Drama. *1849-65* PIPPA PASSES. A DRAMA.

I DEDICATE MY BEST INTENTIONS, IN THIS POEM,
ADMIRINGLY TO THE AUTHOR OF 'ION,'
AFFECTIONATELY TO MR. SERGEANT TALFOURD

R. B.

LONDON: 1841.

dedication *1841* Advertisement. Two or three years ago I wrote a Play, about which the chief matter I much care to recollect at present is, that a Pit-full of goodnatured people applauded it:—ever since, I have been desirous of doing something in the same way that should better reward their attention. What follows I mean for the first of a series of Dramatical Pieces, to come out at intervals, and I amuse myself by fancying that the cheap mode in which they appear will for once help me to a sort of Pit-audience again. Of course such a work must go on no longer than it is liked; and to provide against a certain and but too possible contingency, let me hasten to say now—what, if I were sure of success, I would try to say circumstantially enough at the close—that I dedicate my best intentions most admiringly to the Author of "Ion"—most affectionately to Serjeant Talfourd. ROBERT BROWNING.   *MS* most admiringly .... most affectionately to Mr. Serj⸆ Talfourd. R.B. (lower case; date and place omitted) *1849* (as *MS*, but in small capitals with Serjeant unabbreviated) *1863-68* Serjeant Talfourd. *London*, 1841.

TO THE AUTHOR OF 'ION': Thomas Noon Talfourd (1795-1854), lawyer, MP, and man of letters, was to be knighted when he became a judge in 1849. He was a friend of many writers, including Leigh Hunt and Charles Lamb (whose biographer he became). His play, *Ion*, privately printed in 1835 and published the following year, when Macready produced and acted in it, was regarded by many as a new dawn for the English drama. At the celebrated supper party after the first night Browning met Wordsworth, Landor, Macready, and others. See Griffin and Minchin, pp. 76 ff. With Forster and Procter, Talfourd oversaw the publication of the important two-volume edition of Browning's *Poems* in 1849. The above dedication was added in proof.

PERSONS.

PIPPA.
OTTIMA.
SEBALD.
Foreign Students.
GOTTLIEB.
SCHRAMM.
JULES.
PHENE.
Austrian Police.
BLUPHOCKS.
LUIGI *and his* Mother.
Poor Girls.
MONSIGNOR *and his Attendants.*

PERSONS. {added in *1888* and *1889* only}

PIPPA: 'short for Felippa': see below, II. 372.

PIPPA PASSES.

INTRODUCTION.

New Year's Day at Asolo in the Trevisan.

Scene.—*A large mean airy chamber. A girl,* Pippa, *from the Silk-mills,*
springing out of bed.

Day!
Faster and more fast,
O'er night's brim, day boils at last:
Boils, pure gold, o'er the cloud-cup's brim

s.d. {all editions before *1888* omit the words INTRODUCTION. and Scene.—}

s.d. New Year's Day: Commentators have been troubled by references which seem inconsistent with this time of year. The Ohio editor goes so far as to comment that the reference to the cuckoo at III. 139 'would be more meaningful if it is assumed that B[rowning] means the old New Year's Day, March 25, officially abandoned for January 1 in England in 1752 and in Italy in 1582', but comes to no conclusion; this confuses the adoption of the Gregorian calendar throughout Italy in 1582 with that of 1 January as the start of the year (as against 1 March in Venice and other days in other cities), a process not completed till the end of the eighteenth century. But the action of *Pippa Passes* is set in the Austrian Venetia of Browning's own time. Pettigrew mentions this hypothesis, but observes that Monsignor's remark at IV. 22–4 'indicates that the date is 1 January', taking it (no doubt rightly) to mean that Monsignor had found his brother's murdered body on New Year's Day fourteen years before.

We believe there is no doubt that Browning means 1 January. When Pippa sings '*The year's at the spring*' (I. 221) she is using the word 'spring' as it is used in 1 Sam. 9:26 ('about the spring of the day') and elsewhere, to mean 'The action or time of rising or springing into being or existence': OED II. 5. a., which gives further examples. A careless reading of III. 246, where the first of the three girls says: 'Spring's come and summer's coming', could also mislead, but the context makes it clear that she is wishing a wish, as her two friends have just done at her suggestion. It is not clear what we are to make of the reference to 'The tell-tale cuckoo' at III. 139–40, since Luigi himself believes that his 'mind is touched' (35). Whether or not a swallow might arrive in Venice on New Year's Day (III. 230), we remember that Browning's references to birds (and indeed to flowers) are not always scientifically correct. By this time Browning had visited Italy only once, in 1838, when he had no doubt been struck by the fact that everything is more luxuriant, and 'further on', there than in England.

Asolo: See Introduction, above. Asolo was well known for its silk-mills. The Trevisan March was the name given to the NE part of the Lombard plain: cf. *Sordello*, i. 247 and n.

4 *pure gold*: cf. 'Parting at Morning', 3.

Where spurting and suppressed it lay,   5
For not a froth-flake touched the rim
Of yonder gap in the solid gray
Of the eastern cloud, an hour away;
But forth one wavelet, then another, curled,
Till the whole sunrise, not to be suppressed,   10
Rose, reddened, and its seething breast
Flickered in bounds, grew gold, then overflowed the world.
Oh, Day, if I squander a wavelet of thee,
A mite of my twelve hours' treasure,
The least of thy gazes or glances,   15
(Be they grants thou art bound to or gifts above measure)
One of thy choices or one of thy chances,
(Be they tasks God imposed thee or freaks at thy pleasure)
—My Day, if I squander such labour or leisure,
Then shame fall on Asolo, mischief on me!   20

Thy long blue solemn hours serenely flowing,
Whence earth, we feel, gets steady help and good—
Thy fitful sunshine-minutes, coming, going,
As if earth turned from work in gamesome mood—
All shall be mine! But thou must treat me not   25
As prosperous ones are treated, those who live
At hand here, and enjoy the higher lot,
In readiness to take what thou wilt give,

---

5 *1841-65* lay— *1868* lay;   8 *1841* Of eastern   11 *1841* Rose-reddened,
13 *1841* | Day, if I waste 14 *1841* Aught of my twelve-hours' *MS* twelve-hours
15 *1841* One of thy gazes, one of thy glances,   16 *1841* (Grants thou art bound to,
gifts above measure,)   17 *1841* choices, one *MS* choices, [or] one   18 *1841*
(Tasks God imposed thee, freaks at thy pleasure,)   19 *1841* | Day, if I waste such
20 *1841* | Shame betide Asolo, mischief to me!   21-4 {no equivalent in *1841*}
23 *MS,1849* sunshine minutes,   24 *MS* ⟨That show,⟩ [In which,] earth turns from
1849 In which, earth turns from   25 *1841* But in turn, Day, treat me not
26 *1841* As happy tribes—so happy tribes! who live *MS-1868* As the prosperous are treated,
27 *1841* At hand—the common, other creatures' lot—   28 *1841* Ready to take when
thou

---

8 *an hour away*: an hour ago.   13 *wavelet*: as in Shelley, *Queen Mab*, viii. 24.
20 *Asolo*: stressed on the first syllable.
23 *sunshine-minutes*: cf. Milton, 'L'Allegro', 98: 'on a sunshine holiday'.

And free to let alone what thou refusest;
For, Day, my holiday, if thou ill-usest   30
Me, who am only Pippa,—old-year's sorrow,
Cast off last night, will come again to-morrow:
Whereas, if thou prove gentle, I shall borrow
Sufficient strength of thee for new-year's sorrow.
All other men and women that this earth   35
Belongs to, who all days alike possess,
Make general plenty cure particular dearth,
Get more joy one way, if another, less:
Thou art my single day, God lends to leaven
What were all earth else, with a feel of heaven,—   40
Sole light that helps me through the year, thy sun's!
Try now! Take Asolo's Four Happiest Ones—
And let thy morning rain on that superb
Great haughty Ottima; can rain disturb
Her Sebald's homage? All the while thy rain   45
Beats fiercest on her shrub-house window-pane,
He will but press the closer, breathe more warm
Against her cheek; how should she mind the storm?
And, morning past, if mid-day shed a gloom
O'er Jules and Phene,—what care bride and groom   50
Save for their dear selves? 'T is their marriage-day;
And while they leave church and go home their way,
Hand clasping hand, within each breast would be
Sunbeams and pleasant weather spite of thee.

---

29 *1841* Prepared to pass what   30 *1841* | Day, 'tis but Pippa thou ill-usest
31 *1841* If thou prove sullen, me, whose old year's sorrow   32 *1841* Who except
thee can chase before to-morrow, *MS-1865* to-morrow—   33 *1841* Seest thou, my
day? Pippa's—who mean to borrow   34 *1841* Only of thee strength against new
year's sorrow: 35-42 (no equivalent in *1841*)   40 *MS* heaven;
43 *1841* For let thy morning scowl on   44 *1841* can scowl disturb   45 *1841*
homage? And if noon shed gloom   46-9 (no equivalent in *1841*)   51 *1841*
selves? Then, obscure thy eve   52-5 (no equivalent in *1841*)   53 *MS-1865*
hand,—within   54 *MS-1865* thee!

35 *All other men and women*: ll. 35-42 were no doubt added to emphasize the structure of
the work.
43 *morning*: cf. ll. 49, 55, and 62. Four kinds of love, four times of the day: see 106.
46 *shrub-house*: not in OED: unlikely to be Browning's coinage. Cf. 118.

Then, for another trial, obscure thy eve   55
With mist,—will Luigi and his mother grieve—
The lady and her child, unmatched, forsooth,
She in her age, as Luigi in his youth,
For true content? The cheerful town, warm, close
And safe, the sooner that thou art morose,   60
Receives them. And yet once again, outbreak
In storm at night on Monsignor, they make
Such stir about,—whom they expect from Rome
To visit Asolo, his brother's home,
And say here masses proper to release   65
A soul from pain,—what storm dares hurt his peace?
Calm would he pray, with his own thoughts to ward
Thy thunder off, nor want the angels' guard.
But Pippa—just one such mischance would spoil
Her day that lightens the next twelvemonth's toil   70
At wearisome silk-winding, coil on coil!
      And here I let time slip for nought!
Aha, you foolhardy sunbeam, caught
With a single splash from my ewer!
You that would mock the best pursuer,   75
Was my basin over-deep?
One splash of water ruins you asleep,
And up, up, fleet your brilliant bits
Wheeling and counterwheeling,
Reeling, broken beyond healing: 80
Now grow together on the ceiling!

---

56 *1841* and Madonna grieve   57 *1841* —The mother and the child— *MS*
(Madonna) [The Lady] and   59 *1841* content? And once again, outbreak
60-1 {no equivalent in *1841*}   61 *MS-1865* them!   63 *1841* Such stir to-day
about, who foregoes Rome   *64 {reading of *1841*} *1849–89* brothers'
65 *1841* say there masses   66 *1841* The soul .... that peace?   67-8 {no
equivalent in *1841*}   68 *MS-1865* guard!   70 *1841* Bethink thee, utterly
next   72 *1841* And here am I letting time *MS* here (am) I ⟨letting the⟩ [let] time
73 *1841* | You fool-hardy   75 *1841* that mocked the·   80 *1841* Reeling,
crippled   81 *1841* Grow together .... ceiling,

60 *thou*: her Day.
64 *brother's*: the singular form is correct. Cf. 182-3 below, s.d. before III. 230 and IV. 16,
22, 130.

That will task your wits.
Whoever it was quenched fire first, hoped to see
Morsel after morsel flee
As merrily, as giddily . . .   85
Meantime, what lights my sunbeam on,
Where settles by degrees the radiant cripple?
Oh, is it surely blown, my martagon?
New-blown and ruddy as St. Agnes' nipple,
Plump as the flesh-bunch on some Turk bird's poll!   90
Be sure if corals, branching 'neath the ripple
Of ocean, bud there,—fairies watch unroll
Such turban-flowers; I say, such lamps disperse
Thick red flame through that dusk green universe!
I am queen of thee, floweret!   95
And each fleshy blossom
Preserve I not—(safer
Than leaves that embower it,
Or shells that embosom)
—From weevil and chafer?   100
Laugh through my pane then; solicit the bee;
Gibe him, be sure; and, in midst of thy glee,
Love thy queen, worship me!

---

82 *1841–65* wits!   83 *1841* Whoever it was first quenched fire *MS–1865* Whoever
quenched fire first,   85–6 *1841* As merrily, | As giddily . . . what lights he on—
87 *1841* Where settles himself the cripple?   88 *1841* Oh never surely blown,
89 *1841* New-blown, though!—ruddy as a nipple,   90 *1841,MS* flesh bunch
93 *1841* turban flowers . . I say,   95 *1841* | Queen of thee, floweret, *MS–1863*
floweret;   96 *1841* | Each fleshy   97 *1841* Keep I not, safer   99 *1841*
embosom,   101 *1841* then, solicit the bee,   102–3 *1841* sure, ... glee |
Worship me! |

88 *my martagon?*: a martagon is the Turk's cap lily. Cf. Jonson, *The Sad Shepherd*,
II. viii. 46.
   89 *St. Agnes' nipple*: the story of St Agnes, who died a martyr at thirteen for refusing to
marry, and who remained a virgin in spite of violation, inspired the well-known poems by
Keats and Tennyson.
   90 *flesh-bunch*: no other example of this compound is quoted in OED.
      Turk bird's: turkey's.
   91 *branching*: cf. *Paracelsus*, ii. 164.
   93 *turban-flowers*: the Turk's cap lily is so called from a Turkish word meaning 'a special
form of turban adopted by Sultan Muhammed I': OED.
   100 *weevil and chafer*: destructive types of beetle.

—Worship whom else? For am I not, this day,
Whate'er I please? What shall I please to-day?   105
My morn, noon, eve and night—how spend my day?
To-morrow I must be Pippa who winds silk,
The whole year round, to earn just bread and milk:
But, this one-day, I have leave to go,
And play out my fancy's fullest games;   110
I may fancy all day—and it shall be so—
That I taste of the pleasures, am called by the names
Of the Happiest Four in our Asolo!
See! Up the hill-side yonder, through the morning,
Some one shall love me, as the world calls love: 115
I am no less than Ottima, take warning!
The gardens, and the great stone house above,
And other house for shrubs, all glass in front,
Are mine; where Sebald steals, as he is wont,
To court me, while old Luca yet reposes: 120
And therefore, till the shrub-house door uncloses,
I . . . what now?—give abundant cause for prate
About me—Ottima, I mean—of late,
Too bold, too confident she'll still face down
The spitefullest of talkers in our town.   125
How we talk in the little town below!
    But love, love, love—there's better love, I know!
This foolish love was only day's first offer;
I choose my next love to defy the scoffer:
For do not our Bride and Bridegroom sally   130
Out of Possagno church at noon?

105 *1841* please? Who shall I seem to-day?   106 *1841* | Morn, Noon, Eve, Night—
how must I spend my Day? *MS-1865* My morning, noon, eve, night—   107-13 {no
equivalent in *1841*}   107 *MS* I (am) [must be] Pippa   114 *1841* | Up the
hill-side, thro'   115 *1841* | Love me as I love! | 116 *1841* I am Ottima, take
warning,   117 *1841* And the gardens, and stone   119 *1841* mine, and
Sebald   120 *1841* me, and old . . . . reposes,   123 *1841* Of me (that's
Ottima)—too bold of late,   124 *1841* By far too   125 *1841-63* town— *1865*
town: · 128 *1841* This love's only   129 *1841* | Next love shall defy
130 *1841* not bride and bridegroom

    131 *Possagno church*: Possagno, a village among the Asolan hills some 5 miles N of Asolo
across the Orcana valley, was the birthplace of Antonio Canova: see I. 333 and 367 below,

Their house looks over Orcana valley:
Why should not I be the bride as soon
As Ottima? For I saw, beside,
Arrive last night that little bride—   135
Saw, if you call it seeing her, one flash
Of the pale snow-pure cheek and black bright tresses,
Blacker than all except the black eyelash;
I wonder she contrives those lids no dresses!
—So strict was she, the veil   140
Should cover close her pale
Pure cheeks—a bride to look at and scarce touch,
Scarce touch, remember, Jules! For are not such
Used to be tended, flower-like, every feature,
As if one's breath would fray the lily of a creature?   145
A soft and easy life these ladies lead:
Whiteness in us were wonderful indeed.
Oh, save that brow its virgin dimness,
Keep that foot its lady primness,
Let those ankles never swerve   150
From their exquisite reserve,
Yet have to trip along the streets like me,
All but naked to the knee!
How will she ever grant her Jules a bliss
So startling as her real first infant kiss?   155
Oh, no—not envy, this!

—Not envy, sure!—for if you gave me
Leave to take or to refuse,

133 *1841* Why not be MS Why [should I] not be *1849* Why should I not be
134 *1841* As Ottima? I saw, myself, beside,   135 *1841* that bride—   137–
8 *1841* and blacker tresses | Than . . . not the black eyelash;   139 *1841* A wonder
. . . . dresses   143 *1841* | Remember Jules!—for MS Jules!—for   146–7 (no
equivalent in *1841*)   146 MS–*1863* lead!   147 MS,*1849* indeed—
157 *1841* sure,

and the n. to l. 355. He gave Possagno a splendid new church, the so-called Tempio di
Canova, of which the foundation-stone was laid in 1819. The architectural designs were by
his friend Giovanni Antonio Selva, while he himself was responsible for the sculptural
decoration. For the standard work on Canova, see l. 355 n. below.

149 *lady primness*: for 'lady' meaning 'lady-like' cf. *1 Henry IV*, I. iii. 46.

In earnest, do you think I'd choose
That sort of new love to enslave me?   160
Mine should have lapped me round from the beginning;
As little fear of losing it as winning:
Lovers grow cold, men learn to hate their wives,
And only parents' love can last our lives.
At eve the Son and Mother, gentle pair,   165
Commune inside our turret: what prevents
My being Luigi? While that mossy lair
Of lizards through the winter-time is stirred
With each to each imparting sweet intents
For this new-year, as brooding bird to bird—   170
(For I observe of late, the evening walk
Of Luigi and his mother, always ends
Inside our ruined turret, where they talk,
Calmer than lovers, yet more kind than friends)
—Let me be cared about, kept out of harm,   175
And schemed for, safe in love as with a charm;
Let me be Luigi! If I only knew
What was my mother's face—my father, too!
  Nay, if you come to that, best love of all
Is God's; then why not have God's love befall   180
Myself as, in the palace by the Dome,
Monsignor?—who to-night will bless the home

---

161 *1841* beginning   162 *1849,1863* winning!   163-4 {no equivalent in
1841}   164 *MS,1849* lives: 165 *1841* Why look you! when at eve the pair
MS ⟨So, look you! when at⟩ [At] eve the [son and mother,] gentle Pair,   166 *1841*
turret,   167 *1849-65* while   171-4 {no equivalent in *1841*}
175 *1841* I will be   176 *1841* charm,   177 *1841* I will be Luigi ... if
178 *1841* my father like ... my mother too!   179 *1841* that, the greatest love of all
180 *1841* Is God's: well then, to have   181 *1841* Oneself as   182 *1841*
Where Monsignor to-night

168 *lizards*: see the letter in which Browning acknowledges his 'odd liking for "vermin"',
where he mentions lizards and admits that he loves 'all those wild creatures God "*sets up for
themselves*" so independently of us': Kintner, i. 356.

173 *our ruined turret*: for the 'turret' or ruined castle see Meredith, plate facing p. lii. For
the echo see the opening of Part III, below.

181 *the palace by the Dome*: the campanile of the Duomo (cathedral or principal church) is
clearly visible in the illustration referred to at 173 n. above.

Of his dead brother; and God bless in turn
That heart which beats, those eyes which mildly burn
With love for all men! I, to-night at least,   185
Would be that holy and beloved priest.

Now wait!—even I already seem to share
In God's love: what does New-year's hymn declare?
What other meaning do these verses bear?

All service ranks the same with God: 190
If now, as formerly he trod
Paradise, his presence fills
Our earth, each only as God wills
Can work—God's puppets, best and worst,
Are we; there is no last nor first.   195

Say not "a small event!" Why "small"?
Costs it more pain that this, ye call
A "great event," should come to pass,
Than that? Untwine me from the mass
Of deeds which make up life, one deed   200
Power shall fall short in or exceed!

And more of it, and more of it!—oh yes—
I will pass each, and see their happiness,

183–6 *1841* brother! I to-night at least, | Will be *MS–1868* God will bless   185 *MS–*
1868 men: 186 *1841* Will be *MS* Would [be] that .... priest! *1849–65* priest!
187 *1841* Now wait—even I myself already ought to share   188 *1841* In that—why
else should new year's *MS* In ⟨that⟩ [God's] love: 189 {no equivalent in *1841*}
192 *1841* Paradise, God's presence   193 *1841* earth, and each but as *MS* earth, ⟨then⟩ each
⟨but⟩ [only] as   196 *1841* a small event! Why small? *MS* event"! *1849–68* "small?"
197 *1841* pain this thing ye *1849–68* pain than this,   198 *1841* A great event
200 *1841* deeds that make   202 *1841* it—oh, yes!   203 *MS–1865* pass by, and
203,203a–f *1841* So that my passing, and each happiness | I pass, will be alike important—
prove | That true! oh yes—the brother, | The bride, the lover, and the mother,—|Only to pass
whom will remove— | Whom a mere look at half will cure | The Past, and help me to
endure

190 *All service*: the parallel with *Sordello*, vi. 127–8, is mainly verbal.
199 *Untwine me*: disentangle for me. Cf. Quarles, *Sions Sonets*, ix. 3–4: 'the world cannot
untwine / The joyful union of his heart, and mine': p. 372 in Quarles's *Divine Poems* (1669),
a book owned by Browning and EBB (*Collections*, A 1911). For Browning and Quarles, see
Vol. I, p. 157 n.

And envy none—being just as great, no doubt,
Useful to men, and dear to God, as they!   205
A pretty thing to care about
So mightily, this single holiday!
But let the sun shine! Wherefore repine?
—With thee to lead me, O Day of mine,
Down the grass path grey with dew,   210
Under the pine-wood, blind with boughs,
Where the swallow never flew
Nor yet cicala dared carouse—
No, dared carouse!   [*She enters the street.*

204-5 *1841* The Coming . . . I am just as great, no doubt, | As they! | 208 *1841* |
Why repine? | 209 *1841* me, Day   210 *MS-1868* grass-path
211 *1841* 'Neath the   213 *1841-9* As yet, nor cicale dared *1863* As yet nor cicala
214 *MS-1863* | Dared carouse!

211 *blind*: dark, a sense described in OED as archaic. Cf. *Sordello*, ii. 341 ('a blind retreat').
213 *cicala*: cf. *Sordello*, iii. 260.
214 *No, dared carouse!*: presumably she has just heard the first cicala of the morning.

PART I

MORNING.

SCENE.—*Up the Hill-side, inside the Shrub-house.* LUCA'S, *wife,* OTTIMA,
and her paramour, the German SEBALD.

Sebald [*sings*].

> *Let the watching lids wink!*
> *Day's a-blaze with eyes, think!*
> *Deep into the night, drink!*

Ottima. Night? Such may be your Rhine-land nights
    perhaps;
But this blood-red beam through the shutter's chink   5
—We call such light, the morning: let us see!
Mind how you grope your way, though! How these tall
Naked geraniums straggle! Push the lattice
Behind that frame!—Nay, do I bid you?—Sebald,
It shakes the dust down on me! Why, of course   10
The slide-bolt catches. Well, are you content,
Or must I find you something else to spoil?
Kiss and be friends, my Sebald! Is 't full morning?
Oh, don't speak then!
    Sebald.   Ay, thus it used to be.
Ever your house was, I remember, shut   15
Till mid-day; I observed that, as I strolled
On mornings through the vale here; country girls
Were noisy, washing garments in the brook,

---

2 *1841 think,* — MS *think* —   4–8 *1841* Night? What, a Rhineland night, then? How
these tall | Naked geraniums   6 *MS–1865* morning's: 9 *1841* frame.—
13 *1841* Sebald. Is it *MS–1868* Sebald! Is it   14 *1841,MS* be!

   7 *How these tall*: Elizabeth Barrett, writing to Mary Russell Mitford on 17 July 1841,
asked whether she did not agree 'that there was an occasional *manner*, in the portions most
strictly dramatic, like Landor's, in Landor's dramas, when Landor writes best', quoting ll. 7–
13. 'Is'nt that Landor? Is'nt it his very trick of phrase?': Raymond and Sullivan, i. 239 (cf.
ii. 122).

Hinds drove the slow white oxen up the hills:
But no, your house was mute, would ope no eye.   20
And wisely: you were plotting one thing there,
Nature, another outside. I looked up—
Rough white wood shutters, rusty iron bars,
Silent as death, blind in a flood of light.
Oh, I remember!—and the peasants laughed   25
And said, "The old man sleeps with the young wife."
This house was his, this chair, this window—his.
    Ottima. Ah, the clear morning! I can see St. Mark's;
That black streak is the belfry. Stop: Vicenza
Should lie . . . there's Padua, plain enough, that blue!   30
Look o'er my shoulder, follow my finger!
    Sebald.   Morning?
It seems to me a night with a sun added.
Where's dew, where's freshness? That bruised plant, I
       bruised
In getting through the lattice yestereve,
Droops as it did. See, here's my elbow's mark   35
I' the dust o' the sill.
    Ottima.   Oh, shut the lattice, pray!
    Sebald. Let me lean out. I cannot scent blood here,
Foul as the morn may be.
                There, shut the world out!
How do you feel now, Ottima? There, curse
The world and all outside! Let us throw off   40
This mask: how do you bear yourself? Let's out

19 *1841* Herds drove   20 *1841-9* eye— *1863-8* eye!   22 *1841-63* outside:
24 *1841* light, *MS,1849* light;   26 *1841-9* wife!"   27 *MS-1868* his!
29 *1841* belfry—stop: 30 *1841* blue.   31 *1841-9* finger— *1863* finger.
32 *1841-9* added: 33 *1841-9* dew? where's   36 *1841,MS* In the dust on
37 *1868* out!

    28 *I can see St. Mark's*: St Mark's Cathedral in Venice, more than 30 miles SE of Asolo.
Vicenza and Padua are not quite so far, lying SW and S respectively. Throughout his life
Browning often remembered the view from Asolo: 'on a clear day you can see much farther
than Venice', he wrote in 1889: 'I mentioned some of the dim spots pointed out to my faith
as Towns . . . . . . *do* —go there and get all the good out of the beautiful place I used to dream
about so often in old days': Meredith, p. 97.
    41 *mask*: pretence. Cf. 158.

With all of it.

    Ottima.   Best never speak of it.

    Sebald. Best speak again and yet again of it,
Till words cease to be more than words. "His blood,"
For instance—let those two words mean "His blood"   45
And nothing more. Notice, I'll say them now,
"His blood."

    Ottima.   Assuredly if I repented
The deed—

    Sebald. Repent? Who should repent, or why?
What puts that in your head? Did I once say
That I repented?

    Ottima.   No, I said the deed . . .   50

    Sebald. "The deed" and "the event"—just now it was
"Our passion's fruit"—the devil take such cant!
Say, once and always, Luca was a wittol,
I am his cut-throat, you are . . .

    Ottima.   Here's the wine;
I brought it when we left the house above,   55
And glasses too—wine of both sorts. Black? White then?

    Sebald. But am not I his cut-throat? What are you?

    Ottima. There trudges on his business from the Duomo
Benet the Capuchin, with his brown hood
And bare feet; always in one place at church,   60
Close under the stone wall by the south entry.
I used to take him for a brown cold piece
Of the wall's self, as out of it he rose
To let me pass—at first, I say, I used:
Now, so has that dumb figure fastened on me,   65

42 *1841–68* it!   51 *1841* event"—and just   54 *1841–68* Here is
58 *1849,1863* There,   61 *1841,1849* entry;

   53 *wittol*: 'a tame cuckold': Johnson.

   56 *wine of both sorts. Black?*: Pettigrew and Collins observe that 'Ottima, like the Mac-
beths, tends to avoid words that bear too directly on the murder'. But in Italian 'vino nero' is
sometimes used to mean 'red wine'; and cf. l. 5 above.

   58 *the Duomo*: cf. note to Introduction, 181.

   59 *Benet the Capuchin*: Benedict, abbreviated as in Bene't Street, Cambridge. The
Capuchins are an order of friars, an offshoot from the Franciscans aiming at an even
greater strictness. They wear a brown habit, and used to walk barefoot.

I rather should account the plastered wall
A piece of him, so chilly does it strike.
This, Sebald?
    Sebald.   No, the white wine—the white wine!
Well, Ottima, I promised no new year
Should rise on us the ancient shameful way;   70
Nor does it rise. Pour on! To your black eyes!
Do you remember last damned New Year's day?
    Ottima. You brought those foreign prints. We looked at
       them
Over the wine and fruit. I had to scheme
To get him from the fire. Nothing but saying   75
His own set wants the proof-mark, roused him up
To hunt them out.
    Sebald.   'Faith, he is not alive
To fondle you before my face.
    Ottima.   Do you
Fondle me then! Who means to take your life
For that, my Sebald?
    Sebald.   Hark you, Ottima!   80
One thing to guard against. We'll not make much
One of the other—that is, not make more
Parade of warmth, childish officious coil,
Than yesterday: as if, sweet, I supposed
Proof upon proof were needed now, now first,   85
To show I love you—yes, still love you—love you
In spite of Luca and what's come to him
—Sure sign we had him ever in our thoughts,
White sneering old reproachful face and all!
We'll even quarrel, love, at times, as if   90

---

70 *1841–65* way;   71 *1841* rise—pour on— *1849–68* rise: 77 *1841* Faith,
78 *1849–65* face!   79 *1841* then: 80 *1841–63* Ottima,   81 *1841–65*
One thing's to   85 *1841–63* proof was needed   86 *1841* I love you—still love
you—   87 *1841* him.   89 *1841* all—

  76 *the proof-mark*: Browning's father was an enthusiastic and knowledgeable collector of
prints: see Maynard, pp. 406–7 n. 2. A proof (trial impression) is more valuable than subse-
quent impressions.
  83 *coil*: fuss.

We still could lose each other, were not tied
By this: conceive you?
    Ottima.   Love!
    Sebald.   Not tied so sure.
Because though I was wrought upon, have struck
His insolence back into him—am I
So surely yours?—therefore forever yours?   95
    Ottima. Love, to be wise, (one counsel pays another)
Should we have—months ago, when first we loved,
For instance that May morning we two stole
Under the green ascent of sycamores—
If we had come upon a thing like that   100
Suddenly . . .
    Sebald.   "A thing"—there again—"a thing!"
    Ottima. Then, Venus' body, had we come upon
My husband Luca Gaddi's murdered corpse
Within there, at his couch-foot, covered close—
Would you have pored upon it? Why persist   105
In poring now upon it? For 't is here
As much as there in the deserted house:
You cannot rid your eyes of it. For me,
Now he is dead I hate him worse: I hate . . .
Dare you stay here? I would go back and hold   110
His two dead hands, and say, "I hate you worse,
"Luca, than . . ."
    Sebald.   Off, off—take your hands off mine,
'T is the hot evening—off! oh, morning is it?
    Ottima. There's one thing must be done; you know what
        thing.
Come in and help to carry. We may sleep   115
Anywhere in the whole wide house to-night.

92 *1841,1849* Love— . . . .sure— *1863-8* sure!   108 *1841,1849* it: 111 *1841-*
65 say, I   112 *1841-65* than   *1841* mine!

    93 *wrought upon*: stirred up.   99 *ascent*: 'An eminence, or high place': Johnson.
    102 *Venus' body*: this melodramatic oath seems not to derive from Italian. It may be an
ironical adaptation of 'corpo di Bacco'.
    104 *couch-foot*: the only example in OED is from l. 200 of 'Doctor ——': *Dramatic Idyls:
Second Series*. Cf. Donne, 'A Nocturnal, upon S. Lucy's Day', 7.

   Sebald. What would come, think you, if we let him lie
Just as he is? Let him lie there until
The angels take him! He is turned by this
Off from his face beside, as you will see.   120
   Ottima. This dusty pane might serve for looking glass.
Three, four—four grey hairs! Is it so you said
A plait of hair should wave across my neck?
No—this way.
   Sebald.   Ottima, I would give your neck,
Each splendid shoulder, both those breasts of yours,   125
That this were undone! Killing! Kill the world,
So Luca lives again!—ay, lives to sputter
His fulsome dotage on you—yes, and feign
Surprise that I return at eve to sup,
When all the morning I was loitering here—   130
Bid me despatch my business and begone.
I would . . .
   Ottima. See!
   Sebald.   No, I'll finish. Do you think
I fear to speak the bare truth once for all?
All we have talked of, is, at bottom, fine
To suffer; there's a recompense in guilt;   135
One must be venturous and fortunate:
What is one young for, else? In age we'll sigh
O'er the wild reckless wicked days flown over;
Still, we have lived: the vice was in its place.
But to have eaten Luca's bread, have worn   140
His clothes, have felt his money swell my purse—
Do lovers in romances sin that way?

---

119 *1841–63* him: 122 *1841* is   124 *1841–63* way!   126 *1841* |This
were undone! Killing?—Let the world die   *1849–68* Killing?   127 *1841,1849* Ay,
129 *1841–65* I returned at   132 *1849–68* finish!   135 *1841* in that:
139 {no equivalent in *1841*} *1849,1863* lived!   142 {no equivalent in *1841*}

   119 *He is turned*: Porter and Clarke refer to 'a well-known superstition that the face of a
murdered man always looks skyward for vengeance'.
   122 *Three, four—four grey hairs!*: another possible echo from Donne: see 'The Canoniza-
tion', 3: 'My five grey hairs, or ruined fortune flout.'
   139 *the vice was in its place*: cf. 'The Statue and the Bust', 248.

Why, I was starving when I used to call
And teach you music, starving while you plucked me
These flowers to smell!
    Ottima.   My poor lost friend!
    Sebald.   He gave me   145
Life, nothing less: what if he did reproach
My perfidy, and threaten, and do more—
Had he no right? What was to wonder at?
He sat by us at table quietly:
Why must you lean across till our cheeks touched?   150
Could he do less than make pretence to strike?
'T is not the crime's sake—I'd commit ten crimes
Greater, to have this crime wiped out, undone!
And you—O how feel you? Feel you for me?
    Ottima. Well then, I love you better now than ever,   155
And best (look at me while I speak to you)—
Best for the crime; nor do I grieve, in truth,
This mask, this simulated ignorance,
This affectation of simplicity,
Falls off our crime; this naked crime of ours   160
May not now be looked over: look it down!
Great? let it be great; but the joys it brought,
Pay they or no its price? Come: they or it!
Speak not! The past, would you give up the past
Such as it is, pleasure and crime together?   165
Give up that noon I owned my love for you?
The garden's silence: even the single bee
Persisting in his toil, suddenly stopped,
And where he hid you only could surmise

144-5 *1841* you pluck'd | Me flowers to smell!   149 (no equivalent in *1841*)
151 *1841,1849* strike me?   152 *1849,1863* not for the   154 *1841-65* you?
feel   166 *1841,1849* you—   167 *1863-8* silence!   168 *1841,1849*
stopt *1863,1865* stopt; *1868* stopped:

    161 *looked over*: overlooked.
        look it down!: cf. 'live it down'.
    167 *the single bee*: cf. *Sordello*, vi. 621—2: 'By this, the hermit-bee has stopped / His day's
toil at Goito'. See too Kintner, i. 357, and *Pauline*, 439.

By some campanula chalice set a-swing.   170
Who stammered—"Yes, I love you"?
    Sebald.   And I drew
Back; put far back your face with both my hands
Lest you should grow too full of me—your face
So seemed athirst for my whole soul and body!
    Ottima. And when I ventured to receive you here,   175
Made you steal hither in the mornings—
    Sebald.   When
I used to look up 'neath the shrub-house here,
Till the red fire on its glazed windows spread
To a yellow haze?
    Ottima.   Ah—my sign was, the sun
Inflamed the sere side of yon chestnut-tree   180
Nipped by the first frost.
    Sebald.   You would always laugh
At my wet boots: I had to stride thro' grass
Over my ankles.
    Ottima.   Then our crowning night!
    Sebald. The July night?
    Ottima.   The day of it too, Sebald!
When heaven's pillars seemed o'erbowed with heat,   185
Its black-blue canopy suffered descend
Close on us both, to weigh down each to each,
And smother up all life except our life.
So lay we till the storm came.
    Sebald.   How it came!
    Ottima. Buried in woods we lay, you recollect;   190
Swift ran the searching tempest overhead;
·And ever and anon some bright white shaft
Burned thro' the pine-tree roof, here burned and there,

---

170 *1841-63* campanula's   *1849* a-swing *1863-8* a-swing: *171 (editors' emen-
dation) *1841* As he clung there—"Yes, I love you." *1849* As he clung . . . . you!" *1863-89*
you?"   183 *1841,1849* night—   185 *1849,1863* When the heaven's
186 *1841-63* canopy seemed let descend   193 *1841-65* Burnt . . . . burnt

170 *a-swing*: this antedates the first example in OED.
185 *heaven's pillars*: cf. Job 26:11.
186 *Its black-blue canopy*: cf. *Hamlet*, II. ii. 299-300.

As if God's messenger thro' the close wood screen
Plunged and replunged his weapon at a venture,   195
Feeling for guilty thee and me: then broke
The thunder like a whole sea overhead—
    Sebald. Yes!
    Ottima.   —While I stretched myself upon you, hands
To hands, my mouth to your hot mouth, and shook
All my locks loose, and covered you with them—   200
You, Sebald, the same you!
    Sebald.   Slower, Ottima!
    Ottima. And as we lay—
    Sebald.   Less vehemently! Love me!
Forgive me! Take not words, mere words, to heart!
Your breath is worse than wine! Breathe slow, speak slow!
Do not lean on me!
    Ottima.   Sebald, as we lay,   205
Rising and falling only with our pants,
Who said, "Let death come now! 'T is right to die!
"Right to be punished! Nought completes such bliss
"But woe!" Who said that?
    Sebald.   How did we ever rise?
Was't that we slept? Why did it end?
    Ottima.   I felt you   210
Taper into a point the ruffled ends
Of my loose locks 'twixt both your humid lips.
My hair is fallen now: knot it again!
    Sebald. I kiss you now, dear Ottima, now and now!
This way? Will you forgive me—be once more   215
My great queen?
    Ottima.   Bind it thrice about my brow;

198 *1841* Yes.   200 *1841* them.   201 *1841,1849* you— .... Ottima— *1863*
Ottima—   202 *1841* vehemently— Love me— *1849* me—   203 *1841,1849*
me—take .... heart— *1863,1865* take   204 *1841* wine—breathe slow, speak slow—
1849 speak slow— *1863-8* wine.   205 *1841* me—   207 *1841* now—'tis
1863,1865 't is   208 *1841,1849* punished—nought *1863,1865* nought   210-
11 *1841* I felt | You tapering to a   211 *1849* Fresh tapering to a *1863,1865* Tapering
into   212 *1841-63* lips—   213 *1841* (My .... again). *1849,1863* (My ....
again!)   214 *1841* and now;   215 *1841* will

Crown me your queen, your spirit's arbitress,
Magnificent in sin. Say that!
   Sebald.   I crown you
My great white queen, my spirit's arbitress,
Magnificent . . .   220
       [*From without is heard the voice of* PIPPA, *singing—*

        The year's at the spring
        And day's at the morn;
        Morning's at seven;
        The hill-side's dew-pearled;
        The lark's on the wing;   225
        The snail's on the thorn:
        God's in his heaven—
        All's right with the world!

                            [PIPPA *passes.*

   Sebald. God's in his heaven! Do you hear that? Who
    spoke?
You, you spoke!
   Ottima.   Oh—that little ragged girl!   230
She must have rested on the step: we give them
But this one holiday the whole year round.
Did you ever see our silk-mills—their inside?
There are ten silk-mills now belong to you.
She stoops to pick my double heartsease . . . Sh!   235
She does not hear: call you out louder!
   Sebald.   Leave me!
Go, get your clothes on—dress those shoulders!
   Ottima.   Sebald?
   Sebald. Wipe off that paint! I hate you.

---

s.d., 221 *1841* †[*Without.*]† The   225 *1841* wing,   230 *1841* girl: *1865*
spoke   231–2 *1841* we give | Them but one   233 *1841* e'er
236 *1841,1849* hear—you call out   237 *1841* shoulders.   238 *1841–65* paint.
. . . . you!

   221 *at the spring*: at its beginning. Cf. p. 21 n. above.
   224 *dew-pearled*: no other example in OED, but 'dew-impearled' occurs in Drayton's
sonnet 'Cleere Ankor', 8: see *Complete Works*, ed. J. W. Hebel and others (5 vols., 1961), i. 104.
See too Tennyson's 'Ode to Memory', 14.
   235 *double heartsease*: a kind of pansy.

Ottima.   Miserable!

Sebald. My God, and she is emptied of it now!
Outright now!—how miraculously gone   240
All of the grace—had she not strange grace once?
Why, the blank cheek hangs listless as it likes,
No purpose holds the features up together.
Only the cloven brow and puckered chin
Stay in their places: and the very hair,   245
That seemed to have a sort of life in it,
Drops, a dead web!
    Ottima.   Speak to me—not of me!
    Sebald. —That round great full-orbed face, where not an
        angle
Broke the delicious indolence—all broken!
    Ottima. To me—not of me! Ungrateful, perjured cheat!   250
A coward too: but ingrate's worse than all.
Beggar—my slave—a fawning, cringing lie!
Leave me! Betray me! I can see your drift!
A lie that walks and eats and drinks!
    Sebald.   My God!
Those morbid olive faultless shoulder-blades—   255
I should have known there was no blood beneath!
    Ottima. You hate me then? You hate me then?
    Sebald.   To think
She would succeed in her absurd attempt,
And fascinate by sinning, show herself
Superior—guilt from its excess superior   260
To innocence! That little peasant's voice
Has righted all again. Though I be lost,
I know which is the better, never fear,
Of vice or virtue, purity or lust,
Nature or trick! I see what I have done,   265

239 *1841-65* God!   250 *1841* Ungrateful—to me—not of me—perjured cheat! *1849*
cheat—   251 *1841* all: *1849-68* all!   253 *1841,1849* drift—   257 *1841*
then? you   259 *1841* fascinate with sin! and show *1849, 1863* sinning; and show *1865,*
1868 sinning, and show   261 *1841,1849* Innocence.   265 *1841,1849* trick—

    255 *morbid*: here used, as by critics of art, with a reminiscence of Italian *morbido* and
morbidezza: soft, tender, delicate, lascivious.

Entirely now! Oh I am proud to feel
Such torments—let the world take credit thence—
I, having done my deed, pay too its price!
I hate, hate—curse you! God's in his heaven!
   Ottima.   —Me!
Me! no, no, Sebald, not yourself—kill me!   270
Mine is the whole crime. Do but kill me—then
Yourself—then—presently—first hear me speak!
I always meant to kill myself—wait, you!
Lean on my breast—not as a breast; don't love me
The more because you lean on me, my own   275
Heart's Sebald! There, there, both deaths presently!
   Sebald. My brain is drowned now—quite drowned: all I
      feel
Is . . . is, at swift-recurring intervals,
A hurry-down within me, as of waters
Loosened to smother up some ghastly pit: 280
There they go—whirls from a black fiery sea!
   Ottima. Not me—to him, O God, be merciful!

Talk by the way, while PIPPA *is passing from the hill-side to Orcana.
Foreign Students of painting and sculpture, from Venice, assembled
opposite the house of* JULES, *a young French statuary, at Possagno.*

   1*st Student.* Attention! My own post is beneath this window, but
the pomegranate clump yonder will hide three or four of you with a
285 little squeezing, and Schramm and his pipe must lie flat in the
balcony. Four, five—who's a defaulter? We want everybody, for

266 *1841* now.   267 *1841* credit that   271 *1841-63* —do   272 *1841-*
63 speak—   276 *1841*   Sebald.   279 *1841-63* A hurrying-down
281 *1841* sea.   *1865* They they go— *1868* They—they go—   282 *1849-65* Not to
me, God—to him be merciful!   s.d. *1841 Talk by the way in the mean time. Foreign* Stu-
dents *of* . . . . *Statuary. 1849, 1863 Statuary.*   283 *1841* Attention: 286-9 *1841*
defaulter? Jules . . . . bride. 2 *Stu.* The poet's away—

   279 *a hurry-down*: apparently Browning's coinage. Cf. Carlyle, *The French Revolution*,
Book I, ch. vi: 'destruction all round him, and the rushing-down of worlds': Centenary ed.,
iv. 46.
   s.d. *statuary*: sculptor.

Jules must not be suffered to hurt his bride when the jest's found out.

2nd Student. All here! Only our poet's away—never having much meant to be present, moonstrike him! The airs of that fellow, that 290 Giovacchino! He was in violent love with himself, and had a fair prospect of thriving in his suit, so unmolested was it,—when suddenly a woman falls in love with him, too; and out of pure jealousy he takes himself off to Trieste, immortal poem and all: whereto is this prophetical epitaph appended already, as Bluphocks 295 assures me,—"*Here a mammoth-poem lies, Fouled to death by butterflies.*" His own fault, the simpleton! Instead of cramp couplets, each like a knife in your entrails, he should write, says Bluphocks, both classically and intelligibly.—*Æsculapius, an Epic. Catalogue of the drugs: Hebe's plaister—One strip Cools your lip. Phœbus' emulsion—One bottle* 300 *Clears your throttle. Mercury's bolus—One box Cures* . . .

3rd Student. Subside, my fine fellow! If the marriage was over by ten o'clock, Jules will certainly be here in a minute with his bride.

2nd Student. Good!—only, so should the poet's muse have been universally acceptable, says Bluphocks, *et canibus nostris* . . . and 305 Delia not better known to our literary dogs than the boy Giovacchino!

---

290 *1841* be here, moonstrike   290-1 (*1841* omits "The airs . . . . Giovacchino!")
291 *1841* in love with   292-3 *1841* suit, when suddenly   293 *1841* woman
fell in . . . . too,   295-6 *1841* Bluphocks assured me:— "*The author on the author. Here
so and so, the mammoth, lies, Fouled*   300 *1841* lip;   301 *1841* throttle;
302 *1841* fellow;   304 *1841* 2 *Stu.* So should   304-6 *1841* been acceptable,
says Bluphocks, and Delia . . . . our dogs than the boy.

290 *moonstrike*: probably Browning's coinage, from 'moonstruck'.

295 *Bluphocks*: 'The name means *Blue-Fox*, and is a skit on the *Edinburgh Review*, which is bound in a cover of blue and fox': Furnivall, quoted in Berdoe.

296 *butterflies*: giddy triflers, light-weight critics.

297 *cramp*: obscure, crabbed.

299 *Æsculapius*: the god of Medicine. The students 'are laughing at Giovacchino for having run away from love as if it could be cured by treatment like a disease, and they propose his love poem should be an epic with Æsculapius for the hero, with catalogues of drugs for his cure': Porter and Clarke. Hebe was the Greek goddess of youth, Phoebus the god of poetry: as messenger of the gods, Mercury was associated with love-affairs.

301 *One box Cures* . . .: the pox, for which mercury was the regular prescription.

305 *et canibus nostris*: even to our dogs. Virgil's *Third Eclogue*, 66-7: 'But my flame Amyntas comes to me unsought, so that now Delia is not better known to my dogs.'

1st Student. To the point, now. Where's Gottlieb, the new-
comer? Oh,—listen, Gottlieb, to what has called down this piece of
310 friendly vengeance on Jules, of which we now assemble to witness
the winding-up. We are all agreed, all in a tale, observe, when Jules
shall burst out on us in a fury by and by: I am spokesman—the verses
that are to undeceive Jules bear my name of Lutwyche—but each
professes himself alike insulted by this strutting stone-squarer, who
315 came alone from Paris to Munich, and thence with a crowd of us to
Venice and Possagno here, but proceeds in a day or two alone
again—oh, alone indubitably!—to Rome and Florence. He, forsooth,
take up his portion with these desolate, brutalized, heartless
bunglers!—so he was heard to call us all: now, is Schramm brutal-
320 ized, I should like to know? Am I heartless?

Gottlieb. Why, somewhat heartless; for, suppose Jules a coxcomb
as much as you choose, still, for this mere coxcombry, you will have
brushed off—what do folks style it?—the bloom of his life. Is it too
late to alter? These love-letters now, you call his—I can't laugh at
325 them.

4th Student. Because you never read the sham letters of our indit-
ing which drew forth these.

Gottlieb. His discovery of the truth will be frightful.

4th Student. That's the joke. But you should have joined us at the
330 beginning: there's no doubt he loves the girl—loves a model he
might hire by the hour!

Gottlieb. See here! "He has been accustomed," he writes, "to have

---

308–9 *1841* Gottlieb? Oh, listen, Gottlieb—What called   311–13 *1841* We are all
in a tale, observe, when Jules bursts out on us by and bye: I shall be spokesman, but each
315 *1841–63* came singly from   *1841* Munich, thence   316–17 *1841* alone,—
oh! alone indubitably—   317–18 *1841* He take   319–20 *1841* bunglers! (Is
Schramm brutalized? Am I heartless?)   321–2 *1841* for, coxcomb as much as you
choose, you will   324 *1841* These letters, now . . . . his. I   330–2 *1841* the
girl. *Gott.* See here:

311 *all in a tale* : we shall all tell the same story. Cf. *Much Ado about Nothing*, IV. ii. 28: 'they
are both in a tale'.

314 *stone-squarer*: the word occurs in I Kgs. 5:18. A stone-cutter, and so a pejorative term
for a sculptor. Canova's father and grandfather had in fact been stone-cutters.

321 *a coxcomb* : W. J. Fox described the youthful Browning as 'just a trifle of a dandy,
addicted to lemon-coloured kid-gloves and such things: quite the "glass of fashion and the
mould of form"': see Maynard, 129.

323 *the bloom of his life* : cf. *Much Ado about Nothing*, v. i. 76.

"Canova's women about him, in stone, and the world's women
"beside him, in flesh; these being as much below, as those above, his
"soul's aspiration: but now he is to have the reality." There you laugh   335
again! I say, you wipe off the very dew of his youth.

    1st Student. Schramm! (Take the pipe out of his mouth, some-
body!) Will Jules lose the bloom of his youth?

    Schramm. Nothing worth keeping is ever lost in this world: look at
a blossom—it drops presently, having done its service and lasted its   340
time; but fruits succeed, and where would be the blossom's place
could it continue? As well affirm that your eye is no longer in your
body, because its earliest favourite, whatever it may have first loved to
look on, is dead and done with—as that any affection is lost to the soul
when its first object, whatever happened first to satisfy it, is super-   345
seded in due course. Keep but ever looking, whether with the body's
eye or the mind's, and you will soon find something to look on! Has a
man done wondering at women?—there follow men, dead and alive,
to wonder at. Has he done wondering at men?—there's God to won-
der at: and the faculty of wonder may be, at the same time, old and   350
tired enough with respect to its first object, and yet young and fresh
sufficiently, so far as concerns its novel one. Thus ...

    1st Student. Put Schramm's pipe into his mouth again! There, you
see! Well, this Jules ... a wretched fribble—oh, I watched his dis-
portings at Possagno, the other day! Canova's gallery—you know: 355

335 *1841* have" ... There *1849* have the real." ... There *1863* have the real." There
336 *1841* again! You wipe   337-8 *1841* Schramm (take .... somebody), will
1863,1865 somebody.)   340-2 *1841* presently and fruits succeed; as well affirm
343-4 *1841* favourite is dead   345-6 *1841* object is superseded   346-7 *1841*
course. Has   348 *1841-63* There   349 *1841-63* There's   350-1 *1841*
time grey enough   351-2 *1841* its last object, and yet green sufficiently
352 *1841* one: thus ...   353 *1841* again—   354 *1841* well   *1849* this—
Jules   355-6 *1841* day! The Model-Gallery—you know: he marches

    333 *Canova's women*: Antonio Canova, who had died in 1822, was the most celebrated of
modern sculptors. Towards the end of his life he had become 'what would now be called the
cult-hero of revolutionary movements that were just beginning to gather force': Licht, p. 24
(see 355 n., below). Browning had been particularly eager to see his work when he first
visited Italy, but told Fanny Haworth that he had been 'disappointed in one thing, Canova'
(*Letters*, p. 2). At this time others were beginning to share this disappointment.
    354 *fribble*: trifler. Under 'Fribble' Johnson quotes *The Spectator* [no. 288]: 'A *fribbler*, is
one who professes rapture for the woman, and dreads her consent.'
    355 *Canova's gallery*: the Gipsoteca (gallery of plaster casts) is a museum annex built in
the garden of the house where Canova was born. 'In it are assembled all the original plasters

there he marches first resolvedly past great works by the dozen
without vouchsafing an eye: all at once he stops full at the *Psiche-
fanciulla*—cannot pass that old acquaintance without a nod of
encouragement—"In your new place, beauty? Then behave yourself
360 as well here as at Munich—I see you!" Next he posts himself deliber-
ately before the unfinished *Pietà* for half an hour without moving,
till up he starts of a sudden, and thrusts his very nose into—I say,
into—the group; by which gesture you are informed that precisely
the sole point he had not fully mastered in Canova's practice was a
365 certain method of using the drill in the articulation of the knee-
joint—and that, likewise, has he mastered at length! Good-bye,
therefore, to poor Canova—whose gallery no longer needs detain his
successor Jules, the predestinated novel thinker in marble!

    5th Student. Tell him about the women: go on to the women!

370   *1st Student.* Why, on that matter he could never be supercilious
enough. How should we be other (he said) than the poor devils you
see, with those debasing habits we cherish? He was not to wallow in
that mire, at least: he would wait, and love only at the proper time,
and meanwhile put up with the *Psiche-fanciulla.* Now, I happened to
375 hear of a young Greek—real Greek—girl at Malamocco; a true

360 *1841* Next posts   363 *1841* which you   364 *1841* in Canova was
366 *1841* that, even, has   367-8 *1841* to Canova—whose gallery no longer contains
Jules, *1849* longer need detain   368 *1841* predestinated thinker   369 *1841*
to the women.   371 *1841* other than   373 *1841* would love at   *375
[reading of *1849*] *1841,1863–89* real Greek girl   375-7 *1841* Malamocco, ...
Alciphron hair like sea-moss—you know! White

and all the terra-cotta sketches that were in Canova's possession at the time of his death':
Canova, photographs by David Finn, text by Fred Licht (Abbeville Press, NY, 1983), p. 268.
They were moved to Possagno from Rome by Canova's half-brother in 1836. The 'original
lighting and arrangement of sculptures in Canova's studio [were] closely reproduced': ibid.
226. Before his visit Browning probably consulted *The Works of Antonio Canova*, with
engravings by Henry Moses and a biographical memoir by Count Cicognara (2 vols., 1824).

    361 *the unfinished Pietà*: the stone version of this mourning female figure was left un-
finished at Canova's death, 'and is probably the work of his disciples': Licht, p. 95.

    364–5 *a certain method of using the drill*: Canova left less to his assistants than many sculp-
tors. In particular, 'His work on the tomb of Clement XIV was so intense and so arduous
that Canova suffered a severe deformation of the ribs due to his constant use of the running
drill, which had to be pressed full force against the stone with his chest': Licht, p. 20.

    374 *the Psiche-fanciulla*: the celebrated statue of Psyche as a young girl holding a butterfly
(in Greek ψυχή means both 'soul' and 'butterfly'). The original version was in a private col-
lection in England, but Canova executed a second, which came into the possession of the
Queen of Bavaria. This explains the reference to Munich.

    375 *Malamocco*: an island near Venice.

Islander, do you see, with Alciphron's "hair like sea-moss"—
Schramm knows!—white and quiet as an apparition, and fourteen
years old at farthest,—a daughter of Natalia, so she swears—that hag
Natalia, who helps us to models at three *lire* an hour. We selected
this girl for the heroine of our jest. So first, Jules received a scented 380
letter—somebody had seen his Tydeus at the Academy, and my pic-
ture was nothing to it: a profound admirer bade him persevere—
would make herself known to him ere long. (Paolina, my little
friend of the *Fenice*, transcribes divinely.) And in due time, the
mysterious correspondent gave certain hints of her peculiar 385
charms—the pale cheeks, the black hair—whatever, in short, had
struck us in our Malamocco model: we retained her name, too—
Phene, which is, by interpretation, sea-eagle. Now, think of Jules
finding himself distinguished from the herd of us by such a
creature! In his very first answer he proposed marrying his moni- 390
tress: and fancy us over these letters, two, three times a day, to
receive and despatch! I concocted the main of it: relations were in
the way—secrecy must be observed—in fine, would he wed her on
trust, and only speak to her when they were indissolubly united?
St—st—Here they come!   395

    6th Student. Both of them! Heaven's love, speak softly, speak
within yourselves!

378 *1841* farthest; daughter, so she swears, of that hag   379-80 *1841* hour. So first
382 *1841* to it—bade   384-8 *1841* friend, transcribes divinely.) Now think
393 *1841* observed—would   395-6 *1841* St—St! 6 *Stu.* Both   396 *1841*
softly!

    376 *"hair like sea-moss"*: 'He is beautiful, mother, beautiful, the sweetest thing, and his locks
are curlier than sea-moss': Alciphron, Letter 11 (iii. 1), in *The Letters of Alciphron, Aelian and
Philostratus*, tr. A. R. Benner and F. H. Fobes (Loeb, 1962). We owe this reference to Hood.
    378 *a daughter of Natalia*: Natalia is not Phene's mother. Cf. Introduction, 177-8, and
II. 248-9.
    381 *Tydeus*: a valiant but savage warrior mentioned in the *Iliad*, v. 801.
    the Academy: the Venetian Accademia, an important gallery to which the young
Canova had submitted a piece.
    384 *the Fenice*: the most fashionable theatre in Venice for opera and drama, frequented
by Byron, who considered it much superior to the theatres of London. See several refer-
ences in his *Letters and Journals*.
    388 *Phene . . . sea-eagle*: in the *Odyssey* (iii. 372) Athene, patroness of Jules's art, trans-
figures herself into a φήνη.
    390-1 *he proposed marrying his monitress*: a curious anticipation of Browning's own court-
ship, though in that the first letter was written by himself.

5th Student. Look at the bridegroom! Half his hair in storm and half in calm,—patted down over the left temple,—like a frothy cup
400 one blows on to cool it: and the same old blouse that he murders the marble in.

2nd Student. Not a rich vest like yours, Hannibal Scratchy!—rich, that your face may the better set it off.

6th Student. And the bride! Yes, sure enough, our Phene! Should
405 you have known her in her clothes? How magnificently pale!

Gottlieb. She does not also take it for earnest, I hope?

1st Student. Oh, Natalia's concern, that is! We settle with Natalia.

6th Student. She does not speak—has evidently let out no word. The only thing is, will she equally remember the rest of her lesson,
410 and repeat correctly all those verses which are to break the secret to Jules?

Gottlieb. How he gazes on her! Pity—pity!

1st Student. They go in: now, silence! You three,—not nearer the window, mind, than that pomegranate: just where the little girl,
415 who a few minutes ago passed us singing, is seated!

398 *1841* Bridegroom—half   400 *1849,1863* it!   400-1 *1841* blouse he....
in! *1849, 1863* in!   402 *1841* Scratchy, rich   403 *1849* off!   404-
5 *1841* And the bride—and the bride—how magnificently pale!   407 *1841* is; we
408-13 *1841* word. *Gott.* How he gazes on her! 1 *Stu.* They .... silence!   413-
15 *1841* [omits 'You three,—.... seated!']

402 *Hannibal Scratchy*: Annibale Caracci (1560-1609), a painter best known for the Far-
nese Gallery in Rome.

PART II

NOON.

SCENE.—*Over Orcana. The house of* JULES, *who crosses its threshold with* PHENE: *she is silent, on which* JULES *begins—*

Do not die, Phene! I am yours now, you
Are mine now; let fate reach me how she likes,
If you'll not die: so, never die! Sit here—
My work-room's single seat. I over-lean
This length of hair and lustrous front; they turn   5
Like an entire flower upward: eyes, lips, last
Your chin—no, last your throat turns; 't is their scent
Pulls down my face upon you. Nay, look ever
This one way till I change, grow you—I could
Change into you, beloved!

                You by me,   10
And I by you; this is your hand in mine,
And side by side we sit: all's true. Thank God!
I have spoken: speak you!

                O my life to come!
My Tydeus must be carved that's there in clay;
Yet how be carved, with you about the room?   15
Where must I place you? When I think that once
This room-full of rough block-work seemed my heaven
Without you! Shall I ever work again,
Get fairly into my old ways again,
Bid each conception stand while, trait by trait,   20

1 *1841,1849* Phene—   4 *1841* I do lean over   8 *1849, 1863* you!
9 *1841* That one   10 *1841* beloved! Thou by   11 *1841* by thee—this is thy
hand   13 *1841* speak thou!—O   14 *1841* clay,   15 *1841* And how
. . . . the chamber? *1849, 1863* the chamber?

s.d. *Orcana*: see Introduction, 131 n.
  5 *This length of hair*: cf. *Pauline*, 1 ff.
   lustrous front: cf. Keats, 'Ode to a Nightingale', 29.
  14 *My Tydeus*: see I. 381 n.
  17 *block-work*: to block out means 'To sketch out, mark out roughly': OED.

My hand transfers its lineaments to stone?
Will my mere fancies live near you, their truth—
The live truth, passing and repassing me,
Sitting beside me?
                    Now speak!
                              Only first,
See, all your letters! Was't not well contrived?   25
Their hiding-place is Psyche's robe; she keeps
Your letters next her skin: which drops out foremost?
Ah,—this that swam down like a first moonbeam
Into my world!
               Again those eyes complete
Their melancholy survey, sweet and slow,   30
Of all my room holds; to return and rest
On me, with pity, yet some wonder too:
As if God bade some spirit plague a world,
And this were the one moment of surprise
And sorrow while she took her station, pausing   35
O'er what she sees, finds good, and must destroy!
What gaze you at? Those? Books, I told you of;
Let your first word to me rejoice them, too:
This minion, a Coluthus, writ in red
Bistre and azure by Bessarion's scribe—   40
Read this line . . . no, shame—Homer's be the Greek
First breathed me from the lips of my Greek girl!
This Odyssey in coarse black vivid type
With faded yellow blossoms 'twixt page and page,

---

22 *1841* Will they, my fancies,   *1841-63* my truth—   25 *1841* | Your letters to
me—was't   26 *1841* A hiding-place in Psyche's robe—there lie   27 *1841*
Next to her skin your letters: which comes foremost?   28 *1841* Good—this
29-37 *1841* world. Those? Books I told you of.   39 *1841* minion of Coluthus,
42 {no equivalent in *1841*}   43 *1841-63* My Odyssey   44 *1841* page;

   26 *Psyche's robe*: see I. 357—60. The drapery of the work was much admired.
   39 *minion*: 'A favourite; a darling': Johnson.
      Coluthus: 'a native of Lycopolis in Egypt, who wrote a short poem on the rape of
Helen, in imitation of Homer . . . The composition remained long unknown, till it was dis-
covered . . . in the 15th century, by the learned cardinal Bessarion': Lemprière.
   40 *bistre*: a yellowish-brown to dark-brown colour.

To mark great places with due gratitude;   45
"He said, and on Antinous directed
"A bitter shaft" . . . a flower blots out the rest!
Again upon your search? My statues, then!
—Ah, do not mind that—better that will look
When cast in bronze—an Almaign Kaiser, that,   50
Swart-green and gold, with truncheon based on hip.
This, rather, turn to! What, unrecognized?
I thought you would have seen that here you sit
As I imagined you,—Hippolyta,
Naked upon her bright Numidian horse.   55
Recall you this then? "Carve in bold relief"—
So you commanded—"carve, against I come,
"A Greek, in Athens, as our fashion was,
"Feasting, bay-filleted and thunder-free,
"Who rises 'neath the lifted myrtle-branch.   60
"'Praise those who slew Hipparchus!' cry the guests,

46 {roman type in *1841*}   47 *1841* shaft"—then blots a flower the rest!
48 {no equivalent in *1841*}   52 *1841* to . . but a check already—   53 *1841* Or
you had recognized that   55 *1841-65* horse!   56 *1841* —Forget you . . . .
"carve   57 *1841* you command me—"carve   58-9 *1841* A Greek, bay-
filleted and thunder-free,   59 *1849* bay-filletted   60 *1841* Rising beneath
. . . . branch, *1849-65* branch: 61 *1841* Whose turn arrives to praise Harmodius."—
Praise him! *1849-65* Hipparchus,'   61-3 {direct speech in italics in *1849-65*}

46 "He said: Odyssey, xxii. 10.   50 Almaign: German.
51 truncheon: a short staff, in token of office, as in Sordello, i. 289.
54 Hippolyta: 'called also Antiope, a queen of the Amazons, given in marriage to
Theseus by Hercules, who had conquered her, and taken away her girdle': Lemprière.
55 Numidian: the Numidians, from Algiers and neighbouring regions of inland Africa,
were famous for their horses and horsemanship: they 'rode without saddles or bridles':
Lemprière.
56 "Carve in bold relief: one of the letters tells Jules to carve a statue representing a group
of Greeks, led by 'The Praiser', toasting Harmodius and Aristogiton. Cf. 61, below.
59 bay-filleted and thunder-free: W. P. Ker pointed out the relevance of Childe Harold's Pil-
grimage, iv. 364-5: '. . . the true laurel-wreath which Glory weaves / Is of the tree no bolt of
thunder cleaves': NQ, Series Ten (1904), i. 504. Hobhouse's note on the passage mentions
that 'Tiberius never failed to wear a wreath of laurel when the sky threatened a thunder-
storm', as a protection.
61 'Praise those who slew Hipparchus!': Hipparchus was, with his brother Hippias, a tyrant
of Athens. 'The seduction of a sister of Harmodius raised him many enemies, and he was at
last assassinated by a desperate band of conspirators, with Harmodius and Aristogiton at
their head': Lemprière. Many drinking-songs commemorated the event. See, e.g., that
quoted by Athenæus in The Deipnosophists, tr. C. B. Gulick (Loeb ed., 7 vols.), vii (1941,

"'While o'er thy head the singer's myrtle waves
"'As erst above our champion: stand up, all!'"
See, I have laboured to express your thought.
Quite round, a cluster of mere hands and arms,   65
(Thrust in all senses, all ways, from all sides,
Only consenting at the branch's end
They strain toward) serves for frame to a sole face,
The Praiser's, in the centre: who with eyes
Sightless, so bend they back to light inside   70
His brain where visionary forms throng up,
Sings, minding not that palpitating arch
Of hands and arms, nor the quick drip of wine
From the drenched leaves o'erhead, nor crowns cast off,
Violet and parsley crowns to trample on—   75
Sings, pausing as the patron-ghosts approve,
Devoutly their unconquerable hymn.
But you must say a "well" to that—say "well!"
Because you gaze—am I fantastic, sweet?
Gaze like my very life's-stuff, marble—marbly   80
Even to the silence! Why, before I found
The real flesh Phene, I inured myself
To see, throughout all nature, varied stuff
For better nature's birth by means of art:

62-4 {no equivalent in *1841*}   63 *1849, 1863* our champions': stand   64 *1849-*
65 thought!   66 *1841* Thrust   67 *1841,1849* branches'   68 *1841*
strain towards, serves   69 *1841* (Place your own face)—the Praiser's, who with eyes
71a *1841* (Gaze—I am your Harmodius dead and gone,)   72 *1841* minding nor the
palpitating   74 *1841* nor who cast   75 *1841* Their violet crowns for him to
trample on—   77 *1849, 1863* hymn!   78 *1841* say "well"   81 *1841*
silence—and before   84 *1863,1865* art.

repr. 1961), 222-5: 'In a myrtle-branch I will carry my sword, as did Harmodius and
Aristogiton, when they slew the tyrant and made Athens a city of equal rights'. See our Vol.
II, p. 529, for another quotation from the same work. There is a reference to a youth
waiting to kill a tyrant in *Paracelsus*, ii. 427-30.

    66 *all senses*: all directions. Cf. French *sens*.   67 *consenting*: coming together.
    71 *visionary forms*: those of the 'patron-ghosts' (76), i.e. the friends of Liberty.
    75 *parsley crowns*: 'the leaves of a species of parsley (*Apium graveolens*, our celery), much
used by the ancients in garlands on account of their strong fragrance, especially in
drinking-bouts': Porter and Clarke.
    84 *For better nature's birth*: Aristotelian: 'Art, therefore, in imitating the universal imitates
the ideal': S. H. Butcher, *Aristotle's Theory of Poetry and Fine Art* (2nd ed., 1898), p. 152.

With me, each substance tended to one form 85
Of beauty—to the human archetype.
On every side occurred suggestive germs
Of that—the tree, the flower—or take the fruit,—
Some rosy shape, continuing the peach,
Curved beewise o'er its bough; as rosy limbs, 90
Depending, nestled in the leaves; and just
From a cleft rose-peach the whole Dryad sprang.
But of the stuffs one can be master of,
How I divined their capabilities!
From the soft-rinded smoothening facile chalk 95
That yields your outline to the air's embrace,
Half-softened by a halo's pearly gloom;
Down to the crisp imperious steel, so sure
To cut its one confided thought clean out
Of all the world. But marble!—'neath my tools 100
More pliable than jelly—as it were
Some clear primordial creature dug from depths
In the earth's heart, where itself breeds itself,
And whence all baser substance may be worked;
Refine it off to air, you may,—condense it 105
Down to the diamond;—is not metal there,
When o'er the sudden speck my chisel trips?
—Not flesh, as flake off flake I scale, approach,
Lay bare those bluish veins of blood asleep?
Lurks flame in no strange windings where, surprised 110
By the swift implement sent home at once,
Flushes and glowings radiate and hover
About its track?
          Phene? what—why is this?

---

87 *1841* And every   88 *1841* flower—why, take   90 *1841* bough,
92 *1841* Dryad sprung! *1849* sprang!   94 *1841* capabilities   97 {no equiva-
lent in *1841*}   100 *1841,1849* world: but   102 *1841* from deep
107 *1841–63* sudden specks my   109 *1841* those bluish veins

    87 *suggestive germs*: cf. Wordsworth, *The Excursion*, iv. 861 ff.
    90 *beewise*: not in OED.   92 *Dryad*: wood-nymph.
    95 *smoothening*: OED notes that the word was 'In frequent use *c* 1820–30, esp. by
Landor'.

That whitening cheek, those still dilating eyes!
Ah, you will die—I knew that you would die!   115

    PHENE *begins, on his having long remained silent.*

Now the end's coming; to be sure, it must
Have ended sometime! Tush, why need I speak
Their foolish speech? I cannot bring to mind
One half of it, beside; and do not care
For old Natalia now, nor any of them.   120
Oh, you—what are you?—if I do not try
To say the words Natalia made me learn,
To please your friends,—it is to keep myself
Where your voice lifted me, by letting that
Proceed: but can it? Even you, perhaps,   125
Cannot take up, now you have once let fall,
The music's life, and me along with that—
No, or you would! We'll stay, then, as we are:
Above the world.
              You creature with the eyes!
If I could look for ever up to them,   130
As now you let me,—I believe, all sin,
All memory of wrong done, suffering borne,
Would drop down, low and lower, to the earth
Whence all that's low comes, and there touch and stay
—Never to overtake the rest of me,   135
All that, unspotted, reaches up to you,
Drawn by those eyes! What rises is myself,
Not me the shame and suffering; but they sink,
Are left, I rise above them. Keep me so,
Above the world!
           But you sink, for your eyes   140

114 (no equivalent in *1841*)   117 *1841* Tush—I will not speak   118 *1841*
speech—   119 *1841* Half—so the whole were best unsaid—what care *1849, 1863* it,
besides; and   120 *1841* I for Natalia now, or all of them?   121 *1841* you?—I
do not attempt   122 *1841* Natalia bade me   123 *1841* friends, that I may
keep   124 *1841* letting you *1849, 1863* letting it   125 *1841* can you?—even
127 *1841* with it?   128 *1841* would .. we'll .... are *1849* are   129-39 (no
equivalent in *1841*)   132 *1849, 1863* done or suffering   137 *1849, 1863* Not
so   140 *1841* world—Now you sink—

Are altering—altered! Stay —"I love you, love" . . .
I could prevent it if I understood
More of your words to me: was't in the tone
Or the words, your power?
                        Or stay—I will repeat
Their speech, if that contents you! Only change   145
No more, and I shall find it presently
Far back here, in the brain yourself filled up.
Natalia threatened me that harm should follow
Unless I spoke their lesson to the end,
But harm to me, I thought she meant, not you.   150
Your friends,—Natalia said they were your friends
And meant you well,—because, I doubted it,
Observing (what was very strange to see)
On every face, so different in all else,
The same smile girls like me are used to bear,   155
But never men, men cannot stoop so low;
Yet your friends, speaking of you, used that smile,
That hateful smirk of boundless self-conceit
Which seems to take possession of the world
And make of God a tame confederate,   160
Purveyor to their appetites . . . you know!
But still Natalia said they were your friends,
And they assented though they smiled the more,
And all came round me,—that thin Englishman
With light lank hair seemed leader of the rest;   165
He held a paper—"What we want," said he,
Ending some explanation to his friends—
"Is something slow, involved and mystical,

141 *1841* Are altered . . altering—stay—"I love you, love you,"— *1849, 1863* you, love you"
. . .   *142 {reading of *1841,1849*} *1863-89* understood: 144 *1841,1849* Of
the voice, your power? Stay, stay, I   145 *1841* that affects you! only
147 *1841* up: 148 *1841* Natalia said (like Lutwyche) harm would follow *1849,*
1863 harm would follow   150 *1841* thought, not you: and so   151-76 {no
equivalent in *1841*}   155 *1849, 1863* like us are   159 *1849, 1863* of this world
160 *1849, 1863* God their tame   162 *1849, 1863* But no—Natalia *1865* But no:
Natalia   163 *1849-65* assented while they

   151 *Your friends*: note the addition of ll. 151-76, to clarify matters for the reader.

"To hold Jules long in doubt, yet take his taste
"And lure him on until, at innermost   170
"Where he seeks sweetness' soul, he may find—this!
"—As in the apple's core, the noisome fly:
"For insects on the rind are seen at once,
"And brushed aside as soon, but this is found
"Only when on the lips or loathing tongue."   175
And so he read what I have got by heart:
I'll speak it,—"Do not die, love! I am yours."
No—is not that, or like that, part of words
Yourself began by speaking? Strange to lose
What cost such pains to learn! Is this more right?   180

I am a painter who cannot paint;
In my life, a devil rather than saint;
In my brain, as poor a creature too:
No end to all I cannot do!
Yet do one thing at least I can—   185
Love a man or hate a man
Supremely: thus my lore began.
Through the Valley of Love I went,
In the lovingest spot to abide,
And just on the verge where I pitched my tent,   190
I found Hate dwelling beside.
(Let the Bridegroom ask what the painter meant,
Of his Bride, of the peerless Bride!)
And further, I traversed Hate's grove,
In the hatefullest nook to dwell;   195
But lo, where I flung myself prone, couched Love

170 *1849, 1863* on, so that, at   177 *1841* die, Phene, I am yours" .. *1849–68* yours"
. . .   178 *1841* Stop—is .... of what *1849, 1863* Stop—is   179 *1841* You
spoke? 'Tis not my fault—that I should lose   180 *1841* pains acquiring! is this right?
181–4 (no equivalent in *1841*)   182 *1849–68* saint,   185 *1841* The Bard said,
do one thing I can—   185–99 (roman type in *1841*)   186 *1841* man and hate
187 *1849 my love began.*   189 *1841* In its lovingest .... abide; *1849, 1863 In its loving-*
est   191 *1841* Dwelt Hate beside—   192 *1841* (And the bridegroom asked
what the bard's smile meant   193 *1841* Of his bride.)| 194 *1841* Next Hate
I traversed, the Grove,   195 *1841–63* in its hatefullest (in italics in
1849,1863)   196 *1841* And lo,

172 *noisome* : 'Noxious; . . . unwholesome': Johnson.
181 *I* : i.e. Lutwyche.   187 *Lore* : learning, education.

Where the shadow threefold fell.
(The meaning—those black bride's-eyes above,
Not a painter's lip should tell!)

"And here," said he, "Jules probably will ask,   200
"'You have black eyes, Love,—you are, sure enough,
"'My peerless bride,—then do you tell indeed
"'What needs some explanation! What means this?'"
—And I am to go on, without a word—

> *So, I grew wise in Love and Hate,*   205
> *From simple that I was of late.*
> *Once, when I loved, I would enlace*
> *Breast, eyelids, hands, feet, form and face*
> *Of her I loved, in one embrace—*
> *As if by mere love I could love immensely!*   210
> *Once, when I hated, I would plunge*
> *My sword, and wipe with the first lunge*
> *My foe's whole life out like a sponge—*
> *As if by mere hate I could hate intensely!*
> *But now I am wiser, know better the fashion*   215
> *How passion seeks aid from its opposite passion:*
> *And if I see cause to love more, hate more*
> *Than ever man loved, ever hated before—*
> *And seek in the Valley of Love,*
> *The nest, or the nook in Hate's Grove,*   220

197 *1841* | Next cell. | *1849, 1863 the deepest shadow fell.*   198-9 *1841* (For not I,
said the bard, but those black bride's eyes above | Should tell!)   199 *1849, 1863 Not
the painter's*   200 *1841* (Then Lutwyche said you probably would ask,   201-
3 (in italics with double quotation marks in *1849-65*)   202 *1841* My beautiful
bride—do you, as he sings, tell *1849, 1863* bride,—so do   203 *1841* some exposition—
what is this?" *1849-65 explanation*—   204 *1841* word,)   205-6 (no equivalent
in *1841*)   205 *1849, 1863 grew wiser in*   207-33 (roman type in *1841*)
207 *1849-68 For once,*   210 (no equivalent in *1841*)   211 *1841-68 And when*
213 *1841, 1863* a spunge—   214-16 (no equivalent in *1841*)   216 *1849 pas-
sion,*   217 *1841* —But if I would love and hate more *1849, 1863 more, or hate*
218 *1841* man hated or loved before— *1849-65 That ever*   219 *1841* Would seek
220 *1841* The spot, or in Hatred's grove *1849, 1863 The spot, or the spot in*

197 *Where the shadow threefold fell*: a suggestion of 'the eternal triangle'.
216 *How passion seeks aid*: a variant on the theme of Catullus, lxxxv, 'Odi et amo': 'I hate
and love. Why I do so, perhaps you ask. I know not, but I feel it, and I am in torment.'

Where my soul may surely reach
The essence, nought less, of each,
The Hate of all Hates, the Love
Of all Loves, in the Valley or Grove,—
I find them the very warders   225
Each of the other's borders.

When I love most, Love is disguised
In Hate; and when Hate is surprised
In Love, then I hate most: ask
How Love smiles through Hate's iron casque,   230
Hate grins through Love's rose-braided mask,—
And how, having hated thee,
I sought long and painfully
To reach thy heart, nor prick
The skin but pierce to the quick—   235
Ask this, my Jules, and be answered straight
By thy bride—how the painter Lutwyche can hate!

JULES *interposes.*

Lutwyche! Who else? But all of them, no doubt,
Hated me: they at Venice—presently
Their turn, however! You I shall not meet: 240
If I dreamed, saying this would wake me.
                                          Keep
What's here, the gold—we cannot meet again,

221 *1841* The spot where my soul may reach *1849, 1863 may the sureliest reach*   222a-f
1841 (Here he said, if you interrupted me | With, "There must be some error,—who induced
you | To speak this jargon?"—I was to reply | Simply—"Await till . . . until . ." I must say | Last
rhyme again—) | . . The essence, nought less, of each—   223 *1841-63* Hates, or the (in
italics in *1849,1863*   224 *1841* in its glen or its grove, *1849, 1863 in its*
Valley   227 *1841* So most I love when Love's disguised *1849, 1863 I love most, when*
Love   228 *1841* In Hate's garb—'tis when Hate's surprised   229 *1841* In
Love's weed that I   230 *1841* How Love can smile thro' Hate's barred iron casque,
231 *1841* Hate grin thro'   231a-c *1841* Of thy bride, Giulio! (Then you, "Oh, not
mine— | Preserve the real name of the foolish song!" | But I must answer, "Giulio—Jules—'tis
Jules!)   232 *1841* Thus, I, Jules, hating thee   233 *1841* Sought long and pain-
fully...   234-7 {no equivalent in *1841*}   234 *1849, 1863 To wound thee, and not*
prick   238 *1841,1849* Lutwyche—who   239 *1841*   me—them   at
240 *1841* For them, however!   241 *1841* saying that would   *1849-65* me!
242 *1841* here—this too—we *1849, 1863* here, this gold—

230 *casque* : a helmet which covers part of the face.

Consider! and the money was but meant
For two years' travel, which is over now,
All chance or hope or care or need of it.   245
This—and what comes from selling these, my casts
And books and medals, except . . . let them go
Together, so the produce keeps you safe
Out of Natalia's clutches! If by chance
(For all's chance here) I should survive the gang   250
At Venice, root out all fifteen of them,
We might meet somewhere, since the world is wide.

                [From without is heard the voice of PIPPA, *singing—*

    Give her but a least excuse to love me!
    When—where—
    How—can this arm establish her above me,   255
    If fortune fixed her as my lady there,
    There already, to eternally reprove me?
        ("Hist!"—said Kate the Queen;
        But "Oh!"—cried the maiden, binding her tresses,
        "'T is only a page that carols unseen,   260
        "Crumbling your hounds their messes!")

    Is she wronged?—To the rescue of her honour,
    My heart!
    Is she poor?—What costs it to be styled a donor?
    Merely an earth to cleave, a sea to part.   265
    But that fortune should have thrust all this upon her!
        ("Nay, list!"—bade Kate the Queen;
        And still cried the maiden, binding her tresses,

---

243 *1841-65* Consider—   245 *1841-63* it!   s. d., 253 *1841* †[*Without*]† Give
253-7, 262-6 {roman type in *1841*; refrain in italics; stanzas numbered 1. and 2.}
256 *1841* fixed my lady   258 *1841* (Hist, *1849-65* ("Hist"—   259 {no equi-
valent in *1841*} *1849-68* "Oh—"   260 *1841* —Only a   261 *1841* messes!)
262 *1841* She's wronged?—   264 *1841* She's poor?—   265 *1841* An earth's to
cleave, a sea's to part! *1849, 1863* an earth's to . . . . a sea's to   267 *1841* (Nay, list, *1849-*
65 list,"—   268 {no equivalent in *1841*}

   258 *Kate the Queen* : Caterina Cornaro (1454–1510), Queen of Cyprus, who was forced
to abdicate and to return to Venice in 1489. She was a beautiful woman, loved by the
people. The castle and town of Asolo were conferred on her for life, and there she sur-
rounded herself with a brilliant court.   261 *messes* : portions of food.

> "'T is only a page that carols unseen,
> "Fitting your hawks their jesses!")   270
>
> [PIPPA passes.

JULES *resumes.*

What name was that the little girl sang forth?
Kate? The Cornaro, doubtless, who renounced
The crown of Cyprus to be lady here
At Asolo, where still her memory stays,
And peasants sing how once a certain page   275
Pined for the grace of her so far above
His power of doing good to, "Kate the Queen—
"She never could be wronged, be poor," he sighed,
"Need him to help her!"
                                   Yes, a bitter thing
To see our lady above all need of us;   280
Yet so we look ere we will love; not I,
But the world looks so. If whoever loves
Must be, in some sort, god or worshipper,
The blessing or the blest one, queen or page,
Why should we always choose the page's part?   285
Here is a woman with utter need of me,—
I find myself queen here, it seems!
                                   How strange!
Look at the woman here with the new soul,
Like my own Psyche,—fresh upon her lips
Alit, the visionary butterfly,   290

---

269 *1841 Only a*   270 *1841 jesses!*)— [*1841* omits 'JULES resumes.']   271 {no
equivalent in *1841*}   272 *1841 Kate? Queen Cornaro*   273 *1841 |Cyprus to
live and die the lady here*   274 *1841 At Asolo—and whosoever loves   1849, 1863*
still the peasants keep   275 *1849, 1863 Her memory; and songs tell how many a
page*   275–82 {no equivalent in *1841*}   276 *1849–65 of one so*
277 *1849, 1863 to, as a queen— 1865 to, "She, the queen—*   279 *1849, 1863 "For
him*   285–6 {no equivalent in *1841*}   288–97 {no equivalent in *1841*}
289 *1849, 1863 own Psyche's,—fresh*

  269 *a page*: cf. *Paracelsus*, i. 816–18.
  270 *jesses*: 'Short straps of leather tied about the legs of a hawk, with which she is held on
the fist': Johnson.
  287 *I find myself queen here*: he is in the higher position, Phene in the humbler.
  290 *the visionary butterfly*: cf. I. 374 n., above.

Waiting my word to enter and make bright,
Or flutter off and leave all blank as first.
This body had no soul before, but slept
Or stirred, was beauteous or ungainly, free
From taint or foul with stain, as outward things   295
Fastened their image on its passiveness:
Now, it will wake, feel, live—or die again!
Shall to produce form out of unshaped stuff
Be Art—and further, to evoke a soul
From form be nothing? This new soul is mine!   300

Now, to kill Lutwyche, what would that do?—save
A wretched dauber, men will hoot to death
Without me, from their hooting. Oh, to hear
God's voice plain as I heard it first, before
They broke in with their laughter! I heard them   305
Henceforth, not God.
                              To Ancona—Greece—some isle!
I wanted silence only; there is clay
Everywhere. One may do whate'er one likes
In Art: the only thing is, to make sure
That one does like it—which takes pains to know.   310
    Scatter all this, my Phene—this mad dream!
Who, what is Lutwyche, what Natalia's friends,
What the whole world except our love—my own,
Own Phene? But I told you, did I not,
Ere night we travel for your land—some isle   315
With the sea's silence on it? Stand aside—
I do but break these paltry models up

---

298 *1841* of shapelessness   300 *1841* mine—   303-6 *1841* Without me. To
Ancona—Greece—some isle!   *1849-65* their laughter—Oh,   308 *1841,1849*
Every where.   309 *1841* to be sure   312 *1841* what Natalia—|

294-5 *free / From taint*: cf. Keats, *The Eve of St. Agnes*, 225.
298 *to produce form*: referring to the Scholastic notion (derived from Aristotle) that a por-
tion of matter becomes a thing by having a particular form or shape.
305 *They broke in with their laughter*: cf. 'Pictor Ignotus', 41 ff.
306 *Ancona*: a town on the east coast of Italy which is the principal port for Greece.

To begin Art afresh. Meet Lutwyche, I—
And save him from my statue meeting him?
Some unsuspected isle in the far seas!   320
Like a god going through his world, there stands
One mountain for a moment in the dusk,
Whole brotherhoods of cedars on its brow:
And you are ever by me while I gaze
—Are in my arms as now—as now—as now!   325
Some unsuspected isle in the far seas!
Some unsuspected isle in far-off seas!

Talk by the way, while PIPPA *is passing from Orcana to the Turret. Two or three of the Austrian Police loitering with* BLUPHOCKS, *an English vagabond, just in view of the Turret.*

*Bluphocks.** So, that is your Pippa, the little girl who passed us singing? Well, your Bishop's Intendant's money shall be honestly
330 earned:—now, don't make me that sour face because I bring the

---

* "He maketh his sun to rise on the evil and on the good, and sendeth rain on the just and on the unjust."

318 *1841-63* afresh. Shall I meet Lutwyche, | 319 *1841* my statue's meeting
320 *1888,1889* (some copies) Some unspected isle   321 *1841* world, I trace
324 *1841* I trace   s.d. *1841 way in the mean time. Two*   328-33 (no equivalent
in *1841*; Bluphocks's speech begins '*Oh! were but*')

318 *Meet Lutwyche*: i.e. in a duel.
327 *Some unsuspected isle*: see Shelley's Advertisement to *Epipsychidion*, which begins: 'The Writer of the following lines died at Florence, as he was preparing for a voyage to one of the wildest of the Sporades.' On 28 March 1842 EBB heard from John Kenyon that Browning desired '(if any loosening of family ties sh.d give him to himself) to go to a Greek island & live & die in the sunshine': Raymond and Sullivan, i. 377.
It is curious that DeVane does not mention the Jules/Phene episode in his essay 'The Virgin and the Dragon' (1947: repr. in Drew).
s.d. *the Austrian Police*: the Congress of Vienna (which in general revived the pre-Napoleonic fragmentation of Italy) had restored in Venetia the Austrian rule to which Bonaparte, having extinguished the Republic, had assigned it in 1797 and from which he had reclaimed it eight years later for incorporation into the Kingdom of Italy. Browning deeply sympathized with those who were fighting for Italian independence: see, e.g., 'The Italian in England'.
328 *Bluphocks*: see I. 295 n. Browning's footnote quotes Matt. 5:45.
So, that is your Pippa: note the addition of ll. 328-33, which clarify the action.
329 *your Bishop's Intendant's money*: an Intendant was a high administrative official. The Bishop's Intendant appears in Part IV.

Bishop's name into the business; we know he can have nothing to do
with such horrors: we know that he is a saint and all that a bishop
should be, who is a great man beside. *Oh were but every worm a maggot,*
Every fly a grig, Every bough a Christmas faggot, Every tune a jig! In fact, I
have abjured all religions; but the last I inclined to, was the 335
Armenian: for I have travelled, do you see, and at Koenigsberg,
Prussia Improper (so styled because there's a sort of bleak hungry
sun there), you might remark over a venerable house-porch, a
certain Chaldee inscription; and brief as it is, a mere glance at it used
absolutely to change the mood of every bearded passenger. In they 340
turned, one and all; the young and lightsome, with no irreverent
pause, the aged and decrepit, with a sensible alacrity: 't was the
Grand Rabbi's abode, in short. Struck with curiosity, I lost no time
in learning Syriac—(these are vowels, you dogs,—follow my stick's
end in the mud—*Celarent, Darii, Ferio!*) and one morning presented 345
myself, spelling-book in hand, a, b, c,—I picked it out letter by
letter, and what was the purport of this miraculous posy? Some
cherished legend of the past, you'll say—*"How Moses hocus-pocussed*
Egypt's land with fly and locust,"—or, *"How to Jonah sounded harshish,*
Get thee up and go to Tarshish,"—or, *"How the angel meeting Balaam,* 350
Straight his ass returned a salaam," In no wise! *"Shackabrack—Boach—*
somebody or other—Isaach, Re-cei-ver, Pur-cha-ser and Ex-chan-ger of—

333 *1849, 1863* man besides. Oh! *1841* | Oh! *1865* Oh!   341 *1841,1849* all,
343 *1841* short. I lost   344 Syriac—(vowels,   346–7 *1841* c,—what was
348 *1841-65 hocus-pocust*   351 *1841* salaam,"—in *1849* salaam;"—in

333 *Oh were*: i.e. all is not as it should be.

334 *a grig*: a small creature, sometimes taken to be a grasshopper.

335-6 *the Armenian*: the Armenian Church is one of the oriental Christian communities.

336 *Koenigsberg*: then the capital of East Prussia, which was called Prussia Proper.

339 *Chaldee*: 'The language of the Chaldeans: also the biblical "Syriac" or Aramaic': OED.

345 *Celarent, Darii, Ferio!*: in his pretence of learning, Bluphocks is quoting part of a mnemonic (he omits the first word, 'Barbara') used for teaching syllogistic theory. He may have come on it in any book on logic, e.g. Richard Whately's *Elements of Logic*, 1826. Browning's father seems to have known Whately: see *Collections*, A 680.

347 *posy*: motto, inscription.

348 *"How Moses*: Exod. 10:12 ff. tells how Moses, at the commandment of the Lord, devastated Egypt with a plague of locusts: 'hocus-pocused': tricked, transformed as if by juggling.

349 *"How to Jonah*: Bluphocks is confused: Jonah 1:2-3 describes how the Lord ordered Jonah to go to Nineveh; but he disobediently went to Joppa, and set sail for Tarshish.   350 *"How the angel*: Numb. 22:22 ff.

Stolen Goods"! So, talk to me of the religion of a bishop! I have
renounced all bishops save Bishop Beveridge—mean to live so—
355 and die—*As some Greek dog-sage, dead and merry, Hellward bound in
Charon's wherry, With food for both worlds, under and upper, Lupine-seed
and Hecate's supper, And never an obolus* . . . (Though thanks to you,
or this Intendant through you, or this Bishop through his Intend-
ant—I possess a burning pocketful of *zwanzigers*) . . . *To pay the*
360 *Stygian Ferry!*

    1st Policeman. There is the girl, then; go and deserve them the
moment you have pointed out to us Signor Luigi and his mother.
[*To the rest.*] I have been noticing a house yonder, this long while:
not a shutter unclosed since morning!

365   *2nd Policeman.* Old Luca Gaddi's, that owns the silk-mills here:
he dozes by the hour, wakes up, sighs deeply, says he should like
to be Prince Metternich, and then dozes again, after having bidden

---

*353 (editors' emendation) *1841* goods." *1849–89* Goods!"   *1841* of obliging a
356 *1841* Charon's ferry—With   357 *1841* obolus .. (it might be got in somehow)
*Tho' Cerberus should gobble us—To pay the Stygian ferry—*or you might say, *Never an obol To
pay for the cobl. . . .†* Though   359–63 *1841* pocket-full of *zwanzigers.* 1 Pol. I
have been   364 *1841* morning.

   354 *Bishop Beveridge:* a punning reference to William Beveridge (1637–1708), a prolific
writer whose works include a Latin treatise on 'the Oriental Tongues, especially Hebrew,
Chaldee, Syriac, and Samaritan, together with a Grammar of the Syriac Language'. The
DNB notes that 'In 1687–8 he joined with Dr. Horneck and others in forming religious
societies for "reformation of manners"' and quotes a contemporary censure that he
delights 'in jingle and quibbling, affects a tune and rhyme in all he says, and rests argu-
ment upon nothing but words and sounds'. Johnson, who liked it (Boswell, *Life*, ed.
G. Birkbeck Hill and L. F. Powell, i (1934), 251), notes in his *Dictionary* that 'Bishop' is 'A
cant word for a mixture of wine, oranges, and sugar'.

   355 *dog-sage:* not in OED. The Cynics were Greek philosophers whose name derives
from the Greek for 'dog', in allusion to their churlish and satirical manner. Charon was a
god of Hell who conducted the souls of the dead across the Styx and Acheron to the
infernal regions, for the fee of an obolos (penny). See Lucian, *Dialogues of the Dead*, in
vol. vii (1961) of the Loeb ed., pp. 8 ff.: 'Charon and Menippus'.

   356 *Lupine-seed and Hecate's supper:* both occur in the Dialogue just mentioned.
Lupine-seed is nutritious. Dogs, lambs and honey were generally offered to Hecate
(Proserpine), who was queen of the infernal regions.

   359 *coble* (*1841*): a small rowing boat with a flat bottom used for crossing rivers.

   359 *zwanzigers:* Austrian coins: the payment for his evil deeds, money which is burn-
ing a hole in his pocket.

   359–63 . . . *To pay* . . . [*To the rest.*]: added after *1841*, to clarify the meaning. We see
that Bluphocks is an informer.

   367 *Prince Metternich:* the Chancellor of Austria, hated by all liberal Italians. Cf. 'An
Italian in England', 19 and 121 ff.

young Sebald, the foreigner, set his wife to playing draughts.
Never molest such a household, they mean well.

Bluphocks. Only, cannot you tell me something of this little 370
Pippa, I must have to do with? One could make something of that
name. Pippa—that is, short for Felippa—rhyming to *Panurge consults
Hertrippa—Believest thou, King Agrippa?* Something might be done
with that name.

2nd Policeman. Put into rhyme that your head and a ripe musk- 375
melon would not be dear at half a *zwanziger!* Leave this fooling,
and look out; the afternoon's over or nearly so.

3rd Policeman. Where in this passport of Signor Luigi does our
Principal instruct you to watch him so narrowly? There? What's
there beside a simple signature? (That English fool's busy watch- 380
ing.)

2nd Policeman. Flourish all round—"Put all possible obstacles in
his way;" oblong dot at the end—"Detain him till further advices
reach you;" scratch at bottom—"Send him back on pretence of
some informality in the above;" ink-spirt on right-hand side 385
(which is the case here)—"Arrest him at once." Why and where-
fore, I don't concern myself, but my instructions amount to this:
if Signor Luigi leaves home to-night for Vienna—well and good,
the passport deposed with us for our *visa* is really for his own use,
they have misinformed the Office, and he means well; but let him 390
stay over to-night—there has been the pretence we suspect, the

368 *1841-63* draughts: 370-1 *1841* Only tell me who this little Pippa is I must
have to do with—one   372 *1841* Felippa—*Panurge*   373 *1841-65* Believ'st
375 *1841* 2 *Pol.* Your head   376-7 *1841* this fool, and   378-9 *1841* does
the principal   380-1 *1841* That .... watching.   385 *1841* above."
386 *1841,1849* once,"

372 *Panurge consults Hertrippa*: Porter and Clarke point out that this is a reference to
the passage in Rabelais where Panurge seeks the advice of Herr Trippa, the magician and
physician, about his marriage: *Gargantua and Pantagruel*, Book III, ch. xxv. Much is said
about cuckoldry in this chapter, in which (commentators agree) Rabelais is mocking
Cornelius Agrippa, from whom Browning had taken a quotation to place at the begin-
ning of *Pauline*.

373 *Believest thou, King Agrippa?*: 'King Agrippa, believest thou the prophets? I know
that thou believest': Acts 26:27.

385 *informality*: minor irregularity. OED cites Clarendon, *Letter to the Lord Treasurer*,
i. 125: 'I thought the informality was that ... it was not countersigned by you.'

389 *deposed*: deposited.

accounts of his corresponding and holding intelligence with the
Carbonari are correct, we arrest him at once, to-morrow comes
Venice, and presently Spielberg. Bluphocks makes the signal, sure
395 enough! That is he, entering the turret with his mother, no doubt.

392–3 *the Carbonari*: the Carbonari (literally 'charcoal-burners') were the members of a
secret society in Italy in the early part of the century. Even if it did not actively contri-
bute to the revolutionary movements of 1848–9 and later, the society prepared the way
for the Risorgimento.

394 *Spielberg*: the dreaded Austrian prison. Silvio Pellico, whose *Memoirs* will certainly
have been known to Browning (there is an allusion to them at III. 19, below), was im-
prisoned in I Piombi in Venice (cf. *Sordello*, iii. 876), and then in 'the dreaded fortress of
Spielberg . . . the most terrific prison under the Austrian monarchy': *My Imprisonments:
Memoirs of Silvio Pellico*, tr. Thomas Roscoe (1833), p. 137.

PART III

EVENING.

SCENE.—*Inside the Turret on the Hill above Asolo.* LUIGI *and his* Mother
entering.

   Mother. If there blew wind, you'd hear a long sigh, easing
The utmost heaviness of music's heart.
   Luigi. Here in the archway?
   Mother.   Oh no, no—in farther,
Where the echo is made, on the ridge.
   Luigi.   Here surely, then.
How plain the tap of my heel as I leaped up!   5
Hark—"Lucius Junius!" The very ghost of a voice
Whose body is caught and kept by . . . what are those?
Mere withered wallflowers, waving overhead?
They seem an elvish group with thin bleached hair
That lean out of their topmost fortress—look   10
And listen, mountain men, to what we say,
Hand under chin of each grave earthy face.
Up and show faces all of you!—"All of you!"

s.d. *1841-63* Turret. LUIGI   3 *1841* in further.   4 *1841* then!
5 *1841* up: 5a *1841* Aristogeiton! "ristogeiton"–plain   6 *1841* Was't not?
Lucius Junius! The . . . . voice– *1849-65* "*Lucius Junius!*"   7 *1841* Whose flesh is
caught and kept by those withered wall-flowers,   8 (no equivalent in *1841*)
9 *1841* Or by the elvish   10 *1841-63* Who lean   *1849, 1863* fortress—looking
11-12 *1841* men and women, to what | We say—chins under each   11 *1849, 1863*
And listening, mountain   12 *1849, 1863* Hands under   *1841-68* face:
13 *1849-65* "*All of you!*"

    4 *the echo*: in 1878 Browning described his return to 'this—to me—memorable place
after above forty years absence . . . It was *too* strange when we reached the ruined tower
on the hill-top yesterday, and I said "Let me try if the echo still exists which I discovered
here (you can produce it from only *one* particular spot on a remainder of brick-work)—
and thereupon it answered me plainly as ever, after all the silence"': *Learned Lady: Letters
from Robert Browning to Mrs. Thomas FitzGerald*, ed. Edward C. McAleer (Cambridge,
Mass., 1966), p. 68.
    6 "*Lucius Junius!*": Lucius Junius Brutus, the founder of the Roman Republic. Cf. *Sor-
dello*, iv. 981 and n., and vi. 455.
    13 "*All of you!*": this use of the echo is not uncommon in earlier poetry. See e.g. *The
Poems of Sir Philip Sidney*, ed. William A. Ringler, Jr. (1962), pp. 62 ff.

That's the king dwarf with the scarlet comb; old Franz,
Come down and meet your fate? Hark—"Meet your fate!"   15
   Mother. Let him not meet it, my Luigi—do not
Go to his City! Putting crime aside,
Half of these ills of Italy are feigned:
Your Pellicos and writers for effect,
Write for effect.
   Luigi.   Hush! Say A. writes, and B.   20
   Mother. These A.s and B.s write for effect, I say.
Then, evil is in its nature loud, while good
Is silent; you hear each petty injury,
None of his virtues; he is old beside,
Quiet and kind, and densely stupid. Why   25
Do A. and B. not kill him themselves?
   Luigi.   They teach
Others to kill him—me—and, if I fail,
Others to succeed; now, if A. tried and failed,
I could not teach that: mine's the lesser task.
Mother, they visit night by night . . .
   Mother.   —You, Luigi?   30
Ah, will you let me tell you what you are?
   Luigi. Why not? Oh, the one thing you fear to hint,
You may assure yourself I say and say
Ever to myself! At times—nay, even as now
We sit—I think my mind is touched, suspect   35
All is not sound: but is not knowing that,

14 *1841* king with the scarlet comb: come down!—"Come down." *1849, 1863* the king's
dwarf . . . . comb; now hark—   15 (no equivalent in *1841*) *1849-68* fate! Hark
1849-65 "*Meet your fate!*"   16 *1841* Do not kill that Man, my   17 *1841* to
the City!   21 *1841,1849* A's and B's *1863,1865* A.'s and B.'s   24 *1841-63*
his daily virtues; he is old, | 25 *1841,1849* stupid—why   26 *1841* A and B
28 *1841* A   29 *1841* not do that: . . . . *lesser*   34 *1841* Often to myself; at
times—nay, now—as now *1849-65* myself;

   14 *the king dwarf*: elves were supposed to be diminutive and usually malicious crea-
tures inhabiting unfrequented places.
   old Franz: Franz I of Austria was a strict absolutist. Guided by Metternich, he was
one of the partners in the Holy Alliance, repressing all liberal tendencies.
   17 *his City!*: Vienna, where Franz died in 1835.
   19 *your Pellicos*: see II. 394 n. above.

What constitutes one sane or otherwise?
I know I am thus—so, all is right again.
I laugh at myself as through the town I walk,
And see men merry as if no Italy   40
Were suffering; then I ponder—"I am rich,
"Young, healthy; why should this fact trouble me,
"More than it troubles these?" But it does trouble.
No, trouble's a bad word: for as I walk
There's springing and melody and giddiness,   45
And old quaint turns and passages of my youth,
Dreams long forgotten, little in themselves,
Return to me—whatever may amuse me:
And earth seems in a truce with me, and heaven
Accords with me, all things suspend their strife,   50
The very cicala laughs "There goes he, and there!
"Feast him, the time is short; he is on his way
"For the world's sake: feast him this once, our friend!"
And in return for all this, I can trip
Cheerfully up the scaffold-steps. I go   55
This evening, mother!
    Mother.   But mistrust yourself—
Mistrust the judgment you pronounce on him!
    Luigi. Oh, there I feel—am sure that I am right!
    Mother. Mistrust your judgment then, of the mere means
To this wild enterprise. Say, you are right,—   60
How should one in your state e'er bring to pass
What would require a cool head, a cold heart,
And a calm hand? You never will escape.
    Luigi. Escape? To even wish that, would spoil all.

38 *1841–65* again!   40 *1841* see the world merry   41 *1841* —I
42 *1841* healthy, happy, why   43 *1841* these? *1849* does trouble me! *1863,1865*
trouble!   48 *1841* may recreate me,   51 *1841* very cicales laugh . . . . and
there— *1849* very cicalas laugh *1863* very cicale laugh   55 *1841* scaffold-steps:
56 *1841* mother.   57 *1841–65* him.   58 *1841* right.   60 *1841–63*
Of this wild enterprise: *1865,1868* enterprise   64 *1841* Escape—to wish that even
would spoil all! *1849, 1863* Escape—

    50 *all things suspend their strife*: cf. Shelley, *Prometheus Unbound*, III. iv. 77.
    51 *cicales* (*1841*): incorrect, since 'cicale' is plural.
    61 *in your state*: see ll. 35–6 above.

The dying is best part of it. Too much
Have I enjoyed these fifteen years of mine,
To leave myself excuse for longer life:
Was not life pressed down, running o'er with joy,
That I might finish with it ere my fellows
Who, sparelier feasted, make a longer stay?   70
I was put at the board-head, helped to all
At first; I rise up happy and content.
God must be glad one loves his world so much.
I can give news of earth to all the dead
Who ask me:—last year's sunsets, and great stars   75
Which had a right to come first and see ebb
The crimson wave that drifts the sun away—
Those crescent moons with notched and burning rims
That strengthened into sharp fire, and there stood,
Impatient of the azure—and that day   80
In March, a double rainbow stopped the storm—
May's warm slow yellow moonlit summer nights—
Gone are they, but I have them in my soul!
    Mother. (He will not go!)
    Luigi.   You smile at me? 'T is true,—
Voluptuousness, grotesqueness, ghastliness,   85
Environ my devotedness as quaintly
As round about some antique altar wreathe
The rose festoons, goats' horns, and oxen's skulls.
    Mother. See now: you reach the city, you must cross
His threshold—how?
    Luigi.   Oh, that's if we conspired!   90
Then would come pains in plenty, as you guess—
But guess not how the qualities most fit

65–6 *1841* it—I have | Enjoyed these fifteen years of mine too much
73 *1841,1849* much— *1863,1865* much!   76 *1841–68* That had   84 *1841*
me—I know *1849, 1863* me!   90 *1841* we conspire!   91 *1841* Then come
the pains in plenty you foresee   92 *1841* —Who guess   *1841,1849* qualities
required

    66 *fifteen years*: note his youth. See Introduction, 57, where he is called a 'child'.
    68 *pressed down*: Luke 6:38.
    86 *Environ my devotedness*: cf. John Foxe, *Actes and Monuments (The Book of Martyrs)*
(1563), iii. 297: 'Hypocrisie, arrogancy, and obstinate security environ me.'

For such an office, qualities I have,
Would little stead me, otherwise employed,
Yet prove of rarest merit only here.   95
Every one knows for what his excellence
Will serve, but no one ever will consider
For what his worst defect might serve: and yet
Have you not seen me range our coppice yonder
In search of a distorted ash?—I find   100
The wry spoilt branch a natural perfect bow.
Fancy the thrice-sage, thrice-precautioned man
Arriving at the palace on my errand!
No, no! I have a handsome dress packed up—
White satin here, to set off my black hair;   105
In I shall march—for you may watch your life out
Behind thick walls, make friends there to betray you;
More than one man spoils everything. March straight—
Only, no clumsy knife to fumble for.
Take the great gate, and walk (not saunter) on   110
Thro' guards and guards—I have rehearsed it all
Inside the turret here a hundred times.
Don't ask the way of whom you meet, observe!
But where they cluster thickliest is the door
Of doors; they'll let you pass—they'll never blab   115
Each to the other, he knows not the favourite,
Whence he is bound and what's his business now.
Walk in—straight up to him; you have no knife:
Be prompt, how should he scream? Then, out with you!
Italy, Italy, my Italy!   120
You're free, you're free! Oh mother, I could dream

---

94 *1841* stead us otherwise   95 *1841-63* merit here—here only.   96 *1841*
his excellences   98 *1841* worst defects might   100 *1841-65* ash?—it hap-
pens   101 *1841-65* spoilt branch's a *1841* bow: *1849-65* bow!   103 *1841*
the city on   104 *1841* No, no—   105 *1841,1849* hair— *1863,1865* hair.
107 *1841* walls—binding friends to   109 *1841,1849* for—   112 *1841,1849*
times— *1863,1865* times!   113 *1841,1849* observe,   117 *1841,1849* now—
121 *1841* free—Oh . . . . I believed

120 *Italy, Italy, my Italy!*: cf. 'De Gustibus', 39.

They got about me—Andrea from his exile,
Pier from his dungeon, Gualtier from his grave!
    Mother. Well, you shall go. Yet seems this patriotism
The easiest virtue for a selfish man   125
To acquire: he loves himself—and next, the world—
If he must love beyond,—but nought between:
As a short-sighted man sees nought midway
His body and the sun above. But you
Are my adored Luigi, ever obedient   130
To my least wish, and running o'er with love:
I could not call you cruel or unkind.
Once more, your ground for killing him!—then go!
    Luigi. Now do you try me, or make sport of me?
How first the Austrians got these provinces . . .   135
(If that is all, I'll satisfy you soon)
—Never by conquest but by cunning, for
That treaty whereby . . .
    Mother.   Well?
    Luigi.   (Sure, he's arrived,
The tell-tale cuckoo: spring's his confidant,
And he lets out her April purposes!)   140
Or . . . better go at once to modern time,
He has . . . they have . . . in fact, I understand
But can't restate the matter; that's my boast:
Others could reason it out to you, and prove
Things they have made me feel.
    Mother.   Why go to-night?   145
Morn's for adventure. Jupiter is now
A morning-star. I cannot hear you, Luigi!
    Luigi. "I am the bright and morning-star," saith God—

---

124 *1841* go. If patriotism were not   126 *1841* acquire! . . . . and then, the *1849–*
65 acquire!   132 *1841,1849* Unkind!   133 *1863,1865* him?
134 *1841–63* you ask me,   137 *1841* by warfare but by treaty, for
141 *1841–63* modern times—   148 *1841–65* God saith—

  122–3 *Andrea . . . Pier . . . Gualtier*: fellow conspirators against the tyranny of Austria.
  138 *That treaty*: Austria conquered much of Northern Italy in 1813. By the Congress
of Vienna (1814–15) Austria was permitted to retain its hold on Lombardy and Venetia.
  148 *"I am*: Rev. 22:16.

And, "to such an one I give the morning-star."
The gift of the morning-star! Have I God's gift   150
Of the morning-star?
    Mother.   Chiara will love to see
That Jupiter an evening-star next June.
    Luigi. True, mother. Well for those who live through
       June!
Great noontides, thunder-storms, all glaring pomps
That triumph at the heels of June the god   155
Leading his revel through our leafy world.
Yes, Chiara will be here.
    Mother.   In June: remember,
Yourself appointed that month for her coming.
    Luigi. Was that low noise the echo?
    Mother.   The night-wind.
She must be grown—with her blue eyes upturned   160
As if life were one long and sweet surprise:
In June she comes.
    Luigi.   We were to see together
The Titian at Treviso. There, again!
        [*From without is heard the voice of* PIPPA, *singing—*

    A king lived long ago,
    In the morning of the world,   165
    When earth was nigher heaven than now:

*149 (reading of *1868*) *1841* And, "such .... star!" *1849-65* star!" *1888,1889* star.
150 *1841-65* star—have   153 *1841* live June over.   155 *1841-65* Which
triumph   *1849* of sovereign June   *1863* of the God June   156 *1849* his
glorious revel thro' our world.   162 *1841* We are to   163 *1841* Treviso—
there   s.d., 164 *1841* †[*Without*]† A   164-77 (roman type in *1841*)

   149 *"to such an one*: Rev. 2:26-8.
   154-5 *pomps / That triumph at the heels of June the god*: Luigi is thinking of a triumphal
procession ('Triumph') of the kind familiar in mythological paintings.
   156 *our leafy world*: cf. Keats, 'Sleep and Poetry', 119.
   163 *The Titian*: 'The Annunciation', in the Cathedral.
   164 *A king lived long ago*: this poem had been published, in a slightly different text,
the *Monthly Repository* for November 1835: see our Vol. I, pp. 530-1. As John Grube has
written ('Browning's "The King", UTQ 37 (1967-8), 69-72), its use here 'throws light on
Browning's view of revolutionary activity, and the connection he made between the
human sacrifices of primitive religions and the human sacrifices demanded by a modern
revolution'.

And the king's locks curled,
Disparting o'er a forehead full
As the milk-white space 'twixt horn and horn
Of some sacrificial bull—   170
Only calm as a babe new-born:
For he was got to a sleepy mood,
So safe from all decrepitude,
Age with its bane, so sure gone by,
(The gods so loved him while he dreamed)   175
That, having lived thus long, there seemed
No need the king should ever die.

Luigi. No need that sort of king should ever die!

Among the rocks his city was:
Before his palace, in the sun,   180
He sat to see his people pass,
And judge them every one
From its threshold of smooth stone.
They haled him many a valley-thief
Caught in the sheep-pens, robber-chief   185
Swarthy and shameless, beggar-cheat,
Spy-prowler, or rough pirate found
On the sea-sand left aground;
And sometimes clung about his feet,
With bleeding lip and burning cheek,   190
A woman, bitterest wrong to speak
Of one with sullen thickset brows:
And sometimes from the prison-house
The angry priests a pale wretch brought,
Who through some chink had pushed and pressed   195
On knees and elbows, belly and breast,
Worm-like into the temple,—caught

174 *1849 From age*   178 *1841* dic.   179–203 (roman type in *1841*)
179 *1841* †[*Without.*]† Among *1849* †[*From without.*]† Among   187 *1841* or some
pirate   189 *1841* Sometimes there clung   193 *1841* Sometimes from out
the   196 *1841* Knees and

178 *that sort of king*: Luigi's interjection emphasizes the difference between an ideal
kingdom and his own country under the domination of Franz.

He was by the very god,
Who ever in the darkness strode
Backward and forward, keeping watch   200
O'er his brazen bowls, such rogues to catch!
These, all and every one,
The king judged, sitting in the sun.

Luigi. That king should still judge sitting in the sun!

His councillors, on left and right,   205
Looked anxious up,—but no surprise
Disturbed the king's old smiling eyes
Where the very blue had turned to white.
'T is said, a Python scared one day
The breathless city, till he came,   210
With forky tongue and eyes on flame,
Where the old king sat to judge alway;
But when he saw the sweepy hair
Girt with a crown of berries rare
Which the god will hardly give to wear   215
To the maiden who singeth, dancing bare
In the altar-smoke by the pine-torch lights,
At his wondrous forest rites,—
Seeing this, he did not dare
Approach that threshold in the sun,   220
Assault the old king smiling there.
Such grace had kings when the world begun!

[PIPPA *passes.*

Luigi. And such grace have they, now that the world ends!

198 *1849, 1863 At last there by*   201 *1841* catch: 202 *1849, 1863 And these,*
204 *1841* sun.   205–21 {roman type in *1841*}   205 *1841* †[*Without.*]† His
1849 †[*From without.*]† His   209 *1841* A python passed one day   210 *1841*
The silent streets—until he came,   *212 {reading of DC and all versions except
1888} 1888* alway, *1841* king judged alway;   218a–d *1841* But which the God's self
granted him | For setting free each felon limb | Because of earthly murder done | Faded till
other hope was none;— | 221 *1841* there. †[PIPPA *passes.*   222–8 {no equiva-
lent in *1841*}

   209 *'T is said* : in Greek mythology the Python was a monster which guarded the oracle
of Delphi. The word was later used of any monster.
   223 *now that the world ends!* : in this latter age the ruler is the Python, whom some brave
patriot must slay.

The Python at the city, on the throne,
And brave men, God would crown for slaying him,   225
Lurk in bye-corners lest they fall his prey.
Are crowns yet to be won in this late time,
Which weakness makes me hesitate to reach?
'T is God's voice calls: how could I stay? Farewell!

Talk by the way, while PIPPA *is passing from the Turret to the*
Bishop's Brother's House, close to the Duomo S. Maria. Poor
Girls sitting on the steps.

    1st Girl. There goes a swallow to Venice—the stout
       seafarer!   230
Seeing those birds fly, makes one wish for wings.
Let us all wish; you wish first!
    2nd Girl.   I? This sunset
To finish.
    3rd Girl. That old—somebody I know,
Greyer and older than my grandfather,
To give me the same treat he gave last week—   235
Feeding me on his knee with fig-peckers,
Lampreys and red Breganze-wine, and mumbling
The while some folly about how well I fare,
Let sit and eat my supper quietly:
Since had he not himself been late this morning   240
Detained at—never mind where,—had he not . . .
"Eh, baggage, had I not!"—
    2nd Girl.   How she can lie!
    3rd Girl. Look there—by the nails!
    2nd Girl.   What makes your fingers red?

224 *1849, 1863* Python in the   227 *1849* late trial,   229 *1841* Farewell,
farewell—how could I stay? Farewell! *1849* calls,   s.d. *1841 way in the mean time.*
Poor Girls sitting on the steps of MONSIGNOR'S *brother's house, close to the Duomo S. Maria.*
231 {no equivalent in *1841*}   232 *1841* first.   234 {no equivalent in *1841*}
239 {no equivalent in *1841*} *1849–65* To be let eat   242 *1841* Eh, ... not!—
243 *1841,1849*   nails—

    s.d. *the Duomo S. Maria* : see above, Introduction, 181 n.
    233 *That old* : 'That' is demonstrative.   236 *fig-peckers* : Italian *beccafico* (pl. *beccafichi*).
    237 *Breganze-wine* : Breganze is nearby.

3rd Girl. Dipping them into wine to write bad words with
On the bright table: how he laughed!
  1st Girl.   My turn.   245
Spring's come and summer's coming. I would wear
A long loose gown, down to the feet and hands,
With plaits here, close about the throat, all day;
And all night lie, the cool long nights, in bed;
And have new milk to drink, apples to eat,   250
Deuzans and junetings, leather-coats .. ah, I should say,
This is away in the fields—miles!
  3rd Girl.   Say at once
You'd be at home: she'd always be at home!
Now comes the story of the farm among
The cherry orchards, and how April snowed   255
White blossoms on her as she ran. Why, fool,
They've rubbed the chalk-mark out, how tall you were,
Twisted your starling's neck, broken his cage,
Made a dung-hill of your garden!
  1st Girl.   They, destroy
My garden since I left them? well—perhaps!   260
I would have done so: so I hope they have!
A fig-tree curled out of our cottage wall;
They called it mine, I have forgotten why,
It must have been there long ere I was born:
Cric–cric—I think I hear the wasps o'erhead   265
Pricking the papers strung to flutter there
And keep off birds in fruit-time—coarse long papers,
And the wasps eat them, prick them through and through.
  3rd Girl. How her mouth twitches! Where was I?—before
She broke in with her wishes and long gowns   270
And wasps—would I be such a fool!—Oh, here!

245 *1841,1849* turn: 246 *1841-63* coming: 256 *1841-63* ran:
*257 (reading of *1841-68*) *1888,1889* were *1849, 1863* rubbed out the chalk-mark of
how   259 *1841-63* garden—   264 *1841* born,   265 *1841* Criq—
criq— *1849* Cric—cric—   269 *1841*   where was I before

 251 *Deuzans and junetings, leather-coats*: three types of apple. Browning will have met
'the lasting deuzan' in Quarles, *Emblems*, Book V, Emblem ii, 23. Whether or not that
word was still in common use, 'Leather-coat' (*2 Henry IV*, v. iii. 41) and 'jenneting' were.

This is my way: I answer every one
Who asks me why I make so much of him—
(If you say, "you love him"—straight "he'll not be gulled!")
"He that seduced me when I was a girl   275
"Thus high—had eyes like yours, or hair like yours,
"Brown, red, white,"—as the case may be: that pleases!
See how that beetle burnishes in the path!
There sparkles he along the dust: and, there—
Your journey to that maize-tuft spoiled at least!   280
    1st Girl. When I was young, they said if you killed one
Of those sunshiny beetles, that his friend
Up there, would shine no more that day nor next.
    2nd Girl. When you were young? Nor are you young, that's
        true.
How your plump arms, that were, have dropped away!   285
Why, I can span them. Cecco beats you still?
No matter, so you keep your curious hair.
I wish they'd find a way to dye our hair
Your colour—any lighter tint, indeed,
Than black: the men say they are sick of black,   290
Black eyes, black hair!
    4th Girl.   Sick of yours, like enough.
Do you pretend you ever tasted lampreys
And ortolans? Giovita, of the palace,
Engaged (but there's no trusting him) to slice me
Polenta with a knife that had cut up   295
An ortolan.

274 *1841* (Say, you love him—he'll not be gulled, he'll say) *1849–65* you love him *1849*
gulled")   278 *1841,1849* (See .... path- *1863* path—   279 *1849, 1863*
dust!   280 *1841–63* maize-tuft's spoilt *1865* spoilt   *1849* least!)
283 *1841* day or next.   284 *1841–63* true!   286 *1841–65* them!
291 *1841* hair! 3 *Girl.* .... enough, *1849–65* enough!   295 *1849*   that
has cut
___

278 *burnishes*: intransitive: 'To grow bright or glossy': Johnson. See Christopher Smart,
A Song to David, st. lxi: 'the crocus burnishes'. On Browning and Smart see Vol. I, p. 197,
l. 770 n.
    286 *span*: get my hand round.   287 *curious*: 'Elegant; neat': Johnson.
    293 *ortolans*: the Italian mode of cooking these small birds, considered a great delicacy,
is described in the Prologue to *Ferishtah's Fancies*.
    295 *Polenta*: a kind of pudding, made chiefly of maize flour.

2nd Girl. Why, there! Is not that Pippa
We are to talk to, under the window,—quick,—
Where the lights are?
    1st Girl.   That she? No, or she would sing.
For the Intendant said . . .
    3rd Girl.   Oh, you sing first!
Then, if she listens and comes close . . I'll tell you,—   300
Sing that song the young English noble made,
Who took you for the purest of the pure,
And meant to leave the world for you—what fun!
    2nd Girl [*sings*].

> *You'll love me yet!—and I can tarry*
>   *Your love's protracted growing:*   305
> *June reared that bunch of flowers you carry,*
>   *From seeds of April's sowing.*
>
> *I plant a heartful now: some seed*
>   *At least is sure to strike,*
> *And yield—what you'll not pluck indeed,*   310
>   *Not love, but, may be, like.*
>
> *You'll look at least on love's remains,*
>   *A grave's one violet:*
> *Your look?—that pays a thousand pains.*
>   *What's death? You'll love me yet!*   315

    3rd Girl [*to* PIPPA *who approaches*]. Oh, you may come
closer—we shall not eat you! Why, you seem the very person
that the great rich handsome Englishman has fallen so
violently in love with. I'll tell you all about it.

---

296 *1841* is   298 *1841-63* are? 1 *Girl.* No—or   *1849-65* sing;   298–
9 *1841* sing | —For   304–15 [roman type in *1841-65*]   310 *1841* not care,
indeed,   311 *1841* To pluck, but . . . . like *1849-65* like!   312 *1841* To
look upon . . my whole remains,   317 [section ends with 'eat you!' in *1841*]
319 *1849, 1863* with!

    297 *We are to talk to*: to forward the Intendant's plot.
    309 *strike*: take root.
    317–19 *Why, you seem . . . all about it*: obviously added to clarify the action.
    318 *handsome Englishman*: Bluphocks.

PART IV

NIGHT.

Scene.—*Inside the Palace by the Duomo.* Monsignor, *dismissing his*
Attendants.

Monsignor. Thanks, friends, many thanks! I chiefly desire life
now, that I may recompense every one of you. Most I know some-
thing of already. What, a repast prepared? *Benedicto benedicatur* ...
ugh, ugh! Where was I? Oh, as you were remarking, Ugo, the
5 weather is mild, very unlike winter-weather: but I am a Sicilian,
you know, and shiver in your Julys here. To be sure, when 't was
full summer at Messina, as we priests used to cross in procession
the great square on Assumption Day, you might see our thickest
yellow tapers twist suddenly in two, each like a falling star, or sink
10 down on themselves in a gore of wax. But go, my friends, but go!
[*To the* Intendant.] Not you, Ugo! [*The others leave the apartment.*] I
have long wanted to converse with you, Ugo.

Intendant. Uguccio—

Monsignor. . .'guccio Stefani, man! of Ascoli, Fermo and Fos-
15 sombruno;—what I do need instructing about, are these accounts
of your administration of my poor brother's affairs. Ugh! I shall
never get through a third part of your accounts: take some of these
dainties before we attempt it, however. Are you bashful to that
degree? For me, a crust and water suffice.

s.d. *1841 The palace by*   1-2 *1841* thanks. I desire life now chiefly that *1849-65*
thanks.   3 *1841* already. *Benedicto*   6 *1841,1849* here: 11 *1841*
apartment, where a table with refreshments is prepared.]† I   12 *1841-65* Ugo!
18 *1841,1849* however:

    3 *Benedicto benedicatur*: a traditional grace: Blessing on the Blessed One.

    8 *Assumption Day*: 15 August, celebrated as the anniversary of the assumption of the
body of the Virgin Mary into heaven.

    10 *gore*: clot.   11 *Intendant*: see II. 329 n., above.

    13 *Uguccio*: Ugo wishes Monsignor to call him by the intimate or familiar form of his
name.

    14-15 *Ascoli, Fermo and Fossombruno*: Ascoli Piceno, 53 miles S of Ancona, is an episcopal
see, and capital of the province of the same name. Fermo, some 20 miles to the N, is a
smaller town near the sea. Fossombruno (Fossombrone) is a few miles from Urbino, NE by
E of Arezzo.

Intendant. Do you choose this especial night to question me?   20

Monsignor. This night, Ugo. You have managed my late brother's affairs since the death of our elder brother: fourteen years and a month, all but three days. On the Third of December, I find him . . .

Intendant. If you have so intimate an acquaintance with your 25 brother's affairs, you will be tender of turning so far back: they will hardly bear looking into, so far back.

Monsignor. Ay, ay, ugh, ugh,—nothing but disappointments here below! I remark a considerable payment made to yourself on this Third of December. Talk of disappointments! There was a young 30 fellow here, Jules, a foreign sculptor I did my utmost to advance, that the Church might be a gainer by us both: he was going on hopefully enough, and of a sudden he notifies to me some marvellous change that has happened in his notions of Art. Here's his letter,—"He never had a clearly conceived Ideal within his brain till 35 to-day. Yet since his hand could manage a chisel, he has practised expressing other men's Ideals; and, in the very perfection he has attained to, he foresees an ultimate failure: his unconscious hand will pursue its prescribed course of old years, and will reproduce with a fatal expertness the ancient types, let the novel one appear 40 never so palpably to his spirit. There is but one method of escape: confiding the virgin type to as chaste a hand, he will turn painter instead of sculptor, and paint, not carve, its characteristics,"—strike out, I dare say, a school like Correggio: how think you, Ugo?

Intendant. Is Correggio a painter?   45

Monsignor. Foolish Jules! and yet, after all, why foolish? He may—probably will—fail egregiously; but if there should arise a new painter, will it not be in some such way, by a poet now, or a musician (spirits who have conceived and perfected an Ideal through some other channel), transferring it to this, and escaping our 50

23 *1841* days. The 3rd *1849, 1863* 3rd   30 *1841–63* 3rd   34 *1841–63* art;
41 *1841,1849* spirit: 42–3 *1841* hand, he will paint, not   48–9 *1841* way—a
poet . . . . spirits   50 *1841* channel,

37 *in the very perfection* : cf. 'Andrea del Sarto', e.g. 98–9.

44 *Correggio* : Antonio Allegri (1489?-1534), described by E. H. Gombrich as 'The painter who was looked upon by later generations as the most "progressive" and most daring innovator of the whole period': *The Story of Art* (1956), p. 245.

conventional roads by pure ignorance of them; eh, Ugo? If you have
no appetite, talk at least, Ugo!

    Intendant. Sir, I can submit no longer to this course of yours.
First, you select the group of which I formed one,—next you thin it
55 gradually,—always retaining me with your smile,—and so do you
proceed till you have fairly got me alone with you between four
stone walls. And now then? Let this farce, this chatter end now:
what is it you want with me?

    Monsignor. Ugo!
60   *Intendant.* From the instant you arrived, I felt your smile on me as
you questioned me about this and the other article in those papers—
why your brother should have given me this villa, that *podere*,—and
your nod at the end meant,—what?

    Monsignor. Possibly that I wished for no loud talk here. If once
65 you set me coughing, Ugo!—

    Intendant. I have your brother's hand and seal to all I possess: now
ask me what for! what service I did him—ask me!

    Monsignor. I would better not: I should rip up old disgraces, let
out my poor brother's weaknesses. By the way, Maffeo of Forli
70 (which, I forgot to observe, is your true name), was the interdict
ever taken off you, for robbing that church at Cesena?

    Intendant. No, nor needs be: for when I murdered your brother's
friend, Pasquale, for him . . .

    Monsignor. Ah, he employed you in that business, did he? Well, I
75 must let you keep, as you say, this villa and that *podere*, for fear the
world should find out my relations were of so indifferent a stamp?
Maffeo, my family is the oldest in Messina, and century after cen-
tury have my progenitors gone on polluting themselves with every
wickedness under heaven: my own father . . . rest his soul!—I have, I
80 know, a chapel to support that it may rest: my dear two dead

51 *1841* them,   53 *1841–63* yours: 57 *1841,1849* walls:
59 *1841,1849* Ugo . . .   62 *1841* this manor, that liberty,—and   64 *1841*
here—if *1849, 1863* here: if   68 *1841,1849* I had better   74 *1841* that
matter, did   75 *1841* this manor and that liberty, for   76 *1841* stamp: *1849*
stamp!   80 *1841* it may: my

    62 *podere* : farm, agricultural estate.
    69 *Forli* : Forli, a city some 40 miles SE of Bologna.
    71 *Cesena* : a small town about 12 miles from Forli.

brothers were,—what you know tolerably well; I, the youngest,
might have rivalled them in vice, if not in wealth: but from my boy-
hood I came out from among them, and so am not partaker of their
plagues. My glory springs from another source; or if from this, by
contrast only,—for I, the bishop, am the brother of your employers, 85
Ugo. I hope to repair some of their wrong, however; so far as my
brother's ill-gotten treasure reverts to me, I can stop the con-
sequences of his crime: and not one *soldo* shall escape me. Maffeo,
the sword we quiet men spurn away, you shrewd knaves pick up
and commit murders with; what opportunities the virtuous forego, 90
the villanous seize. Because, to pleasure myself apart from other
considerations, my food would be millet-cake, my dress sackcloth,
and my couch straw,—am I therefore to let you, the offscouring of
the earth, seduce the poor and ignorant by appropriating a pomp
these will be sure to think lessens the abominations so unaccount- 95
ably and exclusively associated with it? Must I let villas and *poderi* go
to you, a murderer and thief, that you may beget by means of them
other murderers and thieves? No—if my cough would but allow me
to speak!

    Intendant. What am I to expect? You are going to punish me?   100
    Monsignor. —Must punish you, Maffeo. I cannot afford to cast
away a chance. I have whole centuries of sin to redeem, and only a
month or two of life to do it in. How should I dare to say . . .
    Intendant. "Forgive us our trespasses"?
    Monsignor. My friend, it is because I avow myself a very worm, 105
sinful beyond measure, that I reject a line of conduct you would

---

82 *1841-63* wealth,   84 *1841* source,   *87 {reading of *1841-68*} *1888,1889*
brothers'   88 *1841* crime,   93 *1841* let the off-scouring   94 *1841*
the ignorant by   96 *1841* let manors and liberties go *1849* and *poderes* go
100 *1841-65* you   *103 {reading of DC and all versions except *1888*} *1888* to {space}
it in. *1841-65* in!   104 *1841* trespasses." *1849* trespasses"—

83 *I came out*: 'Wherefore come out from among them, and be ye separate, saith the
Lord, and touch not the unclean thing; and I will receive you': 2 Cor. 6:17.

83-4 *partaker of their plagues*: 'And I heard another voice from heaven, saying, Come out
of her, my people, that ye be not partakers of her sins, and that ye receive not of her
plagues': Rev. 18:4.

104 *"Forgive us our trespasses"*: Matt. 6:12 (Tyndale's version, in the Book of Common
Prayer). The Intendant wishes the Monsignor to remember a further clause of the Lord's
Prayer: Matt. 6:14.

applaud perhaps. Shall I proceed, as it were, a-pardoning?—I?—who
have no symptom of reason to assume that aught less than my
strenuousest efforts will keep myself out of mortal sin, much less
110 keep others out. No: I do trespass, but will not double that by allow-
ing you to trespass.

    Intendant. And suppose the villas are not your brother's to give,
nor yours to take? Oh, you are hasty enough just now!

    Monsignor. 1, 2—N° 3!—ay, can you read the substance of a letter,
115 N° 3, I have received from Rome? It is precisely on the ground there
mentioned, of the suspicion I have that a certain child of my late
elder brother, who would have succeeded to his estates, was mur-
dered in infancy by you, Maffeo, at the instigation of my late
younger brother—that the Pontiff enjoins on me not merely the
120 bringing that Maffeo to condign punishment, but the taking all
pains, as guardian of the infant's heritage for the Church, to recover
it parcel by parcel, howsoever, whensoever, and wheresoever.
While you are now gnawing those fingers, the police are engaged in
sealing up your papers, Maffeo, and the mere raising my voice
125 brings my people from the next room to dispose of yourself. But I
want you to confess quietly, and save me raising my voice. Why,
man, do I not know the old story? The heir between the succeeding
heir, and this heir's ruffianly instrument, and their complot's effect,
and the life of fear and bribes and ominous smiling silence? Did you
130 throttle or stab my brother's infant? Come now!

    Intendant. So old a story, and tell it no better? When did such an
instrument ever produce such an effect? Either the child smiles in

---

107 *1841,1849* perhaps: 112-13 *1841* give, or yours   115-16 *1841* is on the
ground I there mention of   118-19 *1841-68* late brother—   121 *1841-63* of
that infant's   128 *1841-65* and that heir's   *130 {reading of DC and all
versions except *1888*} *1888* now

    107 *a-pardoning*: this use of 'a-' with a gerund is obsolete and Scots, according to OED.
    108 *symptom*: vestige.
    109 *mortal sin*: sin 'Inferring divine condemnation': Johnson.
    116-17 *a certain child of my late elder brother*: in fact Pippa is Monsignor's niece.
    122 *parcel by parcel*: every part of it. Like the following words, this reproduces legal
jargon.
    127 *between*: apparently meaning 'in the way of', i.e. between the deceased and the
ultimate heir.
    128 *complot*: as in Shakespeare, *Richard III*, III. i. 192.
    131-2 *When did such an instrument*: the ruffian never does what he has undertaken to do.

his face; or, most likely, he is not fool enough to put himself in the
employer's power so thoroughly: the child is always ready to
produce—as you say—howsoever, wheresoever, and whensoever.   135

Monsignor. Liar!

Intendant. Strike me? Ah, so might a father chastise! I shall sleep
soundly to-night at least, though the gallows await me to-morrow;
for what a life did I lead! Carlo of Cesena reminds me of his con-
nivance, every time I pay his annuity; which happens commonly   140
thrice a year. If I remonstrate, he will confess all to the good
bishop—you!

Monsignor. I see through the trick, caitiff! I would you spoke
truth for once. All shall be sifted, however—seven times sifted.

Intendant. And how my absurd riches encumbered me! I dared   145
not lay claim to above half my possessions. Let me but once
unbosom myself, glorify Heaven, and die!

Sir, you are no brutal dastardly idiot like your brother I fright-
ened to death: let us understand one another. Sir, I will make away
with her for you—the girl—here close at hand; not the stupid ob-   150
vious kind of killing; do not speak—know nothing of her nor of me!
I see her every day—saw her this morning: of course there is to be no
killing; but at Rome the courtesans perish off every three years, and
I can entice her thither—have indeed begun operations already.
There's a certain lusty blue-eyed florid-complexioned English   155
knave, I and the Police employ occasionally. You assent, I perceive—
no, that's not it—assent I do not say—but you will let me convert my
present havings and holdings into cash, and give me time to cross
the Alps? 'T is but a little black-eyed pretty singing Felippa, gay silk-
winding girl. I have kept her out of harm's way up to this present;   160
for I always intended to make your life a plague to you with her. 'T
is as well settled once and for ever. Some women I have procured
will pass Bluphocks, my handsome scoundrel, off for somebody;

133 *1841-63* face,   139 *1841* lead?   140-1 *1841,1849* annuity (which ....
year).   144 *1841,1849* once;   151 *1841* her or me. *1849, 1863* her or me!
152-3 *1841* is no killing;   154-5 *1841* already—there's   156 *1841* I employ
158 *1841* give time   161 *1841-65* her!   162 *1841* forever: *1849, 1863* for
ever: 163 *1841* somebody,

134-5 *to produce*: to be produced.
140 *his annuity*: i.e. bribe.

and once Pippa entangled!—you conceive? Through her singing? Is
165 it a bargain?

[*From without is heard the voice of* PIPPA, *singing—*

Overhead the tree-tops meet,
Flowers and grass spring 'neath one's feet;
There was nought above me, nought below,
My childhood had not learned to know:
For, what are the voices of birds   170
—Ay, and of beasts,—but words, our words,
Only so much more sweet?
The knowledge of that with my life begun.
But I had so near made out the sun,
And counted your stars, the seven and one,   175
Like the fingers of my hand:
Nay, I could all but understand
Wherefore through heaven the white moon ranges;
And just when out of her soft fifty changes
No unfamiliar face might overlook me—   180
Suddenly God took me.

[PIPPA *passes.*

Monsignor [*springing up*]. My people—one and all—all—within
there! Gag this villain—tie him hand and foot! He dares . . . I know
not half he dares—but remove him—quick! *Miserere mei, Domine!*
185 Quick, I say!

164-5 *1841* conceive? | *Mon.* Why, if she sings, one might . . . | †[*Without.*]† Over-head
166-81 [roman type in *1841*]   168-9 [no equivalent in *1841*]   168 *1849,*
1863 me, and nought   169 *1849* know!   170 *1841* What are
171 *1841* and beasts, too—but   173 *1841* That knowledge with . . . . begun! *1849-*
65 begun!   175 *1841* Could count your stars, ... One!   177 *1841* Nay,
could   178 *1841* How and wherefore the moon ranges—   183 *1841* foot:

175 *the seven and one* : probably, as Porter and Clarke suggested, the Pleiades (commonly
referred to as seven, though only six are visible to the average naked eye) and Aldebaran, a
bright red star which is chief of the neighbouring group, the Hyades.

184 *Miserere mei, Domine!* : Lord have mercy upon me! Ps. 50 (AV 51):1, in the Vulgate
version).

SCENE.—PIPPA's *chamber again. She enters it.*

The bee with his comb,
The mouse at her dray,
The grub in his tomb,
Wile winter away;   190
But the fire-fly and hedge-shrew and lob-worm, I pray,
How fare they?
Ha, ha, thanks for your counsel, my Zanze!
"Feast upon lampreys, quaff Breganze"—
The summer of life so easy to spend,   195
And care for to-morrow so soon put away!
But winter hastens at summer's end,
And fire-fly, hedge-shrew, lob-worm, pray,
How fare they?
No bidding me then to . . . what did Zanze say?   200
"Pare your nails pearlwise, get your small feet shoes
"More like" . . . (what said she?)—"and less like canoes!"
How pert that girl was!—would I be those pert
Impudent staring women! It had done me,
However, surely no such mighty hurt   205
To learn his name who passed that jest upon me:
No foreigner, that I can recollect,
Came, as she says, a month since, to inspect

189 *1841–68* in its tomb   192 *1841* Where be they   193 *1841* thanks my
Zanze— *1849, 1863* ha, best thanks . . . . Zanze—   194 *1841* "Feed on lampreys,
1849–68 quaff the Breganze"—   195 *1841–63* of life's so   *1841* spend!
196 {no equivalent in *1841*}   199 *1841* Where be they   200 *1841* bidding
you then   *1849–65* she say?   202 *1841–65* like . . (what . . . . she?)—and . . . .
canoes—"   203 *1841* Pert as a sparrow . . . would   204 *1841* staring
wretches! it *1849–65* it   206 *1841* me.—

188 *dray*: nest (usually of a squirrel).
189 *The grub*: 'The larva of an insect, esp. of a beetle; a caterpillar, maggot; also (now
dial.), a worm': OED. Cf. *Romeo and Juliet*, v. iii. 125–6.
191 *hedge-shrew*: '? the shrew-mouse', OED, which has no other example.
    lob-worm: 'A large earthworm used for bait by anglers': OED. Ll. 191–2 are a clear
reminiscence of the story of the ant and the grasshopper, which Browning may first have
encountered in Croxall's edition of *Æsop's Fables* (1722 and many reprints). Cf. *Life*, 26–7,
and our note to *Strafford* IV. i. 56 (Vol. II, p. 113). Browning will also have known La Fon-
taine's fable, 'La Cigale et la Fourmi' (*Fables*, I. i).
202 *"and less like canoes!"*: possibly a reminiscence of Marvell, 'Upon Appleton House',
771–2.

Our silk-mills—none with blue eyes and thick rings
Of raw-silk-coloured hair, at all events.   210
Well, if old Luca keep his good intents,
We shall do better, see what next year brings.
I may buy shoes, my Zanze, not appear
More destitute than you perhaps next year!
Bluph . . . something! I had caught the uncouth name   215
But for Monsignor's people's sudden clatter
Above us—bound to spoil such idle chatter
As ours: it were indeed a serious matter
If silly talk like ours should put to shame
The pious man, the man devoid of blame,   220
The . . . ah but—ah but, all the same,
No mere mortal has a right
To carry that exalted air;
Best people are not angels quite:
While—not the worst of people's doings scare   225
The devil; so there's that proud look to spare!
      Which is mere counsel to myself, mind! for
I have just been the holy Monsignor:
And I was you too, Luigi's gentle mother,
And you too, Luigi!—how that Luigi started   230
Out of the turret—doubtlessly departed
On some good errand or another,
For he passed just now in a traveller's trim,
And the sullen company that prowled
About his path, I noticed, scowled   235
As if they had lost a prey in him.
And I was Jules the sculptor's bride,

210 1841-65 Of English-coloured hair,   211 1841-63 Luca keeps his
212 1841 brings— 1849-68 brings!   214 1841 So destitute, perhaps,
215 1841 Bluf—something—   218-19 (no equivalent in 1841)   223 1841 ·
carrry   225 1841 not worst people's   226 1841,1849 The devils; so
226-7 1841 that regard to spare! | Mere counsel   227 1865 mind: 228 1841
been Monsignor! 1849-65 Monsignor!   229 1841 too, mother,   232 1841
some love-errand   233-6 (no equivalent in 1841)   233 1849 he past just

  211 old Luca: Ottima's husband, who owned silk-mills: see I. 233-4 above.
  233 in a traveller's trim: cf. Wordsworth, 'The Idiot Boy', 37: 'in travelling trim'.

And I was Ottima beside,
And now what am I?—tired of fooling.
Day for folly, night for schooling!   240
New year's day is over and spent,
Ill or well, I must be content.
    Even my lily's asleep, I vow:
Wake up—here's a friend I've plucked you:
Call this flower a heart's-ease now!   245
Something rare, let me instruct you,
Is this, with petals triply swollen,
Three times spotted, thrice the pollen;
While the leaves and parts that witness
Old proportions and their fitness,   250
Here remain unchanged, unmoved now;
Call this pampered thing improved now!
Suppose there's a king of the flowers
And a girl-show held in his bowers—
"Look ye, buds, this growth of ours,"   255
Says he, "Zanze from the Brenta,
"I have made her gorge polenta
"Till both cheeks are near as bouncing
"As her . . . name there's no pronouncing!
"See this heightened colour too,   260
"For she swilled Breganze wine
"Till her nose turned deep carmine;
"'T was but white when wild she grew.
"And only by this Zanze's eyes
"Of which we could not change the size,   265
"The magnitude of all achieved
"Otherwise, may be perceived."

239 *1841-65* fooling!   240 *1841* schooling—   241 *1841* over—over!
242 {no equivalent in *1841*} *1849, 1863* content!   244 *1841* friend I pluckt you.
245 *1841* See—call this a *1849, 1863* See—call   248 *1841-65* pollen,
250 *1841-63* The old   252 *1849* So call *1863* So, call   263 *1841-65* grew!
266 *1841-63* of what's achieved   267 *1841* Elsewhere may be perceived!" *1849,
1863* perceived!"

240 *night for schooling!*: see Tilley, N 174: 'Night is the mother of counsels.'
245 *heart's-ease*: pansy, as at I. 235.

Oh what a drear dark close to my poor day!
How could that red sun drop in that black cloud?
Ah Pippa, morning's rule is moved away,   270
Dispensed with, never more to be allowed!
Day's turn is over, now arrives the night's.
Oh lark, be day's apostle
To mavis, merle and throstle,
Bid them their betters jostle   275
From day and its delights!
But at night, brother howlet, over the woods,
Toll the world to thy chantry;
Sing to the bats' sleek sisterhoods
Full complines with gallantry: 280
Then, owls and bats,
Cowls and twats,
Monks and nuns, in a cloister's moods,
Adjourn to the oak-stump pantry!
                    [*After she has begun to undress herself.*
Now, one thing I should like to really know: 285

269 *1841-63* cloud!   271 *1841* allowed. *1849* allowed,   272 *1841* turn's
over—now's the night's—   277 *1849, 1863* Howlet, far over   281-2 {one line
in *1841-68*}   285 *1841* like really to know:

   270 *morning's rule*: her holiday freedom.
   274 *mavis, merle and throstle*: Harrison rules that '"mavis", properly the throstle, Brown-
ing seems wrongly to have identified with mistle-thrush' (p. 294). 'Merle' is an old name for
the blackbird. Scott often mentions mavis and merle together, as in *The Lady of the Lake*,
IV. xii. 2.
   277 *howlet*: as in *The Pilgrim's Progress*, ii. 189, and *Ivanhoe*, ch. xxvii.
   280 *complines*: 'The last act of worship at night, by which the service of the day is com-
pleted': Johnson.
   282 *twats*: Browning replied to a query from Furnivall on this word: 'In the Royalist
rhymes entitled "Vanity of Vanities, or Sir Harry Vane's Picture" . . . occur these lines

           "'Tis said they will give him a Cardinal's hat:
           They sooner will give him an old nun's twat!"

The ballad is partly quoted in the Appendix to Forster's Life of Vane, but the above lines are
left out—I remember them, however, and the word struck me as a distinctive part of a nun's
attire that might fitly pair off with the cowl appropriated to a monk': *Trumpeter*, p. 135.
Browning may have come on the version of the lines in *Rump: or an Exact Collection of the
Choycest Poems and Songs relating to the Late Times* (2 vols., 1662). In fact 'twat' means the
female genitals, which Furnivall clearly refrained from mentioning. As Peterson remarks,
'RB's embarrassing mistake was duly recorded in the *Oxford English Dictionary*, probably by
FJF—but long after Browning's death.

How near I ever might approach all these
I only fancied being, this long day:
—Approach, I mean, so as to touch them, so
As to ... in some way ... move them—if you please,
Do good or evil to them some slight way.   290
For instance, if I wind
Silk to-morrow, my silk may bind

        [Sitting on the bedside.

And border Ottima's cloak's hem.
Ah me, and my important part with them,
This morning's hymn half promised when I rose!   295
True in some sense or other, I suppose.

        [As she lies down.

God bless me! I can pray no more to-night.
No doubt, some way or other, hymns say right.

   All service ranks the same with God—
   With God, whose puppets, best and worst,   300
   Are we: there is no last nor first.

        [She sleeps.

---

287 *1841,1849* day— *1863* day! 292 *1841* to-morrow, silk may 293 *1841*–
63 And broider · 294 *1841* important passing them 296a *1849, 1863*
Though I passed by them all, and felt no sign. 297 *1841* me tho' I cannot pray to-
night. 299 *1841–63* service is the 300 *1841 Whose puppets,* 301 *1841*
Are we ...... |

 295 *this morning's hymn*: Introduction, 190 ff.
 301 *There is no last nor first*: cf. 'The Boy and the Angel', first published in *Hood's
Magazine* in August 1844.

INTRODUCTION TO *KING VICTOR AND KING CHARLES*

THE first reference to this play occurs in an important letter to Fanny Haworth, now known to have been written on 1 July 1837, in which Browning told her that he was 'going ... to begin thinking about a Tragedy (an Historical one, so I shall want heaps of criticisms on "Strafford")'.[1] In 1839 he submitted *King Victor and King Charles*[2] to Macready, who returned from a rehearsal at the Haymarket Theatre on 21 August to find Browning waiting for him, and noted in his *Diaries*: 'was kept by him long; but he left me where he found me. His object, if he exactly knew it, was to learn from me whether, if he wrote a really good play, it would have a secure chance of acceptance. I told him certainly, and after much vague conversation, he left me to read and rest as I could.'[3] No doubt the play was already nearly completed, since on 5 September Macready read it and concluded that it was 'a *great mistake*'. He called Browning into his room 'and most explicitly told him so, and gave him [his] reasons for coming to such a conclusion'. On 20 September Forster called on Macready and told him of 'Browning's intemperance about his play which he read to Fox, Forster, etc.'. *King Victor* is next mentioned in the *Diaries* on 5 May 1840: a busy day on which Macready attended one of Carlyle's lectures, acted Hamlet 'in a most real and effective manner', and then talked with 'Alexander Dumas' about his projected translation of *Macbeth*. After all this Browning arrived 'to speak about his play'. On 31 July he gave it to Macready, who commented in his *Diaries*: '[it] *does not look well*'. On 12 August

Browning called, and walked out with me on my way to the theatre. As he accompanied me he talked of his play and of *Sordello*, and I most honestly told him my opinion on both, expressing myself most anxious, as I am, that he should justify the expectations formed of him, but that he could not do so by placing himself in opposition to the world. He wished me to have his play done for nothing. I explained to him that Mr. Webster *would not* do it; we talked to the Haymarket, and in parting I promised to read it again.

---

[1] *Correspondence*, iii. 256.

[2] Since Victor's wife (dead before the action of the play begins) was a grand-daughter of Charles I, Browning may well have read about Victor and Savoy in the course of his work on *Strafford*.

[3] *Diaries*, ii. 22, 23, 24, 59, 72, 73.

About 30 December 1841, having obviously abandoned hope of a production, Browning told Fanny Haworth that he was 'going to print "Victor" ... by Feb'', adding enigmatically, 'and there is one thing not so badly painted there'.[1] The play was published on 12 March 1842. About 26 April, regretting the delay in the production of *A Blot in the 'Scutcheon*, 'which was to have been my *Second Number* of Plays', Browning told Macready that he had 'now ... published a very indifferent substitute, whose success will be problematical enough'.[2]

In his preliminary Note Browning refers to four accounts of the career of Victor Amadeus II of Savoy,[3] and makes a gesture towards further 'memoirs, correspondence, and relations of the time'. In fact he owes little to Voltaire's page on the subject, in his 'Précis du siècle de Louis XV', and very little to 'the fifth of Lord Orrery's Letters from Italy'. His main sources, apart from three articles in the *Biographie universelle* (the huge compendium already plundered for *Paracelsus* and *Sordello*), are Condorcet's commentary on Voltaire, and particularly the *Mémoires historiques* of the Abbé Roman, who claims to present a particularly reliable account of the abdication of Victor based on 'authentic memoirs'. Roman writes: 'The conversations which we have had with the old courtiers and the best informed men in Turin, during our residence in that city, provided us with insights which the manuscripts alone would not have afforded us'.[4] It is unlikely that Browning made any considerable use of further source-material.

He must have been attracted by the different interpretations of his *dramatis personae* in the various accounts. Voltaire describes Victor as a man 'whose indecisiveness had passed for policy', stating that he 'abdicated by one caprice ... and repented by another'.[5] For him Victor was a monarch who had become 'weary of affairs and of himself' and Charles a son who 'would have acquired a glory above crowns, by returning to his

---

[1] *Letters*, p. 7.   [2] *New Letters*, p. 25.
[3] See p. 100 below. For a good recent account see Geoffrey Symcox, *Victor Amadeus II: Absolutism in the Savoyard State 1675–1730* (1983). Symcox points out that it is misleading to refer to the territories which Victor ruled simply as 'the duchy of Savoy', since 'their real centre lay across the Alps in the Piedmontese plain of north-western Italy' (p. 7). His observation that 'the small size of the state he ruled makes it a purer "laboratory" specimen of absolutism than larger states like France' helps to explain the interest of Victor to Browning, who had been concerned, from his early poetry onwards, with the question where power should reside and what sort of man should be 'King': a subject discussed by Carlyle in the sixth of his lectures *On Heroes and Hero-Worship*, delivered 22 May 1840. Browning contrasts Victor and his son, for his own purposes, in a manner which departs widely from historical fact: see Jeremy Black, '*King Victor and King Charles*: the Historical Background', BSN (Spring 1984), pp. 39 ff.   [4] Roman, pp. 257–8.   [5] pp. 38–9.

father the crown which he had given him—if his father alone had asked it back from him, and if the circumstances of the time had permitted him to do so'. Voltaire admits that this had been out of the question, since it was reported to be Victor's ambitious mistress who desired to reign.

In his much more detailed account Condorcet tells us that Victor foresaw for Europe several years of peace, followed by another war during which he did not wish his country to be ruled either by an inexperienced young prince or by an old man weakened by age and infirmities.[1] After the abdication, according to Condorcet, D'Ormea decided to gain control. Suspecting that Victor had formed a plan to remount the throne—a plan which would have proved fatal to his own schemes—he persuaded Charles to have his father arrested in the middle of the night, as he lay in bed in the arms of his wife. Condorcet asserts that no evidence of such a plan on Victor's part was ever discovered, and insists that it is a duty to oppose all calumnies. 'Victor had been accused of being changeable, his wife of being ambitious—and both of a project to disturb their country in order to satisfy their ambition';[2] but in fact they were the victims of the treacherous D'Ormea, as Charles realized when it was too late.

In the long article on Victor in the *Biographie universelle*[3] Sismondi rejects the view that he had abdicated in desperation, to escape from an impossible situation between France and Austria, and suggests that he was satiated with power—or was perhaps imitating Christina of Sweden, Casimir of Poland, and Philip II of Spain, three other sovereigns who had abdicated. Like Voltaire and Orrery, Sismondi ascribes Victor's attempt to regain the throne to boredom and to the persuasions of the ambitious woman whom he had married. Admitting that Victor had been a subtle politician, he stresses the great benefits which he had conferred on his country.

It was only in Roman that Browning found an essential element of his play: the theory that Victor's abdication had from the first been a ruse. Roman's portrayal of 'Ce prince dissimulé'[4] is unambiguous throughout. He insists that Victor had chosen the side of France from pure self-interest, disregarding 'justice, honour [and] the faithful observance of treaties': a gamble which had proved unsuccessful. Victor's next move had been a calculated one: he 'only deprived himself of his sovereignty to shelter it from the storm, and to resume it when calm was re-established'.

---

[1] pp. 40 n.–42 n.   [2] Ibid., p. 43.
[3] Vol. xlviii (1827), 383–96. The article is by Sismondi: quotations from it in subsequent notes cite it as 'Sismondi'.
[4] Roman, pp. 260, 260, 257, 269, 260.

He planned to wait until 'the quarrel between the Emperor and the King of Spain should be terminated' before he could take any measures to regain his crown. Having a low opinion of the abilities of Charles, he intended him to be no more than a temporary regent. According to Roman, Victor believed that the Bourbons were 'too generous for the weight of their indignation and their vengeance to fall on a young prince who had just ascended the throne and who could not have had a hand in the projects of his father'. 'At this moment', he adds significantly, 'Victor forgot his Machiavelli.' It is as a Machiavellian schemer that Browning portrays Victor. The principal theme of the play is the contrast between two conceptions of kingship.[1]

Browning's representation of Charles as a man of 'extreme and painful sensibility, prolonged immaturity of powers, earnest good purpose and vacillating will' differs greatly from that which is to be found in the article on him in the *Biographie universelle*[2] and owes a great deal to Roman. Roman makes it clear that Victor had greatly preferred his elder son (whom Browning renames 'Philip'), a bold and lively young man with many of his father's qualities who had died of sunstroke at the age of seventeen. Victor did not love Charles, 'whom he found unresponsive, timid, modest, thrifty and withdrawn',[3] and lacking in any sign of brilliance. '"Off with you," said his father the King one day, "you will never be good for anything but for being the head of a religious order."' In Charles Victor found 'the submission of a son; unwillingness to take up the sceptre, and eagerness to lay it down at the first sign of his father's wish': a character perfectly suited to his schemes. Roman does not doubt the sincerity of Charles's desire that his father should retain the throne, nor does he suggest that there was any dissimulation in his expressions of unwillingness to rule. He states that Charles wished to resign the throne the following year, when his father asked him to do so—but that he was dissuaded by his advisers. He portrays Charles as a sensitive man who

---

[1] See *King Victor*, II. 147, *King Charles*, I. 310 ff., and *King Charles*, II. 50 ff., where the reformed D'Ormea is speaking: 'A temper / Like Victor's may avail to keep a state; / He terrifics men and they fall not off; / Good to restrain: best, if restraint were all. / But, with the silent circle round him, ends / Such sway: our King's begins precisely there.'

[2] viii (1813), 159–60. According to this article, Charles deliberately kept clear of political affairs in his youth, 'and to avoid alarming the easily offended and ambitious character of his father, forced himself to dissemble his natural talents for war and politics—talents easily developed in him by excellent masters'. Charles 'appeared indifferent to fame and power', seeming to take the title of King against his own desire. The article goes on to emphasize that he proved an effective and excellent monarch. A modern historian may see him as continuing his father's work.

[3] Roman, pp. 261–4.

would weep, later in his life, when he came in sight of the château of Moncalier or of anything else that reminded him of 'the last miseries of his father'.[1]

Polyxena, whose 'noble and right woman's manliness' does so much to help Charles to develop in the course of Browning's play, owes no more than her name to any of his sources: she is wholly his own creation.

For the Machiavellian character of D'Ormea Browning drew mainly on Condorcet and on an article in vol. xxxii of the *Biographie*.[2] Whereas Voltaire makes no mention of him, Condorcet tells us that he was one of the advisers whom Victor recommended to his son when he abdicated: 'This minister', Condorcet continues, 'had rendered him the service of terminating certain differences with the court of Rome which had continued for a large part of his reign, and of obtaining from Rome a concordat more favourable than Victor could have hoped for. He did not know [however] that Ormea had lavished money on Cardinal Coscia, . . . who governed Pope Benedict XIII',[3] with the result that Coscia had deceived the Pope for the benefit of Savoy. Condorcet tells us that when D'Ormea was recalled from Rome and appointed a minister of state, he planned to become master from the moment of his arrival. It was he who was responsible for Charles's subsequent treatment of his father: he was 'le vrai coupable'.[4] Browning's attempt to show D'Ormea's development from 'ill-considered rascality' to his 'subsequent better-advised rectitude' is entirely his own conception.

While the Countess of Sebastian never appears on the stage, she has a role of some importance in the background of the play, as she had in history. Voltaire describes her as Victor's 'maîtresse devenue sa femme'.[5] Condorcet says that while the Countess and Victor had long been friends, he had never been her lover. Sismondi hints that she had been his mistress. Roman, like Orrery, tells us that they had become lovers when he was a young prince and she a beauty of fifteen, and that their love was said to have had 'des suites trop sensibles', which explains Browning's reference to her son.[6] About her character there is little difference of opinion. Roman describes her development in one concise sentence: 'The young and beautiful Cumiane had been tender and sensitive; the countess of Saint Sebastian was an intriguer; the marchioness of Spigo set no limits to her ambition; she coveted the throne.'[7]

---

[1] Ibid., pp. 282–3.   [2] pp. 145–7.

[3] Condorcet, p. 40 n.   [4] Ibid., p. 43 n.

[5] Voltaire, p. 38; Condorcet, p. 40; *Biographie universelle*, xlviii, p. 393a; Roman, p. 266.

[6] *King Victor*, I. 272.   [7] Roman, p. 268.

No manuscript of *King Victor and King Charles* is known to be extant. After its appearance as the second of the *Bells and Pomegranates* the play was included in each collected edition, but not extensively revised. After *1849* Browning almost consistently changed the pronunciation of the name 'D'Ormea', expanding it from two to three syllables and shifting the stress from the first syllable to the second: so altering the metre of every line in which the name appears. This revision, together with 'sir' for 'sire' and 'Chambery' for 'Chamberri', accounts in places for up to a fifth of the substantive changes after the first edition. Neither of the changes which Browning made in the Brigham Young copy of *Bells and Pomegranates* ('striped' for 'stripped' at *King Victor*, II. 345 and 'how'er' for 'however' at *King Charles*, II. 98) found its way into later editions. The six emendations made by Browning in the Dykes Campbell copy of *1888* are adopted in the present edition.[1] In other places we have seldom departed from our copy-text, although we have occasionally preferred an earlier reading where the punctuation of *1888* is defective[2] or where Browning or his compositor wavered over a tricky spelling, as in *King Victor*, II. 331.

---

[1] These include 'give a pretext' for 'give pretext' in *King Charles*, I. 31, which was made incorrectly in *1889*.

[2] e.g. *King Victor*, II. 194.

KING VICTOR & KING CHARLES;

A TRAGEDY.

title *1842* BELLS AND POMEGRANATES. Nᵒ· II—KING VICTOR AND KING CHARLES. BY ROBERT BROWNING, Author of "Paracelsus." LONDON: EDWARD MOXON, DOVER STREET. MDCCCXLII. *1849-68* CHARLES. A Tragedy.

NOTE.

So far as I know, this Tragedy is the first artistic consequence of what Voltaire termed "a terrible event without consequences;" and although it professes to be historical, I have taken more pains to arrive at the history than most readers would thank me for particularizing: since acquainted,
5 as I will hope them to be, with the chief circumstances of Victor's remarkable European career—nor quite ignorant of the sad and surprising facts I am about to reproduce (a tolerable account of which is to be found, for instance, in Abbé Roman's *Récit*, or even the fifth of Lord Orrery's Letters from Italy)—I cannot expect them to be versed, nor desirous of becoming
10 so, in all the detail of the memoirs, correspondence, and relations of the time. From these only may be obtained a knowledge of the fiery and audacious temper, unscrupulous selfishness, profound dissimulation, and singular fertility in resources, of Victor—the extreme and painful sensibility, prolonged immaturity of powers, earnest good purpose and vacil-
15 lating will of Charles—the noble and right woman's manliness of his wife—and the ill-considered rascality and subsequent better-advised rectitude of D'Ormea. When I say, therefore, that I cannot but believe my statement (combining as it does what appears correct in Voltaire and plausible in Condorcet) more true to person and thing than any it has
20 hitherto been my fortune to meet with, no doubt my word will be taken, and my evidence spared as readily.

R. B.

London: 1842.

1842 ADVERTISEMENT. So *1849–68* {no heading}   1 *1842–63* first artistical con-
sequence   7 *1842–63* reproduce (tolerable accounts of   9 *1842* versed, or
desirous   10 *1842–63* the   details   of   22 *1849* {no   signature}
23 *1842,1849*
{no dateline}

   2 *"a terrible event"*: 'Ce fut un terrible événement qui n'eut aucune suite': 'Précis du siècle
de Louis XV': *Œuvres* (70 vols., Strasburg, 1784–5), xxii. 39.
   8 *Abbé Roman's Récit*: *Mémoires historiques et inédits sur les révolutions arrivées en Danemarck et
en Suède . . .; suivis . . . d'un récit historique sur l'abdication de Victor Amédée, roi de Savoie*, by the
Abbé Roman (Paris, 1807).
   Lord Orrery's Letters: *Letters from Italy, in the Years 1754 and 1755*, by the late Rt. Hon.
John Earl of Corke and Orrery (1773), pp. 46–53.
   19 *Condorcet*: Condorcet's long note appears on pp. 39–43 of the edition of Voltaire
mentioned above.

PERSONS.

Victor Amadeus, *first King of Sardinia.*
Charles Emmanuel, *his son, Prince of Piedmont.*
Polyxena, *wife of Charles.*
D'Ormea, *minister.*

Scene.—*The Council Chamber of Rivoli Palace, near Turin, communicating with a Hall at the back, an Apartment to the left, and another to the right of the stage.*

Time, 1730–1731.

KING VICTOR & KING CHARLES.

FIRST YEAR, 1730.—KING VICTOR.

PART I.

CHARLES, POLYXENA.

Charles. You think so? Well, I do not.
Polyxena.   My beloved,
All must clear up; we shall be happy yet:
This cannot last for ever—oh, may change
To-day or any day!
Charles.   —May change? Ah yes—
May change!
Polyxena.   Endure it, then.
Charles.   No doubt, a life   5
Like this drags on, now better and now worse.
My father. may . . . may take to loving me;
And he may take D'Ormea closer yet
To counsel him;—may even cast off her
—That bad Sebastian; but he also may   10
. . . Or no, Polyxena, my only friend,
He may not force you from me?
Polyxena.   Now, force me
From you!—me, close by you as if there gloomed
No Sebastians, no D'Ormeas on our path—
At Rivoli or Turin, still at hand,   15
Arch-counsellor, prime confidant . . . force me!
Charles. Because I felt as sure, as I feel sure

---

6 *1842,1849* worse;   8 *1842,1849* take, too, D'Ormea   14 *1842* No D'Or-
meas, no Sebastians on

8 *D'Ormea* : trisyllabic, with the stress on the second syllable. See p. 98, above.
10 *Sebastian* : see Introduction, p. 97.

We clasp hands now, of being happy once.
Young was I, quite neglected, nor concerned
By the world's business that engrossed so much   20
My father and my brother: if I peered
From out my privacy,—amid the crash
And blaze of nations, domineered those two.
'T was war, peace—France our foe, now—England, friend—
In love with Spain—at feud with Austria! Well—   25
I wondered, laughed a moment's laugh for pride
In the chivalrous couple, then let drop
My curtain—"I am out of it," I said—
When . . .
    Polyxena. You have told me, Charles.
    Charles.   Polyxena—
When suddenly,—a warm March day, just that!   30
Just so much sunshine as the cottage child
Basks in delighted, while the cottager
Takes off his bonnet, as he ceases work,
To catch the more of it—and it must fall
Heavily on my brother! Had you seen   35
Philip—the lion-featured! not like me!
    Polyxena. I know—
    Charles.   And Philip's mouth yet fast to mine,
His dead cheek on my cheek, his arm still round
My neck,—they bade me rise, "for I was heir
To the Duke," they said, "the right hand of the Duke:"   40

23 *1842,1849* two;   24 *1842* England's friend—   29 *1868* Charles!
30-3 *1842* that | Sunshine the cottager's child basks in—he | Takes   31 *1849-65* the
cottager's child   35 *1842-65* brother . . . had   40 *1842-63* Duke;" *1865*
Duke."

    20 *the world's business*: as in *Sordello*, i. 624.
    24 *'T was war, peace*: see Introduction. The reference is to the war of the Spanish Succes-
sion, concluded in 1713. Charles had been born in 1701. Victor's elder son (also Victor Ama-
deus) died in 1715: to avoid confusion, Browning changes his name to Philip (l. 36 below).
    27 *chivalrous*: brave, adventurous. Johnson, who states that the word is 'Out of use',
stresses the first syllable. Here the stress is on the second, as in *An Universal Etymological
English Dictionary*, by N. Bailey, 14th ed., 1751.
    34 *it must fall*: the sun. 'Il mourut . . . d'un coup de soleil': Roman, p. 264. In Condorcet
no cause of his death is given: in the article on Victor in *Biographie universelle*, xlviii, the
death is said to have been due to smallpox.

Till then he was my father, not the Duke.
So . . . let me finish . . . the whole intricate
World's-business their dead boy was born to, I
Must conquer,—ay, the brilliant thing he was,
I, of a sudden must be: my fault, my follies,   45
—All bitter truths were told me, all at once,
To end the sooner. What I simply styled
Their overlooking me, had been contempt:
How should the Duke employ himself, forsooth,
With such an one, while lordly Philip rode   50
By him their Turin through? But he was punished,
And must put up with—me! 'T was sad enough
To learn my future portion and submit.
And then the wear and worry, blame on blame!
For, spring-sounds in my ears, spring-smells about,   55
How could I but grow dizzy in their pent
Dim palace-rooms at first? My mother's look
As they discussed my insignificance,
She and my father, and I sitting by,—
I bore; I knew how brave a son they missed: 60
Philip had gaily run state-papers through,
While Charles was spelling at them painfully!
But Victor was my father spite of that.
"Duke Victor's entire life has been," I said,
"Innumerable efforts to one end;   65
"And on the point now of that end's success,
"Our Ducal turning to a Kingly crown,
"Where's time to be reminded 't is his child

---

41 *1842–68* Duke!   59 *1842,1849* (She . . . . by,)—   61 *1842–65* gaily passed
state-papers o'er,   64–9 *1842* {no quotation marks}

    44 *the brilliant thing*: '*Victor Amédée* avait un fils aîné, qui rempli de qualités aimables en faisait espérer de brillantes': Condorcet, p. 39 n.
    57 *My mother's look*: Victor's first wife Anne, daughter of the Duke of Orléans and granddaughter of Charles I, died in 1728.
    67 "*Our Ducal turning to a Kingly crown*: Duke of Savoy from the age of seven, Victor became King of Sicily in 1713 and King of Sardinia in 1720. Sismondi tells us that 'his greatest ambition was the title of king': *Biographie universelle*, xlviii. 390b. The ambition had long characterized his family: ibid., 392b. Cf. Marlowe, *Tamburlaine the Great*, Part I, II. vii. 29.

"He spurns?" And so I suffered—scarcely suffered,
Since I had you at length!
   Polyxena.   —To serve in place   70
Of monarch, minister, and mistress, Charles.
   Charles. But, once that crown obtained, then was't not like
Our lot would alter? "When he rests, takes breath,
"Glances around, sees who there's left to love—
"Now that my mother's dead, sees I am left—   75
"Is it not like he'll love me at the last?"
Well, Savoy turns Sardinia; the Duke's King:
Could I—precisely then—could you expect
His harshness to redouble? These few months
Have been . . . have been . . . Polyxena, do you   80
And God conduct me, or I lose myself!
What would he have? What is 't they want with me?
Him with this mistress and this minister,
—You see me and you hear him; judge us both!
Pronounce what I should do, Polyxena!   85
   Polyxena. Endure, endure, beloved! Say you not
He is your father? All's so incident
To novel sway! Beside, our life must change:
Or you'll acquire his kingcraft, or he'll find
Harshness a sorry way of teaching it.   90
I bear this—not that there's so much to bear.
   Charles. You bear? Do not I know that you, tho' bound
To silence for my sake, are perishing
Piecemeal beside me? And how otherwise

---

69 *1842* suffered . . hardly suffered, *1849* suffered . . yet scarce suffered, *1863* suffered—
yet scarce suffered,   71 *1863-8* Charles!   73–6 *1842* {no quotation marks}
74 *1842-68* around, and sees who's left   76 *1842* Was it not like he'd love {some
copies of *1888, 1889* lack initial quotation marks}   77 *1842,1849* Well: . . . . King!
87 *1842-65* That he's your   89 *1842* he'll learn   90 *1842* His own's a
92 *1842-65* bear it? Don't I   94 *1842-63* otherwise?

   70 *I had you at length!*: Victor's younger son married Polixène-Christine of Hesse-
Rheinsfeld in 1724, his first wife having died the previous year.

   79 *His harshness to redouble?*: Condorcet, pp. 39–40 n.

   83 *this mistress*: Browning follows the common belief, rejecting Condorcet's contention
that Sebastian had never been Victor's mistress. See Introduction, p. 97.

When every creephole from the hideous Court   95
Is stopped: the Minister to dog me, here—
The Mistress posted to entrap you, there!
And thus shall we grow old in such a life;
Not careless, never estranged,—but old: to alter
Our life, there is so much to alter!
    Polyxena.   · Come—   100
Is it agreed that we forego complaint
Even at Turin, yet complain we here
At Rivoli? 'T were wiser you announced
Our presence to the King. What's now afoot
I wonder? Not that any more's to dread   105
Than every day's embarrassment: but guess
For me, why train so fast succeeded train
On the high-road, each gayer still than each!
I noticed your Archbishop's pursuivant,
The sable cloak and silver cross; such pomp   110
Bodes . . . what now, Charles? Can you conceive?
    Charles.   · Not I.
    Polyxena. A matter of some moment.
    Charles.   There's our life!
Which of the group of loiterers that stare
From the lime-avenue, divines that I—
About to figure presently, he thinks,   .   115
In face of all assembled—am the one
Who knows precisely least about it?
    Polyxena.   Tush!
D'Ormea's contrivance!
    Charles.   Ay, how otherwise
Should the young Prince serve for the old King's foil?
—So that the simplest courtier may remark   120
'T were idle raising parties for a Prince

---

97 *1865* there. *1868* there?   101 *1842–63* forego complaints   108 *1842–63*
each;   113 *1842–63* that stared

---

   95 *creephole*: 'A hole into which any animal may creep to escape danger': Johnson. Cf.
'Instans Tyrannus', 55.
   102 *Turin*: Victor's capital (stressed on the first syllable).

Content to linger the Court's laughing-stock.
Something, 't is like, about that weary business
    [*Pointing to papers he has laid down, and which* POLYXENA *examines.*
—Not that I comprehend three words, of course,
After all last night's study.
    Polyxena.   The faint heart!   125
Why, as we rode and you rehearsed just now
Its substance . . . (that's the folded speech I mean,
Concerning the Reduction of the Fiefs)
—What would you have?—I fancied while you spoke,
Some tones were just your father's.
    Charles.   Flattery!   130
    Polyxena. I fancied so:—and here lurks, sure enough
My note upon the Spanish Claims! You've mastered
The fief-speech thoroughly: this other, mind,
Is an opinion you deliver,—stay,
Best read it slowly over once to me;   135
Read—there's bare time; you read it firmly—loud
—Rather loud, looking in his face,—don't sink
Your eye once—ay, thus! "If Spain claims . . ." begin
—Just as you look at me!
    Charles.   At you! Oh truly,
You have I seen, say, marshalling your troops,   140
Dismissing councils, or, through doors ajar,
Head sunk on hand, devoured by slow chagrins
—Then radiant, for a crown had all at once
Seemed possible again! I can behold
Him, whose least whisper ties my spirit fast,   145
In this sweet brow, nought could divert me from
Save objects like Sebastian's shameless lip,

---

122 *1842-63* linger D'Ormea's laughing-stock! *1865,1868* linger D'Ormea's laughing-stock.   123 *1863* business: *1865,1868* business!

  128 *the Reduction of the Fiefs*: the article on D'Ormea in the *Biographie universelle* mentions that he was instrumental in having minutely examined 'les titres en vertu desquels les nobles possédaient quelques fiefs démembrés du domaine de l'état, pour les forcer à restitution, sur de légers vices de forme': xxxii. 145b. 'Reduction' here has the obsolete meaning 'reclamation'.

  132 *the Spanish Claims!*: Roman, pp. 259 ff.

Or worse, the clipped grey hair and dead white face
And dwindling eye as if it ached with guile,
D'Ormea wears . . .
        [*As he kisses her, enter from the* KING's *apartment* D'ORMEA.
            I said he would divert   150
My kisses from your brow!
    D'Ormea [*aside*].   Here! So, King Victor
Spoke truth for once: and who's ordained, but I
To make that memorable? Both in call,
As he declared. Were 't better gnash the teeth,
Or laugh outright now?
    Charles [*to* POLYXENA]. What's his visit for?   155
    D'Ormea [*aside*]. I question if they even speak to me.
    Polyxena [*to* CHARLES].
Face the man! He'll suppose you fear him, else.
[*Aloud.*] The Marquis bears the King's command, no doubt?
    D'Ormea [*aside*]. Precisely!—If I threatened him, perhaps?
Well, this at least is punishment enough!   160
Men used to promise punishment would come.
    Charles. Deliver the King's message, Marquis!
    D'Ormea [*aside*].   Ah—
So anxious for his fate? [*Aloud.*] A word, my Prince,
Before you see your father—just one word
Of counsel!
    Charles. Oh, your counsel certainly!   165
Polyxena, the Marquis counsels us!
Well, sir? Be brief, however!
    D'Ormea.   What? You know
As much as I?—preceded me, most like,
In knowledge! So! ('T is in his eye, beside—
His voice: he knows it, and his heart's on flame   170
Already.) You surmise why you, myself,

150 *1842,1849* Which D'Ormea wears . . .   152 *1842* once,   154 *1842–68*
declared!   156 *1842,1849* if they'll even   157 *1842,1849* Face D'Ormea,
he'll   158 *1842–65* doubt.   165 *1842–63* certainly—   169 *1842,1849*
knowledge?   *1842* 'Tis   171 *1842* Already! *1849–68* Already!)

Del Borgo, Spava, fifty nobles more,
Are summoned thus?
    Charles.   Is the Prince used to know,
At any time, the pleasure of the King,
Before his minister?—Polyxena,   175
Stay here till I conclude my task: I feel
Your presence (smile not) through the walls, and take
Fresh heart. The King's within that chamber?
    D'Ormea [*passing the table whereon a paper lies, exclaims, as he*
        glances at it].   "Spain"!
    Polyxena [*aside to* CHARLES].
Tarry awhile: what ails the minister?
    D'Ormea. Madam, I do not often trouble you.   180
The Prince loathes, and you scorn me—let that pass!
But since it touches him and you, not me,
Bid the Prince listen!
    Polyxena [*to* CHARLES]. Surely you will listen!
—Deceit?—those fingers crumpling up his vest?
    Charles. Deceitful to the very fingers' ends!   185
    D'Ormea [*who has approached them, overlooks the other paper*
    CHARLES *continues to hold*].
My project for the Fiefs! As I supposed!
Sir, I must give you light upon those measures
—For this is mine, and that I spied of Spain,
Mine too!
    Charles. Release me! Do you gloze on me
Who bear in the world's face (that is, the world   190
You make for me at Turin) your contempt?

---

*178 (editors' emendation) *1842* Spain! *1849–89* "Spain!"   181 *1842–68* you loathe
me—   *1842,1849* pass;   183 *1865,1868* will listen   191 *1842–65* You've
made for

   172 *Del Borgo*: 'On the 3rd of September 1730, he [Victor] summoned to the château of
Rivoli the knights of the Annonciade, the ministers of state, the presidents of the supreme
courts, and all the great men, without anyone—but for the Prince of Piedmont and the
Marquis del Borgo—being informed of the reason for this extraordinary convocation':
Sismondi, p. 393a. Cf. Roman, pp. 264–5. 'Spava' does not occur in any of the sources
named by Browning.
   189 *gloze on me*: use fair words to me.

—Your measures?—When was not a hateful task
D'Ormea's imposition? Leave my robe!
What post can I bestow, what grant concede?
Or do you take me for the King?
    D'Ormea.   Not I!   195
Not yet for King,—not for, as yet, thank God,
One who in . . . shall I say a year, a month?
Ay!—shall be wretcheder than e'er was slave
In his Sardinia.—Europe's spectacle
And the world's bye-word! What? The Prince aggrieved   200
That I excluded him our counsels? Here
                        [*Touching the paper in* CHARLES's *hand.*
Accept a method of extorting gold
From Savoy's nobles, who must wring its worth
In silver first from tillers of the soil,
Whose hinds again have to contribute brass   205
To make up the amount: there's counsel, sir,
My counsel, one year old; and the fruit, this—
Savoy's become a mass of misery
And wrath, which one man has to meet—the King:
You're not the King! Another counsel, sir!   210
Spain entertains a project (here it lies)
Which, guessed, makes Austria offer that same King
Thus much to baffle Spain; he promises;

192 *1865,1868*—Your measure?—When was not any hateful *1842-63* was any hateful
193 *1842-63* Not D'Ormea's   199 *1842-68* Sardinia,—   201 *1842,1849*
That I've excluded   206 *1842-68* sir!

    202 *extorting gold*: the article on D'Ormea in the *Biographie universelle* tells us that 'The
operations which he suggested and carried out, as director of finance, made him a crowd of
enemies': xxxii. 145b.
    211 *Spain entertains a project*: 'events having made it probable that the Bourbons would
return to Italy again, Victor and all the other European cabinets became anxious at the
prospect. Victor received propositions from both France and Austria to join with them in
case of a rupture. After having wavered between them for some time, he finally made
secret engagements with both. In June, 1730, he received from the Emperor of Austria a
sum of money, with the promise that he and his descendants should be governors of Milan
in perpetuo if he would never separate his interests from those of Austria. A few days after,
the Spanish Minister, having had a secret audience with him, made him flattering offers, if
he would declare himself for the Bourbons': Porter and Clarke.
    212 *makes Austria offer*: Roman, pp. 259-60.

Then comes Spain, breathless lest she be forestalled,
Her offer follows; and he promises . . .   215
    Charles. —Promises, sir, when he has just agreed
To Austria's offer?
    D'Ormea.   That's a counsel, Prince!
But past our foresight, Spain and Austria (choosing
To make their quarrel up between themselves
Without the intervention of a friend)   220
Produce both treaties, and both promises . . .
    Charles. How?
    D'Ormea.   Prince, a counsel! And the fruit of that?
Both parties covenant afresh, to fall
Together on their friend, blot out his name,
Abolish him from Europe. So, take note,   225
Here's Austria and here's Spain to fight against:
And what sustains the King but Savoy here,
A miserable people mad with wrongs?
You're not the King!
    Charles.   Polyxena, you said
All would clear up: all does clear up to me.   230
    D'Ormea. Clear up! 'T is no such thing to envy, then?
You see the King's state in its length and breadth?
You blame me now for keeping you aloof
From counsels and the fruit of counsels? Wait
Till I explain this morning's business!
    Charles [*aside*].   No—   235
Stoop to my father, yes,—D'Ormea, no:
—The King's son, not to the King's counsellor!
I will do something, but at least retain
The credit of my deed. [*Aloud*]. Then it is this
You now expressly come to tell me?
    D'Ormea.   This   240

215 *1842* follows,   216 *1842-68* he before agreed   218 *1842* Austria,
choosing   220 *1842* friend,   226 *1842-68* against,   230 *1842-68*
me!   231 *1842-63* Clears up? *1865,1868* Clear up?   235 *1842,1849* I've
explained this   236 *1842,1849* yes,—to D'Ormea, *1842* no!   239 *1842-68*
deed!   *1842,1849* Then, D'Ormea, this

    229 *you said* : l. 2 above.

To tell! You apprehend me?
   Charles.   Perfectly.
Further, D'Ormea, you have shown yourself,
For the first time these many weeks and months,
Disposed to do my bidding?
   D'Ormea.   From the heart!
   Charles. Acquaint my father, first, I wait his pleasure: 245
Next . . . or, I'll tell you at a fitter time.
Acquaint the King!
   D'Ormea [*aside*]. If I 'scape Victor yet!
First, to prevent this stroke at me: if not,—
Then, to avenge it! [*To* CHARLES.] Gracious sir, I go.   [*Goes.*
   Charles. God, I forbore! Which more offends, that man   250
Or that man's master? Is it come to this?
Have they supposed (the sharpest insult yet)
I needed e'en his intervention? No!
No—dull am I, conceded,—but so dull,
Scarcely! Their step decides me.
   Polyxena.   How decides?   255
   Charles. You would be freed D'Ormea's eye and hers?
—Could fly the court with me and live content?
So, this it is for which the knights assemble!
The whispers and the closeting of late,
The savageness and insolence of old,   260
—For this!
   Polyxena. What mean you?
   Charles.   How? You fail to catch
Their clever plot? I missed it, but could you?
These last two months of care to inculcate
How dull I am,—D'Ormea's present visit
To prove that, being dull, I might be worse   265
Were I a King—as wretched as now dull—

---

242 *1842,1849* And further,   *245 (reading of *1842-68*) *1888,1889* pleasure
249 *1842* s.d. †[*Exit.*   252 *1842* yet!)   256 *1842-63* be free from D'Ormea's
264 *1842,1849* am,—with D'Ormea's

   259 *the closeting*: 'private conferences, which were then called closetings': Hume, *History of England* (1806 ed.), v. lxx. 264.

You recognize in it no winding up
Of a long plot?
    Polyxena.   Why should there be a plot?
    Charles. The crown's secure now; I should shame the
      crown—
An old complaint; the point is, how to gain   270
My place for one, more fit in Victor's eyes,
His mistress the Sebastian's child.
    Polyxena.   In truth?
    Charles. They dare not quite dethrone Sardinia's Prince:
But they may descant on my dulness till
They sting me into even praying them   275
Grant leave to hide my head, resign my state,
And end the coil. Not see now? In a word,
They'd have me tender them myself my rights
As one incapable;—some cause for that,
Since I delayed thus long to see their drift!   280
I shall apprise the King he may resume
My rights this moment.
    Polyxena.   Pause! I dare not think
So ill of Victor.
    Charles.   Think no ill of him!
    Polyxena. —Nor think him, then, so shallow as to suffer
His purpose be divined thus easily.   285
And yet—you are the last of a great line;
There's a great heritage at stake; new days
Seemed to await this newest of the realms
Of Europe:—Charles, you must withstand this!
    Charles.   Ah—

---

270 *1842* to save   271 {no equivalent in *1842*}   272 *1842* My place for his
Sebastian's   *1849, 1863* mistress',   276 *1842-65* For leave   277 *1842* see
that? In   282 *1842,1849* Pause—

   272 *the Sebastian's child*: cf. Introduction, p. 97. There is no suggestion in history, or in
this play, that Victor had any such intention.
   277 *the coil*: the trouble, as in *Sordello*, i. 379, and *The Ring and the Book*, x. 2043.
   287 *new days*: Browning probably assumes that his readers are aware of the highly suc-
cessful and beneficent reign of Victor's son and successor, as summarized (for example) in
the article on Charles-Emmanuel III in *Biographie universelle*, viii. 159-60.

You dare not then renounce the splendid Court   290
For one whom all the world despises? Speak!
   Polyxena. My gentle husband, speak I will, and truth.
Were this as you believe, and I once sure
Your duty lay in so renouncing rule,
I could . . . could? Oh what happiness it were—   295
To live, my Charles, and die, alone with you!
   Charles. I grieve I asked you. To the presence, then!
By this, D'Ormea acquaints the King, no doubt,
He fears I am too simple for mere hints,
And that no less will serve than Victor's mouth   300
Demonstrating in council what I am.
I have not breathed, I think, these many years!
   Polyxena. Why, it may be!—if he desire to wed
That woman, call legitimate her child.
   Charles. You see as much? Oh, let his will have way!   305
You'll not repent confiding in me, love?
There's many a brighter spot in Piedmont, far,
Than Rivoli. I'll seek him: or, suppose
You hear first how I mean to speak my mind?
—Loudly and firmly both, this time, be sure!   310
I yet may see your Rhine-land, who can tell?
Once away, ever then away! I breathe.
   Polyxena. And I too breathe.
   Charles.   Come, my Polyxena!

298 *1842,1849* D'Ormea acquaints the King by this, no doubt,   301 *1842–63*
Teaching me in full council   303 *1842,1849* he desires to   304 *1842–65*
woman and legitimate   313 *1842–63* breathe!   *1842* s.d. †[*Exeunt.*

KING VICTOR.

Part II.

Enter King Victor, *bearing the Regalia on a cushion, from his apartment.*
He calls loudly.

Victor. D'Ormea!—for patience fails me, treading thus
Among the obscure trains I have laid,—my knights
Safe in the hall here—in that anteroom,
My son,—D'Ormea, where? Of this, one touch—

[*Laying down the crown.*

This fireball to these mute black cold trains—then   5
Outbreak enough!
[*Contemplating it.*] To lose all, after all!
This, glancing o'er my house for ages—shaped,
Brave meteor, like the crown of Cyprus now,
Jerusalem, Spain, England, every change
The braver,—and when I have clutched a prize   10
My ancestry died wan with watching for,
To lose it!—by a slip, a fault, a trick
Learnt to advantage once and not unlearned
When past the use,—"just this once more" (I thought)
"Use it with Spain and Austria happily,   15
"And then away with trick!" An oversight
I'd have repaired thrice over, any time
These fifty years, must happen now! There's peace
At length; and I, to make the most of peace,
Ventured my project on our people here,   20
As needing not their help: which Europe knows,
And means, cold-blooded, to dispose herself

---

2 *1842-63* the trains that I   3 {no equivalent in *1842*}   4 *1842,1849* son,—
and D'Ormea   5 *1842-63* then!   19 *1842* make of peace the most,

5 *black cold trains*: Johnson defines 'train' as 'the line of powder leading to the mine'.
7 *glancing o'er my house for ages*: see *King Victor*, 1, 67 n. above.

(Apart from plausibilities of war)
To crush the new-made King—who ne'er till now
Feared her. As Duke, I lost each foot of earth   25
And laughed at her: my name was left, my sword
Left, all was left! But she can take, she knows,
This crown, herself conceded . . . That's to try,
Kind Europe! My career's not closed as yet!
This boy was ever subject to my will,   ·   30
Timid and tame—the fitter! D'Ormea, too—
What if the sovereign also rid himself
Of thee, his prime of parasites?—I delay!
D'Ormea!   [*As* D'ORMEA *enters, the* KING *seats himself.*
       My son, the Prince—attends he?
    D'Ormea.   Sir,
He does attend. The crown prepared!—it seems   35
That you persist in your resolve.
       Victor.   Who's come?
The chancellor and the chamberlain? My knights?
    D'Ormea. The whole Annunziata. If, my liege,
Your fortune had not tottered worse than now . . .
    Victor. Del Borgo has drawn up the schedules? mine—   40
My son's, too? Excellent! Only, beware
Of the least blunder, or we look but fools.
First, you read the Annulment of the Oaths;   ·
Del Borgo follows . . . no, the Prince shall sign;
Then let Del Borgo read the Instrument: 45
On which, I enter.
    D'Ormea.   Sir, this may be truth;
You, sir, may do as you affect—may break

23 *1842* (Apart the plausibilities   32 *1842–63* sovereign's also rid of thee
33 *1842–63* His prime of parasites?—Yet I delay!   34 *1842–63* he? Sire,
39 *1842–63* Your fortunes had   41 *1842* Excellent.   42 *1842* or but fools
we look.   46 *1842–63* enter.—Sire, this   47 *1842–63* You, sire, may

  23 *plausibilities of war*: perhaps 'plausible threats of war'. In *La Saisiaz*, l. 399, 'plausibilit-
ies of trust' seems to mean 'things it is plausible to trust in'.
  31 *Timid and tame*: 'Ce prince était froid, timide, modeste': Roman, p. 263.
  38 *The whole Annunziata*: 'les chevaliers de l'ordre de l'Annonciade': Roman, p. 264. The
Annunziata, the highest Italian Order of Chivalry, was instituted in 1362 by Amedeo VI of
Savoy, and renewed in 1515.   47 *affect*: please.

Your engine, me, to pieces: try at least
If not a spring remain worth saving! Take
My counsel as I've counselled many times!   50
What if the Spaniard and the Austrian threat?
There's England, Holland, Venice—which ally
Select you?
    Victor.   Aha! Come, D'Ormea,—"truth"
Was on your lip a minute since. Allies?
I've broken faith with Venice, Holland, England   55
—As who knows if not you!
    D'Ormea.   But why with me
Break faith—with one ally, your best, break faith?
    Victor. When first I stumbled on you, Marquis—'t was
At Mondovi—a little lawyer's clerk . . .
     D'Ormea. Therefore your soul's ally!—who brought you
       through   60
Your quarrel with the Pope, at pains enough—
Who simply echoed you in these affairs—
On whom you cannot therefore visit these
Affairs' ill-fortune—whom you trust to guide
You safe (yes, on my soul) through these affairs!   65
     Victor. I was about to notice, had you not
Prevented me, that since that great town kept
With its chicane D'Ormea's satchel stuffed
And D'Ormea's self sufficiently recluse,
He missed a sight,—my naval armament   70

---

49 *1842-63* spring remains worth   *1842* saving! Bid   50 *1842* Me counsel
53 *1842,1849* Come, my D'Ormea,   55 *1842-63* England.   56 *1842* But not
with   57 *1842* Broke faith . . . . best, broke faith.   58-9 *1842* Marquis—(at |
Mondovi 'twas,—a   . . . .   clerk . . .)   59 *1863,1865*   lawyer's-clerk . . .
62 *1842,1849* Who've simply   64 *1842-63* you'll trust   65 *1842-63* soul) in
these   67 *1842* since Mondovi kept   68 *1842,1849* chicane my D'Ormea's

    51 *the Spaniard and the Austrian*: Roman, p. 260.

    59 *at Mondovi*: according to the article on D'Ormea in the *Biographie universelle*, xxxii.
145a, Victor found D'Ormea, a man of humble family from Mondovi, serving as a judge at
Carmagnola. Condorcet says he was 'tiré de la misère'.

    68 *chicane*: chicanery, the abuse of legal forms: 'The art of protracting a contest by petty
objection and artifice': Johnson. Cf. 'Before', 31.

When I burned Toulon. How the skiff exults
Upon the galliot's wave!—rises its height,
O'ertops it even; but the great wave bursts,
And hell-deep in the horrible profound
Buries itself the galliot: shall the skiff   75
Think to escape the sea's black trough in turn?
Apply this: you have been my minister
—Next me, above me possibly;—sad post,
Huge care, abundant lack of peace of mind;
Who would desiderate the eminence?   80
You gave your soul to get it; you'd yet give
Your soul to keep it, as I mean you shall,
D'Ormea! What if the wave ebbed with me?
Whereas it cants you to another crest;
I toss you to my son; ride out your ride!   85
    D'Ormea. Ah, you so much despise me?
    Victor.   You, D'Ormea?
Nowise: and I'll inform you why. A king
Must in his time have many ministers,
And I've been rash enough to part with mine
When I thought proper. Of the tribe, not one   90
(... Or wait, did Pianezze?—ah, just the same!)
Not one of them, ere his remonstrance reached
The length of yours, but has assured me (commonly
Standing much as you stand,—or nearer, say,
The door to make his exit on his speech)   95
—I should repent of what I did. D'Ormea,

---

83 *1842,1849* My D'Ormea!   84 *1842,1849* to another's crest   86 *1842–63*
me then? You,   96 *1842* –"I .... did:" now, D'Ormea, *1849* did: now, D'Ormea,
1863 did:

   71 *When I burned Toulon*: an exaggeration. In the summer of 1707 a force of Savoyard,
Imperial, and hired contingents, under the command of Victor and Prince Eugene,
besieged Toulon. They were unsuccessful, but the defenders of Toulon were obliged to
scuttle the warships in the harbour to protect them from bombardment.
    exults: rises exultantly. Cf. Pope, *Windsor-Forest*, 112.
   72 *the galliot's wave*: a galliot is 'a small, swift galley': Johnson.   84 *cants*: tosses.
   91 *Pianezze*: Sismondi names the Marquis of Pianezze as one of two counsellors who
persuaded Victor, as a very young man, briefly to imprison his own mother: p. 383b. Victor
soon repented, and arrested the two men.

Be candid, you approached it when I bade you
Prepare the schedules! But you stopped in time,
You have not so assured me: how should I
Despise you then?

Enter CHARLES.

   Victor [*changing his tone*]. Are you instructed? Do   100
My order, point by point! About it, sir!
   D'Ormea. You so despise me! [*Aside.*] One last stay
     remains—
The boy's discretion there.
          [*To* CHARLES.]   For your sake, Prince,
I pleaded, wholly in your interest,
To save you from this fate!
   Charles [*aside*].   Must I be told   105
The Prince was supplicated for—by him?
   Victor [*to* D'ORMEA]. Apprise Del Borgo, Spava, and the
     rest,
Our son attends them; then return.
   D'Ormea.   One word!
   Charles [*aside*]. A moment's pause and they would drive
     me hence,
I do believe!
   D'Ormea [*aside*]. Let but the boy be firm!   110
   Victor. You disobey?
   Charles [*to* D'ORMEA]. You do not disobey
Me, at least? Did you promise that or no?
   D'Ormea. Sir, I am yours: what would you? Yours am I!
   Charles. When I have said what I shall say, 't is like
Your face will ne'er again disgust me. Go!   115
Through you, as through a breast of glass, I see.

---

97 *1842,1849* (Be   98 *1842,1849*   time)   102 *1842,1849*   me?
108 *1842* word ... *1849* word.   112 *1842,1849* Mc, D'Ormea? Did
113 *1842* am I.

  102 *stay*: 'prop; support': Johnson.
  116 *as through a breast of glass* : cf. the opening of a letter by Pope: 'The old project of a window in the bosom, to render the soul of man visible': *The Works*, with notes and illustrations by Joseph Warton and others (9 vols., 1822), vii. 323 (*Correspondence*, ed. G. Sherburn, ii. 23).

And for your conduct, from my youth till now,
Take my contempt! You might have spared me much,
Secured me somewhat, nor so harmed yourself:
That's over now. Go, ne'er to come again!   120
    D'Ormea. As son, the father—father as, the son!
My wits! My wits!   [*Goes.*
    Victor [*seated*]. And you, what meant you, pray,
Speaking thus to D'Ormea?
    Charles.   Let us not
Waste words upon D'Ormea! Those I spent
Have half unsettled what I came to say.   125
His presence vexes to my very soul.
    Victor. One called to manage a kingdom, Charles, needs
       heart
To bear up under worse annoyances
Than seems D'Ormea—to me, at least.
    Charles [*aside*].   Ah, good!
He keeps me to the point. Then be it so.   130
[*Aloud.*] Last night, sir, brought me certain papers—these—
To be reported on,—your way of late.
Is it last night's result that you demand?
    Victor. For God's sake, what has night brought forth?
       Pronounce
The . . . what's your word?—result!
    Charles.   Sir, that had proved   135
Quite worthy of your sneer, no doubt:—a few
Lame thoughts, regard for you alone could wring,
Lame as they are, from brains like mine, believe!
As 't is, sir, I am spared both toil and sneer.
These are the papers.
    Victor.   Well, sir? I suppose   140

121 *1842* s.d. †[*Exit.*   123 *1842–63* By speaking   124 *1842–68* Weary our-
selves with D'Ormea! Those few words   127 *1842–63* manage kingdoms, Charles,
129 *1842–63* Than D'Ormea seems—to   130 *1842–68* point!   131 *1842–63*
night, sire, brought   135 *1842–63* result! Sire, that   136 *1842,1849* your
sneers, no   138 *1842* believe.   *139 (reading of *1842–68*, DC, *1889*) *1888*
sneer   *1842–63* 'tis, sire, I   140 *1842,1849* There are
   132 *your way of late*: see Condorcet, pp. 39 n.–40 n.

You hardly burned them. Now for your result!

   Charles. I never should have done great things of course,
But . . . oh my father, had you loved me more!

    Victor. Loved? [*Aside.*] Has D'Ormea played me false, I
      wonder?

[*Aloud.*] Why, Charles, a king's love is diffused—yourself   145
May overlook, perchance, your part in it.
Our monarchy is absolutest now
In Europe, or my trouble's thrown away.
I love, my mode, that subjects each and all
May have the power of loving, all and each,   150
Their mode: I doubt not, many have their sons
To trifle with, talk soft to, all day long:
I have that crown, this chair, D'Ormea, Charles!

   Charles. 'Tis well I am a subject then, not you.

   Victor [*aside*]. D'Ormea has told him everything.

                  [*Aloud.*] Aha!   155
I apprehend you: when all's said, you take
Your private station to be prized beyond
My own, for instance?

   Charles.   —Do and ever did
So take it: 't is the method you pursue
That grieves . . .

    Victor.   These words! Let me express, my friend,   160
Your thoughts. You penetrate what I supposed
Secret. D'Ormea plies his trade betimes!
I purpose to resign my crown to you.

   Charles. To me?

141 *1842* result.   143 *1849* more . . .   144 *1842–63* Loved you? †[*Aside.*]†
Has   148 *1842,1849* away: 153 *1842–65* chair, and D'Ormea,   *1842*
Charles.   159–60 *1842* method that aggrieves . . . | These words! these words! Let
161 *1842–65* Your thought. You   162 *1842–63* A secret.

  143 *had you loved me more!*: 'Victor did not love his son Charles Emmanuel, and had a low
opinion of him': Roman, p. 263.

  147 *Our monarchy is absolutest*: see Introduction, above, p. 94 n³.

  149 *my mode*: in my way.

  163 *I purpose to resign*: cf. the abrupt way in which Taurello Salinguerra hands over his
power to Sordello: *Sordello*, v. 719 ff.

Victor.   Now,—in that chamber.

Charles.   You resign
The crown to me?

    Victor.   And time enough, Charles, sure?   165
Confess with me, at four-and-sixty years
A crown's a load. I covet quiet once
Before I die, and summoned you for that.

    Charles. 'T is I will speak: you ever hated me.
I bore it,—have insulted me, borne too—   170
Now you insult yourself; and I remember
What I believed you, what you really are,
And cannot bear it. What! My life has passed
Under your eye, tormented as you know,—
Your whole sagacities, one after one,   175
At leisure brought to play on me—to prove me
A fool, I thought and I submitted; now
You'd prove . . . what would you prove me?

    Victor.   This to me?
I hardly know you!

    Charles.   Know me? Oh indeed
You do not! Wait till I complain next time   180
Of my simplicity!—for here's a sage
Knows the world well, is not to be deceived,
And his experience and his Macchiavels,
D'Ormeas, teach him—what?—that I this while
Have envied him his crown! He has not smiled,   185
I warrant,—has not eaten, drunk, nor slept,
For I was plotting with my Princess yonder!
Who knows what we might do or might not do?
Go now, be politic, astound the world!
That sentry in the antechamber—nay,   190

164 *1842-63* Now— *1865* Now: *1868* Now   169 *1842-68* me,   171 *1842-*
63 yourself,   176-7 *1842* to bear on me—to prove | Me—fool,
184 *1842,1849* His D'Ormeas,   186 *1842* drunk, or slept   190 *1842* the
antichamber . . nay

   175 *sagacities*: this antedates the earliest example of the plural in OED, which is from
Carlyle's *Reminiscences* (2 vols., 1881), i. 103 (written 1866).
   183 *his Macchiavels*: see Roman, quoted on p. 97 above.

The varlet who disposed this precious trap

[Pointing to the crown.

That was to take me—ask them if they think
Their own sons envy them their posts!—Know me!
   Victor. But you know me, it seems: so, learn in brief
My pleasure. This assembly is convened . . .   195
   Charles. Tell me, that woman put it in your head!
You were not sole contriver of the scheme,
My father!
   Victor.   Now observe me, sir! I jest
Seldom—on these points, never. Here, I say,
The knights assemble to see me concede,   200
And you accept, Sardinia's crown.
   Charles.   Farewell!
'T were vain to hope to change this: I can end it.
Not that I cease from being yours, when sunk
Into obscurity: I'll die for you,
But not annoy you with my presence. Sir,   205
Farewell! Farewell!

Enter D'ORMEA.

   D'Ormea [*aside*]. Ha, sure he's changed again—
Means not to fall into the cunning trap!
Then Victor, I shall yet escape you, Victor!
   Victor [*suddenly placing the crown upon the head of* CHARLES].
D'Ormea, your King!
       [*To* CHARLES.] My son, obey me! Charles,
Your father, clearer-sighted than yourself,   210
Decides it must be so. 'Faith, this looks real!
My reasons after; reason upon reason
After: but now, obey me! Trust in me!
By this, you save Sardinia, you save me!

*194 {reading of *1842-68*} *1888,1889* brief.   196 *1842* Tell me Sebastian put
1842-63 head—   199 *1842* Here to witness   200 *1842* (I say they are assem-
bled) me concede,   · 204 *1842* I'd die   205 *1842,1849* presence—Sire, *1863*
presence. Sire,   207 *1842,1849* trap—   214 *1842* save Savoy, my subjects, me!

191 *disposed* : placed, arranged.
214 *you save Sardinia* : in 1726-7 Pope Benedict had recognized Victor Amadeus as King

Why, the boy swoons! [*To* D'ORMEA.] Come this side!   215
D'Ormea [*as* CHARLES *turns from him to* VICTOR].
                                                      You persist?
    Victor. Yes, I conceive the gesture's meaning. 'Faith,
He almost seems to hate you: how is that?
Be re-assured, my Charles! Is't over now?
Then, Marquis, tell the new King what remains
To do! A moment's work. Del Borgo reads   220
The Act of Abdication out, you sign it,
Then I sign; after that, come back to me.
    D'Ormea. Sir, for the last time, pause!
    Victor.   Five minutes longer
I am your sovereign, Marquis. Hesitate—
And I'll so turn those minutes to account   225
That . . . Ay, you recollect me! [*Aside.*] Could I bring
My foolish mind to undergo the reading
That Act of Abdication!
                    [*As* CHARLES *motions* D'ORMEA *to precede him.*
                    Thanks, dear Charles!
                              [CHARLES *and* D'ORMEA *retire.*
    Victor. A novel feature in the boy,—indeed
Just what I feared he wanted most. Quite right,   230
This earnest tone: your truth, now, for effect!
It answers every purpose: with that look,
That voice,—I hear him: "I began no treaty,"
(He speaks to Spain), "nor ever dreamed of this
"You show me; this I from my soul regret;   235
"But if my father signed it, bid not me
"Dishonour him—who gave me all, beside:"
And, "True," says Spain, "'t were harsh to visit that

215 *1842*   swoons.   218 *1842*   Charles.   223 *1842–63*   Sire,   for
230 *1842* Just that I   237 *1842,1849*   beside."   238 *1842–63* And, "truth,"
says
_____
of Sardinia and agreed that he would have the undisputed right to appoint bishops to all the
dioceses there. Early in 1730, however, Benedict's successor Clement XII set about under-
mining these arrangements.

    220 *Del Borgo reads*: Roman, p. 265, *Biographie universelle*, xlviii. 393a.
    233 *"I began no treaty"*: see Introduction, p. 96.

"Upon the Prince." Then come the nobles trooping:
"I grieve at these exactions—I had cut   240
"This hand off ere impose them; but shall I
"Undo my father's deed?"—and they confer:
"Doubtless he was no party, after all;
"Give the Prince time!"
                              Ay, give us time, but time!
Only, he must not, when the dark day comes,   245
Refer our friends to me and frustrate all.
We'll have no child's play, no desponding fits,
No Charles at each cross turn entreating Victor
To take his crown again. Guard against that!

                    Enter D'ORMEA.

Long live King Charles!
                         No—Charles's counsellor!   250
Well, is it over, Marquis? Did I jest?
    D'Ormea. "King Charles"! What then may you be?
    Victor.   Anything!
A country gentleman that, cured of bustle,
Now beats a quick retreat toward Chambery,
Would hunt and hawk and leave you noisy folk   255
To drive your trade without him. I'm Count Remont—
Count Tende—any little place's Count!

---

241 *1842* ere imposed them;   247 *1842-65* desponding-fits,   249 *1842* [no
s.d.]   250 *1842* Long live King Charles!—*Enter* D'ORMEA. King Charles's counsel-
lor!   *252 [editors' emendation] *1842* King Charles! .... Anything. *1849-89*
Charles!"   253 *1842-63* that's cured   254 *1842-63* And beats   *1842*
retreat towards Chamberri   255 *1842-63* To hunt

246 *frustrate*: stressed on the first syllable, as in Johnson, and elsewhere in Browning.
253 *A country gentleman*: 'un gentilhomme de province': Sismondi, p. 393b.
254 *Chambery*: Roman, p. 266.
256 *Count Remont*: obviously a fictitious personage.
257 *Count Tende*: the Pass of Tenda was one of the Alpine passes the control of which
gave importance to the Dukes of Savoy. 'Victor had assumed the fictitious name Conte di
Tenda on a secret diplomatic mission to Venice in 1687': Ohio, following the Marchesa
Vitelleschi, *The Romance of Savoy: Victor Amadeus II. and his Stuart Bride* (2 vols., 1905), i. 249.
Three sixteenth-century noblemen with this title are mentioned in the *Biographie univer-
selle*, vol. xlv.

D'Ormea. Then Victor, Captain against Catinat
At Staffarde, where the French beat you; and Duke
At Turin, where you beat the French; King late   260
Of Savoy, Piedmont, Montferrat, Sardinia,
—Now, "any little place's Count"—
   Victor.   Proceed!
D'Ormea. Breaker of vows to God, who crowned you first;
Breaker of vows to man, who kept you since;
Most profligate to me who outraged God   265
And man to serve you, and am made pay crimes
I was but privy to, by passing thus
To your imbecile son—who, well you know,
Must—(when the people here, and nations there,
Clamour for you the main delinquent, slipped   270
From King to—"Count of any little place")
Must needs surrender me, all in his reach,—
I, sir, forgive you: for I see the end—
See you on your return—(you will return)—
To him you trust, a moment . . .
   Victor.   Trust him? How?   275
My poor man, merely a prime-minister,

---

259 *1842* you,   262 *1842* {no quotation marks} Proceed.   263 *1842* first,
264 *1842* since,   269 *1842* when   271 *1842-68* {no quotation marks}
1842 place   272 *1842-63* —Surrender me, all left within his reach,—
275 *1842-63* trust in for the moment . . . *Vic.* How? *1865,1868* trust thus for the moment
. . . *Vic.* Trust him? How?   276 *1842,1849* Trust in him? (merely *1863* Trust in
him? merely

   258 *Captain against Catinat*: Sismondi describes how, on 18 August 1690, Victor attacked
the French commander Catinat, and was lured into an ambush near La Staffarde: although
he fought valiantly, he was severely defeated.
   259-60 *Duke / At Turin*: as Duke of Savoy, Victor successfully covered the retreat of the
French after the battle of Chiari, in 1701.
   261 *Montferrat*: by the Treaty of Utrecht, as a note to Sismondi's article points out
(390b-391a), 'The Duke of Savoy gained the Isle of Sicily, to which was attached the title of
King, the object of his ambition; and was restored to the possession of all that France had
taken from him ten years before . . . His territory was considerably increased on the side of
the Dauphiné and on that of Lombardy; and Montferrat, cause of so many wars, was
returned to him in its entirety.'
   268 *imbecile*: less strong than in modern English: 'weak; feeble': Johnson, who puts the
stress on the second syllable, as it is here.
   274 *(you will return)*: see Introduction, p. 95.

Make me know where my trust errs!

    D'Ormea.   In his fear,

His love, his——but discover for yourself

What you are weakest, trusting in!

    Victor.   Aha,

D'Ormea, not a shrewder scheme than this   280

In your repertory? You know old Victor—

Vain, choleric, inconstant, rash—(I've heard

Talkers who little thought the King so close)

Felicitous now, were 't not, to provoke him

To clean forget, one minute afterward,   285

His solemn act, and call the nobles back

And pray them give again the very power

He has abjured?—for the dear sake of what?

Vengeance on you, D'Ormea! No: such am I,

Count Tende or Count anything you please,   290

—Only, the same that did the things you say,

And, among other things you say not, used

Your finest fibre, meanest muscle,—you

I used, and now, since you will have it so,

Leave to your fate—mere lumber in the midst,   295

You and your works. Why, what on earth beside

Are you made for, you sort of ministers?

    D'Ormea. Not left, though, to my fate! Your witless son

Has more wit than to load himself with lumber:

He foils you that way, and I follow you.   300

    Victor. Stay with my son—protect the weaker side!

    D'Ormea. Ay, to be tossed the people like a rag,

And flung by them for Spain and Austria's sport,

---

277 *1842,1849* This D'Ormea!) How trust in him? *D'O.* In *1863* This D'Ormea! How trust
in him? *D'O.* In   278 *1842-1863* His love,—but pray discover
280 *1842,1849* My D'Ormea,   286 *1842,1849* act—to call   288 *1849,1863*
abjured!—   *1842-63* —what?   289 *1842-63* you! No, D'Ormea: such
298 *1842* —Left, though, at Chamberri? Your   302 *1842-63* Ay, be tossed to the
303 *1842-63* them to Spain and Austria—so

    278 *his*— : presumably Charles's sense of duty: see 334–5 below.

    281 *repertory* : stressed on the second syllable, as in the first edition of Johnson (1755): by
the ninth edition (1806) the stress has moved to the first syllable.

Abolishing the record of your part
In all this perfidy!

   Victor.   Prevent, beside,   305
My own return!

   D'Ormea.   That's half prevented now!
'T will go hard but you find a wondrous charm
In exile, to discredit me. The Alps,
Silk-mills to watch, vines asking vigilance—
Hounds open for the stag, your hawk's a-wing—   310
Brave days that wait the Louis of the South,
Italy's Janus!

   Victor.   So, the lawyer's clerk
Won't tell me that I shall repent!

   D'Ormea.   You give me
Full leave to ask if you repent?

   Victor.   Whene'er
Sufficient time's elapsed for that, you judge!   315

                     [*Shouts inside* "KING CHARLES!"

   D'Ormea. Do you repent?

   Victor [*after a slight pause*]. . . . I've kept them waiting? Yes!
Come in, complete the Abdication, sir!   [*They go out.*

Enter POLYXENA.

   Polyxena. A shout! The sycophants are free of Charles!
Oh is not this like Italy? No fruit
Of his or my distempered fancy, this,   320
But just an ordinary fact! Beside,
Here they've set forms for such proceedings; Victor
Imprisoned his own mother: he should know,
If any, how a son's to be deprived

306 *1842* now.   307 *1842,1849* you'll find
elapse for   *1842* judge. s.d. *1842–68* CHARLES."
1842 †[*Exeunt*.   318 *1842–68* shout?
   315 *1865,1868* Sufficient time
   316 *1842* Yes.   317 s.d.

   310 *open*: give tongue, as in *The Merry Wives of Windsor*, IV. ii. 174–5: 'if I cry out thus upon no trail, never trust me when I open again'.
   311 *the Louis of the South*: the sources agree in stressing Victor's ambition of emulating Louis XIV, in marriage as in other respects.
   312 *Italy's Janus!*: because, like the Roman deity, he faces in two directions.
   323 *Imprisoned his own mother*: see 91 n. above.

Of a son's right. Our duty's palpable.   325
Ne'er was my husband for the wily king
And the unworthy subjects: be it so!
Come you safe out of them, my Charles! Our life
Grows not the broad and dazzling life, I dreamed
Might prove your lot; for strength was shut in you   330
None guessed but I—strength which, untrammelled once,
Had little shamed your vaunted ancestry—
Patience and self-devotion, fortitude,
Simplicity and utter truthfulness
—All which, they shout to lose!
                             So, now my work   335
Begins—to save him from regret. Save Charles
Regret?—the noble nature! He's not made
Like these Italians: 't is a German soul.

                        CHARLES *enters crowned.*
Oh, where's the King's heir? Gone!—the Crown Prince?
    Gone!—
Where's Savoy? Gone!—Sardinia? Gone! But Charles   340
Is left! And when my Rhine-land bowers arrive,
If he looked almost handsome yester-twilight
As his grey eyes seemed widening into black
Because I praised him, then how will he look?
Farewell, you stripped and whited mulberry-trees   345
Bound each to each by lazy ropes of vine!
Now I'll teach you my language: I'm not forced
To speak Italian now, Charles?
               [*She sees the crown.*] What is this?
Answer me—who has done this? Answer!
    Charles.   He!
I am King now.
    Polyxena.   Oh worst, worst, worst of all!   350

327 *1842* so.   *331 [reading of *1868*] *1842-65* untrammeled *1888,1889* untra-
melled   338 *1842-63* Like the Italians: 339 *1842-65* Gone:— .... Gone—
1868 Gone:— .... Gone:—   340 *1842-68* Savoy? Gone:—   349 *1842* He:
   331 *untrammelled once* : once it had been untrammelled.
   338 *a German soul* : Polyxena was from Hesse-Rheinsfeld.

Tell me! What, Victor? He has made you King?
What's he then? What's to follow this? You, King?
    Charles. Have I done wrong? Yes, for you were not by!
    Polyxena. Tell me from first to last.
    Charles.   Hush—a new world
Brightens before me; he is moved away   355
—The dark form that eclipsed it, he subsides
Into a shape supporting me like you,
And I, alone, tend upward, more and more
Tend upward: I am grown Sardinia's King.
    Polyxena. Now stop: was not this Victor, Duke of Savoy   360
At ten years old?
    Charles.   He was.
    Polyxena.   And the Duke spent
Since then, just four-and-fifty years in toil
To be—what?
    Charles.   King.
    Polyxena.   Then why unking himself?
    Charles. Those years are cause enough.
    Polyxena.   The only cause?
    Charles. Some new perplexities.
    Polyxena.   Which you can solve   365
Although he cannot?
    Charles.   He assures me so.
    Polyxena. And this he means shall last—how long?
    Charles.   How long?
Think you I fear the perils I confront?
He's praising me before the people's face—
My people!
    Polyxena. Then he's changed—grown kind, the King?   370
Where can the trap be?
    Charles.   Heart and soul I pledge!

---

351 *1842–63* me—   357 *1842* like yours,   364 *1842* Those ten and four-
and-fifty years. *Pol.* Those only?   371 *1842,1849* (Where . . . . be?)   *1842* Heart
and soul—and soul,

356 *it*: the new world.
358 *I . . . tend upward*: cf. *Paracelsus*, v. 742 and 881, and *Sordello*, vi. 803.
363 *unking*: as in *Strafford*, v. ii. 148.

My father, could I guard the crown you gained,
Transmit as I received it,—all good else
Would I surrender!
    Polyxena.   Ah, it opens then
Before you, all you dreaded formerly?   375
You are rejoiced to be a king, my Charles?
    Charles. So much to dare? The better;—much to dread?
The better. I'll adventure though alone.
Triumph or die, there's Victor still to witness
Who dies or triumphs—either way, alone!   380
    Polyxena. Once I had found my share in triumph, Charles,
Or death.
    Charles. But you are I! But you I call
To take, Heaven's proxy, vows I tendered Heaven
A moment since. I will deserve the crown!
    Polyxena. You will. [*Aside.*] No doubt it were a glorious
        thing   385
For any people, if a heart like his
Ruled over it. I would I saw the trap.

Enter VICTOR.

'T is he must show me.
    Victor.   So, the mask falls off
An old man's foolish love at last. Spare thanks!
I know you, and Polyxena I know.   390
Here's Charles—I am his guest now—does he bid me
Be seated? And my light-haired blue-eyed child
Must not forget the old man far away
At Chambery, who dozes while she reigns.
    Polyxena. Most grateful shall we now be, talking least   395
Of gratitude—indeed of anything
That hinders what yourself must need to say
To Charles.

---

373 *1842* Deliver it as I received it, all | 380 *1842* alone.   382 *1842* are me!
But   387 *1842-65* trap!   389 *1842-63* last!   *1842,1849* thanks— *1863*
thanks: 394 *1842* At Chamberri, who . . . . reigns?   397 *1842-63* must have
to

    Charles. Pray speak, sir!
    Victor.   'Faith, not much to say:
Only what shows itself, you once i' the point
Of sight. You're now the King: you'll comprehend   400
Much you may oft have wondered at—the shifts,
Dissimulation, wiliness I showed.
For what's our post? Here's Savoy and here's Piedmont,
Here's Montferrat—a breadth here, a space there—
To o'ersweep all these, what's one weapon worth?   405
I often think of how they fought in Greece:
(Or Rome, which was it? You're the scholar, Charles!)
You made a front-thrust? But if your shield too
Were not adroitly planted, some shrewd knave
Reached you behind; and him foiled, straight if thong   410
And handle of that shield were not cast loose,
And you enabled to outstrip the wind,
Fresh foes assailed you, either side; 'scape these,
And reach your place of refuge—e'en then, odds
If the gate opened unless breath enough   415
Were left in you to make its lord a speech.
Oh, you will see!
    Charles.   No: straight on shall I go,
Truth helping; win with it or die with it.
    Victor. 'Faith, Charles, you're not made Europe's fighting-
      man!
The barrier-guarder, if you please. You clutch   420
Hold and consolidate, with envious France
This side, with Austria that, the territory

398 *1842-63*   speak, sire! 'Faith,   399 *1842-63* itself, once in the
1865,1868 in the   400 *1842-68* You are now   *406 {reading of DC, *1889*}
1842-88   Greece   407 *1842*   Charles)   416 *1842-63*   Was   left
419 *1842*   fighting-man.   420 *1842-63*   Its   barrier- ....   You   hold,
421 *1842-63* Not take—consolidate, with envious French   422 *1842* side and Aus-
trians that, these territories *1849, 1863* with Austrians that, these territories

   399-400 *you once i'the point* / *Of sight*: once you are in the right position to see.
   410 *him foiled*: absolute: when he was foiled.
   412 *to outstrip the wind*: see Dryden's translation of the *Æneid*, v. 153 and xii. 519.
   414-15 *odds* / *If*: it was a toss-up whether.
   420 *barrier-guarder*: not in OED.

I held—ay, and will hold . . . which *you* shall hold
Despite the couple! But I've surely earned
Exemption from these weary politics,   425
—The privilege to prattle with my son
And daughter here, though Europe wait the while.
   Polyxena. Nay, sir,—at Chambery, away for ever,
As soon you will be, 't is farewell we bid you:
Turn these few fleeting moments to account!   430
'T is just as though it were a death.
   Victor.   Indeed!
   Polyxena [*aside*]. Is the trap there?
   Charles.   Ay, call this parting—death!
The sacreder your memory becomes.
If I misrule Sardinia, how bring back
My father?
   Victor. I mean . . .
   Polyxena [*who watches* VICTOR *narrowly this while*].
                  Your father does not mean   435
You should be ruling for your father's sake:
It is your people must concern you wholly
Instead of him. You mean this, sir? (He drops
My hand!)
   Charles. That people is now part of me.
   Victor. About the people! I took certain measures   440
Some short time since . . . Oh, I know well, you know
But little of my measures! These affect
The nobles; we've resumed some grants, imposed

---

423 *1842* you   425 {no equivalent in *1842*}   427 *1842* daughter tho' the
world should wait *1849* Europe waits the   428 *1842-63* Nay, sire at   *1842* at
Chamberri, away   429 *1842-63* you'll be, 'tis a farewell . . . . you!
435,435a *1842-63* father? No—that thought shall ever urge me.| *Vic.* I do not mean . . . *Pol.*
[s.d.] Your father does not mean   436 *1842-63* That you are ruling
438 *1842-63* You meant this, sire? (He   441 *1842-63* I'm aware you
442 *1842-63* measures—

  439 *That people*: 'Wholly devoted to his people, he reformed abuses, rectified the
administration of justice, the collection of taxes and the management of financial affairs,
and re-established order and discipline among his troops': *Biographie universelle*, viii. 159b.
Cf. *Sordello*, vi. 120: 'The People were himself'.
  443 *we've resumed some grants*: see *King Victor*, I. 128 n.

A tax or two: prepare yourself, in short,
For clamour on that score. Mark me: you yield   445
No jot of aught entrusted you!
    Polyxena.   No jot
You yield!
    Charles. My father, when I took the oath,
Although my eye might stray in search of yours,
I heard it, understood it, promised God
What you require. Till from this eminence   450
He move me, here I keep, nor shall concede
The meanest of my rights.
    Victor [*aside*].   The boy's a fool!
—Or rather, I'm a fool: for, what's wrong here?
To-day the sweets of reigning: let to-morrow
Be ready with its bitters.

                Enter D'ORMEA.

                There's beside   455
Somewhat to press upon your notice first.
    Charles. Then why delay it for an instant, sir?
That Spanish claim perchance? And, now you speak,
—This morning, my opinion was mature,
Which, boy-like, I was bashful in producing   460
To one I ne'er am like to fear in future!
My thought is formed upon that Spanish claim.
    Victor. Betimes indeed. Not now, Charles! You require
A host of papers on it.
    D'Ormea [*coming forward*]. Here they are.
[*To* CHARLES.] I, sir, was minister and much beside   465
Of the late monarch; to say little, him
I served: on you I have, to say e'en less,
No claim. This case contains those papers: with them

---

445 *1842,1849* For clamours on   *1842-63* score: 446 *1842-63* of what's
entrusted   451 *1842-63* He moves me,   452 *1842* fool.   457 *1842-*
63 instant, sire?   461 *1842* To you—I   463 *1842,1849* (Betimes indeed.)
1863 indeed!   *1842-63* Charles.   465 *1842-68* I was the minister

458 *That Spanish claim* : as at I. 132 above.

I tender you my office.
   Victor [*hastily.*]   Keep him, Charles!
There's reason for it—many reasons: you   470
Distrust him, nor are so far wrong there,—but
He's mixed up in this matter—he'll desire
To quit you, for occasions known to me:
Do not accept those reasons: have him stay!
   Polyxena [*aside*]. His minister thrust on us!
   Charles [*to* D'ORMEA].   Sir, believe,   475
In justice to myself, you do not need
E'en this commending: howsoe'er might seem
My feelings toward you, as a private man,
They quit me in the vast and untried field
Of action. Though I shall myself (as late   480
In your own hearing I engaged to do)
Preside o'er my Sardinia, yet your help
Is necessary. Think the past forgotten
And serve me now!
   D'Ormea.   I did not offer you
My service—would that I could serve you, sir!   485
As for the Spanish matter . . .
   Victor.   But despatch
At least the dead, in my good daughter's phrase,
Before the living! Help to house me safe
Ere with D'Ormea you set the world a-gape!
Here is a paper—will you overlook   490
What I propose reserving for my needs?
I get as far from you as possible:
Here's what I reckon my expenditure.
   Charles [*reading*]. A miserable fifty thousand crowns—

477 *1842,1849* commending: whatsoe'er might be *1863* commending: whatso'er might
478 *1842* feelings towards you   485 *1842-63* My services— . . . . sire!   486
1863-68 But dispatch   489 *1842-63* Ere you and D'Ormea set   492 *1842-*
63 possible.   493 *1842,1849* There's what   *494 (reading of DC, *1889*)*
1842 crowns. *1849-68* crowns! *1888* crowns

   469 *Keep him, Charles!*: for Victor's advice see *Biographie universelle*, xxxii. 146a and Con-
dorcet, p. 40.

   494 *fifty thousand crowns*: as in Condorcet and Sismondi. In Roman his pension is 10,000
crowns.

Victor. Oh, quite enough for country gentlemen!   495
Beside the exchequer happens . . . but find out
All that, yourself!
 Charles [*still reading*]. "Count Tende"—what means this?
 Victor. Me: you were but an infant when I burst
Through the defile of Tende upon France.
Had only my allies kept true to me!   500
No matter. Tende's, then, a name I take
Just as . . .
 D'Ormea. —The Marchioness Sebastian takes
The name of Spigno.
 Charles.   How, sir?
 Victor [*to* D'ORMEA]. Fool! All that
Was for my own detailing. [*To* CHARLES.] That anon!
 Charles [*to* D'ORMEA]. Explain what you have said, sir!
 D'Ormea.   I supposed   505
The marriage of the King to her I named,
Profoundly kept a secret these few weeks,
Was not to be one, now he's Count.
 Polyxena [*aside*].   With us
The minister—with him the mistress!
 Charles [*to* VICTOR].   No—
Tell me you have not taken her—that woman   510
To live with, past recall!
 Victor.   And where's the crime . . .
 Polyxena [*to* CHARLES]. True, sir, this is a matter past recall
And past your cognizance. A day before,
And you had been compelled to note this: now,—
Why note it? The King saved his House from shame: 515
What the Count did, is no concern of yours.
 Charles [*after a pause*]. The Spanish claim, D'Ormea!

497 *1842* yourself. Cha. (s.d.) Count Tende—what is this? 516 *1842-63* Count
does is .517 *1842-63* Spanish business, D'Ormea!

 499 *the defile of Tende*: see 257 n., above.
 503 *The name of Spigno*: as in Orrery: 'Spigo' in Roman (p. 268), 'Spino' in Sismondi
(p. 393b).
 506 *The marriage of the King*: Browning follows Sismondi and Condorcet in placing the
marriage before the abdication: in Roman it occurs afterwards.

Victor.   Why, my son,
I took some ill-advised . . . one's age, in fact,
Spoils everything: though I was overreached,
A younger brain, we'll trust, may extricate   520
Sardinia readily. To-morrow, D'Ormea,
Inform the King!
      D'Ormea [without regarding VICTOR, *and leisurely*].
                              Thus stands the case with Spain:
When first the Infant Carlos claimed his proper
Succession to the throne of Tuscany . . .
      Victor. I tell you, that stands over! Let that rest!   525
There is the policy!
      Charles [to D'ORMEA]. Thus much I know,
And more—too much: the remedy?
      D'Ormea.   Of course!
No glimpse of one.
      Victor.   No remedy at all!
It makes the remedy itself—time makes it.
      D'Ormea [to CHARLES].
But if . . .
      Victor [still more hastily].
            In fine, I shall take care of that: 530
And, with another project that I have . . .
      D'Ormea [turning on him].
                  Oh, since Count Tende means to take again
King Victor's crown!—
      Polyxena [throwing herself at VICTOR's *feet*].
                        E'en now retake it, sir!
Oh speak! We are your subjects both, once more!
Say it—a word effects it! You meant not,   535
Nor do mean now, to take it: but you must!
'T is in you—in your nature—and the shame's
Not half the shame 't would grow to afterwards!
      Charles. Polyxena!
      Polyxena.   A word recalls the knights—

526 *1842* policy.   533 *1842–63* it, sirc!   538 *1842–63* to afterward!
    521 *Sardinia* : see note to l. 214 above.

Say it! What's promising and what's the past?   540
Say you are still King Victor!
   D'Ormea.   Better say
The Count repents, in brief!   [VICTOR *rises.*
   Charles.   With such a crime
I have not charged you, sir!
   Polyxena.   (Charles turns from me!)

SECOND YEAR, 1731.—KING CHARLES.

Part I.

Enter Queen Polyxena *and* D'Ormea.—*A pause.*

Polyxena. And now, sir, what have you to say?
D'Ormea.   Count Tende . . .
Polyxena. Affirm not I betrayed you; you resolve
On uttering this strange intelligence
—Nay, post yourself to find me ere I reach
The capital, because you know King Charles   5
Tarries a day or two at Evian baths
Behind me:—but take warning,—here and thus
                              [*Seating herself in the royal seat.*
I listen, if I listen—not your friend.
Explicitly the statement, if you still
Persist to urge it on me, must proceed: 10
I am not made for aught else.
D'Ormea.   Good! Count Tende . . .
Polyxena. I, who mistrust you, shall acquaint King Charles
Who even more mistrusts you.
D'Ormea.   Does he so?
Polyxena. Why should he not?
D'Ormea.   Ay, why not? Motives, seek
You virtuous people, motives! Say, I serve   15
God at the devil's bidding—will that do?
I'm proud: our people have been pacified,
Really I know not how—
Polyxena.   By truthfulness.
D'Ormea. Exactly; that shows I had nought to do
With pacifying them. Our foreign perils   20

11 *1842* Good: 18 *1842,1849* (Really . . . . how)—   20 *1842,1849* them: {u
of our *turned in 1842*}

4 *post* : 'To travel with speed': Johnson.
6 *at Evian baths* : according to Sismondi, after a distressing visit to his father Charles and
his wife went to the Bath at Évian, 'where he intended to spend several weeks': p. 394a.

Also exceed my means to stay: but here
'T is otherwise, and my pride's piqued. Count Tende
Completes a full year's absence: would you, madam,
Have the old monarch back, his mistress back,
His measures back? I pray you, act upon   25
My counsel, or they will be.
    Polyxena.   When?
    D'Ormea.   Let's think.
Home-matters settled—Victor's coming now;
Let foreign matters settle—Victor's here
Unless I stop him; as I will, this way.
    Polyxena [*reading the papers he presents*].
If this should prove a plot 'twixt you and Victor?   30
You seek annoyances to give a pretext
For what you say you fear.
    D'Ormea.   Oh, possibly!
I go for nothing. Only show King Charles
That thus Count Tende purposes return,
And style me his inviter, if you please!   35
    Polyxena. Half of your tale is true; most like, the Count
Seeks to return: but why stay you with us?
To aid in such emergencies.
    D'Ormea.   Keep safe
Those papers: or, to serve me, leave no proof
I thus have counselled! When the Count returns,   40
And the King abdicates, 't will stead me little
To have thus counselled.
    Polyxena.   The King abdicate!
    D'Ormea. He's good, we knew long since—wise, we
        discover—
Firm, let us hope:—but I'd have gone to work
With him away. Well!
    [CHARLES *without.*] In the Council Chamber?   45

22-3 *1842* piqued. Would you, madam,   28 *1842-63* here: *31 (reading of
DC) *1842,1849* give him pretext   *1863-88* give pretext *1889* give the pretext
32 *1842-68* fear!   35 *1842-65* please.   37 *1842* Would come: but where-
fore are you left with us?   40 *1842-65* counselled: 45 *1842* And he away.

    21 *to stay*: to put an end to.

D'Ormea. All's lost!

Polyxena.   Oh, surely not King Charles! He's changed—
That's not this year's care-burthened voice and step:
'T is last year's step, the Prince's voice!

    D'Ormea.   I know.

                             [Enter CHARLES:—D'ORMEA *retiring a little.*

    Charles. Now wish me joy, Polyxena! Wish it me
The old way!   *[She embraces him.*

        There was too much cause for that!   50
But I have found myself again. What news
At Turin? Oh, if you but felt the load
I'm free of—free! I said this year would end
Or it, or me—but I am free, thank God!

    Polyxena. How, Charles?

    Charles.   You do not guess? The day I found   55
Sardinia's hideous coil, at home, abroad,
And how my father was involved in it,—
Of course, I vowed to rest and smile no more
Until I cleared his name from obloquy.
We did the people right—'t was much to gain   60
That point, redress our nobles' grievance, too—
But that took place here, was no crying shame:
All must be done abroad,—if I abroad
Appeased the justly-angered Powers, destroyed
The scandal, took down Victor's name at last   65
From a bad eminence, I then might breathe
And rest! No moment was to lose. Behold
The proud result—a Treaty, Austria, Spain
Agree to—

    D'Ormea [*aside*]. I shall merely stipulate

---

46 *1842*   lost.   47 *1842*   care—burthened   48 *1849-65*   know!
51 *1842,1849* again! What's news *1863* again!   ·   55 *1842* guess!   58 *1842-63*
rest or smile   59 *1842-63* I freed his   64 *1842* Appease the . . . . destroy
65 *1842* scandal, take down   66 *1842* then may breathe   67 *1842* lose:

    56 *coil*: trouble. Cf. *King Victor*, I. 277 n.   62 *that*: i.e. that which.
    66 *bad eminence*: as in *Paradise Lost*, ii. 6.
    68 *a Treaty*: in 1731, by the second Treaty of Vienna, disputes about the Spanish succession were terminated.

For an experienced headsman.
    Charles.   Not a soul   70
Is compromised: the blotted past's a blank:
Even D'Ormea escapes unquestioned. See!
It reached me from Vienna; I remained
At Evian to despatch the Count his news;
'T is gone to Chambery a week ago—   75
And here am I: do I deserve to feel
Your warm white arms around me?
    D'Ormea [coming forward].   He knows that?
    Charles. What, in Heaven's name, means this?
    D'Ormea.   He knows that matters
Are settled at Vienna? Not too late!
Plainly, unless you post this very hour   80
Some man you trust (say, me) to Chambery
And take precautions I acquaint you with,
Your father will return here.
    Charles.   Are you crazed,
D'Ormea? Here? For what? As well return
To take his crown!
    D'Ormea.   He will return for that.   85
    Charles [to POLYXENA]. You have not listened to this man?
    Polyxena.   He spoke
About your safety—and I listened.
               [*He disengages himself from her arms.*
    Charles [to D'ORMEA].   What

---

72 *1842,1849* Even D'Ormea will escape unquestioned.   73 *1842* This reached
74 *1863–8* to dispatch the   75 *1842* to Chamberri a   81 *1842* to Cham-
berri,   82 *1849* I'll acquaint   83 *1842,1849* here. *Cha.* Is he crazed,
84 *1842,1849* This D'Ormea?   85 *1842* He does return

    70 *headsman*: executioner.

    74 *to despatch the Count his news*: the article on D'Ormea in the *Biographie universelle*, xxxii.
146a, mentions that for a long time Charles made a point of keeping his father well
informed, but that D'Ormea opposed this practice and eventually managed to put an end
to it.

    77 *He knows that?*: 'In the month of August 1731, Victor learned that the Emperor
agreed to allow Don Carlos to enter Italy with 6000 Spanish troops. He imparted this news
to the marchioness [of Spigo]: she could not conceal her joy': Roman, p. 270. There
ensued Victor's attempt to return as King.

Apprised you of the Count's intentions?
 D'Ormea.   **Me?**
His heart, sir; you may not be used to read
Such evidence however; therefore read   90
      [*Pointing to* POLYXENA'S *papers.*
My evidence.
 Charles [*to* POLYXENA]. Oh, worthy this of you!
And of your speech I never have forgotten,
Though I professed forgetfulness; which haunts me
As if I did not know how false it was;
Which made me toil unconsciously thus long   95
That there might be no least occasion left
For aught of its prediction coming true!
And now, when there is left no least occasion
To instigate my father to such crime—
When I might venture to forget (I hoped)   100
That speech and recognize Polyxena—
Oh worthy, to revive, and tenfold worse,
That plague! D'Ormea at your ear, his slanders
Still in your hand! Silent?
 Polyxena.   As the wronged are.
 Charles. And you, D'Ormea, since when have you
  presumed   105
To spy upon my father? I conceive
What that wise paper shows, and easily.
Since when?
 D'Ormea. The when and where and how belong
To me. 'T is sad work, but I deal in such.
You ofttimes serve yourself; I'd serve you here: 110
Use makes me not so squeamish. In a word,

---

89 *1842-63* heart, sire; you 95 *1842* toil inconsciously thus 97 *1842* For
what your speech predicted coming true! 100 *1842* I hoped, 103 *1842-63*
plague now! D'Ormea *105 (reading of *1842-68*) *1888,1889* since when you have
presumed *1842,1849* And, D'Ormea, *1863* And pray, D'Ormea,
106 *1842,1849* (I 107 *1842,1849* easily.)

 95 *inconsciously* (1842): OED gives three examples of 'inconscious', from the seventeenth
and eighteenth centuries. Its only examples of 'inconsciously' are from *Sordello* (1840-65),
vi. 148, and *Red Cotton Night-Cap Country*, iii. 386.

Since the first hour he went to Chambery,
Of his seven servants, five have I suborned.

    Charles. You hate my father?

    D'Ormea.   Oh, just as you will!

                                 [*Looking at* POLYXENA.

A minute since, I loved him—hate him, now!   115
What matter?—if you ponder just one thing:
Has he that treaty?—he is setting forward
Already. Are your guards here?

    Charles.   Well for you
They are not! [*To* POLYXENA.]. Him I knew of old, but you—
To hear that pickthank, further his designs!   [*To* D'ORMEA.
Guards?—were they here, I'd bid them, for your trouble   121
Arrest you.

    D'Ormea. Guards you shall not want. I lived
The servant of your choice, not of your need.
You never greatly needed me till now
That you discard me. This is my arrest.   125
Again I tender you my charge—its duty
Would bid me press you read those documents.
Here, sir!   [*Offering his badge of office.*

    Charles [*taking it*]. The papers also! Do you think
I dare not read them?

    Polyxena.   Read them, sir!

    Charles.   They prove,
My father, still a month within the year   130
Since he so solemnly consigned it me,
Means to resume his crown? They shall prove that,
Or my best dungeon . . .

    D'Ormea.   Even say, Chambery!

---

112 *1842* to Chamberri,   114 *1842* will.   116 *1842–63* What matters?—If
1849 you'll ponder   *1842* thing.   119 *1842* I have none! {s.d.} Him
128 *1842–63* Here, sire! {s.d.} The   *132 {reading of *1842–68*} *1888,1889* that.
133 *1842*   say Chamberri!

   120 *pickthank*: 'An officious fellow . . . ; a whispering parasite': Johnson. Cf. *1 Henry IV*,
III. ii. 25. In *The Pilgrim's Progress*, Pickthank bears witness that Faithful has spoken ill of
Beelzebub (pp. 94–5 in the ed. of J. B. Wharey, rev. R. Sharrock, 1960).
   132 *to resume his crown?*: see Introduction, pp. 94 ff.

'T is vacant, I surmise, by this.
    Charles.   You prove
Your words or pay their forfeit, sir. Go there!   135
Polyxena, one chance to rend the veil
Thickening and blackening 'twixt us two! Do say,
You'll see the falsehood of the charges proved!
Do say, at least, you wish to see them proved
False charges—my heart's love of other times!   140
    Polyxena. Ah, Charles!
    Charles [*to* D'ORMEA]. Precede me, sir!
    D'Ormea.   And I'm at length
A martyr for the truth! No end, they say,
Of miracles. My conscious innocence!
    [*As they go out, enter—by the middle door, at which he pauses—* VICTOR.
    Victor. Sure I heard voices? No. Well, I do best
To make at once for this, the heart o' the place.   145
The old room! Nothing changed! So near my seat,
D'Ormea?
                [*Pushing away the stool which is by the* KING'S *chair.*
        I want that meeting over first,
I know not why. Tush, he, D'Ormea, slow
To hearten me, the supple knave? That burst
Of spite so eased him! He'll inform me . . .
                    What?   150
Why come I hither? All's in rough: let all
Remain rough. There's full time to draw back—nay,
There's nought to draw back from, as yet; whereas,
If reason should be, to arrest a course
Of error—reason good, to interpose   155
And save, as I have saved so many times,
Our House, admonish my son's giddy youth,
Relieve him of a weight that proves too much—

---

137 *1842* two.   144 *1842-65* No!   148 *1842-63* Tush, D'Ormea won't be
slow   149 *1842-63* knave!   152 *1842-63* rough;   157 *1842* My
house—
   151 *All's in rough*: merely sketched out. Cf. *Sordello*, ii. 467.

Now is the time,—or now, or never.

                                              'Faith,
This kind of step is pitiful, not due   160
To Charles, this stealing back—hither, because
He's from his capital! Oh Victor! Victor!
But thus it is. The age of crafty men
Is loathsome; youth contrives to carry off
Dissimulation; we may intersperse   165
Extenuating passages of strength,
Ardour, vivacity, and wit—may turn
E'en guile into a voluntary grace:
But one's old age, when graces drop away
And leave guile the pure staple of our lives—   170
Ah, loathsome!

                     Not so—or why pause I? Turin
Is mine to have, were I so minded, for
The asking; all the army's mine—I've witnessed
Each private fight beneath me; all the Court's
Mine too; and, best of all, D'Ormea's still   175
D'Ormea and mine. There's some grace clinging yet.
Had I decided on this step, ere midnight
I'd take the crown.

                     No. Just this step to rise
Exhausts me. Here am I arrived: the rest
Must be done for me. Would I could sit here   180
And let things right themselves, the masque unmasque
Of the old King, crownless, grey hair and hot blood—
The young King, crowned, but calm before his time,
They say,—the eager mistress with her taunts,—

162 *1842* Victor—Victor—   163 *1842,1849* is: 175 *1842–63* all, my
D'Ormea's   176 *1842–63* His D'Ormea; no! There's   178 *1842–65* No!
179 *1842,1849* me!   182 *1842,1849* the King, crownless,   *1842–63* grey hairs
and   184 *1842,1849* eager woman with

160 *not due* : not fair.
162 *He's from his capital!*: 'The young monarch, an hour after receiving information [of
his father's return], takes horse, crosses the Little St Bernard Pass, and reaches the capital
with a small retinue on the very day when his father was coming down to the chateau at
Rivoli': Sismondi, p. 394a.
183 *calm before his time*: cf. *King Victor*, II. 31 and n.

And the sad earnest wife who motions me   185
Away—ay, there she knelt to me! E'en yet
I can return and sleep at Chambery
A dream out.
                    Rather shake it off at Turin,
King Victor! Say: to Turin—yes, or no?
    'T is this relentless noonday-lighted chamber,   190
Lighted like life but silent as the grave,
That disconcerts me. That's the change must strike.
No silence last year! Some one flung doors wide
(Those two great doors which scrutinize me now)
And out I went 'mid crowds of men—men talking,   195
Men watching if my lip fell or brow knit,
Men saw me safe forth, put me on my road:
That makes the misery of this return.
Oh had a battle done it! Had I dropped,
Haling some battle, three entire days old,   200
Hither and thither by the forehead—dropped
In Spain, in Austria, best of all, in France—
Spurned on its horns or underneath its hooves,
When the spent monster went upon its knees
To pad and pash the prostrate wretch—I, Victor,   205
Sole to have stood up against France, beat down
By inches, brayed to pieces finally
In some vast unimaginable charge,
A flying hell of horse and foot and guns
Over me, and all's lost, for ever lost,   210
There's no more Victor when the world wakes up!
Then silence, as of a raw battle-field,

185 *1842* who beckons me   ·187 *1842* at Chamberri   189 *1842-63* Victor!
Is't ·to   191 (no equivalent in *1842*)   192-3 *1842* me. Some one
192 *1849* me! There must be the change— *1863* me! There the *1865,1868* me. There the
194 *1842* doors that scrutinise   196 *1842,1849* brow changed; *1863,1865* knit;
198 *1842-63* return!   201 *1842* forehead—sunk   204 *1842,1849* monster
goes upon   208 *1842,1849* By some

   205 *To pad and pash*: to beat down and crush. Cf. 'Childe Roland', 130-1: 'Whose savage
trample thus could pad the dank / Soil to a plash?'
   207 *brayed to pieces*: cf. *Sordello*, i. 68: 'Braying a Persian shield'.
   212 *raw*: recent, unhealed (cf. 'raw wound').

Throughout the world. Then after (as whole days
After, you catch at intervals faint noise
Through the stiff crust of frozen blood)—there creeps   215
A rumour forth, so faint, no noise at all,
That a strange old man, with face outworn for wounds
Is stumbling on from frontier town to town,
Begging a pittance that may help him find
His Turin out; what scorn and laughter follow   220
The coin you fling into his cap! And last,
Some bright morn, how men crowd about the midst
O' the market-place, where takes the old king breath
Ere with his crutch he strike the palace-gate
Wide ope!
    To Turin, yes or no—or no?   225

    Re-enter CHARLES *with papers.*

 Charles. Just as I thought! A miserable falsehood
Of hirelings discontented with their pay
And longing for enfranchisement! A few
Testy expressions of old age that thinks
To keep alive its dignity o'er slaves   230
By means that suit their natures!
    [*Tearing them.*] Thus they shake
My faith in Victor!
        [*Turning, he discovers* VICTOR.
 Victor [*after a pause*]. Not at Evian, Charles?
What's this? Why do you run to close the doors?
No welcome for your father?
 Charles [*aside*].   Not his voice!
What would I give for one imperious tone   235
Of the old sort! That's gone for ever.
 Victor.   Must
I ask once more . . .
 Charles.   No—I concede it, sir!

213 *1842* whole weeks 215 *1842* blood)—to creep 217 *1842* man, face
220 *1842* out; laughter and scorn to follow 221 *1842,1849* cap: 222 *1842*
morn, to see crowds about 223 *1842-68* Of the *1842* old man breath

You are returned for ... true, your health declines;
True, Chambery's a bleak unkindly spot;
You'd choose one fitter for your final lodge—   240
Veneria, or Moncaglier—ay, that's close
And I concede it.
    Victor.   I received advices
Of the conclusion of the Spanish matter,
Dated from Evian Baths ...
    Charles.   And you forbore
To visit me at Evian, satisfied   245
The work I had to do would fully task
The little wit I have, and that your presence
Would only disconcert me—
    Victor.   Charles?
    Charles.   —Me, set
For ever in a foreign course to yours,
And ...
        Sir, this way of wile were good to catch,   250
But I have not the sleight of it. The truth!
Though I sink under it! What brings you here?
    Victor. Not hope of this reception, certainly,
From one who'd scarce assume a stranger mode
Of speech, did I return to bring about   255
Some awfulest calamity!
    Charles.   —You mean,
Did you require your crown again! Oh yes,
I should speak otherwise! But turn not that
To jesting! Sir, the truth! Your health declines?
Is aught deficient in your equipage?   260

---

239 *1842* True, Chamberri's a   *241 {reading of *1842-68*, DC, *1889*} *1888* closed
244 *1842* baths.—   256 *1842* calamity.   257 *1842* again:

   241 *Veneria, or Moncaglier*: one of the family palaces was at Venaria Reale, just outside
Turin. In his account of the meeting of Victor and Charles, Sismondi mentions that
'Victor-Amédée complaining that the air of Savoy was unfavourable to his health, his son
immediately ordered that the chateau of Montcalier should be prepared for his reception':
p. 394a–b. Cf. Roman, p. 271.
   250 *this way of wile*: this cunning way of behaving. Cf. *Strafford*, vi. ii. 14: 'this way of
blood'.

Wisely you seek myself to make complaint,
And foil the malice of the world which laughs
At petty discontents; but I shall care
That not a soul knows of this visit. Speak!
    Victor [*aside*]. Here is the grateful much-professing son   265
Prepared to worship me, for whose sole sake
I think to waive my plans of public good!
[*Aloud.*] Nay, Charles, if I did seek to take once more
My crown, were so disposed to plague myself,
What would be warrant for this bitterness?   270
I gave it—grant I would resume it—well?
    Charles. I should say simply—leaving out the why
And how—you made me swear to keep that crown:
And as you then intended . . .
    Victor.   Fool! What way
Could I intend or not intend? As man,   275
With a man's will, when I say "I intend,"
I can intend up to a certain point,
No farther. I intended to preserve
The crown of Savoy and Sardinia whole:
And if events arise demonstrating   280
The way, I hoped should guard it, rather like
To lose it . . .
    Charles.   Keep within your sphere and mine!
It is God's province we usurp on, else.
Here, blindfold through the maze of things we walk
By a slight clue of false, true, right and wrong;   285
All else is rambling and presumption. I
Have sworn to keep this kingdom: there's my truth.
    Victor. Truth, boy, is here, within my breast; and in
Your recognition of it, truth is, too;

---

262 *1842* which seizes   263 *1842* On petty   266 *1842,1849* Who was to
worship me, and for whose sake   267 *1842* I near had waived my   269 *1842*
crown, and were disposed   273 *1868* crown   276 *1842,1849* man's life,
when   278 *1842-68* No further. I   280 *1842* arise to demonstrate
281 *1842,1849* way I took to keep it, rather's like   285 *1842,1849* slight thread of
285a *1842* Truth here for us—truth everywhere for God:

280 *demonstrating*: stressed on the second syllable, as in Johnson.

And in the effect of all this tortuous dealing   290
With falsehood, used to carry out the truth,
—In its success, this falsehood turns, again,
Truth for the world. But you are right: these themes
Are over-subtle. I should rather say
In such a case, frankly,—it fails, my scheme: 295
I hoped to see you bring about, yourself,
What I must bring about. I interpose
On your behalf—with my son's good in sight—
To hold what he is nearly letting go,
Confirm his title, add a grace perhaps.   300
There's Sicily, for instance,—granted me
And taken back, some years since: till I give
That island with the rest, my work's half done.
For his sake, therefore, as of those he rules . . .
    Charles. Our sakes are one; and that, you could not say,   305
Because my answer would present itself
Forthwith:—a year has wrought an age's change.
This people's not the people now, you once
Could benefit; nor is my policy
Your policy.
    Victor [*with an outburst*]. I know it! You undo   310
All I have done—my life of toil and care!
I left you this the absolutest rule
In Europe: do you think I sit and smile,
Bid you throw power to the populace—
See my Sardinia, that has kept apart,   315
Join in the mad and democratic whirl
Whereto I see all Europe haste full tide?
England casts off her kings; France mimics England:

292 *1842* falsehood is again   293 *1842-68* world!   297 *1842-63* about:
307 *1842-63* change: 313 *1842-68* I will sit still   314 *1842-68* And see you
throw all power   *1842* the people— *1849, 1863* power off to the people—
315 *1842-68* has stood apart,

    291 *used to carry out the truth* : cf. *Sordello*, iii. 793 ff.
    301 *Sicily* : Sicily, granted to Victor in 1713, had been taken back by the Emperor as a
consequence of Victor's defeat in 1718.
    312 *the absolutest rule* : see Introduction, pp. 94 n.

This realm I hoped was safe. Yet here I talk,
When I can save it, not by force alone,   320
But bidding plagues, which follow sons like you,
Fasten upon my disobedient . . .
            [*Recollecting himself.*] Surely
I could say this—if minded so—my son?
    Charles. You could not. Bitterer curses than your curse
Have I long since denounced upon myself   325
If I misused my power. In fear of these
I entered on those measures—will abide
By them: so, I should say, Count Tende . . .
    Victor.   No!
But no! But if, my Charles, your—more than old—
Half-foolish father urged these arguments,   330
And then confessed them futile, but said plainly
That he forgot his promise, found his strength
Fail him, had thought at savage Chambery
Too much of brilliant Turin, Rivoli here,
And Susa, and Veneria, and Superga—   335
Pined for the pleasant places he had built
When he was fortunate and young—
    Charles.   My father!
    Victor. Stay yet!—and if he said he could not die
Deprived of baubles he had put aside,
He deemed, for ever—of the Crown that binds   340
Your brain up, whole, sound and impregnable,
Creating kingliness—the Sceptre too,
Whose mere wind, should you wave it, back would beat
Invaders—and the golden Ball which throbs
As if you grasped the palpitating heart   345
Indeed o' the realm, to mould as choose you may!
—If I must totter up and down the streets

319 *1842–68* safe!   324 *1842–65* not!   333 *1842* savage Chamberri
338 *1842–65* yet—   346 *1849–68* as you may choose!

329–30 *more than old— / Half-foolish father*: cf. *King Lear*, IV. vii. 60.

335 *And Susa*: Victor lost Susa to the French in 1704. For Veneria see 241 n., above.
Victor built a basilica at Superga, east of Turin, in gratitude for a victory against France.

My sires built, where myself have introduced
And fostered laws and letters, sciences,
The civil and the military arts!   350
Stay, Charles! I see you letting me pretend
To live my former self once more—King Victor,
The venturous yet politic: they style me
Again, the Father of the Prince: friends wink
Good-humouredly at the delusion you   355
So sedulously guard from all rough truths
That else would break upon my dotage!—You—
Whom now I see preventing my old shame—
I tell not, point by cruel point, my tale—
For is 't not in your breast my brow is hid?   360
Is not your hand extended? Say you not . . .

       Enter D'ORMEA, *leading in* POLYXENA.
    Polyxena [advancing and withdrawing CHARLES—*to* VICTOR].
In this conjuncture even, he would say
(Though with a moistened eye and quivering lip)
The supplicant is my father. I must save
A great man from himself, nor see him fling   365
His well-earned fame away: there must not follow
Ruin so utter, a break-down of worth
So absolute: no enemy shall learn,
He thrust his child 'twixt danger and himself,
And, when that child somehow stood danger out,   370
Stole back with serpent wiles to ruin Charles
—Body, that's much,—and soul, that's more—and realm,
That's most of all! No enemy shall say . . .

    D'Ormea. Do you repent, sir?
    Victor [resuming himself]   D'Ormea? This is well!

350 *1842,1849* arts—   351 *1842-65* Charles—   354 *1842* friends winking
355 *1842* delusion you're   356 *1842* So sedulous in guarding from sad truth,
357 *1842,1849* upon the dotage!—   364 *1842-63* father—

    349 *And fostered laws and letters*: 'He had a very wise code of laws drawn up, which
received his name . . . His regulations on public education gave new life to the love of solid
learning. Although he himself was not learned, he protected science and literature': foot-
note to Sismondi's article, p. 392b.
    374 s.d. *[resuming himself]*: becoming himself again.

Worthily done, King Charles, craftily done!   375
Judiciously you post these, to o'erhear
The little your importunate father thrusts
Himself on you to say!—Ah, they'll correct
The amiable blind facility
You show in answering his peevish suit.   380
What can he need to sue for? Thanks, D'Ormea!
You have fulfilled your office: but for you,
The old Count might have drawn some few more livres
To swell his income! Had you, lady, missed
The moment, a permission might be granted   385
To buttress up my ruinous old pile!
But you remember properly the list
Of wise precautions I took when I gave
Nearly as much away—to reap the fruits
I should have looked for!
    Charles.   Thanks, sir: degrade me,   390
So you remain yourself! Adieu!
    Victor.   I'll not
Forget it for the future, nor presume
Next time to slight such mediators! Nay—
Had I first moved them both to intercede,
I might secure a chamber in Moncaglier   395
—Who knows?
    Charles.   Adieu!
    Victor.   You bid me this adieu
With the old spirit?
    Charles.   Adieu!
    Victor.   Charles—Charles!
    Charles.   Adieu!

378 *1842-63* say! Ay, they'll   380 *1842-68* You showed in   *1842,1849* suit:
381 *1842-68* for? Bravely, D'Ormea,   382 *1842-68* Have you fulfilled
385 *1842,1849* permission had been granted   *1863-8* permission would be
386 *1842-63* To build afresh my   *1842,1849* pile—   387 *1842-68* you remem-
bered properly   388 *1863,1865* I took   390 *1842* I ever looked *1863-8* I
might have looked   391 *1842-65* yourself.   393 *1842,1849* such potent
mediators!   395 *1842,1849* might have had a   397 *1842,1849* Charles—
Charles—

376 *Judiciously you post these*: cf. II. ii. 157, below.

[Victor *goes.*

  Charles. You were mistaken, Marquis, as you hear.
'T was for another purpose the Count came.
The Count desires Moncaglier. Give the order!   400
    D'Ormea [*leisurely*]. Your minister has lost your
        confidence,
Asserting late, for his own purposes,
Count Tende would . . .
    Charles [*flinging his badge back*]. Be still the minister!
And give a loose to your insulting joy;
It irks me more thus stifled than expressed: 405
Loose it!
    D'Ormea. There's none to loose, alas! I see
I never am to die a martyr.
    Polyxena.   Charles!
    Charles. No praise, at least, Polyxena—no praise!

1842 s.d. †[*Exit* Victor.   398 *1842-68* hear!   403 *1842,1849* still our minis-
ter!   *1863* minister   405 *1842-63* expressed.   407 *1842,1849* martyr!
408 s.d. †[*1842 Exeunt Omnes.*

KING CHARLES.

Part II.

D'ORMEA, *seated, folding papers he has been examining.*

This at the last effects it: now, King Charles
Or else King Victor—that's a balance: but now,
D'Ormea the arch-culprit, either turn
O' the scale,—that's sure enough. A point to solve,
My masters, moralists, whate'er your style!   5
When you discover why I push myself
Into a pitfall you'd pass safely by,
Impart to me among the rest! No matter.
Prompt are the righteous ever with their rede
To us the wrongful; lesson them this once!   10
For safe among the wicked are you set,
D'Ormea! We lament life's brevity,
Yet quarter e'en the threescore years and ten,
Nor stick to call the quarter roundly "life."
D'Ormea was wicked, say, some twenty years;   15
A tree so long was stunted; afterward,
What if it grew, continued growing, till
No fellow of the forest equalled it?
'T was a stump then; a stump it still must be:
While forward saplings, at the outset checked,   20
In virtue of that first sprout keep their style
Amid the forest's green fraternity.
Thus I shoot up to surely get lopped down
And bound up for the burning. Now for it!

---

s.d. *1842,1849* Night.—D'ORMEA   2 *1842,1849* balance: now   3 *1842-63*
For D'Ormea   5 *1842,1849* whate'er's your   10 *1842-63* the wicked—lesson
12 *1842,1849* Old D'Ormea. *1863* D'Ormea.   19 *1842-65* a shrub then—a shrub it

5 *style*: title.
9 *rede*: advice.
10 *To us the wrongful*: OED describes as obsolete this use of the word applied to people.

Enter CHARLES *and* POLYXENA *with* Attendants.

D'Ormea |*rises*|. Sir, in the due discharge of this my office—   25
This enforced summons of yourself from Turin,
And the disclosure I am bound to make
To-night,—there must already be, I feel,
So much that wounds . . .
    Charles.   Well, sir?
    D'Ormea.   —That I, perchance,
May utter also what, another time,   30
Would irk much,—it may prove less irksome now.
    Charles. What would you utter?
    D'Ormea.   That I from my soul
Grieve at to-night's event: for you I grieve,
E'en grieve for . . .
    Charles.   Tush, another time for talk!
My kingdom is in imminent danger?
    D'Ormea.   Let   35
The Count communicate with France—its King,
His grandson, will have Fleury's aid for this,
Though for no other war.
    Charles.   First for the levies:
What forces can I muster presently?
                 [D'ORMEA *delivers papers which* CHARLES *inspects.*
    Charles. Good—very good. Montorio . . . how is this?   40
—Equips me double the old complement
Of soldiers?
    D'Ormea. Since his land has been relieved

---

37 *His grandson* : 'The King of France, Louis XV, grandson of Victor by the Duchess of
Burgundy, initially espoused his quarrel, and advanced 25,000 men to the frontiers of
Dauphiné. But, having been informed of the true reasons which influenced King Charles,
and having learned that he had just signed a treaty with the Emperor, [he] recalled his
army': Roman, p. 279. Voltaire denies as 'très-faux' the story that Louis XV wished to side
with his father against the son, 'as has been said in the memoirs of that period'. Cf. Condor-
cet, pp. 42–3.
    Fleury's aid : Guillaume-François Joly de Fleury, 'procureur-genéral' to the King.
    40 *Montorio* : a nobleman not mentioned in the sources which Browning names.

From double imposts, this he manages:
But under the late monarch . . .
    Charles.   Peace! I know.
Count Spava has omitted mentioning   45
What proxy is to head these troops of his.
    D'Ormea. Count Spava means to head his troops himself.
Something to fight for now; "Whereas," says he,
"Under the sovereign's father" . . .
    Charles.   It would seem
That all my people love me.
    D'Ormea.   Yes.
          [*To* POLYXENA *while* CHARLES *continues to inspect the papers.*
                        A temper   50
Like Victor's may avail to keep a state;
He terrifies men and they fall not off;
Good to restrain: best, if restraint were all.
But, with the silent circle round him, ends
Such sway: our King's begins precisely there.   55
For to suggest, impel and set at work,
Is quite another function. Men may slight,
In time of peace, the King who brought them peace:
In war,—his voice, his eyes, help more than fear.
They love you, sir!
    Charles [*to* Attendants]. Bring the regalia forth!   60
Quit the room! And now, Marquis, answer me!
Why should the King of France invade my realm?
    D'Ormea. Why? Did I not acquaint your Majesty
An hour ago?
    Charles.   I choose to hear again
What then I heard.
    D'Ormea.   Because, sir, as I said,   65
Your father is resolved to have his crown

---

43 *1842–68* double impost this   44 *1842–63* Peace.   48 *1842,1849* Some-
thing's to   53 *1842–63* all: 55 *1842–63* sway.   58 *1842* who brings
them   60 *1842–63* you, sire! Bring . . . . forth.   61 *1842–65* room.   *1842–*
63 me—   65 *1842–63* Because, sire, as   66 *1842,1849* have the crown

  43 *double imposts*: see above, *King Victor*, II. 440 ff.
  45 *Count Spava*: cf. *King Victor*, I. 172 n.

At any risk; and, as I judge, calls in
The foreigner to aid him.
  Charles.   And your reason
For saying this?
  D'Ormea [*aside*]. Ay, just his father's way!
[*To* CHARLES.] The Count wrote yesterday to your forces'
  Chief,   70
Rhebinder—made demand of help—
  Charles.   To try
Rhebinder—he's of alien blood: aught else?
  D'Ormea. Receiving a refusal,—some hours after,
The Count called on Del Borgo to deliver
The Act of Abdication: he refusing,   75
Or hesitating, rather—
  Charles.   What ensued?
  D'Ormea. At midnight, only two hours since, at Turin,
He rode in person to the citadel
With one attendant, to Soccorso gate,
And bade the governor, San Remi, open—   80
Admit him.
  Charles. For a purpose I divine.
These three were faithful, then?
  D'Ormea.   They told it me.
And I—
  Charles. Most faithful—

---

67 *1842* risk,   68 *1842,1849* These foreigners to   75 *1842* he refused,
76 *1842* Or hesitated, rather—   79 *1849–68* to the Soccorso   82 *1842–68* me:

71 *Rhebinder*: Condorcet (p. 40 n.) mentions that Victor recommended 'Rebender, a German general whom he had just made Marshal' to Charles at the same time as he recommended D'Ormea.

74 *The Count called on Del Borgo*: 'Victor . . . went so far as to ask the minister Del Borgo for the act of his abdication, charging him to inform his son of his determination to resume the reins of government. The minister, full of confusion and embarrassment, but not daring to expose himself by a refusal to the fury of the old monarch, promised to bring him this act the following day': Sismondi, p. 394b. Roman (pp. 273–4) gives a similar account.

78 *He rode*: Victor 'went to present himself at the sally port of the citadel of Turin. He demanded entry. An officer there informed the Baron Saint-Remi, who was the Governor. He arrived at all speed, not knowing what to think of this step on the part of the former King. The Prince wished to enter. The baron respectfully refused to have the port opened': Roman, p. 275. Sismondi gives a similar account: p. 394b.

D'Ormea.   Tell it you—with this
Moreover of my own: if, an hour hence,
You have not interposed, the Count will be   85
O' the road to France for succour.
    Charles.   Very good!
You do your duty now to me your monarch
Fully, I warrant?—have, that is, your project
For saving both of us disgrace, no doubt?
    D'Ormea. I give my counsel,—and the only one.   90
A month since, I besought you to employ
Restraints which had prevented many a pang:
But now the harsher course must be pursued.
These papers, made for the emergency,
Will pain you to subscribe: this is a list   95
Of those suspected merely—men to watch;
This—of the few of the Count's very household
You must, however reluctantly, arrest;
While here's a method of remonstrance—sure
Not stronger than the case demands—to take   100
With the Count's self.
    Charles.   Deliver those three papers.
    Polyxena [*while* CHARLES *inspects them—to* D'ORMEA].
Your measures are not over-harsh, sir: France
Will hardly be deterred from her intents
By these.
    D'Ormea. If who proposes might dispose,
I could soon satisfy you. Even these,   105

86 *1842-63* Upon his road . . . . succour. Good! *1865,1868* On his road   89 *1842-63*
disgrace, past doubt?   90 *1842* I have my counsel, which is the *1849* I have my
93 *1842* must have its way.   97 *1849, 1863* household.   99 *1842,1849* (sure
100 *1842,1849* demands)   103 *1842-63* from coming hither   104 *1842-63*
these. What good of my proposing measures   105 *1842-63* Without a chance of
their success? E'en these

    93 *the harsher course* : the article on Charles in the *Biographie universelle* mentions that in
self-defence he ordered rigorous measures to be taken 'contre quelques grands de la cour':
viii. 159a. Roman tells us that Victor's confessor 'and more than fifty persons of distinction
were arrested at the same time. The governor, the intendant of Chambéri, Count Saint-
Georges, the principal president of the senate, were summoned. The count was imprisoned
in the citadel and interrogated. The count of Cumiane, brother of the marchioness and her
confidant, confessed everything, and obtained his pardon': p. 278.

Hear what he'll say at my presenting!
   Charles [*who has signed them*].   There!
About the warrants! You've my signature.
What turns you pale? I do my duty by you
In acting boldly thus on your advice.
   D'Ormea [*reading them separately*]. Arrest the people I
     suspected merely?   110
   Charles. Did you suspect them?
   D'Ormea.   Doubtless: but—but—sir,
This Forquieri's governor of Turin,
And Rivarol and he have influence over
Half of the capital! Rabella, too?
Why, sir—
   Charles. Oh, leave the fear to me!
   D'Ormea [*still reading*].   You bid me   115
Incarcerate the people on this list?
Sir—
   Charles. But you never bade arrest those men,
So close related to my father too,
On trifling grounds?
   D'Ormea.   Oh, as for that, St. George,
President of Chambery's senators,   120
Is hatching treason! still—
          [*More troubled.*] Sir, Count Cumiane
Is brother to your father's wife! What's here?
Arrest the wife herself?
   Charles.   You seem to think
A venial crime this plot against me. Well?

---

106 *1842–65* presenting.   111 *1842–63* but—sire,   112 *1842–65* Turin;
114 *1842–65* capital.—   115 *1842–63* Why, sire—Oh,   *1842,1849* to me.
117 *1842–63* Sire—Why, you   120 *1842* of Chamberri's senators,
121 *1842,1849* treason—but— †[*Still more troubled.*]† Sire, Count *1863* treason! but— [rest
of line as *1842,1849*]   123 *1849, 1863* to think it   124 *1842*   It
venial crime to plot *1849,1863*   crime to plot

   112 *Forquieri*: Condorcet mentions that '*Fosquieri*, Governor of Turin, has been seduced
[by Victor], as well as the Marquis of *Rivarol*': 41 n. Browning, or his printer, mistook the
name.
    114 *Rabella*: he is not mentioned in any of the sources named by Browning.
    119 *St. George*: named by Roman, p. 278.   121 *Count Cumiane*: cf. 93 n., above.

D'Ormea [*who has read the last paper*].
Wherefore am I thus ruined? Why not take   125
My life at once? This poor formality
Is, let me say, unworthy you! Prevent it
You, madam! I have served you, am prepared
For all disgraces: only, let disgrace
Be plain, be proper—proper for the world   130
To pass its judgment on 'twixt you and me!
Take back your warrant, I will none of it!
　　Charles. Here is a man to talk of fickleness!
He stakes his life upon my father's falsehood;
I bid him . . .
　　D'Ormea. Not you! Were he trebly false,   135
You do not bid me . . .
　　Charles.　　　　Is't not written there?
I thought so: give—I'll set it right.
　　D'Ormea.　　　　　　Is it there?
Oh yes, and plain—arrest him now—drag here
Your father! And were all six times as plain,
Do you suppose I trust it?
　　Charles.　　　　Just one word!   140
You bring him, taken in the act of flight,
Or else your life is forfeit.
　　D'Ormea.　　　　Ay, to Turin
I bring him, and to-morrow?
　　Charles.　　　　　　Here and now!
The whole thing is a lie, a hateful lie,
As I believed and as my father said.   145
I knew it from the first, but was compelled
To circumvent you; and the great D'Ormea,
That baffled Alberoni and tricked Coscia,

132 *1842-63*　it.　　134 *1842*　falsehood,　　138 *1842-63*　him—now
140 *1842,1849*　I'd trust　　143 *1842-63*　him?　　147 *1842-63*　the crafty
D'Ormea,

141 *You bring him* : 'The King, with tears in his eyes, . . . signed the order which the Mar-
quis d'Ormea went to carry out': Sismondi, p. 394b.
148 *Alberoni . . . Coscia* : 'The Cardinal Alberoni . . . endeavoured to recover, by arms or
by acts of treason, the parts of the former Spanish monarchy of which the Treaty of

The miserable sower of such discord
'Twixt sire and son, is in the toils at last.   150
Oh I see! you arrive—this plan of yours,
Weak as it is, torments sufficiently
A sick old peevish man—wrings hasty speech,
An ill-considered threat from him; that's noted;
Then out you ferret papers, his amusement   155
In lonely hours of lassitude—examine
The day-by-day report of your paid spies--
And back you come: all was not ripe, you find,
And, as you hope, may keep from ripening yet,
But you were in bare time! Only, 't were best   160
I never saw my father—these old men
Are potent in excuses: and meanwhile,
D'Ormea's the man I cannot do without!
   Polyxena. Charles—
   Charles.   Ah, no question! You against me too!
You'd have me eat and drink and sleep, live, die   165
With this lie coiled about me, choking me!
No, no, D'Ormea! You venture life, you say,
Upon my father's perfidy: and I
Have, on the whole, no right to disregard
The chains of testimony you thus wind   170

149 *1842* of the discord,   150 *1842-65* last!   151 *1842* see—
154 *1842-63* And ill-considered threats from   157 *1842-63* paid creatures—
162 *1842,1849* and, meantime,   163 *1849* without.   164 *1842-63* You're
for D'Ormea too! *1865* You for D'Ormea too!   165 *1842* sleep, and die
166 *1842,1849* coil'd   167 *1842* no—he's caught. †[*To D'Ormea.*]† You *1849-65*
no— he's caught! {rest of line as *1842*}   170 *1842* you have wound

Utrecht had deprived Philippe V': Sismondi, p. 391b. Cf. the article on Jules Alberoni in
vol. i of the *Biographie universelle*. The article on D'Ormea in vol. xxxii states that he won
Coscia over 'par des présents': p. 145b.

160-1 *'t were best / I never saw my father*: 'In his last days, he [Victor] asked to see his son,
promising not to reproach him at all. D'Ormea had the credit of preventing an interview
which could have destroyed himself by revealing to the King that this whole terrible catas-
trophe was the work of his Minister': Condorcet, p. 43. Roman gives a different account of
the same matter. He tells us that, 'knowing Victor's dissimulation, his eloquence, and his
ascendancy over his son', D'Ormea made the most pressing representations to Charles.
Then he persuaded the Queen to try her eloquence, and 'the tears of a young wife [proved]
more persuasive than political arguments': pp. 281-2.

About me; though I do—do from my soul
Discredit them: still I must authorize
These measures, and I will. Perugia!
          [*Many* Officers *enter.*] Count—
You and Solar, with all the force you have,
Stand at the Marquis' orders: what he bids,   175
Implicitly perform! You are to bring
A traitor here; the man that's likest one
At present, fronts me; you are at his beck
For a full hour! he undertakes to show
A fouler than himself,—but, failing that,   .   180
Return with him, and, as my father lives,
He dies this night! The clemency you blame
So oft, shall be revoked—rights exercised,
Too long abjured.
          [*To* D'ORMEA.] Now sir, about the work!
To save your king and country! Take the warrant!   185
     D'Ormea. You hear the sovereign's mandate, Count
          Perugia?
Obey me! As your diligence, expect
Reward! All follow to Moncaglier!
               Charles [*in great anguish*]. D'Ormea! [D'ORMEA *goes.*
He goes, lit up with that appalling smile!
                         [*To* POLYXENA, *after a pause.*
At least you understand all this?
     Polyxena.   These means   190
Of our defence—these measures of precaution?
     Charles. It must be the best way; I should have else
Withered beneath his scorn.
     Polyxena.   What would you say?
     Charles. Why, do you think I mean to keep the crown,

---

173 *1842* I do. Perugia!   175 *1842–63* Are at   179 *1842–65* hour;   *1842–*
63 show you   182 *1842,1849* you've blamed   184 *1842–63* That I've
abjured.   186 *1842,1849* D'O. †[boldly to PERUGIA.]† You   188 *1842*
Reward.   *1842–68* to Moncaglier! D'Ormea!   s.d. *1842* †[*Exit* D'ORMEA, *cum suis.*
192 *1842–63* way.   194 *1842–68* Why, you don't think

174 *Solar:* Solaro was one of the minor courtiers charged with the custody of Victor.
'Perugia' (l. 173) does not appear in the named sources.

Polyxena?
   Polyxena. You then believe the story   195
In spite of all—that Victor comes?
    Charles.   Believe it?
I know that he is coming—feel the strength
That has upheld me leave me at his coming!
'T was mine, and now he takes his own again.
Some kinds of strength are well enough to have;   200
But who's to have that strength? Let my crown go!
I meant to keep it; but I cannot—cannot!
Only, he shall not taunt me—he, the first . . .
See if he would not be the first to taunt me
With having left his kingdom at a word.   205
With letting it be conquered without stroke,
With . . . no—no—'t is no worse than when he left!
I've just to bid him take it, and, that over,
We'll fly away—fly, for I loathe this Turin,
This Rivoli, all titles loathe, all state.   210
We'd best go to your country—unless God
Send I die now!
    Polyxena.   Charles, hear me!
    Charles.   And again
Shall you be my Polyxena—you'll take me
Out of this woe! Yes, do speak, and keep speaking!
I would not let you speak just now, for fear   215
You'd counsel me against him: but talk, now,
As we two used to talk in blessed times:
Bid me endure all his caprices; take me
From this mad post above him!
    Polyxena.   I believe
We are undone, but from a different cause.   220
All your resources, down to the least guard,

196 *1842* Victor's coming? *Cha.* Coming? *1849-68* Victor's coming?   197 *1842* I
feel that   *203 {reading of *1863-8*} *1842,1849* first— *1888,1889* first . .
205 *1842* kingdom all exposed— *1849, 1863* word— *1865,1868* word,   207 *1842-63*
he left it, *1865* left,   209 *1842* We fly   210 *1842* This Rivoli, and titles
loathe, and state. *1849, 1863* loathe, and state.   212 *1842* now.   214 *1842*
woe.   218-19 *1842* caprices—take | Me from this post   220 *1842* cause:

Are at D'Ormea's beck. What if, the while,
He act in concert with your father? We
Indeed were lost. This lonely Rivoli—
Where find a better place for them?

    Charles [*pacing the room*].   And why   225
Does Victor come? To undo all that's done,
Restore the past, prevent the future! Seat
His mistress in your seat, and place in mine
... Oh, my own people, whom will you find there,
To ask of, to consult with, to care for,   230
To hold up with your hands? Whom? One that's false—
False—from the head's crown to the foot's sole, false!
The best is, that I knew it in my heart
From the beginning, and expected this,
And hated you, Polyxena, because   235
You saw thro' him, though I too saw thro' him,
Saw that he meant this while he crowned me, while
He prayed for me,—nay, while he kissed my brow,
I saw——

    Polyxena. But if your measures take effect,
D'Ormea true to you?

    Charles.   Then worst of all!   240
I shall have loosed that callous wretch on him!
Well may the woman taunt him with his child—
I, eating here his bread, clothed in his clothes,
Seated upon his seat, let slip D'Ormea
To outrage him! We talk—perchance he tears   245

222 *1842–63* Are now at   *1842* beck: *1842,1849* if this while   223 *1842,1849*
He acts in   226 *1842–63* done!   228 *1842* Sebastian in   240 *1842–63*
And D'Ormea's true   244 *1842–63* seat, give D'Ormea leave *1865* seat, let
D'Ormea slip   245 *1842–63* perchance they tear

    227 *Restore the past, prevent the future!*: see Introduction, pp. 94 ff.

    228 *His mistress in your seat*: perhaps suggested by a fact mentioned by Sismondi as
ominous: that when she went to see the Queen, Sebastian 'took an armchair similar to that
of this princess': p. 394b.

    244 *let slip D'Ormea*: cf. *The Taming of the Shrew*, v. ii. 52: 'Lucentio slipp'd me like his
greyhound'.

    245 *To outrage*: 'To injure violently or contumeliously': Johnson.

My father from his bed; the old hands feel
For one who is not, but who should be there,
He finds D'Ormea! D'Ormea too finds him!
The crowded chamber when the lights go out—
Closed doors—the horrid scuffle in the dark—   250
The accursed prompting of the minute! My guards!
To horse—and after, with me—and prevent!
    Polyxena [*seizing his hand*]. King Charles! Pause here upon
       this strip of time
Allotted you out of eternity!
Crowns are from God: you in his name hold yours.   255
Your life's no least thing, were it fit your life
Should be abjured along with rule; but now,
Keep both! Your duty is to live and rule—
You, who would vulgarly look fine enough
In the world's eye, deserting your soul's charge,—   260
Ay, you would have men's praise, this Rivoli
Would be illumined! While, as 't is, no doubt,
Something of stain will ever rest on you;
No one will rightly know why you refused
To abdicate; they'll talk of deeds you could   265
Have done, no doubt,—nor do I much expect
Future achievement will blot out the past,
Envelope it in haze—nor shall we two
Live happy any more. 'T will be, I feel,

248 *1842-63* And he finds   251 *1842* Th'accursed promptings of *1849, 1863*
accursed promptings of   253 *1842* Pause you upon   255 *1842-68* God—in
his name you hold yours.   261 *1842* men's tongues—this   262 *1842* illu-
mined— *1849* illumined: 267 *1842-63* Future achievements will
269 *1842-63* Be happy   *1842,1849* more;

   246 *My father from his bed* : 'several officers entered the King's chamber, secured his per-
son, and conducted him to the chateau of Rivoli. The Marchioness of Spigo was arrested at
the same time, and taken to the chateau of Ceva': Roman, p. 277.
   259 *would vulgarly look fine enough* : this opposes Voltaire's view (see Introduction, p. 96),
and that of Condorcet, who wrote that it was 'unworthy counsellors' who persuaded
Charles that such an action 'would cheapen him in the eyes of the powers and make it seem
that he was incapable of reigning': p. 42. Johnson gives 'among the common people' as one
definition of 'vulgarly'.
   264 *No one will rightly know* : this belief that the truth is unlikely ever to be known may be
found in many places in Browning, e.g. in *Sordello*, vi. 819 ff. Cf. Carlyle, 'On History',
1830 (Centenary ed., xxvii. 87).

Only in moments that the duty's seen   270
As palpably as now: the months, the years
Of painful indistinctness are to come,
While daily must we tread these palace-rooms
Pregnant with memories of the past: your eye
May turn to mine and find no comfort there,   275
Through fancies that beset me, as yourself,
Of other courses, with far other issues,
We might have taken this great night: such bear,
As I will bear! What matters happiness?
Duty! There's man's one moment: this is yours!   280
    [*Putting the crown on his head, and the sceptre in his hand, she*
       places him on his seat: a long pause and silence.

       Enter D'ORMEA *and* VICTOR, *with* Guards.

  Victor. At last I speak; but once—that once, to you!
'T is you I ask, not these your varletry,
Who's King of us?
    Charles [*from his seat*].
               Count Tende . . .
  Victor.   What your spies
Assert I ponder in my soul, I say—
Here to your face, amid your guards! I choose   285
To take again the crown whose shadow I gave—
For still its potency surrounds the weak
White locks their felon hands have discomposed.
Or I'll not ask who's King, but simply, who
Withholds the crown I claim? Deliver it!   290
I have no friend in the wide world: nor France

273 *1842* tread the palace   280 s.d. *1842* D'ORMEA, *cum suis, and* VICTOR. | *1849-68*
and VICTOR. | 281 *1842* you.   285 *1842* guards.   286 *1842* crown I
gave—its shade   290 *1842* crown he claims? Deliver

   273 *these palace-rooms*: Roman (pp. 282-3) and Orrery (p. 46) mention that the château
of Moncalier became an object of aversion to Charles, for the remainder of his life.
   280 *There's man's one moment*: cf. ll. 253-4 above. The insistence that a man must seize his
opportunity is ubiquitous in Browning.
   282 *varletry*: 'Rabble; crowd; populace': Johnson. Cf. *Antony and Cleopatra*, v. ii. 56, and
Sordello, vi. 402.
   288 *felon hands*: cf. Thomson, *Liberty*, iv. 1189.

Nor England cares for me: you see the sum
Of what I can avail. Deliver it!
   Charles. Take it, my father!

                    And now say in turn,
Was it done well, my father—sure not well,   295
To try me thus! I might have seen much cause
For keeping it—too easily seen cause!
But, from that moment, e'en more woefully
My life had pined away, than pine it will.
Already you have much to answer for.   300
My life to pine is nothing,—her sunk eyes
Were happy once! No doubt, my people think
I am their King still . . . but I cannot strive!
Take it!

   Victor [*one hand on the crown* CHARLES *offers, the other on his
     neck*].

        So few years give it quietly,
My son! It will drop from me. See you not?   305
A crown's unlike a sword to give away—
That, let a strong hand to a weak hand give!
But crowns should slip from palsied brows to heads
Young as this head: yet mine is weak enough,
E'en weaker than I knew. I seek for phrases   310
To vindicate my right. 'T is of a piece!
All is alike gone by with me—who beat
Once D'Orleans in his lines—his very lines!
To have been Eugene's comrade, Louis's rival,
And now . . .

   Charles [*putting the crown on him, to the rest*]. The King
     speaks, yet none kneels, I think!   315
   Victor. I am then King! As I became a King
Despite the nations, kept myself a King,

---

303 *1842-63* That I'm their   314 *1842-68* Louis'   315 *1842 him.*]† The

   294 *Take it, my father!*: unhistorical. Browning makes Charles do what Voltaire and Con-
dorcet wish that he had done.
   312-13 *who beat / Once D'Orleans in his lines*: Victor's victory in 1706 is described by Sis-
mondi: pp. 388b-389a. He was helped by Prince Eugene of Savoy.

So I die King, with Kingship dying too
Around me. I have lasted Europe's time.
What wants my story of completion? Where   320
Must needs the damning break show? Who mistrusts
My children here—tell they of any break
'Twixt my day's sunrise and its fiery fall?
And who were by me when I died but they?
D'Ormea there!
>   *Charles.*   What means he?
>   *Victor.*   Ever there!   325
Charles—how to save your story! Mine must go.
Say—say that you refused the crown to me!
Charles, yours shall be my story! You immured
Me, say, at Rivoli. A single year
I spend without a sight of you, then die.   330
That will serve every purpose—tell that tale
The world!
>   *Charles.* Mistrust me? Help!
>   *Victor.*   Past help, past reach!
'T is in the heart—you cannot reach the heart:
This broke mine, that I did believe, you, Charles,
Would have denied me and disgraced me.
>   *Polyxena.*   Charles   335
Has never ceased to be your subject, sir!
He reigned at first through setting up yourself
As pattern: if he e'er seemed harsh to you,
'T was from a too intense appreciation
Of your own character: he acted you—   340

319 1842–68 me! .... time!   *321 1849–65* show!   *325 1842–63* Who?—
D'Ormea   *326 (reading of DC,1889)* 1842–68 go! *1888* go   *1842–68* story?
327 1842–63 me—   *330 1842* you and die— *1849–68* die—   *335 1842–68*
denied and so disgraced   *336 1842* subject, sire— *1849, 1863* subject, sire!

318 *with Kingship dying*: a prominent theme in Carlyle's sixth lecture 'On Heroes and
Hero-Worship', delivered on 22 May 1840: 'In rebellious ages, when Kingship itself seems
dead and abolished, Cromwell, Napoleon, step-forth again as Kings': *Works* (Centenary
ed.), v. 204.

327 *say that you refused the crown*: historically, Charles did. Cf. Introduction, p. 95.

337–8 *through setting up yourself / As pattern*: the article on Charles in the *Biographie univer-
selle* stresses that Charles was a most effective ruler: viii. 159a.

Ne'er for an instant did I think it real,
Nor look for any other than this end.
I hold him worlds the worse on that account;
But so it was.
    Charles [*to* POLYXENA]. I love you now indeed.
[*To* VICTOR.] You never knew me.
    Victor.   Hardly till this moment,   345
When I seem learning many other things
Because the time for using them is past.
If 't were to do again! That's idly wished.
Truthfulness might prove policy as good
As guile. Is this my daughter's forehead? Yes: 350
. I've made it fitter now to be a queen's
Than formerly: I've ploughed the deep lines there
Which keep too well a crown from slipping off.
No matter. Guile has made me King again.
Louis—'t was in King Victor's time:—long since ,   355
When Louis reigned and, also, Victor reigned.
How the world talks already of us two!
God of eclipse and each discoloured star,
Why do I linger then?
               Ha! Where lurks he?
D'Ormea! Nearer to your King! Now stand!   360
           [*Collecting his strength as* D'ORMEA *approaches.*
You lied, D'Ormea! I do not repent.   [*Dies.*

---

342 *1842,1849* Or look   344 *1842* {no s.d.} *1842-68* indeed!   345 *1842-68*
me!   353 *1842* That keep   *1842-65* off!   355-6 {roman type in *1842*}
360 *1842-63* D'Ormea! Come nearer   361 *1842-63* But you lied,

   346 *When I seem learning* : Browning was deeply interested in the view of life which may
present itself to a dying man. See *Paracelsus*, i. 765 ff., v. 487 ff., and v. 507-9; and cf. Ian
Jack, *Browning's Major Poetry* (1973), pp. 198 ff.

   356 *and, also, Victor reigned* : it was Victor's ambition to be regarded as comparable to his
enemy, Louis XIV. See Sismondi, p. 393a.

INTRODUCTION TO
DRAMATIC LYRICS

W E have already quoted the letter of 9 March 1840 in which Browning told Eliza Flower that he intended 'to song-write, play-write forthwith'.[1] During the next two years he published two plays and meditated others, but apart from the lyrics and lyrical passages in *Pippa Passes* he printed nothing resembling a lyric or song. On 22 May 1842, however, he told Alfred Domett that he was going to publish 'a few songs and small poems which Moxon advised me to do for popularity's sake!'--the exclamation-mark no doubt revealing a certain embarrassment at avowing such an aim.[2]

Moxon cannot have known many earlier short poems of Browning's, when he made his momentous suggestion. He knew the four strange lyrics in *Paracelsus*, and the five pieces which had appeared in the *Monthly Repository* between October 1834 and May 1836. While he may have seen one or two other pieces in manuscript, there is no evidence that he did, and Browning was later to tell Elizabeth Barrett that 'nobody ever sees what I do till it is printed'.[3]

Neither the title of the third of the *Bells and Pomegranates* nor the laconic 'Advertisement' prefixed to it offered the prospective reader much assistance. Almost the only unambiguously lyrical pieces in the little pamphlet are the 'Cavalier Tunes'—which may explain why these slight things are given pride of place. When, in 1863, Browning attempted to classify his shorter poems, only six pieces (the 'Cavalier Tunes', the poem later called 'Soliloquy of the Spanish Cloister', 'Cristina', and 'Through the Metidja') were classified as Lyrics: half a dozen of the shortest and least important of the poems. Eight were classified as Romances, an acknowledgement that narrative is more important than Lyric in this collection. In 1842 'Lyrics' means no more than 'short poems'.

In reading most collections of short poems we sense that the poet has given some thought to the arrangement of the individual pieces, but no principle of sequence is evident in *Dramatic Lyrics*, while the late addition of 'The Pied Piper' makes it clear that he had not calculated how many poems he required to fill sixteen pages. The perplexity of early readers—the reviewer in the *Athenæum* commented that the collection contained

---

[1] *Correspondence*, iv. 256. [2] *Browning and Domett*, p. 36. [3] Kintner, i. 55.

'mere fragments ... apparently thoughts jotted down for after use—or rejected from their places in longer pieces' and referred to them as '*disjecta membra*'[1]—is easier to understand when we read the poems as they first appeared. Eight of the thirteen poems which follow the initial trio are presented as pairs. The poem which we know as 'My Last Duchess' appears simply as 'I.—Italy' in a pair of poems entitled 'Italy and France', its companion being the future 'Count Gismond'. 'Incident of the French Camp' is here the first of two poems with the general heading 'Camp and Cloister', itself entitled 'I.—Camp. (*French.*)': it is paired with the future 'Soliloquy of the Spanish Cloister'. 'Johannes Agricola in Meditation' is the first of two 'Madhouse Cells' (the name of Agricola being nowhere mentioned), 'Porphyria's Lover' being the other (equally without an individual title). 'In a Gondola' is so named, but when we read it as it appears here, with no indication when the man is speaking and when the woman—or even of the fact that the man has been '*surprised, and stabbed*' before he speaks the last seven lines—even this straightforward piece becomes relatively obscure.

The dates of composition span the period from 1835 (or 1834) to 1842, in which last year at least four or five of the poems were written: see the individual introductions. Elizabeth Barrett was one of a very small number of readers who saw the high merit of the collection—Joseph Arnould was another.[2] Browning himself was pleased with the pamphlet, as the letter which accompanied a presentation copy for Alfred Domett makes clear: 'With this you get some more verses of mine,' he wrote on 13 December 1842, '—I shall have more ready ere long, I hope—and better.'[3] Three years later he was to publish *Dramatic Romances and Lyrics*.[4]

Something of the process by which *1842* was prepared for publication can be seen in the first and second proofs presented by Browning to Thomas Powell and now at Harvard. The first proof is dated, in the author's hand, 'New Cross. Hatcham Surrey Nov: 11: 1842 Friday.' It lacks 'The Pied Piper' and has only fourteen pages. Most of Browning's markings correct printer's errors, but he also adds an exclamation-mark at the end of the last line of 'Through the Metidja', and notes 'M.S. cuckoldy' at the bottom of p. 1—perhaps an indication that he regretted the revision

---

[1] *Athenæum*, 1843, p. 385a.

[2] For Elizabeth Barrett's views see, in particular, Raymond and Sullivan, ii. 121-2 and 162. For Arnould's praise, in verse, see Donald Smalley, 'Joseph Arnould and Robert Browning: New Letters ... and a Verse Epistle': PMLA 80 (1965), 90 ff.

[3] *Browning and Domett*, p. 48.

[4] For a more general discussion of this pamphlet, see Ian Jack, 'Browning's *Dramatic Lyrics* (1842)', in BIS 15 (1987).

which he had made by erasure in the second (Yale) manuscript. A stage-direction—'(he is stabbed by one of the Three)'—is inserted before the last seven lines of 'In a Gondola', but there is no sign of it in the second proof. In l. 106 'Paul's cloak' replaces 'Gian's cloak', so adding another character to the shadowy cast. On p. 7 Browning added a very rough sketch of an angel to illustrate 'In a Gondola', 87–99, and on p. 12 a doodle of a flower to illustrate the 'ray-like florets' in 'Rudel to the Lady of Tripoli'.

It was in the second proof that Browning first saw 'The Pied Piper' in print. He revised the dedication from '*To Mr. C., the Younger*', changed 'spoil' to 'shock' at l. 282, and completed the last word of the poem which had been imperfectly printed. While these changes appear in the published text, his alteration of 'abide' to 'reside' in l. 23 of 'Through the Metidja' was missed, and Browning had to make it by hand in the copies he presented to Powell and to Domett. In the latter he also corrected l. 116 of 'Count Gismond' from 'we too' to 'we two', and added (in pencil) 'He' and 'She' to the appropriate sections of 'In a Gondola'.

In the Brigham Young copy we find the revisions from 'abide' to 'reside' and from 'We too' to 'We two', and two further revisions which were to appear in *1849*: in l. 83 of 'Count Gismond' we find 'I was bid' instead of 'me he bid', while l. 32 of 'Cristina' becomes 'Away the rest have trifled'. Line 14 of 'Marching Along' has 'Hazlerig, Hollis and' in place of 'Serve Hazelrig', an intermediate reading. At no stage did Browning notice that p. 8 of the second proof was wrongly numbered 7, as in *1842*.

When the poems in *Dramatic Lyrics* were reprinted in later collections (as all of them were) other revisions were of course introduced. Two lines in 'Count Gismond' marred by inadvertent internal rhymes (54 and 94) were improved, for example, while the last line of 'Artemis Prologizes' was revised from 'In fitting silence the event await' to the memorable form in which we read it, 'Await, in fitting silence, the event'.

All but two of Browning's corrections to *1888* appear, identically, in the Dykes Campbell copy and the Brown University list and were made in *1889*. The exceptions are the commas after 'else', which Browning wanted to remove from the ends of ll. 13 and 15 of 'Give a Rouse' (correction in Brown University only) and which we have retained. We have also made some minor punctuation changes and have restored a couple of earlier readings: in 'Waring' l. 121 and 'Cristina', l. 63. The pamphlet was published in the last week of November, 1842.

DRAMATIC LYRICS

title *1842* BELLS AND POMEGRANATES. Nᵒ· III.–DRAMATIC LYRICS. BY ROBERT BROWNING. Author of "Paracelsus." LONDON: EDWARD MOXON, DOVER STREET. MDCCCXLII.

ADVERTISEMENT.

Such Poems as the following come properly enough, I
suppose, under the head of "Dramatic Pieces;" being, though
for the most part Lyric in expression, always Dramatic in
principle, and so many utterances of so many imaginary per-
sons, not mine.

R. B.

ADVERTISEMENT.: we give this as it appears in *1842*, on the verso of the title-page,
facing the first page of the text. There is nothing similar in *Dramatic Romances and Lyrics*,
1845. In *1849*, when the contents of the pamphlets of *1842* and *1845* were printed together
as part of vol. ii of the *Poems*, under the title 'Dramatic Romances and Lyrics', the text of the
former Advertisement appears (without Browning's initials) as a footnote asterisked to
'Cavalier Tunes' but obviously intended to apply to the 'Dramatic Romances and Lyrics' as
a whole. In the first volume of *The Poetical Works* (3 vols., 1863), of which the title is *Lyrics,
Romances, Men, and Women*, the footnote appears in the same way, but begins: 'Such Poems
as the majority in this volume might also come' and has 'often Lyric' instead of 'for the
most part Lyric'. There is also a note opposite the first page of the text: 'In this Volume are
collected and redistributed the pieces first published in 1842, 1845, and 1855, respectively,
under the titles of "Dramatic Lyrics," "Dramatic Romances," and "Men and Women." Part
of these were inscribed to my dear friend John Kenyon: I hope the whole may obtain the
honour of an association with his memory. R.B.'

In the third volume of *1868*, which contains the 'Dramatic Lyrics', the revised footnote
is given again, while the note on the opposite page is slightly altered to read: 'In a late edi-
tion were collected and redistributed the pieces first published in 1842, 1845 and 1855,
respectively . . . It is not worth while to disturb this arrangement' (p. 74). There is no note to
the 'Dramatic Romances' in vol. iv or to the 'Men and Women' poems in vol. v.

In *1888-9* the revised footnote appears once again, under the first page of 'Cavalier
Tunes' (which are given with the other 'Dramatic Lyrics', in vol. vi). The further note about
the 'late edition' now disappears. There is no note in vol. iv (which includes the 'Men and
Women' poems) or vol. v (which includes the 'Dramatic Romances').

CAVALIER TUNES

THERE are two manuscripts of the first two poems, one on the two sides of a small leaf in the Robert H. Taylor Collection at Princeton, and the other (which has all three poems) at Yale. The Princeton manuscript, which has important variants, was unknown to DeVane, Pettigrew, and others. Whereas it has no watermark, the first of the three leaves at Yale has an 1836 watermark. They are no doubt later than the leaf at Princeton: the Yale version of 'Marching Along' is much closer to *1842*, and shows the interesting erasure of 'cuckoldy' (in favour of 'crop-headed') in the second line.

DeVane states that the poems 'were probably written during the summer of 1842, and were intended to mark the second centenary of the beginning of the Civil Wars', which is possible. The fact that the later versions bear an 1836 watermark, however, would be consistent with a date of composition close to that of the publication of *Strafford* in 1837.

Some of the echoes of Scott were noted by R. L. Lowe in NQ for 1 March 1952, pp. 103–4. The 'Tunes' were set to music by Stanford in 1882 (cf. *Learned Lady*, pp. 144–5 n.).

1849 Dramatic Romances and Lyrics; 1863 Lyrics; 1868– Dramatic Lyrics.

CAVALIER TUNES.

I. MARCHING ALONG.

I.

KENTISH Sir Byng stood for his King,
Bidding the crop-headed Parliament swing:
And, pressing a troop unable to stoop
And see the rogues flourish and honest folk droop,
Marched them along, fifty-score strong,   5
Great-hearted gentlemen, singing this song.

II.

God for King Charles! Pym and such carles
To the Devil that prompts 'em their treasonous parles!
Cavaliers, up! Lips from the cup,
Hands from the pasty, nor bite take nor sup   10

---

collective title (not in *Princeton*)   footnote (see p. 178 above) title *Princeton* Kentish Sir
Byng.   1 *Princeton* for the king—*Yale* for (the) [his] King,   2 *Princeton* the
cuckoldy Parliament *Yale* the [crop-headed] Parliament   3 *Princeton* troop dis-
dainful to   4 *Princeton* flourish while honest   7 *Princeton* and his snarls
8 *Princeton* that pricks on such pestilent carles!

1 *Kentish Sir Byng*: Kent was predominantly Royalist in sympathy, 'and never ceased to
be a source of anxiety to the Parliament, until the day when it welcomed Charles II back to
its shores': *The Victoria County History, Kent*, iii. 308. 'Sir Byng' has no particular original.

2 *crop-headed*: OED has no other instance of this compound. In Scott's *Woodstock*, how-
ever, a Royalist refers to 'crop-eared canting villains' (ch. ii, para. 33).

  cuckoldy (Princeton): cf. *Woodstock*, ch. i, para. 8 from the end: 'the old cuckoldy priest
of Godstow'; and *Peveril of the Peak*, ch. vi, para. 16: 'the cuckoldy Roundhead'. The word is
simply a term of abuse.

3 *pressing a troop*: Johnson's twelfth definition of the verb is 'To force into military
service'. Here the sense of compulsion seems to be absent.

7 *God for King Charles!*: a phrase of the time: cf. *Prince Rupert his Declaration* (1642), p. 5:
'The Lord prosper the works of their hands who stand for God and King Charles.'

  carles: 'A mean, rude, rough, brutal man': Johnson. The word occurs in Scott, e.g. in
the 'Glee for King Charles' in *Woodstock*, ch. ii.

10 *nor bit take nor sup*: a common phrase: see e.g. *Old Mortality*, ch. vi, para. 5 from end.

Till you're—
   CHORUS.—*Marching along, fifty-score strong,*
       Great-hearted gentlemen, singing this song.

III.

Hampden to hell, and his obsequies' knell
Serve Hazelrig, Fiennes, and young Harry as well!
England, good cheer! Rupert is near!   15
Kentish and loyalists, keep we not here
   CHORUS.—*Marching along, fifty-score strong,*
       Great-hearted gentlemen, singing this song?

IV.

Then, God for King Charles! Pym and his snarls
To the Devil that pricks on such pestilent carles!   20
Hold by the right, you double your might;
So, onward to Nottingham, fresh for the fight,

11 *Princeton* Cho) Till you're marching... *Yale-1849* (no line division)   *13 (reading
of *Princeton, Yale, 1842-65*, DC,BrU,*1889*) *1868,1888* knell.   14 *Princeton, Yale, 1842*
Serve Rudyard, and Fiennes, *Princeton* well: 15 *Princeton* Rupert, good cheer! suc-
cour is near—   19 *Princeton* God for King Charles! Pym and such carles *Yale* ⟨So⟩
[Then], God   20 *Princeton* that taught him his treasonous parles!   21 *Prince-
ton* God will require who stands for the right— *Yale* might,   22 *Princeton* Then on-
ward *Yale* ⟨Then⟩ [So], onward

    13 *Hampden* : John Hampden, a close associate of Sir John Eliot; the 'wonderful influence'
of his character is mentioned in the biography in vol. iii of John Forster's *Eminent British
Statesmen.* He was one of the five members whom Charles tried to impeach in 1842. He is a
character in Browning's *Strafford.*
    14 *Hazelrig* : Sir Arthur Hesilrige or Haselrig was associated with the introduction of the
bill of attainder against Strafford. On 3 January 1642 he was one of the Five Members
impeached by the King.
    Rudyard (Princeton): Benjamin Rudyard attacked the King's evil counsellors in the
Long Parliament. He is a character in Browning's *Strafford.*
    Fiennes : Nathaniel Fiennes made a famous speech for the abolition of episcopacy in
1641. He too is a character in *Strafford.*
    young Harry : Henry Vane, a religious enthusiast who adopted puritan views. He and his
father are characters in *Strafford,* while Forster's fourth volume contains his Life.
    15 *Rupert* : Prince Rupert joined Charles at Nottingham in July 1642. Appointed general
of the horse, he was described as being 'like a perpetual motion... in a short time heard of at
many places at a great distance' (DNB xlix. 406b). On 23 September he gained the first victory
of the war, against Nathaniel Fiennes at Worcester.
    16 *loyalists* : the word seems to have appeared during the Civil War. OED knows of no
example before 1647.
    20 *pricks on* : a Shakespearian phrase: see e.g. *Othello,* III. iii. 415.
    22 *Nottingham* : Charles raised his standard at Nottingham on 22 August 1842.

CHORUS.—*March we along, fifty-score strong,*
Great-hearted gentlemen, singing this song!

II. GIVE A ROUSE.

I.

King Charles, and who'll do him right now?
King Charles, and who's ripe for fight now?
Give a rouse: here's, in hell's despite now,
King Charles!

II.

Who gave me the goods that went since?   5
Who raised me the house that sank once?
Who helped me to gold I spent since?
Who found me in wine you drank once?
　　　CHORUS.—*King Charles, and who'll do him right now?*
　　　　　　King Charles, and who's ripe for fight now?   10
　　　　　　Give a rouse: here's, in hell's despite now,
　　　　　　King Charles!

III.

To whom used my boy George quaff else,
By the old fool's side that begot him?
For whom did he cheer and laugh else,   15
While Noll's damned troopers shot him?

---

*23 {reading of DC,BrU and all versions except *1888*} *1888* fifty score
II. 1-2 {lines transposed in *Princeton*}　　　7 *Princeton* Who found me in gold
8 *Princeton* Who kept me　　　9-12 *Princeton* Ch. / King Charles—and who's ripe for
fight now? &c.　　　13 *Princeton* my son George

　　II. Title: a 'Rouse' is a bumper or toast. Cf. *Othello*, II. iii. 60.
　　5 *since*: later, or long since.
　　8 *found me in wine*: 'To supply; to furnish; as, he *finds* me in money and in victuals': John-
son, 'To Find', 17.
　　16 *Noll's damned troopers*: at the beginning of the nineteenth chapter of *Woodstock* Sir
Henry Lee tells his daughter to join him in 'A health to King Charles!' It is poor ale, but 'the
toast will excuse the liquor, had Noll himself brewed it'. The 1811 *Dictionary of the Vulgar
Tongue* still contains the word, with the explanation: 'Old Noll; Oliver Cromwell'.

CHORUS.—*King Charles, and who'll do him right now?*
King Charles, and who's ripe for fight now?
Give a rouse: here's, in hell's despite now,
King Charles!   20

III. BOOT AND SADDLE.

I.

Boot, saddle, to horse, and away!
Rescue my castle before the hot day
Brightens to blue from its silvery grey,
    CHORUS.—*Boot, saddle, to horse, and away!*

II.

Ride past the suburbs, asleep as you'd say;   5
Many's the friend there, will listen and pray
"God's luck to gallants that strike up the lay—
    CHORUS.—*"Boot, saddle, to horse, and away!"*

III.

Forty miles off, like a roebuck at bay,
Flouts Castle Brancepeth the Roundheads' array: 10
Who laughs, "Good fellows ere this, by my fay,
    CHORUS.—*"Boot, saddle, to horse, and away!"*

IV.

Who? My wife Gertrude; that, honest and gay,
Laughs when you talk of surrendering, "Nay!
"I've better counsellors; what counsel they?   15
    CHORUS.—*"Boot, saddle, to horse, and away!"*

17-20 *Princeton* Ch. / King Charles—and who's &c.
III. title *Yale, 1842* My wife Gertrude.   10 *Yale* ⟨Barham⟩ [Brancepeth]
12 *Yale away*"? *1842-68 away*?"   14 *Yale* "Nay⟨!⟩[:]

III. 1 *Boot, saddle*: 'sound, boot and saddle—to horse and away': *Woodstock*, ch. i, para.7 from the end. The speaker there is an Independent preacher exhorting his auditors to follow Cromwell. The phrase occurs again in ch. xiv, para. 13 from the end.

10 *Castle Brancepeth*: there is a castle in Brancepeth, though the greater part of it is nineteenth-century. Brancepeth is not in Kent, however, but 4 miles SW of Durham. Barham is a village in Kent, 6 miles SE of Canterbury, but it has no castle.   11 *by my fay*: by my faith.

MY LAST DUCHESS

FERRARA

THE poem was published in *Dramatic Lyrics* as the first of two poems bearing the title 'ITALY AND FRANCE'. In *1849* the general title was dropped, in favour of the two titles with which we are familiar. In *1863* and subsequently the poems were separated.

If Browning had not added 'Ferrara' to the title in *1849* it is unlikely that an original for the Duke would have been sought for. But he did, and in 1936 Louis S. Friedland successfully disposed of the claim that the Duke was based on Vespasiano Gonzaga, Duke of Sabbioneta, and made out a case for Alfonso II, Duke of Ferrara 1559–97.[1] Friedland points to the importance of Ferrara and the Este family in *Sordello*, and rightly suggests that Browning is likely to have read the entry on Alfonso II (though it is not 'long') in one of the articles on the family in the *Biographie universelle*.[2] In 1558 Alfonso (who was to prove the last of the Este line) married Lucrezia, younger daughter of Cosimo I de' Medici: a political marriage to a girl just fourteen. On the third day after the wedding he left on political business, and did not return for almost two years. When Lucrezia died, at the age of seventeen, there were the usual rumours of poison. A highly cultivated man, for whose court Tasso wrote his *Aminta* and Guarini his *Pastor Fido*, the Duke was noted, even in that society, for his pride. He first met his second wife, Barbara of Austria, in an elaborately contrived encounter at Innsbruck. Friedland mentions that the chief of her escort on that occasion was Nikolaus Madruz, and states that while Madruz represented his master's overlord, Maximilian II, he 'took his instructions from Ferdinand, Count of Tyrol ... to whom he was directly responsible' (p. 682). Friedland conjectures that it is Madruz whom Browning's Duke is addressing.

We notice a certain inconsistency in Friedland's statements about the Duchess. On p. 673 he states that it 'appears quite possible' that Browning was thinking of Lucrezia, but on p. 683 he claims that 'We can no longer be in doubt ... as to the identity of the Last Duchess'—though he admits that he cannot point to Browning's 'immediate sources'. The article in the *Biographie universelle* merely names Lucrezia as the first of Alfonso's three wives.

[1] 'Ferrara and *My Last Duchess*', SP 33 (1936), 656 ff.
[2] Vol. xiii (1815), pp. 376b–377a. The article is by Sismondi.

When the poem was first published Browning cannot have expected his readers to associate it with any particular Duke and Duchess, or with any particular city. Even when he named Ferrara, he can hardly have expected them to associate it with any particular episode. While Friedland may well be right in his conjectures, it is also possible that 'Ferrara' was simply added as a general stage-direction. Our notes to ll. 3, 22, 45, and 56 may support such a conclusion. No particular painting has seriously been suggested in relation to the poem, and we notice that 'a day' is a most improbable period for the painting of such a portrait. Browning's habit, from boyhood, of sitting for a long time—'a good hour'[1]—studying some painting which interested him may well have led, by way of a number of examples of Italian portraiture, to the triumph of this poem.

A more immediate stimulus may have been a piece in Tennyson's two-volume *Poems* of 1842, a collection which we know that Browning studied with care.[2] 'The Gardener's Daughter; or The Pictures', a monologue by a sentimental old painter addressed to two young men on the circumstances in which he had met his late wife, concludes as follows:

> But this whole hour your eyes have been intent
> On that veil'd picture—veil'd, for what it holds
> May not be dwelt on by the common day.
> This prelude has prepared thee. Raise thy soul;
> Make thine heart ready with thine eyes: the time
> Is come to raise the veil.
>   Behold her there,
> As I beheld her ere she knew my heart,
> My first, last love; the idol of my youth,
> The darling of my manhood, and, alas!
> Now the most blessed memory of mine age.   (264–73)

Tennyson's blameless old widower may have helped suggest to Browning the cold Renaissance aristocrat whose possible historical identity has proved so tantalizing to scholars.

Such a possibility tends to support DeVane's conjecture that this poem was published 'in the summer or early fall of 1842'.

1849 Dramatic Romances and Lyrics; 1863 Romances; 1868– Dramatic Romances.

---

[1] Kintner, i. 509.

[2] *Browning and Domett*, pp. 40–1 (13 July 1842). We know that the poem greatly impressed Browning's friend Arnould, and that it was mentioned when Browning and Tennyson met at a later time. Cf. Ian Jack, *Browning's Major Poetry*, p. 92.

MY LAST DUCHESS.

FERRARA

THAT's my last Duchess painted on the wall,
Looking as if she were alive. I call
That piece a wonder, now: Frà Pandolf's hands
Worked busily a day, and there she stands.
Will't please you sit and look at her? I said   5
"Frà Pandolf" by design, for never read
Strangers like you that pictured countenance,
The depth and passion of its earnest glance,
But to myself they turned (since none puts by
The curtain I have drawn for you, but I)   10
And seemed as they would ask me, if they durst,
How such a glance came there; so, not the first
Are you to turn and ask thus. Sir, 't was not
Her husband's presence only, called that spot
Of joy into the Duchess' cheek: perhaps   15
Frà Pandolf chanced to say "Her mantle laps
"Over my lady's wrist too much," or "Paint
"Must never hope to reproduce the faint

title *1842* ITALY AND FRANCE. I.–ITALY.   2 *1842–65* alive;

3 *Frà Pandolf's hands*: Frà, Brother (It.) As Friedland comments (p. 678), the name Pandolf
'is not unknown in the annals of Italian art', but no particular artist is indicated here.

5–6 *I said / "Frà Pandolf" by design*: to the question 'By what design?' Browning answered:
'To have some occasion for telling the story, and illustrating part of it': see 'Robert Brown-
ing's Answers to Questions concerning some of his Poems', by A. Allen Brockington,
reprinted from the *Cornhill Magazine* for March 1914, p. 316, in *New Poems*, pp. 174 ff. It is
possible that the Duke mentions that the artist was a religious to rebut any suspicion that he
himself was jealous. On the other hand, as Dr J. B. Bullen has pointed out to us, a book
reviewed by Browning in July 1842 contains the following observation: 'It is not undeserving
of remark, that this [entering a religious order] was not an uncommon mode of escaping
punishment for love offences in that age. Alessandro Pandolfo, threatened on account of his
passion for Leonora di Toledo de' Medici, turned capuchin': *Conjectures and Researches con-
cerning the Love Madness and Imprisonment of Torquato Tasso*, by Richard Henry Wilde (2 vols.,
New York 1842), i. 186 n. The review has been reprinted as *Browning's Essay on Chatterton* by
Donald Smalley (Cambridge, Mass., 1948).

"Half-flush that dies along her throat:" such stuff
Was courtesy, she thought, and cause enough   20
For calling up that spot of joy. She had
A heart—how shall I say?—too soon made glad,
Too easily impressed; she liked whate'er
She looked on, and her looks went everywhere.
Sir, 't was all one! My favour at her breast,   25
The dropping of the daylight in the West,
The bough of cherries some officious fool
Broke in the orchard for her, the white mule
She rode with round the terrace—all and each
Would draw from her alike the approving speech,   30
Or blush, at least. She thanked men,—good! but thanked
Somehow—I know not how—as if she ranked
My gift of a nine-hundred-years-old name
With anybody's gift. Who'd stoop to blame
This sort of trifling? Even had you skill   35
In speech—(which I have not)—to make your will
Quite clear to such an one, and say, "Just this
"Or that in you disgusts me; here you miss,
"Or there exceed the mark"—and if she let
Herself be lessoned so, nor plainly set   40
Her wits to yours, forsooth, and made excuse,
—E'en then would be some stooping; and I choose
Never to stoop. Oh sir, she smiled, no doubt,
Whene'er I passed her; but who passed without
Much the same smile? This grew; I gave commands;   45

30 *1842* the forward speech,   31 *1842-65* good;   36 *1842* not)—could make
42 *1842-63* stooping,

22 *too soon made glad*: 'Was she in fact shallow and easily and equally well pleased with any
favour', Browning was asked (cf. n. to 5–6 above), 'or did the Duke so describe her as a super-
cilious cover to real and well justified jealousy?' He answered: 'As an excuse—mainly to him-
self—for taking revenge on one who had unwittingly wounded his absurdly pretentious
vanity, by failing to recognise his superiority in even the most trifling matters.'

30 *the approving speech*: note revision.

40–1 *set/Her wits to yours*: a phrase which occurs in Shakespeare, e.g. in *Troilus and Cressida*,
II. i. 84.

45 *I gave commands*: when Hiram Corson asked what this meant Browning answered: 'I
meant that the commands were that she should be put to death.' After a pause, however, he

Then all smiles stopped together. There she stands
As if alive. Will't please you rise? We'll meet
The company below, then. I repeat,
The Count your master's known munificence
Is ample warrant that no just pretence   50
Of mine for dowry will be disallowed;
Though his fair daughter's self, as I avowed
At starting, is my object. Nay, we'll go
Together down, sir. Notice Neptune, though,
Taming a sea-horse, thought a rarity,   55
Which Claus of Innsbruck cast in bronze for me!

54 *1842-65* sir!   56 *1842-65* me.

added, 'with a characteristic dash of expression, and as if the thought had just started in his
mind, "Or he might have had her shut up in a convent"': *An Introduction to the Study of Robert
Browning's Poetry* (3rd ed., Boston 1899), p. viii. As Corson remarks, when he wrote the
poem Browning 'may not have thought definitely what the commands were . . . This was all
his art purpose required.' Browning's second thoughts perhaps suggest that he had not been
following a specific source.

    56 *Claus of Innsbruck*: see Introduction, above, for one possible reason for the mention
of Innsbruck. Browning visited the city, as he told Fanny Haworth (*Letters*, p. 3), on his way
home from Italy in 1838. If, like most travellers, he visited the celebrated Hofkirche, he
will have seen the huge bronze statues which surround the tomb of the Emperor Maxi-
milian I. The statues represent historical and 'historical' figures (one is King Arthur), and
none of them is the work of a 'Claus'. Nikolaus Türing built the church, however. It is suf-
ficient that Innsbruck is celebrated for sculpture in iron and bronze.

COUNT GISMOND

AIX IN PROVENCE

S E E introduction to 'My Last Duchess'. With this poem, too, the addition of a place was an afterthought, probably intended to indicate a contrasting attitude to women rather than any particular historical original. In the fifteenth century Aix was the centre of the brilliant court of René, Count of Provence. The interest in tournaments in England about this time is epitomized by the tournament held at Eglinton Castle by the thirteenth Earl in 1839, in which the future Napoleon III took part, and Lady Seymour was Queen of Beauty. Disraeli was to give an account of the event in *Endymion*. The tournament in *Ivanhoe* is clearly an influence on this poem, not least in the conception of 'the false knight' (92). There is no evidence to date the composition of the poem.

John V. Hagopian ('The Mask of Browning's Countess Gismond', PQ 40, 1961, pp. 153–5: cf. John W. Tilton and R. Dale Tuttle, SP 59, 1962, pp. 83–95) seems responsible for the influential notion that the speaker is a liar, and far from innocent: a view which would surely have astonished Browning. In his 'Ariosto and Browning: A Reexamination of "Count Gismond"', VP 11 (1973), pp. 15–25, Frank Allen is much too dogmatic when he states that 'Browning undoubtedly created the poem using as sources the Genevra–Airodant episode of Ariosto's *Orlando Furioso* and, to a lesser degree, the Hero–Claudio episode of Shakespeare's *Much Ado about Nothing*.'

1849 Dramatic Romances and Lyrics; 1863 Romances; 1868– Dramatic Romances.

COUNT GISMOND.

AIX IN PROVENCE

I.

CHRIST God who savest man, save most
  Of men Count Gismond who saved me!
Count Gauthier, when he chose his post,
  Chose time and place and company
To suit it; when he struck at length   5
My honour, 't was with all his strength.

II.

And doubtlessly ere he could draw
  All points to one, he must have schemed!
That miserable morning saw
  Few half so happy as I seemed,   10
While being dressed in queen's array
To give our tourney prize away.

III.

I thought they loved me, did me grace
  To please themselves; 't was all their deed;
God makes, or fair or foul, our face;   15
  If showing mine so caused to bleed
My cousins' hearts, they should have dropped
A word, and straight the play had stopped.

IV.

They, too, so beauteous! Each a queen
  By virtue of her brow and breast;   20

title *1842* II.—FRANCE.   1 *1849* savest men, save   6 *1842* My honor's face
'twas with full strength.   13 *1842* thought all loved   18 *1842* and all the

  7-8 *draw / All points to one*: cf. Donne, *The First Anniversary*, 222: 'To draw, and fasten
sundred points in one'.
  13 *did me grace*: a phrase used by Shakespeare, e.g. in *Sonnets* 28 (10) and 132 (11).
  14 *their deed*: their doing.

Not needing to be crowned, I mean,
  As I do. E'en when I was dressed,
Had either of them spoke, instead
Of glancing sideways with still head!

V.

But no: they let me laugh, and sing   25
  My birthday song quite through, adjust
The last rose in my garland, fling
  A last look on the mirror, trust
My arms to each an arm of theirs,
And so descend the castle-stairs—   30

VI.

And come out on the morning-troop
  Of merry friends who kissed my cheek,
And called me queen, and made me stoop
  Under the canopy—(a streak
That pierced it, of the outside sun,   35
Powdered with gold its gloom's soft dun)—

VII.

And they could let me take my state
  And foolish throne amid applause
Of all come there to celebrate
  My queen's-day—Oh I think the cause   40
Of much was, they forgot no crowd
Makes up for parents in their shroud!

VIII.

However that be, all eyes were bent
  Upon me, when my cousins cast
Theirs down; 't was time I should present   45
  The victor's crown, but . . . there, 't will last

26 *1842* through;   43 *1842* Howe'er that be, when eyes *1849, 1863* Howe'er
44 *1842* me, both my   46 *1842* The victor with his . . . there,

33 *And called me queen*: cf. *Ivanhoe*, ch. xiii, para. 9: 'the destined Queen of the day had
arrived upon the field'.
43-4 *all eyes were bent / Upon me*: cf. Southey, *Joan of Arc*, iv. 62: 'Every eye on her was bent'.

No long time . . . the old mist again
Blinds me as then it did. How vain!

IX.

See! Gismond's at the gate, in talk
  With his two boys: I can proceed.   50
Well, at that moment, who should stalk
  Forth boldly—to my face, indeed—
But Gauthier, and he thundered "Stay!"
And all stayed. "Bring no crowns, I say!

X.

"Bring torches! Wind the penance-sheet   55
  "About her! Let her shun the chaste,
"Or lay herself before their feet!
  "Shall she whose body I embraced
"A night long, queen it in the day?
"For honour's sake no crowns, I say!"   60

XI.

I? What I answered? As I live,
  I never fancied such a thing
As answer possible to give.
  What says the body when they spring
Some monstrous torture-engine's whole   65
Strength on it? No more says the soul.

---

48 *1842* me .. but the true mist was rain.   52 *1842* Forth calmly (to . . . . indeed)
1849-65 (to . . . . indeed)   54 *1842* And all did stay. "No crowns, I say!" *1849* say!"
62 *1842* I never thought there was such thing

  51-2 *who should stalk / Forth boldly*: in his *Diary* for 30 April 1878 (ed. E. A. Horsman, 1953) Domett wrote of a visit to Browning: 'I spoke strongly against some slight alterations Browning had made in the late or latest edition of his Poems, in the ballad of Count Gismond.' Quoting part of st. ix from memory, and italicizing 'did' in l. 54, he continued: 'The third line—destroying and cheating all the impetuosity of the verse, the regular sledge-hammer rhythmic beat of the iambics—he has actually altered . . . An inconceivably blundering correction *possibly* made to avoid the double rhyme, "stay" and "say", in one line, which could only be perceptible to a stupid, utterly unimpassioned reader.' 'Browning agreed with me,' he concluded; 'I suppose sincerely, since the thing is so obvious and indisputable.' No revision was made, however.

XII.

Till out strode Gismond; then I knew
    That I was saved. I never met
His face before, but, at first view,
    I felt quite sure that God had set   70
Himself to Satan; who would spend
A minute's mistrust on the end?

XIII.

He strode to Gauthier, in his throat
    Gave him the lie, then struck his mouth
With one back-handed blow that wrote   75
    In blood men's verdict there. North, South,
East, West, I looked. The lie was dead,
And damned, and truth stood up instead.

XIV.

This glads me most, that I enjoyed
    The heart of the joy, with my content   80
In watching Gismond unalloyed
    By any doubt of the event:
God took that on him—I was bid
Watch Gismond for my part: I did.

XV.

Did I not watch him while he let   85
    His armourer just brace his greaves,
Rivet his hauberk, on the fret
    The while! His foot . . . my memory leaves

70 *1863* God hath set   *74 {reading of DC,BrU and all versions except *1888*} *1888*
mout   80 *1842* joy, nor my   81 *1842* Gismond was alloyed
83 *1842* him—me he bid

    73-4 *in his throat / Gave him the lie* : a combination of two idioms, 'to give the lie to' and 'to
lie in the throat'.
    80 *The heart of the joy* : for this use of 'heart' cf. *The Merry Wives of Windsor*, II. ii. 202, and
Twelfth Night, I. v. 179.   82 *the event* : the outcome.
    86 *greaves* : 'Armour for the legs': Johnson.
    87 *hauberk* : 'A coat of mail; a breastplate': Johnson.
    on the fret : impatient. The Ohio editor strangely supposes that this is a reference to
'frets, or interlacings' holding together the chain mail.

No least stamp out, nor how anon
He pulled his ringing gauntlets on.   90

XVI.

And e'en before the trumpet's sound
    Was finished, prone lay the false knight,
Prone as his lie, upon the ground:
    Gismond flew at him, used no sleight
O' the sword, but open-breasted drove   95
Cleaving till out the truth he clove.

XVII.

Which done, he dragged him to my feet
    And said "Here die, but end thy breath
"In full confession, lest thou fleet
    "From my first, to God's second death!   100
"Say, hast thou lied?" And, "I have lied
"To God and her," he said, and died.

XVIII.

Then Gismond, kneeling to me, asked
    —What safe my heart holds, though no word
Could I repeat now, if I tasked   105
    My powers for ever, to a third
Dear even as you are. Pass the rest
Until I sank upon his breast.

XIX.

Over my head his arm he flung
    Against the world; and scarce I felt   110

92 *1842* finished there lay prone the Knight,   94 *1842* My Knight flew
95 *1842-68* Of the

   100 *God's second death* : damnation. Cf. Donne, *The First Anniversary*, 450–1, where the poet
refers to Elizabeth Drury's 'second birth, / That is, thy death'.

   107 *as you are* : see 125.

   109 *Over my head his arm he flung* : a protective gesture which reminds us of the relationship
of this poem to Browning's favourite Andromeda myth. 'Count Gismond was the Perseus to
rescue the maligned lady of the romance': DeVane, 'The Virgin and the Dragon' (Drew,
p. 99). The speaker is an orphan (41–2).

His sword (that dripped by me and swung)
  A little shifted in its belt:
For he began to say the while
How South our home lay many a mile.

XX.

So 'mid the shouting multitude   115
  We two walked forth to never more
Return. My cousins have pursued
  Their life, untroubled as before
I vexed them. Gauthier's dwelling-place
God lighten! May his soul find grace!   120

XXI.

Our elder boy has got the clear
  Great brow; tho' when his brother's black
Full eye shows scorn, it . . . Gismond here?
  And have you brought my tercel back?
I just was telling Adela   125
How many birds it struck since May.

---

111 *1842,1849* that . . . . swung,   112 *1842* belt, *1849* belt,—   116 *1842* we too walked

124 *tercel* : 'The male of any kind of hawk; in Falconry esp. of the peregrine falcon . . . and the goshawk': OED.

125 *I just was telling Adela* : the speaker's motherly fib (she does not choose to tell her young son the real subject of the conversation) has led to a misreading of the poem which makes the speaker a 'guilty woman': cf. Introduction. Note ll. 49–50, however.

INCIDENT OF THE FRENCH CAMP

IN *1842* this and the following poem are entitled only 'CAMP AND CLOISTER. I.—Camp. (*French.*)' and 'II.—Cloister. (*Spanish.*)'. From *1849* the poems have had their present titles. From *1863* they have been separated.

The French stormed Ratisbon (Regensburg in Bavaria) on 23 April 1809, in an important engagement in which they were pursuing the Austrian army. After a partial breach in the walls had been effected, Scott tells us, the musket-fire was so fierce that 'There was at length difficulty in finding volunteers to renew the attack, when the impetuous Lannes, by whom they were commanded, seized a ladder, and rushed forward to fix it himself against the walls. "I will show you," he exclaimed, "that your general is still a grenadier." The example prevailed, the wall was surmounted, and the combat was continued or renewed in the streets of the town': *Life of Napoleon* (*The Miscellaneous Prose Works of Sir Walter Scott*, vol. xiii, p. 179). For Lannes see n. to l. 11 below.

Mrs Orr tells us, probably on Browning's authority, that 'The story is true; but its actual hero was a man' (*Handbook*, p. 300). Stories about Napoleon are innumerable, and there are many about this siege; but none at all close to this has so far been found. DeVane points out that interest in Napoleon was stimulated by the second funeral when his body was reburied in Paris in December 1841. Browning's father mentioned a juvenile production by his son 'On Bonaparte', which he considered 'remarkably beautiful': *Life*, p. 32.

The manuscript of the first stanza in the British Library (Kelley and Coley, E 193) seems to have been prepared for *1868*, since it is headed 'Dramatic Romances' and inscribed on the back '(follow Colombe's Birthday)'. It has no comma after l. 2.

1849 Dramatic Romances and Lyrics; 1863 Romances; 1868– Dramatic Romances.

INCIDENT OF THE FRENCH CAMP.

I

You know, we French stormed Ratisbon:
  A mile or so away,
On a little mound, Napoleon
  Stood on our storming-day;
With neck out-thrust, you fancy how,   5
  Legs wide, arms locked behind,
As if to balance the prone brow
  Oppressive with its mind.

II.

Just as perhaps he mused "My plans
  "That soar, to earth may fall,   10
"Let once my army-leader Lannes
  "Waver at yonder wall,"—
Out 'twixt the battery-smokes there flew
  A rider, bound on bound
Full-galloping; nor bridle drew   15
  Until he reached the mound.

III.

Then off there flung in smiling joy,
  And held himself erect
By just his horse's mane, a boy:
  You hardly could suspect—   20
(So tight he kept his lips compressed,
  Scarce any blood came through)
You looked twice ere you saw his breast
  Was all but shot in two.

title *1842* CAMP AND CLOISTER. I.—CAMP. (*French.*)   3 *1842,1849* Napoléon

8 *Oppressive*: heavy, weighed down.
  11 *Lannes*: Jean Lannes, one of Napoleon's most devoted generals and one of the first
eighteen *maréchaux de l'Empire* created by him, died later in 1809, at the battle of Essling.
  13 *battery-smokes*: volumes or clouds of smoke rising from the gun-batteries. For the
plural see OED 'Smoke', sb. 2.

IV.

"Well," cried he, "Emperor, by God's grace　　　　　25
　　"We've got you Ratisbon!
"The Marshal's in the market-place,
　　"And you'll be there anon
"To see your flag-bird flap his vans
　　"Where I, to heart's desire,　　　　　30
"Perched him!" The chief's eye flashed; his plans
　　Soared up again like fire.

V.

The chief's eye flashed; but presently
　　Softened itself, as sheathes
A film the mother-eagle's eye　　　　　35
　　When her bruised eaglet breathes;
"You're wounded!" "Nay," the soldier's pride
　　Touched to the quick, he said:
"I'm killed, Sire!" And his chief beside
　　Smiling the boy fell dead.　　　　　40

37 *1842-65* "Nay," his soldier's
　　29 *your flag-bird*: the flag with Napoleon's device, the eagle.
　　　vans: wings.
　　34-5 *as sheathes / A film*: as a film sheathes.

SOLILOQUY OF THE
SPANISH CLOISTER

FOR the first two printings of this poem, see the introduction to 'Incident of the French Camp'. In *1863* Browning made a trio of 'The Flower's Name', 'Sibrandus Schafnaburgensis', and this, printing them among the Lyrics, as 'Garden Fancies': from *1868* the poem has stood on its own.

The date of composition is unknown. The poem is often associated with Browning's visit to Italy in 1838, but it is noteworthy that in 1834 he had referred to 'Spain—another of my loves'. In a letter to Ripert-Monclar he told him that since he had last seen him he had 'learned Spanish enough [to] be able to read "the majestic Tongue which Calderon along the desert flung!–"', continuing: 'I am more & more possessed by a perfect antipathy for the North & its sights & sounds—which is strange truly, but real—I *will* not learn German for instance—& can't help learning Spanish!'[1]

1849 Dramatic Romances and Lyrics; 1863 Lyrics; 1868– Dramatic Lyrics.

SOLILOQUY OF THE SPANISH CLOISTER.

I.

GR-R-R—there go, my heart's abhorrence!
  Water your damned flower-pots, do!
If hate killed men, Brother Lawrence,
  God's blood, would not mine kill you!
What? your myrtle-bush wants trimming?   5
  Oh, that rose has prior claims—
Needs its leaden vase filled brimming?
  Hell dry you up with its flames!

---

title *1842* II.—CLOISTER. (*Spanish.*)

[1]. *Correspondence*, iii. 111. The quotation is from Shelley's 'Letter to Maria Gisborne', 180–1.

II.

At the meal we sit together:
  Salve tibi! I must hear   10
Wise talk of the kind of weather,
  Sort of season, time of year:
Not a plenteous cork-crop: scarcely
  Dare we hope oak-galls, I doubt:
What's the Latin name for "parsley"?   15
  What's the Greek name for Swine's Snout?

III.

Whew! We'll have our platter burnished,
  Laid with care on our own shelf!
With a fire-new spoon we're furnished,
  And a goblet for ourself,   20
Rinsed like something sacrificial
  Ere 't is fit to touch our chaps—
Marked with L. for our initial!
  (He-he! There his lily snaps!)

IV.

Saint, forsooth! While brown Dolores   25
  Squats outside the Convent bank
With Sanchicha, telling stories,
  Steeping tresses in the tank,

---

17 *1842* Phew! We'll   24 *1842,1849* (He, he!

  10 *Salve tibi*: a standard greeting, e.g. 'How are you?'

  14 *oak-galls*: galls or excrescences 'produced on various species of oak by the punctures of various gall-flies' (OED): they are useful for making ink and for various other manufactures.

  15 *"parsley"*: *apium* or (from the Greek) *petroselinum*.

  16 *Swine's Snout*: ὑός or ὕειον ῥύγχος. For the name 'Swine's snout' or *Rostrum porcinum* for the dandelion see Richard C. A. Prior, *On the Popular Names of British Plants* (1863), p. 222 (cit. OED s.v. swine). Here the phrase is abusive, however, as in 'Lady *Swin-snout*, his yeolow-fac'd Mistres': Thomas Nashe, *Pierce Penilesse*, in *The Works*, ed. R. B. McKerrow, rev. F. P. Wilson (5 vols., 1958), i. 169.

  19 *fire-new*: a compound which occurs four times in Shakespeare, e.g. in *Richard III*, I. iii. 256.

  22 *chaps*: 'The mouth of a beast of prey . . . used in contempt for the mouth of a man': Johnson.

Blue-black, lustrous, thick like horsehairs,
  —Can't I see his dead eye glow,   30
Bright as 't were a Barbary corsair's?
  (That is, if he'd let it show!)

V.

When he finishes refection,
  Knife and fork he never lays
Cross-wise, to my recollection,   35
  As do I, in Jesu's praise.
I the Trinity illustrate,
  Drinking watered orange-pulp—
In three sips the Arian frustrate;
  While he drains his at one gulp.   40

VI.

Oh, those melons? If he's able
  We're to have a feast! so nice!
One goes to the Abbot's table,
  All of us get each a slice.
How go on your flowers? None double?   45
  Not one fruit-sort can you spy?
Strange!—And I, too, at such trouble,
  Keep them close-nipped on the sly!

---

30 *1842* eye grow   32 *1842* That .... show.   34 *1842* fork across he lays
35 *1842* Never,   to   40 *1842–65* gulp!   41 *1842–65* melons!
42 *1842–68* feast;   48 *1842,1849* Keep 'em close—

    31 *a Barbary corsair's*: Johnson defines a corsair as 'A pirate; one who professes to scour the sea, and seize merchants.' The Barbary coast referred to the Saracen countries along the north of Africa.

    36 *As do I, in Jesu's praise*: cf. Stendhal, *Le Rouge et le Noir*, ch. 26: 'Julien n'aspira pas d'emblée, comme les autres séminaristes qui servaient de modèle aux autres, à faire à chaque instant des actions *significatives*, c'est-à-dire prouvant un genre de perfection chrétienne. Au séminaire, il est une façon de manger un œuf à la coque, qui annonce les progrès faits dans la vie dévote.' The resemblance is probably accidental, since it is in 1847 that EBB tells Miss Mitford that Browning and she are reading the book together: *Letters of EBB*, i. 319.

    37 *illustrate*: stressed on the second syllable, as in Johnson.

    39 *the Arian*: Arians denied that Christ was consubstantial with God. The speaker here is emphasizing his orthodox belief in the Trinity.

VII.

There's a great text in Galatians,
   Once you trip on it, entails   50
Twenty-nine distinct damnations,
   One sure, if another fails:
If I trip him just a-dying,
   Sure of heaven as sure can be,
Spin him round and send him flying   55
   Off to hell, a Manichee?

VIII.

Or, my scrofulous French novel
   On grey paper with blunt type!
Simply glance at it, you grovel
   Hand and foot in Belial's gripe: 60

52 *1842,1849* fails.   60 *1842* gripe.

49 *a great text in Galatians*: in 1888, in reply to a letter from the Revd James Graham now
lost, Browning wrote: 'I really believe that when I try to put myself in the place of any
ignorant person who figures in a poem, I adopt his very ignorance,' and states that he will
'try to remove' two biblical blunders pointed out by his correspondent. He continues: 'The
same lapse of memory would seem to occur in the case of the Text from Galatians, but I
was not careful to be correct': David George, 'Four New Browning Letters', SIB (Spring
1974), p. 62. If the letter had been published earlier a great deal of fruitless scholarly
enquiry might have been avoided. There is no such text in Galatians, but Deut. 28 has
twenty-nine verses (16–44) of curses on the disobedient. As R. A. Pearsall remarked
('Browning's Texts in Galatians and Deuteronomy', MLQ (1952), 256–8), marginal refer-
ences in the Douay and King James versions of the Bible point out that in Galatians Paul is
quoting from this part of Deuteronomy, and this provides the required link. In Galatians
Paul emphasizes the futility of trying to live by 'law' or a prescribed code, and insists that
man should live by faith; the epistle ends with a repeated warning that its readers should
not put their trust in religious observances.
   Browning removed one of the two 'Biblical blunders' ('Hophni' for 'Uzzah' in *The Ring
and the Book*, iv. 834), but left the other ('Saint Paul' for 'Saint James' in 'The Heretic's
Tragedy', 3). It is sometimes difficult to be sure when Browning blundered, when (as here)
he 'was not careful to be correct', and when (as he once explained) a blunder was deliberate,
because he was writing dramatically: as in his use of 'High Priest' for 'Chief Rabbi' in
'Filippo Baldinucci on the Privilege of Burial', st. xxvi. See the article cited above, p. 68. An
extreme example of a deliberate, 'dramatic', error is the dying Bishop's reference to 'Saint
Praxed at his sermon on the mount' in 'The Bishop Orders his Tomb', 95. Cf., too, *A Blot in
the 'Scutcheon*, II. 177 and n.
   53 *just a-dying*: cf. *Hamlet*, III. iii. 88 ff.
   56 *a Manichee*: a heretic. 'The special feature of the system which the name chiefly sug-
gests to modern readers is the dualistic theology, according to which Satan was represented
as co-eternal with God': OED.

If I double down its pages
  At the woeful sixteenth print,
When he gathers his greengages,
  Ope a sieve and slip it in't?

IX.

Or, there's Satan!—one might venture   65
  Pledge one's soul to him, yet leave
Such a flaw in the indenture
  As he'd miss till, past retrieve,
Blasted lay that rose-acacia
  We're so proud of! *Hy, Zy, Hine* . . .   70
'St, there's Vespers! *Plena gratiâ*
  Ave, Virgo! Gr-r-r—you swine!

---

65 *1842* Or, the Devil!—one   66 *1842* soul yet slily leave   71 *1842* St
*1842*P¹ʼ² *gratia*

69 *rose-acacia*: *Robinia hispida*, a tree with rose-coloured flowers; the American moss-
locust.

70 *Hy, Zy, Hine* . . .: no one has proved the meaning of these words. In VP 1 (1963), 158–
60 Patrick W. Gainer argued for the view that the speaker is mocking the sound of the
chapel bell. He went so far as to check 'the tones of the chapel bells of several monasteries'.
He found them to be 'not lower than A-440', and argued that 'the speaker's distortion
would raise the pitch at least a third' (giving a musical illustration). In '"Hy, Zy, Hine" and
Peter of Abano', VP 12 (1974), 165–9 James F. Loucks argued that the words represent the
beginning of an imprecation, quoting nonsense-words from the 'Exorcismus spiritu[u]m
aereorum' of Abano, which include 'Hy' and 'Hyn'.

71–2 *Plena gratiâ / Ave, Virgo!*: 'Ave, gratia plena' is the address to the Virgin in Luke 1: 28
(the Annunciation), in the Vulgate text. The Angelus, a devotional exercise said at morning,
noon, and evening at the sound of a bell rung for the purpose, traditionally takes the form
of three Ave Marias, each introduced by a versicle (e.g. 'Angelus Domini nuntiavit Mariæ
. . . Ave Maria' etc.). Cf. Charles T. Phipps, SJ, in VP 7 (1969), 158–9. The Ave Maria does
not form a major part of Vespers, however—if indeed it is included at all. But the use of the
Ave Maria as an unsympathetic stereotype of Catholic ceremony is long-standing: see *The
Faerie Queene*, I. i. xxxv. 9, for example. The confused order of the words and the substitu-
tion of the word 'Virgo' for 'Maria' are no doubt introduced deliberately, as part of the
characterization of the speaker.

IN A GONDOLA

ABOUT 30 December 1841 Browning told Fanny Haworth that he had called on Forster 'the other day—and he pressed me into committing verse on the instant, not the minute, in Maclise's behalf—who has wrought a divine Venetian work, it seems, for the British Institution—Forster described it well—but I could do nothing better than this wooden ware (All the "properties", as we say, were given—and the problem was how to caloguize them in rhyme and unreason)'. After quoting the seven lines with which 'In a Gondola' begins, he added: 'Singing and stars and night and Venice streets in depths of shade and space are "properties", do you please to see. And now tell me, is this below the average of Catalogue original poetry? Tell me—for to that end, of being told, I write it. (It is, I suppose in print now and past help).'[1]

The catalogue was published about 5 February, when the exhibition opened. On p. 17, where Maclise's painting is no. 255 ('A Serenade', 5 feet by 3 feet 8 inches), the lines are printed, as by '*Robert Browning, Author of Paracelsus,* &c.' In the second part of a two-part review of the exhibition which appeared in *The Art-Union. A Monthly Journal of the Fine Arts* on 1 April 'A Serenade' is one of the paintings singled out for notice: Browning's lines are quoted.[2] After the notice the anonymous author writes: 'We have quoted the passage pictured, less to justify the somewhat fantastic air and character of the cavalier, than as an example of exceedingly rich and graceful versification from the pen of a poet, kindred to Maclise in imagination and mind.' While a number of the other paintings are accompanied by lines of verse, this seems the only one with lines written for the occasion. It is clear that Browning's friends, remembering how impressed he had been by Venice, were doing what they could to promote his interest.

When he saw the picture Browning 'thought the Serenader too jolly somewhat for the notion I got from Forster', adding: 'I took up the subject in my own way.'[3]

---

[1] *Letters*, p. 7. Browning knew Maclise, having met him through Forster. Dickens liked the colour of the sky in 'A Serenade': see his letter to Maclise, 22 July 1844 (*The Letters of Charles Dickens*, The Pilgrim Edition, vol. iv, ed. Kathleen Tillotson, 1977, p. 159).

[2] p. 76. The word 'me' is omitted from l. 3.

[3] *Trumpeter*, p. 24. The painting, now at Baylor, is reproduced in the *Browning Newsletter* for Fall 1970 (p. 21).

It will be noticed that Browning developed from his original seven lines a Dramatic Scene of the kind already exemplified in *Pippa Passes*, with which ll. 37–48 may be compared.

In *1842* there are no indications of when the man is speaking, or when the woman. Even the fact that the man has been '*surprised, and stabbed*' before he speaks the last seven lines is not indicated. This rendered the poem obscure. Michael Meredith, who remarks that the earlier text, 'more intense and more confused, better conveys the impact Venice made on Browning in 1838', reprints it on pp. 181 ff. of *More than Friend*.

1849 Dramatic Romances and Lyrics; 1863 Romances; 1868– Dramatic Romances.

IN A GONDOLA.

He sings.

I SEND my heart up to thee, all my heart
   In this my singing.
For the stars help me, and the sea bears part;
   The very night is clinging
Closer to Venice' streets to leave one space   5
   Above me, whence thy face
May light my joyous heart to thee its dwelling-place.

She speaks.

Say after me, and try to say
My very words, as if each word
Came from you of your own accord,   10
In your own voice, in your own way:
"This woman's heart and soul and brain
"Are mine as much as this gold chain
"She bids me wear; which" (say again)

{*1842* has sections numbered in roman numerals where other versions have *He sings. She speaks.* etc.}   2 *1842,1849,1865* singing! *1863* singing   9 *1842P*¹ ⟨Thy⟩ [My] words as *1842* My words as   12–17 {*1842* has italics where other versions have quotation marks, throughout}

1 *I send my heart up*: cf. *Paracelsus*, i. 203.   3 *bears part*: in my singing.

"I choose to make by cherishing   15
"A precious thing, or choose to fling
"Over the boat-side, ring by ring."
And yet once more say . . . no word more!
Since words are only words. Give o'er!

Unless you call me, all the same,   20
Familiarly by my pet name,
Which if the Three should hear you call,
And me reply to, would proclaim
At once our secret to them all.
Ask of me, too, command me, blame—   25
Do, break down the partition-wall
'Twixt us, the daylight world beholds
Curtained in dusk and splendid folds!
What's left but—all of me to take?
I am the Three's: prevent them, slake   30
Your thirst! 'T is said, the Arab sage,
In practising with gems, can loose
Their subtle spirit in his cruce
And leave but ashes: so, sweet mage,
Leave them my ashes when thy use   35
Sucks out my soul, thy heritage!

He sings.

I.

Past we glide, and past, and past!
  What's that poor Agnese doing

19-20 *1842-65* (no space between sections)   24 *1842,1849* all: 26 *1842,*
1849 Do   28 *1842-65* folds.   29-36 *1842* (printed as separate section, num-
bered III.)   30 *1842* Three's,

    22 *the Three*: 'He and the Couple', as the original version of 104 makes clear: her hus-
band and her brothers Paul and Gian.
    30 *prevent*: 'To go before; to be before': Johnson.
    30-1 *slake / your thirst!*: as in 'Too Late', 135-6.
    31 *the Arab sage*: cf. *Sordello*, iv. 600.   32 *practising*: working, experimenting with.
    33 *cruce*: crucible, as in *Sordello*, vi. 300. Cf. vi. 98, 'mage'.
    36 *Sucks out my soul*: cf. Marlowe, *Dr Faustus*, l. 1771: 'Her lips sucke forth my soule'.

Where they make the shutters fast?
  Grey Zanobi's just a-wooing   40
To his couch the purchased bride:
  Past we glide!

II.

Past we glide, and past, and past!
  Why's the Pucci Palace flaring
Like a beacon to the blast?   45
  Guests by hundreds, not one caring
If the dear host's neck were wried:
  Past we glide!

She sings.

I.

The moth's kiss, first!
Kiss me as if you made believe   50
You were not sure, this eve,
How my face, your flower, had pursed
Its petals up; so, here and there
You brush it, till I grow aware
Who wants me, and wide ope I burst.   55

II.

The bee's kiss, now!
Kiss me as if you entered gay
My heart at some noonday,
A bud that dares not disallow
The claim, so all is rendered up,   60
And passively its shattered cup
Over your head to sleep I bow.

---

54 *1842* | Brush it,   55 *1849, 1863* wide open burst.   62 *1849* bow

44 *the Pucci Palace*: probably fictitious.

47 *wried*: wrung.

49 *The moth's kiss*: cf. Shelley, 'The Sensitive Plant', ii. 50-1: 'soft moths that kiss / The sweet lips of the flowers, and harm not'.

He sings.

I.

What are we two?
I am a Jew,
And carry thee, farther than friends can pursue,   65
To a feast of our tribe;
Where they need thee to bribe
The devil that blasts them unless he imbibe
Thy . . . Scatter the vision for ever! And now,
As of old, I am I, thou art thou!   70

II.

Say again, what we are?
The sprite of a star,
I lure thee above where the destinies bar
My plumes their full play
Till a ruddier ray   75
Than my pale one announce there is withering away
Some . . . Scatter the vision for ever! And now,
As of old, I am I, thou art thou!

He muses.

Oh, which were best, to roam or rest?
The land's lap or the water's breast?   80
To sleep on yellow millet-sheaves,
Or swim in lucid shallows just
Eluding water-lily leaves,
An inch from Death's black fingers, thrust

66 *1842,1849* tribe,   69 *1842,1849* Thy . . . Shatter the   71 *1842* But again,
*77 (reading of *1842–68*) *1888,1889* Some . . (reading of *1842–65*) *1868–89* now.   *1849*
Some . . . Shatter the

66 *a feast of our tribe*: perhaps the *Seder*, a communal meal on the eve of the Passover,
which roughly coincides with Easter.

69 *Thy* . . .: the missing word is no doubt 'blood', with reference to the 'blood libel' that
Jews killed Christian children as sacrificial victims, particularly at Passover. Cf. Chaucer,
'The Prioress's Tale'.

80 *the water's breast*: cf. Shelley, 'To Jane: The Recollection', 78: 'the dark water's breast'.

To lock you, whom release he must;   85
Which life were best on Summer eves?

He speaks, musing.

Lie back; could thought of mine improve you?
From this shoulder let there spring
A wing; from this, another wing;
Wings, not legs and feet, shall move you!   90
Snow-white must they spring, to blend
With your flesh, but I intend
They shall deepen to the end,
Broader, into burning gold,
Till both wings crescent-wise enfold   95
Your perfect self, from 'neath your feet
To o'er your head, where, lo, they meet
As if a million sword-blades hurled
Defiance from you to the world!

Rescue me thou, the only real!   100
And scare away this mad ideal
That came, nor motions to depart!
Thanks! Now, stay ever as thou art!

Still he muses.

I.

What if the Three should catch at last
Thy serenader? While there's cast   105
Paul's cloak about my head, and fast
Gian pinions me, Himself has past

---

87 *1842* could I improve you?   88 *1842P*[1] let ⟨thou⟩ [there] spring   104 *1842*
| He and the Couple catch at last   105 *1842* serenader;   106 *1842P*[1] ⟨Gian's⟩
[Paul's] cloak

   95 *both wings crescent-wise*: cf. *Sordello*, vi. 14–16 and 568–70. The image, no doubt from
the visual arts, made a deep appeal to Browning.   100 *real*: reality.
   107 *Himself*: her husband. The word is still used in this sense in country parts of Scotland and Ireland.

His stylet thro' my back; I reel;
And . . . is it thou I feel?

II.

They trail me, these three godless knaves,   110
Past every church that sains and saves,
Nor stop till, where the cold sea raves
By Lido's wet accursed graves,
They scoop mine, roll me to its brink,
And . . . on thy breast I sink!   115

She replies, musing.

Dip your arm o'er the boat-side, elbow-deep,
As I do: thus: were death so unlike sleep,
Caught this way? Death's to fear from flame or steel,
Or poison doubtless; but from water—feel!

Go find the bottom! Would you stay me? There!   120
Now pluck a great blade of that ribbon-grass
To plait in where the foolish jewel was,
I flung away: since you have praised my hair,
'T is proper to be choice in what I wear.

---

109 *1842* it Thee I   110 *1842* me, do these godless   *111 {reading of *1842–*
65} *1868–89* that saints and   119 *1842* doubtless,

  108 *stylet*: stiletto.
  111 *that sains and saves*: the later 'saints' is almost certainly an error, overlooked by
Browning. Pettigrew is right, the Ohio editor wrong. Cf. Praed, 'The Legend of the
Drachenfels', 45: 'Mary, Mother, sain and save'. OED quotes the line in its earlier form,
pointing out that 'sain' occurs 'especially in conjunction with "save"': 'sain', *v.* 2b. In *An
Etymological Dictionary of the Scottish Language* (Edinburgh, 2 vols., 1808) John Jamieson has a
full treatment of the word, pointing out the original meaning 'To make the sign of the
cross'. Cf. German 'segnet'.
  113 *By Lido's wet accursed graves*: 'Ancient Jewish tombs are there, moss-grown and half
covered with sand. The place is desolate and very gloomy': Berdoe, p. 217: 'accursed'
because unsanctified.
  117 *were death so unlike sleep*: the affinity between the two is a constant thought in
Shelley. See, e.g., *Adonais*, vii. 7 and *The Cenci*, v. iii. 138 and v. iv. 114. In classical
mythology, Death and Sleep are twins.

He speaks.

Row home? must we row home? Too surely 125
Know I where its front's demurely
Over the Giudecca piled;
Window just with window mating,
Door on door exactly waiting,
All's the set face of a child: 130
But behind it, where's a trace
Of the staidness and reserve,
And formal lines without a curve,
In the same child's playing-face?
No two windows look one way 135
O'er the small sea-water thread
Below them. Ah, the autumn day
I, passing, saw you overhead!
First, out a cloud of curtain blew,
Then a sweet cry, and last came you— 140
To catch your lory that must needs
Escape just then, of all times then,
To peck a tall plant's fleecy seeds,
And make me happiest of men.
I scarce could breathe to see you reach 145
So far back o'er the balcony
To catch him ere he climbed too high
Above you in the Smyrna peach
That quick the round smooth cord of gold,
This coiled hair on your head, unrolled, 150
Fell down you like a gorgeous snake
The Roman girls were wont, of old,
When Rome there was, for coolness' sake

125 *1842* Must we, must we *Home*? Too surely   133 *1842* | Formal lines
141 *1842-65* your loory that   147-8 *1849, 1863* (To .... peach)

127 *the Giudecca* : the Giudecca canal, between the main part of the city and the island
called Giudecca (formerly Spinalunga). Browning refers to 'the dead black Giudecca' and
its seaweed in *Sordello*, iii. 693.
141 *lory* : a type of parrot, or bird of similar appearance.
148 *the Smyrna peach* : peach-tree.

To let lie curling o'er their bosoms.
Dear lory, may his beak retain   155
Ever its delicate rose stain
As if the wounded lotus-blossoms
Had marked their thief to know again!

Stay longer yet, for others' sake
Than mine! What should your chamber do?   160
—With all its rarities that ache
In silence while day lasts, but wake
At night-time and their life renew,
Suspended just to pleasure you
Who brought against their will together   165
These objects, and, while day lasts, weave
Around them such a magic tether
That dumb they look: your harp, believe,
With all the sensitive tight strings
Which dare not speak, now to itself   170
Breathes slumberously, as if some elf
Went in and out the chords, his wings
Make murmur wheresoe'er they graze,
As an angel may, between the maze
Of midnight palace-pillars, on   .   175
And on, to sow God's plagues, have gone
Through guilty glorious Babylon.
And while such murmurs flow, the nymph

154 *1842* To place within their   155 *1842-65* Dear loory, may   158 *1842* |
Marked their   165 *1842* That brought reluctantly together *1849* —That brought
1863 That brought   167 *1842* Round them   168 *1849-65* That they look
dumb: your   170 *1842-63* That dare   171 *1842,1849* Breathes slumbrously
as   172 *1842* out tall chords   173 *1842* Get murmurs from whene'er they
graze,   174 *1842* As may an angel thro' the maze   175 *1842* Of pillars on
God's quest have gone   176 (no equivalent in *1842*)   177 *1842* At guilty

161 *its rarities*: the objects which she has collected. The fancy that the lady's favourite
possessions come to life at night, and live a life of their own (during the day they are held
together by 'a magic tether'), is reminiscent of children's stories.

176 *to sow God's plagues*: cf. e.g. Jer. 50: 13 ff. Cf. *Sordello*, i. 592 ff.

177 *Through guilty glorious Babylon*: 'glorious' primarily in the first sense in Johnson:
'Boastful; proud; haughty; ostentatious'. Browning may be remembering John Martin's
once-celebrated painting, 'The Fall of Babylon'.

Bends o'er the harp-top from her shell
As the dry limpet for the lymph   180
Come with a tune he knows so well.
And how your statues' hearts must swell!
And how your pictures must descend
To see each other, friend with friend!
Oh, could you take them by surprise,   185
You'd find Schidone's eager Duke
Doing the quaintest courtesies
To that prim saint by Haste-thee-Luke!
And, deeper into her rock den,
Bold Castelfranco's Magdalen   190
You'd find retreated from the ken
Of that robed counsel-keeping Ser—
As if the Tizian thinks of her,

---

182 *1842* how the statues'   183 *1842* how the pictures   188 *1842,1849*
Luke: 193 *1842* her!

180 *lymph*: water.

182–3 *your statues . . . your pictures*: cf. the description of Leigh Hunt's study in Keats, 'Sleep and Poetry', 354 ff.

186 *Schidone's eager Duke*: Bartolommeo Schidone or Schidoni (1560–1616) was born at Modena and brought up under the Caracci, though he seems rather to have modelled himself on Raphael and Correggio. This is an imaginary painting.

188 *that prim saint by Haste-thee-Luke!*: Browning explained the allusion, in response to a question from Furnivall, in 1882: '"Luca-fa-presto," as Luca Giordano was styled—somewhat disparagingly—from his expeditious way of working': *Trumpeter*, p. 50. According to Michael Bryan's *A Biographical and Critical Dictionary of Painters and Engravers* (2 vols., 1816), i. 476, 'Such was the demand for his drawings and sketches, that his father continually urged him to despatch, by repeating to him, *Luca fa presto*, by which appellation he is sometimes designated.' Bryan gives his dates as 1632–1705.

190 *Bold Castelfranco's Magdalen*: Giorgio Barbarelli, commonly known as Giorgione, was born at Castelfranco, near Trevigi, about 1478. According to Bryan he was 'the first of the Venetian painters that broke through the timid and constrained style to which the art was confined at the time of the Bellini'. He died in 1510. Titian greatly admired him.

192 *Ser*: not 'seer' (Pettigrew), but Master or gentleman, as in *Luria*, I. 21. '*Ser* is commonly used by Boccaccio and others for *Messer*', Landor noted on the first page of 'Chaucer, Boccaccio, and Petrarca': *Imaginary Conversations of Literary Men and Statesmen*, 2nd ser., I. 207 n.

193 *the Tizian*: unlike the other pictures described, this may be based on a particular original, Titian's portrait of Jacopo Strada, in which the art-dealer (or 'Antiquarius', as he preferred to term himself) is portrayed, richly dressed, holding a statuette of Venus above a table on which we see part of a sculptured torso, several gold coins, and a letter. Browning may well have seen an engraving of this celebrated portrait, and be spinning a story from it. He may have known that Titian regarded Strada as a pretentious humbug.

And is not, rather, gravely bent
On seeing for himself what toys   195
Are these, his progeny invent,
What litter now the board employs
Whereon he signed a document
That got him murdered! Each enjoys
Its night so well, you cannot break   200
The sport up, so, indeed must make
More stay with me, for others' sake.

She speaks.

I.

To-morrow, if a harp-string, say,
Is used to tie the jasmine back
That overfloods my room with sweets,   205
Contrive your Zorzi somehow meets
My Zanze! If the ribbon's black,
The Three are watching: keep away!

II.

Your gondola—let Zorzi wreathe
A mesh of water-weeds about   210
Its prow, as if he unaware
Had struck some quay or bridge-foot stair!
That I may throw a paper out
As you and he go underneath.

There's Zanze's vigilant taper; safe are we.   215
Only one minute more to-night with me?

194 *1842* As if he is not rather bent   195 *1842* On trying for   201 *1842* so,
for others' sake   202 *1842* Than mine, your stay must longer make!
206 *1842* Be sure that Zorzi   207 *1842–65* Zanze: 208 *1842* I use, they're
watching; keep away. *1849–65* away.   212 *1842–65* stair;   215 *1842–63* we!

205 *overfloods*: first used, according to OED, by Byron, in *Sardanapalus*, v. i. 194.
207 *My Zanze!*: a common name, which also occurs in *Sordello*, iii. 879, and in *Pippa Passes*, iv. 256 etc.
210 *water-weeds*: no earlier instance in OED.

Resume your past self of a month ago!
Be you the bashful gallant, I will be
The lady with the colder breast than snow.
Now bow you, as becomes, nor touch my hand   220
More than I touch yours when I step to land,
And say, "All thanks, Siora!"—

                        Heart to heart
And lips to lips! Yet once more, ere we part,
Clasp me and make me thine, as mine thou art!

                         [He is surprised, and stabbed.
It was ordained to be so, sweet!—and best   225
Comes now, beneath thine eyes, upon thy breast.
Still kiss me! Care not for the cowards! Care
Only to put aside thy beauteous hair
My blood will hurt! The Three, I do not scorn
To death, because they never lived: but I   230
Have lived indeed, and so—(yet one more kiss)—can die!

219 *1842-63* snow: 222 *1842* All thanks, Siora ... *1849* All thanks, Siora!—
223 *1842* lips! Once, ere   224 *1842* | Make me s.d. *1842P¹* [(he is stabbed by one of
the Three)] *1842P²,1842* (no s.d.) *1863-68* He   225 *1842* It was to be so, Sweet,
1849-65 Sweet,—   226 *1842* Comes 'neath thine   *1842-63* eyes, and on thy
229 *1842* hurt.   231 *1842* die.

    217 *Resume*: revert to, become again.
    222 *Siora*: Signora. Cf. 'Ser' in 192.
    229 *The Three*: as in 22.
    231 *can die!*: 'Was *she* true, or in the conspiracy?', Browning was strangely asked. He
replied, 'Out of it'. See *New Poems*, p. 176.

ARTEMIS PROLOGIZES

B R O W N I N G referred to the composition of this poem in a letter and in a
note on the proofs. In the letter, written to Julia Wedgwood in 1864, he
recalled having been ill—'something unpleasant in the head'—when, 'one
Good *Saturday*', he was reading the revise of *Pippa Passes*. 'I wrote in bed
such a quantity of that "Hippolytus", of which I wrote down the prologue,
but forgot the rest, though the resuscitation-scene which was to have
followed, would have improved matters'.[1] The 'Good *Saturday*' of 1841
was 10 April. The note on the proofs is as follows:

I had better say perhaps that the above is nearly all retained of a tragedy I
composed, much against my endeavour, while in bed with a fever two years ago:
it went farther into the story of Hippolytus and Acrisia; but when I got well,
putting only thus much down at once, I soon forgot the remainder—which came
nearer the mark, I think.[2]

In the second proof the last seven words were deleted, and in that form the
note was printed by Mrs Orr in her *Life*. Since it is likely that the date
given to Julia Wedgwood is accurate, 'two years ago' seems to refer to a
period of little more than eighteen months.[3] Mrs Orr provides a useful
account of the poem in her *Handbook* :

This was suggested by the 'Hippolytos' of Euripides; and destined to become part
of a larger poem, which should continue its story. For, according to the legend,
Hippolytos having perished through the anger of Aphrodite (Venus), was revived
by Artemis (Diana), though only to disappoint her affection by falling in love with
one of her nymphs, Aricia. Mr. Browning imagines that she has removed him in
secret to her own forest retreat, and is nursing him back to life by the help of
Asclepios; and the poem is a monologue in which she describes what has passed,
from Phædra's self-betrayal to the present time. Hippolytos still lies unconscious;
but the power of the great healer has been brought to bear upon him, and the
unconsciousness seems only that of sleep. Artemis is *awaiting the event*.
    The ensuing chorus of nymphs, the awakening of Hippolytos, and with it the
stir of the new passion within him, had already taken shape in Mr. Browning's
mind. Unfortunately, something put the inspiration to flight, and it did not
return.[4]

---

[1] Wedgwood, p. 102.   [2] Note on first proof.
[3] Pettigrew follows DeVane (who gives no authority) in stating that the illness occurred
in December 1840 and January 1841. This is inconsistent with the letter to Julia Wedg-
wood, however.   [4] pp. 119–20; *Life*, p. 121 n.

'When Mr. Browning gave me these supplementary details for the *Handbook*,' Mrs Orr wrote in a footnote to the passage in the *Life* in which she quotes the note which Browning wrote on the proofs, 'he spoke as if his illness had interrupted the work, not preceded its conception. The real fact is, I think, the more striking.' By this last sentence she must mean that she believed that Browning had not begun work on the projected play before he fell ill. It seems likely that he had thought of such a thing, and perhaps begun planning it, but had written little if any of it. How much he 'composed' we cannot know, but a good deal more had certainly 'taken shape in [his] mind'.

No other poem of Browning's contains so many echoes and other literary references.

Browning's 'passion' for Greek literature had been evident as early as *Pauline*. In 1845 he told Elizabeth Barrett that 'once upon a time' he had hoped to 'restore' one of the lost plays of the Promethean trilogy of Æschylus.[1] He had always a particular interest in Euripides. The present poem may be compared with the Prologue spoken by Aphrodite at the beginning of the *Hippolytus*, and with the Euripidean opening of *Comus*. When Arnold described it as 'one of the very best antique fragments I know', he was echoing Mrs Orr's 'an original fragment in the classic manner'.[2] DeVane refers the reader to the description of Artemis in the *Parleyings* ('With Gerard de Lairesse', ix).

1849 Dramatic Romances and Lyrics; 1863 Men, and Women; 1868– Men and Women.

---

[1] Kintner, i. 37; *Correspondence*, iii. 265. Cf. 'Bishop Blougram's Apology', 184.
[2] *Letters of Matthew Arnold 1848–1888*, ed. George W. E. Russell (2 vols., 1895), i. 61; *Handbook*, p. 119.

ARTEMIS PROLOGIZES.

I AM a goddess of the ambrosial courts,
And save by Here, Queen of Pride, surpassed
By none whose temples whiten this the world.
Through heaven I roll my lucid moon along;
I shed in hell o'er my pale people peace;   5
On earth I, caring for the creatures, guard
Each pregnant yellow wolf and fox-bitch sleek,
And every feathered mother's callow brood,
And all that love green haunts and loneliness.
Of men, the chaste adore me, hanging crowns   10
Of poppies red to blackness, bell and stem,
Upon my image at Athenai here;
And this dead Youth, Asclepios bends above,
Was dearest to me. He, my buskined step
To follow through the wild-wood leafy ways,   15
And chase the panting stag, or swift with darts
Stop the swift ounce, or lay the leopard low,

title *1842,1849* ARTEMIS PROLOGUIZES.   4 *1842* roll its lucid   5 *1842*
In Hades shed o'er   13 *1842* Of such this Youth,   14 *1842* me, and my

   Title: Artemis is the Greek equivalent of Diana in Roman mythology. She is the goddess
of hunting, and of chastity. 'She was supposed to be the same as the moon, and Proserpine
or Hecate' (Lemprière). She cared for animals, and for women in childbirth. The Greek
προλογίζειν is used by the scholiasts on the tragedians to mean 'to speak a prologue'. It first
occurs in English in the induction to *Four Plays in One*, by Beaumont and Fletcher (1608).
   1 *ambrosial courts*: cf. *Comus*, 16: 'ambrosial weeds'.
   2 *Here*: Here is the Ionic form of Hera, who corresponds to the Roman Juno, Queen of
the Gods.
   3 *this the world*: cf. *Comus*, 5–6: 'this dim spot, / Which men call earth'.
   4 *lucid*: 'Shining; bright; glittering': Johnson.
   8 *And every feathered mother's callow brood*: cf. *Paradise Lost*, vii. 418–20: 'Their brood . . .
Their callow young, but feathered soon'.   12 *Athenai*: Athens.
   13 *this dead Youth*: according to some accounts, Asclepios (Æsculapius, god of medicine)
healed Hippolytus: see, e.g., *Æneid* vii. 765 ff.
   14 *my buskined step*: buskins are half-boots reaching to the calf or knee. They were part
of the traditional portrayal of Artemis.
   15 *the wild-wood leafy ways*: cf. *Cymbeline*, IV. ii. 393: 'With wild wood-leaves'.
   17 *the swift ounce*: 'The ounce . . . is much less than the panther': Goldsmith, *Natural History* (1776), iii. 255.

Neglected homage to another god:
Whence Aphrodite, by no midnight smoke
Of tapers lulled, in jealousy despatched   20
A noisome lust that, as the gadbee stings,
Possessed his stepdame Phaidra for himself
The son of Theseus her great absent spouse.
Hippolutos exclaiming in his rage
Against the fury of the Queen, she judged   25
Life insupportable; and, pricked at heart
An Amazonian stranger's race should dare
To scorn her, perished by the murderous cord:
Yet, ere she perished, blasted in a scroll
The fame of him her swerving made not swerve.   30
And Theseus read, returning, and believed,
And exiled, in the blindness of his wrath,
The man without a crime who, last as first,
Loyal, divulged not to his sire the truth.
Now Theseus from Poseidon had obtained   35
That of his wishes should be granted three,
And one he imprecated straight—"Alive
"May ne'er Hippolutos reach other lands!"
Poseidon heard, ai ai! And scarce the prince

18 *1842* He paid not homage   22 *1842* for the child   23 *1842* Of Theseus
her great husband then afar.   24 *1842* But when Hippolutos exclaimed with rage
25 *1842,1849* the miserable Queen,   26 *1842* Intolerable life, and, *1849* insupport-
able,   27 *1842* race had right   30 *1842,1849* swerve,   *31 (editors'
emendation)   *1863–89* Theseus, *1842* Which Theseus saw, returning, *1849* Which
Theseus read,   32 *1842* So, in the blindness of his wrath, exiled *1849* So, exiled
35 *1842* But Theseus   37 *1842* And this one imprecated now—alive *1849* And this
he . . . . —alive *1863,1865* —alive   38 *1842–65* May . . . . lands!

21 *noisome*: 'Noxious; mischievous; unwholesome': Johnson.
    the gadbee: gadfly (Gk. οἶστρος). Hood points out the parallel in Æschylus, *Prometheus Bound*, 566 and 878–80, describing how Io (as a heifer) was persecuted by Juno, who sent a gadfly to torment her. Cf. *Sordello*, ii. 773–4. The Greek word can also mean a sting, any-thing that drives one mad; and hence any mad desire, insane passion, frenzy. See Euripides, *Orestes*, 791, *Bacchæ*, 665.
22 *his stepdame Phaidra*: see introduction.
28 *the murderous cord*: hearing of the death of Hippolytus, Phædra hanged herself.
30 *swerving*: sinning.
35 *Poseidon*: the Greek name for Neptune, king of the sea.
37 *imprecated*: prayed.   39 *ai ai!*: alas! (Gk).

Had stepped into the fixed boots of the car   40
That give the feet a stay against the strength
Of the Henetian horses, and around
His body flung the rein, and urged their speed
Along the rocks and shingles of the shore,
When from the gaping wave a monster flung   45
His obscene body in the coursers' path.
These, mad with terror, as the sea-bull sprawled
Wallowing about their feet, lost care of him
That reared them; and the master-chariot-pole
Snapping beneath their plunges like a reed,   50
Hippolutos, whose feet were trammelled fast,
Was yet dragged forward by the circling rein
Which either hand directed; nor they quenched
The frenzy of their flight before each trace,
Wheel-spoke and splinter of the woeful car,   55
Each boulder-stone, sharp stub and spiny shell,
Huge fish-bone wrecked and wreathed amid the sands
On that detested beach, was bright with blood
And morsels of his flesh: then fell the steeds
Head-foremost, crashing in their mooned fronts,   60
Shivering with sweat, each white eye horror-fixed.
His people, who had witnessed all afar,
Bore back the ruins of Hippolutos.
But when his sire, too swoln with pride, rejoiced

---

43 *1842-63* the reins, and   45 *1842P*¹ ⟨Than⟩ [When] from   46 *1842* path:
1849 path!   51 *1842* were trammeled sure, *1849-65* were trammeled fast,
53 *1849* nor was quenched   54 *1849* of that flight   56 *1842* And boulder-
stone,

   40 *the fixed boots*: cf. Euripides, *Hippolytus*, 1189.
   42 *the Henetian horses*: cf. Euripides, *Hippolytus*, 231.
   47 *the sea-bull*: the bull from the sea. Cf. Euripides, *Hippolytus*, 1214.
   48 *Wallowing about their feet*: cf. *Paradise Lost* vii. 409-11: 'on smooth the seal, / And
bended dolphins play: part huge of bulk / Wallowing unwieldy'.
   54 *trace*: the leather strap by which the collar of a horse is connected with the cross-bar
which is fixed across the head of the shafts.
   56 *stub*: the stump of a tree or bush.
      spiny: sharp, jagged.
   60 *mooned fronts*: the crescent-shaped fronts of the chariots. Cf. *Sordello*, v. 15.
   63 *the ruins of Hippolutos*: cf. *Julius Caesar*, iii. i. 257.

(Indomitable as a man foredoomed) 65
That vast Poseidon had fulfilled his prayer,
I, in a flood of glory visible,
Stood o'er my dying votary and, deed
By deed, revealed, as all took place, the truth.
Then Theseus lay the woefullest of men, 70
And worthily; but ere the death-veils hid
His face, the murdered prince full pardon breathed
To his rash sire. Whereat Athenai wails.

So I, who ne'er forsake my votaries,
Lest in the cross-way none the honey-cake 75
Should tender, nor pour out the dog's hot life;
Lest at my fane the priests disconsolate
Should dress my image with some faded poor
Few crowns, made favours of, nor dare object
Such slackness to my worshippers who turn 80
Elsewhere the trusting heart and loaded hand,
As they had climbed Olumpos to report
Of Artemis and nowhere found her throne—
I interposed: and, this eventful night,—
(While round the funeral pyre the populace 85
Stood with fierce light on their black robes which bound
Each sobbing head, while yet their hair they clipped

---

65 *1842* Indomitable .... foredoomed,   73 *1842* sire. Whence now Athenai
73-4 {no paragraph division in *1842-65*}   74 *1842* But I,   77 *1842* fane dis-
consolate the priests   81 *1849-65* The trusting heart and loaded hand elsewhere,
82 *1849* climbed Oulumpos to   85 *1842-65* While   86 *1842* Stand with
1842,1849 robes that blind   *1863,1865* robes to blind   87 *1842* they clip

   65 *Indomitable*: here, foolishly stubborn.
   66 *vast*: because Poseidon is god of the sea.
   67 *glory visible*: Artemis/Diana is usually portrayed with a crescent ('glory') over her head.
   71 *worthily*: deservedly, as in *Paradise Lost*, xi. 524.
   73 *Whereat Athenai wails*: cf. *Samson Agonistes*, 1752: 'Whence Gaza mourns'.
   75 *in the cross-way*: Diana 'was called Trivia when worshipped in the cross-ways where her statues were generally erected': Lemprière.
   79 *object*: cf. Latin *obicere*: reproach my worshippers with such slackness.
   82 *As*: as if (archaic).
   87 *their hair they clipped*: in mourning. Cf. *Sordello*, ii. 714 n.

O'er the dead body of their withered prince,
And, in his palace, Theseus prostrated
On the cold hearth, his brow cold as the slab   90
'T was bruised on, groaned away the heavy grief—
As the pyre fell, and down the cross logs crashed
Sending a crowd of sparkles through the night,
And the gay fire, elate with mastery,
Towered like a serpent o'er the clotted jars   95
Of wine, dissolving oils and frankincense,
And splendid gums like gold),—my potency
Conveyed the perished man to my retreat
In the thrice-venerable forest here.
And this white-bearded sage who squeezes now   100
The berried plant, is Phoibos' son of fame,
Asclepios, whom my radiant brother taught
The doctrine of each herb and flower and root,
To know their secret'st virtue and express
The saving soul of all: who so has soothed   105
With lavers the torn brow and murdered cheeks,
Composed the hair and brought its gloss again,
And called the red bloom to the pale skin back,
And laid the strips and jagged ends of flesh
Even once more, and slacked the sinew's knot   110
Of every tortured limb—that now he lies
As if mere sleep possessed him underneath
These interwoven oaks and pines. Oh cheer,
Divine presenter of the healing rod,
Thy snake, with ardent throat and lulling eye,   115

91 *1842* 'Tis bruised on, groans away   97 *1842–65* gold,—

94 *elate*: with a reminiscence of L. *elatus* high, as in *Sordello*, i. 904.

95 *clotted jars*: the meaning is probably that the jars cohered, in the fierce heat.

99 *thrice-venerable*: very venerable: cf. *2 Henry VI*, III. ii. 157.

101 *of fame*: famous. Cf. *Twelfth Night*, III. iii. 23: 'the things of fame / That do renown this city'.   103 *The doctrine*: knowledge.

106 *lavers*: i.e. vessels for washing, or perhaps the process of washing itself: see OED, sense 3. Cf. 'lavers' in *Samson Agonistes* 1727.

113 *Oh cheer*: greetings! Cf. 116.

115 *Thy snake*: 'Serpents are more particularly sacred to him, not only as the ancient physicians used them in their prescriptions, but because also they are considered as the

Twines his lithe spires around! I say, much cheer!
Proceed thou with thy wisest pharmacies!
And ye, white crowd of woodland sister-nymphs,
Ply, as the sage directs, these buds and leaves
That strew the turf around the twain! While I   120
Await, in fitting silence, the event.

121 *1842* In fitting silence the event await.

symbol of prudence and foresight so necessary in the medical profession': Lemprière on
Æsculapius.

117 *pharmacies*: OED gives 'A medicine or medicinal potion' as one meaning of 'pharm-
acy', but describes it as obsolete and rare, instancing only Chaucer, *The Knight's Tale*, 1855.

119 *Ply*: busy yourself with.

120 *the twain*: Artemis and Hippolytus.

121 *the event*: the outcome, as in *Comus*, 410.

WARING

As Pettigrew mentions, Browning wrote 'Alfred Domett or' above the title of the poem, in the second set of proofs. From the first the identity of 'Waring' was recognized by Browning's friends: '"Waring" delighted us all very much', Joseph Arnould wrote to Domett in the spring of 1843, 'for we recognised in it a fancy portrait of a very dear friend.'[1] The best background is the letters printed in *Robert Browning and Alfred Domett*. Griffin and Minchin tell us that Waring was the name of a King's Messenger whom Browning had met during his brief visit to Russia in 1834.[2] We note that the narrator of Part I wonders whether Waring may be in Russia, while the narrator of Part II describes how he saw him in a small boat at Trieste (like Browning himself, Domett had recently visited Italy).[3]

Domett, who was a year older than Browning, came from an adventurous family. His father, whom he described as 'devoted to the sea ... a thorough sailor to the backbone',[4] entered the navy at the age of twelve, then moved to the merchant navy, and prospered, sending two of his sons to the school in Camberwell which Browning attended. In 1833 he published *Poems*. The two men may first have met two years later, when Domett returned from a prolonged journey to Canada and North America.[5] That same year he entered the Middle Temple, and Browning inscribed a copy of *Paracelsus* to him.[6] In 1837 he contributed verse to *Blackwood's*, while in 1839, after a visit to Italy, he published *Venice. A Poem*. The two men were members of a group of friends who met for talk on a wide range of subjects: a good account of 'The Colloquials', as they sometimes called themselves, may be found in Maynard, pp. 97 ff. and 104 ff. Domett's annotations in his copy of *Sordello*, many of which have been printed in our second volume, reveal him as one of the poem's most determined and successful readers.

While much in the poem is fanciful—Domett did not leave England as suddenly as Waring, he left in spring, not in December, while his destination was known to his friends—a great deal was inspired by Browning's interpretation of Domett's character. The two men were close friends:

---

[1] *Browning and Domett*, p. 62.   [2] p. 63.   [3] See n. to l. 220.
[4] *The Diary of Alfred Domett*, ed. E. A. Horsman (1953), p. 108.
[5] See *The Canadian Journal of Alfred Domett*, ed. E. A. Horsman and Lillian Rea Benson (London, Canada, 1955).
[6] Kelley and Coley, E 318.

Browning told Fanny Haworth that he experienced 'real sorrow of heart' when Domett left.[1] In 1848 he addressed Domett in an unusually personal poem, 'The Guardian Angel. A Picture at Fano': 'Where are you, dear old friend? / How rolls the Wairoa at your world's far end? / This is Ancona, yonder is the sea.'

When Matthew Arnold's brother Tom met Domett in New Zealand he described him as 'full of suppressed energy . . . no dreamer, no waverer, but a fiery resolute man of action, capable of making his weight felt and his will prevail'.[2] For a short time he was Prime Minister of New Zealand. He returned to England in 1871, and published a poem about New Zealand the following year, *Ranolf and Amohia*, in which he described Browning as 'Subtlest Asserter of the Soul in Song'.[3] In 1877 he dedicated a collection of poems old and new to his friend,[4] including in it 'Lines sent to Robert Browning, . . . on a certain critique on "Pippa Passes"'.

1849 Dramatic Romances and Lyrics; 1863 Romances; 1868–Dramatic Romances.

WARING.

I.

I.

WHAT's become of Waring
Since he gave us all the slip,
Chose land-travel or seafaring,
Boots and chest or staff and scrip,
Rather than pace up and down   5
Any longer London town?

title *1842P*[2] ('Alfred Domett or' added above title)

4 *staff and scrip* : appropriate to a pilgrim or other traveller by land, as a sea-chest was to a seafarer.

[1] *New Letters*, p. 27. Cf. Domett's parting letter to Browning; in *The Diary*, p. 14.
[2] Quoted by Maynard, p. 100.
[3] There was a 2nd ed., rev., 2 vols., 1883.
[4] In the dedication Browning is described as 'A mighty poet and a subtle-souled psychologist.'

II.

Who'd have guessed it from his lip
Or his brow's accustomed bearing,
On the night he thus took ship
Or started landward?—little caring   10
For us, it seems, who supped together
(Friends of his too, I remember)
And walked home thro' the merry weather,
The snowiest in all December.
I left his arm that night myself   15
For what's-his-name's, the new prose-poet
Who wrote the book there, on the shelf—
How, forsooth, was I to know it
If Waring meant to glide away
Like a ghost at break of day?   20
Never looked he half so gay!

III.

He was prouder than the devil:
How he must have cursed our revel!
Ay and many other meetings,
Indoor visits, outdoor greetings,   25
As up and down he paced this London,
With no work done, but great works undone,
Where scarce twenty knew his name.
Why not, then, have earlier spoken,
Written, bustled? Who's to blame   30
If your silence kept unbroken?

10 *1842* landward,   14 *1842* | Snowiest in   *1842,1849* December;
17 *1842–63* That wrote

11 *For us . . . who supped together*: see introduction.
14 *December*: Domett set off on 30 April.
16 *For what's-his-name's*: conceivably Thomas Powell (on whom see Maynard) whose
Poems were published by Effingham Wilson (the publisher of *Paracelsus*) in 1842. Among
the 'Miscellaneous Poems' in the volume there occurs 'The Death of Adam. (A Dream.)',
which is in prose. Powell gave Browning a copy: Kelley and Coley, A 1889.
27 *With no work done*: 'tell me how you are, where you are, what you do and mean to
do—and to do in our way, for live properly you cannot without writing, and to write a book
now will take one at least the ten or dozen years you portion out for your stay abroad':
Browning and Domett, pp. 34–5 (22 May 1842).

"True, but there were sundry jottings,
"Stray-leaves, fragments, blurrs and blottings,
"Certain first steps were achieved
"Already which"—(is that your meaning?)   35
"Had well borne out whoe'er believed
"In more to come!" But who goes gleaning
. Hedgeside chance-blades, while full-sheaved
Stand cornfields by him? Pride, o'erweening
Pride alone, puts forth such claims   40
O'er the day's distinguished names.

IV.

Meantime, how much I loved him,
I find out now I've lost him.
I who cared not if I moved him,
Who could so carelessly accost him,   45
Henceforth never shall get free
Of his ghostly company,
His eyes that just a little wink
As deep I go into the merit
Of this and that distinguished spirit—   50
His cheeks' raised colour, soon to sink,
As long I dwell on some stupendous
And tremendous (Heaven defend us!)
Monstr'-inform'-ingens-horrend-ous
Demoniaco-seraphic   55
Penman's latest piece of graphic.

32–5,36–7 {no quotation marks in *1842*}   37 *1842* come: 43 *1842–63* him:
45 *1842* —Could so   46 *1842* | Never shall   48 *1842* And eyes
53 *1842* tremendous (God defend

33 *blurrs and blottings*: cf. Quarles, *Enchiridion*, III. xiii: 'He that cleanses a blot with blotted fingers makes a greater blurre.' For Browning and Quarles see our Vol. II, p. 301 n. 129. In 'A Reverie' (1825) Domett had described himself 'Mingling and mangling bits of rhymes / And changing each a thousand times.'

42 *how much I loved him*: in his first letter to New Zealand Browning took the opportunity of writing 'freely what, I dare say, I said niggardly enough—my real love for you—better love than I supposed I was fit for': *Browning and Domett*, p. 33.

54 *Monstr'-inform'-ingens-horrend-ous*: recalling Polyphemus, the one-eyed monster, in the *Æneid*: 'monstrum horrendum, informe, ingens': iii. 658.

56 *graphic*: drawing, or writing.

Nay, my very wrist grows warm
With his dragging weight of arm.
E'en so, swimmingly appears,
Through one's after-supper musings,   60
Some lost lady of old years
With her beauteous vain endeavour
And goodness unrepaid as ever;
The face, accustomed to refusings,
We, puppies that we were ... Oh never   65
Surely, nice of conscience, scrupled
Being aught like false, forsooth, to?
Telling aught but honest truth to?
What a sin, had we centupled
Its possessor's grace and sweetness!   70
No! she heard in its completeness
Truth, for truth's a weighty matter,
And, truth at issue, we can't flatter!
Well, 't is done with; she's exempt
From damning us thro' such a sally;   75
And so she glides, as down a valley,
Taking up with her contempt,
Past our reach; and in, the flowers
Shut her unregarded hours.

v.

Oh, could I have him back once more,   80
This Waring, but one half-day more!
Back, with the quiet face of yore,
So hungry for acknowledgment
Like mine! I'd fool him to his bent.
Feed, should not he, to heart's content?   85
I'd say, "to only have conceived,

58 *1842-63* arm!   *73 [reading of *1842-49*] *1863-89* And truth, at issue,
84 *1842-65* bent!

61 *Some lost lady*: a woman who had been jilted, or perhaps betrayed.
69 *had we centupled*: even if we had centupled.
77 *Taking up*: perhaps 'going her way'.
84 *I'd fool him to his bent*: cf. *Hamlet*, III. ii. 374.

"Planned your great works, apart from progress,
"Surpasses little works achieved!"
I'd lie so, I should be believed.
I'd make such havoc of the claims   90
Of the day's distinguished names
To feast him with, as feasts an ogress
Her feverish sharp-toothed gold-crowned child!
Or as one feasts a creature rarely
Captured here, unreconciled   95
To capture; and completely gives
Its pettish humours licence, barely
Requiring that it lives.

VI.

Ichabod, Ichabod,
The glory is departed!   100
Travels Waring East away?
Who, of knowledge, by hearsay,
Reports a man upstarted
Somewhere as a god,
Hordes grown European-hearted,   105
Millions of the wild made tame
On a sudden at his fame?
In Vishnu-land what Avatar?
Or who in Moscow, toward the Czar,

---

87 *1842* "Your great works, tho' they never progress, *1849* "Your great works, tho' they
ne'er make progress, *1863,1865* (as *1849* but with "though" and "never" uncontracted)
88 *1842–65* "Surpasses all we've yet achieved!"   93 *1842–65* Her sharp-toothed
*97 (reading of *1842–65*) *1868–89* humours license, barely   109 *1842* Or, North in

88 *"Surpasses little works achieved!"*: cf. *Sordello*, iii. 622 ff., particularly 629–30: 'his lay was
but an episode / In the bard's life'.

92 *as feasts an ogress*: apparently a reference to a children's story.

97 *barely*: merely.

99 *Ichabod*: 1 Sam. 4: 21: 'And she named the child I-chabod, saying, The glory is
departed from Israel.'   105 *European-hearted*: i.e. 'civilized'.

108 *In Vishnu-land what Avatar?*: what reincarnation of Waring has occurred in the land
of the Hindus? (Vishnu, one of the principal Hindu deities; avatar, the descent of a deity to
earth in human form.) India was one of the attractive parts of the Empire for a man of
ability and ambition. A close friend of Browning and Domett, Joseph Arnould, was to go
there as Judge of the Supreme Court at Bombay in 1859.

With the demurest of footfalls   110
Over the Kremlin's pavement bright
With serpentine and syenite,
Steps, with five other Generals
That simultaneously take snuff,
For each to have pretext enough   115
And kerchiefwise unfold his sash
Which, softness' self, is yet the stuff
To hold fast where a steel chain snaps,
And leave the grand white neck no gash?
Waring in Moscow, to those rough   120
Cold northern natures borne perhaps,
Like the lambwhite maiden dear
From the circle of mute kings
Unable to repress the tear,
Each as his sceptre down he flings,   125
To Dian's fane at Taurica,
Where now a captive priestess, she alway
Mingles her tender grave Hellenic speech
With theirs, tuned to the hailstone-beaten beach
As pours some pigeon, from the myrrhy lands   130
Rapt by the whirlblast to fierce Scythian strands
Where breed the swallows, her melodious cry

110 *1842* Who, with the gentlest of   112 *1842* and siennite,   114 *1842*
Who simultaneously   115 *1842* That each may have   116 *1842,1849* To
kerchiefwise unfurl his *1863* To kerchiefwise   120 *1842* In Moscow, Waring to
*121 (reading of *1842–68*) *1888,1889* born   *1842* Cold natures   122 *1842*
maiden, (clear   123 *1842* Thro' the   125 *1842* flings),   126 *1842* To
the Dome at   127 *1842* a priestess, she

112 *serpentine and syenite*: two types of ornamental stone, the latter allied to granite.
119 *And leave . . . no gash*: Tsar Paul had been assassinated in 1801.
120 *Waring in Moscow*: see Introduction, above.
122 *the lambwhite maiden*: Hood points out that 'Browning's lines build a picture round
the facts recounted in the speech of the Messenger' in Euripides, *Iphigenia at Aulis*, 1540 ff.
126 *Taurica*: the Crimean peninsula, joined by an isthmus to the ancient Scythia. For the
priestess, cf. Euripides, *Iphigenia among the Taurians*.
130 *myrrhy*: no earlier example in OED.
131 *whirlblast*: a word first used by Wordsworth, according to OED, and then by Coler-
idge and Shelley.
          Scythian: in classical literature Scythia refers to all regions to the N and NE of the
Black Sea.

Amid their barbarous twitter!
In Russia? Never! Spain were fitter!
Ay, most likely 't is in Spain   135
That we and Waring meet again
Now, while he turns down that cool narrow lane
Into the blackness, out of grave Madrid
All fire and shine, abrupt as when there's slid
Its stiff gold blazing pall   140
From some black coffin-lid.
Or, best of all,
I love to think
The leaving us was just a feint;
Back here to London did he slink,   145
And now works on without a wink
Of sleep, and we are on the brink
Of something great in fresco-paint:
Some garret's ceiling, walls and floor,
Up and down and o'er and o'er   150
He splashes, as none splashed before
Since great Caldara Polidore.
Or Music means this land of ours
Some favour yet, to pity won
By Purcell from his Rosy Bowers,—   155
"Give me my so-long promised son,
"Let Waring end what I begun!"
Then down he creeps and out he steals
Only when the night conceals

---

139 *1868* when their's slid   145 *1842,1849* slink;   152 *1842,1849* Polidore:
153-7 (no equivalent in *1842*)

148 *something great in fresco-paint*: a tolerable drawing by Domett forms the frontispiece
to *The Canadian Journal* (see Introduction).

152 *Caldara Polidore*: Polidoro da Caravaggio (1495-1543). An engraving of his Andro-
meda hung in Browning's room: see *Pauline*, 656 ff. and accompanying n. in our Vol. I.
Maynard reproduces the picture on his pp. 160-1.

155 *his Rosy Bowers*: 'From rosie Bow'rs' was printed in *Orpheus Britannicus* (1698), with
the heading: 'This was the last Song that Mr Purcell set, it being in his Sickness': *Grove's Dic-
tionary of Music and Musicians*, 5th ed. (ed. Eric Blom, 9 vols.), vi (1966), p. 1001a. The song
was for 'Don Quixote, part iii', which was produced in 1695, the year of Purcell's death.

His face; in Kent 't is cherry-time, .   160
Or hops are picking: or at prime
Of March he wanders as, too happy,
Years ago when he was young,
Some mild eve when woods grew sappy
And the early moths had sprung   165
To life from many a trembling sheath
Woven the warm boughs beneath;
While small birds said to themselves
What should soon be actual song,
And young gnats, by tens and twelves,   170
Made as if they were the throng
That crowd around and carry aloft
The sound they have nursed, so sweet and pure,
Out of a myriad noises soft,
Into a tone that can endure   175
Amid the noise of a July noon
When all God's creatures crave their boon,
All at once and all in tune,
And get it, happy as Waring then,
Having first within his ken   180
What a man might do with men:
And far too glad, in the even-glow,
To mix with the world he meant to take
Into his hand, he told you, so—
And out of it his world to make,   185
To contract and to expand
As he shut or oped his hand.
Oh Waring, what's to really be?
A clear stage and a crowd to see!
Some Garrick, say, out shall not he   190
The heart of Hamlet's mystery pluck?

---

162 *1842* he steals as when, too happy,   164 *1842* woods were sappy,
167 *1842* beneath,   181 *1842,1849* men,   183 *1849* with your world

181 *What a man might do with men*: see Introduction.
190 *Garrick*: David Garrick (1717–79). Hamlet was one of his most celebrated roles.
191 *The heart of Hamlet's mystery pluck*: *Hamlet*, III. ii. 357.

Or, where most unclean beasts are rife,
Some Junius—am I right?—shall tuck
His sleeve, and forth with flaying-knife!
Some Chatterton shall have the luck   195
Of calling Rowley into life!
Some one shall somehow run a muck
With this old world for want of strife
Sound asleep. Contrive, contrive
To rouse us, Waring! Who's alive?   200
Our men scarce seem in earnest now.
Distinguished names!—but 't is, somehow,
As if they played at being names
Still more distinguished, like the games
Of children. Turn our sport to earnest   205
With a visage of the sternest!
Bring the real times back, confessed
Still better than our very best!

                        II.

                        I.

"WHEN I last saw Waring . . ."
(How all turned to him who spoke!   210
You saw Waring? Truth or joke?
In land-travel or sea-faring?)

194 *1842,1849* and out with   199 *1842,1849* asleep: 201 *1842,1849* now:
202 *1842* names,   208 *1842* than the very   210 *1842-65* spoke—

192 *unclean beasts*: a biblical phrase (e.g. Lev. 5: 2) here probably referring to politics.

193 *Some Junius*: used generically for a fearless exposer of abuses. The *Letters of Junius* appeared in a periodical in 1769-72, and in many editions thereafter. The pseudonymous author was probably Sir Philip Francis.

194 *flaying-knife*: this is the only example in OED.

195 *Some Chatterton*: Browning's deep interest in Thomas Chatterton led him to write an anonymous article in the *Foreign Quarterly Review* for July 1842: it has since been edited by Donald Smalley as *Browning's Essay on Chatterton* (Cambridge, Mass., 1948). 'Rowley' was a fictitious mediaeval poet whose poems Chatterton himself composed.

198-9 *this old world . . . Sound asleep*: in his letters to Domett Browning complains of 'a creeping, magnetic, assimilating influence nothing can block out' in the old world: perhaps New Zealand will prove better. See e.g. *Browning and Domett*, p. 35.

210 *him who spoke!*: another member of the group of friends now speaks.

II.

"We were sailing by Triest
"Where a day or two we harboured:
"A sunset was in the West,   215
"When, looking over the vessel's side,
"One of our company espied
"A sudden speck to larboard.
"And as a sea-duck flies and swims
"At once, so came the light craft up,   220
"With its sole lateen sail that trims
"And turns (the water round its rims
"Dancing, as round a sinking cup)
"And by us like a fish it curled,
"And drew itself up close beside,   225
"Its great sail on the instant furled,
"And o'er its thwarts a shrill voice cried,
"(A neck as bronzed as a Lascar's)
"'Buy wine of us, you English Brig?
"'Or fruit, tobacco and cigars?   230
"'A pilot for you to Triest?
"'Without one, look you ne'er so big,
"'They'll never let you up the bay!
"'We natives should know best.'
"I turned, and 'just those fellows' way,'   235
"Our captain said, 'The 'long-shore thieves
"'Are laughing at us in their sleeves.'

227 *1842–65* its planks, a

213 *Triest*: on his first voyage to Italy in 1838 Browning noted in his diary, of which the
relevant pages are in the library of the University of Toronto, that his boat 'Arrived at
Trieste' on 30 May, and '—anchored 4 p m.' The next day he 'Left by . . . boat for Venice,
10½ p m'.

218 *larboard*: the port or left-hand side of a vessel, when one is facing the nose or bow.

220 *the light craft*: cf. 'the fisher's lonely bark' in Domett's poem, *Venice*. The second part
of 'Waring' was no doubt suggested by Domett's recent visit to Italy.

221 *lateen sail*: 'A triangular sail suspended by a long yard at an angle of about 45 degrees
to the mast': OED.

227 *thwarts*: the thwarts are the seats on which the rowers sit, and hence the side of the
boat.

228 *Lascar*: an Indian sailor.

III.

"In truth, the boy leaned laughing back;
"And one, half-hidden by his side
"Under the furled sail, soon I spied,   240
"With great grass hat and kerchief black,
"Who looked up with his kingly throat,
"Said somewhat, while the other shook
"His hair back from his eyes to look
"Their longest at us; then the boat,   245
"I know not how, turned sharply round,
"Laying her whole side on the sea
"As a leaping fish does; from the lee
"Into the weather, cut somehow
"Her sparkling path beneath our bow   250
"And so went off, as with a bound,
"Into the rosy and golden half
"O' the sky, to overtake the sun
"And reach the shore, like the sea-calf
"Its singing cave; yet I caught one   255
"Glance ere away the boat quite passed,
"And neither time nor toil could mar
"Those features: so I saw the last
"Of Waring!"—You? Oh, never star
Was lost here but it rose afar!   260
Look East, where whole new thousands are!
In Vishnu-land what Avatar?

245 *1842* us; and the   248 *1842P*[1] leaping ⟨first⟩ [fish] does   250 *1842-63*
bow;   252 *1842,1849* the rose and   253 *1842-68* "Of the

241 *"With great grass hat*: Domett seems to have liked large hats: see the watercolour drawing reproduced opposite p. 32 of *Browning and Domett*.
248-9 *from the lee / Into the weather*: into the wind.
254 *sea-calf*: seal.
262 *In Vishnu-land what Avatar?*: cf. 108 and n. above.

RUDEL TO THE LADY OF TRIPOLI

WE DO not know when this poem was written, but Browning will have come on Rudel in the course of his work on *Sordello*, so we may assume as likely a date between the spring of 1840 and the autumn of 1842. Of the various accounts of the troubadour which he knew, that in Sismondi's *Historical View of the Literature of the South of Europe* may be quoted:

The knights, who had returned from the Holy Land, spoke with enthusiasm of a Countess of Tripoli, who had extended to them the most generous hospitality, and whose grace and beauty equalled her virtues. Geoffrey Rudel, hearing this account, fell deeply in love with her, without having ever seen her; and prevailed upon one of his friends, Bertrand d'Allamanon, a Troubadour like himself, to accompany him to the Levant. In 1162, he quitted the court of England, whither he had been conducted by Geoffrey the brother of Richard I., and embarked for the Holy Land. On his voyage, he was attacked by a severe illness, and had lost the power of speech, when he arrived at the port of Tripoli. The countess, being informed that a celebrated poet was dying of love for her, on board a vessel which was entering the roads, visited him on shipboard, took him kindly by the hand, and attempted to cheer his spirits.[1]

Rudel was able to thank her, 'and to declare his passion', before he died. The Countess raised a tomb of porphyry to his memory in Tripoli. Sismondi quotes Rudel's verses *'on distant love'*, which are the inspiration of Browning's poem. A generally similar account of Rudel is given in a book which we know Browning to have possessed, *The Literary History of the Troubadours . . . Collected and Abridged* from the larger work by the Abbé Millot by Mrs Dobson.[2]

Browning alters the story considerably. His Rudel has not set out for Tripoli, nor does he plan such a journey: instead he addresses a 'Pilgrim' and asks him to take the message of his love to the lady. Neither the symbolism of the first part of the poem, nor the device described in the third, derives from his sources.

According to DeVane, Browning 'uses the characteristic troubadour device of portraying the love of Rudel by the symbolic use of flowers. Rudel is the sun-flower, turning to the sun which represents love. But the

---

[1] We quote from the translation by Thomas Roscoe (4 vols., 1823), i. 104–5. In 1836 John Graham had published a commonplace poem on the subject, *Geoffrey Rudel; or, The Pilgrim of Love.*
[2] Kelley and Coley, A 1377. Cf. our Vol. II, p. 173.

sun has little effect upon the Mount, which represents his lady, cold and lofty as the convention of courtly love demanded.' In what is almost the only full attempt to discuss the matter, Eleanor Cook understandably finds it impossible to 'make the lady and the Mount correspond'.[1] She concludes that 'the lady is the sun', and the Mount the lady's husband. The symbolism of the sunflower is clear (see ll. 24–6). We believe that the sun symbolizes sexual passion. It seems likely that the title of Rudel's most celebrated poem, 'Amor de Lonh', provides the necessary clue to the meaning of the Mount, which represents love which is distant and unattainable, that extreme of romantic or courtly love which has been called 'by many a name'.

The poem is the work of a man who had studied the Troubadours in some detail: it is also the work of a lifelong reader of Quarles. It owes something to the tradition of the emblem book, in which the sunflower frequently occurs as the emblem of fidelity. It is interesting that in the third section Rudel should refer to weaving his 'device', since, as Rosemary Freeman informs us, 'Emblem books were useful . . . to embroiderers and tapestry makers.'[2]

In *1842* the poem is the first of the two yoked as 'Queen-Worship', the second being 'Cristina'. In *1849* the two appear without the joint title.

1849 Dramatic Romances and Lyrics; 1863 Men, and Women; 1868– Men and Women.

RUDEL TO THE LADY OF TRIPOLI.

I.

I KNOW a Mount, the gracious Sun perceives
First, when he visits, last, too, when he leaves
The world; and, vainly favoured, it repays
The day-long glory of his steadfast gaze

title *1842* QUEEN-WORSHIP. I.–RUDEL AND THE LADY OF TRIPOLI.
1 *1842* the Sun perceives   3 *1842* and it repays   4 *1842* his gaze

[1] *Browning's Lyrics: An Exploration* (Toronto, 1974), p. 83.
[2] *English Emblem Books* (1948), p. 93. On pp. 25 ff. Dr Freeman points out the importance of the sunflower, mentions that 'The Marigold, Sunflower, Heliotrope and Girasole were regarded as interchangeable terms in the seventeenth century', and reminds us that the flower 'was commonly supposed to turn about on its stalk in accordance with the movement of the sun', which rendered it the perfect image of faithfulness.

By no change of its large calm front of snow.   5
And underneath the Mount, a Flower I know,
He cannot have perceived, that changes ever
At his approach; and, in the lost endeavour
To live his life, has parted, one by one,
With all a flower's true graces, for the grace   10
Of being but a foolish mimic sun,
With ray-like florets round a disk-like face.
Men nobly call by many a name the Mount
As over many a land of theirs its large
Calm front of snow like a triumphal targe   15
Is reared, and still with old names, fresh names vie,
Each to its proper praise and own account:
Men call the Flower the Sunflower, sportively.

II.

Oh, Angel of the East, one, one gold look
Across the waters to this twilight nook,   20
—The far sad waters, Angel, to this nook!

III.

Dear Pilgrim, art thou for the East indeed?
Go!—saying ever as thou dost proceed,
That I, French Rudel, choose for my device
A sunflower outspread like a sacrifice   25
Before its idol. See! These inexpert
And hurried fingers could not fail to hurt
The woven picture; 't is a woman's skill
Indeed; but nothing baffled me, so, ill

5 *1842* calm steadfast front of snow.   6 *1842* | A Flower I know,   8 *1842*
approach,   15 *1842* Calm steadfast front like   16 *1842-63* fresh ones vie,
26 *1842* idol:

   7 *He* : the Sun.
   12 *With ray-like florets* : OED defines 'floret' as 'One of the little flowers that go to make
up a composite flower.' In the margin of the first proof Browning jotted a doodle (rather
than an illustration) of a sunflower.
   19 *Angel of the East* : the Lady.
   22 *Dear Pilgrim* : there is no hint of his identity, but cf. Bertrand d'Allamanon (see Intro-
duction).

Or well, the work is finished. Say, men feed   30
On songs I sing, and therefore bask the bees
On my flower's breast as on a platform broad:
But, as the flower's concern is not for these
But solely for the sun, so men applaud
In vain this Rudel, he not looking here   35
But to the East—the East! Go, say this, Pilgrim dear!

32 *1842* On the flower's

CRISTINA

THE remarkable assertion by Thomas Powell that this poem represents the meditations of a young man who had fallen in love with Queen Victoria seems to have led admirers of Browning to ask who 'Cristina' was, since we find Furnivall stating that 'The queen intended was Cristina of Spain: the young man was or went mad.'[1] Berdoe gives a similar account: 'Maria Christina of Naples is the lady of the poem. She was born in 1806, and in 1829 became the fourth wife of Ferdinand VII ... of Spain. She became Regent of Spain on the death of her husband, in 1833. Her daughter was Queen Isabella II. She was the dissolute mother of a still more dissolute daughter.'[2] Berdoe goes on to quote Lord Malmesbury's *Memoirs of an Ex-Minister*, where we read that Cristina 'was said at the time to be the cause of more than one inflammable victim languishing in prison for having too openly admired this royal coquette'.[3] One of her contemporaries described her eyes as 'thirsting for pleasure'.[4]

There were so many rumours about her behaviour that Pettigrew's suggestion that the poem may have been written in 1840, since in that year 'her secret marriage to one Muñoz was revealed', cannot be conclusive; but it is probable, in any case, that 'Cristina' was written about that time.

In *1842* this followed 'Rudel and the Lady of Tripoli' as the second of the 'Queen-Worship' poems. In *1849* the joint-title disappeared.

In *Selections from the Poetical Works of Robert Browning*, made by the poet himself in 1872, this poem is printed as thirty-two lines, each stanza containing four lines of eight trochaic feet. In *A History of English Prosody*, iii (2nd ed., 1923), 223-4, George Saintsbury stated, somewhat misleadingly, that 'the poet was in two minds about his metre'. Saintsbury preferred the version in short lines.

1848 Dramatic Romances and Lyrics; 1863 Lyrics; 1868– Dramatic Lyrics.

---

[1] p. 114 in the miscellaneous volume of *Browning Society Papers* published by the Society in 1881: cf. p. 158.
[2] p. 120.
[3] 3rd ed. (2 vols., 1884), i. 30.
[4] Edmund B. d'Auvergne, *A Queen at Bay* (1910), p. 219.

CRISTINA.

I.

She should never have looked at me
   If she meant I should not love her!
There are plenty . . . men, you call such,
   I suppose . . . she may discover
All her soul to, if she pleases,   5
   And yet leave much as she found them:
But I'm not so, and she knew it
   When she fixed me, glancing round them.

II.

What? To fix me thus meant nothing?
   But I can't tell (there's my weakness)   10
What her look said!—no vile cant, sure,
   About "need to strew the bleakness
"Of some lone shore with its pearl-seed,
   "That the sea feels"—no "strange yearning
"That such souls have, most to lavish   15
   "Where there's chance of least returning."

III.

Oh, we're sunk enough here, God knows!
   But not quite so sunk that moments,
Sure tho' seldom, are denied us,
   When the spirit's true endowments   20
Stand out plainly from its false ones,
   And apprise it if pursuing

---

title *1842* QUEEN-WORSHIP. II.—CRISTINA.   1 *1842* should not have
2 *1842* her: 3 *1842* There's plenty   6 *1842* them.   10 *1842,1849*
tell . . . . weakness . .   11 *1842* said: 21 *1842* Stand plain out from

   4 *discover*: reveal.

   8 *fixed me*: gazed fixedly at me.

   11 *no vile cant*: cf. the banal conceptions of the poetaster Eglamor, in *Sordello*, ii. 4 ff., ii.
177 ff., and vi. 1 ff.

   17 *sunk*: 'Degraded or reduced in status or value': OED, 'Sunk', *ppl. a.* 2b.

   22 *if*: whether it is.

Or the right way or the wrong way,
   To its triumph or undoing.

IV.

There are flashes struck from midnights,   25
   There are fire-flames noondays kindle,
Whereby piled-up honours perish,
   Whereby swollen ambitions dwindle,
While just this or that poor impulse,
   Which for once had play unstifled,   30
Seems the sole work of a life-time
   That away the rest have trifled.

V.

Doubt you if, in some such moment,
   As she fixed me, she felt clearly,
Ages past the soul existed,   35
   Here an age 't is resting merely,
And hence fleets again for ages,
   While the true end, sole and single,
It stops here for is, this love-way,
   With some other soul to mingle?   40

VI.

Else it loses what it lived for,
   And eternally must lose it;
Better ends may be in prospect,
   Deeper blisses (if you choose it),

---

23 *1842* | The right   28 *1842-65* Whereby swoln ambitions   29 *1842*
While this   32 *1842* | Away the   37 *1842* | Hence, fleets   *1842,1849* ages:
38 *1842* And the   44 *1842,1849* if . . . . it,   .

26 *fire-flames*: as in Coleridge, 'A Day Dream', 26.

30 *unstifled*: OED cites Edward Young, *Night Thoughts*, ii. 121, as the only example before this.

32 *the rest*: the other impulses, which are in reality less important.

39 *love-way*: this compound appears to be Browning's coinage.

40 *With some other soul to mingle*: cf. Donne, 'To Sir Henry Wotton', 1: 'Sir, more than kisses, letters mingle Soules'. As W. Milgate points out (*The Satires . . . of John Donne*, 1967, p. 226), the notion of souls mingling may be traced back to an epigram in the Greek Anthology attributed to Plato.

But this life's end and this love-bliss   45
    Have been lost here. Doubt you whether
This she felt as, looking at me,
    Mine and her souls rushed together?

VII.

Oh, observe! Of course, next moment,
    The world's honours, in derision,   50
Trampled out the light for ever:
    Never fear but there's provision
Of the devil's to quench knowledge
    Lest we walk the earth in rapture!
—Making those who catch God's secret   55
    Just so much more prize their capture!

VIII.

Such am I: the secret's mine now!
    She has lost me, I have gained her;
Her soul's mine: and thus, grown perfect,
    I shall pass my life's remainder.   60
Life will just hold out the proving
    Both our powers, alone and blended:
And then, come the next life quickly!
    This world's use will have been ended.

---

48 *1863,1865* together.   55 *1842* catch the secret   56 *1842–68* capture.
58 *1842,1849* her!   60 *1842,1849* remainder,   61 *1842* That just holds out
62 *1842* | Our powers   *63 [reading of *1849–68*] *1842,1888,1889* come next
1842 quickly,   64 *1842* This life will have been ended!

52 *provision:* i.e. the devil has taken precautions.
59 *grown perfect:* a phrase sometimes used in religious writings.
61 *will just hold out:* will offer no more than.

JOHANNES AGRICOLA IN MEDITATION

LIKE the following poem, this was first published in the *Monthly Reposi-tory* for January 1836, with the signature 'Z.'[1] Its title was 'Johannes Agricola', and it had the following epigraph:

'ANTINOMIANS, so denominated for rejecting the Law as a thing of no use under the Gospel dispensation: they say, that good works do not further, nor evil works hinder salvation; that the child of God cannot sin, that God never chas-tiseth him, that murder, drunkenness, &c. are sins in the wicked but not in him, that the child of grace being once assured of salvation, afterwards never doubteth . . . . . . that God doth not love any man for his holiness, that sanctification is no evidence of justification, &c. Pontanus, in his Catalogue of Heresies, says John Agricola was the author of this sect, A.D. 1535.'—*Dictionary of all Religions*, 1704.[2]

In *1842* the two poems are headed 'Madhouse Cells', I and II, without individual titles, and fill the two columns of p. 13. In *1849* the titles are 'I.—Madhouse Cell. / Johannes Agricola in Meditation' and 'II.—Madhouse Cell. / Porphyria's Lover'. From *1863* the poems were separated.

The two poems must have been written by about the end of 1835. Anne Ritchie states that 'Porphyria's Lover' was written in Russia in 1834.[3] Unfortunately her book is highly unreliable, as the statement on the pre-vious page that Browning 'went to Italy when he was twenty years of age' makes clear. Griffin and Minchin seem to claim that both poems were written in St Petersburg.[4] Since Browning's 'total stay in Russia could not have been much more than two weeks',[5] and since they give no authority for the assertion, this seems unlikely, though Browning was capable of

[1] pp. 45-6.
[2] The full title of the book, which is commonly ascribed to Defoe, reads: *Dictionarium Sacrum seu Religiosum. / A Dictionary of All Religions, Ancient and Modern.* A copy inscribed 'Robert Browning' is listed by Kelley and Coley as A 1371. It is of interest that Browning will have found virtually the same entry (with the same date, '1535') in another book in his father's library, *The Great Historical . . . Dictionary . . . Revis'd, Corrected and Enlarg'd* by Jeremy Collier, vol. i (2nd ed., 1701): Kelley and Coley, A 685. Browning told Furnivall that he had 'read it right through when [he] was a boy': *Trumpeter*, p. 101. His quotation omits adultery, which is mentioned between murder and drunkenness in both the *Dictionarium* and in Collier.
[3] *Records of Tennyson, Ruskin and Browning* (2nd ed., 1893), p. 221.
[4] Their wording may be ambiguous, however: 'Browning . . . speaks of having shown Fox other poems—probably *Johannes Agricola* and *Porphyria's Lover*, written in St. Peters-burg, and both first printed in the *Repository* of 1836' (p. 73).
[5] Maynard, p. 420 n. 246.

very rapid composition. Perhaps he made a definite statement on the matter in his old age. It is clear that the second of the two poems must have been written as a companion to the first; but we do not know for certain which was written first,[1] or even if they were written at the same time. The unusual verse form (stanzas of five lines rhyming *ababb*) may have caught Browning's eye in Tennyson's *Poems* of 1832 ('1833'): we notice that 'aloof' and 'reproof' are the rhyme-words of the first and third lines of the second poem in the volume.[2]

DeVane believes that 'Johannes Agricola' may have been 'an offshoot of Browning's studies for *Paracelsus*' (in which case it could not have been written before the winter of 1834). That is very possible, but his argument on the matter is seriously confused.[3] Pettigrew and Collins are misled by DeVane and oddly use the allegation that Browning 'changed the date in his quotation from 1538 to 1535', without explanation, to support 1835 as the date of composition.

1849 Dramatic Romances and Lyrics; 1863 Romances; 1868– Men and Women.

---

[1] Probability seems to favour 'Johannes Agricola', however, since the verse-form is more freely used in 'Porphyria's Lover'. 'Porphyria' is printed first in the *Monthly Repository*, but that may not have been Browning's decision.

[2] 'To —', beginning 'All good things have not kept aloof. Tennyson did not republish the poem in full until 1872, when he placed it among his 'Juvenilia' and provided a different first line. See *The Poems*, ed. Christopher Ricks (1969), p. 350. In 1842 Browning deplored the fact that Tennyson had omitted several of his earlier poems from the two-volume edition which he published in that year: *Browning and Domett*, p. 41.

[3] First, DeVane claims that 'Browning has slightly garbled the text of the *Dictionary*... The date actually ascribed by Potanus [*sic*] in his *Catalogus praecipuorum ... haereticorum* is 1538.' Browning is not quoting from Pontanus (Ioannes Pontanus of Frankfurt an der Oder), however, but from the *Dictionary of All Religions*.

Secondly, DeVane states that Browning encountered Agricola during his work for *Paracelsus*, in a 'section' added to Melchior Adam's *Vitæ Germanorum Medicorum* giving the lives of lawyers. This is wrong, as is the date DeVane assigns to the *Vitæ*. It is true, as has been shown in an article by Ian Jack in BIS 15 (1987), that Agricola is the subject of an entry in another compendium by Melchior Adam, *Vitæ Germanorum Theologorum*, and that in it his association with a sect called the 'Antinomi' is dated to the year 1538; but there is no evidence that Browning knew this book, and the strongest possible evidence that he knew the *Dictionary of All Religions* and *The Great Historical ... Dictionary*.

JOHANNES AGRICOLA IN MEDITATION.

THERE's heaven above, and night by night
   I look right through its gorgeous roof;
No suns and moons though e'er so bright
   Avail to stop me; splendour-proof
   I keep the broods of stars aloof: 5
For I intend to get to God,
   For 't is to God I speed so fast,
For in God's breast, my own abode,
   Those shoals of dazzling glory, passed,
   I lay my spirit down at last.   10
I lie where I have always lain,
   God smiles as he has always smiled;
Ere suns and moons could wax and wane,
   Ere stars were thundergirt, or piled
   The heavens, God thought on me his child;   15
Ordained a life for me, arrayed
   Its circumstances every one
To the minutest; ay, God said
   This head this hand should rest upon
   Thus, ere he fashioned star or sun.   20
And having thus created me,
   Thus rooted me, he bade me grow,
Guiltless for ever, like a tree

title *1836* JOHANNES AGRICOLA. *1842* MADHOUSE CELLS. I. *1849* I.–MADHOUSE
CELL. JOHANNES AGRICOLA IN MEDITATION.   1 *1836* above:
7 *1836* fast!   9 *1836–49* glory past,   15 *1836,1842* child,   20 *1836*
sun!

   2 *its gorgeous roof* : cf. Shelley, *Alastor*, 96: 'the varying roof of heaven'.

   4 *splendour-proof* : the only other compound in OED is from Shelley, *Epipsychidion*, 81:
'The splendour-winged stars'.

   5 *aloof* : cf. Richard Corbett, 'Iter Boreale', 269: 'Wee care not for those glorious Lamps
aloofe', referring to the stars.

   13 *Ere suns and moons could wax and wane* : cf. Cowper, *Expostulation*, 324–5: 'States thrive
or wither, as moons wax and wane, / Ev'n as his will and his decrees ordain'.

   14 *thundergirt* : there is no other example of this compound in OED.

That buds and blooms, nor seeks to know
   The law by which it prospers so: 25
But sure that thought and word and deed
   All go to swell his love for me,
Me, made because that love had need
   Of something irreversibly
   Pledged solely its content to be.   30
Yes, yes, a tree which must ascend,
   No poison-gourd foredoomed to stoop!
I have God's warrant, could I blend
   All hideous sins, as in a cup,
   To drink the mingled venoms up,   35
Secure my nature will convert
   The draught to blossoming gladness fast:
While sweet dews turn to the gourd's hurt,
   And bloat, and while they bloat it, blast,
   As from the first its lot was cast.   40
For as I lie, smiled on, full-fed
   By unexhausted power to bless,
I gaze below on hell's fierce bed,
   And those its waves of flame oppress,
   Swarming in ghastly wretchedness;   45
Whose life on earth aspired to be
   One altar-smoke, so pure!—to win
If not love like God's love for me,
   At least to keep his anger in;
   And all their striving turned to sin.   50
Priest, doctor, hermit, monk grown white
   With prayer, the broken-hearted nun,

---

25 *1836,1842* A law   29 *1836-68* something irrevocably   32 *1836* stoop:
*35 [reading of *1836-63*] *1865-89* up;   37 *1842-65* fast,   42 *1836* With
unexhausted blessedness,—   45 *1836,1842* wretchedness,   46 *1836* Whose
like on   48 *1836-63* love to me,   49 *1836* in ... *1842,1849* in,
50 *1836-49* sin!   52 *1836* prayer:

   32 *poison-gourd*: not in OED.
   35 *up,*: the semicolon substituted for the comma from *1865* obscures the syntax.

The martyr, the wan acolyte,
   The incense-swinging child,—undone
   Before God fashioned star or sun!   55
God, whom I praise; how could I praise,
   If such as I might understand,
Make out and reckon on his ways,
   And bargain for his love, and stand,
   Paying a price, at his right hand?   60

<hr>

53 *1836* wan accolyte,   author's signature [*1836* only] Z.

   53 *acolyte* : 'One of the lowest order in the Romish church, whose office is to prepare the elements for the offices, to light the church, &c.': Johnson.

PORPHYRIA'S LOVER

ON the question of date, and the publishing history of this poem, see the introduction to 'Johannes Agricola in Meditation'.

In an important essay, 'Browning and the Dramatic Monologue', Michael Mason has pointed out that one source of 'Porphyria's Lover' is a poem by B. W. Procter ('Barry Cornwall'), *Marcian Colonna*.[1] Having murdered his mistress, Colonna sat beside her body 'as a nurse might do', 'And saw, and felt her sweet forgiving smile'. We hear that 'She died, and spoke no word', that 'Death and Fate / Had done what might be then', and that 'No bitterness, nor hate, nor dread was there'. *Marcian Colonna* ends with intimations of mortality absent from 'Porphyria's Lover': we hear that the girl's mouth 'had fallen low', and that she 'Lay changed to clay, and perish'd'.

Browning's more important source, as Mason pointed out, was a passage in *Blackwood's Magazine* acknowledged by Procter. 'Extracts from Gosschen's Diary' purports to be transcribed from a manuscript written by a German priest who had ministered to a young man condemned to death for the murder of his mistress. Here is an extract:

Do you think there was no pleasure in murdering her? I grasped her by that radiant, golden hair,—I bared those snow-white breasts,—I dragged her sweet body towards me, and, as God is my witness, I stabbed, and stabbed her with this very dagger, ten, twenty, forty times, through and through her heart. She never so much as gave one shriek, for she was dead in a moment,—but she would not have shrieked had she endured pang after pang, for she saw my face of wrath turned upon her,—she knew that my wrath was just, and that I did right to murder her who would have forsaken her lover in his insanity.

I laid her down upon a bank of flowers,—that were soon stained with her blood. I saw the dim blue eyes beneath the half-closed lids,—that face so changeful in its living beauty was now fixed as ice, and the balmy breath came from her sweet lips no more. My joy, my happiness, was perfect.[2]

While Browning owes relatively little to John Wilson (whom we now know to have been the writer of the 'Diary'), what he does owe is

---

[1] Mason's essay appeared in Isobel Armstrong (ed.), *Robert Browning* (Writers and their Background, 1974). The relevant passage begins on p. 255. Browning had known Procter for some time, and was to dedicate *Colombe's Birthday* to him. Our quotations are from section xvi of the poem.

[2] *Blackwood's Magazine*, August 1818, p. 597b.

important. Wilson's protagonist is, and knows himself to be, insane. 'Who else loved her so well as to shed her innocent blood?', he asks.[1] He has been Maria's lover or 'husband', it is not clear which.[2] He believes that he has been 'foredoomed' to sin and Hell (a direct contrast with 'Johannes Agricola'). Speaking to the priest, he says: 'well did I know that death cannot so change the heart that once had life, as to obliterate from THINE [the dead girl's] the merciful love of me!' He does not desire the forgiveness of God.

The priest's statement that there was in the murderer 'a strange and fearful mixture of good and evil' makes it clear that he was the sort of man who would have interested Browning, who was to confess to Julia Wedgwood that he did 'unduly like the study of morbid cases of the soul'.[3]

The poem may be compared with 'The Sisters', a monologue by a female murderer in Tennyson's *Poems* of 1832. It will be noticed that the five-line stanza is more freely used in 'Porphyria's Lover' than in 'Johannes Agricola'.

1849 Dramatic Romances and Lyrics; 1863 Romances; 1868– Dramatic Romances.

PORPHYRIA'S LOVER.

THE rain set early in to-night,
　　The sullen wind was soon awake,
It tore the elm-tops down for spite,
　　And did its worst to vex the lake:
　　I listened with heart fit to break,　　　　　　　　5
When glided in Porphyria; straight
　　She shut the cold out and the storm,
And kneeled and made the cheerless grate
　　Blaze up, and all the cottage warm;
　　Which done, she rose, and from her form　　　10

title *1836* PORPHYRIA. *1842* MADHOUSE CELLS. II. *1849* II.–MADHOUSE CELL. PORPHYRIA'S LOVER. 1 *1836* to-night: 4 *1842–68* lake, *5 (reading of *1836,1842*) *1849* break; *1863–89* break.

4 *to vex the lake*: cf. Shelley, *The Revolt of Islam*, 2888–9: 'some calm wave / Vexed into whirlpools'.

[1] p. 597a, followed by other quotations from pp. 596–8.
[2] See pp. 597b and 598a. 　　　　　　　　　　[3] *Wedgwood*, p. 158.

Withdrew the dripping cloak and shawl,
   And laid her soiled gloves by, untied
Her hat and let the damp hair fall,
   And, last, she sat down by my side
   And called me. When no voice replied,   15
She put my arm about her waist,
   And made her smooth white shoulder bare,
And all her yellow hair displaced,
   And, stooping, made my cheek lie there,
   And spread, o'er all, her yellow hair,   20
Murmuring how she loved me—she
   Too weak, for all her heart's endeavour,
To set its struggling passion free
   From pride, and vainer ties dissever,
   And give herself to me for ever.   25
But passion sometimes would prevail,
   Nor could to-night's gay feast restrain
A sudden thought of one so pale
   For love of her, and all in vain:
   So, she was come through wind and rain.   30
Be sure I looked up at her eyes
   Happy and proud; at last I knew
Porphyria worshipped me; surprise
   Made my heart swell, and still it grew
   While I debated what to do.   35
That moment she was mine, mine, fair,
   Perfectly pure and good: I found
A thing to do, and all her hair
   In one long yellow string I wound
   Three times her little throat around,   40
And strangled her. No pain felt she;
   I am quite sure she felt no pain.
As a shut bud that holds a bee,
   I warily oped her lids: again
   Laughed the blue eyes without a stain.   45

12 *1836* by;   25 *1836–49* ever: 26 *1836* prevail;   30 *1836,1842* And
she   32 *1836–49* Proud, very proud;

And I untightened next the tress
    About her neck; her cheek once more
Blushed bright beneath my burning kiss:
    I propped her head up as before,
    Only, this time my shoulder bore   50
Her head, which droops upon it still:
    The smiling rosy little head,
So glad it has its utmost will,
    That all it scorned at once is fled,
    And I, its love, am gained instead!   55
Porphyria's love: she guessed not how
    Her darling one wish would be heard.
And thus we sit together now,
    And all night long we have not stirred,
    And yet God has not said a word!   60

50 *1836-65 my*   52 *1836* head!   53 *1836* will;   55 *1836* instead,
58 *1836* now: author's signature [*1836* only] Z.

46 *untightened* : this is the only use of the word known to OED, which, however, cites its
occurrence in *The New and Complete Dictionary* of John Ash, 1775.

THROUGH THE METIDJA TO
ABD-EL-KADR

IN *Dramatic Lyrics* the date '1842' is part of the title, so drawing attention to the contemporary reference of the poem. It disappeared after *1868*.

The Metija, near Algiers, is an alluvial plain which is a feature of the generally mountainous coastal region of Algeria. The gifted Abd al-Qādir (Servant of the Mighty One), proclaimed emir at Mascara in 1832, 're-united under his sway the tribes that had hitherto been divided, and infused a unique spirit into their resistance. For fifteen years he held the French in check, treating on terms of equality with their government.'[1] As Berdoe pointed out, the poem is inspired by an incident in the war when the Duc d'Aumale fell on the emir's camp and took several thousand prisoners, Abd-el-Kadr himself escaping with difficulty. Although the speaker would not be a fit inmate for a 'Madhouse Cell', the poem presents us—as Mrs Orr observed[2]—with the 'mystic fancies' which pass through the mind of a devout Muslim. It was no doubt written in June 1842 (when the newspapers contained numerous accounts of the fighting in Algeria) or soon afterwards. Browning remained keenly interested in Abd-el-Kadr. When, early in 1848, he surrendered to the French 'under an express promise that he should be sent either to Alexandria or to St. Jean d'Acre', but was kept as a prisoner in France, EBB wrote to Mrs Martin: 'my husband is furious about the treatment of Abd-el-Kader, so I hear a good deal about him'.[3]

Domett wrote that the poem 'was composed on horseback', adding: 'Browning, who in young days looked delicate in health (nothing like so strong and sturdy as he looks now) had been ordered to take "horse-exercise," so was riding every day.'[4] Like 'How they brought the Good News', this poem is predominantly anapaestic. The first line is repeated as the first, fourth, and eighth line of each stanza, so occurring fifteen times. There is only one rhyme-sound throughout, which occurs (medial rhymes included) sixty-four times. Of the thirteen monosyllabic words under 'IDE' in the *Dictionary of Rhymes* at the end of the second volume of

[1] *Encyclopædia Britannica*, i. 651.
[2] *Handbook*, p. 304.
[3] *Letters of EBB* i. 388.
[4] *Diary*, p. 96.

The Art of English Poetry, by Edward Bysshe (8th ed., 2 vols., 1737), only
'bide' is absent.[1]

1849 Dramatic Romances and Lyrics; 1863 Lyrics; 1868– Dramatic Lyrics.

THROUGH THE METIDJA TO ABD-EL-KADR.

I.

As I ride, as I ride,
With a full heart for my guide,
So its tide rocks my side,
As I ride, as I ride,
That, as I were double-eyed,   5
He, in whom our Tribes confide,
Is descried, ways untried
As I ride, as I ride.

II.

As I ride, as I ride
To our Chief and his Allied,   10
Who dares chide my heart's pride
As I ride, as I ride?
Or are witnesses denied—
Through the desert waste and wide
Do I glide unespied   15
As I ride, as I ride?

title *1842-68* .... KADR. 1842.

  3 *tide*: cf. Cowper, 'Retirement', 453: 'the tide of life'.

  5 *as I were double-eyed*: as if I had 'the second sight', or more than usual spiritual vision.
OED has no example of the compound in this sense.

  6 *He*: Allah, whose prophet is Mohammed.

  [1] In *A History of English Prosody*, iii (2nd ed., 1923), 223, George Saintsbury describes the
poem as 'an almost impudent but thoroughly successful experiment in monorhyme',
adding: 'nothing but the clang of the *i* will do'. He greatly prefers this poem to 'How they
brought the Good News', and observes that 'The thing is virtually and schematically in
single-foot lines . . .'.

III.

As I ride, as I ride,
When an inner voice has cried,
· The sands slide, nor abide
(As I ride, as I ride)
O'er each visioned homicide
That came vaunting (has he lied?)
To reside—where he died,
As I ride, as I ride.

IV.

As I ride, as I ride,   25
Ne'er has spur my swift horse plied,
Yet his hide, streaked and pied,
As I ride, as I ride,
Shows where sweat has sprung and dried,
—Zebra-footed, ostrich-thighed—   30
How has vied stride with stride
As I ride, as I ride!

V.

As I ride, as I ride,
Could I loose what Fate has tied,
Ere I pried, she should hide   35
(As I ride, as I ride)
All that's meant me—satisfied

---

23 *1842P²* To ⟨ab⟩[rc]side *1842P¹,1842* To abide—where   36 *1842,1849* As . . . .
ride,

---

21 *visioned homicide*: cf. Scott, *Cadyow Castle*, l. 114, where a horseman is described as
riding headlong 'As one some vision'd sight that saw'. Browning's speaker is thinking of the
French killers who come to fight his leader.
  23 *To reside*: it is curious that the correction from 'abide' in the second set of proofs went
unregarded in *1842*. Browning wished to avoid the repetition from 19.
  30 *Zebra-footed, ostrich-thighed*: compounds no doubt invented by Browning.
  34 *what Fate has tied*: presumably the future.
  37 *All that's meant me*: all that I am.

When the Prophet and the Bride
Stop veins I'd have subside
As I ride, as I ride!   40

---

38 *the Bride*: as a young man Muhammad married Khadija, a widow fifteen years older
than himself, but the reference here is probably to a member of his harem, Ayesha, whom
he married after the Flight to Yathrib, when she was very young. He is said to have died in
her arms.

39 *stop veins*: cf. l. 2, above.

THE PIED PIPER OF HAMELIN

THIS poem was added to the *Dramatic Lyrics* at the last moment, as is shown by its absence from the first of the two surviving proofs of the pamphlet.[1] An ambiguous sentence in *A Browning Handbook* (p. 128) led Pettigrew and Collins to suppose that DeVane believed there to be a holograph manuscript of the poem: there is none, so far as we are aware, and such was not DeVane's meaning. DeVane does err, however, in stating that the disappearance of two lines between *1842* and *1849* is the only considerable change in the text: no lines 'disappeared', while 28–9 and 48–51 were added in *1849*.

Browning explained the origin of the poem to Furnivall in 1881. 'The "W.M. the younger" was poor William Macready's eldest son—dead, a few years ago. He had a talent for drawing, and asked me to give him some little thing to illustrate; so, I made a bit of a poem out of an old account of the death of the Pope's legate at the Council of Trent—which he made such clever drawings for, that I tried a more picturesque subject, the Piper. I still possess the half dozen of the designs he gave me.'[2] The first draft of the earlier poem, dated February 1841, survives in the Browning family's copy of *The Wonders of the Little World*, by Nathaniel Wanley.[3] In an undated letter, perhaps written in the spring of that year, the boy told Browning that he 'liked exceedingly the Cardinal and the dog', hoped that the poet would be pleased with his drawings, and told him that he could not 'go to school because my cough is so bad'.[4] Willie's second letter is dated 18 May 1842 and reports that he has 'finished the rest of the illustration of the Pied Piper': he hopes that Browning will like what he has done, but is 'sorry to say' that he does not think the new drawings 'so good as the Council chamber, or the other one that I did'.

It appears likely that Browning wrote 'The Pied Piper' in April 1842. He did not intend to publish it, but when Moxon found that there was

---

[1] See p. 175 above.

[2] *Trumpeter*, p. 27. The drawings, four for the poem about the Cardinal, and three for 'The Pied Piper', are now at Baylor.

[3] 'The Cardinal and the Dog' was published by Browning at the end of his life, in *Asolando* (1889, '1890').

[4] The boy's two letters were published in the TLS for 15 September 1921 (p. 596), by C. Elkin Mathews, who judged from the 'boyish text hand of the writer' that the first letter was 'written a year or so earlier than the other'. We are told that Browning 'carefully treasured the boy's letters'.

insufficient material for this third of the *Bells* Browning sent him the poem, encouraged by the admiration of his sister Sarianna and of Alfred Domett.[1]

The question of sources has often been discussed. Furnivall initially stated that the story 'is taken from one of the famous *Familiar Letters* of James Howell,—Section VI. Letter XLVII'.[2] He obviously went on to consult Browning, however, for among the 'Additions' to his Bibliography, having given a long quotation from Verstegan's *Restitution of Decayed Intelligence* (see below), he states categorically that 'the poet had never seen V. before his poem was written. He got the story from North Wanley's *Wonders of the Little World* (fol. 1678) and the authorities there cited.'[3] The error 'North' for 'Nath.' suggests that Furnivall misread a letter from Browning. The copy of Wanley survives, in the possession of Dr Philip Kelley, and 'Pied Piper 598' is one of the numerous jottings which Browning made by way of index. Here is the passage, from Book VI, Chap. 19. 28:

At *Hammel*, a Town in the Dutchy of *Brunswick*, in the year of Christ 1284. upon the 26. day of *June*, the Town being grievously troubled with Rats and Mice, there came to them a Piper, who promised upon a certain rate to free them from them all; it was agreed, he went from street to street, and playing upon his Pipe, drew after him out of the Town all that kind of Vermine, and then demanding his wages was denied it. Whereupon he began another tune, and there followed him one hundred and thirty Boys to a Hill called *Koppen*, situate on the North by the Road, where they perished, and were never seen after. This Piper was called the pyed Piper, because his cloaths were of several colours. This story is writ and religiously kept by them in their Annals at *Hammel*, read in their Books, and painted in their Windows, and in their Churches, of which I am a witness by my own sight. Their elder Magistrates, for the confirmation of the truth of this, are wont to write in conjunction in their publick Books, such a year of Christ, and such a year of the Transmigration of the children, &c. It's also observed in the memory of it, that in the street he passed out of, no Piper be admitted to this day. The street is called *Burgelosestrasse*; if a Bride be in that street, till she is gone out of it there is no dancing to be suffered.[4]

---

[1] *Life*, p. 122. Mr Michael Meredith draws our attention to an unpublished letter from Sarianna to Mrs Miller Morrison, dated 29 August 1899: 'is there any of his poems really popular?', she asks, 'except, perhaps, the Pied Piper—for which he may thank me and Alfred Domett, as he himself did not think it worth publishing'. The letter is at the Humanities Research Center in Texas.

[2] *A Bibliography of Robert Browning* (2nd ed., 1881), p. 113.

[3] Ibid. (in a later section dated 31 December), pp. 158-9.

[4] We quote from the folio edition, which Browning owned. For 'the authorities there cited' see below.

To explain why we agree with others who have examined the matter that Browning's most important source was in fact Verstegan, in spite of his own denial, it will be best to quote the relevant passage:

And now hath one digression drawn on another, for beeing by reason of speaking of these Saxons of *Transiluania*, put in mynd of a most true & maruelous strange accident that hapned in *Saxonie* not many ages past, I cannot omit for the strangenes thereof briefly heer by the way to set it down. There came into the town of *Hamel* in the countrey of *Brunswyc* an od kynd of compagnion, who for the fantastical cote which hee wore beeing wrought with sundry colours, was called the pyed pyper; for a pyper hee was, besydes his other qualities. This fellow forsooth offred the townsmen for a certain somme of mony to rid the town of all the rattes that were in it (for at that tyme the burgers were with that vermin greatly annoyed) The accord in fyne beeing made; the pyed pyper with a shril pype went pyping through the streets, and foorthwith the rattes came all running out of the howses in great numbers after him; all which hee led vnto the riuer of *Weaser* and therein drowned them. This donne, and no one rat more perceaued to bee left in the town; he afterward came to demaund his reward according to his bargain, but beeing told that the bargain was not made with him in good earnest, to wit, with an opinion that euer hee could bee able to do such a feat: they cared not what they accorded vnto, when they imagyned it could neuer bee deserued, and so neuer to bee demaunded: but neuerthelesse seeing hee had donne such an vnlykely thing in deed, they were content to giue him a good reward; & so offred him far lesse then hee lookt for: but hee therewith discontented, said he would haue his ful recompence according to his bargain, but they vtterly denying to giue it him, hee threatened them with reuenge; they bad him do his wurst, wherevpon he betakes him again to his pype, & going through the streets as before, was followed of a number of boyes out at one of the gates of the citie, and coming to a litle hil, there opened in the syde thereof a wyde hole, into the which himself and all the children beeing in number one hundreth & thirty, did enter; and beeing entred, the hil closed vp again, and became as before. A boy that beeing lame & came somwhat lagging behynd the rest, seeing this that hapned, returned presently back & told what hee had seen; foorthwith began great lamentation among the parents for their children, and men were sent out with all dilligence, both by land & by water to enquyre yf ought could bee heard of them, but with all the enquyrie they could possibly vse, nothing more then is aforesaid could of them bee vnderstood. In memorie whereof it was then ordayned, that from thence-foorth no drum, pype or other instrument, should be sounded in the street leading to the gate through which they passed; nor no osterie to bee there holden. And it was also established, that from that tyme forward in all publyke wrytings that should bee made in that town, after the date therein set down of the yeare of our Lord, the date of the yeare of the going foorth of their children should bee added, the which they haue accordingly euer

since continued. And this great wonder hapned on the 22. day of Iuly, in the yeare
of our Lord one thowsand three hundreth seauentie, and six.

The occasion now why this matter came vnto my remembrance in speaking of
Transiluania, was, for that some do reporte that there are diuers found among the
Saxons in *Transiluania* that haue lyke surnames vnto diuers of the burgers of
Hamel, and wil seem thereby to inferr, that this iugler or pyed pyper, might by
negromancie haue transported them thether, but this carieth litle apparence of
truthe; because it would haue bin almost as great a wonder vnto the Saxons of
Transiluania to haue had so many strange children brought among them, they
knew not how, as it was to those of *Hamel* to lose them: & they could not but
haue kept memorie of so strange a thing, yf in deed any such thing had there
hapned.[1]

The most thorough study of the sources remains an article by Arthur
Dickson published in 1926.[2] Dickson mentions five features common to
Browning and Verstegan which are not to be found in Howell or Wanley:
the date, 22 July 1376; the challenge to the Piper to 'do his worst'; the lame
boy; the statement that no tavern was allowed in the street; and the men-
tion of the belief that the children may have been carried off to Transyl-
vania. We may add that Verstegan and Browning name the river and use
the word 'shrill' to describe the piping.

Dickson also mentions two points common to Browning and Wanley
which are not to be found in Verstegan: the fact that the hill into which
the children disappeared is named (though differently); and the statement
that the story of the Piper is painted in their windows and churches. If
evidence for Browning's knowledge of Wanley were required, this would
serve.

In view of Browning's emphatic (though misleading) reference to
Wanley, Dickson investigated the authorities named by him, with which
Browning seemed to claim acquaintance. They are '*Wier*.[3] *de præstig.
Dæmon. li.* l. *c.* 16. p. 47. *Schot. phys. curios.* l. 3. *c.* 24. *p.* 519', and Howell.
Having investigated several editions of *De Præstigiis Dæmonum*, he found a
full account of the Piper in that published in Basle in 1583. Neither in
this book nor in the *Physica Curiosa* of P. G. Schott (various eds., Herbipoli,
i.e. Würzburg) did he find even one of the points of agreement between

---

[1] Richard Verstegan, *A Restitution of Decayed Intelligence* (Antwerp, 1605). There were
several editions, so that the book is not rare. 'Verstegan' was the alias of Richard Rowlands
(fl. 1565–1620), a recusant antiquary who wrote a number of books: one may consult the
DNB, and A. G. Petti, *The Letters and Despatches*, 1959.

[2] 'Browning's Source for *The Pied Piper of Hamelin*': *Studies in Philology*, 23, no. 3 (July,
1926), 327–36.

[3] Johann Wier, or 'Wicrius'.

Verstegan and Browning. He points out, justly, that Schott's 'Köpffelberg' is closer to Browning's 'Koppelberg' than Wanley's 'hill called Koppen', and concludes: 'It is possible, then—I think, hardly more—that Browning used Schott.'

Dickson lists more than a dozen further versions of the story which he examined. He points out that only two (to which we add a third, below) have the date 22 July 1376, and that one of these (J. Pomarius, *Chronica der Sachsen und Nidersachsen*, Wittenberg, 1588) is one of Verstegan's sources, while the other (P. Heylyn, *Cosmographie*, 5th ed., London, 1677) is the work of an author who acknowledges Verstegan as an authority. Dickson leans toward the possibility that Browning also used or remembered Prosper Mérimée's *Chronique du temps de Charles IX* (Paris, 1829), but the evidence seems to us completely unconvincing.[1]

Dickson mentions other versions which he had been unable to consult, one or two of them 'German authors' referred to by Browning's father.[2] While it is easy to add to this list, only one omitted book seems of any importance: otherwise Occam's razor may be used, and we may safely conclude that while it is perfectly possible that Browning took some detail from a source other than Verstegan, supplemented by Wanley, there is no evidence that he did, and it could not have been an important one.

The book which was unknown to Dickson was *The Great Historical . . . Dictionary*, 2nd ed., 'Revis'd, Corrected and Enlarg'd' by Jeremy Collier (1701), which Browning told Furnivall that he had 'read . . . right through when [he] was a boy', adding that his father gave it to him 'many years after'.[3] We have the best evidence, therefore, that Browning read this version of the story at an early and impressionable age:

HAMELEN, Lat. *Hamila*, a Town of *Lower Saxony* in *Germany*, under the Duke of *Hanouer*. It lies properly in the Dukedom of *Brunswick*, between *Heildesheim* on the East, and *Paderborne* on the West, being 26 Miles S. of *Hamburg*, and 20 S.E. of *Bremen*, and Watered by the River *Weser*. It is famous for the wonderful Accident said to have happened here *July* 22. 1376; for being incredibly troubled with Rats, a Musician (whom they call'd the *Py'd-Piper*) offer'd to destroy 'em for a certain Summ which was agreed upon. Then the Piper tuning his Pipes, all the Rats in the Town danced after him as he cross'd the River, and were drowned. This done, he demanded his Pay, but was denied. Whereupon

---

[1] Little more (in fact) than that Mérimée describes the Piper as tall, swarthy, gaunt ('grand . . . , basané, see'): see Dickson, p. 335.

[2] See pp. 520-1 below.

[3] *Trumpeter*, p. 101. Cf. Kelley and Coley, A 685.

striking up a new Fit of Mirth, all the Children of the Town (Male and Female) were so much charmed therewith, that they followed him to a neighbouring Hill, which opening, swallowed all up but one that lagged behind, and according to some, they were seen again in Transilvania. In memory of this Tragedy, it was Ordered, That in all publick Writings, after the Date of our Saviours Nativity, this of their Childrens being swallowed up, should be added.

We note that this account gives the name as 'Hamelen' (Verstegan has 'Hamel' and Wanley 'Hammel', a detail for which Dickson believed Browning to be indebted to Howell);[1] and that Collier names the river as the 'Weser' (Verstegan has 'Weaser', while there is no river in Wanley).

We can go further back, however, since Griffin and Minchin tell us, no doubt on good authority, that 'The story . . . was familiar to him even before he had learned to read, for it was a favourite with his legend-loving father, who, devoted as he was to children, versified and illustrated the tale with pen and pencil for other small folk than those of his own family.'[2] Whether or not Robert Browning senior 'versified and illustrated the tale' when he first told it to his son we do not know: the important thing is that Browning knew the story from a very early time.

By a fortunate chance three versions of the Pied Piper story by Browning's father survive. The first, which is merely an abandoned beginning, has only sixty-six lines, and ends with the following note: 'I began this not knowing that Robert had written on this subject—Having heard him mention it—I stopped short. I never saw his manuscript till some weeks afterwards. R.B. 2nd March. 1843. To Miss Earles.' We do not know how much later he wrote the two completed versions.

We give these versions in Appendix A. The fragment does not reach the appearance of the Piper. It is notable for the mention of 'proofs of this narration' near the end:

> Yet there are *Schochius**—*Erithius**
> And *Kirkmaleus** lying by us.
>   And 'twere absurd
> Of men so well known, learn'd & pious
>   To doubt the word.

A note explaining the asterisks reads: 'German authors who have written upon this subject.' In the Appendix we tentatively identify them, and

---

[1] Dickson, p. 330. Browning may well have known Howell from an early time. Kelley and Coley, A 1261, is inscribed by EBB and himself, without a date. L. 284 may be indebted to Howell: 'They wrote the story on a column.'

[2] p. 21.

observe that it seems unlikely that Browning's father had read them through.

An obvious difference between his father's telling of the story and his own is that in the former the Mayor and townspeople fear from the beginning that the Piper is a practitioner of black magic, and therefore in league with the Devil. Near the end we hear how the children 'follow'd him with pleasure— / But with a tinge of mirth— / Different from what's seen on earth— / Smiling ghastly—staring wild— / Leaping madly—roaring loud / Each a monster—not a child.'[1] There is an element of the macabre in this version of the story which we do not find in Browning's, but which is latent or patent in many of the older versions. Further, we notice that in one version 'The loveliest children in the place'—these at least who are named—are all girls, 'Maries & Kates ... Sarahs, & Susans—Essies— Bessies!', a fact sufficiently explained when we learn that this was written for girls. There is no mention of the threat to the Piper to do his worst, and no boy (or girl) who is left behind.

1849 Dramatic Romances and Lyrics; 1863 Romances; 1868– Dramatic Romances.

THE PIED PIPER OF HAMELIN;

A CHILD'S STORY.

(WRITTEN FOR, AND INSCRIBED TO, W. M. THE YOUNGER.)

I.

HAMELIN Town's in Brunswick,
　By famous Hanover city;
The river Weser, deep and wide,
Washes its wall on the southern side;
A pleasanter spot you never spied;　　　　　　5

---

dedication [in italics in *1842*] *1842*P² *to*, ⟨*Mr. C.*⟩ [*W.M.*] *the*

　4 *on the southern side*: Hamlen is in the south-west of Hanover, at the confluence of the Weser and the Hamel.

¹ Ll. 266 ff.

But, when begins my ditty,
Almost five hundred years ago,
To see the townsfolk suffer so
From vermin, was a pity.

II.

Rats!   10
They fought the dogs and killed the cats,
   And bit the babies in the cradles,
And ate the cheeses out of the vats,
   And licked the soup from the cooks' own ladles,
Split open the kegs of salted sprats,   15
Made nests inside men's Sunday hats,
And even spoiled the women's chats
     By drowning their speaking
     With shrieking and squeaking
In fifty different sharps and flats.   20

III.

At last the people in a body
    To the Town Hall came flocking:
"'T is clear," cried they, "our Mayor's a noddy;
    "And as for our Corporation—shocking
"To think we buy gowns lined with ermine   25
"For dolts that can't or won't determine
"What's best to rid us of our vermin!
"You hope, because you're old and obese,
"To find in the furry civil robe ease?
"Rouse up, sirs! Give your brains a racking   30
"To find the remedy we're lacking,
"Or, sure as fate, we'll send you packing!"
At this the Mayor and Corporation
Quaked with a mighty consternation.

---

13 *1842* And eat the   14 *1849* the cook's own   23-32 (no quotation marks
in *1842*)   27 *1842* What's like to   28-9 (no equivalent in *1842*)
*34 (reading of *1842-68*,DC,BrU,*1889*) *1888* consternation

IV.

An hour they sat in council,   35
  At length the Mayor broke silence:
"For a guilder I'd my ermine gown sell,
  "I wish I were a mile hence!
"It's easy to bid one rack one's brain—
"I'm sure my poor head aches again,   40
"I've scratched it so, and all in vain.
"Oh for a trap, a trap, a trap!"
Just as he said this, what should hap
At the chamber door but a gentle tap?
"Bless us," cried the Mayor, "what's that?"   45
(With the Corporation as he sat,
Looking little though wondrous fat;
Nor brighter was his eye, nor moister
Than a too-long-opened oyster,
Save when at noon his paunch grew mutinous   50
For a plate of turtle green and glutinous)
"Only a scraping of shoes on the mat?
"Anything like the sound of a rat
"Makes my heart go pit-a-pat!"

V.

"Come in!"—the Mayor cried, looking bigger: 55
And in did come the strangest figure!
His queer long coat from heel to head
Was half of yellow and half of red,
And he himself was tall and thin,
With sharp blue eyes, each like a pin,   60
And light loose hair, yet swarthy skin,
No tuft on cheek nor beard on chin,

---

stanza IV. *1888,1889* v.   37–42 [no quotation marks in *1842*]   *45 [reading of all versions except *1888*] *1888* that?' [no quotation marks in *1842*]   48–51 [no equivalent in *1842*]   52–5 [no quotation marks in *1842*]   53 *1842* Any thing   *55 [reading of *1842–68*,DC,BrU,*1889*] *1888* bigger   58 *1842–63* red;   *61 [reading of *1842–68*,DC,BrU,*1889*] *1888* skin

    37 *guilder*: a gold coin formerly current in the Netherlands and parts of Germany.

But lips where smiles went out and in;
There was no guessing his kith and kin:
And nobody could enough admire   65
The tall man and his quaint attire.
Quoth one: "It's as my great-grandsire,
"Starting up at the Trump of Doom's tone,
"Had walked this way from his painted tomb-stone!"

VI.

He advanced to the council-table: 70
And, "Please your honours," said he, "I'm able,
"By means of a secret charm, to draw
    "All creatures living beneath the sun,
    "That creep or swim or fly or run,
"After me so as you never saw!   75
"And I chiefly use my charm
"On creatures that do people harm,
"The mole and toad and newt and viper;
"And people call me the Pied Piper."
(And here they noticed round his neck   80
    A scarf of red and yellow stripe,
To match with his coat of the self-same cheque;
    And at the scarf's end hung a pipe;
And his fingers, they noticed, were ever straying
As if impatient to be playing   85
Upon this pipe, as low it dangled
Over his vesture so old-fangled.)
"Yet," said he, "poor piper as I am,
"In Tartary I freed the Cham,

---

64 *1842–63* kin!   66 *1842–63* attire: 67–9, 71–9 {no quotation marks in
1842}   88–96 {no quotation marks in *1842*}

   65 *admire*: 'To regard with wonder': Johnson.

   74 *that creep*: cf. Gen. 1: 20 ff.; Schiller, *Wilhelm Tell*, III. i. 12: 'Was da kreucht und
fleucht' (All that creeps and flies).

   82 *cheque*: an old spelling.

   87 *old-fangled*: apparently Browning's coinage, by analogy with 'new-fangled'.

   89 *the Cham*: 'An obsolete form of KHAN formerly commonly applied to the rulers of
the Tartars and Mongols': OED.

"Last June, from his huge swarms of gnats; 90
"I eased in Asia the Nizam
    "Of a monstrous brood of vampyre-bats:
"And as for what your brain bewilders,
    "If I can rid your town of rats
"Will you give me a thousand guilders?" 95
"One? fifty thousand!"—was the exclamation
Of the astonished Mayor and Corporation.

VII.

Into the street the Piper stept,
    Smiling first a little smile,
As if he knew what magic slept 100
    In his quiet pipe the while;
Then, like a musical adept,
To blow the pipe his lips he wrinkled,
And green and blue his sharp eyes twinkled,
Like a candle-flame where salt is sprinkled; 105
And ere three shrill notes the pipe uttered,
You heard as if an army muttered;
And the muttering grew to a grumbling;
And the grumbling grew to a mighty rumbling;
And out of the houses the rats came tumbling. 110
Great rats, small rats, lean rats, brawny rats,
Brown rats, black rats, grey rats, tawny rats,
Grave old plodders, gay young friskers,
    Fathers, mothers, uncles, cousins,
Cocking tails and pricking whiskers, 115
    Families by tens and dozens,

---

97 *1868* Corporation

91 *the Nizam*: 'The hereditary title of the rulers of Hyderabad': OED.

103 *wrinkled*: in Southey's 'The Cataract of Lodore. Described in Rhymes for the Nursery', l. 103 reads: 'And sprinkling and twinkling and wrinkling', and l. 106: 'And grumbling and rumbling and tumbling' (cf. Browning's ll. 108–110). Browning probably knew this poem, and another by Southey, 'God's Judgement on a Wicked Bishop', which has a long epigraph from Coryat's *Crudities* and tells the story of how a cruel bishop was eaten alive by mice or (according to 'Other authors') by rats.

Brothers, sisters, husbands, wives—
Followed the Piper for their lives.
From street to street he piped advancing,
And step for step they followed dancing,   120
Until they came to the river Weser,
    Wherein all plunged and perished!
—Save one who, stout as Julius Cæsar,
Swam across and lived to carry
    (As he, the manuscript he cherished)   125
To Rat-land home his commentary:
Which was, "At the first shrill notes of the pipe,
"I heard a sound as of scraping tripe,
"And putting apples, wondrous ripe,
"Into a cider-press's gripe: 130
"And a moving away of pickle-tub-boards,
"And a leaving ajar of conserve-cupboards,
"And a drawing the corks of train-oil-flasks,
"And a breaking the hoops of butter-casks:
"And it seemed as if a voice   135
    "(Sweeter far than by harp or by psaltery
"Is breathed) called out, 'Oh rats, rejoice!
    "'The world is grown to one vast drysaltery!

---

122 *1842,1849* perished   126 *1842,1849* commentary,   127-45 (no quotation marks in *1842*)   136 *1842* (Sweeter than by harp or by psaltery *1849-65* by harp   137-40 (no single quotation marks in *1849-65*)   138 *1842* grown one

123 *stout as Julius Cæsar*: as Lemprière records, the *Commentaries* on the Gallic wars were 'nearly lost; and when Caesar saved his life in the bay of Alexandria, he was obliged to swim from his ship, with his arms in one hand and his commentaries in the other'. The story is likely to have been familiar to Willie Macready, since selections from Caesar are often read by beginners at Latin.

132 *conserve-cupboards*: cupboards for 'preserves', jam and other dainties made from fruit cooked with sugar.

133 *train-oil-flasks*: train-oil is made by boiling the blubber of whales. It was used for lamps and for other purposes.

136 *by harp or by psaltery*: harp and psaltery (an ancient stringed instrument similar to the lyre) are associated in the Psalms, e.g. Ps. 57: 8.

138 *drysaltery*: a drysalter's wares included oils, sauces, pickles, tinned meats, etc. As Pettigrew and Collins note, this antedates the first occurrence of the word in OED, that in *Dombey and Son* (May 1847). No doubt the word was already in common use.

"'So munch on, crunch on, take your nuncheon,
"'Breakfast, supper, dinner, luncheon!'   140
"And just as a bulky sugar-puncheon,
"All ready staved, like a great sun shone
"Glorious scarce an inch before me,
"Just as methought it said, 'Come, bore me!'
"—I found the Weser rolling o'er me."   145

VIII.

You should have heard the Hamelin people
Ringing the bells till they rocked the steeple.
"Go," cried the Mayor, "and get long poles,
"Poke out the nests and block up the holes!
"Consult with carpenters and builders,   150
"And leave in our town not even a trace
"Of the rats!"—when suddenly, up the face
Of the Piper perked in the market-place,
With a, "First, if you please, my thousand guilders!"

IX.

A thousand guilders! The Mayor looked blue;   155
So did the Corporation too.
For council dinners made rare havoc
With Claret, Moselle, Vin-de-Grave, Hock;

---

141 *1842* as one bulky   142 *1842* Ready staved,   144 {no single quotation
marks in *1849–65*)   147 *1842,1849* steeple;   148–52, 154 {no quotation
marks in *1842*}   154 *1865* guilders!

139 *nuncheon*: 'A piece of victuals eaten between meals': Johnson. Cf. *Hudibras*, I. i. 344:
'They took their Breakfasts or their Nuncheons.' Browning knew Butler's poem well: cf.
Kintner, i. 20 and 546, and one of his notes on *Paracelsus* (our Vol. I, p. 509). Reviewing
Dramatic Lyrics in *The Examiner*, John Forster wrote: 'for the neatness of his rhymes in his
lighter efforts, we think that Butler would have hugged him': *Critical Heritage*, p. 83.
141 *sugar-puncheon*: a puncheon was normally a liquid-measure, varying from 72 to 120
gallons. The word was archaic by 1842.
142 *staved*: casked.
144 *bore*: breach.
153 *perked*: Johnson defines the verb as meaning 'To hold up the head with an affected
briskness.'
158 *Vin-de-Grave*: Graves, a wine from the Bordeaux district.

And half the money would replenish
Their cellar's biggest butt with Rhenish.   160
To pay this sum to a wandering fellow
With a gipsy coat of red and yellow!
"Beside," quoth the Mayr with a knowing wink,
"Our business was done at the river's brink;
"We saw with our eyes the vermin sink,   165
"And what's dead can't come to life, I think.
"So, friend, we're not the folks to shrink
"From the duty of giving you something for drink,
"And a matter of money to put in your poke;
"But as for the guilders, what we spoke   170
"Of them, as you very well know, was in joke.
"Beside, our losses have made us thrifty.
"A thousand guilders! Come, take fifty!"

x.

The Piper's face fell, and he cried
"No trifling! I can't wait, beside!   175
"I've promised to visit by dinnertime
"Bagdat, and accept the prime
"Of the Head-Cook's pottage, all he's rich in,
"For having left, in the Caliph's kitchen,
"Of a nest of scorpions no survivor: 180
"With him I proved no bargain-driver,
"With you, don't think I'll bate a stiver!
"And folks who put me in a passion
"May find me pipe after another fashion."

163–73, 175–84 {no quotation marks in *1842*}   172 *1842,1849* thrifty;
173 *1863* fifty!   184 *1849, 1863* pipe to another
    164 *done*: completed, finished with.
    169 *poke*: 'A pocket; a small bag': Johnson.
    177 *the prime*: 'The best part': Johnson, who quotes Swift, 'To a Lady', 127–30: 'Give no
more to every guest, / Than he's able to digest: / Give him always of the prime; / And but
little at a time.'
    178 *pottage*: 'Any thing boiled or decocted for food': Johnson.
    182 *bate a stiver*: 'To bate: to lessen a demand', Johnson, who defines a stiver as 'A Dutch
coin about the value of a halfpenny.'

XI.

"How?" cried the Mayor, "d'ye think I brook   185
"Being worse treated than a Cook?
"Insulted by a lazy ribald
"With idle pipe and vesture piebald?
"You threaten us, fellow? Do your worst,
"Blow your pipe there till you burst!"   190

XII.

Once more he stept into the street
   And to his lips again
   Laid his long pipe of smooth straight cane;
And ere he blew three notes (such sweet
Soft notes as yet musician's cunning   195
   Never gave the enraptured air)
There was a rustling that seemed like a bustling
Of merry crowds justling at pitching and hustling,
Small feet were pattering, wooden shoes clattering,
Little hands clapping and little tongues chattering,   200
And, like fowls in a farm-yard when barley is scattering,
Out came the children running.
All the little boys and girls,
With rosy cheeks and flaxen curls,
And sparkling eyes and teeth like pearls,   205
Tripping and skipping, ran merrily after
The wonderful music with shouting and laughter.

XIII.

The Mayor was dumb, and the Council stood
As if they were changed into blocks of wood,
Unable to move a step, or cry   210

---

185 *1842-63* I'll brook   191 *1842-63* strcct; *1865,1868* strcct,   196 *1842*
th'enraptured   185-90 {no quotation marks in *1842*}

   198 *justling*: jostling (Johnson gives both spellings).

     pitching and hustling: 'When they hustle, all the halfpence pitched at the mark arc thrown into a hat held by the player who claims the first chance': Joseph Strutt, *The Sports and Pastimes of the People of England*, 1801 (cd. of 1875), III. vii. 15, cited in OED.

To the children merrily skipping by,
—Could only follow with the eye
That joyous crowd at the Piper's back.
But how the Mayor was on the rack,
And the wretched Council's bosoms beat,   215
As the Piper turned from the High Street
To where the Weser rolled its waters
Right in the way of their sons and daughters!
However he turned from South to West,
And to Koppelberg Hill his steps addressed,   220
And after him the children pressed;
Great was the joy in every breast.
"He never can cross that mighty top!
"He's forced to let the piping drop,
"And we shall see our children stop!"   225
When, lo, as they reached the mountain-side,
A wondrous portal opened wide,
As if a cavern was suddenly hollowed;
And the Piper advanced and the children followed,
And when all were in to the very last,   230
The door in the mountain-side shut fast.
Did I say all? No! One was lame,
    And could not dance the whole of the way;
And in after years, if you would blame
    His sadness, he was used to say,—   235
"It's dull in our town since my playmates left!
"I can't forget that I'm bereft
"Of all the pleasant sights they see,
"Which the Piper also promised me.
"For he led us, he said, to a joyous land,   240
"Joining the town and just at hand,

212 *1849–65* And could   220 *1842* to Coppelburg Hill   223–5 (no quota-
tion marks in *1842*)   226 *1842–63* the mountain's side   236–55 (no quota-
tion marks in *1842*)   239 *1842,1849* me;

   219 *from South to West*: Browning is not aiming at geographical exactitude.
   220 *Koppelberg Hill*: 'the Koppelberg is not one of the imposing hills by which Hameln is
surrounded, but no more than a slight elevation of the ground, barely high enough to hide
the children from view as they left the town': *Encyclopædia Britannica*, xii. 876b.

"Where waters gushed and fruit-trees grew
"And flowers put forth a fairer hue,
"And everything was strange and new;
"The sparrows were brighter than peacocks here,   245
"And their dogs outran our fallow deer,
"And honey-bees had lost their stings,
"And horses were born with eagles' wings:
"And just as I became assured
"My lame foot would be speedily cured,   250
"The music stopped and I stood still,
"And found myself outside the hill,
"Left alone against my will,
"To go now limping as before,
"And never hear of that country more!"   255

XIV.

Alas, alas for Hamelin!
    There came into many a burgher's pate
    A text which says that heaven's gate
    Opes to the rich at as easy rate
As the needle's eye takes a camel in!   260
The mayor sent East, West, North and South,
To offer the Piper, by word of mouth,
    Wherever it was men's lot to find him,
Silver and gold to his heart's content,
If he'd only return the way he went,   265
    And bring the children behind him.
But when they saw 't was a lost endeavour,
And Piper and dancers were gone for ever,
They made a decree that lawyers never
    Should think their records dated duly   270
If, after the day of the month and year,

244 *1842* every thing   249 *1842* I felt assured   252 *1889* hill.
259 *1842* easy a rate

248 *horses . . . with eagles' wings*: like the hippogriffs of fable, which had the head and wings of an eagle and the body and hindquarters of a horse.
258 *a text*: Matt. 19: 24.
269 *a decree*: see Verstegan and Wanley, as quoted in Introduction.

These words did not as well appear,
"And so long after what happened here
    "On the Twenty-second of July,
"Thirteen hundred and seventy-six:"   275
And the better in memory to fix
The place of the children's last retreat,
They called it, the Pied Piper's Street—
Where any one playing on pipe or tabor
Was sure for the future to lose his labour.   280
Nor suffered they hostelry or tavern
    To shock with mirth a street so solemn;
But opposite the place of the cavern
    They wrote the story on a column,
And on the great church-window painted   285
The same, to make the world acquainted
How their children were stolen away,
And there it stands to this very day.
And I must not omit to say
That in Transylvania there's a tribe   290
Of alien people who ascribe
The outlandish ways and dress
On which their neighbours lay such stress,
To their fathers and mothers having risen
Out of some subterraneous prison   295
Into which they were trepanned
Long time ago in a mighty band
Out of Hamelin town in Brunswick land,
But how or why, they don't understand.

                              xv.

So, Willy, let me and you be wipers   300
Of scores out with all men—especially pipers!

---

274 *1849-68* Júly,   282 *1842P²* To ⟨spoil⟩ [shock] with   287 *1842-63* away;
291 *1842-68* people that ascribe   300 *1842,1849* let you and me be
301 *1842-65* pipers:

  279 *any one playing on pipe or tabor*: see pp. 258-9 above.
  285 *And on the great church-window painted*: cf. Wanley, quoted on p. 258 above.
  296 *trepanned*: ensnared.

And, whether they pipe us free fróm rats or fróm mice,
If we've promised them aught, let us keep our promise!

302 *1842* they rid us from rats or from *1849, 1863* from rats   303 *1842P²* our
pro[mise.] *1842-65* promise.

303 *let us keep our promise!*: years later Browning was irritated by a suggestion that the
moral of the poem referred to his own relations with Macready: 'It would perhaps have
been better to see no "sly hit" in what was merely the obvious moral of a poem meant for a
little boy. His father never broke a promise with me nor,—I am sure,—with anybody else. I
certainly had a difference with him on quite another matter—but long after the "Pied
Piper" was written': letter to H. Courthope Bowen, dated 'Nov. 7. '81', in the possession of
Mr Michael Meredith.

INTRODUCTION TO *THE RETURN OF THE DRUSES*

In the letter to Fanny Haworth written on 1 July 1837 from which we have already quoted on p. 93, Browning told her that he 'had chosen a splendid subject' for the further tragedy which he had had 'in prospect' when he 'learned that a magazine for next, *this* month, will have a *scene* founded on my story: vulgarizing or doing no good to it', with the result that he 'thr[e]w it up'. Now, therefore, he was looking for another theme, 'a subject of the most wild and passionate love, to contrast with the one I mean to have ready in a short time'. He continued: 'I have many half-conceptions, floating fancies: give me your notion of a thorough self-devotement, self-forgetting; should it be a woman who loves thus, or a man? What circumstances will best draw out, set forth this feeling? Think for me . . .'[1] Kelley and Hudson have identified the original 'splendid subject', the Death of Marlowe, on which R. H. Horne published a Dramatic Scene in the *Monthly Repository* for August 1837. Mrs Orr no doubt had Browning's own authority for identifying the alternative subject as *The Return of the Druses*.[2] We do not know how early Browning began work on this play, but 'Mansoor the Hierophant' was one of the three dramas advertised as 'Nearly Ready' at the end of *Sordello*, in March 1840.[3] In the letter to Domett written during the same month, in which he denied being 'difficult on system', Browning told him that he was busy on the plays he had advertised, and assured him that they should 'be plain enough if my pains are not thrown away—and, in lieu of Sir Philip and his like, Stokes may assure himself that I see him (first row of the pit, under the second oboe, hat between legs, play-bill on a spike, and a "comforter" round his throat "because of the draught from the stage"), and unless he leaves off sucking his orange at the

---

[1] *Correspondence*, iii. 256–7.

[2] *Life*, p. 97.

[3] '"Mansoor" was one of the names of the third Fatemite Caliph, Biamrallah,' Browning explained to Gosse many years later '—but the word "Hierophant" was used inadvertently. I changed the title to "The Return of the Druses," and the name to "Djabal." It is very good of you to care about the circumstance': *Letters*, p. 187. Browning also told Gosse that *King Victor and King Charles* and *The Return of the Druses* were 'concluded before 1840': *Personalia*, p. 47. Griffin and Minchin state that *The Blot in the 'Scutcheon* and *The Return of the Druses* 'are each said to have been written in five days' (p. 108). The evidence about the former is more persuasive: see p. 357, below.

pathetic morsels of my play, I hold them nought'.[1] It is clear that Browning was still eager for theatrical success.

In April or May, as it seems, he wrote to Macready: 'What you say puts fresh heart into me—I am sure you will like this last labour of mine, and mean therefore to spend a day or two in making a fair copy of it, the M.S. I should have read being a portentous scribble. Most likely you will receive it on Saturday Night.'[2] We do not know exactly what happened next, but in a letter conjecturally dated June 1840 Browning told Macready that he had 'considerably altered and, I hope, improved' the play: 'the three acts are now five, as you advised, and *go* the better for it—such as they are I will send them as soon as I can'. He delivered the play on 31 July, on which day Macready noted, in the privacy of his *Diaries*, that it *'does not look well'*.[3] On 3 August he read it, 'and with the deepest concern I yield to the belief that he will *never write again*—to any purpose', adding: 'I fear his intellect is not quite clear. I do not know how to write to Browning.' Nine days later Browning called and walked with him to the theatre, talking of *The Return of the Druses* and of *Sordello*: 'I most honestly told him my opinion on both, expressing myself most anxious, as I am, that he should justify the expectations formed of him, but that he could not do so by placing himself in opposition to the world.' Macready added: 'He wished me to have his play done for nothing. I explained to him that Mr. Webster would not do it; we talked to the Haymarket, and in parting I promised to read it again.' The result appears from Browning's letter of 9 August:

So once again, dear Macready, I have failed to please you! The Druses *return*, in another sense than I had hoped; for though, to confess a truth, I have worked from the beginning somewhat in the spirit of the cucumber-dresser in the old story (the doctor, you remember, bids such an one "slice a plate full—salt it, pepper it, add oil, vinegar &c &c and then .. throw all behind the fire")—spite of this, I *did* rather fancy that you would have "sympathized" with Djabal in the main scenes of my play; and your failing to do so is the more decisive against it, that I really had you *here*, in this little room of mine, while I wrote bravely away—*here* were you, propping the weak, pushing the strong parts (such I thought there might be!)—now majestically motionless, and now "laying about as busily, as the Amazonian dame Penthesilé"—and *here*, please the fates, shall you again & again give breath and blood to some thin creation of mine yet unevoked—but *elsewhere—enfoncé!* Your other objections I think less material—

---

[1] *Browning and Domett*, pp. 29–30. Sir Philip Sidney is taken as the type of the intelligent spectator, as contrasted with the plebeian Stokes. Cf. *Sordello*, i. 68 ff.

[2] *Correspondence*, iv. 268–9; *New Letters*, p. 20.

[3] *Diaries*, ii. 72, 73.

that the auditory, for instance, know nothing of the Druzes and their doings *until I tell them* (which is the very office I take on myself) that they are men & women oppressed and outraged in such and such ways and desirous of being rid of their oppressor and outrager: if the auditory thus far instructed (and I considered that point sufficiently made out) call for a previous acquaintance with the Druzes before they will go along with such a desire .. are they not worthy compatriots of the Hyde-park gentleman who "could not think of pulling a man out of the Serpentine to whom he had not been previously introduced"?[1]

Browning argues against Macready's 'misgivings' and maintains that if he were in his place 'it should be my first condition with a playwright that his piece should be new, essentially new for better or for worse . . . If it did not fail .. were it even some poor *Return of the Druzes*, it would be something yet unseen, in however poor a degree—something, therefore, to go and see.' In a postscript Browning told Macready that he did not wish his play to be forwarded to Benjamin Nottingham Webster, the manager of the Haymarket Theatre, and added that he would call for his manuscript 'some morning this week'. Four days later he did call, before the unfortunate Macready had finished his bath, 'and really *wearied* me with his obstinate faith in his poem of *Sordello*, and of his eventual celebrity, and also with his self-opinionated persuasions upon his *Return of the Druses*. I fear he is for ever gone . . . Browning accompanied me to the theatre, at last consenting to leave the MS. with me for a second perusal.'[2] On 15 September Macready brought himself to read as much as he could of this 'mystical, strange and heavy play', and concluded: 'It is not good.' 'Wrote to him', he confided in his *Diaries*, 'and, offering to do all in my power, gave him my reconsidered opinion.' We next hear of the play on 22 May 1842, when Browning told Domett that he was going to 'print the Eastern play' he might remember hearing about.[3] In January of the following year *The Return of the Druses*, which was never acted in Browning's lifetime, was published as the fourth of the *Bells and Pomegranates*.

Browning's choice of subject-matter was unusual, but hardly unexampled. Byron, who never forgot Mme de Staël's advice to 'Stick to the East', had been fascinated by the pages of the *Travels* of Edward Daniel Clarke devoted to the Druzes: 'I doat upon the *Druses*,' he told Clarke when he thanked him for a copy of his second volume, 'but who

[1] *Correspondence*, iv. 294.
[2] *Diaries*, ii. 76, 80.
[3] *Browning and Domett*, p. 36.

the deuce are they with their Pantheism? I shall never be easy till I ask *them the question.*[1] Clarke had described the Druses as

A sect of Arabs inhabiting the environs of Mount Libanus; so called from their founder, surnamed *El Durzi*, who came from Persia into Egypt in the year 1020 ... Niebuhr and Volney have given a full account of their history. It has been ignorantly supposed that they are the offspring of a colony of French Crusaders; but their name occurs in the Itinerary of Benjamin of Tudela, written anterior to the Crusades ... Pococke fell into the error of their Christian origin. 'If any account', says he, 'can be given of the original of the Druses, it is, that they are the remains of the Christian armies in the Holy War.'[2]

While there is no evidence that Browning knew Clarke's book, we can be certain that he turned to the *Biographie universelle*[3] and to *The Decline and Fall of the Roman Empire*. Griffin and Minchin go so far as to state that the former 'suggested the idea of *The Return of the Druses*.'[4] Here is what Browning will have found, in the nineteenth volume:

HAKEM (Biamr-Allah), *Abou Aly Mansour*, third Fatemite khalif of Egypt, succeeded his father Azyz-billah in ... 996 [999], at the age of only eleven. This personage is celebrated in history for the uninterrupted succession of cruelties and extravagances which filled his reign. A capricious and ferocious despot, he did not know how to deserve the love of any of his subjects, and made himself detested by all ... The Christians suffered a great deal under the reign of Hakem ... The excess of the evils to which they were subjected decided the eastern Christians to implore their western brothers for rescue, and was the first motive which led to the crusades. The Popes likewise, in the arguments which they utilized to bring about the sacred war, did not forget to paint these calamities in terms both eloquent and true. Hakem disappeared [in March 1021], after a reign of twenty-five years and one month. It has been maintained that his sister had occasioned his death; but the most reliable historians state that he was assassinated by a man from Saïd ... Who would have believed that a monster like Hakem could become the object of a religious cult? Hamza-ben-Aly claimed that this khalif had been raised to heaven, and that he would return one day to reign over the whole earth: he made this dogma the foundation-stone of the sect of the Druses, of which some remains still exist today in Syria.

[1] *Byron's Letters and Journals*, ed. Leslie A. Marchand (12 vols., 1973–82), iii. 101 and ii. 181. By the beginning of the 1840s, in spite of Macready's objection that 'the auditory ... know nothing of the Druzes and their doings', the troubles in Lebanon and the unhappy condition of the Druses were often mentioned in the English press.

[2] *Travels in Various Countries of Europe and Africa*, Part II, Sect. i (1812), p. 367 n.

[3] Cf. pp. 95–7 above. Browning will also have read about the Druses in *The Great Historical ... Dictionary*, by Jeremy Collier (cf. pp. 244 n., 261–2). The account in the *Dictionary of All Religions*, from which he took the epigraph for 'Johannes Agricola', is merely a conflation of the two entries in Collier.   [4] Griffin and Minchin, p. 25.

Browning is also sure to have read of the Druses in Gibbon, whose account of them could well have suggested that they would form an eligible subject for a play which is, as Mrs Orr described it, 'fictitious in plot, but historical in character'.[1] Gibbon's passage on the Fatimite caliphs is to be found in the penultimate paragraph of ch. LVII of *The Decline and Fall*:

The third of these Fatimite caliphs was the famous Hakem, a frantic youth, who was delivered by his impiety and despotism from the fear either of God or man; and whose reign was a wild mixture of vice and folly ... At first the caliph declared himself a zealous mussulman, the founder or benefactor of moschs and colleges ... But his vanity was soon flattered by the hope of introducing a new religion: he aspired above the fame of a prophet, and styled himself the visible image of the most high God, who, after nine apparitions on earth, was at length manifest in his royal person. At the name of Hakem, the lord of the living and the dead, every knee was bent in religious adoration: his mysteries were performed on a mountain near Cairo: sixteen thousand converts had signed his profession of faith; and at the present hour, a free and warlike people, the Druses of mount Libanus, are persuaded of the life and divinity of a madman and tyrant.

Gibbon goes on to write of 'the inconstancy or repentance of Hakem', recording that, after his assassination, 'The succeeding caliphs resumed the maxims of religion and policy', 'a free toleration' again being granted. 'The religion of the Druses', he comments in a characteristic footnote, 'is concealed by their ignorance and hypocrisy. Their secret doctrines are confined to the elect who profess a contemplative life; and the vulgar Druses, the most indifferent of men, occasionally conform to the worship of the Mahometans and Christians of their neighbourhood. The little that is, or deserves to be, known, may be seen in the industrious Niebuhr ..., and the second volume of the recent and instructive Travels of M. de Volney.'

It is all but certain that Browning consulted Volney's book, *Voyage en Syrie et en Égypte*,[2] in which prominence is given to the myth that the Druses were descended from French Crusaders. Volney describes the visit to the court of the Medici made by Fakr-el-din in the early years of the seventeenth century:

The arrival of an Oriental prince in Italy, did not fail to attract the public attention. Enquiry was made into his nation, and the origin of the Druzes became popular topics [sic] of research. Their history and religion were found to be so

---

[1] *Handbook*, p. 60.

[2] Volney's book was published in two volumes in Paris in 1787. We quote from the English translation, *Travels through Syria and Egypt*, published in London in two volumes the same year. The above quotation is from ii. 43-4. Volney ascribes to the Druses 'a truly republican spirit'.

little known as to leave it a matter of doubt whether they should be classed with the Mahometans or Christians. The Crusades were called to mind, and it was soon suggested that a people who had taken refuge in the mountains, and were enemies to the natives, could be no other than the offspring of the Crusaders.

This idle conceit was too favourable to Fakr-el-din for him to endeavour to disprove it: he was artful enough, on the contrary, to pretend he was related to the house of Lorraine; and the missionaries and merchants, who promised themselves a new opening for conversions and commerce, encouraged his pretensions. When an opinion is in vogue, every one discovers new proofs of its certainty. The learned in etymology, struck with the resemblance of the names, insisted, that *Druzes* and *Dreux* must be the same word, and, on this foundation, formed the system of a pretended colony of French Crusaders, who, under the conduct of a Comte *de Dreux*, had formed a settlement in Lebanon.

We do not know whether Browning consulted Carsten Niebuhr's book (available in French as *Voyage en Arabie & en d'autres Pays circonvoisins,* Amsterdam and Utrecht, 1780), but it is highly probable that he had looked into Lamartine's *Souvenirs, impressions, pensées et paysages, pendant un voyage en Orient* (4 vols., Paris 1835), since in the year of its publication we find him telling Amédée de Ripert-Monclar that it was 'making a noise here just now';[1] but Lamartine includes no information which was not available to Browning elsewhere.[2]

No manuscript of *The Return of the Druses* appears to survive. The play, which Browning reprinted in *1849* and subsequent collected editions, presents hardly any textual difficulties. In *1843* 'Loÿs' and 'Maäni' have diaeresis marks, as an aid to pronunciation. These disappear in all later editions: the change is not recorded in our textual notes.

The three emendations in the Dykes Campbell copy have been adopted in this edition.[3] At I. 311 an obvious misprint in *1888* and *1889* is corrected.

---

[1] *Correspondence*, iii. 144.

[2] As DeVane points out, the article in the *Biographie universelle* refers to the *Chrestomathie Arabe* of Silvestre de Sacy (Paris 1806). There is nothing in the play, however, which is clearly from de Sacy.

[3] These include the grammatically dubious 'pursuant of' (I. 131), which Browning preferred to the earlier 'pursuant to'. In the Brigham Young copy of *Bells and Pomegranates* Browning picked up the misprint 'stay' for 'slay' (II. 307), which was duly corrected in *1849*. There are no changes to *The Return of the Druses* in the Texas annotated copy of *1843*.

THE RETURN OF THE DRUSES

A TRAGEDY

title *1843*   BELLS AND POMEGRANATES. Nᵒ· IV.—THE RETURN OF THE DRUSES. A Tragedy. IN FIVE ACTS. BY ROBERT BROWNING. Author of "Paracelsus." LONDON: EDWARD MOXON, DOVER STREET. MDCCCXLIII.

PERSONS.

The Grand-Master's Prefect.
The Patriarch's Nuncio.
The Republic's Admiral.
LOYS DE DREUX, *Knight-Novice.*
Initiated Druses —DJABAL, KHALIL, ANAEL, MAANI,
    KARSHOOK, RAGHIB, AYOOB, *and others.*
Uninitiated Druses.
Prefect's Guard. Nuncio's Attendants. Admiral's Force.

TIME, 14—

PLACE.—*An Islet of the Southern Sporades, colonized by Druses of Lebanon, and garrisoned by the Knights-Hospitallers of Rhodes.*

SCENE.—*A Hall in the Prefect's Palace.*

{no italics in *1843–68*}

PERSONS: The first three represent respectively the Grand-Master of the Knights Hospitallers (whose chief seat was at Rhodes, at the time of the action of the play), the Church, and the Venetian Republic.

Initiated Druses: see Introduction, p. 281.

PLACE: the colonization of 'An Islet of the Southern Sporades' by the Druses is unhistorical. The reference is to the islands since 1912 termed the Southern Dodecanese, e.g. Rhodes, Nissyros, Symi, and Kastellorizo to the south. Apart from Rhodes, they are 'islets' with castles on them and a history of innumerable invasions. The islands now called the Sporades—Skiathos, Skopelos, etc.—were formerly called the Northern Sporades.

The supposed writer of Shelley's *Epipsychidion* died as he 'was preparing for a voyage to one of the wildest of the Sporades': Browning himself was attracted by the idea of escaping 'to a Greek island'. Cf. *Pippa Passes*, above, note to II. 327.

THE RETURN OF THE DRUSES.

ACT I.

Enter stealthily KARSHOOK, RAGHIB, AYOOB *and other initiated* Druses, *each as he enters casting off a robe that conceals his distinctive black vest and white turban; then, as giving a loose to exultation,—*

Karshook. The moon is carried off in purple fire:
Day breaks at last! Break glory, with the day,
On Djabal's dread incarnate mystery
Now ready to resume its pristine shape
Of Hakeem, as the Khalif vanished erst   5
In what seemed death to uninstructed eyes,
On red Mokattam's verge—our Founder's flesh,
As he resumes our Founder's function!
    Raghib.   —Death
Sweep to the Christian Prefect that enslaved

---

3 *1843* On Djabal, ready to resume his shape   4 (no equivalent in *1843*)
6 (no equivalent in *1843*)   7 *1843* Mokattam's brow—our

s.d. KARSHOOK: in 1854 Browning wrote a poem entitled 'Ben Karshook's Wisdom', which he did not include in his collected editions: see *New Poems*, pp. 27–8. He explained to Furnivall that the name is the Hebrew word for a thistle: *Trumpeter*, p. 24.

white turban: 'Those who compose [this class] are to the rest of the nation what the *initiated* were to the *profane*; they assume the name of *Okkals*, which means spiritualists [religious], and bestow on the vulgar the epithet of *Djâhel*, or *ignorant*... These are distinguishable by the White Turban they affect to wear, as a symbol of their purity': Volney, ii. 59. Cf. Niebuhr, p. 349.

5 *Hakeem*: 'They have one or two books which they conceal with the greatest care; but chance has deceived their jealousy; for, in a civil war, which happened six or seven years ago, the Emir Yousef, who is *Djâhel*, or ignorant, found one among the pillage of one of their oratories. I am assured, by persons who have read it, that it contains only a mystic jargon, the obscurity of which, doubtless, renders it valuable to adepts. Hakem Bamr-ellah is there spoken of, by whom they mean God, incarnated in the person of the Calif': Volney, ii. 60–1. Cf. Introduction, above.

7 *On red Mokattam's verge*: Hakem (Biamr-Allah), the third Fatemite khalif, is said to have been killed on Mount Mokattam (near Cairo), when it was red with the setting sun: see an Arabic writer cited by Volney, ii. 37.

9 *the Christian Prefect*: this is unhistorical.

So long us sad Druse exiles o'er the sea!   10
    Ayoob. Most joy be thine, O Mother-mount! Thy brood
Returns to thee, no outcasts as we left,
But thus—but thus! Behind, our Prefect's corse;
Before, a presence like the morning—thine,
Absolute Djabal late,—God Hakeem now   15
That day breaks!
    Karshook.   Off then, with disguise at last!
As from our forms this hateful garb we strip,
Lose every tongue its glozing accent too,
Discard each limb the ignoble gesture! Cry,
'T is the Druse Nation, warders on our Mount   20
Of the world's secret, since the birth of time,
—No kindred slips, no offsets from thy stock,
No spawn of Christians are we, Prefect, we
Who rise . . .
    Ayoob.   Who shout . . .
    Raghib.   Who seize, a first-fruits, ha—
Spoil of the spoiler! Brave!
    [*They begin to tear down, and to dispute for, the decorations of the hall.*
    Karshook.   Hold!
    Ayoob.   —Mine, I say;   25
And mine shall it continue!
    Karshook.   Just this fringe!
Take anything beside! Lo, spire on spire,
Curl serpentwise wreathed columns to the top
O' the roof, and hide themselves mysteriously
Among the twinkling lights and darks that haunt   30
Yon cornice! Where the huge veil, they suspend
Before the Prefect's chamber of delight,

15 *1843* late, and Hakeem   *24 [reading of *1843-68*] *1888,1889* shout . .
26 *1843* Just that fringe!   29 *1843-68* Of the   31 *1843* cornice,—

    11 *Mother-mount!*: Mount Lebanon, the central mountain-mass of Syria.
    18 *glozing*: specious, as in *Paracelsus*, iv. 629.
    21 *the birth of time*: cf. Shelley, *Alastor*, 128.
    22 *slips, . . . offsets*: twigs and sprouts or shoots of a plant.
    28 *serpentwise wreathed columns*: Browning will have been aware that serpent-worship had prevailed in Lebanon.

Floats wide, then falls again as if its slave,
The scented air, took heart now, and anon
Lost heart to buoy its breadths of gorgeousness   35
Above the gloom they droop in—all the porch
Is jewelled o'er with frostwork charactery;
And, see, yon eight-point cross of white flame, winking
Hoar-silvery like some fresh-broke marble stone:
Raze out the Rhodian cross there, so thou leav'st me   40
This single fringe!
  Ayoob.   Ha, wouldst thou, dog-fox? Help!
—Three hand-breadths of gold fringe, my son was set
To twist, the night he died!
  Karshook.   Nay, hear the knave!
And I could witness my one daughter borne,
A week since, to the Prefect's couch, yet fold   45
These arms, be mute, lest word of mine should mar
Our Master's work, delay the Prefect here
A day, prevent his sailing hence for Rhodes—
How know I else?—Hear me denied my right
By such a knave!
  Raghib [*interposing*]. Each ravage for himself!   50
Booty enough! On, Druses! Be there found
Blood and a heap behind us; with us, Djabal
Turned Hakeem; and before us, Lebanon!
Yields the porch? Spare not! There his minions dragged
Thy daughter, Karshook, to the Prefect's couch!   55
Ayoob! Thy son, to soothe the Prefect's pride,
Bent o'er that task, the death-sweat on his brow,
Carving the spice-tree's heart in scroll-work there!
Onward in Djabal's name!

33.*1849* (as   36 *1849* in)   37 *1843* with frosted charactery,
38 *1843* A Rhodian eight-point 39 *1843* Hoar-silvered like 40 *1843* the
Prefect's Cross *1849* the Rhodian's Cross 41 *1843* That single 55 *1843*
couch: 56 *1843* Ayoob, 58 *1843* there:

 37 *frostwork charactery*: cf. Shelley, *Hellas*, 416: 'frostwork diadems like dew'.
 38 *yon eight-point cross*: the Knights Hospitallers of St John of Jerusalem, who captured
Rhodes in 1309, wore a white cross with eight points on a black ground.
 41 *dog-fox*: cf. *Troilus and Cressida*, v. iv. 12.
 52 *Blood and a heap*: a bloody heap (by hendiadys).

As the tumult is at height, enter KHALIL. *A pause and silence.*

Khalil.   Was it for this,
Djabal hath summoned you? Deserve you thus   60
A portion in to-day's event? What, here—
When most behoves your feet fall soft, your eyes
Sink low, your tongues lie still,—at Djabal's side,
Close in his very hearing, who, perchance,
Assumes e'en now God Hakeem's dreaded shape,—   65
Dispute you for these gauds?
    Ayoob.   How say'st thou, Khalil?
Doubtless our Master prompts thee! Take the fringe,
Old Karshook! I supposed it was a day . . .
    Khalil. For pillage?
    Karshook.   Hearken, Khalil! Never spoke
A boy so like a song-bird; we avouch thee   70
Prettiest of all our Master's instruments
Except thy bright twin-sister; thou and Anael
Challenge his prime regard: but we may crave
(Such nothings as we be) a portion too
Of Djabal's favour; in him we believed,   75
His bound ourselves, him moon by moon obeyed,
Kept silence till this daybreak—so, may claim
Reward: who grudges me my claim?
    Ayoob.   To-day
Is not as yesterday!
    Raghib.   Stand off!
    Khalil.   Rebel you?
Must I, the delegate of Djabal, draw   80
His wrath on you, the day of our Return?
    Other Druses. Wrench from their grasp the fringe!
        Hounds! must the earth
Vomit her plagues on us thro' thee?—and thee?
Plague me not, Khalil, for their fault!
    Khalil.   Oh, shame!

65 *1843* now lost Hakeem's   80 *1843* of Hakeem, draw   82 *1843* from his
grasp   *1843-68* fringe! Hound! must

·59 s.d. The dramatic effect is intensified by Khalil's youth.

Thus breaks to-day on you, the mystic tribe   85
Who, flying the approach of Osman, bore
Our faith, a merest spark, from Syria's ridge
Its birthplace, hither! "Let the sea divide
"These hunters from their prey," you said; "and safe
"In this dim islet's virgin solitude   90
"Tend we our faith, the spark, till happier time
"Fan it to fire; till Hakeem rise again,
"According to his word that, in the flesh
"Which faded on Mokattam ages since,
"He, at our extreme need, would interpose,   95
"And, reinstating all in power and bliss,
"Lead us himself to Lebanon once more."
Was't not thus you departed years ago,
Ere I was born?
    Druses.   'T was even thus, years ago.
    Khalil. And did you call—(according to old laws   100
Which bid us, lest the sacred grow profane,
Assimilate ourselves in outward rites
With strangers fortune makes our lords, and live
As Christian with the Christian, Jew with Jew,
Druse only with the Druses)—did you call   105
Or no, to stand 'twixt you and Osman's rage
(Mad to pursue e'en hither thro' the sea
The remnant of our tribe), a race self-vowed
To endless warfare with his hordes and him,
The White-cross Knights of the adjacent Isle?   110
    Kharshook. And why else rend we down, wrench up, rase
      out?

---

86 *1843* That, flying   88 *1843* hither: 88-9, 89-97 {no quotation marks in
1843-65}   *91 {reading of *1868*} *1888,1889* 'Tend   92 *1843* fire; again till
Hakeem rise   100 *1843* you not—(according   108 *1843-63* of your tribe

    86 *Osman* : the founder of the Ottoman empire in Asia.
    90 *this dim islet's virgin solitude* : cf. *Pauline*, 331: 'the dim clustered isles in the blue sea'.
    95 *extreme* : stressed on the first syllable. See *Pauline*, 908 and n.
    102 *Assimilate ourselves in outward rites* : see Volney, ii. 61-2, Niebuhr, pp. 352-3, and
Gibbon's comment on the matter, on p. 281 above.

These Knights of Rhodes we thus solicited
For help, bestowed on us a fiercer pest
Than aught we fled—their Prefect; who began
His promised mere paternal governance   115
By a prompt massacre of all our Sheikhs
Able to thwart the Order in its scheme
Of crushing, with our nation's memory,
Each chance of our return, and taming us
Bondslaves to Rhodes for ever—all, he thinks   120
To end by this day's treason.
    Khalil.   Say I not?
You, fitted to the Order's purposes,
Your Sheikhs cut off, your rites, your garb proscribed,
Must yet receive one degradation more;
The Knights at last throw off the mask—transfer,   125
As tributary now and appanage,
This islet they are but protectors of,
To their own ever-craving liege, the Church,
Who licenses all crimes that pay her thus.
You, from their Prefect, were to be consigned   130
(Pursuant of I know not what vile pact)
To the Knights' Patriarch, ardent to outvie
His predecessor in all wickedness.
When suddenly rose Djabal in the midst,
Djabal, the man in semblance, but our God   135
Confessed by signs and portents. Ye saw fire
Bicker round Djabal, heard strange music flit

---

112 *1843* The Knights   115 (no equivalent in *1843*)   116 *1843* By massacre,
who thinks to end to-day   117 (no equivalent in *1843*) ·   118 *1843* By
treachery, a scheme of theirs for crushing   *1849, 1863*   our nationalities,
120 *1843* ever. *Kha*. Say I not?   121 (no equivalent in *1843*)   123 *1843–68*
off, your very garb   125–9 (no equivalent in *1843*)   128 *1849, 1863* ever-
craving lord, the   129 *1849, 1863* Which licenses   *1849* pay it thus— *1863* pay
it thus.   *131 (reading of DC,*1889*) (no equivalent in *1843*) *1849* Pursuant to I
1863–88 (Pursuant to I   *1849* pact,   133 *1843,1849* wickedness;
134 *1843* rose Hakeem in   135 *1843* our Khalif

136–7 *Ye saw fire / Bicker round Djabal*: cf. *Paradise Lost*, vi. 766: 'Of smoke and bickering
flame'. Johnson gives 'To quiver; to play backward and forward' as the meaning of 'bicker'.

Bird-like about his brow?
Druses.   We saw—we heard!
Djabal is Hakeem, the incarnate Dread,
The phantasm Khalif, King of Prodigies!   140
    Khalil. And as he said has not our Khalif done,
And so disposed events (from land to land
Passing invisibly) that when, this morn,
The pact of villany complete, there comes
This Patriarch's Nuncio with this Master's Prefect   145
Their treason to consummate,—each will face
For a crouching handful, an uplifted nation:
For simulated Christians, confessed Druses:
And, for slaves past hope of the Mother-mount,
Freedmen returning there 'neath Venice' flag;   150
That Venice which, the Hospitallers' foe,
Grants us from Candia escort home at price
Of our relinquished isle, Rhodes counts her own—
Venice, whose promised argosies should stand
Toward harbour: is it now that you, and you,   155
And you, selected from the rest to bear
The burthen of the Khalif's secret, further
To-day's event, entitled by your wrongs,
And witness in the Prefect's hall his fate—
That you dare clutch these gauds? Ay, drop them!
    Karshook.   True,   160
Most true, all this; and yet, may one dare hint,
Thou art the youngest of us?—though employed
Abundantly as Djabal's confidant,

---

138 *1843* heard.   139–40 (no equivalent in *1843*)   141 *1843-68* said hath
not   *1843* done?   142 *1843* —Not so   143 *1843* Going invisibly)
145 *1865* with his Master's   146 *1843* To consummate their treason, each
151 *1843* —Venice, which, these proud Hospitallers' foe,   153–4 *1843* relinquished
islet—Venice, brothers, | Whose promised argosies should stand by this   155 *1843*
Towards the harbour: is it now that you, | *1849-68* Toward the harbour: 156 *1843*
to carry

146 *to consummate* : stressed on the second syllable, as in Johnson and in *Paracelsus*, ii. 475.
152 *Candia* : the Venetian capital of Crete, now Iraklion.
154 *stand* : in Johnson's meaning no. 32, 'To hold a course at sea'.

Transmitter of his mandates, even now.
Much less, whene'er beside him Anael graces   165
The cedar throne, his queen-bride, art thou like
To occupy its lowest step that day!
Now, Khalil, wert thou checked as thou aspirest,
Forbidden such or such an honour,—say,
Would silence serve so amply?
          Khalil.   Karshook thinks   170
I covet honours? Well, nor idly thinks.
Honours? I have demanded of them all
The greatest.
          Karshook. I supposed so.
          Khalil.   Judge, yourselves!
Turn, thus: 't is in the alcove at the back
Of yonder columned porch, whose entrance now   175
The veil hides, that our Prefect holds his state,
Receives the Nuncio, when the one, from Rhodes,
The other lands from Syria; there they meet.
Now, I have sued with earnest prayers . . .
          Karshook.   For what
Shall the Bride's brother vainly sue?
          Khalil.   That mine—   180
Avenging in one blow a myriad wrongs
—Might be the hand to slay the Prefect there!
Djabal reserves that office for himself.   [*A silence.*
Thus far, as youngest of you all, I speak
—Scarce more enlightened than yourselves; since, near   185
As I approach him, nearer as I trust
Soon to approach our Master, he reveals
Only the God's power, not the glory yet.
Therefore I reasoned with you: now, as servant
To Djabal, bearing his authority,   190

164 *1843,1849* now: 168 *1843* And, Khalil, wert thou plucked as
171 *1843-68* thinks!   173 *1843-68* greatest!   176 *1843,1849* state;
182 *1843* hand that slays the   184 *1843* I spoke   188 *1843* the Khalif's
power, not glory yet: *1849* yet:

     166 *the cedar throne*: from biblical times Lebanon has been famous for its cedars.

Hear me appoint your several posts! Till noon
None see him save myself and Anael: once
The deed achieved, our Khalif, casting off
The embodied Awe's tremendous mystery,
The weakness of the flesh disguise, resumes   195
His proper glory, ne'er to fade again.

Enter a Druse.

 The Druse. Our Prefect lands from Rhodes!—without a
  sign
That he suspects aught since he left our Isle;
Nor in his train a single guard beyond
The few he sailed with hence: so have we learned   200
From Loys.
 Karshook. Loys? Is not Loys gone
For ever?
 Ayoob. Loys, the Frank Knight, returned?
 The Druse. Loys, the boy, stood on the leading prow
Conspicuous in his gay attire, and leapt
Into the surf the foremost. Since day-dawn   205
I kept watch to the Northward; take but note
Of my poor vigilance to Djabal!
 Khalil.   Peace!
Thou, Karshook, with thy company, receive
The Prefect as appointed: see, all keep
The wonted show of servitude: announce   210
His entry here by the accustomed peal
Of trumpets, then await the further pleasure
Of Djabal! (Loys back, whom Djabal sent
To Rhodes that we might spare the single Knight
Worth sparing!)

---

192 *1843,1849* None sees him 193 *1843* Khalif will appear. 194–6 (no
equivalent in *1843*) 201 *1843,1849* From Loys . . . 204 *1843* attire—has
leapt 205 *1843* surf already: since *1849* foremost:

 202 *the Frank knight*: see Introduction, p. 280 above. OED defines 'Frank' as 'A name
given by the nations bordering on the Levant to an individual of Western nationality.'
 205 *day-dawn*: first recorded in Coleridge, *Remorse*, IV. ii. 53.

Enter a second Druse.

The Druse. I espied it first! Say, I   215
First spied the Nuncio's galley from the South!
Said'st thou a Crossed-keys' flag would flap the mast?
It nears apace! One galley and no more.
If Djabal chance to ask who spied the flag,
Forget not, I it was!
    Khalil.   Thou, Ayoob, bring   220
The Nuncio and his followers hither! Break
One rule prescribed, ye wither in your blood,
Die at your fault!

Enter a third Druse.

    The Druse.   I shall see home, see home!
—Shall banquet in the sombre groves again!
Hail to thee, Khalil! Venice looms afar;   225
The argosies of Venice, like a cloud,
Bear up from Candia in the distance!
    Khalil.   Joy!
Summon our people, Raghib! Bid all forth!
Tell them the long-kept secret, old and young!
Set free the captive, let the trampled raise   230
Their faces from the dust, because at length
The cycle is complete, God Hakeem's reign
Begins anew! Say, Venice for our guard,
Ere night we steer for Syria! Hear you, Druses?
Hear you this crowning witness to the claims   235
Of Djabal? Oh, I spoke of hope and fear,
Reward and punishment, because he bade
Who has the right; for me, what should I say
But, mar not those imperial lineaments,

215 *1843* espied him first!   224 *1843* again.   230 *1843* the captives, have
the *1849–68* the captives, let   232 *1843* complete, and Hakeem's   236 *1843*
Djabal!

  217 *a Crossed-keys' flag*: the Papal flag, with the keys of heaven and hell.
  222 *wither*: 'To waste, or pine away': Johnson.
  232 *The cycle is complete*: cf. *Sordello*, v. 539 (and note), and 941. Cf. II. 143 and 228, below.

No majesty of all that rapt regard   240
Vex by the least omission! Let him rise
Without a check from you!
    Druses.   Let Djabal rise!

          Enter LOYS.—*The* Druses *are silent.*

    Loys. Who speaks of Djabal?—for I seek him, friends!
[*Aside.*] *Tu Dieu!* 'T is as our Isle broke out in song
For joy, its Prefect-incubus drops off   245
To-day, and I succeed him in his rule!
But no—they cannot dream of their good fortune!
[*Aloud.*] Peace to you, Druses! I have tidings for you
But first for Djabal: where's your tall bewitcher,
With that small Arab thin-lipped silver-mouth?   250
    Khalil [*aside to* KARSHOOK]. Loys, in truth! Yet Djabal can-
    not err!
    Karshook [*to* KHALIL]. And who takes charge of Loys?
    That's forgotten,
Despite thy wariness! Will Loys stand
And see his comrades slaughtered?
    Loys [*aside*].   How they shrink
And whisper, with those rapid faces! What?   255
The sight of me in their oppressors' garb
Strikes terror to the simple tribe? God's shame
On those that bring our Order ill repute!
· But all's at end now; better days begin
For these mild mountaineers from over-sea: 260
The timidest shall have in me no Prefect
To cower at thus! [*Aloud.*] I asked for Djabal—
    Karshook [*aside*].   Better
One lured him, ere he can suspect, inside

---

254 *1843–65* his comrade slaughtered?   255 *1843* What!   257 *1843* tribe!
    244 *Tu Dieu!*: Thou, O God!
    250 *silver-mouth*: i.e. eloquent mouth. Cf. Shakespeare, *Pericles*, v. i. 106–9: 'My dearest
wife was like this maid, . . . as silver-voiced', Shelley, *Epipsychidion*, 301, and *Sordello*, i. 68–9.
    255 *those rapid faces*: cf. Shelley, *The Revolt of Islam*, 1162: 'with rapid lips'.
    260 *these mild mountaineers*: 'They have no knowledge of . . . any thing which constitutes
the art of war': Volney, ii. 71. In fact, however, the Druses are by no means 'mild'.

The corridor; 't were easy to despatch
A youngster. [*To* Loys.] Djabal passed some minutes since   265
Thro' yonder porch, and . . .
    Khalil [*aside*].   Hold! What, him despatch?
The only Christian of them all we charge
No tyranny upon? Who,—noblest Knight
Of all that learned from time to time their trade
Of lust and cruelty among us,—heir   270
To Europe's pomp, a truest child of pride,—
Yet stood between the Prefect and ourselves
From the beginning? Loys, Djabal makes
Account of, and precisely sent to Rhodes
For safety? I take charge of him!
                [*To* Loys.] Sir Loys,—   275
    Loys. There, cousins! Does Sir Loys strike you dead?
    Khalil [*advancing*]. Djabal has intercourse with few or
      none
Till noontide: but, your pleasure?
    Loys.   "Intercourse
"With few or none"?—(Ah, Khalil, when you spoke
I saw not your smooth face! All health!—and health   280
To Anael! How fares Anael?)—"Intercourse
"With few or none"? Forget you, I've been friendly
With Djabal long ere you or any Druse?
—Enough of him at Rennes, I think, beneath
The Duke my father's roof! He'd tell by the hour,   285
With fixed white eyes beneath his swarthy brow,
Plausiblest stories . . .
    Khalil.   Stories, say you?—Ah,
The quaint attire!
    Loys.   My dress for the last time!

---

264 *1843* easy then despatch   *266 {reading of *1843-68*} *1888,1889* porch . .
271 *1843-63* Europe's pomps, a   275 *1843* I have charge   *279 {editors'
emendation} *1843-89* none?"   *282 {editors' emendation} *1843-89* none?"
288 *1843* time.

273-4 *Loys, Djabal makes / Account of* : Loys, whom Djabal values highly. Cf. Ps. 144: 3.
284 *Rennes* : formerly the capital of Brittany.

How sad I cannot make you understand,
This ermine, o'er a shield, betokens me   290
Of Bretagne, ancientest of provinces
And noblest; and, what's best and oldest there,
See, Dreux', our house's blazon, which the Nuncio
Tacks to an Hospitaller's vest to-day!
    Khalil. The Nuncio we await? What brings you back   295
From Rhodes, Sir Loys?
    Loys.   How you island-tribe
Forget the world's awake while here you drowse!
What brings me back? What should not bring me, rather!
Our Patriarch's Nuncio visits you to-day—
Is not my year's probation out? I come   300
To take the knightly vows.
    Khalil.   What's that you wear?
    Loys. This Rhodian cross? The cross your Prefect wore.
You should have seen, as I saw, the full Chapter
Rise, to a man, while they transferred this cross
From that unworthy Prefect's neck to . . . (fool—   305
My secret will escape me!) In a word,
My year's probation passed, a Knight ere eve
Am I; bound, like the rest, to yield my wealth
To the common stock, to live in chastity,
(We knights espouse alone our Order's fame)   310
—Change this gay weed for the black white-crossed gown,
And fight to death against the Infidel
—Not, therefore, against you, you Christians with
Such partial difference only as befits
The peacefullest of tribes. But Khalil, prithee,   315
Is not the Isle brighter than wont to-day?
    Khalil. Ah, the new sword!
    Loys.   See now! You handle sword

---

297 *1865,1868* the world awake   298 *1843-68* rather?   299 {no equivalent
in *1843*}   307 *1843,1849* probation's passed   *311 {reading of *1843-68*}
1888,1889 the back white-crossed   312 *1843* Infidel.   315 *1843-68* tribes!

293 *Dreux'*: possessive.
311 *this gay weed*: as in *Sordello*, iii. 545.

As 't were a camel-staff. Pull! That's my motto,
Annealed *"Pro fide,"* on the blade in blue.
    Khalil. No curve in it? Surely a blade should curve.   320
    Loys. Straight from the wrist! Loose—it should poise itself!
    Khalil [*waving with irrepressible exultation the sword*]. We are
    a nation, Loys, of old fame
Among the mountains! Rights have we to keep
With the sword too!
[*Remembering himself.*] But I forget—you bid me
Seek Djabal?
    Loys.   What! A sword's sight scares you not?   325
(The People I will make of him and them!
Oh let my Prefect-sway begin at once!)
Bring Djabal—say, indeed, that come he must!
    Khalil. At noon seek Djabal in the Prefect's Chamber,
And find . . . [*Aside.*] Nay, 't is thy cursed race's token,   330
Frank pride, no special insolence of thine!
[*Aloud.*] Tarry, and I will do your bidding, Loys!
[*To the rest aside.*] Now, forth you! I proceed to Djabal
    straight.
Leave this poor boy, who knows not what he says!
Oh will it not add joy to even thy joy,   335
Djabal, that I report all friends were true?
                   [KHALIL *goes, followed by the* Druses.
    Loys. Tu Dieu! How happy I shall make these Druses!
Was't not surpassingly contrived of me
To get the long list of their wrongs by heart,
Then take the first pretence for stealing off   340
From these poor islanders, present myself
Sudden at Rhodes before the noble Chapter,
And (as best proof of ardour in its cause
Which ere to-night will have become, too, mine)

---

318 *1843* camel's   staff!   *1849–68*   camel-staff!   320 *1843–68*   curve!
332 *1843–65* Loys.   334 {no equivalent in *1843*} *1849–65* says.   335 *1843*
Oh, adds it not a joy   336 s.d. *1843* †[*Exit* KHALIL, *followed*

   319 *"Pro fide"*: 'For the Faith.'
   320 *Surely a blade should curve*: unlike the straight blades used by the 'Franks'.

Acquaint it with this plague-sore in its body,   345
This Prefect and his villanous career?
The princely Synod! All I dared request
Was his dismissal; and they graciously
Consigned his very office to myself—
Myself may cure the Isle diseased!

          And well   350
For them, they did so! Since I never felt
How lone a lot, tho' brilliant, I embrace,
Till now that, past retrieval, it is mine.
To live thus, and thus die! Yet, as I leapt
On shore, so home a feeling greeted me   355
That I could half believe in Djabal's story,
He used to tempt my father with, at Rennes—
And me, too, since the story brought me here—
Of some Count Dreux and ancestor of ours
Who, sick of wandering from Bouillon's war,   360
Left his old name in Lebanon.

             Long days
At least to spend in the Isle! and, my news known
An hour hence, what if Anael turn on me
The great black eyes I must forget?

               Why, fool,
Recall them, then? My business is with Djabal,   365
Not Anael! Djabal tarries: if I seek him?—
The Isle is brighter than its wont to-day.

---

347 *1843* dared to ask   350 *1843-63* may heal whate'er's diseased! And good
353 *1843* past retrieve, the lot is   357-8 (no equivalent in *1843*)   363 *1843-*
63 Anael turns on   367 *1843-68* to-day!   s.d. *1843* †[*Exit.*

   345 *this plague-sore*: cf. *King Lear*, II. iv. 223.

   359 *Of some Count Dreux*: see Introduction, p. 282 above.

   360 *Bouillon's war*: the First Crusade, at the end of the eleventh century. Godfrey of
Bouillon was the first of the crusading princes to arrive at Constantinople.

ACT II.

Enter DJABAL.

Djabal. That a strong man should think himself a God!
I—Hakeem? To have wandered through the world,
Sown falsehood, and thence reaped now scorn, now faith,
For my one chant with many a change, my tale
Of outrage, and my prayer for vengeance—this   5
Required, forsooth, no mere man's faculty,
Nought less than Hakeem's? The persuading Loys
To pass probation here; the getting access
By Loys to the Prefect; worst of all,
The gaining my tribe's confidence by fraud   10
That would disgrace the very Frank,—a few
Of Europe's secrets which subdue the flame,
The wave,—to ply a simple tribe with these,
Took Hakeem?
           And I feel this first to-day!
Does the day break, is the hour imminent   15
When one deed, when my whole life's deed, my deed
Must be accomplished? Hakeem? Why the God?
Shout, rather, "Djabal, Youssof's child, thought slain
"With his whole race, the Druses' Sheikhs, this Prefect
"Endeavoured to extirpate--saved, a child,   20
"Returns from traversing the world, a man,
"Able to take revenge, lead back the march
"To Lebanon"—so shout, and who gainsays?

---

1 [no equivalent in *1843*]   5 *1843* vengeance—took   6 [no equivalent in
1843]   7 *1843* No less than Hakeem? *1849–68* Nor less   11 *1843–63* very
Franks, a   12 *1843–63* secrets that subdue   17 *1843* Hakeem? What of
Hakeem?

2 *Hakeem*: God incarnate: cf. n. to I. 5 above.
20 *extirpate*: stressed on the second syllable, as in Johnson.
    saved, a child: cf. the manner in which the infant Sordello was saved: *Sordello*, ii. 325 ff.

But now, because delusion mixed itself
Insensibly with this career, all's changed!   25
Have I brought Venice to afford us convoy?
"True—but my jugglings wrought that!" Put I heart
Into our people where no heart lurked?—"Ah,
"What cannot an impostor do!"
                                        Not this!
Not do this which I do! Not bid avaunt   30
Falsehood! Thou shalt not keep thy hold on me!
—Nor even get a hold on me! 'T is now—
This day—hour—minute—'t is as here I stand
On the accursed threshold of the Prefect,
That I am found deceiving and deceived!   35
And now what do I?—hasten to the few
Deceived, ere they deceive the many—shout,
"As I professed, I did believe myself!
"Say, Druses, had you seen a butchery—
"If Ayoob, Karshook saw—Maani there   40
"Must tell you how I saw my father sink;
"My mother's arms twine still about my neck;
"I hear my brother shriek, here's yet the scar
"Of what was meant for my own death-blow—say,
"If you had woke like me, grown year by year   45
"Out of the tumult in a far-off clime,
"Would it be wondrous such delusion grew?
"I walked the world, asked help at every hand;
"Came help or no? Not this and this? Which helps
"When I returned with, found the Prefect here,   50
"The Druses here, all here but Hakeem's self,
"The Khalif of the thousand prophecies,
"Reserved for such a juncture,—could I call
"My mission aught but Hakeem's? Promised Hakeem

27, 28-9 {no quotation marks in *1843*}   38-61 {no quotation marks in *1843-63*}
43 *1843-65* brother's shriek,   47 *1843* wondrous that delusions grew?
52 {no equivalent in *1843*}

26 *brought*: persuaded.
27 *jugglings*: cf. *Pauline*, 681 and n.
39 *a butchery*: cf. Shelley, *The Revolt of Islam*, 2439.

"More than performs the Djabal—you absolve?   55
"—Me, you will never shame before the crowd
"Yet happily ignorant?—Me, both throngs surround,
"The few deceived, the many unabused,
"—Who, thus surrounded, slay for you and them
"The Prefect, lead to Lebanon? No Khalif,   60
"But Sheikh once more! Mere Djabal—not" . . .

                    Enter KHALIL *hastily.*

    Khalil.   —God Hakeem!
'T is told! The whole Druse nation knows thee, Hakeem,
As we! and mothers lift on high their babes
Who seem aware, so glisten their great eyes,
Thou hast not failed us; ancient brows are proud;   65
Our elders could not earlier die, it seems,
Than at thy coming! The Druse heart is thine!
Take it! my lord and theirs, be thou adored!
    Djabal [*aside*]. Adored!—but I renounce it utterly!
    Khalil. Already are they instituting choirs   70
And dances to the Khalif, as of old
'T is chronicled thou bad'st them.
    Djabal [*aside*].   I abjure it!
'T is not mine—not for me!
    Khalil.   Why pour they wine
Flavoured like honey and bruised mountain-herbs,
Or wear those strings of sun-dried cedar-fruit?   75
Oh, let me tell thee—Esaad, we supposed
Doting, is carried forth, eager to see
The last sun rise on the Isle: he can see now!
The shamed Druse women never wept before:
They can look up when we reach home, they say.   80

57 *1843* surround! *1849-68* surround   58 (no equivalent in *1843*)   61 *1843*
more! Djabal—no longer . . . (s.d.) *Kha.* —Hakeem!   s.d. *1868 hastily*   65 *1843-68*
proud!   72 *1843* chronicled you bade them.   74 *1843-63* mountain herbs?
76 *1843* tell you—Esaad, 78 *1843* The sun rise

Smell!—sweet cane, saved in Lilith's breast thus long—
Sweet! it grows wild in Lebanon. And I
Alone do nothing for thee! 'T is my office
Just to announce what well thou know'st—but thus
Thou bidst me. At this self-same moment tend   85
The Prefect, Nuncio and the Admiral
Hither by their three sea-paths: nor forget
Who were the trusty watchers!—thou forget?
Like me, who do forget that Anael bade . . .
    Djabal [*aside*]. Ay, Anael, Anael—is that said at last?   90
Louder than all, that would be said, I knew!
What does abjuring mean, confessing mean,
To the people? Till that woman crossed my path,
On went I, solely for my people's sake:
I saw her, and I then first saw myself,   95
And slackened pace: "if I should prove indeed
"Hakeem—with Anael by!"
    Khalil [*aside*].   Ah, he is rapt!
Dare I at such a moment break on him
Even to do my sister's bidding? Yes:
The eyes are Djabal's and not Hakeem's yet,   100
Though but till I have spoken this, perchance.
    Djabal [*aside*]. To yearn to tell her, and yet have no one
Great heart's word that will tell her! I could gasp
Doubtless one such word out, and die.
                [*Aloud.*] You said
That Anael . . .
    Khalil.   . . . Fain would see thee, speak with thee,   105
Before thou change, discard this Djabal's shape

---

83 *1843* for you! 'Tis   84 *1843* well you know; but   85 *1843* You bid me.
88 *1843* watchers!—You forget?   95 *1843* and myself too saw I first, *1849, 1863*
and I first saw too myself,   97 *1843* Anael here!" (Ah, ... rapt!)   98 *1843*
on you   99 *1843–63* Yes!   100 *1843–63* yet!   104 *1843–63* die!
105 *1843* see you, speak with you,   106 *1843* Before you change,

    81 *sweet cane, saved in Lilith's breast*: identified by Porter and Clarke as *Acorus calamus*
which, 'when trodden on, smells like incense'. According to the Talmud, Lilith was Adam's
first wife. See the poem, 'Adam, Lilith, and Eve', in *Jocoseria* (1883).
    87 *sea-paths*: as in Milton's translation of Ps. 8: 22.

She knows, for Hakeem's shape she is to know.
Something to say that will not from her mind!
I know not what—"Let him but come!" she said.
   Djabal [*half-apart*]. My nation—all my Druses—how fare
     they?   110
Those I must save, and suffer thus to save,
Hold they their posts? Wait they their Khalif too?
   Khalil. All at the signal pant to flock around
That banner of a brow!
   Djabal [*aside*].   And when they flock,
Confess them this: and after, for reward,   115
Be chased with howlings to her feet perchance!
—Have the poor outraged Druses, deaf and blind,
Precede me there, forestall my story there,
Tell it in mocks and jeers!
                    I lose myself.
Who needs a Hakeem to direct him now?   120
I need the veriest child—why not this child?
                     [*Turning abruptly to* KHALIL.
You are a Druse too, Khalil; you were nourished
Like Anael with our mysteries: if she
Could vow, so nourished, to love only one
Who should avenge the Druses, whence proceeds   125
Your silence? Wherefore made you no essay,
Who thus implicitly can execute
My bidding? What have I done, you could not?
Who, knowing more than Anael the prostration
Of our once lofty tribe, the daily life   130
Of this detested . . .
              Does he come, you say,
This Prefect? All's in readiness?
   Khalil.   The sword,
The sacred robe, the Khalif's mystic tiar,

107 *1843,1849* know: 108 *1843-63* Something's to . . . . mind: 109 *1843*
now how—"Let   115 *1843* Confess to them, and   116 *1843-68* perchance?
119 *1843,1849* jeers—   *1843-68* myself!   125 *1843-63* should revenge the
129 *1843* And, knowing   131 *1843* (Does

133 *tiar*: tiara.

Laid up so long, are all disposed beside
The Prefect's chamber.

    Djabal.   —Why did you despair?   135
    Khalil. I know our nation's state? Too surely know,
As thou who speak'st to prove me! Wrongs like ours
Should wake revenge: but when I sought the wronged
And spoke,—"The Prefect stabbed your son—arise!
"Your daughter, while you starve, eats shameless bread   140
"In his pavilion—then arise!"—my speech
Fell idly: 't was, "Be silent, or worse fare!
"Endure till time's slow cycle prove complete!
"Who mayst thou be that takest on thee to thrust
"Into this peril—art thou Hakeem?" No!   145
Only a mission like thy mission renders
All these obedient at a breath, subdues
Their private passions, brings their wills to one.

    Djabal. You think so?
    Khalil.   Even now—when they have witnessed
Thy miracles—had I not threatened all   150
With Hakeem's vengeance, they would mar the work,
And couch ere this, each with his special prize,
Safe in his dwelling, leaving our main hope
To perish. No! When these have kissed thy feet
At Lebanon, the past purged off, the present   155
Clear,—for the future, even Hakeem's mission
May end, and I perchance, or any youth,
Shall rule them thus renewed.—I tutor thee!

    Djabal. And wisely. (He is Anael's brother, pure
As Anael's self.) Go say, I come to her.   160
Haste! I will follow you.   [KHALIL *goes.*
             Oh, not confess

134 *1843* long, all are disposed   135 *1843* chamber.)   136 *1843* state.
137 *1843* As you, who speak to .... like theirs   143 *1868* complete;
144 *1843* tak'st   146 *1843* like your mission   148 *1843-68* one!
150 *1843* Your miracles   *1843-63* threatened them   151 *1843-63* the whole,
152 *1843,1849* And lie ere   154 *1843-68* perish!   *1843* kissed your feet
157 *1843* any child,   158 *1843* Could rule *1849, 1863* Can rule   *1843-68* I talk
to thee!   159 *1863-8* He   160 *1863,1865* self! *1868* self.   161 s.d.
1843 †[*Exit* KHALIL.

To these, the blinded multitude—confess,
Before at least the fortune of my deed
Half-authorize its means! Only to her
Let me confess my fault, who in my path   165
Curled up like incense from a Mage-king's tomb
When he would have the wayfarer descend
Through the earth's rift and bear hid treasure forth!
How should child's-carelessness prove manhood's crime
Till now that I, whose lone youth hurried past,   170
Letting each joy 'scape for the Druses' sake,
At length recover in one Druse all joy?
Were her brow brighter, her eyes richer, still
Would I confess. On the gulf's verge I pause.
How could I slay the Prefect, thus and thus?   175
Anael, be mine to guard me, not destroy!   [*Goes.*

Enter ANAEL, *and* MAANI *who is assisting to array her in the ancient dress
of the Druses.*

    Anael. Those saffron vestures of the tabret-girls!
Comes Djabal, think you?
    Maani.   Doubtless Djabal comes.
    Anael. Dost thou snow-swathe thee kinglier, Lebanon,
Than in my dreams?—Nay all the tresses off   180
My forehead! Look I lovely so? He says
That I am lovely.
    Maani.   Lovely: nay, that hangs
Awry.

168 *1843-63* and take hid treasure up.   169 *1843-68* When should my first child's-
carelessness have stopped   170 *1843-68* If not when I,   172 *1843-68*
length recovered in   *1843-63* all joys?   174 *1843-68* confess!
176 *1843* Be thou my guardian, not destroyer, Anael! †[*Exit.*   181 *1843,1849* fore-
head   182 *1843,1849* Lovely! nay

    166 *incense from a Mage-king's tomb*: Porter and Clarke point out the reference to 'the
Oriental superstition that the ashes of magicians exhale perfume revealing tombs where
treasures are hid'.
    177 *Those saffron vestures of the tabret-girls!*: cf. 245-7, below. Anael is thinking of
Lebanon. Johnson defines 'tabret' as 'A Tabour', citing Gen. 31: 27.
    179 *snow-swathe*: for the 'snow of Lebanon' see Jer. 18: 14. Cf. *Pauline*, 953. Browning
cannot have considered how an actor could speak this line.
    kinglier: Marlowe uses 'kingly' as an adverb in *I Tamburlaine*, 1. vii. 29.

Anael. You tell me how a khandjar hangs?
The sharp side, thus, along the heart, see, marks
The maiden of our class. Are you content   185
For Djabal as for me?
    Maani.   Content, my child.
    Anael. Oh mother, tell me more of him! He comes
Even now—tell more, fill up my soul with him!
    Maani. And did I not ... yes, surely ... tell you all?
    Anael. What will be changed in Djabal when the Change   190
Arrives? Which feature? Not his eyes!
    Maani.   'T is writ
Our Hakeem's eyes rolled fire and clove the dark
Superbly.
    Anael. Not his eyes! His voice perhaps?
Yet that's no change; for a grave current lived
—Grandly beneath the surface ever lived,   195
That, scattering, broke as in live silver spray
While ... ah, the bliss ... he would discourse to me
In that enforced still fashion, word on word!
'T is the old current which must swell thro' that,
For what least tone, Maani, could I lose?   200
'T is surely not his voice will change!
                      —If Hakeem
Only stood by! If Djabal, somehow, passed
Out of the radiance as from out a robe;
Possessed, but was not it!
                He lived with you?
Well—and that morning Djabal saw me first   205
And heard me vow never to wed but one
Who saved my People—on that day ... proceed!
    Maani. Once more, then: from the time of his return
In secret, changed so since he left the Isle

---

183 *1843* a kandjar hangs?   187 *1843,1849* him.   192 *1843* Our Khalif's
eyes   *197 {reading of *1843-68*} *1888,1889* While .. ah, the bliss .. he
199 *1843* current that must   206 *1843-63* heard my vow   207 *1843* People
first—that

183 *a khandjar*: an Eastern dagger.

That I, who screened our Emir's last of sons,   210
This Djabal, from the Prefect's massacre
—Who bade him ne'er forget the child he was,
—Who dreamed so long the youth he might become—
I knew not in the man that child; the man
Who spoke alone of hope to save our tribe,   215
How he had gone from land to land to save
Our tribe—allies were sure, nor foes to dread.
And much he mused, days, nights, alone he mused:
But never till that day when, pale and worn
As by a persevering woe, he cried   220
"Is there not one Druse left me?"—and I showed
The way to Khalil's and your hiding-place
From the abhorred eye of the Prefect here,
So that he saw you, heard you speak—till then,
Never did he announce—(how the moon seemed   225
To ope and shut, the while, above us both!)
—His mission was the mission promised us;
The cycle had revolved; all things renewing,
He was lost Hakeem clothed in flesh to lead
His children home anon, now veiled to work   230
Great purposes: the Druses now would change!
   Anael. And they have changed! And obstacles did sink,
And furtherances rose! And round his form
Played fire, and music beat her angel wings!
My people, let me more rejoice, oh more   235
For you than for myself! Did I but watch
Afar the pageant, feel our Khalif pass,
One of the throng, how proud were I—tho' ne'er
Singled by Djabal's glance! But to be chosen
His own from all, the most his own of all,   240
To be exalted with him, side by side,

---

213 *1843* he had become—   215 *1843–63* of hopes to   217 *1843–68* dread;
231 *1843,1849* change.   237 *1843* feel the Khalif   241 *1843–68* side.

  228 *The cycle had revolved*: cf. I. 232 and II. 143 above.
  234 *fire, and music*: cf. I. 136–8 above.
  239 *Singled*: singled out, as in *3 Henry VI*, II. iv. 1.

Lead the exulting Druses, meet ... ah, how
Worthily meet the maidens who await
Ever beneath the cedars—how deserve
This honour, in their eyes? So bright are they   245
Who saffron-vested sound the tabret there,
The girls who throng there in my dream! One hour
And all is over: how shall I do aught
That may deserve next hour's exalting?—How?—

                      [*Suddenly to* MAANI.

Mother, I am not worthy him! I read it   250
Still in his eyes! He stands as if to tell me
I am not, yet forbears. Why else revert
To one theme ever?—how mere human gifts
Suffice him in myself—whose worship fades,
Whose awe goes ever off at his approach,   255
As now, who when he comes ...

            [DJABAL *enters.*] Oh why is it
I cannot kneel to you?
    Djabal.   Rather, 't is I
Should kneel to you, my Anael!
    Anael.   Even so!
For never seem you—shall I speak the truth?—
Never a God to me! 'T is the Man's hand,   260
Eye, voice! Oh do you veil these to our people,
Or but to me? To them, I think, to them!
And brightness is their veil, shadow—my truth!
You mean that I should never kneel to you
—So, thus I kneel!
    Djabal [*preventing her*]. No—no!

             [*Feeling the khandjar as he raises her.*
             Ha, have you chosen ...   265
    Anael. The khandjar with our ancient garb. But, Djabal,

243 *1843* who have watched   246 *1843-63* That saffron-vestured sound the tabrets
there—   247 *1843-63* my dreams! One   250 *1849, 1863* worthy of him!
252 *1843-63* forbears!   255 *1843* goes off ever at   256 *1843* now, that as he
1849, 1863 now, that when he   s.d. *1849, 1863* †[*As* DJABAL   262 *1843* me?
Them, let me think,   265 *1843-68* —So I will kneel!

   263 *brightness is their veil*: cf. Shelley, *Prometheus Unbound*, III. i. 34.

Change not, be not exalted yet! Give time
That I may plan more, perfect more! My blood
Beats, beats!
  [*Aside.*]   Oh must I then—since Loys leaves us
Never to come again, renew in me   270
These doubts so near effaced already—must
I needs confess them now to Djabal?—own
That when I saw that stranger, heard his voice,
My faith fell, and the woeful thought flashed first
That each effect of Djabal's presence, taken   275
For proof of more than human attributes
In him, by me whose heart at his approach
Beat fast, whose brain while he was by swam round,
Whose soul at his departure died away,
—That every such effect might have been wrought   280
In other frames, tho' not in mine, by Loys
Or any merely mortal presence? Doubt
Is fading fast; shall I reveal it now?
How shall I meet the rapture presently,
With doubt unexpiated, undisclosed?   285
  Djabal [*aside*]. Avow the truth? I cannot! In what words
Avow that all she loved in me was false?
—Which yet has served that flower-like love of hers
To climb by, like the clinging gourd, and clasp
With its divinest wealth of leaf and bloom.   290
Could I take down the prop-work, in itself
So vile, yet interlaced and overlaid
With painted cups and fruitage—might these still
Bask in the sun, unconscious their own strength
Of matted stalk and tendril had replaced   295
The old support thus silently withdrawn!
But no; the beauteous fabric crushes too.

267 *1843* yet—   268 *1843-65* more.   271 *1843,1849* Those doubts
273 *1843* I Loÿs saw and Loÿs heard,   281 *1843-63* In others' frames,
284 *1843* And yet to be rewarded presently *1849, 1863* How can I be rewarded presently,
285 *1843* undisclosed!   287 *1843-63* she loves in *1865* she love in
290 *1843* bloom:

'T is not for my sake but for Anael's sake
I leave her soul this Hakeem where it leans.
Oh could I vanish from her, quit the Isle!   300
And yet—a thought comes: here my work is done
At every point; the Druses must return—
Have convoy to their birth-place back, whoe'er
The leader be, myself or any Druse—
Venice is pledged to that; 't is for myself,   305
For my own vengeance in the Prefect's death,
I stay now, not for them: to slay or spare
The Prefect, whom imports it save myself?
He cannot bar their passage from the Isle;
What would his death be but my own reward?   310
Then, mine I will forego. It is foregone!
Let him escape with all my House's blood!
Ere he can reach land, Djabal disappears,
And Hakeem, Anael loved, shall, fresh as first,
Live in her memory, keeping her sublime   315
Above the world. She cannot touch that world
By ever knowing what I truly am,
Since Loys,—of mankind the only one
Able to link my present with my past,
My life in Europe with my Island life,   320
Thence, able to unmask me,—I've disposed
Safely at last at Rhodes, and . . .

Enter KHALIL.

Khalil.   Loys greets thee!
Djabal. Loys? To drag me back? It cannot be!
Anael [*aside*]. Loys! Ah, doubt may not be stifled so!
Khalil. Can I have erred that thou so gazest? Yes,   325
I told thee not in the glad press of tidings

299 *1843-68* leans!   300 {no equivalent in *1843*} *1849, 1863* from them—quit
303-4, 306 {no equivalent in *1843*}   307 *1843* to stay or   309 {no equivalent
in *1843*}   313 *1843* Ere he can land I will have disappeared,   320 *1843* That
life .... with this Island life,   322 *1843* greets you!   324a,b *1843* Doubt
must be quite destroyed or quite confirmed, | Must find day somehow, live or dead. 'Tis
well!   325 *1843* that you so gaze on me?   326 *1843* True, I forgot, in

Of higher import, Loys is returned
Before the Prefect, with, if possible,
Twice the light-heartedness of old. As though
On some inauguration he expects,   330
To-day, the world's fate hung!
    Djabal.   —And asks for me?
    Khalil. Thou knowest all things. Thee in chief he greets,
But every Druse of us is to be happy
At his arrival, he declares: were Loys
Thou, Master, he could have no wider soul   335
To take us in with. How I love that Loys!
    Djabal [*aside*]. Shame winds me with her tether round and
        round.
    Anael [*aside*]. Loys? I take the trial! it is meet,
The little I can do, be done; that faith,
All I can offer, want no perfecting   340
Which my own act may compass. Ay, this way
All may go well, nor that ignoble doubt
Be chased by other aid than mine. Advance
Close to my fear, weigh Loys with my Lord,
The mortal with the more than mortal gifts!   345
    Djabal [*aside*]. Before, there were so few deceived! and
        now
There's doubtless not one least Druse in the Isle
But, having learned my superhuman claims,
And calling me his Khalif-God, will clash
The whole truth out from Loys at first word!   350
While Loys, for his part, will hold me up,
With a Frank's unimaginable scorn
Of such imposture, to my people's eyes!

329 *1843* old. You'd think ·   331 *1843* hung.   332 *1843* Ah, you know all
1843-63 things!   333 *1843* every body else is   335 *1843* Thou, Khalif, he
337 *1843* {no s.d.} *1849-68* round!   338 *1843* trial: meet it is   342 *1843*
ignoble spot   343 *1843* mine. Best go   345 *1843-63* mortal's .... mortal's
346 *1843* deceived,   348 *1843,1849* (having   349 *1843* Khalif now) will
1849 Kalif-God)   351 *1843* And Loÿs,   353 *1843* Of this imposture, ...
eyes,   353a *1843* To Khalil's eyes, to Anael's eyes! Oh, how
    349 *clash*: beat.

Could I but keep him longer yet awhile
From them, amuse him here until I plan   355
How he and I at once may leave the Isle!
Khalil I cannot part with from my side—
My only help in this emergency:
There's Anael!
    Anael.   Please you?
    Djabal.   Anael—none but she!
[*To* ANAEL.] I pass some minutes in the chamber there,   360
Ere I see Loys: you shall speak with him
Until I join you. Khalil follows me.
    Anael [*aside*]. As I divined: he bids me save myself
Offers me a probation—I accept.
Let me see Loys!
    Loys [*without*]. Djabal!
    Anael [*aside*].   'T is his voice.   365
The smooth Frank trifler with our people's wrongs,
The self-complacent boy-inquirer, loud
On this and that inflicted tyranny,
—Aught serving to parade an ignorance
Of how wrong feels, inflicted! Let me close   370
With what I viewed at distance: let myself
Probe this delusion to the core!
    Djabal.   He comes.
Khalil, along with me! while Anael waits
Till I return once more—and but once more.

---

354 *1843* —How hold him longer yet a little while *1849* but hold him   356 *1843*-
63 Isle?   357-8 {no equivalent in *1843*}   359 *1843* (Anael only!) Anael,
1849 (Anael .... she!)   360 *1843* {no s.d.} I would pass some few minutes here
within   362 *1843* you and declare the end.   364 *1843* Allows me the proba-
tion—*1843-63* accept!   371 *1843* distance, and, myself, *1849* distance; *1863* dis-
tance!   372 *1843-63* comes!   373 *1863* me;   374 *1843-68* more!
s.d. *1843* †[*Exeunt* DJABAL and KHALIL. *Manet* ANAEL.

    355 *amuse* : 'entertain with tranquillity': Johnson.

ACT III.

ANAEL *and* LOYS.

Anael. Here leave me! Here I wait another. 'T was
For no mad protestation of a love
Like this you say possesses you, I came.
　　Loys. Love? how protest a love I dare not feel?
Mad words may doubtless have escaped me: you　　　　5
Are here—I only feel you here!
　　Anael.　　　　　　　No more!
　　Loys. But once again, whom could you love? I dare,
Alas, say nothing of myself, who am
A Knight now, for when Knighthood we embrace,
Love we abjure: so, speak on safely: speak,　　　　10
Lest I speak, and betray my faith! And yet
To say your breathing passes through me, changes
My blood to spirit, and my spirit to you,
As Heaven the sacrificer's wine to it—
This is not to protest my love! You said　　　　15
You could love one . . .
　　Anael.　　　　　One only! We are bent
To earth—who raises up my tribe, I love;
The Prefect bows us—who removes him; we
Have ancient rights—who gives them back to us,
I love. Forbear me! Let my hand go!
　　Loys.　　　　　　Him　　　　20
You could love only? Where is Djabal? Stay!
[*Aside.*] Yet wherefore stay? Who does this but myself?

---

4 *1843-63* Love—
now, and when
15 *1843,1849* love?　　7 *1843* Say but again,
11 *1843* faith so? Sure *1849* faith so! Sure *1863* faith.
17 *1843* To the earth—　　8 *1843* Alas!　　9 *1843*
18 *1843* Prefect bends us—
22 *1843* [no s.d.]

　　12-13 *changes / My blood to spirit*: cf. Donne, 'The Extasie', 61-2: 'As our love labours to
beget / Spirits'.　　14 *As Heaven the sacrificer's wine*: in the Communion service.
　　18 *bows*: transitive, as in *Samson Agonistes*, 698.
　　who removes him: i.e. I love the man who removes him.

Had I apprised her that I come to do
Just this, what more could she acknowledge? No,
She sees into my heart's core! What is it   25
Feeds either cheek with red, as June some rose?
Why turns she from me? Ah fool, over-fond
To dream I could call up . . .
                                        . . . What never dream
Yet feigned! 'T is love! Oh Anael speak to me!
Djabal—
        Anael. Seek Djabal by the Prefect's chamber   30
At noon!   [*She paces the room.*
        Loys [*aside*]. And am I not the Prefect now?
Is it my fate to be the only one
Able to win her love, the only one
Unable to accept her love? The past
Breaks up beneath my footing: came I here   35
This morn as to a slave, to set her free
And take her thanks, and then spend day by day
Content beside her in the Isle? What works
This knowledge in me now? Her eye has broken
The faint disguise away: for Anael's sake   40
I left the Isle, for her espoused the cause
Of the Druses, all for her I thought, till now,
To live without!
                —As I must live! To-day
Ordains me Knight, forbids me . . . never shall
Forbid me to profess myself, heart, arm,   45
Thy soldier!
        Anael.   Djabal you demanded, comes.
        Loys [*aside*]. What wouldst thou, Loys? See him? Nought
        beside
Is wanting: I have felt his voice a spell

24 *1843,1849* No!   25 *1843,1849* core: 30 *1843-65* Djabal!
31 *1843 Loÿs.* And   38 *1843* Beside her in the Isle content? What   39 *1843-*
63 now!   43 *1843* live: 46 *1843* you awaited, comes! *1849-68* comes!
47 *1843* [no s.d.]

 25 *my heart's core*: as in *Hamlet*, III. ii. 71.
 34-5 *The past* / *Breaks up*: cf. *Pauline* 395-6.

From first to last. He brought me here, made known
The Druses to me, drove me hence to seek   50
Redress for them; and shall I meet him now,
When nought is wanting but a word of his,
To—what?—induce me to spurn hope, faith, pride,
Honour away,—to cast my lot among
His tribe, become a proverb in men's mouths,   55
Breaking my high pact of companionship
With those who graciously bestowed on me
The very opportunities I turn
Against them! Let me not see Djabal now!
  Anael. The Prefect also comes.
  Loys [*aside*].   Him let me see,   60
Not Djabal! Him, degraded at a word,
To soothe me,—to attest belief in me—
And after, Djabal! Yes, ere I return
To her, the Nuncio's vow shall have destroyed
This heart's rebellion, and coerced this will   65
For ever.
              Anael, not before the vows
Irrevocably fix me . . .
                    Let me fly!
The Prefect, or I lose myself for ever!   [*Goes.*
  Anael. Yes, I am calm now; just one way remains—
One, to attest my faith in him: for, see   70
I were quite lost else: Loys, Djabal, stand
On either side—two men! I balance looks
And words, give Djabal a man's preference,
No more. In Djabal, Hakeem is absorbed!
And for a love like this, the God who saves   75
My race, selects me for his bride? One way!

59 *1843* Against them. Löys, they procured thee, think, *1849* them.   59a *1843* What
now procures her love! Not Djabal now!   60 *1843–68* comes!   *1843* [no s.d.]
62 *1843,1849* To please me,—   66 *1843* not until the   67 *1843* me leave her!
68 *1843* ever. †[*Exit.*   70 *1843* So I attest   71 *1843* I am quite lost now: Löys
and Djabal stand   74 *1843* more. The Khalif is absorbed in Djabal!   75 *1843*
Is it for a love like this that he who saves   76 *1849–65* bride!

  55 *become a proverb*: biblical, as in Deut. 28: 37.

Enter DJABAL.

Djabal [to himself]. No moment is to waste then; 't is
   resolved.
If Khalil may be trusted to lead back
My Druses, and if Loys can be lured
Out of the Isle—if I procure his silence,   80
Or promise never to return at least,—
All's over. Even now my bark awaits:
I reach the next wild islet and the next,
And lose myself beneath the sun for ever.
And now, to Anael!
    Anael.   Djabal, I am thine!   85
    Djabal. Mine? Djabal's?—As if Hakeem had not been?
    Anael. Not Djabal's? Say first, do you read my thought?
Why need I speak, if you can read my thought?
    Djabal. I do not, I have said a thousand times.
    Anael. (My secret's safe, I shall surprise him yet!)   90
Djabal, I knew your secret from the first:
Djabal, when first I saw you . . . (by our porch
You leant, and pressed the tinkling veil away,
And one fringe fell behind your neck—I see!)
. . . I knew you were not human, for I said   95
"This dim secluded house where the sea beats
"Is heaven to me—my people's huts are hell
"To them; this august form will follow me,
"Mix with the waves his voice will,—I have him;
"And they, the Prefect! Oh, my happiness   100
"Rounds to the full whether I choose or no!
"His eyes met mine, he was about to speak,
"His hand grew damp—surely he meant to say
"He let me love him: in that moment's bliss
"I shall forget my people pine for home—   105

77 *1843* to sparc then; *1843-65* resolved!   79 *1843-63* The Druses,
80 *1843* Isle—can I   82 *1843-65* over!   *1843* bark is ready;   84 *1843*
myself thus in the   *1843-65* ever!   84a,b *1843* Anacl remains now.—Think! She
loved in me | But Hakeem—Hakeem's vanished; and on Djabal   85 *1843* Had never
glanced— *An.* Djabal, I am thinc own!   87, 88 *1843-63* my thoughts?
99 *1843* will, him have I   100 *1843-68* Prefect;   101 *1843* I chose or

"They pass and they repass with pallid eyes!"
I vowed at once a certain vow; this vow—
Not to embrace you till my tribe was saved.
Embrace me!

    Djabal [*apart*]. And she loved me! Nought remained
But that! Nay, Anael, is the Prefect dead?   110

    Anael. Ah, you reproach me! True, his death crowns all,
I know—or should know: and I would do much,
Believe! but, death! Oh, you, who have known death,
Would never doom the Prefect, were death fearful
As we report!

            Death!—a fire curls within us   115
From the foot's palm, and fills up to the brain,
Up, out, then shatters the whole bubble-shell
Of flesh, perchance!

            Death!—witness, I would die,
Whate'er death be, would venture now to die
For Khalil, for Maani—what for thee?   120
Nay but embrace me, Djabal, in assurance
My vow will not be broken, for I must
Do something to attest my faith in you,
Be worthy you!

    Djabal [*avoiding her*]. I come for that—to say
Such an occasion is at hand: 't is like   125
I leave you—that we part, my Anael,—part
For ever!

    Anael. We part? Just so! I have succumbed,—
I am, he thinks, unworthy—and nought less
Will serve than such approval of my faith.
Then, we part not! Remains there no way short   130
Of that? Oh not that!

            Death!—yet a hurt bird

---

109 s.d. *1843* †[*Shrinking.*]†   112 *1843* know—I should   113 *1843* Believe—
1843-63 but, death—   120 *1843* For Maäni—for Khalil—but, for him?—
124 *1849, 1863* worthy of you!   127 *1843* succumbed, he thinks,
129 *1843-63* faith!   130 *1843* not! Yet remains

116 *the foot's palm* : OED describes the use of 'palm' for the sole of the foot as rare: 'Palm',
sb. 2c.

Died in my hands; its eyes filmed—"Nay, it sleeps,"
I said, "will wake to-morrow well." 't was dead.

    Djabal. I stand here and time fleets. Anael—I come
To bid a last farewell to you: perhaps   135
We never meet again. But, ere the Prefect
Arrive . . .

             Enter KHALIL, *breathlessly.*

Khalil. He's here! The Prefect! Twenty guards,
No more: no sign he dreams of danger. All
Awaits thee only. Ayoob, Karshook, keep
Their posts—wait but the deed's accomplishment   140
To join us with thy Druses to a man.
Still holds his course the Nuncio—near and near
The fleet from Candia steering.

    Djabal [*aside*].   All is lost!
—Or won?

    Khalil.   And I have laid the sacred robe,
The sword, the head-tiar, at the porch—the place   145
Commanded. Thou wilt hear the Prefect's trumpet.

    Djabal. Then I keep Anael,—him then, past recall,
I slay—'t is forced on me. As I began
I must conclude—so be it!

    Khalil.   For the rest,
Save Loys, our foe's solitary sword,   150
All is so safe that . . . I will ne'er entreat
Thy post again of thee: tho' danger none,
There must be glory only meet for thee

---

132 *1843* my arms its—   133 *1843-63* dead!   135-6 *1843* you—we never |
Perhaps shall meet again—but,   137 *1843* Arrives ... †[*Enter*   139 *1843*
Awaits you only—   141 *1843* with your Druses   *1843-68* man!
143 *1843,1849* Candia's steering!   144 *1843-63* sacred robes,   145 *1843*
porch as 'twas   146 *1843* Commanded—You will hear   147 *1843* Anael, I
keep them, him then, past retrieve,   148 *1843-68* me!   150 *1843* (Save
Loÿs, but a solitary sword) *1849* (Save .... sword)   152 *1843* Your post again of
you—tho' danger's none, *1849* danger's none,   153 *1843* for you

  150 *sword* : swordsman, soldier.

In slaying the Prefect.

    Anael [*aside*].   And 't is now that Djabal
Would leave me!—in the glory meet for him!   155

    Djabal. As glory, I would yield the deed to you
Or any Druse; what peril there may be,
I keep. [*Aside.*] All things conspire to hound me on.
Not now, my soul, draw back, at least! Not now!
The course is plain, howe'er obscure all else.   160
Once offer this tremendous sacrifice,
Prevent what else will be irreparable,
Secure these transcendental helps, regain
The Cedars—then let all dark clear itself!
I slay him!

    Khalil. Anael, and no part for us!   165
[*To* DJABAL.] Hast thou possessed her with . . .

    Djabal [*to* ANAEL].   Whom speak you to?
What is it you behold there? Nay, this smile
Turns stranger. Shudder you? The man must die,
As thousands of our race have died thro' him.
One blow, and I discharge his weary soul   170
From the flesh that pollutes it! Let him fill
Straight some new expiatory form, of earth
Or sea, the reptile or some aëry thing:
What is there in his death?

    Anael.   My brother said,
Is there no part in it for us?

    Djabal.   For Khalil,—   175
The trumpet will announce the Nuncio's entry;
Here, I shall find the Prefect hastening
In the Pavilion to receive him—here

---

154 *1843-68* Prefect! *1843* [no s.d.]   157 *1843,1849* any one; what
158 *1843* [no s.d.] *1843-68* on!   164 *1843* all this clear   170 *1843* A blow,
171 *1843* The body that pollutes it— *1849* it— *1863* it;   172 *1843* Some new

    164 *The Cedars*: see l. 166 n.

    172 *some new expiatory form*: an allusion to the alleged belief of some of the Druses in
metempsychosis. 'The Christians, who live in their country, pretend [claim] that several of
them believe in Metempsychosis': Volney, ii. 61.

I slay the Prefect; meanwhile Ayoob leads
The Nuncio with his guards within: once these   180
Secured in the outer hall, bid Ayoob bar
Entry or egress till I give the sign
Which waits the landing of the argosies
You will announce to me: this double sign
That justice is performed and help arrived,   185
When Ayoob shall receive, but not before,
Let him throw ope the palace doors, admit
The Druses to behold their tyrant, ere
We leave for ever this detested spot.
Go, Khalil, hurry all! No pause, no pause!   190
Whirl on the dream, secure to wake anon!
    Khalil. What sign? and who the bearer?
    Djabal.   Who shall show
My ring, admit to Ayoob. How she stands!
Have I not . . . I must have some task for her.
Anael, not that way! 'T is the Prefect's chamber!   195
Anael, keep you the ring—give you the sign!
(It holds her safe amid the stir.) You will
Be faithful?
    Anael [*taking the ring*]. I would fain be worthy. Hark!
                                     [*Trumpet without.*

    Khalil. He comes.
    Djabal.   And I too come.
    Anael.   One word, but one!
Say, shall you be exalted at the deed?   200
Then? On the instant?
    Djabal.   I exalted? What?
He, there—we, thus—our wrongs revenged, our tribe
Set free? Oh, then shall I, assure yourself,
Shall you, shall each of us, be in his death   204

---

180 *1843* once he   184 *1843* Yourself announce: when he receives my sign
185–6 {no equivalent in *1843*}   190 *1843,1849* all—   192 *1843* sign? *Dja*.
Whoe'er shall show my ring admit   193 *1843* To Ayoob and the Nuncio. How
195 *1843* Anael! . . . . way! That's the *1849–65* Anael!   *1843* chamber. *1863* chamber
198 *1843* worthy you! | *1849–68* worthy of you! | 199 *1843–68* comes! . . . . come!
203 *1843,1849* free—

Exalted!

Khalil. He is here.

Djabal.   Away—away!   [*They go.*

Enter the PREFECT *with* Guards, *and* LOYS.

The Prefect [*to* Guards]. Back, I say, to the galley every
          guard!
That's my sole care now; see each bench retains
Its complement of rowers; I embark
O' the instant, since this Knight will have it so.
Alas me! Could you have the heart, my Loys!   210
[*To a* Guard *who whispers.*]
Oh, bring the holy Nuncio here forthwith!   [*The* Guards *go.*
Loys, a rueful sight, confess, to see
The grey discarded Prefect leave his post,
With tears i' the eye! So, you are Prefect now?
You depose me—you succeed me? Ha, ha!   215
          Loys. And dare you laugh, whom laughter less becomes
Than yesterday's forced meekness we beheld . . .
          Prefect. —When you so eloquently pleaded, Loys,
For my dismissal from the post? Ah, meek
With cause enough, consult the Nuncio else!   220
And wish him the like meekness: for so staunch
A servant of the Church can scarce have bought
His share in the Isle, and paid for it, hard pieces!
You've my successor to condole with, Nuncio!
I shall be safe by then i' the galley, Loys!   225
          Loys. You make as you would tell me you rejoice
To leave your scene of . . .
          Prefect.   Trade in the dear Druses?
Blood and sweat traffic? Spare what yesterday

*205 {reading of *1843-68*,DC,*1889*} *1888* Away—away   *1843-68* here!   s.d.
1843 †[*Exeunt.*   210 *1843-68* Loys?   211 s.d. *1843* †[*Exeunt* Guards.

          223 *hard pieces!*: in hard cash, as distinct from promissory notes, etc. See OED 'hard', *adj.*,
I. 2.
          228 *Blood and sweat traffic*: having been despatched to St Kitts as a young man, Brown-
ing's father 'conceived such a hatred to the slave-system in the West Indies . . . that he relin-
quished every prospect' and returned to England, 'to his father's profound astonishment
and rage': Kintner, ii. 1005-6.

We heard enough of! Drove I in the Isle
A profitable game? Learn wit, my son,   230
Which you'll need shortly! Did it never breed
Suspicion in you, all was not pure profit,
When I, the insatiate . . . and so forth—was bent
On having a partaker in my rule?
Why did I yield this Nuncio half the gain,   235
If not that I might also shift—what on him?
Half of the peril, Loys!
   Loys.   Peril?
   Prefect.   Hark you!
I'd love you if you'd let me—this for reason,
You save my life at price of . . . well, say risk
At least, of yours. I came a long time since   240
To the Isle; our Hospitallers bade me tame
These savage wizards, and reward myself—
   Loys. The Knights who so repudiate your crime?
   Prefect. Loys, the Knights! we doubtless understood
Each other; as for trusting to reward   245
From any friend beside myself . . . no, no!
I clutched mine on the spot, when it was sweet,
And I had taste for it. I felt these wizards
Alive—was sure they were not on me, only
When I was on them: but with age comes caution: 250
And stinging pleasures please less and sting more.
Year by year, fear by fear! The girls were brighter
Than ever ('faith, there's yet one Anael left,
I set my heart upon—Oh, prithee, let
That brave new sword lie still!)—These joys looked brighter,   255
But silenter the town, too, as I passed.
With this alcove's delicious memories
Began to mingle visions of gaunt fathers,
Quick-eyed sons, fugitives from the mine, the oar,

---

229 *1843-68* We had enough   234 *1843* having an associate in   244 *1843*
Knights—we doubtless understand   254 *1843* upon)—   255 *1843* still!—
These joys were brighter,   258 *1843* Yet to be mingled visions

Stealing to catch me. Brief, when I began   260
To quake with fear—(I think I hear the Chapter
Solicited to let me leave, now all
Worth staying for was gained and gone!)—I say,
Just when, for the remainder of my life,
All methods of escape seemed lost—that then   265
Up should a young hot-headed Loys spring,
Talk very long and loud,—in fine, compel
The Knights to break their whole arrangement, have me
Home for pure shame—from this safehold of mine
Where but ten thousand Druses seek my life,   270
To my wild place of banishment, San Gines
By Murcia, where my three fat manors lying,
Purchased by gains here and the Nuncio's gold,
Are all I have to guard me,—that such fortune
Should fall to me, I hardly could expect.   275
Therefore I say, I'd love you.
   Loys.   Can it be?
I play into your hands then? Oh no, no!
The Venerable Chapter, the Great Order
Sunk o' the sudden into fiends of the pit?
But I will back—will yet unveil you!
   Prefect.   Me?   280
To whom?—perhaps Sir Galeas, who in Chapter
Shook his white head thrice—and some dozen times
My hand next morning shook, for value paid!
To that Italian saint, Sir Cosimo?—

---

260 *1843-68* me: 264 *1843* That when   265 *1843* lost—just then
275 *1843-68* expect!   276 *1843-68* you!   283 *1843,1849* hand this morning
1843 paid? *1849* paid

   259 *Quick-eyed sons*: cf. 'The Bishop Orders his Tomb', 104.

   271-2 *San Gines / By Murcia*: a village near the bay of Murcia, near Cartagena.

   278 *Chapter*: 'A duly constituted general meeting or assembly of the canons of a col-
legiate or cathedral church, of the members of any monastic or religious order, or of an
order of knights, for consultation and transaction of the affairs of their order': OED
sb. 4.

   284 *Sir Cosimo*: Cosimo de Medici: an allusion to the visit of Fakr-el-din to the court of
the Medici in Florence, at the beginning of the seventeenth century. See Volney, ii. 41 ff.

Indignant at my wringing year by year   285
A thousand bezants from the coral-divers,
As you recounted; felt the saint aggrieved?
Well might he—I allowed for his half-share
Merely one hundred. To Sir ...
   Loys.   See! you dare
Inculpate the whole Order; yet should I,   290
A youth, a sole voice, have the power to change
Their evil way, had they been firm in it?
Answer me!
   Prefect.   Oh, the son of Bretagne's Duke,
And that son's wealth, the father's influence, too,
And the young arm, we'll even say, my Loys,   295
—The fear of losing or diverting these
Into another channel, by gainsaying
A novice too abruptly, could not influence
The Order! You might join, for aught they cared,
Their red-cross rivals of the Temple! Well,   300
I thank you for my part, at all events.
Stay here till they withdraw you! You'll inhabit
My palace—sleep, perchance, in the alcove
Whither I go to meet our holy friend.
Good! and now disbelieve me if you can,—   305
This is the first time for long years I enter
Thus [*lifts the arras*] without feeling just as if I lifted
The lid up of my tomb.
   Loys.   They share his crime!
God's punishment will overtake you yet.

287 *1843-65* felt he not aggrieved?   289 *1843-68* hundred!   301 *1843-65*
events!   303 *1843,1849* This palace—   *1843* in this alcove; *1849* in this alcove,
304 {no equivalent in *1843*} *1849-65* Where now I   *1849, 1863* friend:
308 *1843-65* tomb!   309 *1843-65* yet!

  286 *bezants*: valuable coins, of gold or silver.

  290 *Inculpate*: stressed on the second syllable.

  300 *Their red-cross rivals of the Temple*: the Knights Templar were members of a military
and religious order founded in the early twelfth century for the protection of the Holy
Sepulchre and of Christian pilgrims visiting the Holy Land. Their name derives from their
occupation of a building on or close to the site of the Temple of Solomon in Jerusalem.
They were suppressed in 1312.

Prefect. Thank you it does not! Pardon this last flash: 310
I bear a sober visage presently
With the disinterested Nuncio here—
His purchase-money safe at Murcia, too!
Let me repeat—for the first time, no draught
Coming as from a sepulchre salutes me.   315
When we next meet, this folly may have passed,
We'll hope. Ha, ha!   [*Goes through the arras.*
    Loys.   Assure me but . . . he's gone!
He could not lie. Then what have I escaped,
I, who had so nigh given up happiness
For ever, to be linked with him and them!   320
Oh, opportunest of discoveries! I
Their Knight? I utterly renounce them all!
Hark! What, he meets by this the Nuncio? Yes,
The same hyæna groan-like laughter! Quick—
To Djabal! I am one of them at last,   325
These simple-hearted Druses—Anael's tribe!
Djabal! She's mine at last. Djabal, I say!   [*Goes.*

311 *1843* a graver visage   317 s.d. *1843* †[*Exit thro'*   318 *1843–65* lie! . . . .
escaped!   319 *1843,1849* who have so   323 *1843* Nuncio? Quick
324 (no equivalent in *1843*)   326 *1843,1849* Those simple-hearted   327 s.d.
1843 †[*Exit.*

ACT IV.

Enter DJABAL.

Djabal. Let me but slay the Prefect. The end now!
To-morrow will be time enough to pry
Into the means I took: suffice, they served,
Ignoble as they were, to hurl revenge
True to its object.   [*Seeing the robe, etc. disposed.*
              Mine should never so   5
Have hurried to accomplishment! Thee, Djabal,
Far other mood befitted! Calm the Robe
Should clothe this doom's awarder!
                  [*Taking the robe.*] Shall I dare
Assume my nation's Robe? I am at least
A Druse again, chill Europe's policy   10
Drops from me: I dare take the Robe. Why not
The Tiar? I rule the Druses, and what more
Betokens it than rule?—yet—yet—   [*Lays down the tiar.*
[*Footsteps in the alcove.*] He comes!   [*Taking the sword.*
If the Sword serve, let the Tiar lie! So, feet
Clogged with the blood of twenty years can fall   15
Thus lightly! Round me, all ye ghosts! He'll lift . . .
Which arm to push the arras wide?—or both?
Stab from the neck down to the heart—there stay!
Near he comes—nearer—the next footstep! Now!
                  [*As he dashes aside the arras,* ANAEL *is discovered.*
Ha! Anael! Nay, my Anael, can it be?   20
Heard you the trumpet? I must slay him here,
And here you ruin all. Why speak you not?
Anael, the Prefect comes! [ANAEL *screams.*] So slow to feel
'T is not a sight for you to look upon?
A moment's work—but such work! Till you go,   25

5 s.d. *1843–63 the robes, &c.*   7 *1843–63* other moods befitted!   8 *1843* awar-
der. {s. d.} Well, I   9 *1843* Robe.   11 *1843* Robe: 14 *1843–63* sword
serves, let   *16 {reading of *1843–68*} *1888,1889* lift . .   23 *1843–63* So late to

I must be idle—idle, I risk all!   [*Pointing to her hair.*
Those locks are well, and you are beauteous thus,
But with the dagger 't is, I have to do!
    Anael. With mine!·
    Djabal.   Blood—Anael?
    Anael.   Djabal, 't is thy deed!
It must be! I had hoped to claim it mine—   30
Be worthy thee—but I must needs confess
'T was not I, but thyself . . . not I have . . . Djabal!
Speak to me!
    Djabal.   Oh, my punishment!
    Anael.   Speak to me
While I can speak! touch me, despite the blood!
When the command passed from thy soul to mine,   35
I went, fire leading me, muttering of thee,
And the approaching exaltation,—"make
"One sacrifice!" I said,—and he sat there,
Bade me approach; and, as I did approach,
Thy fire with music burst into my brain.   40
'T was but a moment's work, thou saidst—perchance
It may have been so! Well, it is thy deed.
    Djabal. It is my deed.
    Anael.   His blood all this!—this! and . . .
And more! Sustain me, Djabal! Wait not—now
Let flash thy glory! Change thyself and me!   45
It must be! Ere the Druses flock to us!
At least confirm me! Djabal, blood gushed forth—
He was our tyrant—but I looked he'd fall
Prone as asleep—why else is death called sleep?
Sleep? He bent o'er his breast! 'T is sin, I know,—   50
Punish me, Djabal, but wilt thou let him?

---

29 *1843 An.* Mine—Look! *Dja.* Blood—   30 *1843,1849* be—   33 *1843,1849*
me!   34 *1843,1849* speak—   37-8 {no quotation marks in *1843-63*}
40 *1843,1849* brain— *1863-68* brain: 42, 43 *1843-68* deed!   44 *1843-65*
more—   *1843,1849* Djabal—   47 *1863,1865* Djabal!   50 *1843* his neck—
'Tis *1849* breast—

    40 *Thy fire with music*: see I. 136-8.

Be it thou that punishest, not he—who creeps
On his red breast—is here! 'T is the small groan
Of a child—no worse! Bestow the new life, then!
Too swift it cannot be, too strange, surpassing!   55
                    [*Following him as he retreats.*
Now! Change us both! Change me and change thou!
    Djabal [*sinks on his knees*].   Thus!
Behold my change! You have done nobly. I!—
    Anael. Can Hakeem kneel?
    Djabal.   No Hakeem, and scarce Djabal!
I have dealt falsely, and this woe is come.
No—hear me ere scorn blast me! Once and ever,   60
The deed is mine. Oh think upon the past!
    Anael [*to herself*]. Did I strike once, or twice, or many
        times?
    Djabal. I came to lead my tribe where, bathed in glooms,
Doth Bahumid the Renovator sleep:
Anael, I saw my tribe: I said, "Without   65
"A miracle this cannot be"—I said
"Be there a miracle!"—for I saw you.
    Anael. His head lies south the portal.
    Djabal.   —Weighed with this
The general good, how could I choose my own?
What matter was my purity of soul?   70
Little by little I engaged myself—
Heaven would accept me for its instrument,
I hoped: I said Heaven had accepted me.
    Anael. Is it this blood breeds dreams in me? Who said

53 *1843,1849* here—   55 s.d. *1843-68* him *up and down.*   56 *1865* both!
Chance me   57 *1843-68* nobly!   58 *1843,1849* Hakeem, but mere Djabal!
59 *1843* have spoke falsely, *1843-68* have spoken falsely,   60 *1843-63* scorn blasts
me!   61 *1843,1849* mine .. *1863-8* mine!   62 *1843* (Did .... times?)
67 *1843-68* you!   68 *1843* (His .... portal!) *Dja.* —To this end *1849-68* portal!
69 [no equivalent in *1843*] *1849* own,   70 *1843* What was I with my
73 *1843* said it had   *1843-68* me!

64 *Bahumid the Renovator*: Moktana Baha ud-Din was one of the great propagators of the
Druse faith: his writings were known from Constantinople to the borders of India. He tried
to prove that the Christian Messiah reappeared as Hamza.
    69 *The general good*: cf. *Paracelsus*, i. 304.

You were not Hakeem? And your miracles—   75
The fire that plays innocuous round your form?

                             [*Again changing her whole manner.*

Ah, thou wouldst try me—thou art Hakeem still!
   Djabal. Woe—woe! As if the Druses of the Mount
(Scarce Arabs, even there, but here, in the Isle,
Beneath their former selves) should comprehend   80
The subtle lore of Europe! A few secrets
That would not easily affect the meanest
Of the crowd there, could wholly subjugate
The best of our poor tribe. Again that eye?
   Anael [*after a pause springs to his neck*].
Djabal, in this there can be no deceit!   85
Why, Djabal, were you human only,—think,
Maani is but human, Khalil human,
Loys is human even—did their words
Haunt me, their looks pursue me? Shame on you
So to have tried me! Rather, shame on me   90
So to need trying! Could I, with the Prefect
And the blood, there—could I see only you?
—Hang by your neck over this gulf of blood?
Speak, I am saved! Speak, Djabal! Am I saved?
   [*As* DJABAL *slowly unclasps her arms, and puts her silently from*
      him,
Hakeem would save me. Thou art Djabal. Crouch!   95
Bow to the dust, thou basest of our kind!
The pile of thee, I reared up to the cloud—
Full, midway, of our fathers' trophied tombs,
Based on the living rock, devoured not by
The unstable desert's jaws of sand,—falls prone.   100
Fire, music, quenched: and now thou liest there
A ruin, obscene creatures will moan through.

---

77 *1843* Ah, you would try me—you are Hakeem   79 *1863,1865* —Scarce
80 *1863,1865* selves—   84 *1843-68* tribe!   94 s.d. *1843-68* him.
95 *1843-68* me!.... Djabal!   100 *1843-68* prone!   102 *1843-68* through!

   97 *The pile of thee, I reared up* : cf. *Paradise Regained*, iv. 546-7. Johnson defines 'Pile' as 'An edifice; a building.'

—Let us come, Djabal!
   Djabal.   Whither come?
   Anael.   At once—
Lest so it grow intolerable. Come!
Will I not share it with thee? Best at once!   105
So, feel less pain! Let them deride,—thy tribe
Now trusting in thee,—Loys shall deride!
Come to them, hand in hand, with me!
   Djabal.   Where come?
   Anael. Where?—to the Druses thou hast wronged! Confess,
Now that the end is gained—(I love thee now—)   110
That thou hast so deceived them—(perchance love thee
Better than ever.) Come, receive their doom
Of infamy! O, best of all I love thee!
Shame with the man, no triumph with the God,
Be mine! Come!
   Djabal.   Never! More shame yet? and why?   115
Why? You have called this deed mine—it is mine!
And with it I accept its circumstance.
How can I longer strive with fate? The past
Is past: my false life shall henceforth show true.
Hear me! The argosies touch land by this;   120
They bear us to fresh scenes and happier skies.
What if we reign together?—if we keep
Our secret for the Druses' good?—by means
Of even their superstition, plant in them
New life? I learn from Europe: all who seek   125
Man's good must awe man, by such means as these.
We two will be divine to them—we are!
All great works in this world spring from the ruins

107 *1843* thee,—even Löys deride!   111 *1843* them .. (better love thee
112 *1843* Perchance than ever:) *1849-68* ever!)   113 *1843* infamy ... (Oh, *1849*
infamy—(Oh,   115 *1843,1849* mine!)   *119 (reading of *1863-8*,DC) *1849*
true— *1888* tur *1889* true   *1843* henceforth come true—   120 *1843,1849* me:
121 (no equivalent in *1843*) *1849* skies; *1863-8* skies: 124 *1843* Of their gross
superstition   125 *1843* I am from   126 *1843* man: .... these,
127a,b *1843* Let them conceive the rest—and I will keep them | Still safe in ignorance of all
the past—

Of greater projects—ever, on our earth,
Babels men block out, Babylons they build.   130
I wrest the weapon from your hand! I claim
The deed! Retire! You have my ring—you bar
All access to the Nuncio till the forces
From Venice land.
     Anael.   Thou wilt feign Hakeem then?
     Djabal [*putting the Tiara of Hakeem on his head*].
And from this moment that I dare ope wide   135
Eyes that till now refused to see, begins
My true dominion: for I know myself,
And what I am to personate. No word?

                          [ANAEL *goes.*

'T is come on me at last! His blood on her—
What memories will follow that! Her eye,   140
Her fierce distorted lip and ploughed black brow!
Ah, fool! Has Europe then so poorly tamed
The Syrian blood from out thee? Thou, presume
To work in this foul earth by means not foul?
Scheme, as for heaven,—but, on the earth, be glad   145
If a least ray like heaven's be left thee!
                       Thus
I shall be calm—in readiness—no way
Surprised.   [A *noise without.*
        This should be Khalil and my Druses.
Venice is come then! Thus I grasp thee, sword!
Druses, 't is Hakeem saves you! In! Behold   150
Your Prefect!

     Enter LOYS. DJABAL *hides the khandjar in his robe.*

---

130 *1849* Men block out Babels, to build Babylons.   134 *1843* land! *An.* You will
feign *1849-68* land!   s.d. *1843* †[*Puts the Tiar of 1849,1863 the Tiar of*   136 *1843*
that refused till now to   137 *1843-65* dominion!   138 *[reading of 1843-65]*
1868-89 am I   *1843* †[*Exit* ANEAL.   140 *1843* Such memories   141 *1843*
And her distorted   *1843,1849* brow—   146 *1843* If but a ray   148 *1843-68*
Druses!   151 *1843* The Prefect! . . . . well met Djabal!—but he's close at hand,

   130 *block out*: plan. For Babel and Babylon see Gen. 11: 1-9; *Bābel* is the Hebrew for
Babylon.

Loys. Oh, well found, Djabal!—but no time for words.
You know who waits there?   [*Pointing to the alcove.*
                         Well!—and that 't is there
He meets the Nuncio? Well? Now, a surprise—
He there—
  Djabal. I know—
  Loys.   —is now no mortal's lord,   155
Is absolutely powerless—call him, dead—
He is no longer Prefect—you are Prefect!
Oh, shrink not! I do nothing in the dark,
Nothing unworthy Breton blood, believe!
I understood at once your urgency   160
That I should leave this isle for Rhodes; I felt
What you were loath to speak—your need of help.
I have fulfilled the task, that earnestness
Imposed on me: have, face to face, confronted
The Prefect in full Chapter, charged on him   165
The enormities of his long rule; he stood
Mute, offered no defence, no crime denied.
On which, I spoke of you, and of your tribe,
Your faith so like our own, and all you urged
Of old to me: I spoke, too, of your goodness,   170
Your patience—brief, I hold henceforth the Isle
In charge, am nominally lord,—but you,
You are associated in my rule—
Are the true Prefect! Ay, such faith had they
In my assurance of your loyalty   175
(For who insults an imbecile old man?)
That we assume the Prefecture this hour.
You gaze at me? Hear greater wonders yet—

---

153 s.d. *1843* †[*Points to* . . . . *Well;*   154 *1843-68* Well!   155 *1843-63* lord.
162 *1843,1849* help;   166 *1843* What you have told and I have seen; he stood
167 *1843,1849* denied;   168 *1843* your Druses'   169 *1843* Slight difference
in faith from us .. all   *1843,1849* you've urged   170 *1843,1849* So oft to
171 *1843* And patience—   172 *1843* nominally Prefect, but | *1849, 1863* nominally
Prefect,—but you,   174 *1843* You are the Prefect!   177 *1843-68* hour!
178 *1843* me! A greater wonder yet— *1849-68* me!

169 *Your faith so like our own*: see Introduction, pp. 281-2.

I cast down all the fabric I have built.
These Knights, I was prepared to worship . . . but   180
Of that another time; what's now to say,
Is—I shall never be a Knight! Oh, Djabal,
Here first I throw all prejudice aside,
And call you brother! I am Druse like you:
My wealth, my friends, my power, are wholly yours,   185
Your people's, which is now my people: for
There is a maiden of your tribe, I love—
She loves me—Khalil's sister—
    Djabal.   Anael?
    Loys.   Start you?
Seems what I say, unknightly? Thus it chanced:
When first I came, a novice, to the isle . . .   190

       Enter one of the NUNCIO's Guards *from the alcove.*

    Guard. Oh horrible! Sir Loys! Here is Loys!
And here—   [*Others enter from the alcove.*
[*Pointing to* DJABAL.] Secure him, bind him—this is he!
                      [*They surround* DJABAL.
    Loys. Madmen—what is't you do? Stand from my friend,
And tell me!
    Guard.   Thou canst have no part in this—
Surely no part! But slay him not! The Nuncio   195
Commanded, slay him not!
    Loys.   Speak, or . . .

    Guard.   The Prefect
Lies murdered there by him thou dost embrace.
    Loys. By Djabal? Miserable fools! How Djabal?
[*A* Guard *lifts* DJABAL's *robe* ; DJABAL *flings down the khand-
    jar.*
    Loys [*after a pause*]. Thou hast received some insult worse
    than all,

179 *1843* See me throw down this fabric *1849–68* I throw down *1849, 1863* all this fabric
1843–68 built!   *180 {editors' emendation} *1843–68* worship . . *1888,1889* worship
. . . .†   184 *1843–68* you!   189 *1843* What I say seems unknightly?
192 *1843* Djabal! †[*Others*   194 *1843* Guards. Thou   195 *1843–65* part—

Some outrage not to be endured—
          [*To the Guards.*] Stand back!   200
He is my friend—more than my friend. Thou hast
Slain him upon that provocation.
    Guard.   No!
No provocation! 'T is a long devised
Conspiracy: the whole tribe is involved.
He is their Khalif—'t is on that pretence—   205
Their mighty Khalif who died long ago,
And now comes back to life and light again!
All is just now revealed, I know not how,
By one of his confederates—who, struck
With horror at this murder, first apprised   210
The Nuncio. As 't was said, we find this Djabal
Here where we take him.
    Djabal [*aside*].   Who broke faith with me?
    Loys [*to* DJABAL]. Hear'st thou? Speak! Till thou speak, I
      keep off these,
Or die with thee. Deny this story! Thou
A Khalif, an impostor? Thou, my friend,   215
Whose tale was of an inoffensive tribe,
With . . . but thou know'st—on that tale's truth I pledged
My faith before the Chapter: what art thou?
    Djabal. Loys, I am as thou hast heard. All's true.
No more concealment! As these tell thee, all   220
Was long since planned. Our Druses are enough
To crush this handful: the Venetians land
Even now in our behalf. Loys, we part.
Thou, serving much, wouldst fain have served me more;
It might not be. I thank thee. As thou hearest,   225
We are a separated tribe: farewell!
    Loys. Oh where will truth be found now? Canst thou so

201 *1843-68* friend! Thou   202 *1843* provocation! *Guards.* No! *1849-68* provoca-
tion!   204 *1843* involved— *1849* involved: 206-7 {no equivalent in *1843*}
207 *1849, 1863* now is come to   *1849-68* again—   210 *1843* murder, has
apprized   212 *1843* Who breaks faith   216 *1843* inoffensive race. *1849-68*
inoffensive race,   219 *1843-68* true!   223 *1843-65* we part here! *1868* we
part!   224 *1843* Thou hast served much,

Belie the Druses? Do they share thy crime?
Those thou professest of our Breton stock,
Are partners with thee? Why, I saw but now   230
Khalil, my friend: he spoke with me—no word
Of this! and Anael—whom I love, and who
Loves me—she spoke no word of this.
    Djabal.   Poor boy!
Anael, who loves thee? Khalil, fast thy friend?
We, offsets from a wandering Count of Dreux?   235
No: older than the oldest, princelier
Than Europe's princeliest race, our tribe: enough
For thine, that on our simple faith we found
A monarchy to shame your monarchies
At their own trick and secret of success.   240
The child of this our tribe shall laugh upon
The palace-step of him whose life ere night
Is forfeit, as that child shall know, and yet
Shall laugh there! What, we Druses wait forsooth
The kind interposition of a boy   245
—Can only save ourselves if thou concede?
—Khalil admire thee? He is my right-hand,
My delegate!—Anael accept thy love?
She is my bride!
    Loys.   Thy bride? She one of them?
    Djabal. My bride!
    Loys.   And she retains her glorious eyes!   250
She, with those eyes, has shared this miscreant's guilt!
Ah—who but she directed me to find
Djabal within the Prefect's chamber? Khalil
Bade me seek Djabal there, too. All is truth.
What spoke the Prefect worse of them than this?   255
Did the Church ill to institute long since

228 *1843* Druses?—This not thy sole crime?   229 *1849–65* thou professedst of
233 *1843–68* this!   237 *1843–68* princeliest tribe are we. Enough   238 *1843–*
68 For thee, that   245 *1843,1849* boy?   246 *1843–63* ourselves when thou
concedest?   254 *1843* there! Too true it is! *1849, 1863* too! All is true! *1865,1868*
too! ... . truth!

235 *offsets*: sprouts, descendants (as at I. 22).

Perpetual warfare with such serpentry?
And I—have I desired to shift my part,
Evade my share in her design? 'T is well.

    Djabal. Loys, I wronged thee—but unwittingly: 260
I never thought there was in thee a virtue
That could attach itself to what thou deemest
A race below thine own. I wronged thee, Loys,
But that is over: all is over now,
Save the protection I ensure against   265
My people's anger. By their Khalif's side,
Thou art secure and mayst depart: so, come!

    Loys. Thy side? I take protection at thy hand?

             Enter other Guards.

    Guards. Fly with him! Fly, Sir Loys! 'T is too true:
And only by his side thou mayst escape.   270
The whole tribe is in full revolt: they flock
About the palace—will be here—on thee—
And there are twenty of us, we the Guards
O' the Nuncio, to withstand them! Even we
Had stayed to meet our death in ignorance,   275
But that one Druse, a single faithful Druse,
Made known the horror to the Nuncio. Fly!
The Nuncio stands aghast. At least let us
Escape thy wrath, O Hakeem! We are nought
In thy tribe's persecution! [*To* Loys.] Keep by him!   280
They hail him Hakeem, their dead Prince returned:
He is their God, they shout, and at his beck
Are life and death!

    Loys [*springing at the khandjar* DJABAL *had thrown down, seizes
        him by the throat*].

257 *1843,1849* serpentry   258 *1843,1849* As these? Have   259 *1843-68*
well!   260 *1843-68* I have wronged   *1843* unwittingly.   264 *1843* over.
All   269 *1843* fly, my Master! 'tis too true! *1849-68* true!   270 *1843*
escape— *1849-68* escape!   273 *1843* us, with the   274 *1843-68* Of the
1843 them! Fly!—below   275-7 [no equivalent in *1843*]   277 *1849* Nuncio!
279 *1843-63* Escape their wrath   281 [no equivalent in *1843*]

    257 *serpentry*: Browning had found the word in Keats, *Endymion*, i. 821: 'Left by men-
slugs and human serpentry.' He used it again in *The Ring and the Book*, xii. 561.

Thus by his side am I!
Thus I resume my knighthood and its warfare,
Thus end thee, miscreant, in thy pride of place!   285
Thus art thou caught. Without, thy dupes may cluster:
Friends aid thee, foes avoid thee,—thou art Hakeem,
How say they?—God art thou! but also here
Is the least, youngest, meanest the Church calls
Her servant, and his single arm avails   290
To aid her as she lists. I rise, and thou
Art crushed. Hordes of thy Druses flock without:
Here thou hast me, who represent the Cross,
Honour and Faith, 'gainst Hell, Mahound and thee.
Die! [DJABAL *remains calm.*] Implore my mercy, Hakeem, that
          my scorn   295
May help me! Nay, I cannot ply thy trade;
I am no Druse, no stabber: and thine eye,
Thy form, are too much as they were—my friend
Had such. Speak! Beg for mercy at my foot!

          [DJABAL *still silent.*

Heaven could not ask so much of me—not, sure,   300
So much. I cannot kill him so.
          [*After a pause.*] Thou art
Strong in thy cause, then—dost outbrave us, then.
Heardst thou that one of thine accomplices,
Thy very people, has accused thee? Meet
His charge! Thou hast not even slain the Prefect   305
As thy own vile creed warrants. Meet that Druse!
Come with me and disprove him—be thou tried
By him, nor seek appeal! Promise me this,
Or I will do God's office. What, shalt thou

284 *1843-65* warfare!   286 *1843-63* caught!   *1843-68* cluster,
287 *1843* art Khalif,   289 *1843-65* least, meanest, youngest the   292 *1843-
68* crushed!   *1865* without!   294 *1843-68* thee!   295 *1843* mercy, Kha-
lif, that   299 *1843-63,1868* such! *1865* such;   301 *1843-68* much! .... so!
{no s.d. in *1843-68*}   302 *1843-68* then! .... then!   306 *1843* that charge—
1849, 1863 Druse—   308 *1843* appeal—this promise me—   *1849, 1863* appeal—
309 *1843-68* office!

294 *Mahound*: 'The "false prophet" Mohammed': OED.

Boast of assassins at thy beck, yet truth   310
Want even an executioner? Consent,
Or I will strike—look in my face—I will!
    Djabal. Give me again my khandjar, if thou darest!
                                    [LOYS *gives it.*
Let but one Druse accuse me, and I plunge
This home. A Druse betray me? Let us go!   315
[*Aside.*] Who has betrayed me?   [*Shouts without.*
                    Hearest thou? I hear
No plainer than long years ago I heard
That shout—but in no dream now. They return!
Wilt thou be leader with me, Loys? Well.

ACT V.

The Uninitiated Druses, *filling the hall tumultuously, and speaking together.*

Here flock we, obeying the summons. Lo, Hakeem hath appeared, and the Prefect is dead, and we return to Lebanon! My manufacture of goats' fleece must, I doubt, soon fall away there. Come, old Nasif—link thine arm in mine—we fight, if needs be.
5 Come, what is a great fight-word?—"Lebanon"? (My daughter—my daughter!)—But is Khalil to have the office of Hamza?—Nay, rather, if he be wise, the monopoly of henna and cloves. Where is Hakeem?—The only prophet I ever saw, prophesied at Cairo once, in my youth: a little black Copht, dressed all in black too, with a
10 great stripe of yellow cloth flapping down behind him like the back-fin of a water-serpent. Is this he? Biamrallah! Biamreh! HAKEEM!

Enter the NUNCIO, *with* Guards.

Nuncio [*to his* Attendants].
Hold both, the sorcerer and this accomplice
Ye talk of, that accuseth him! And tell
Sir Loys he is mine, the Church's hope: 15
Bid him approve himself our Knight indeed!

---

s.d. *1843-63* Druses, *covering the stage tumultuously,*   *5 {editors' emendation}
1849-89 "Lebanon?" {no quotation marks in *1843*}   15 *1843* hope!

  5 *fight-word*: a compound not in OED.
  6 *the office of Hamza*: 'Hamza-ben-Ahmud, propagated [the Druse beliefs] with an inde-
fatigable zeal in Egypt, in Palestine, and along the coast of Syria': Volney, ii. 38.
  9 *a little black Copht*: the Copts ('Cophts' often in the seventeenth and eighteenth cen-
turies) are native Egyptian Christians. Volney gives an account of them, i. 78 ff. Browning
could have found a fuller description in *An Account of the Manners and Customs of the Modern
Egyptians*, by Edward William Lane (2 vols., 1836), ii. 308 ff.
  11-12 *Biamrallah! Biamreh!* HAKEEM!: in ascending order. An impostor called
Mohammad-ben-Ismael flattered the third Fatimite Khalif by maintaining that he was
God incarnate; 'and, instead of his name *Hakem-b'amr-ellah*, which signifies, governing by
the order of God, he called him *Hakem-b'amr-eh*, governing by his own order': Volney, ii. 37.
Cf. 41, below.
  16 *approve*: prove.

Lo, this black disemboguing of the Isle!
[*To the* Druses.] Ah children, what a sight for these old eyes
That kept themselves alive this voyage through
To smile their very last on you! I came   20
To gather one and all you wandering sheep
Into my fold, as though a father came . . .
As though, in coming, a father should . . .
                                   [*To his* Guards.] (Ten, twelve
—Twelve guards of you, and not an outlet? None?
The wizards stop each avenue? Keep close!)   25
[*To the* Druses.] As if one came to a son's house, I say,
So did I come—no guard with me—to find . . .
Alas—alas!
      A Druse. Who is the old man?
      Another.   Oh, ye are to shout!
Children, he styles you.
      Druses.   Ay, the Prefect's slain!
Glory to the Khalif, our Father!
      Nuncio.   Even so   30
I find, (ye prompt aright) your father slain.
While most he plotted for your good, that father
(Alas, how kind, ye never knew)—lies slain.
[*Aside.*] (And hell's worm gnaw the glozing knave—with me,
For being duped by his cajoleries!   35
Are these the Christians? These the docile crew
My bezants went to make me Bishop o'er?)
[*To his* Attendants, *who whisper.*] What say ye does this
         wizard style himself?
Hakeem? Biamrallah? The third Fatemite?
What is this jargon? He—the insane Khalif,   40
Dead near three hundred years ago, come back
In flesh and blood again?

---

20 *1865,1868* on ye! I   30 *1843–68* so!   31 *1843* ye . . . . aright,   *1843–65*
slain; *1868* slain!   33 *1843,1849* (Alas!   *1843* slain— *1849–68* slain!

   34 *glozing* : specious, as at I. 18 above.   37 *bezants* : see III. 286 n.
   41 *Dead near three hundred years ago* : see p. 284 above, where '14—' is given as the time of
the action of the play.

Druses.   He mutters! I hear ye?
He is blaspheming Hakeem. The old man
Is our dead Prefect's friend. Tear him!
    Nuncio.   Ye dare not.
I stand here with my five-and-seventy years,   45
The Patriarch's power behind me, God's above.
Those years have witnessed sin enough; ere now
Misguided men arose against their lords,
And found excuse; but ye, to be enslaved
By sorceries, cheats—alas! the same tricks, tried   50
On my poor children in this nook o' the earth,
Could triumph, that have been successively
Exploded, laughed to scorn, all nations through:
"*Romaioi, Ioudaioi te kai proselutoi ,*
"Cretes and Arabians"—you are duped the last.   55
Said I, refrain from tearing me? I pray ye
Tear me! Shall I return to tell the Patriarch
That so much love was wasted—every gift
Rejected, from his benison I brought,
Down to the galley-full of bezants, sunk   60
An hour since at the harbour's mouth, by that . . .
That . . . never will I speak his hated name!
[*To his* Servants.] What was the name his fellow slip-fetter
Called their arch-wizard by? [*They whisper.*] Oh, Djabal was't.
    Druses. But how a sorcerer? false wherein?
    Nuncio.   (Ay, Djabal!)   65
How false? Ye know not, Djabal has confessed . . .
Nay, that by tokens found on him we learn . . .
What I sailed hither solely to divulge—

---

44 *1843-68* friend! . . . . not!   45 *1843* five-and-sixty years,   46 *1843-65*
behind, and God's above me! *1868* above!   51 *1843-68* of the   *54 {reading
of *1849*} *1843, 1863-89 Ioudaioite kai*   55 *1843-68* last!   63 *1863,1865 was*
64 *1843 whisper.*]† One Djabal was't? *1863-8* was't?

    54 "*Romaioi* : 'strangers of Rome, Jews and proselytes': Acts 2: 10, in a transliteration of
the Greek text. The reference is to the speaking in many tongues at Pentecost.
    55 "*Cretes and Arabians* : the beginning of the following verse in Acts.
    63 *slip-fetter* : not in OED, but probably not Browning's coinage. OED has 'slip-gibbet',
described as 'now *dial.* '.

How by his spells the demons were allured
To seize you: not that these be aught save lies   70
And mere illusions. Is this clear? I say,
By measures such as these, he would have led you
Into a monstrous ruin: follow ye?
Say, shall ye perish for his sake, my sons?
  Druses. Hark ye!
  Nuncio.   —Be of one privilege amerced?   75
No! Infinite the Patriarch's mercies are!
No! With the Patriarch's licence, still I bid
Tear him to pieces who misled you! Haste!
  Druses. The old man's beard shakes, and his eyes are white fire!
After all, I know nothing of Djabal beyond what Karshook says; he 80
knows but what Khalil says, who knows just what Djabal says him-
self. Now, the little Copht Prophet, I saw at Cairo in my youth,
began by promising each bystander three full measures of wheat . . .

    Enter KHALIL *and the initiated* DRUSES.

  Khalil. Venice and her deliverance are at hand:
Their fleet stands through the harbour. Hath he slain   85
The Prefect yet? Is Djabal's change come yet?
  Nuncio [*to* Attendants].
What's this of Venice? Who's this boy?
     [Attendants *whisper.*]
       One Khalil?
Djabal's accomplice, Loys called, but now,
The only Druse, save Djabal's self, to fear?
[*To the Druses.*] I cannot hear ye with these aged ears: 90
Is it so? Ye would have my troops assist?
Doth he abet him in his sorceries?
Down with the cheat, guards, as my children bid!
    [*They spring at* KHALIL; *as he beats them back,*

---

76 *1843-63* mercies be! 77 *1849-65* I bid ye 79 *1843* white! After
80 *1843* Karshook says, *1849, 1863* Khalil says; 83 *1843* bystander . . . |
84 *1843-68* hand! 85 *1843-68* harbour! 93 s.d. *1843 back.*]†

 75 *amerced*: fined, deprived. Cf. *Paradise Lost*, i. 609.
 85 *stands*: holds its course (as at I. 154-5).

Stay! No more bloodshed! Spare deluded youth!
Whom seek'st thou? (I will teach him)—whom, my child?   95
Thou know'st not what these know, what these declare.
I am an old man as thou seest—have done
With life; and what should move me but the truth?
Art thou the only fond one of thy tribe?
'T is I interpret for thy tribe.
    Khalil.   Oh, this   100
Is the expected Nuncio! Druses, hear—
Endure ye this? Unworthy to partake
The glory Hakeem gains you! While I speak,
The ships touch land: who makes for Lebanon?
They plant the winged lion in these halls!   105
    Nuncio [*aside*]. If it be true! Venice? Oh, never true!
Yet Venice would so gladly thwart our Knights,
So fain get footing here, stand close by Rhodes!
Oh, to be duped this way!
    Khalil.   Ere he appear
And lead you gloriously, repent, I say!   110
    Nuncio [*aside*]. Nor any way to stretch the arch-wizard
        stark
Ere the Venetians come? Cut off the head,
The trunk were easily stilled. [*To the* Druses.] He? Bring him
        forth!
Since so you needs will have it, I assent.
You'd judge him, say you, on the spot—confound   115
The sorcerer in his very circle? Where's

94 *1843–63* Stay—....bloodshed—   96 *1843–63* Thou knowest not   *1843* know,
and just have told. *1849* know, have just told me.   98 *1843,1849* With earth, and
1863 With earth; and   100 *1843–68* tribe!   103 *1843* you! Why, by this
105 *1843–63* They'll plant   106 *1843* {no s.d.} (If   107 *1843* thwart the
Knights,   108 *1843–68* And fain   *1843,1849* here so close   109 *1843*
way!)   *1843–63* he appears   110 *1843–63* To lead   111 *1843* {no s.d.}
(Oh, any *1849* †[*Aside*.]† Oh, any   112 *1843,1849* come! Were he cut off | *1863*
come? Be he cut off, | 113 *1843–63* The rest were   *1843* easily tamed.) {no s.d.}
He? *1849–65* easily tamed. †[*To*   114 *1843–68* assent!   115 *1843–68* spot?
    99 *fond* : foolish.
    105 *the winged lion* : the symbol of Venice. Cf. 387 below.
    116 *The sorcerer in his very circle* : alluding to the belief that a magician or wizard is

Our short black-bearded sallow friend who swore
He'd earn the Patriarch's guerdon by one stab?
Bring Djabal forth at once!
   Druses.   Ay, bring him forth!
The Patriarch drives a trade in oil and silk,   120
And we're the Patriarch's children—true men, we!
Where is the glory? Show us all the glory!
   Khalil. You dare not so insult him! What, not see . . .
(I tell thee, Nuncio, these are uninstructed,
Untrusted: they know nothing of our Khalif!)   125
—Not see that if he lets a doubt arise
'T is but to give yourselves the chance of seeming
To have some influence in your own Return!
That all may say ye would have trusted him
Without the all-convincing glory—ay,   130
And did! Embrace the occasion, friends! For, think—
What wonder when his change takes place? But now
For your sakes, he should not reveal himself.
No: could I ask and have, I would not ask
The change yet!

               Enter DJABAL *and* LOYS.

           Spite of all, reveal thyself!   135
I had said, pardon them for me—for Anael—
For our sakes pardon these besotted men—
Ay, for thine own—they hurt not thee! Yet now
One thought swells in me and keeps down all else.
This Nuncio couples shame with thee, has called   140
Imposture thy whole course, all bitter things
Has said: he is but an old fretful man!
Hakeem—nay, I must call thee Hakeem now—
Reveal thyself! See! Where is Anael? See!

---

117 *1843–68* who said   120 *1843,1849* silk— *1863,1865* silk: *123 (reading
of *1868*) *1843–65,1888,1889* see . .   128 *1843* return!   129 *1843–65* say they
would   132 *1843–65* What merit when   133 *1843–68* himself!
134 *1843* have.   139 *1843,1849* else!   144 *1843* See, Druses! (Anael?)—See!

invulnerable in his magic circle. Cf. Dryden, 'Prologue to *The Tempest*', 19–20: 'But Shake-
speare's magic could not copied be; / Within that circle none durst walk but he'.

Loys [*to* DJABAL]. Here are thy people. Keep thy word to
    me!   145
Djabal. Who of my people hath accused me?
Nuncio.   So!
So this is Djabal, Hakeem, and what not?
A fit deed, Loys, for thy first Knight's day!
May it be augury of thy after-life!
Ever prove truncheon of the Church as now   150
That, Nuncio of the Patriarch, having charge
Of the Isle here, I claim thee [*turning to* DJABAL] as these bid
    me,
Forfeit for murder done thy lawful prince,
Thou conjurer that peep'st and mutterest!
Why should I hold thee from their hands? (Spells, children?   155
But hear how I dispose of all his spells!)
Thou art a prophet?—wouldst entice thy tribe
From me?—thou workest miracles? (Attend!
Let him but move me with his spells!) I, Nuncio . . .
    Djabal. . . . Which how thou camest to be, I say not now,   160
Though I have also been at Stamboul, Luke!
Ply thee with spells, forsooth! What need of spells?
If Venice, in her Admiral's person, stoop
To ratify thy compact with her foe,
The Hospitallers, for this Isle—withdraw   165
Her warrant of the deed which reinstates
My people in their freedom, tricked away
By him I slew,—refuse to convoy us
To Lebanon and keep the Isle we leave—
Then will be time to try what spells can do!   170

---

145 *1843-68* people!   146 *1843* accused his Khalif?| 150 *1843,1849* Ever be
truncheon   153 *1843* prince!   *1849-65* murder on thy   154 (no equiva-
lent in *1843*)   *1863,1865* peepest and   158 *1843-65* Away?—thou
160 *1843,1849* thou cam'st to   162 *1843* thee, Luke Mystocthydi, with my spells?
163 *1843* person, choose   164 *1849, 1863* her foes,   167 *1843* in its free-
dom,   169 *1843* Afar to Lebanon at price of the Isle,   170 *1843* —Then time
to try what miracles may do!

    150 *truncheon* : cudgel.
    161 *Stamboul* : Istanbul, Constantinople.
    162 *Luke Mystocthydi* (*1843*): Luke the Initiate (Gk. μύστης, initiate).

Dost thou dispute the Republic's power?
  Nuncio.   Lo ye!
He tempts me too, the wily exorcist!
No! The renowned Republic was and is
The Patriarch's friend: 't is not for courting Venice
That I—that these implore thy blood of me.   175
Lo ye, the subtle miscreant! Ha, so subtle?
Ye, Druses, hear him. Will ye be deceived?
How he evades me! Where's the miracle
He works? I bid him to the proof—fish up
Your galley-full of bezants that he sank!   180
That were a miracle! One miracle!
Enough of trifling, for it chafes my years.
I am the Nuncio, Druses! I stand forth
To save you from the good Republic's rage
When she shall find her fleet was summoned here   185
To aid the mummeries of a knave like this.
                    [*As the* DRUSES *hesitate, his* Attendants *whisper.*
Ah, well suggested! Why, we hold the while
One who, his close confederate till now,
Confesses Djabal at the last a cheat,
And every miracle a cheat. Who throws me   190
His head? I make three offers, once I offer,—
And twice . . .
  Djabal.   Let who moves perish at my foot!
  Khalil. Thanks, Hakeem, thanks! Oh, Anael, Maani,
Why tarry they?
  Druses [*to each other*]. He can! He can! Live fire—
[*To the* NUNCIO.] I say he can, old man! Thou know'st him
    not.   195
Live fire like that thou seest now in his eyes,

---

172 (no equivalent in *1843*)   175 *1843–68* me!   177 *1843–68* him!
180 *1843–65* he sunk!   182 *1843,1849* my age—   183 *1843* stand here
184 *1843* Republic's wrath   185 *1843* summoned just   186 *1843* of this
wizard here! *1849* of this crafty knave! *1863–68* this!   187 *1843,1849* hold this
while   190 *1843–68* cheat!   192 *1843* foot?   195 s.d. *1865,1868*
NUNCIO,]†   *1843,1849* (I . . . . not.)   196 (no equivalent in *1843*)

    182 *chafes*: irritates, angers.

Plays fawning round him. See! The change begins.
All the brow lightens as he lifts his arm.
Look not at me! It was not I!
    Djabal.   What Druse
Accused me, as he saith? I bid each bone   200
Crumble within that Druse! None, Loys, none
Of my own people, as thou said'st, have raised
A voice against me.
    Nuncio [*aside*].   Venice to come! Death!
    Djabal [*continuing*]. Confess and go unscathed, however
        false!
Seest thou my Druses, Luke? I would submit   205
To thy pure malice did one Druse confess!
How said I, Loys?
    Nuncio [*to his* Attendants *who whisper*].
                  Ah, ye counsel so?
[*Aloud.*] Bring in the witness, then, who, first of all,
Disclosed the treason! Now I have thee, wizard!
Ye hear that? If one speaks, he bids you tear him   210
Joint after joint: well then, one does speak! One,
Befooled by Djabal, even as yourselves,
But who hath voluntarily proposed
To expiate, by confessing thus, the fault
Of having trusted him.   [*They bring in a veiled* Druse.
    Loys.   Now, Djabal, now!   215
    Nuncio. Friend, Djabal fronts thee! Make a ring, sons.
      Speak!
Expose this Djabal—what he was, and how:
The wiles he used, the aims he cherished: all,
Explicitly as late 't was spoken to these
My servants: I absolve and pardon thee.   220

197 *1843* fire plays round him—See! The change begins? *1849–68* begins!   198 (no
equivalent in *1843*) *1849–68* arm!   200 *1843* Accuseth me,   204 *1843* Now
speak and go unscathed, how false soe'er!   206 *1843* one least Druse speak!
209 *1843* Told this man's treasons! Now I have thee, Djabal!   212 *1843* Whom I
have not as yet e'en spoken with,   216 *1843,1849* fronts you! (Make   *1843*
sons!)—Say *1849* sons!) *1863–8* sons!—   217 *1843* The course of Djabal;
219 *1843,1849* late you spoke to   *1843* these!   220 (no equivalent in *1843*)
1849 pardon you.

Loys. Thou hast the dagger ready, Djabal?
Djabal.   Speak,
Recreant!
Druses. Stand back, fool! farther! Suddenly
You shall see some huge serpent glide from under
The empty vest, or down will thunder crash!
Back, Khalil!
Khalil.   I go back? Thus go I back!   225
[*To* ANAEL.] Unveil! Nay, thou shalt face the Khalif! Thus!
   [*He tears away* ANAEL's *veil;* DJABAL *folds his arms and bows his head;*
   the Druses *fall back;* LOYS *springs from the side of* DJABAL *and the*
   NUNCIO.
Loys. Then she was true—she only of them all!
True to her eyes—may keep those glorious eyes,
And now be mine, once again mine! Oh, Anael!
Dared I think thee a partner in his crime—   230
That blood could soil that hand? nay, 't is mine—Anael,
—Not mine?—who offer thee before all these
My heart, my sword, my name—so thou wilt say
That Djabal, who affirms thou art his bride,
Lies—say but that he lies!
Djabal.   Thou, Anael?   235
  Loys. Nay, Djabal, nay, one chance for me—the last!
Thou hast had every other; thou hast spoken
Days, nights, what falsehood listed thee—let me
Speak first now; I will speak now!
Nuncio.   Loys, pause!
Thou art the Duke's son, Bretagne's choicest stock,   240
Loys of Dreux, God's sepulchre's first sword:
This wilt thou spit on, this degrade, this trample
To earth?

---

230 *1843* crime?   232 *1843* Mine now? Who   234 *1843* This Djabal,
235 *1863* Lies! say   239 *1843* first—I will speak—Anael!—*Nuncio.*
240 *1843-68* son, Breton's choicest   241 *1843* Loÿs de Dreux—

  238 *listed*: pleased.
  241 *sword*: swordsman, soldier, as at III. 150 above, and 366 below.

Loys [*to* ANAEL]. Who had foreseen that one day, Loys
Would stake these gifts against some other good
In the whole world? I give them thee! I would   245
My strong will might bestow real shape on them,
That I might see, with my own eyes, thy foot
Tread on their very neck! 'T is not by gifts
I put aside this Djabal: we will stand—
We do stand, see, two men! Djabal, stand forth!   250
Who's worth her, I or thou? I—who for Anael
Uprightly, purely kept my way, the long
True way—left thee each by-path, boldly lived
Without the lies and blood,—or thou, or thou?
Me! love me, Anael! Leave the blood and him!   255
[*To* DJABAL.] Now speak—now, quick on this that I have
     said,—
Thou with the blood, speak if thou art a man!
     Djabal [*to* ANAEL]. And was it thou betrayedst me? 'T is
          well!
I have deserved this of thee, and submit.
Nor 't is much evil thou inflictest: life   260
Ends here. The cedars shall not wave for us:
For there was crime, and must be punishment.
See fate! By thee I was seduced, by thee
I perish: yet do I—can I repent?
I with my Arab instinct, thwarted ever   265
By my Frank policy,—and with, in turn,
My Frank brain, thwarted by my Arab heart—
While these remained in equipoise, I lived

---

243 *1843 Loÿs*. (no s.d.) Ah, who had said, "One day this Loÿs *1849-65 Loys*. †[*to* AN.]† Ah,
who had foreseen, "One day, Loys   244 *1843-65* "Will stake   245 *1843-65*
"In . . . . world?"—   252 *1843* Kept tamely, soberly my *1849* Kept, purely, uprightly
my   253 *1843* by-path—kept   255 *1843* Come out of this blood! Love me,
Anael, leave him! *1849,1863* I! Love   256 *1843* quick upon what I
258 *1843* Ah, was . . . . me? Then, speak!   259 *1843* 'Tis well—I have deserved
this—I submit— *1849* submit: 263 *1843,1849* seduced— *1863,1865* seduced; *1868*
seduced!   264 *1843* repent!   265 *1843* with an Arab   266 *1843* and,
in its turn, *1849* and, within turn,   267 *1843* A Frank

   253 *by-path* : for the pejorative sense cf. *2 Henry IV*, IV. v. 185.
   256 *quick on this* : immediately after this.

—Nothing; had either been predominant,
As a Frank schemer or an Arab mystic,   270
I had been something;—now, each has destroyed
The other—and behold, from out their crash,
A third and better nature rises up—
My mere man's-nature! And I yield to it:
I love thee, I who did not love before!   275
    Anael. Djabal!
    Djabal.   It seemed love, but it was not love:
How could I love while thou adoredst me?
Now thou despisest, art above me so
Immeasurably! Thou, no other, doomest
My death now; this my steel shall execute   280
Thy judgment; I shall feel thy hand in it.
Oh luxury to worship, to submit,
Transcended, doomed to death by thee!
    Anael.   My Djabal!
    Djabal. Dost hesitate? I force thee then. Approach,
Druses! for I am out of reach of fate;   285
No further evil waits me. Speak the doom!
Hear, Druses, and hear, Nuncio, and hear, Loys!
    Anael. HAKEEM!   *[She falls dead.*
                [The Druses *scream, grovelling before him.*
    Druses. Ah Hakeem!—not on me thy wrath!
Biamrallah, pardon! never doubted I!
Ha, dog, how sayest thou?
    [They surround and seize the NUNCIO *and his* Guards. LOYS *flings*
    himself upon the body of ANAEL, *on which* DJABAL *continues to gaze*
    as stupefied.
    Nuncio.   Caitiffs! Have ye eyes?   290
Whips, racks should teach you! What, his fools? his dupes?
Leave me! Unhand me!

276 {no equivalent in *1843*} *1849* Djabal—   *1849, 1863* but true love it was not—
277 *1843* Ana. Djabal— Dja. ... How   279 *1843-63* Immeasurably—
281 *1843-68* it!   283 *1843* To be transcended,....thee!| 284 *1843 An.* My
Djabal! *Dja.* Dost   *1843-68* then!   286 *1843* evil can befall me—Speak!| *1849,*
1863 the truth!   289 *1843,1849* pardon—   290 *1843-65* Ah, dog,   s.d.
1843 †*[They seize and surround the*

Khalil [approaching DJABAL *timidly].*
                              Save her for my sake!
She was already thine; she would have shared
To-day thine exaltation: think, this day
Her hair was plaited thus because of thee!   295
Yes, feel the soft bright hair—feel!
    Nuncio [struggling with those who have seized him].
                                              What, because
His leman dies for him? You think it hard
To die? Oh, would you were at Rhodes, and choice
Of deaths should suit you!
    Khalil [bending over ANAEL's *body].*
                              Just restore her life!
So little does it! there— the eyelids tremble!   300
'T was not my breath that made them: and the lips
Move of themselves. I could restore her life!
Hakeem, we have forgotten—have presumed
On our free converse: we are better taught.
See, I kiss—how I kiss thy garment's hem   305
For her! She kisses it—Oh, take her deed
In mine! Thou dost believe now, Anael?—See,
She smiles! Were her lips open o'er the teeth
Thus, when I spoke first? She believes in thee!
Go not without her to the cedars, lord!   310
Or leave us both—I cannot go alone!
I have obeyed thee, if I dare so speak:
Hath Hakeem thus forgot all Djabal knew?
Thou feelest then my tears fall hot and fast
Upon thy hand, and yet thou speakest not?   315
Ere the Venetian trumpet sound—ere thou
Exalt thyself, O Hakeem! save thou her!

294 *1843-63* think!   295 *1843,1849* thee— *1863* thee.   300 *1843,1849* it—
307 *1843,1849* mine—   308 *1843* smiles! was her lip ope thus o'er
309 *1843* When first I spoke? She doth believe in thee!   *1849* So, when
310 *1843* Cedars, Hakeem!   311 *1843* alone—   312 *1843* I must say so—
1849 dare say so—   315 *1843,1849* not!   317 *1843,1849* save her—save her!

    297 *leman* : mistress, beloved.
    300 *the eyelids tremble!* : cf. *King Lear*, v. iii. 261 ff. and 310-11.

Nuncio. And the accursed Republic will arrive
And find me in their toils—dead, very like,
Under their feet!
                        What way—not one way yet   320
To foil them? None?   [*Observing* DJABAL's *face.*
                    What ails the Khalif? Ah,
That ghastly face! A way to foil them yet!
[*To the* Druses.] Look to your Khalif, Druses! Is that face
God Hakeem's? Where is triumph,—where is . . . what
Said he of exaltation—hath he promised   325
So much to-day? Why then, exalt thyself!
Cast off that husk, thy form, set free thy soul
In splendour! Now, bear witness! here I stand—
I challenge him exalt himself, and I
Become, for that, a Druse like all of you!   330
    The Druses. Exalt thyself! Exalt thyself, O Hakeem!
    Djabal [*advances*]. I can confess now all from first to last.
There is no longer shame for me. I am . . .
    [*Here the Venetian trumpet sounds: the* Druses *shout,* DJABAL's *eye
        catches the expression of those about him, and, as the old dream comes
        back, he is again confident and inspired.*
—Am I not Hakeem? And ye would have crawled
But yesterday within these impure courts   335
Where now ye stand erect! Not grand enough?
—What more could be conceded to such beasts
As all of you, so sunk and base as you,
Than a mere man? A man among such beasts
Was miracle enough: yet him you doubt,   340
Him you forsake, him fain would you destroy—
With the Venetians at your gate, the Nuncio
Thus—(see the baffled hypocrite!) and, best
The Prefect there!
    Druses.   No, Hakeem, ever thine!

322 *1843-63* face— *1865* face?   324 *1843* A Khalif's? Where   326 *1843*
thyself?   328 *1843* splendour: *1843,1849* witness—
331 *1843,1849* thyself—exalt   333 s.d. *1843-68 shout: his eye*   334 *1843-*
65 not   339 *1843* But a

Nuncio. He lies—and twice he lies—and thrice he lies!   345
Exalt thyself, Mahound! Exalt thyself!

Djabal. Druses! we shall henceforth be far away—
Out of mere mortal ken—above the cedars—
But we shall see ye go, hear ye return,
Repeopling the old solitudes,—through thee,   350
My Khalil! Thou art full of me: I fill
Thee full—my hands thus fill thee! Yestereve,
—Nay, but this morn, I deemed thee ignorant
Of all to do, requiring word of mine
To teach it: now, thou hast all gifts in one,   355
With truth and purity go other gifts,
All gifts come clustering to that. Go, lead
My people home whate'er betide!
          [*Turning to the* Druses.] Ye take
This Khalil for my delegate? To him
Bow as to me? He leads to Lebanon—   360
Ye follow? '

Druses. We follow! Now exalt thyself!

Djabal [*raises* Loys]. Then to thee, Loys! How I wronged
          thee, Loys!
Yet, wronged, no less thou shalt have full revenge,
Fit for thy noble self, revenge—and thus.
Thou, loaded with such wrongs, the princely soul,   365
The first sword of Christ's sepulchre—thou shalt
Guard Khalil and my Druses home again!
Justice, no less, God's justice and no more,
For those I leave! To seeking this, devote
Some few days out of thy Knight's brilliant life: 370
And, this obtained them, leave their Lebanon,
My Druses' blessing in thine ears—(they shall
Bless thee with blessing sure to have its way)

347 *1843-65* away!   354 *1843-63* requiring words of   356 *1843-63* gifts!
357 *1843,1849* that—   *1863* that!   362 *1843* How have I   364 *1843,1849*
thus: 365 *1843-63* with these wrongs,   370 *1843,1849* life,
373 *1843* thee a blessing

347 *we*: the royal plural.
369-70 *To seeking this, devote / Some few days*: cf. *Paracelsus,* i. 474 ff.

—One cedar-blossom in thy ducal cap,
One thought of Anael in thy heart,—perchance,   375
One thought of him who thus, to bid thee speed,
His last word to the living speaks! This done,
Resume thy course, and, first amidst the first
In Europe, take my heart along with thee!
Go boldly, go serenely, go augustly—   380
What shall withstand thee then?
            [*He bends over* ANAEL.] And last to thee!
Ah, did I dream I was to have, this day,
Exalted thee? A vain dream: hast thou not
Won greater exaltation? What remains
But press to thee, exalt myself to thee?   385
Thus I exalt myself, set free my soul!
    [*He stabs himself. As he falls, supported by* KHALIL *and* LOYS, *the*
        Venetians *enter; the* ADMIRAL *advances.*
    Admiral. God and St. Mark for Venice! Plant the Lion!
    [*At the clash of the planted standard, the* Druses *shout and move tumul-*
        tuously forward, LOYS *drawing his sword.*
Djabal [*leading them a few steps between* KHALIL *and* LOYS].
On to the Mountain! At the Mountain, Druses!
                                    [*Dies.*

---

378 *1843-68* first amid the   381 *1843,1849* what can withstand   386 s.d.
1843 himself— *1865,1868* himself;   388 *1849* Mountain. At

INTRODUCTION TO *A BLOT IN THE 'SCUTCHEON*

A Blot in the 'Scutcheon was both produced and published on 11 February 1843. We know a good deal about its earlier history, although some details are uncertain. In a preliminary form it may well have been written very rapidly, since Browning told Julia Wedgwood that he had 'conceived the whole' of it 'and put it down easily in five days', and repeated this to Gosse many years later.[1] We do not know when this first sketch was written. The letter in which Browning announced his new work to Macready is undated:

'The luck of the third adventure' is proverbial— I have written a spick & span new Tragedy—(a sort of compromise between my own notion & yours—as I understand it, at least—) and will read it to you if you care to be bothered so far— there is *action* in it, drabbing, stabbing, et autres gentillesses,—who knows but the Gods may mean me good even yet?—Only, make no scruple of saying flatly that you cannot spare the time, if engagements of which I know nothing but fancy a great deal, should claim every couple of hours in the course of this week.[2]

The first reference to the play in Macready's *Diaries* occurs in the entry for 26 September 1841: 'Forster importuned me after dinner to read Browning's tragedy, which I did. He had taken *enough* wine, and was rather exaggerating in his sensibility and praise. I was not prepared, and could not do justice to it in reading.'[3] Macready accepted *A Blot* before he left the Haymarket theatre for Drury Lane after 7 December. Our account of what happened then is by Browning: 'When the Drury Lane season began, Macready informed me that he should act the play when he had brought out two others—"The Patrician's Daughter," and "Plighted Troth:" having done so, he wrote to me that the former had been unsuccessful in money-drawing, and the latter had "smashed his arrangements altogether:" but he would still produce my play.'[4] Browning adds that he had no notion that it would have been 'a proper thing, in such a case, to "release him from his promise"'.

---

[1] *Wedgwood*, p. 102; *Personalia*, p. 61. Griffin and Minchin mention a similar report about *The Return of the Druses* (see p. 227 n[3] above); but in the case of *A Blot in the 'Scutcheon* we have Browning's own repeated statement.   [2] *Correspondence*, iv. 293.

[3] *Diaries*, ii. 143. Subsequent quotations may be found under their dates.

[4] *Life*, p. 111. *The Patrician's Daughter* was by John Westland Marston, *Plighted Troth* by the Revd. C. F. Darley (brother of George Darley).

The failure of *Plighted Troth* occurred on 20 April 1842. Soon after that Browning wrote to Macready:

I have forborne troubling you about my Play from a conviction that you would do the very best possible for us both in that matter: but as the Season is drawing (I suppose) to an end, and no piece is at present announced in the Bills, it has struck me that in all likelihood the failure of *Plighted Troth* may render it inexpedient in your opinion to venture on a fresh Trial this Campaign; and I stand, if I remember rightly, next in succession on your List. I need not say that I would not for the world be the cause of any considerable anxiety to you . . much less of loss in any shape—and that I shall therefore most entirely acquiesce in whatever you consider expedient to be done, or left undone.—But, here is my case—that quiet, generally-intelligible, and (for me!) popular sort of thing, was to have been my *Second Number* of Plays—on your being gracious to it, I delayed issuing any farther attempts for nearly a year—and now have published a very indifferent substitute,[1] whose success will be problematical enough. I have nothing by me at all fit to be substituted for the work in your hands. Will you have the kindness to say if I am mistaken in my conjecture as to your intentions?—And if you will at all object to my withdrawing it, in that case, and printing it at once—the booksellers' season being now in the prime?[2]

According to Browning, Macready replied to the effect that the failure of *Plighted Troth* 'had frightened him into shutting the house earlier than he had meant. Nothing new this season, therefore, but next, &c. &c. &c.' Browning continued: 'I shall go to the end of this year, as I now go on—shall print the Eastern play you may remember hearing about—finish a wise metaphysical play . . . , and print a few songs and small poems which Moxon advised me to do for popularity's sake! These things done (and my play out), I shall have tried an experiment to the end, and be pretty well contented either way.'[3]

Macready was not allowed to forget *A Blot in the 'Scutcheon*. On 17 July he told Bulwer Lytton that he had high hopes of a play 'with scenes of great passion by Browning'.[4] Later in the year Forster showed the manuscript to Dickens, who replied, on 25 November:

Browning's play has thrown me into a perfect passion of sorrow. To say that there is anything in its subject save what is lovely, true, deeply affecting, full of the best emotion, the most earnest feeling, and the most true and tender source of interest, is to say that there is no light in the sun, and no heat in blood. It is full

[1] *King Victor and King Charles*.
[2] *New Letters*, pp. 25–6.
[3] *Browning and Domett*, p. 36. The 'wise metaphysical play' seems to have been *A Soul's Tragedy*.
[4] Quoted in Charles H. Shattuck, *Bulwer and Macready* (Urbana, Ill., 1958), p. 212.

of genius, natural and great thoughts, profound, and yet simple and beautiful in its vigour. I know nothing that is so affecting, nothing in any book I have ever read, as Mildred's recurrence to that 'I was so young—I had no mother.' I know no love like it, no passion like it, no moulding of a splendid thing after its conception, like it. And I swear it is a tragedy that MUST be played; and must be played, moreover, by Macready. There are some things I would have changed if I could (they are very slight, mostly broken lines); and I assuredly would have the old servant *begin his tale upon the scene*; and be taken by the throat, or drawn upon, by his master, in its commencement. But the tragedy I never shall forget, or less vividly remember than I do now. And if you tell Browning that I have seen it, tell him that I believe from my soul there is no man living (and not many dead) who could produce such a work.[1]

This remarkable testimonial, which Forster did not show to Browning,[2] no doubt carried a great deal of weight. On 13 December Browning told Domett that 'Macready [was] getting on poorly enough', but added: 'he pledges himself to keep his Theatre open till he has played my Tragedy—I don't know what will be the end of it'.[3] On 25 January 1843 Macready turned his attention to Browning's play, as recorded in the following extracts from his *Diaries*:

January 26th. —Continued the perusal of the *Blot on the Scutcheon* . . . Finished *Blot*, etc. Went over *Athelwold*[4]—will not do at present.

January 28th. —Went to Drury Lane theatre, finishing by the way the *Blot on*, etc. . . . Willmott, to whom, on Anderson's declining, I had entrusted the reading *Blot on*, etc., came and reported to me that they laughed at it, and that Anderson passed his jokes on it—not very decorous for an official! I fear—I fear this young man's head is gone.[5]

January 29th. —Browning called, told him of the reading on Saturday and the conduct of the actors.[6] Advised him as to the alteration of second act.

[1] *The Letters of Charles Dickens* (Pilgrim Edition), iii (1974), ed. Madeline House and others, pp. 381–3. For the recurrent phrase see below, I. iii. 237–8, II. 361, and II. 401.

[2] Whatever his reason, the Pilgrim editors rightly observe that Forster 'can have had no ungenerous motive for withholding it'. When Browning saw what Dickens had written, in 1872, he was unjust to Forster, wrongly claiming that the passage had been 'directed . . . to be shown to myself'. Browning resented, on the other hand, any suggestion that Macready had accepted the play at the instigation of Dickens, insisting that he had accepted it before he left the Haymarket in December 1841, and that Dickens 'was not in England when he did so' (*Life*, p. 111). Dickens did not sail for America until 4 January 1842. The Ohio editor suggests that Browning was referring to Dickens's trip to Scotland in June/July 1841; but that is too early, and 'not in England' seldom bears such an interpretation, even on this side of the Atlantic. Probably Forster showed the play to Dickens because he was afraid that Macready's resolution was wavering.

[3] *Browning and Domett*, p. 48.   [4] By William Smith.

[5] Cf. Macready's comment on reading *The Return of the Druses*, p. 278 above.

[6] It is unlikely that Macready told Browning that his play had been laughed at by the

January 31st. —Went to Drury Lane theatre. Found Browning waiting for me in a state of great excitement. He abused the door-keeper and was in a very great passion. I calmly apologized for having detained him, observing that I had made a great effort to meet him at all. He had not given his *name* to the doorkeeper, who had told him he might walk into the green-room; but his dignity was mortally wounded. I fear he is a very conceited man. Went over his play with him, then looked over part of it. Read it in the room with great difficulty, being *very unwell.*

February 1st. — . . . Read Browning's play. Rose, and read and cut it again. Serle called, and I told him of my inability to meet my work—that I *could not* play this part of Browning's unless the whole work of the theatre stopped, that I thought it best to reduce it to its proper form—three acts, and let Phelps do it on all accounts. He concurred with me . . . I wrote a note to Browning.

Exasperated by Macready's behaviour, Browning 'took the MS. to his publisher Moxon, who also had a quarrel with Macready, and who was therefore only too pleased to coöperate in his confusion'.[1] On 4 February (as it would seem) Browning wrote to Macready that he had received a note from him the previous night, 'and would have called at the Theatre' as suggested, if another engagement had not prevented him. This engagement may well have been with Moxon. 'I will try & attend [the] next Rehearsal', the letter continued. 'As for the play, I must send my copy to press on Monday M^g and correct while the printers have it in hand. One thing, however, I ought to ascertain now—can you tell me (by a couple of lines) how you divide the piece into Acts (for I am *quite* of your opinion that there should be Three only). I think the 1st Act should include the Bedchamber Scene. The 2^d—the two Library Scenes. And the 3^d—what now stand as 4th and 5th. But you shall decide.'[2] On the 4th Macready rehearsed the play. The following day, a Sunday, found him 'dejected, desponding—almost despairing'. On the Monday Phelps was too ill to rehearse, so Macready himself decided to understudy his part. On the 7th he 'Rehearsed Browning's play, with the idea of acting the part of Lord Tresham, if Mr. Phelps should continue ill. Browning came and in better humour than I have lately seen him.' This was perhaps because arrangements for printing the play had been completed. On the 8th Macready 'rehearsed three acts of *Much Ado About Nothing* and the *Blot on the 'Scutcheon* ', adding that he 'began to despair' about Browning's play. On the 9th he 'Resolved to do the part of Tresham for Mr. Phelps, and

actors 'from beginning to end', however, as he wrote in 1884: *Life*, p. 111. See the same book, pp. 117-18, for Helen Faucit's judicious account of the occasion, and her conclusion that 'somehow the mischief proved irreparable, for a few of the actors during the rehearsals chose to continue to misunderstand the text, and never took the interest in the play which they would have done had Mr.Macready read it'.

[1] Gosse, pp. 64-5.   [2] *Checklist,* 43:50.

'began reading the part . . . and cutting it'. The same day (we notice) he acted Othello, 'as *well* as I *could*, but not effectively—at least the audience did not applaud me much', with the result that he was 'dissatisfied with them and [himself]', though he was conscious that he had done his best. Meanwhile, according to Browning's account of the matter, *A Blot in the 'Scutcheon* had been 'printed in a few hours, in a single sheet [16 pages], as part five of *Bells and Pomegranates*, and was in the hands of each of the actors'[1] before he himself reached the theatre. According to Browning's recollection, Phelps waylaid him as he was entering and told him that he was eager to play Tresham after all: that he was better now, and could master the part by sitting up all night. Browning therefore 'took Phelps with him into the green-room, where Macready was already studying the play in its printed form, with the actors around him', and told him that he would be 'very glad to leave it in his hands'. We are told that Macready 'crumpled up the play he was holding in his hand, and threw it to the other end of the room'. The account in his *Diaries* differs only in detail:

February 10th. —Began the consideration and study of the part of Tresham, which was to occupy my single thoughts till accomplished. About a quarter past one a note came from Willmott, informing me that Mr. Phelps would do the part, if he 'died for it,' so that my time had been lost. Arrived I applied to business; offered to give to Browning and Mr. Phelps the benefit of my consideration and study in the cuts, etc. I had made one I thought particularly valuable, not letting Tresham die, but consigning him to a convent. Browning, however, in the worst taste, manner, and spirit, declined any further alterations, expressing himself perfectly satisfied with the manner in which Mr. Phelps executed Lord Tresham. I had no more to say. I could only think Mr. Browning a very disagreeable and offensively mannered person. *Voilà tout!*

Many years later Browning still remembered, with undiminished indignation, that Macready wanted the title changed to *The Sister*:[2] 'Tresham was to announce his intention of going into a monastery! all this, to keep up the belief that Macready, and Macready alone, could produce a veritable "tragedy," unproduced before.' On the 11th (to revert to Macready's *Diaries*) he directed the rehearsal, 'and made many valuable improvements. Browning seemed desirous to explain or qualify the strange carriage and temper of yesterday, and laid much blame on Forster for irritating him'. Macready watched the performance, noting that it 'was badly acted in Phelps's and Mrs. Stirling's parts—pretty well in Anderson's, very well in Helen Faucit's'. He was '*angry* after the play about the call being directed without me'.

[1] Gosse, p. 65; *Life*, p. 112.   [2] *Life*, p. 112.

Browning always insisted that his play had been 'a complete success', though 'deprived of every advantage, in the way of scenery, dresses, and rehearsing'.[1] According to his account of the matter to Gosse,

> He would not allow his parents or his sister to go to the theatre; no tickets were sent to him, but finding that the stage-box was his, not by favor, but by right, he went with no other companion than Mr. Edward Moxon. But his expectations of failure were not realized. Phelps acted magnificently, carrying out the remark of Macready, that the difference between himself and the other actors was that they could do magnificent things now and then, on a spurt, but that he could always command his effects. Anderson, a *jeune premier* of promise, acted the young lover with considerable spirit, although the audience was not quite sure whether to laugh or no when he sang his song, 'There's a Woman like a Dewdrop,' in the act of climbing in at the window. Finally, Miss Helen Faucit almost surpassed herself in Mildred Tresham . . . When the curtain went down, the applause was vociferous. Phelps was called and recalled, and then there rose the cry of 'Author!' To this Mr. Browning remained silent and out of sight.[2]

It is fortunate that we have an account of the three nights of the play's run from a reliable witness who was a devoted admirer of Browning's, Joseph Arnould. He wrote to Alfred Domett, in New Zealand:

> those who knew *Browning* were . . . aware of a little history of bad feeling—intrigue and petty resentment—which I fancy, making all allowance for both sides, amounts to just this. Macready had the usual amount of plays on hand and promises to authors unperformed when you and I witnessed the 'deep damnation of the bringing forth' of 'Plighted Troth.' That shook him a good deal. He might possibly, remembering 'Strafford,' have looked doubtfully at Browning's chance of writing a play that would take, and he brought out two new plays, one of which ('The Patrician's Daughter,' by John W. Marston) had a decent success, while still nothing was heard of Browning's play. Meanwhile judicious friends, as judicious friends will, had a habit of asking Browning when the play was coming out—you can fancy how sensitively Browning would chafe at this. At length the paramount object with him became to have the play played, no matter how, so that it was at once. With these feelings he forced Macready to name an early day for playing it. The day was named, Macready was to take the part of . . . Tresham, which was made for him, and everything was going on swimmingly, when lo! a week or so before the day of representation, Macready declines altogether his part unless the play can be postponed till after Easter [16 April]. Browning, naturally in 'a sulky chafe' at this, declines postponement with haughty coolness; indicates that if Mr. Phelps will take the part he shall be perfectly satisfied; and under this new arrangement, Mr. Phelps having zealously laboured at his part, comes the last rehearsal day. Macready then again appears, hints that he has

---

[1] *Life*, p. 115.   [2] *Personalia*, pp. 66–8.

studied the character, will act the first night. Upon this our Robert does not fall prone at his feet and worship him for his condescending goodness—not that at all does our Robert do, but quite other than that—with laconic brevity he positively declines taking the part from Phelps, dispenses with Macready's aid, &c., and all this in face of a whole green-room. You imagine the fury and whirlwind of our managerial wrath—silent fury, a compressed whirlwind, volcano fires burning white in our pent heart. We say nothing, of course, but we do our spiteful uttermost; we give no orders—we provide paltry machinery—we issue mandates to all our dependent pen-wielders—to all tribes of men who rejoice in suppers and distinguished society.[1]

Arnould enclosed examples of 'their dirty work' in the letter, no doubt including the reviews in the *Athenæum* and the *Spectator*, and then proceeded to give 'an exacter notion of the real reception the piece met with'. According to this,

The first night was magnificent... Poor Phelps did his utmost, Helen Faucit very fairly, and there could be no mistake at all about the honest enthusiasm of the audience. The gallery (and this, of course, was very gratifying, because not to be expected at a play of *Browning*) took all the points quite as quickly as the pit, and entered into the general feeling and interest of the action far more than the boxes—some of whom took it upon themselves to be shocked at being betrayed into so much interest for a young woman who had behaved so improperly as Mildred.

In contrast to this 'triumph', the second night 'was evidently presided over by the spirit of the manager'. Arnould found himself 'one of about sixty or seventy in the pit', yet that seemed a crowd 'when compared to the desolate emptiness of the boxes'. The gallery was again full, however, 'and again among all who were there were the same decided impressions of pity and horror produced'. On the third night Arnould 'again took [his] wife to the boxes', but the theatre presented a depressing sight. 'It was evident at a glance that [this performance] was to be the last. My own delight, and hers too, in the play was increased at this third representation, and would have gone on increasing to a thirtieth; but the miserable, great, chilly house, with its apathy and emptiness, produced on us both the painful sensation which made her exclaim that 'she could cry with vexation' at seeing so noble a play so basely marred.' Arnould's conclusion is an interesting one:

there can be no doubt whatever that the absence of Macready's name from the list of performers of the new play was the means of keeping away numbers from

[1] *Browning and Domett*, pp. 62 ff.—The publication of Macready's *Diaries* in 1912 made it evident that Browning was uncharacteristically ungenerous to Macready. For further evidence of his lack of understanding of Macready's situation and of the weaknesses of his own play, see William Baker, 'Robert Browning on William Charles Macready', *BSN* (December 1978), pp. 12–18.

the house. Whether if he had played and *they* had come the play would have been permanently popular is another question. I don't myself think it would. With some of the grandest situations and finest passages you can conceive, it does undoubtedly want a sustained interest to the end of the third act; in fact the whole of that act on the stage is a falling off from the second act; which I need not tell you is for all purposes of performance the most unpardonable fault. Still, it will no doubt—nay, it must—have done this, viz. produced a higher opinion than ever of Browning's genius and the great things he is yet to do, in the minds not only of a clique, but of the general world of readers. No one now would shake their heads if you said of 'our Robert Browning,' This man will go far yet.[1]

Macready's difficulties with the play continued after the end of its brief run. In the rush to get *A Blot in the 'Scutcheon* on the stage he had over-looked the proper licensing procedure. On 16 February, accordingly, he received the standard warning on the matter, which he passed to Serle, his acting manager, to answer. Serle's somewhat lame excuses and apologies failed to satisfy the Lord Chancellor, who replied with threats of banning and prosecution if any more plays were performed without the proper authorization.[2]

Shortly after the production Helen Faucit asked Browning to write something in her album. On 4 March he complied, sending her the lines printed below, in Appendix B. They were to remain close and affectionate friends. Relations between Browning and Macready were to be very different. Two weeks later Macready noted that he happened to meet Browning, 'who was startled into accosting me, but seeming to remember that he did not intend to do so, started off in great haste'.[3] At a 'dull party' in 1846 Browning did not speak to Macready, which led the latter to comment, 'the *puppy!* etc.' Three years later he observed that, but for *Paracelsus*, he could not think anyone would read Browning's poetry twice 'who had choice of any other poet'. On 7 April 1850 Forster gave him a copy of *Christmas-Eve and Easter-Day*, with 'a sort of regretful message from Browning', but he read it without pleasure, objecting to 'the juxtaposition of vulgar and coarse images and high religious thoughts'. The two men were never again to be friends, though many years later they met 'to shake hands and forgive'.[4] After Macready's death in 1873 and the publication of

---

[1] It is remarkable that Elizabeth Barrett heard John Kenyon's account of the new play almost at once, and was herself impressed when she read it: see Raymond and Sullivan, ii. 173 and 175.

[2] Lord Chamberlain's papers in the Public Record Office: LC 1: 25, 47. See also John Russell Stephens, *The Censorship of English Drama 1824–1901* (Cambridge, 1980), p. 15.

[3] *Diaries*, ii. 198, 340, 432, 464.

[4] Griffin and Minchin, p. 119.

Reminiscences and Selections from his Diary and Letters two years later Browning continued to believe that the chance of his play succeeding had been deliberately jeopardized. The publicity occasioned by the first American production in 1884 led him to write a series of letters to an American correspondent (Frank Hill) in which he gave him his version of events at Drury Lane more than forty years before:

poor Macready's plan was frustrated—and a play,—not with himself as protagonist . . . proved—what Macready himself declared it to be—a 'complete success' . . . There is nothing to wonder at in the absence of any comment upon this discreditable Blot in Macready's 'Scutcheon in the journal of himself or the correspondence of his henchman Forster.[1]

In 1848 Browning gave Phelps permission to mount a new production at Sadler's Wells, stipulating—though without effect—that 'the purity of the text' should be preserved.[2] Joseph Arnould, who attended the first night on 27 November, wrote to Browning to express the 'delight & gratification which we, in common with a crowded audience felt, at the revival of your noble play'. 'It was indeed a grand triumph', he concluded, '& Phelps did his part thoroughly well both as actor & manager. The papers will have informed you of its success since then.'[3] In fact Browning was again disappointed with the reception of his play, which was performed eight times in 1848–9 and has since rarely been acted in the professional theatre.[4]

The Text

The two manuscripts which survive from the first production, Macready's working copy (*MS*) and the Lord Chamberlain's copy (*LC*) show how far the stage version of the play differed from the printed text (*1843*). *MS*, now in the Beinecke Library at Yale, is a fair transcript in the hand of Sarianna Browning, with a few revisions in her hand and a few in

---

[1] Unpublished letter to F. H. Hill, 21 December 1884 (Yale).

[2] *Elizabeth Barrett Browning: Letters to her Sister, 1846–1859*, ed. Leonard Huxley (1929), p. 94.

[3] Letter dated 26 December 1848, printed in the article cited on p. 6, above.

[4] It was with reluctance that Browning allowed cuts and alterations to be made to the text for the play's North American tour, and he was gratified to receive the reviews from Philadelphia, where critics found the changes unnecessary: 'the satisfactory thing', he wrote to Hill on 15 January 1885, 'would have been that the play was given just as the playwright intended'. It was only in the special productions organized through the Browning Society that he felt his intentions had been honoured, and that 'all was done capitally—all that was requisite for getting a fair judgment of the thing': *Trumpeter*, p. 112.

Browning's own. It has also extensive revisions (both in ink and in pencil) in Macready's hand, some of which may have been authorized by Browning: Macready cut (in aggregate) about a quarter of the whole work.[1] Single lines and short passages are often cancelled and then absorbed within longer sections circled and cross-hatched for omission. Even within the cancelled sections alterations are frequently marked. We conclude that Macready worked on the text on at least three occasions, but cannot establish which changes were made on the dates—29 January, 1 and 9 February—indicated in his *Diaries*. In the parts of the play which remain uncut alternative and additional lines are added in his hand, as are stage directions ('sits', 'rises', 'kneeling', 'placing her on the couch', 'door L', etc.) and a reminder to the stage hands: 'see Lamp ready at Blue pane'. Some words and phrases are underlined throughout, perhaps for the prompter's preliminary reading to the cast.

While *MS* was in the hands of Macready, Browning continued to work on his own copy of the play, which has disappeared. It is clear that some of the changes which he made were transferred to *MS*. Others were made only in the printer's copy, so that *MS* and *1843* often diverge. In *MS*, for example, in a passage cancelled by Macready (III. i. 153 in this edition), 'hoof' is altered to 'foot':

The thoughtless ⟨hoof⟩ [foot] upon her life and mine

and this alteration must also have been made in Browning's own manuscript, since it is incorporated in *1843*. At I. i. 29, however, *MS* has 'Let Gerard ⟨be⟩ [sulk] alone—', but Browning seems to have thought better of the alteration: *1843* has simply 'Let Gerard be!' In our textual notes we collate *MS* with the printed editions, recording cuts (but not alterations within cuts) and indicating which of the alterations are in Macready's hand.

LC, now in the British Library, clearly derives from *MS*, though it incorporates only some of the later cuts and changes. It appears to represent an intermediate stage in the process of revision, after Macready had begun work on the manuscript but before the final changes of 9 February. Comparison of the texts at I. iii. 174–7, for instance, shows *LC* incorporating two alterations, one of which was later rescinded, and including two lines ultimately cancelled:

---

[1] See Joseph W. Reed, Jr., 'Browning and Macready: The Final Quarrel': PMLA lxxv (1960), 597–603. Browning later told EBB that 'greater excisions had been determined on' (including that of the whole of the first scene), but 'the appearance of the printed copy had the effect it intended': Kintner, ii. 730. *LC* has been published in facsimile by James Hogg in *Robert Browning and the Victorian Theatre*, vol. ii (Salzburger Studien zur Anglistik und Amerikanistik 4, 1977).

MS	LC	*1843*
174	I was scarce ⟨a⟩ [more than] boy [alteration subsequently deleted]	I was scarce more than boy	I was scarce a boy
175	and you ⟨were infantine⟩ [so young]	And you so young	And you were infantine
176-7	[deleted]	as *1843*	

LC retains the original five-act (seven-scene) structure of *MS*, though the revisions to *MS* indicate that it was to be reorganized into three acts (six scenes), as in all printed versions of the play.

The first printing of *A Blot* (recorded in our textual notes as *1843*[1]) was the only one of the *Bells and Pomegranates* to sell out and be reissued. The new impression, made some time between 1843 and 1846, has forty changes, mainly in accidentals,[1] but perpetuates a few misprints from *1843*[1]. There are no corrections to *A Blot* in either the Brigham Young or the Texas annotated copy of *Bells and Pomegranates*. The play was reprinted in all Browning's subsequent collections, and the song from Act I ('There's a woman like a dew-drop') was included in the 1865 *Selection*. Only one alteration was made by Browning to the Dykes Campbell copy of *1888* and the Brown University list; it was made correctly in *1889* and has been adopted here.

---

[1] See Craig Abbott, 'Revisions in the "Second Edition" of *A Blot in the 'Scutcheon*', *Browning Newsletter* (Spring 1972), pp. 53-5, which gives a virtually complete list of the changes.

A
BLOT IN THE 'SCUTCHEON;

A TRAGEDY.

title *1843* BELLS AND POMEGRANATES. Nº· V.—A BLOT IN THE 'SCUTCHEON. A Tragedy, IN THREE ACTS. BY ROBERT BROWNING, Author of "Paracelsus." LONDON: EDWARD MOXON, DOVER STREET. MDCCCXLIII.

PERSONS.

MILDRED TRESHAM.
GUENDOLEN TRESHAM.
THOROLD, Earl Tresham.
AUSTIN TRESHAM.
HENRY, Earl Mertoun.
GERARD, *and other retainers of* Lord Tresham.

TIME, 17——.

1843 gives the cast for the performance at the Theatre Royal, Drury Lane, February 11 1843, opposite the first page of the text. Mildred Tresham was played by Miss Helen Faucit, Guendolen Tresham by Mrs Stirling, Thorold, Lord Tresham by Mr Phelps, Austin Tresham by Mr Hudson, Henry, Earl Mertoun by Mr Anderson, and Gerard by Mr G. Bennett.
Lord Tresham becomes Earl Tresham in *1868*.

A

BLOT IN THE 'SCUTCHEON.

ACT I.

SCENE I.—*The interior of a lodge in* LORD TRESHAM'S *park. Many* Retainers *crowded at the window, supposed to command a view of the entrance to his mansion.* GERARD, *the warrener, his back to a table on which are flagons, etc.*

1st Retainer. Ay, do! push, friends, and then you'll push
down me!
—What for? Does any hear a runner's foot
Or a steed's trample or a coach-wheel's cry?
Is the Earl come or his least poursuivant?
But there's no breeding in a man of you   5
Save Gerard yonder: here's a half-place yet,
Old Gerard!
        Gerard.   Save your courtesies, my friend.
Here is my place.
        2nd Retainer.   Now, Gerard, out with it!
What makes you sullen, this of all the days
I' the year? To-day that young rich bountiful   10
Handsome Earl Mertoun, whom alone they match
With our Lord Tresham through the country-side,
Is coming here in utmost bravery
To ask our master's sister's hand?

---

s.d. *1865 to com a MS,1843-65* Warrener, sitting alone, his   1 *MS,1843,1849* do—
MS push me down. *1843-65* me.   2-8 *MS* (What .... placc!)   14 *MS* hand.

    s.d. *warrener*: 'An officer employed to watch over the game in a park or preserve. *Obs. exc. Hist.*': OED.

    4 *poursuivant*: attendant. OED mentions this spelling as found in the seventeenth and eighteenth centuries.

    13 *bravery*: 'Splendour; magnificence': Johnson.

Gerard.   What then?

  2nd Retainer. What then? Why, you, she speaks to, if she
    meets   15
Your worship, smiles on as you hold apart
The boughs to let her through her forest walks,
You, always favourite for your no-deserts,
You've heard, these three days, how Earl Mertoun sues
To lay his heart and house and broad lands too   20
At Lady Mildred's feet: and while we squeeze
Ourselves into a mousehole lest we miss
One congee of the least page in his train,
You sit o' one side—"there's the Earl," say I—
"What then?" say you!

  3rd Retainer.   I'll wager he has let   25
Both swans he tamed for Lady Mildred swim
Over the falls and gain the river!

  Gerard.   Ralph,
Is not to-morrow my inspecting day
For you and for your hawks?

  4th Retainer.   Let Gerard be!
He's coarse-grained, like his carved black cross-bow stock.   30
Ha, look now, while we squabble with him, look!
Well done, now—is not this beginning now,
To purpose?

  1st Retainer. Our retainers look as fine—
That's comfort. Lord, how Richard holds himself
With his white staff! Will not a knave behind   35
Prick him upright?

  4th Retainer.   He's only bowing, fool!
The Earl's man bent us lower by this much.

---

24 *MS* you 〈sit〉 [keep] o'   25 *MS,1843-68* then,"   27 *MS* river.
28 *MS* To-morrow's my inspecting-day for you   29 *MS* And for your hawks. 4. Let
Gerard 〈be〉 [sulk] alone—   30 *MS* He's ill-grained,   31 *MS* look ye, while
32-57 *MS* [deleted]   34 *1843,1849* comfort!

  18 *no-deserts*: formerly a common type of formation: see OED, 'No', *a.* II. 5. a.
  22 *mousehole*: a tiny space.
  23 *congee*: a ceremonious bow.
  35 *white staff*: a symbol of office carried by a functionary such as a steward.

1st Retainer. That's comfort. Here's a very cavalcade!

3rd Retainer. I don't see wherefore Richard, and his troop
Of silk and silver varlets there, should find   40
Their perfumed selves so indispensable
On high days, holidays! Would it so disgrace
Our family, if I, for instance, stood—
In my right hand a cast of Swedish hawks,
A leash of greyhounds in my left?—

   Gerard.   —With Hugh   45
The logman for supporter, in his right
The bill-hook, in his left the brushwood-shears!

   3rd Retainer. Out on you, crab! What next, what next?
    The Earl!

   1st Retainer. Oh Walter, groom, our horses, do they match
The Earl's? Alas, that first pair of the six—   50
They paw the ground—Ah Walter! and that brute
Just on his haunches by the wheel!

   6th Retainer.   Ay—ay!
You, Philip, are a special hand, I hear,
At soups and sauces: what's a horse to you?
D' ye mark that beast they've slid into the midst   55
So cunningly?—then, Philip, mark this further;
No leg has he to stand on!

   1st Retainer.   No? That's comfort.

   2nd Retainer. Peace, Cook! The Earl descends. Well,
    Gerard, see
The Earl at least! Come, there's a proper man,
I hope! Why, Ralph, no falcon, Pole or Swede,   60
Has got a starrier eye.

   3rd Retainer.   His eyes are blue:
But leave my hawks alone!

42 *1843* holy days! *1849* holy-days!   47 *1843* shears.   57a *MS* {Macready's hand} [Here Gerard, see—they are coming this way]   58 *MS* Peace, ⟨Cook⟩ [Peace]!
1843 Cook. *MS* descends—Oh Gerard, see   60-2 *MS* ⟨I hope!....alone!⟩

    44 *a cast of Swedish hawks*: Johnson defines 'cast' (15) as 'A flight; a number of hawks dismissed from the fist.'
    45 *A leash of greyhounds*: a group of three greyhounds.
    48 *crab!*: 'A peevish morose person': Johnson.

4th Retainer.   So young, and yet
So tall and shapely!
    5th Retainer.   Here's Lord Tresham's self!
There now—there's what a nobleman should be!
He's older, graver, loftier, he's more like   65
A House's head.
    2nd Retainer. But you'd not have a boy
—And what's the Earl beside?—possess too soon
That stateliness?
    1st Retainer.   Our master takes his hand—
Richard and his white staff are on the move—
Back fall our people—(tsh!—there's Timothy   70
Sure to get tangled in his ribbon-ties,
And Peter's cursed rosette's a-coming off!)
—At last I see our lord's back and his friend's;
And the whole beautiful bright company
Close round them—in they go!
    [*Jumping down from the window-bench, and making for the table and its
        jugs.*]
                              Good health, long life,   75
Great joy to our Lord Tresham and his House!
    6th Retainer. My father drove his father first to court,
After his marriage-day—ay, did he!
    2nd Retainer.   God bless
Lord Tresham, Lady Mildred, and the Earl!
Here, Gerard, reach your beaker!
    Gerard.   Drink, my boys!   80
Don't mind me—all's not right about me—drink!
    2nd Retainer [*aside*]. He's vexed, now, that he let the show
        escape!
[*To* GERARD.] Remember that the Earl returns this way.

---

63 *MS* self.   66 *1843-68* head!   66-8 *MS* ⟨But you'd .... stateliness?⟩
68a *MS* ⟨Macready's hand⟩ ⟨Away, Away⟩ [Hush! they're here, quick to our posts—to our
posts]   69-83 *MS* ⟨deleted⟩   75 s.d. *1843-65 jugs, &c.*   80 *1843-65*
boys: 81 *1843* drink.

Gerard. That way?

2nd Retainer.   Just so.

Gerard.   Then my way's here.   [*Goes.*

2nd Retainer.   Old Gerard

Will die soon—mind, I said it! He was used   85
To care about the pitifullest thing
That touched the House's honour, not an eye
But his could see wherein: and on a cause
Of scarce a quarter this importance, Gerard
Fairly had fretted flesh and bone away   90
In cares that this was right, nor that was wrong,
Such point decorous, and such square by rule—
He knew such niceties, no herald more:
And now—you see his humour: die he will!

1st Retainer. God help him! Who's for the great servants'-
hall   95
To hear what's going on inside? They'd follow
Lord Tresham into the saloon.

3rd Retainer.   I!—

4th Retainer.   I!—

Leave Frank alone for catching, at the door,
Some hint of how the parley goes inside!
Prosperity to the great House once more!   100
Here's the last drop!

1st Retainer.   Have at you! Boys, hurrah!

SCENE II.—*A Saloon in the Mansion.*

Enter LORD TRESHAM, LORD MERTOUN, AUSTIN, *and* GUENDOLEN.

Tresham. I welcome you, Lord Mertoun, yet once more,

---

84 *MS* Th⟨at⟩[is] way?   s.d. *1843* †[*Exit.*   85 *1843* it: 91 *1843*¹ wrong;
92 *MS* This point was decorous and that by rule, *1843–68* Such a point *1843,1849* and such
by rule—   93 *1843,1849* (He .... more)   95–101 *MS* {deleted}
*95 {reading of MS} *1843–1889* 2nd Retainer.   100 *1843–65* more—   101 s.d.
MS,1843 †[*Exeunt.*
    Scene ii.   s.d. *MS* {insertions in Macready's hand} Tresham [leading in] *Lord Mer-*
toun, *1843,1849* MERTOUN;

    92 *decorous*: stressed on the second syllable, as in Johnson.

To this ancestral roof of mine. Your name
—Noble among the noblest in itself,
Yet taking in your person, fame avers,
New price and lustre,—(as that gem you wear,   5
Transmitted from a hundred knightly breasts,
Fresh chased and set and fixed by its last lord,
Seems to re-kindle at the core)—your name
Would win you welcome!—
    Mertoun.   Thanks!
    Tresham.   —But add to that,
The worthiness and grace and dignity   10
Of your proposal for uniting both
Our Houses even closer than respect
Unites them now—add these, and you must grant
One favour more, nor that the least,—to think
The welcome I should give;—'t is given! My lord,   15
My only brother, Austin: he's the king's.
Our cousin, Lady Guendolen—betrothed
To Austin: all are yours.
    Mertoun.   I thank you—less
For the expressed commendings which your seal,
And only that, authenticates—forbids   20
My putting from me . . . to my heart I take
Your praise . . . but praise less claims my gratitude,
Than the indulgent insight it implies
Of what must needs be uppermost with one
Who comes, like me, with the bare leave to ask,   25
In weighed and measured unimpassioned words,
A gift, which, if as calmly 't is denied,
He must withdraw, content upon his cheek,
Despair within his soul. That I dare ask
Firmly, near boldly, near with confidence   30

---

3 *MS* (Noble   5 *MS* New tint and   5–8 *MS* (as . . . . core))   6 *1843* a
thousand knightly   16 *MS* King's: 18 *MS* yours!   20 *MS* (And . . . .
authenticates)   27 *MS,1843* if as quietly denied,   29 *MS,1843,1849* soul:

    7 *chased* : engraved in relief.
    16 *he's the king's* : i.e. he serves the King in the army. Cf. II. 327.

That gift, I have to thank you. Yes, Lord Tresham,
I love your sister—as you'd have one love
That lady . . . oh more, more I love her! Wealth,
Rank, all the world thinks me, they're yours, you know,
To hold or part with, at your choice—but grant   35
My true self, me without a rood of land,
A piece of gold, a name of yesterday,
Grant me that lady, and you . . . Death or life?
    Guendolen [*apart to* AUSTIN].
Why, this is loving, Austin!
    Austin.   He's so young!
    Guendolen. Young? Old enough, I think, to half surmise   40
He never had obtained an entrance here,
Were all this fear and trembling needed.
    Austin.   Hush!
He reddens.
    Guendolen. Mark him, Austin; that's true love!
Ours must begin again.
    Tresham.   We'll sit, my lord.
Ever with best desert goes diffidence.   45
I may speak plainly nor be misconceived.
That I am wholly satisfied with you
On this occasion, when a falcon's eye
Were dull compared with mine to search out faults,
Is somewhat. Mildred's hand is hers to give   50
Or to refuse.
    Mertoun. But you, you grant my suit?
I have your word if hers?
    Tresham.   My best of words
If hers encourage you. I trust it will.
Have you seen Lady Mildred, by the way?
    Mertoun. I . . . I . . . our two demesnes, remember, touch;   55
I have been used to wander carelessly
After my stricken game: the heron roused

31 *MS,1843* you for. Lord Tresham,   33 *1843* her.   33-8 *MS* (wealth . . . .
life?)   34 *1843-65* *me,*   36 *1843-65* *me*   39 *1843-65* *is*
43 *MS* Austin— *1843* Austin, *1889* Austin   55 *MS* touch.

Deep in my woods, has trailed its broken wing
Thro' thicks and glades a mile in yours,—or else
Some eyass ill-reclaimed has taken flight   60
And lured me after her from tree to tree,
I marked not whither. I have come upon
The lady's wondrous beauty unaware,
And—and then . . . I have seen her.
  Guendolen [*aside to* AUSTIN]. Note that mode
Of faltering out that, when a lady passed,   65
He, having eyes, did see her! You hàd said—
"On such a day I scanned her, head to foot;
"Observed a red, where red should not have been,
"Outside her elbow; but was pleased enough
"Upon the whole." Let such irreverent talk   70
Be lessoned for the future!
  Tresham.   What's to say
May be said briefly. She has never known
A mother's care; I stand for father too.
Her beauty is not strange to you, it seems—
You cannot know the good and tender heart,   75
Its girl's trust and its woman's constancy,
How pure yet passionate, how calm yet kind,
How grave yet joyous, how reserved yet free
As light where friends are—how imbued with lore
The world most prizes, yet the simplest, yet   80
The . . . one might know I talked of Mildred—thus
We brothers talk!
  Mertoun. I thank you.
  Tresham.   In a word,

---

58 *MS* in ⟨its⟩ [my] woods   62 *MS* whither . . . *1843,1849* whither . .
64 *MS* Note ⟨that⟩ [his] mode 65 *MS,1843,1849* Of faultering out 66 *MS*
her— 67 *MS* foot, 69 *MS,1843* elbow, 71 *MS* future.
72 *MS* briefly: 79 *1843* how embued with

 59 *thicks*: thickets, described by OED as 'Now rare'.
 60 *eyass*: a young hawk.
  ill-reclaimed: badly trained. Johnson's fourth meaning for the verb is 'To tame'. He
cites Dryden, 'Palamon and Arcite', iii. 89: 'An Eagle well reclaim'd'.
 71 *lessoned*: as in 'My Last Duchess', 40.

Control's not for this lady; but her wish
To please me outstrips in its subtlety
My power of being pleased: herself creates   85
The want she means to satisfy. My heart
Prefers your suit to her as 't were its own.
Can I say more?
    Mertoun.   No more—thanks, thanks—no more!
    Tresham. This matter then discussed . . .
    Mertoun.   —We'll waste no breath
On aught less precious. I'm beneath the roof   90
Which holds her: while I thought of that, my speech
To you would wander—as it must not do,
Since as you favour me I stand or fall.
I pray you suffer that I take my leave!
    Tresham. With less regret 't is suffered, that again   95
We meet, I hope, so shortly.
    Mertoun.   We? again?—
Ah yes, forgive me—when shall . . . you will crown
Your goodness by forthwith apprising me
When . . . if . . . the lady will appoint a day
For me to wait on you—and her.
    Tresham.   So soon   100
As I am made acquainted with her thoughts
On your proposal—howsoe'er they lean—
A messenger shall bring you the result.
    Mertoun. You cannot bind me more to you, my lord.
Farewell till we renew . . . I trust, renew   105
A converse ne'er to disunite again.
    Tresham. So may it prove!
    Mertoun.   You, lady, you, sir, take
My humble salutation!

83–6 *MS* ⟨her wish . . . . satisfy.⟩ [Macready's hand in margin: 'In']   87 *MS* suit as
'twere its own to her—   88 *MS* thanks—no more.   90 *MS* precious!
91 *MS,1843, 1863* That holds   *MS,1843* I think of   92 *MS* To you were idle; as
it must not be,   94 *MS* leave.   100 *MS* her. Tresh. As soon

    87 *Prefers your suit*: as in *Julius Caesar*, III. i. 27–8: 'Let him go / And presently prefer his
suit to Caesar'.

Guendolen and Austin. Thanks!
Tresham.   Within there!
[Servants *enter.* TRESHAM *conducts* MERTOUN *to the door. Meantime*
    AUSTIN *remarks,*

                                                    Well,
Here I have an advantage of the Earl,
Confess now! I'd not think that all was safe   110
Because my lady's brother stood my friend!
Why, he makes sure of her—"do you say, yes—
"She'll not say, no,"—what comes it to beside?
I should have prayed the brother, "speak this speech,
"For Heaven's sake urge this on her—put in this—   115
"Forget not, as you'd save me, t' other thing,—
"Then set down what she says, and how she looks,
"And if she smiles, and" (in an under breath)
"Only let her accept me, and do you
"And all the world refuse me, if you dare!"   120
    Guendolen. That way you'd take, friend Austin? What a
        shame
I was your cousin, tamely from the first
Your bride, and all this fervour's run to waste!
Do you know you speak sensibly to-day?
The Earl's a fool.
    Austin.   Here's Thorold. Tell him so!   125
    Tresham [*returning*]. Now, voices, voices! 'St! the lady's
        first!
How seems he?—seems he not . . . come, faith give fraud
The mercy-stroke whenever they engage!
Down with fraud, up with faith! How seems the Earl?
A name! a blazon! if you knew their worth,   130

109 *MS* | Well—here *1868* an advantge of   110 *1843* now;   *1843-65* I'd *MS* was
gained   111 *MS* friend: *1843-63* friend.   114 *1843-65* I   115 *MS*
"Urge this on her, o'Heaven's name—put in this—   118 *MS* she cares . . and"—(in
1843 smiles," and, in . . . . breath, *1849, 1863* smiles," and   125 *MS* Here's
Tresham: tell him so.   126 *MS* voices—voices—   127-9 *MS* (faith . . . .
faith!)   130 *MS* name, a blazon— . . . . worth!

    128 *mercy-stroke*: coup de grâce.
    130 *a blazon*: a coat of arms.

As you will never! come—the Earl?
   Guendolen.   He's young.
   Tresham. What's she? an infant save in heart and brain.
Young! Mildred is fourteen, remark! And you . . .
Austin, how old is she?
   Guendolen.   There's tact for you!
I meant that being young was good excuse   135
If one should tax him . . .
   Tresham.   Well?
   Guendolen.   —With lacking wit.
   Tresham. He lacked wit? Where might he lack wit, so
     please you?
   Guendolen. In standing straighter than the steward's rod
And making you the tiresomest harangue,
Instead of slipping over to my side   140
And softly whispering in my ear, "Sweet lady,
"Your cousin there will do me detriment
"He little dreams of: he's absorbed, I see,
"In my old name and fame—be sure he'll leave
"My Mildred, when his best account of me   145
"Is ended, in full confidence I wear
"My grandsire's periwig down either cheek.
"I'm lost unless your gentleness vouchsafes" . . .
   Tresham. . . . "To give a best of best accounts, yourself,
"Of me and my demerits." You are right!   150
He should have said what now I say for him.
You golden creature, will you help us all?
Here's Austin means to vouch for much, but you
—You are . . . what Austin only knows! Come up,
All three of us: she's in the library   155
No doubt, for the day's wearing fast. Precede!

---

131 *MS* never: come!   133 *MS* [Macready's hand] is ⟨fourteen⟩ [eighteen], remark!
138 *MS,1843,1849* standing straiter than   139 *MS,1843,1849* tiresomest harangues,
141 *MS* And gently whispering   147 *MS* cheek: 150 *MS* right.
*152 [reading of *MS,1843–63*] *1865–89* Yon golden   153 *MS* much;
154 *MS* knows.   155 *MS* us.

   133 *fourteen* : a little older than Juliet, who has 'not seen the change of fourteen years':
Romeo and Juliet, I. ii. 9. Note Macready's alteration to 'eighteen'.

Guendolen. Austin, how we must—!

Tresham.   Must what? Must speak truth,
Malignant tongue! Detect one fault in him!
I challenge you!

   Guendolen.   Witchcraft's a fault in him,
For you're bewitched.

   Tresham.   What's urgent we obtain   160
Is, that she soon receive him—say, to-morrow—
Next day at furthest.

   Guendolen.   Ne'er instruct me!

   Tresham.   Come!
—He's out of your good graces, since forsooth,
He stood not as he'd carry us by storm
With his perfections! You're for the composed   165
Manly assured becoming confidence!
—Get her to say, "to-morrow," and I'll give you . . .
I'll give you black Urganda, to be spoiled
With petting and snail-paces. Will you? Come!

SCENE III.—MILDRED's *chamber. A painted window overlooks the park.*
MILDRED *and* GUENDOLEN.

   Guendolen. Now, Mildred, spare those pains. I have not
     left
Our talkers in the library, and climbed
The wearisome ascent to this your bower
In company with you,—I have not dared . . .
Nay, worked such prodigies as sparing you   5
Lord Mertoun's pedigree before the flood,

---

158 *MS* detect a fault   159 *MS* you.   161 *MS* soon receives him . .
162 *MS,1843,1849* at farthest.   *MS* ⟨Next⟩ [Ne'er] instruct   164 *MS* He came
not,   167 *MS* to-morrow,   169 s.d. *MS,1843* †[Exeunt.
   Scene iii.   s.d. *MS Mildred's Bedchamber. A MS,1843 window in the background.* MIL-
DRED   1 *MS* pains:

   168 *black Urganda* : a fine horse. Urganda is the name of an enchantress in *Don Quixote*, i,
ch. 5. Keats has 'Urganda's sword' in 'To J. H. Reynolds, Esq.', 29; but the poem was not
published until 1848.
   169 *snail-paces* : probably a nonce-word, from 'snail-paced'.

Which Thorold seemed in very act to tell
—Or bringing Austin to pluck up that most
Firm-rooted heresy—your suitor's eyes,
He would maintain, were grey instead of blue—   10
I think I brought him to contrition!—Well,
I have not done such things, (all to deserve
A minute's quiet cousin's talk with you,)
To be dismissed so coolly.
    Mildred.   Guendolen!
What have I done? what could suggest . . .
    Guendolen.   There, there!   15
Do I not comprehend you'd be alone
To throw those testimonies in a heap,
Thorold's enlargings, Austin's brevities,
With that poor silly heartless Guendolen's
Ill-timed misplaced attempted smartnesses—   20
And sift their sense out? now, I come to spare you
Nearly a whole night's labour. Ask and have!
Demand, be answered! Lack I ears and eyes?
Am I perplexed which side of the rock-table
The Conqueror dined on when he landed first,   25
Lord Mertoun's ancestor was bidden take—
The bow-hand or the arrow-hand's great meed?
Mildred, the Earl has soft blue eyes!
    Mildred.   My brother—
Did he . . . you said that he received him well?
    Guendolen. If I said only "well" I said not much.   30
Oh, stay—which brother?
    Mildred.   Thorold! who—who else?
    Guendolen. Thorold (a secret) is too proud by half,—

---

8 *MS* As bringing   14 *1843–68* coolly!   *1843–65* Guendolen,   15 *MS*
What cause have I . . . what *1843–63* done . . *MS* There! There!   17 *MS* throw these
testimonies   18 *MS* Thorold's orations, Austin's brevity,   21–2 *MS* to
spare | You nearly a night's labour—ask and have—   23 *MS* answered! Have I
24–7 *MS* (deleted)   31 *MS* Thorold—

   27 *The bow-hand* : am I likely to be concerned whether Lord Mertoun's ancestor sat on
the left hand or the right hand of William the Conqueror?

Nay, hear me out—with us he's even gentler
Than we are with our birds. Of this great House
The least retainer that e'er caught his glance   35
Would die for him, real dying—no mere talk:
And in the world, the court, if men would cite
The perfect spirit of honour, Thorold's name
Rises of its clear nature to their lips.
But he should take men's homage, trust in it,   40
And care no more about what drew it down.
He has desert, and that, acknowledgment;
Is he content?
    Mildred.   You wrong him, Guendolen,
    Guendolen. He's proud, confess; so proud with brooding
      o'er
The light of his interminable line,   45
An ancestry with men all paladins,
And women all . . .
    Mildred.   Dear Guendolen, 't is late!
When yonder purple pane the climbing moon
Pierces, I know 't is midnight.
    Guendolen.   Well, that Thorold
Should rise up from such musings, and receive   50
One come audaciously to graft himself
Into this peerless stock, yet find no flaw,
No slightest spot in such an one . . .
    Mildred.   Who finds
A spot in Mertoun?
    Guendolen.   Not your brother; therefore,
Not the whole world.
    Mildred.   I am weary, Guendolen.   55
Bear with me!
    Guendolen. I am foolish.
    Mildred.   Oh no, kind!

33-4 *MS* he's gentler than | We with our birds and flowers; of   39 *MS,1843,1849*
lips: 42-7 *MS* ⟨He . . . . all . .⟩   47 *MS* late.   48 *MS* the evening star
55 *MS,1843-65* I'm   56 *MS* me. . . . . kind: *1843-68* kind—

    39 *clear*: pure.   46 *paladins*: knightly heroes, as in *Sordello*, i. 69.

But I would rest.
   Guendolen.   Good night and rest to you!
I said how gracefully his mantle lay
Beneath the rings of his light hair?
   Mildred.   Brown hair.
   Guendolen. Brown? why, it *is* brown: how could you
    know that?   60
   Mildred. How? did not you—Oh, Austin 't was, declared
His hair was light, not brown—my head!—and look,
The moon-beam purpling the dark chamber! Sweet,
Good night!
   Guendolen. Forgive me—sleep the soundlier for me!
                    [*Going, she turns suddenly.*
                      Mildred!

Perdition! all's discovered! Thorold finds   65
—That the Earl's greatest of all grandmothers
Was grander daughter still—to that fair dame
Whose garter slipped down at the famous dance!   [*Goes.*
   Mildred. Is she—can she be really gone at last?
My heart! I shall not reach the window. Needs   70
Must I have sinned much, so to suffer.
   [*She lifts the small lamp which is suspended before the Virgin's image in*
     the window, and places it by the purple pane.
                    There!
                [*She returns to the seat in front*
Mildred and Mertoun! Mildred, with consent
Of all the world and Thorold, Mertoun's bride!
Too late! 'T is sweet to think of, sweeter still
To hope for, that this blessed end soothes up   75

---

57 *MS,1843,1849* you.   59 *MS* Brown hair— *1843-63* Brown hair!   60 *MS*
is   61 *MS* Know? did   63 *MS* The star beam . . . . chamber.   64 *MS*
night. . . . . me! (*Exit Guendolen.*) *Mildred starts up.* Gone!   65-8 {no equivalent in
MS}   65 *1843,1849*   discovered.—   68 s.d. *1843*   †[*Exit.*
70 *MS,1843,1849* heart— *MS* window: *1843,1849* window!   71 *MS,1843-68* suffer!
s.d. *MS it within the*   73 *MS* world, of Thorold—   74 *MS* late:

   68 *Whose garter slipped down*: since the time of Selden the garter after which the highest
order of knighthood in Great Britain is named has been supposed to have been that of the
Countess of Salisbury, in the reign of Edward III.
   75 *soothes up*: atones for.

The curse of the beginning; but I know
It comes too late: 't will sweetest be of all
To dream my soul away and die upon.   [*A noise without.*
The voice! Oh why, why glided sin the snake
Into the paradise Heaven meant us both?   80
                    [*The window opens softly. A low voice sings.*

There's a woman like a dew-drop, she's so purer than the purest;
And her noble heart's the noblest, yes, and her sure faith's the surest:
And her eyes are dark and humid, like the depth on depth of lustre
Hid i' the harebell, while her tresses, sunnier than the wild-grape,
      cluster,
Gush in golden-tinted plenty down her neck's rose-misted marble: 85
Then her voice's music . . . call it the well's bubbling, the bird's
      warble!

                [*A figure wrapped in a mantle appears at the window.*
And this woman says, "My days were sunless and my nights were
      moonless,
"Parched the pleasant April herbage, and the lark's heart's outbreak
      tuneless,
"If you loved me not!" And I who—(ah, for words of flame!) adore
      her,
Who am mad to lay my spirit prostrate palpably before her—   90
                [*He enters, approaches her seat, and bends over her.*
I may enter at her portal soon, as now her lattice takes me,
And by noontide as by midnight make her mine, as hers she makes
      me!

                [*The* Earl *throws off his slouched hat and long cloak.*

76 MS the ⟨curse⟩ ⟨woe⟩ [grief] of   78 *1843–65* upon! MS {no s.d.}   79 MS
His voice!   79–80 MS ⟨Oh why, ... both?⟩   81–92 {small roman in *1843–*
68}   81 MS, *1843* purest,   84 MS Hid ⟨in{?} thickets⟩ [i' the harebell,] while
85 MS her ⟨white⟩ [neck's] rose-misted   86 MS ⟨Neck; and t⟩ [T]hen . . . . music!
[call it] the   87–92 MS {deleted}   89 *1843–63* her!

    79 *sin the snake*: cf. *Paradise Lost*, xi. 426–7.
    81 *There's a woman like a dew-drop*: in *The Versification of Robert Browning* (Columbus,
Ohio, 1928) H. H. Hatcher stated that this poem and 'Home-Thoughts, from the Sea' have
'the same rhythm and line-length as *A Toccata of Galuppi's*' (p. 182): there is a marked resem-
blance, but the lines of this song are acatalectic, in contrast to those in the other two poems.

My very heart sings, so I sing, Beloved!
   Mildred. Sit, Henry—do not take my hand!
   Mertoun.   'T is mine.
The meeting that appalled us both so much   95
Is ended.
   Mildred. What begins now?
   Mertoun.   Happiness
Such as the world contains not.
   Mildred.   That is it.
Our happiness would, as you say, exceed
The whole world's best of blisses: we—do we
Deserve that? Utter to your soul, what mine   100
Long since, Beloved, has grown used to hear,
Like a death-knell, so much regarded once,
And so familiar now; this will not be!
   Mertoun. Oh, Mildred, have I met your brother's face,
Compelled myself—if not to speak untruth,   105
Yet to disguise, to shun, to put aside
The truth, as—what had e'er prevailed on me
Save you, to venture? Have I gained at last
Your brother, the one scarer of your dreams,
And waking thoughts' sole apprehension too?   110
Does a new life, like a young sunrise, break
On the strange unrest of our night, confused
With rain and stormy flaw—and will you see
No dripping blossoms, no fire-tinted drops
On each live spray, no vapour steaming up,   115
And no expressless glory in the East?
When I am by you, to be ever by you,
When I have won you and may worship you,

93 *MS* [inserted between ll. 92 and 94] I sing because my very heart sings, Mildred!
94 *MS* ⟨Sit⟩, [Dear] Henry. ⟨do .... mine.⟩   *1843-65* hand .... mine!   96 *MS*
Happiness: *104 [reading of *1843-68*] *MS* face, — *1888,1889* face   107-
8 *MS* (as what save you had e'er prevailed | On me to venture—) and thus have I gained
110 *MS* too,—   112 *MS,1843* of the night   116 *MS* East—

  113 *flaw*: 'A sudden gust; a violent blast ... Obsolete': Johnson.
  114 *fire-tinted*: not recorded in OED.
  116 *expressless*: inexpressible, as in Marlowe, *I Tamburlaine*, v.ii. 219.

Oh, Mildred, can you say "this will not be"?
    Mildred. Sin has surprised us, so will punishment.   120
    Mertoun. No—me alone, who sinned alone!
    Mildred.   The night
You likened our past life to—was it storm
Throughout to you then, Henry?
    Mertoun.   Of your life
I spoke—what am I, what my life, to waste
A thought about when you are by me?—you   125
It was, I said my folly called the storm
And pulled the night upon. 'T was day with me—
Perpetual dawn with me.
    Mildred.   Come what, come will,
You have been happy: take my hand!
    Mertoun [*after a pause*].   How good
Your brother is! I figured him a cold—   130
Shall I say, haughty man?
    Mildred.   They told me all.
I know all.
    Mertoun. It will soon be over.
    Mildred.   Over?
Oh, what is over? what must I live through
And say, "'t is over"? Is our meeting over?
Have I received in presence of them all   135
The partner of my guilty love—with brow
Trying to seem a maiden's brow—with lips
Which make believe that when they strive to form
Replies to you and tremble as they strive,
It is the nearest ever they approached   140
A stranger's . . . Henry, yours that stranger's . . . lip—
With cheek that looks a virgin's, and that is . . .

---

119 *MS* This . . . . be? *1849,1868* be?"   120 *1843–68* us;   120–1 *MS* ⟨Sin . . . .
sinned alone.⟩   128 *MS* dawn to me!   129 *MS* ⟨take my hand⟩ *MS,1843* (no
s.d.)   130 *MS* is—   131 *MS* man.   132 *MS* over: Mil. Over!
134 *MS* 'Tis over?— *1843,1849,1868* over?"   136 *MS* my ⟨guilty⟩ love—with brow
[Macready's hand] [, with lips]   137–42 *MS* ⟨deleted⟩   142 *1843–65 is* . . .

Ah God, some prodigy of thine will stop
This planned piece of deliberate wickedness
In its birth even! some fierce leprous spot   145
Will mar the brow's dissimulating! I
Shall murmur no smooth speeches got by heart,
But, frenzied, pour forth all our woeful story,
The love, the shame, and the despair—with them
Round me aghast as round some cursed fount   150
That should spirt water, and spouts blood. I'll not
. . . Henry, you do not wish that I should draw
This vengeance down? I'll not affect a grace
That's gone from me—gone once, and gone for ever!
  Mertoun. Mildred, my honour is your own. I'll share   155
Disgrace I cannot suffer by myself.
A word informs your brother I retract
This morning's offer; time will yet bring forth
Some better way of saving both of us.
  Mildred. I'll meet their faces, Henry!
  Mertoun.   When? to-morrow!   160
Get done with it!
  Mildred. Oh, Henry, not to-morrow!
Next day! I never shall prepare my words
And looks and gestures sooner.—How you must
Despise me!
  Mertoun. Mildred, break it if you choose,
A heart the love of you uplifted—still   165
Uplifts, thro' this protracted agony,
To heaven! but Mildred, answer me,—first pace
The chamber with me—once again—now, say

143 *MS* Oh ⟨God⟩ [Macready's hand] [Heaven!] some *1843–65* God! 144 *MS* deliberate ⟨wickedness⟩ [feigning] 145 *MS,1843–65* even— 145–6 *MS* ⟨some .... dissimulating–⟩ 146 *1843–65* dissimulating— 148 *MS* But [Macready's hand] [Oh—Henry—will you not despise me?] 148–64 *MS* ⟨frenzied .... Despise me!⟩ 150 *1843–68* as men round 160 *1843,1849* faces, Mertoun! .... to-morrow? 163 *1843,1849* sooner!— 167 *MS* Heaven—
167–8 *MS* ⟨first .... now⟩

143 *prodigy* : omen, portent.
145 *some fierce leprous spot* : cf. *Sordello*, i. 567–8 and n.
150 *some cursed fount* : cf. *Sordello*, iv. 89 ff.

Calmly the part, the . . . what it is of me
You see contempt (for you did say contempt)   170
—Contempt for you in! I would pluck it off
And cast it from me!—but no—no, you'll not
Repeat that?—will you, Mildred, repeat that?
　　Mildred. Dear Henry!
　　Mertoun.　　　　　　I was scarce a boy—e'en now
What am I more? And you were infantine   175
When first I met you; why, your hair fell loose
On either side! My fool's-cheek reddens now
Only in the recalling how it burned
That morn to see the shape of many a dream
—You know we boys are prodigal of charms   180
To her we dream of—I had heard of one,
Had dreamed of her, and I was close to her,
Might speak to her, might live and die her own,
Who knew? I spoke. Oh, Mildred, feel you not
That now, while I remember every glance   185
Of yours, each word of yours, with power to test
And weigh them in the diamond scales of pride,
Resolved the treasure of a first and last
Heart's love shall have been bartered at its worth,
—That now I think upon your purity   190
And utter ignorance of guilt—your own
Or other's guilt—the girlish undisguised
Delight at a strange novel prize—(I talk
A silly language, but interpret, you!)
If I, with fancy at its full, and reason   195
Scarce in its germ, enjoined you secrecy,

---

170 *MS* for . . (you did say "contempt" . .)　　171 *MS,1843* in?　　173 *MS* that . .
will　　174 *MS* Henry . . *1843,1849* Henry— *MS* ⟨Macready's hand; addition subse-
quently deleted⟩ scarce ⟨a⟩ [more than] boy　　175 *MS* ⟨Macready's hand⟩ ⟨What
a⟩[A]m I [much] more? and you ⟨were infantine⟩ [so young]　　176-7 *MS* ⟨why . . . .
side⟩　　179 *MS,1843* dream!　　180 *MS* ⟨Macready's hand⟩ know ⟨we boys are⟩
[that youth is] prodigal　　181 *MS* ⟨Macready's hand⟩ her ⟨we⟩ [it] dream[s] of
185 *MS* now, when I　　186-9 *MS* ⟨with power . . . . worth—⟩　　189 *1843*[1]
worth;　　192 *MS* others

187 *diamond scales*: scales exact enough to weigh diamonds.

If you had pity on my passion, pity
On my protested sickness of the soul
To sit beside you, hear you breathe, and watch
Your eyelids and the eyes beneath—if you   200
Accorded gifts and knew not they were gifts—
If I grew mad at last with enterprise
And must behold my beauty in her bower
Or perish—(I was ignorant of even
My own desires—what then were you?) if sorrow—   205
Sin—if the end came—must I now renounce
My reason, blind myself to light, say truth
Is false and lie to God and my own soul?
Contempt were all of this!
    Mildred.   Do you believe . . .
Or, Henry, I'll not wrong you—you believe   210
That I was ignorant. I scarce grieve o'er
The past. We'll love on; you will love me still.
    Mertoun. Oh, to love less what one has injured! Dove,
Whose pinion I have rashly hurt, my breast—
Shall my heart's warmth not nurse thee into strength?   215
Flower I have crushed, shall I not care for thee?
Bloom o'er my crest, my fight-mark and device!
Mildred, I love you and you love me.
    Mildred.   Go!
Be that your last word. I shall sleep to-night.
    Merton. This is not our last meeting?
    Mildred.   One night more.   220
    Mertoun. And then—think, then!
    Mildred.   Then, no sweet courtship-days,
No dawning consciousness of love for us,

---

198 *MS* {Macready's hand} prot⟨racted⟩[ested] sickness   204-6 *MS* ⟨I was . . . .
camc⟩   206 *1843* now rcnouucc {2nd 'u' not turned 'n'}   208 *MS* {Macready's
hand} to ⟨God⟩ [Heaven] and   209 *MS* this. ⟨Do you believe . . .⟩   210-
12 *MS* ⟨Or⟩, Henry, ⟨I'll . . . . love on—⟩   212 *1843-68* past! . . . . still!
216 *MS* {Macready's hand} have ⟨crushed⟩ [bruised], shall   217 *MS* devi⟨s⟩[c]e!
218 *1843-68* me!   221 *MS* then!—think   222 *MS* us!

  217 *Bloom* : imperative.
    fight-mark : this compound is not recorded in OED.

No strange and palpitating births of sense
From words and looks, no innocent fears and hopes,
Reserves and confidences: morning's over!   225
 Mertoun. How else should love's perfected noontide
  follow?
All the dawn promised shall the day perform.
 Mildred. So may it be! but—
        You are cautious, Love?
Are sure that unobserved you scaled the walls?
 Mertoun. Oh, trust me! Then our final meeting's fixed   230
To-morrow night?
 Mildred.   Farewell! Stay, Henry ... wherefore?
His foot is on the yew-tree bough; the turf
Receives him: now the moonlight as he runs
Embraces him—but he must go—is gone.
Ah, once again he turns—thanks, thanks, my Love!   235
He's gone. Oh, I'll believe him every word!
I was so young, I loved him so, I had
No mother, God forgot me, and I fell.
There may be pardon yet: all's doubt beyond.
Surely the bitterness of death is past.   240

---

228 *MS* be.   230 *MS* me. *MS,1843* fixed?   231 *MS* Mil. (*as he retires*) Fare-
well. stay, Henry!   232-6 *MS* (added at end of scene in Macready's hand)
234 *MS* gone!   235 *MS* turns!   236 *MS* gone!   236-40 *MS* (deleted)
240 *1843-68* past!   s.d. *1843* †[*Scene shuts.*

237 *I was so young*: cf. II. 361 and 401, and see Introduction, p. 359.

ACT II.

SCENE—*The Library.*

Enter LORD TRESHAM, *hastily.*

Tresham. This way! In, Gerard, quick!

[*As* GERARD *enters,* TRESHAM *secures the door.*

Now speak! or, wait—

I'll bid you speak directly.   [*Seats himself.*

Now repeat

Firmly and circumstantially the tale

You just now told me; it eludes me; either

I did not listen, or the half is gone   5

Away from me. How long have you lived here?

Here in my house, your father kept our woods

Before you?

Gerard.   —As his father did, my lord.

I have been eating, sixty years almost,

Your bread.

Tresham. Yes, yes. You ever were of all   10

The servants in my father's house, I know,

The trusted one. You'll speak the truth.

Gerard.   I'll speak

God's truth. Night after night . . .

Tresham.   Since when?

Gerard.   At least

A month—each midnight has some man access

To Lady Mildred's chamber.

Tresham.   Tush, "access"—   15

---

s.d. *MS The Library. Enter Lord Tresham hastily—he secures the door to the left, then turning to the right exclaims—*   1 *MS,1843,1849* way—   *MS* Gerard!   s.d. *MS the right door.*)
MS speak—   4 *MS,1843,1849* You've just   6 *MS* you been here?
7 *MS* house?   8 *MS* you.   13 *MS* {Macready's hand} ⟨God's⟩ [Heaven's]
truth: *1843,1849* truth: 14 *MS* ⟨A midnight⟩ [A month]

No wide words like "access" to me!

Gerard.   He runs
Along the woodside, crosses to the South,
Takes the left tree that ends the avenue . . .

   Tresham. The last great yew-tree?

   Gerard.   You might stand upon
The main boughs like a platform. Then he . . .

   Tresham.   Quick!   20

   Gerard. Climbs up, and, where they lessen at the top,
—I cannot see distinctly, but he throws,
I think—for this I do not vouch—a line
That reaches to the lady's casement—

   Tresham.   —Which
He enters not! Gerard, some wretched fool   25
Dares pry into my sister's privacy!
When such are young, it seems a precious thing
To have approached,—to merely have approached,
Got sight of, the abode of her they set
Their frantic thoughts upon. He does not enter?   30
Gerard?

   Gerard. There is a lamp that's full i' the midst,
Under a red square in the painted glass
Of Lady Mildred's . . .

   Tresham.   Leave that name out! Well?
That lamp?

   Gerard.   —Is moved at midnight higher up
To one pane—a small dark-blue pane; he waits   35
For that among the boughs: at sight of that,
I see him, plain as I see you, my lord,
Open the lady's casement, enter there . . .

   Tresham. —And stay?

   Gerard.   An hour, two hours.

16 *1843* me!"   19-20 *MS* {Macready's hand} great ⟨yew⟩ [beech]-tree? ⟨You . . . .
platform—⟩ Tres. Quick! and then?   22 *MS* ⟨I . . . . distinctly⟩   23 *MS* ⟨for
. . . . vouch⟩   25 *MS* Gerrard,   30 *MS* upon; . . . . enter; *1843-68* upon!
31 *MS* Gerard!   *MS,1843-68* in the   33 *MS* out—

16 *wide words*: words which are vague or have a wide meaning and range: a common
usage in the nineteenth century, as OED notes.   35 *a small dark-blue pane*: cf. I. iii. 48.

Tresham.   And this you saw
Once?—twice?—quick!
    Gerard.   Twenty times.
    Tresham.   And what brings you   40
Under the yew-trees?
    Gerard.   The first night I left
My range so far, to track the stranger stag
That broke the pale, I saw the man.
    Tresham.   Yet sent
No cross-bow shaft through the marauder?
    Gerard.   But
He came, my lord, the first time he was seen,   45
In a great moonlight, light as any day,
From Lady Mildred's chamber.
    Tresham [*after a pause*] You have no cause
—Who could have cause to do my sister wrong?
    Gerard. Oh, my lord, only once—let me this once
Speak what is on my mind! Since first I noted   50
All this, I've groaned as if a fiery net
Plucked me this way and that—fire if I turned
To her, fire if I turned to you, and fire
If down I flung myself and strove to die.
The lady could not have been seven years old   55
When I was trusted to conduct her safe
Through the deer-herd to stroke the snow-white fawn
I brought to eat bread from her tiny hand
Within a month. She ever had a smile
To greet me with—she . . . if it could undo   60
What's done, to lop each limb from off this trunk . . .
All that is foolish talk, not fit for you—
I mean, I could not speak and bring her hurt

---

40 *MS* [And] What brings you ⟨there⟩   43 *MS* saw this man—   47 *MS* [no
s.d.] You've   55 *MS* That Lady . . . . been ⟨three⟩ [seven] years   56 *MS* her
thro'   57 *MS* The herd of deer to ⟨see⟩ [stroke] the   58 *MS* eat from out her
59 *MS* month: 61 *MS* trunk!   63 *MS* and do her

    51 *a fiery net*: probably a reminiscence of the shirt of Nessus, which caused the death of
Hercules. See e.g. Sophocles, *Trachiniae*, 1050 ff., and Ovid, *Metamorphoses*, ix. 152 ff.

For Heaven's compelling. But when I was fixed
To hold my peace, each morsel of your food   65
Eaten beneath your roof, my birth-place too,
Choked me. I wish I had grown mad in doubts
What it behoved me do. This morn it seemed
Either I must confess to you, or die:
Now it is done, I seem the vilest worm   70
That crawls, to have betrayed my lady.
    Tresham.   No—
No, Gerard!
    Gerard.   Let me go!
    Tresham.   A man, you say:
What man? Young? Not a vulgar hind? What dress?
    Gerard. A slouched hat and a large dark foreign cloak
Wraps his whole form; even his face is hid;   75
But I should judge him young: no hind, be sure!
    Tresham. Why?
    Gerard.   He is ever armed: his sword projects
Beneath the cloak.
    Tresham.   Gerard,—I will not say
No word, no breath of this!
    Gerard.   Thanks, thanks, my lord!   [*Goes.*
    Tresham [*paces the room. After a pause*].
Oh, thought's absurd!—as with some monstrous fact   80
Which, when ill thoughts beset us, seems to give
Merciful God that made the sun and stars,
The waters and the green delights of earth,
The lie! I apprehend the monstrous fact—
Yet know the maker of all worlds is good,   85
And yield my reason up, inadequate
To reconcile what yet I do behold—

64 *MS,1843,1849* compelling: 68 *1843¹,1868* me to do. *MS* do: 69 *MS*
die.   71 *1843-68* lady!   74 *MS* hat;   76 *MS* sure.   77-8 *1843*
sword | Projects   79 *MS* this. . . . . Lord.   s.d. *MS Exit Gerard. Tresham paces the*
room—⟨*unfaste..; the left door*⟩—*after 1843* †[*Exit.*   80 *MS,1843¹* absurd here! like
some   81 *MS,1843-63* That, when   82 *MS,1843* Merciful Heaven that
84 *MS* lie:

64 *fixed*: resolved. Cf. Shelley, *Prometheus Unbound*, 1. 262.

Blasting my sense! There's cheerful day outside:
This is my library, and this the chair
My father used to sit in carelessly   90
After his soldier-fashion, while I stood
Between his knees to question him: and here
Gerard our grey retainer,—as he says,
Fed with our food, from sire to son, an age,—
Has told a story—I am to believe!   95
That Mildred . . . oh, no, no! both tales are true,
Her pure cheek's story and the forester's!
Would she, or could she, err—much less, confound
All guilts of treachery, of craft, of . . . Heaven
Keep me within its hand!—I will sit here   100
Until thought settle and I see my course.
Avert, oh God, only this woe from me!
    [*As he sinks his head between his arms on the table,* GUENDOLEN's *voice
    is heard at the door.*
Lord Tresham! [*She knocks.*] Is Lord Tresham there?
    [TRESHAM, *hastily turning, pulls down the first book above him and
    opens it.*
    Tresham.   Come in! [*She enters.*
Ha, Guendolen!—good morning.
    Guendolen.   Nothing more?
    Tresham. What should I say more?
    Guendolen.   Pleasant question! more?   105
This more. Did I besiege poor Mildred's brain
Last night till close on morning with "the Earl,"
"The Earl"—whose worth did I asseverate
Till I am very fain to hope that . . . Thorold,
What is all this? You are not well!
    Tresham.   Who, I?   110
You laugh at me.

88 *MS* sense! 'tis cheerful   93 *MS* Gerard the grey   95 *MS* believe—
96 *MS* no, no—   101 *MS,1843-63* thought settles and   102 s.d. *MS table* ⟨*the
scene shuts. Act 3. Scene 1. (The Library as before. Tresham in the same posture*⟩*. Guendolen's voice at
the door to the right*   103 *MS* Tresham here? .... in.   104 *MS,1843-65* Ah
Guendolen— *1868* Guendolen—   106 *MS* more— *1843-63* more!   109 *MS*
hope . . . but, Thorold,

Guendolen.   Has what I'm fain to hope,
Arrived then? Does that huge tome show some blot
In the Earl's 'scutcheon come no longer back
Than Arthur's time?
        Tresham.   When left you Mildred's chamber?
        Guendolen. Oh, late enough, I told you! The main thing   115
To ask is, how I left her chamber,—sure,
Content yourself, she'll grant this paragon
Of Earls no such ungracious . . .
        Tresham.   Send her here!
        Guendolen. Thorold?
        Tresham.   I mean—acquaint her, Guendolen,
—But mildly!
        Guendolen. Mildly?
        Tresham.   Ah, you guessed aright!   120
I am not well: there is no hiding it.
But tell her I would see her at her leisure—
That is, at once! here in the library!
The passage in that old Italian book
We hunted for so long is found, say, found—   125
And if I let it slip again . . . you see,
That she must come—and instantly!
        Guendolen.   I'll die
Piecemeal, record that, if there have not gloomed
Some blot i' the 'scutcheon!
        Tresham.   Go! or, Guendolen,
Be you at call,—with Austin, if you choose,—   130
In the adjoining gallery! There, go!   [GUENDOLEN *goes.*
Another lesson to me! You might bid
A child disguise his heart's sore, and conduct
Some sly investigation point by point
With a smooth brow, as well as bid me catch   135
The inquisitorial cleverness some praise.

115 *MS* you;   116 *1843* left the chamber.   120 *MS* mildly . . . . aright—
123 *MS* once— . . . . Library—   127 *MS* instantly—   129 *MS* 'scutcheon.
Go—   131 *MS,1843* gallery—   s.d. *MS,1843* †[*Exit Guendolen.*
136 *1843-68* praise!

136 *cleverness some praise*: cleverness which some praise.

If you had told me yesterday, "There's one
"You needs must circumvent and practise with,
"Entrap by policies, if you would worm
"The truth out: and that one is—Mildred!" There,   140
There—reasoning is thrown away on it!
Prove she's unchaste . . . why, you may after prove
That she's a poisoner, traitress, what you will!
Where I can comprehend nought, nought's to say,
Or do, or think. Force on me but the first   145
Abomination,—then outpour all plagues,
And I shall ne'er make count of them.

Enter MILDRED.

Mildred.   What book
Is it I wanted, Thorold? Guendolen
Thought you were pale; you are not pale. That book?
That's Latin surely.
  Tresham.   Mildred, here's a line,   150
(Don't lean on me: I'll English it for you)
"Love conquers all things." What love conquers them?
What love should you esteem—best love?
  Mildred.   True love.
  Tresham. I mean, and should have said, whose love is best
Of all that love or that profess to love?   155
  Mildred. The list's so long: there's father's, mother's, hus-
   band's . . .
  Tresham. Mildred, I do believe a brother's love
For a sole sister must exceed them all.
For see now, only see! there's no alloy
Of earth that creeps into the perfect'st gold   160
Of other loves—no gratitude to claim;
You never gave her life, not even aught

---

139 *MS* "Entrap with policies, 140 *MS* Mildred"— 143 *MS* poisoner,
murderess, what you will.   *144 {reading of *MS,1843-68}* *1888,1889* say.
145 *1843-68* think! 147 *MS,1843-68* them! 149 *1843-63* not pale!
150 *MS,1843-63* surely! 158 *1843-63* all! 159 *MS* only see—
160 *MS* the perfectest gold 162 *MS,1843* even the dross

 152 *"Love conquers all things"* : 'Omnia vincit amor': Virgil, *Eclogues*, x. 69.

That keeps life—never tended her, instructed,
Enriched her—so, your love can claim no right
O'er her save pure love's claim: that's what I call   165
Freedom from earthliness. You'll never hope
To be such friends, for instance, she and you,
As when you hunted cowslips in the woods
Or played together in the meadow hay.
Oh yes—with age, respect comes, and your worth   170
Is felt, there's growing sympathy of tastes,
There's ripened friendship, there's confirmed esteem:
—Much head these make against the new-comer!
The startling apparition, the strange youth—
Whom one half-hour's conversing with, or, say,   175
Mere gazing at, shall change (beyond all change
This Ovid ever sang about) your soul
... Her soul, that is,—the sister's soul! With her
'T was winter yesterday; now, all is warmth,
The green leaf's springing and the turtle's voice,   180
"Arise and come away!" Come whither?—far
Enough from the esteem, respect, and all
The brother's somewhat insignificant
Array of rights! All which he knows before,
Has calculated on so long ago!   185
I think such love, (apart from yours and mine,)
Contented with its little term of life,
Intending to retire betimes, aware
How soon the background must be place for it,
—I think, am sure, a brother's love exceeds   190
All the world's love in its unworldliness.

---

165 *MS,1843-65* O'er hers save   166-85 *MS* (you'll never hope .... long ago!)
172 *1843-65* esteem,   177 *1843-63* about!)   178 *1843-65* ... *Her*
186 *MS* think ⟨that⟩ [such] love *1843* think such love   191 *MS* worlds loves in
1843,1849 world's loves in

177 *This Ovid*: Ovid's *Metamorphoses* is the work referred to, a long poem made up of a
great many mythological tales, nearly all of which involve some miraculous change of
form. As always in Ovid, love is a pervasive theme. The implied confusion with Virgil (152)
is to be attributed to the speaker, and not to Browning.
180 *the turtle's voice*: the cooing of the turtle-dove. the emblem of constancy in love.

Mildred. What is this for?

Tresham.   This, Mildred, is it for!
Oh, no, I cannot go to it so soon!
That's one of many points my haste left out—
Each day, each hour throws forth its silk-slight film   195
Between the being tied to you by birth,
And you, until those slender threads compose
A web that shrouds her daily life of hopes
And fears and fancies, all her life, from yours:
So close you live and yet so far apart!   200
And must I rend this web, tear up, break down
The sweet and palpitating mystery
That makes her sacred? You—for you I mean,
Shall I speak, shall I not speak?

    Mildred.   Speak!

    Tresham.   I will.

Is there a story men could—any man   205
Could tell of you, you would conceal from me?
I'll never think there's falsehood on that lip.
Say "There is no such story men could tell,"
And I'll believe you, though I disbelieve
The world—the world of better men than I,   210
And women such as I suppose you. Speak!
[*After a pause.*] Not speak? Explain then! Clear it up then!
    Move
Some of the miserable weight away
That presses lower than the grave! Not speak?
Some of the dead weight, Mildred! Ah, if I   215
Could bring myself to plainly make their charge
Against you! Must I, Mildred? Silent still?

---

192 *MS* it for: *193 (editors' emendation) *MS,1843,1849* Oh, no *1863* Oh; no,
1865-89 Or, no,   197-200 *MS* (until .... apart!) (added over deletion in Mac-
ready's hand: 'In')   204 *MS* speak?—Shall .... Speak—I   207 *1843-63* lip!
212 *MS* (no s.d.) Explain then—clear up all, then— *1843* clear up all, then!   214 *MS*
grave—   217 *MS* you.

    195 *its silk-slight film* : cf. *Sordello*, i. 664 ff. and n.
    198 *shrouds* : conceals, screens.

[*After a pause.*] Is there a gallant that has night by night
Admittance to your chamber?
                    [*After a pause.*] Then, his name!
Till now, I only had a thought for you: 220
But now,—his name!
    Mildred.   Thorold, do you devise
Fit expiation for my guilt, if fit
There be! 'T is nought to say that I'll endure
And bless you,—that my spirit yearns to purge
Her stains off in the fierce renewing fire: 225
But do not plunge me into other guilt!
Oh, guilt enough! I cannot tell his name.
    Tresham. Then judge yourself! How should I act?
        Pronounce!
    Mildred. Oh, Thorold, you must never tempt me thus!
To die here in this chamber by that sword   230
Would seem like punishment: so should I glide,
Like an arch-cheat, into extremest bliss!
'T were easily arranged for me: but you—
What would become of you?
    Tresham.   And what will now
Become of me? I'll hide your shame and mine   235
From every eye; the dead must heave their hearts
Under the marble of our chapel-floor;
They cannot rise and blast you. You may wed
Your paramour above our mother's tomb;
Our mother cannot move from 'neath your foot.   240
We two will somehow wear this one day out:
But with to-morrow hastens here—the Earl!
The youth without suspicion face can come

218 *MS* {no s.d.}   219 *MS* name?   223 *MS* be—   228 *MS* yourself.
.... pronounce.   229 *MS* thus—   232 *MS* bliss—   233 *1843,1849*
me!   237 *MS* floor,   238 *1843-63* you!   239 *MS* tomb,
*241 {reading of *MS,1843-68*} *1888,1889* We too   243 *MS* without a dream, that
faces come *1843* suspicion faces come *1849-68* suspicion that faces come

225 *the fierce renewing fire*: cf. Mal. 3: 2.
236 *heave their hearts*: groan.
243 *suspicion face*: suspicion that a face.

From Heaven, and heart from . . . whence proceed such hearts?
I have despatched last night at your command   245
A missive bidding him present himself
To-morrow—here—thus much is said; the rest
Is understood as if 't were written down—
"His suit finds favour in your eyes." Now dictate
This morning's letter that shall countermand   250
Last night's—do dictate that!
   Mildred.   But, Thorold—if
I will receive him as I said?
   Tresham.   The Earl?
   Mildred. I will receive him.
   Tresham [*starting up*].   Ho there! Guendolen!

         GUENDOLEN *and* AUSTIN *enter.*

And, Austin, you are welcome, too! Look there!
The woman there!
   Austin and Guendolen. How? Mildred?
   Tresham.   Mildred once!   255
Now the receiver night by night, when sleep
Blesses the inmates of her father's house,
—I say, the soft sly wanton that receives
Her guilt's accomplice 'neath this roof which holds
You, Guendolen, you, Austin, and has held   260
A thousand Treshams—never one like her!
No lighter of the signal-lamp her quick
Foul breath near quenches in hot eagerness
To mix with breath as foul! no loosener
O' the lattice, practised in the stealthy tread,   265
The low voice and the noiseless come-and-go!

244 *MS,1843-68* and hearts from . . .   249 *MS* {no quotation marks} *1843,1849*
eyes," *1863-8* eyes:"   252 *1843-65 The Earl?*   253 *1843-63* him! *MS* there—
254 *MS* too—Look there,   255 *MS* Aus. [(both)] How! . . . . once—
259 *MS,1843* roof that holds   261 *MS* her—   260-6 *MS* {deleted}
265 *1843-68* Of the

   244 *whence proceed such hearts?* : cf. *King Lear*, III. vi. 76-7.
   266 *come-and-go* : as in 'The Laboratory', 32, and *The Ring and the Book*, v. 942. (Cf.
French *va-et-vient*.) This antedates the first example of the compound noun in OED
(*Supplement*, i. *A-G*, 1972) by fifty years.

Not one composer of the bacchant's mien
Into—what you thought Mildred's, in a word!
Know her!

   Guendolen. Oh, Mildred, look to me, at least!
Thorold—she's dead, I'd say, but that she stands   270
Rigid as stone and whiter!

   Tresham.   You have heard . . .

   Guendolen. Too much! You must proceed no further.

   Mildred.   Yes—
Proceed! All's truth. Go from me!

   Tresham.   All is truth,
She tells you! Well, you know, or ought to know,
All this I would forgive in her. I'd con   275
Each precept the harsh world enjoins, I'd take
Our ancestors' stern verdicts one by one,
I'd bind myself before them to exact
The prescribed vengeance—and one word of hers,
The sight of her, the bare least memory   280
Of Mildred, my one sister, my heart's pride
Above all prides, my all in all so long,
Would scatter every trace of my resolve.
What were it silently to waste away
And see her waste away from this day forth,   285
Two scathed things with leisure to repent,
And grow acquainted with the grave, and die
Tired out if not at peace, and be forgotten?
It were not so impossible to bear.
But this—that, fresh from last night's pledge renewed   290
Of love with the successful gallant there,
She calmly bids me help her to entice,

---

268 *MS* what we thought Mildred, in   271 *MS* whiter—   272 *MS* much—
. . . . further— *1843-63* further!   273 *MS,1843,1849* Proceed—   *1843-63* All's
truth! Go   *MS* me.   274 *MS* tells you—   275 *MS* her:
283 *MS,1843,1849* Had scattered every   *1843-63* resolve!   284-9 *MS* (deleted)
289 *1843* This were   *1843-63* bear!   292 *MS,1843,1849* She'll calmly bid me

   267 *the bacchant's mien*: the air of a drunken reveller.

   286 *scathed*: blasted, destroyed. Cf. Carlyle, *Sartor Resartus*, II. viii, para. 1: 'the fire-
baptised soul . . . so scathed and thunder-riven' (Centenary ed., i. 136).

Inveigle an unconscious trusting youth
Who thinks her all that's chaste and good and pure,
—Invites me to betray him . . . who so fit   295
As honour's self to cover shame's arch deed?
—That she'll receive Lord Mertoun—(her own phrase)—
This, who could bear? Why, you have heard of thieves,
Stabbers, the earth's disgrace, who yet have laughed,
"Talk not to me of torture—I'll betray   300
"No comrade I've pledged faith to!"—you have heard
Of wretched women—all but Mildreds—tied
By wild illicit ties to losels vile
You'd tempt them to forsake; and they'll reply
"Gold, friends, repute, I left for him, I find   305
"In him, why should I leave him then for gold,
"Repute or friends?"—and you have felt your heart
Respond to such poor outcasts of the world
As to so many friends; bad as you please,
You've felt they were God's men and women still,   310
So, not to be disowned by you. But she
That stands there, calmly gives her lover up
As means to wed the Earl that she may hide
Their intercourse the surelier: and, for this,
I curse her to her face before you all.   315
Shame hunt her from the earth! Then Heaven do right
To both! It hears me now—shall judge her then!
          [*As* MILDRED *faints and falls,* TRESHAM *rushes out.*
    Austin. Stay, Tresham, we'll accompany you!

293 MS an inconscious trusting   295 MS,1843,1849 —Invite me   295-6 MS
⟨(who . . . . arch-deed?)⟩ {added beside deletion in Macready's hand: ⟨'In!'⟩   297 MS
"she'll . . . . Mertoun"—that's her phrase, 1843 Mertoun—(that's her phrase)—
299 MS have said   300 MS,1843 not of tortures to me—I'll   301 MS "No
fellow I've MS,1843 to"—   303 MS,1843 In wild   MS to some vile wretch
304 1843 forsake,   305 MS,1843-63 I have   308 MS,1843 to these poor
311 MS you; 1843-63 you!   314 MS the safelier—and for that 1843 the safelier! and,
for that 1849, 1863 surelier!   315 MS [Macready's hand] I ⟨curse⟩ [cast] her ⟨to her
face⟩ [out from me] before MS,1843-63 all!   316 MS Earth—   317 MS
both—   s.d. (Mildred   318 MS Wait Tresham, ... you—

    303 *losels*: Johnson defines a losel as 'A scoundrel; a sorry worthless fellow', adding that
the word is obsolete. Cf. *Sordello*, iii. 789 and 795.

   Guendolen.   We?
What, and leave Mildred? We? Why, where's my place
But by her side, and where yours but by mine?   320
Mildred—one word? Only look at me, then!
    Austin. No, Guendolen! I echo Thorold's voice.
She is unworthy to behold . . .
    Guendolen.   Us two?
If you spoke on reflection, and if I
Approved your speech—if you (to put the thing   325
At lowest) you the soldier, bound to make
The king's cause yours and fight for it, and throw
Regard to others of its right or wrong,
—If with a death-white woman you can help,
Let alone sister, let alone a Mildred,   330
You left her—or if I, her cousin, friend
This morning, playfellow but yesterday,
Who said, or thought at least a thousand times,
"I'd serve you if I could," should now face round
And say, "Ah, that's to only signify   335
"I'd serve you while you're fit to serve yourself:
"So long as fifty eyes await the turn
"Of yours to forestall its yet half-formed wish,
"I'll proffer my assistance you'll not need—
"When every tongue is praising you, I'll join   340
"The praisers' chorus—when you're hemmed about
"With lives between you and detraction—lives
"To be laid down if a rude voice, rash eye,
"Rough hand should violate the sacred ring
"Their worship throws about you,—then indeed,   345
"Who'll stand up for you stout as I?" If so
We said, and so we did,—not Mildred there
Would be unworthy to behold us both,

320 *MS,1843-65* where's yours   321 *MS,1843,1849* word—   322 *MS* Guen-
dolen— .... voice *1843-63* voice!   325-6 *MS* ..to.... lowest..   327 *MS*
⟨Another's⟩ [The King's] cause yours—to fight   333 *MS,1843,1849* Who've said
MS ⟨at least or thought⟩ [or thought at least] a   337-46 *MS* ("So long .... as I?")
338 *1863,1865* to forestal its

But we should be unworthy, both of us,
To be beheld by—by—your meanest dog,   350
Which, if that sword were broken in your face
Before a crowd, that badge torn off your breast,
And you cast out with hooting and contempt,
—Would push his way thro' all the hooters, gain
Your side, go off with you and all your shame   355
To the next ditch you choose to die in! Austin,
Do you love me? Here's Austin, Mildred,—here's
Your brother says he does not believe half—
No, nor half that—of all he heard! He says,
Look up and take his hand!

    Austin.   Look up and take   360
My hand, dear Mildred!

    Mildred.   I—I was so young!
Beside, I loved him, Thorold—and I had
No mother; God forgot me: so, I fell.

    Guendolen. Mildred!

    Mildred.   Require no further! Did I dream
That I could palliate what is done? All's true.   365
Now, punish me! A woman takes my hand?
Let go my hand! You do not know, I see.
I thought that Thorold told you.

    Guendolen.   What is this?
Where start you to?

    Mildred.   Oh, Austin, loosen me!
You heard the whole of it—your eyes were worse,   370
In their surprise, than Thorold's! Oh, unless
You stay to execute his sentence, loose
My hand! Has Thorold gone, and are you here?

---

351 *MS,1843* your sight   353 *MS,1843-63* with hootings and   356 *MS,
1843,1849* you chose to   *MS* in—   358 *MS,1843* he don't believe one half
359 *MS* he's heard— *1843*¹ he's heard!   361 *MS* Mildred—   361-6 *MS* ⟨I
.... my hand!⟩   363 *1843-63* fell!   366 *1843-63* hand!   367 *MS*
hand—   369 *MS* me—   371 *MS* Thorold's—   373 *MS,1843* Thorold
left and

  364 *Require* : demand.

Guendolen. Here, Mildred, we two friends of yours will
    wait
Your bidding; be you silent, sleep or muse!   375
Only, when you shall want your bidding done,
How can we do it if we are not by?
Here's Austin waiting patiently your will!
One spirit to command, and one to love
And to believe in it and do its best,   380
Poor as that is, to help it—why the world
Has been won many a time, its length and breadth,
By just such a beginning!
    Mildred.   I believe
If once I threw my arms about your neck
And sunk my head upon your breast, that I   385
Should weep again.
    Guendolen.   Let go her hand now, Austin!
Wait for me. Pace the gallery and think
On the world's seemings and realities,
Until I call you.   [AUSTIN *goes.*
    Mildred.   No—I cannot weep.
No more tears from this brain—no sleep—no tears!   390
O Guendolen, I love you!
    Guendolen.   Yes: and "love"
Is a short word that says so very much!
It says that you confide in me.
    Mildred.   Confide!
    Guendolen. Your lover's name, then! I've so much to learn,
Ere I can work in your behalf!
    Mildred.   My friend,   395
You know I cannot tell his name.
    Guendolen.   At least
He is your lover? and you love him too?

---

375 *MS* Your pleasure; be . . . . muse;   378 *MS* will: 383 *MS* beginning.
386 *1843,1849*   again!   *MS,1843–65* Austin.   388 *MS* Of the
389 *MS,1843* †[*Exit Austin.*   *1843–63* weep!   390 *MS* tears.   391 *MS* and
love   392 *MS* much: 394 *MS* then—   395 *MS* behalf—
397 *MS,1843–65 is*

Mildred. Ah, do you ask me that?—but I am fallen
So low!
    Guendolen. You love him still, then?
    Mildred.   My sole prop
Against the guilt that crushes me! I say,   400
Each night ere I lie down, "I was so young—
"I had no mother, and I loved him so!"
And then God seems indulgent, and I dare
Trust him my soul in sleep.
    Guendolen.   How could you let us
E'en talk to you about Lord Mertoun then?   405
    Mildred. There is a cloud around me.
    Guendolen.   But you said
You would receive his suit in spite of this?
    Mildred. I say there is a cloud . . .
    Guendolen.   No cloud to me!
Lord Mertoun and your lover are the same!
    Mildred. What maddest fancy . . .
    Guendolen [*calling aloud*].   Austin! (spare your pains—   410
When I have got a truth, that truth I keep)—
    Mildred. By all you love, sweet Guendolen, forbear!
Have I confided in you . . .
    Guendolen.   Just for this!
Austin!—Oh, not to guess it at the first!
But I did guess it—that is, I divined,   415
Felt by an instinct how it was: why else
Should I pronounce you free from all that heap
Of sins which had been irredeemable?
I felt they were not yours—what other way
Than this, not yours? The secret's wholly mine!   420
    Mildred. If you would see me die before his face . . .
    Guendolen. I'd hold my peace! And if the Earl returns

400–4 MS ⟨I say . . . . in sleep.⟩   401–2 1843 {no quotation marks}   404–
5 MS you let | Us talk   407 MS this—   410 MS {no s.d.} Spare
411 MS truth I grasp.   412 MS forbear—   413 MS you? . . . . this.
415 MS,1843–65 did   416 MS was—how else   418 MS irredeemable
419 {no equivalent in MS}   420 MS Were ⟨they⟩ [this] not ⟨yours⟩ [so]. The . . . .
mine   422 MS peace! ⟨And⟩[What] if

To-night?
 Mildred. Ah Heaven, he's lost!
 Guendolen.   I thought so. Austin!

       Enter AUSTIN.

Oh, where have you been hiding?
 Austin.   Thorold's gone,
I know not how, across the meadow-land.   425
I watched him till I lost him in the skirts
O' the beech-wood.
 Guendolen.   Gone? All thwarts us.
 Mildred.   Thorold too?
 Guendolen. I have thought. First lead this Mildred to her
   room.
Go on the other side; and then we'll seek
Your brother: and I'll tell you, by the way,   430
The greatest comfort in the world. You said
There was a clue to all. Remember, Sweet,
He said there was a clue! I hold it. Come!

423 *MS* Heaven! *1843–63* so!   426 *MS* the skirt   427 *MS,1843–68* Of the
MS beech-wood. All   *MS,1843–63* us!   *MS* too!   430 *MS* brother
433 *1865* Come   s.d. *MS,1843* †[*Exeunt.*

ACT III.

SCENE I.—*The end of the Yew-tree Avenue under* MILDRED's *window. A light seen through a central red pane.*

Enter TRESHAM *through the trees.*

Again here! But I cannot lose myself.
The heath—the orchard—I have traversed glades
And dells and bosky paths which used to lead
Into green wild-wood depths, bewildering
My boy's adventurous step. And now they tend   5
Hither or soon or late; the blackest shade
Breaks up, the thronged trunks of the trees ope wide,
And the dim turret I have fled from, fronts
Again my step; the very river put
Its arm about me and conducted me   10
To this detested spot. Why then, I'll shun
Their will no longer: do your will with me!
Oh, bitter! To have reared a towering scheme
Of happiness, and to behold it razed,
Were nothing: all men hope, and see their hopes   15
Frustrate, and grieve awhile, and hope anew.
But I . . . to hope that from a line like ours
No horrid prodigy like this would spring,
Were just as though I hoped that from these old
Confederates against the sovereign day,   20
Children of older and yet older sires,
Whose living coral berries dropped, as now
On me, on many a baron's surcoat once,

---

1 *MS* myself:—   3 *MS* And bosky wild wood paths   4 *MS* Into wild depths
of green, bewildering   5 *MS* step, *1843,1849* step;   6–11 *MS* ⟨the blackest
. . . . spot.⟩   16 *1843,1849* anew: 20 (no equivalent in *MS*)   21 *MS*
yet older trees—   22–4 *MS* ⟨⟨Whose living . . . . wimple⟩⟩   22 *1843,1849*
⟨Whose

3 *bosky* : wooded.
23 *surcoat* : 'A short coat worn over the rest of the dress': Johnson.

On many a beauty's whimple—would proceed
No poison-tree, to thrust, from hell its root,   25
Hither and thither its strange snaky arms.
Why came I here? What must I do? [*A bell strikes.*] A bell?
Midnight! and 't is at midnight . . . Ah, I catch
—Woods, river, plains, I catch your meaning now,
And I obey you! Hist! This tree will serve.   30

   [*He retires behind one of the trees. After a pause, enter* MERTOUN *cloaked
     as before.*

   Mertoun. Not time! Beat out thy last voluptuous beat
Of hope and fear, my heart! I thought the clock
I' the chapel struck as I was pushing through
The ferns. And so I shall no more see rise
My love-star! Oh, no matter for the past!   35
So much the more delicious task to watch
Mildred revive: to pluck out, thorn by thorn,
All traces of the rough forbidden path
My rash love lured her to! Each day must see
Some fear of hers effaced, some hope renewed: 40
Then there will be surprises, unforeseen
Delights in store. I'll not regret the past.

             [*The light is placed above in the purple pane.*
And see, my signal rises, Mildred's star!
I never saw it lovelier than now
It rises for the last time. If it sets,   45
'T is that the re-assuring sun may dawn.

   [*As he prepares to ascend the last tree of the avenue,* TRESHAM *arrests his
     arm.*

Unhand me—peasant, by your grasp! Here's gold.
'T was a mad freak of mine. I said I'd pluck

24 *1843,1849* wimple)   *1863-8* wimple—   26 MS {deleted}   27 MS
[Here!—and] Why came . . . . do? {illegible deletion; no s.d.} *1843* do!—   29 MS river,
dells, I   30 MS you. . .   *1843-63* serve!   s.d. *1843*[1] *Enter* MERTON *cloaked*
31 MS time?   31-2 MS ⟨Beat out . . . . heart!⟩   33 MS,*1843-68* In the
35 MS star.   36 MS delicious toil to see *1843-68* to see   37 MS to pick out
39 MS to—Each day will see   40 *1843-63* renewed!   42 MS,*1843-63* Past!
s.d. MS {deleted}   43 *1843,1849* rises!   45 *1843,1849* time!   46 MS
may rise. *1843* may rise! *1849* dawn!   47 MS grasp—

   24 *whimple*: hood or veil.

A branch from the white-blossomed shrub beneath
The casement there. Take this, and hold your peace.   50
    Tresham. Into the moonlight yonder, come with me!
Out of the shadow!
    Mertoun.   I am armed, fool!
    Tresham.   Yes,
Or no? You'll come into the light, or no?
My hand is on your throat—refuse!—
    Mertoun.   That voice!
Where have I heard . . . no—that was mild and slow.   55
I'll come with you.   [*They advance.*
    Tresham.   You're armed: that's well. Declare
Your name: who are you?
    Mertoun.   (Tresham!—she is lost!)
    Tresham. Oh, silent? Do you know, you bear yourself
Exactly as, in curious dreams I've had
How felons, this wild earth is full of, look   60
When they're detected, still your kind has looked!
The bravo holds an assured countenance,
The thief is voluble and plausible,
But silently the slave of lust has crouched
When I have fancied it before a man.   65
Your name!
    Mertoun. I do conjure Lord Tresham—ay,
Kissing his foot, if so I might prevail—
That he for his own sake forbear to ask
My name! As heaven's above, his future weal
Or woe depends upon my silence! Vain!   70
I read your white inexorable face.

---

49 *MS* from that white-blossomed   50 *1843-63* there!   51 *MS* yonder!. . . .
me—   52 *MS* fool—   54 *MS* refuse—   55 *1843* *that*
56 *1843-63* you!   s.d. *MS* (*They come to the front of the stage.*)   *1843* †[*They advance to*
the front of the stage. MS well—and now   *1843-68* well. | 57 *MS* Tresham . . . . . .
lost!— *1843* Tresham!. . . . lost!   58 *MS* {Macready's hand} ⟨d⟩[S]o ⟨you know you
bear |⟩ [should felons be]   59–65 *MS* ⟨| Yourself exactly . . . . a man.⟩
*64 {reading of *1843-68*} *1888,1889* crouched.   65 *1843-63* man!   66 *1843-*
68 name?   69 *MS* name. As Heaven is there, his   70 *MS* silence.
70–1 *MS* ⟨Vain!. . . . face.⟩   71 *1843-63* face!

    62 *bravo* : 'A man who murders for hire': Johnson.

Know me, Lord Tresham!   [*He throws off his disguises.*

 Tresham.   Mertoun!

       [*After a pause.*] Draw now!

 Mertoun.   Hear me

But speak first!

 Tresham.   Not one least word on your life!

Be sure that I will strangle in your throat

The least word that informs me how you live   75

And yet seem what you seem! No doubt 't was you

Taught Mildred still to keep that face and sin.

We should join hands in frantic sympathy

If you once taught me the unteachable,

Explained how you can live so, and so lie.   80

With God's help I retain, despite my sense,

The old belief—a life like yours is still

Impossible. Now draw!

 Mertoun.   Not for my sake,

Do I entreat a hearing—for your sake,

And most, for her sake!

 Tresham.   Ha ha, what should I   85

Know of your ways? A miscreant like yourself,

How must one rouse his ire? A blow?—that's pride

No doubt, to him! One spurns him, does one not?

Or sets the foot upon his mouth, or spits

Into his face! Come! Which, or all of these?   90

 Mertoun. 'Twixt him and me and Mildred, Heaven be

   judge!

Can I avoid this? Have your will, my lord!

        [*He draws and, after a few passes, falls.*

72 *MS* {Macready's hand} ⟨Know me⟩ [Draw], Lord Tresham. {s.d.} ⟨Mertoun!⟩ {s.d.} Draw ⟨now⟩ [then]! Hear | 73 *MS* Me speak first—   74–6 *MS* ⟨Be sure .... No doubt⟩   76 *1843* yet are what you are! No   77 *MS* Mildred how to wear that *1843–63* sin!   78–83 *MS* ⟨I should join hands .... Impossible.⟩   80 *1843–63* lie!   81 *1843* I will keep despite   83 *1843–63* Impossible! *MS* draw. 84–5 *MS* ⟨for your sake .... her sake ..⟩ Ah, ⟨what should I⟩   86 *MS* ⟨Know of your ways?⟩ A {Macready's hand} ⟨felon⟩ [miscreant] like yourself—   87 *1843*[1] How most one   *MS,1843* that's great   88 *MS* to him—   89 *MS* One sets 90 *MS,1843* face—*MS,1843–63* come—   92 s.d. *MS draws* — [and] *after*

Tresham. You are not hurt?

Mertoun.   You'll hear me now!

Tresham.   But rise!

Mertoun. Ah, Tresham, say I not "you'll hear me now!"
And what procures a man the right to speak   95
In his defence before his fellow man,
But—I suppose—the thought that presently
He may have leave to speak before his God
His whole defence?

Tresham.   Not hurt? It cannot be!
You made no effort to resist me. Where   100
Did my sword reach you? Why not have returned
My thrusts? Hurt where?

Mertoun.   My lord—

Tresham.   How young he is!

Mertoun. Lord Tresham, I am very young, and yet
I have entangled other lives with mine.
Do let me speak, and do believe my speech!   105
That when I die before you presently,—

Tresham. Can you stay here till I return with help?

Mertoun. Oh, stay by me! When I was less than boy
I did you grievous wrong and knew it not—
Upon my honour, knew it not! Once known,   110
I could not find what seemed a better way
To right you than I took: my life—you feel
How less than nothing were the giving you
The life you've taken! But I thought my way
The better—only for your sake and hers: 115
And as you have decided otherwise,
Would I had an infinity of lives

93 *MS* ⟨You are not hurt?⟩ You'll   *1865* now,   *MS* {Macready's hand} now—[Lord
Tresham] Tres. [Mertoun!] ⟨But⟩ [Oh] rise—   94 *MS* Tresham, said I .... me
speak?"   95–9 *MS* ⟨And what .... defence?⟩   99 *MS* hurt—   102–
6 *MS* ⟨My Lord ...... presently ...⟩   105 *1863,1865* speak!   *1843–65* speech,
108 *MS* {Macready's hand} When ⟨I was less⟩ [scarce more] than boy   110 *MS*
⟨Upon .... not⟩   113 *MS,1843–65* nothing had been giving you   114 *MS*
taken,—   115 *1843–65* hers.   116 *MS,1843* But as

To offer you! Now say—instruct me—think!
Can you, from the brief minutes I have left,
Eke out my reparation? Oh think—think!   120
For I must wring a partial—dare I say,
Forgiveness from you, ere I die?
    Tresham.   I do
Forgive you.
    Mertoun. Wait and ponder that great word!
Because, if you forgive me, I shall hope
To speak to you of—Mildred!
    Tresham.   Mertoun, haste   125
And anger have undone us. 'T is not you
Should tell me for a novelty you're young,
Thoughtless, unable to recall the past.
Be but your pardon ample as my own!
    Mertoun. Ah, Tresham, that a sword-stroke and a drop   130
Of blood or two, should bring all this about!
Why, 't was my very fear of you, my love
Of you—(what passion like a boy's for one
Like you?)—that ruined me! I dreamed of you—
You, all accomplished, courted everywhere,   135
The scholar and the gentleman. I burned
To knit myself to you: but I was young,
And your surpassing reputation kept me
So far aloof! Oh, wherefore all that love?
With less of love, my glorious yesterday   140
Of praise and gentlest words and kindest looks,
Had taken place perchance six months ago.
Even now, how happy we had been! And yet
I know the thought of this escaped you, Tresham!

---

118 *MS* you— .... think— *1865,1868* think   119 *MS,1843-65* from out the
minutes   120 *MS* {Macready's hand} ⟨Make⟩ [Eke] out my reparation— ⟨oh speak—
speak⟩ [do think think]   122 *MS* die.   123-8 *MS* ⟨Oh, wait—ponder ....
past.⟩   128 *1843-63* Past!   130-47 *MS* ⟨Ah Tresham .... Where—where—⟩
133 *1843-63* passion's like   139 *1843,1849* aloof—   141 *1843-63* and gentle
words   142 *1843-65* ago!

   1 30 *sword-stroke* : the only earlier example in OED is from Scott, *Anne of Geierstein*, ch.
vi, para. 20.

Let me look up into your face; I feel   145
'T is changed above me: yet my eyes are glazed.
Where? where?
                    [*As he endeavours to raise himself, his eye catches the lamp.*
                    Ah, Mildred! What will Mildred do?
Tresham, her life is bound up in the life
That's bleeding fast away! I'll live—must live,
There, if you'll only turn me I shall live   150
And save her! Tresham—oh, had you but heard!
Had you but heard! What right was yours to set
The thoughtless foot upon her life and mine,
And then say, as we perish, "Had I thought,
"All had gone otherwise"? We've sinned and die: 155
Never you sin, Lord Tresham! for you'll die,
And God will judge you.
     Tresham.   Yes, be satisfied!
That process is begun.
     Mertoun.   And she sits there
Waiting for me! Now, say you this to her—
You, not another—say, I saw him die   160
As he breathed this, "I love her"—you don't know
What those three small words mean! Say, loving her
Lowers me down the bloody slope to death
With memories . . . I speak to her, not you,
Who had no pity, will have no remorse,   165
Perchance intend her . . . Die along with me,
Dear Mildred! 't is so easy, and you'll 'scape
So much unkindness! Can I lie at rest,
With rude speech spoken to you, ruder deeds
Done to you?—heartless men shall have my heart,   170
And I tied down with grave-clothes and the worm,

149-55 *MS* ⟨I'll live . . . . otherwise"⟩   150 *1843-63* There!   152 *1843-65*
right have you to   155 *1843-68* otherwise."   156 *MS,1843* you   *MS*
Tresham,   157 *MS* {Macready's hand} And ⟨God⟩ [Heaven] will . . . . Yes: be satis-
fied: *1843-63* satisfied—   159 *MS* me— *1843,1849* me.   161 *MS* {Mac-
ready's hand} he ⟨said⟩ [breathed] this *1843,1849* (you   162 *MS* mean— *1843,1849*
mean)   162-74 *MS* ⟨Say how that love . . . . stripe!⟩   170 *1843,1849* you—
1843-65 men to have

Aware, perhaps, of every blow—oh God!—
Upon those lips—yet of no power to tear
The felon stripe by stripe! Die, Mildred! Leave
Their honourable world to them! For God   175
We're good enough, though the world casts us out.
                                        [*A whistle is heard.*
   Tresham. Ho, Gerard!

     Enter GERARD, AUSTIN *and* GUENDOLEN, *with lights.*
                              No one speak! You see what's done.
I cannot bear another voice.
   Mertoun.   There's light—
Light all about me, and I move to it.
Tresham, did I not tell you—did you not   180
Just promise to deliver words of mine
To Mildred?
   Tresham.   I will bear those words to her.
   Mertoun. Now?
   Tresham.   Now. Lift you the body, and leave me
The head.
     [*As they have half raised* MERTOUN, *he turns suddenly.*
   Mertoun. I knew they turned me: turn me not from her!
There! stay you! there!   [*Dies.*
   Guendolen [*after a pause*]. Austin, remain you here   185
With Thorold until Gerard comes with help:
Then lead him to his chamber. I must go
To Mildred.
   Tresham.   Guendolen, I hear each word
You utter. Did you hear him bid me give

---

174 *1843–65* stripe?   *MS* Oh Mildred, leave   175 *MS* them—we're good *1843–
63* them—   176 *MS* Enough for God, {added in Macready's hand above: 'Him'} tho'
. . . . out— *1843–63* out!   s.d. *MS* {deleted}   177 s.d. *MS* (*Enter Gerard, Guendolen
and Austin with 1843–63* done!   178 *1843–63* voice!   180 *MS* did not I tell
183–4 *MS* ⟨Lift you . . . . head.⟩   183 *1843,1849* Now! Lift *1843–63* body, Gerard,
and   184 *MS* ⟨I knew they turned me—⟩ . . . . her—   185 *MS* There—⟨stay
you⟩—there— (*he dies*) (*After a pause—Guendolen says to Austin*) Remain   186 *MS*
help

---

174 *stripe* : strip.

His message? Did you hear my promise? I,   190
And only I, see Mildred.
     Guendolen.   She will die.
     Tresham. Oh no, she will not die! I dare not hope
She'll die. What ground have you to think she'll die?
Why, Austin's with you!
     Austin.   Had we but arrived
Before you fought!
     Tresham.   There was no fight at all.   195
He let me slaughter him—the boy! I'll trust
The body there to you and Gerard—thus!
Now bear him on before me.
     Austin.   Whither bear him?
     Tresham. Oh, to my chamber! When we meet there next,
We shall be friends.   [*They bear out the body of* MERTOUN.
           Will she die, Guendolen?   200
     Guendolen. Where are you taking me?
     Tresham.   He fell just here.
Now answer me. Shall you in your whole life
—You who have nought to do with Mertoun's fate,
Now you have seen his breast upon the turf,
Shall you e'er walk this way if you can help?   205
When you and Austin wander arm-in-arm
Through our ancestral grounds, will not a shade
Be ever on the meadow and the waste—
Another kind of shade than when the night
Shuts the woodside with all its whispers up?   210
But will you ever so forget his breast
As carelessly to cross this bloody turf
Under the black yew avenue? That's well!

191 *1843–63* Mildred!   192 *MS* die—   193–4 *MS* ⟨What ground . . . . you!⟩
195 *1843–63* all!   196–7 *MS* ⟨These boys! . . . . thus—⟩   196 *1843* him—
these boys!—I'll   199 *MS* chamber— *1843,1849* chamber.   200 *MS* s.d. *the*
body—) ⟨Will she die⟩   201 *1843–63* here!   207–8 *MS* ⟨will not . . . . the
waste—⟩   209–10 [no equivalent in *MS*]   210 *1843,1849* up!
211 *MS* [Macready's hand] ⟨But⟩ [Say] will you *MS,1843* forget this night   212 *MS*
As knowingly to *1843–63* As willingly to   213 *MS* ⟨Under . . . . avenue?⟩ That's
well—

You turn your head: and I then?—
   Guendolen.   What is done
Is done. My care is for the living. Thorold,   215
Bear up against this burden: more remains
To set the neck to!
   Tresham.   Dear and ancient trees
My fathers planted, and I loved so well!
What have I done that, like some fabled crime
Of yore, lets loose a Fury leading thus   220
Her miserable dance amidst you all?
Oh, never more for me shall winds intone
With all your tops a vast antiphony,
Demanding and responding in God's praise!
Hers ye are now, not mine! Farewell—farewell!   225

SCENE II.—MILDRED's *chamber.* MILDRED *alone.*

He comes not! I have heard of those who seemed
Resourceless in prosperity,—you thought
Sorrow might slay them when she listed; yet
Did they so gather up their diffused strength
At her first menace, that they bade her strike,   5
And stood and laughed her subtlest skill to scorn.
Oh, 't is not so with me! The first woe fell,
And the rest fall upon it, not on me:
Else should I bear that Henry comes not?—fails
Just this first night out of so many nights?   10
Loving is done with. Were he sitting now,
As so few hours since, on that seat, we'd love

214 *1843–63* head!   *1843–65* I   MS then!   215 *1843–63* done!
216 *MS,1843,1849* this burthen—more   217 *MS,1865* to.   220 *MS,1843*
fury—free to lead   222–4 *MS* (deleted)   225 *MS* mine—Farewell—Farewell.
s.d. *MS,1843* †[*Exeunt.*
   Scene ii.   5 *MS* they stood and bade | 6 *MS* Her strike and   7 *MS*
me—   9 *MS* not—   10 *MS* nights.   11–14 *MS* (deleted)
11 *1843–63* with!

   220 *a Fury*: 'One of the deities of vengeance': Johnson.
   223 *antiphony*: 'Alternate singing or chanting by a choir divided into two parts': OED.

No more—contrive no thousand happy ways
To hide love from the loveless, any more.
I think I might have urged some little point   15
In my defence, to Thorold; he was breathless
For the least hint of a defence: but no,
The first shame over, all that would might fall.
No Henry! Yet I merely sit and think
The morn's deed o'er and o'er. I must have crept   20
Out of myself. A Mildred that has lost
Her lover—oh, I dare not look upon
Such woe! I crouch away from it! 'T is she,
Mildred, will break her heart, not I! The world
Forsakes me: only Henry's left me—left?   25
When I have lost him, for he does not come,
And I sit stupidly . . . Oh Heaven, break up
This worse than anguish, this mad apathy,
By any means or any messenger!
    Tresham [*without*]. Mildred!
    Mildred.   Come in! Heaven hears me!
                    [*Enter* TRESHAM.] You? alone?   30
Oh, no more cursing!
    Tresham.   Mildred, I must sit.
There—you sit!
    Mildred.   Say it, Thorold—do not look
The curse! deliver all you come to say!
What must become of me? Oh, speak that thought
Which makes your brow and cheeks so pale!
    Tresham.   My thought?   35
    Mildred. All of it!
    Tresham.   How we waded—years ago—
After those water-lilies, till the plash,
I know not how, surprised us; and you dared

14 *1843–63* more!   17 *1843–63* no!   20–4 *MS* ⟨I must . . . . not I!⟩
30 *MS* in— . . . . me.   s.d. *MS,1843,1849* †[*Tresham enters*]†   *MS* You! alone!
31 *MS* ⟨Oh no more cursing!⟩   33 *MS,1843–63* curse—   *MS* say—
35 *MS,1843–68* and cheek so   36 *MS* {Macready's hand} we ⟨waded⟩ [sported] years
37 *MS* {Macready's hand} ⟨After⟩ [among] the water lilies *1843* After the water-lilies
38 *1843* us

Neither advance nor turn back: so, we stood
Laughing and crying until Gerard came—   40
Once safe upon the turf, the loudest too,
For once more reaching the relinquished prize!
How idle thoughts are, some men's, dying men's!
Mildred,—
    Mildred. You call me kindlier by my name
Than even yesterday: what is in that?   45
    Tresham. It weighs so much upon my mind that I
This morning took an office not my own!
I might . . . of course, I must be glad or grieved,
Content or not, at every little thing
That touches you. I may with a wrung heart   50
Even reprove you, Mildred; I did more:
Will you forgive me?
    Mildred.   Thorold? do you mock?
Or no . . . and yet you bid me . . . say that word!
    Tresham. Forgive me, Mildred!—are you silent, Sweet?
    Mildred [*starting up*]. Why does not Henry Mertoun come
        to-night?   55
Are you, too, silent?
    [*Dashing his mantle aside, and pointing to his scabbard, which is empty.*
                Ah, this speaks for you!
You've murdered Henry Mertoun! Now proceed!
What is it I must pardon? This and all?
Well, I do pardon you—I think I do.
Thorold, how very wretched you must be!   60
    Tresham. He bade me tell you . . .
    Mildred.   What I do forbid
Your utterance of! So much that you may tell
And will not—how you murdered him . . . but, no!
You'll tell me that he loved me, never more

---

39 *1843,1849* back,   40 *MS* crying, you, till Gerard   41-2 *MS* (deleted)
43 *MS* men's.   46 *MS* It is so   47 *MS* own.—   52 *MS,1843* You
must forgive *MS* me. *1843* me! *MS* mock   53 *MS* . . No—no   *56 (reading
of *MS,1843-68,*DC,BrU,*1889*) *1888* for you *1843-65* Are you,   57 *MS* Mertoun—
59 *MS* you (with all my heart) [I think I do.]   62 *MS* of: *1843 may*

Than bleeding out his life there: must I say   65
"Indeed," to that? Enough! I pardon you.
   Tresham. You cannot, Mildred! for the harsh words, yes:
Of this last deed Another's judge: whose doom
I wait in doubt, despondency and fear.
   Mildred. Oh, true! There's nought for me to pardon! True!   70
You loose my soul of all its cares at once.
Death makes me sure of him for ever! You
Tell me his last words? He shall tell me them,
And take my answer—not in words, but reading
Himself the heart I had to read him late,   75
Which death . . .
   Tresham.   Death? You are dying too? Well said
Of Guendolen! I dared not hope you'd die:
But she was sure of it.
   Mildred.   Tell Guendolen
I loved her, and tell Austin . ...
   Tresham.   Him you loved:
And me?
   Mildred. Ah, Thorold! Was't not rashly done   80
To quench that blood, on fire with youth and hope
And love of me—whom you loved too, and yet
Suffered to sit here waiting his approach
While you were slaying him? Oh, doubtlessly
You let him speak his poor confused boy's-speech   85
—Do his poor utmost to disarm your wrath
And respite me!—you let him try to give
The story of our love and ignorance,
And the brief madness and the long despair—
You let him plead all this, because your code   90

---

66 *MS* Enough—   *MS,1843-65* you!   67 *MS* Mildred—   70 *MS* true—it
is not mine to pardon—you   71 *MS* Have loosed my *1843-63* You loosed my
72 *MS* forever—*you 1843-63* You   73 *MS,1843-63 He*   75 *MS* him once—
77 *MS* die.   79 *MS* I love[d] her .... you love[d]—   80 *MS* Oh Thorold
82 *MS* of me—of me you loved, I think, *1843* me, *you* loved I think, and yet
83 *MS* Yet suffered to sit waiting   84 *MS* him—   85 *MS* confused love-
speech,   87 *MS* me—   88 *MS,1843-63* our loves, and   89 *MS* [Mac-
ready's hand] long (repentance) [despair]

Of honour bids you hear before you strike:
But at the end, as he looked up for life
Into your eyes—you struck him down!
    Tresham.   No! No!
Had I but heard him—had I let him speak
Half the truth—less—had I looked long on him   95
I had desisted! Why, as he lay there,
The moon on his flushed cheek, I gathered all
The story ere he told it: I saw through
The troubled surface of his crime and yours
A depth of purity immovable,   100
Had I but glanced, where all seemed turbidest
Had gleamed some inlet to the calm beneath;
I would not glance: my punishment's at hand.
There, Mildred, is the truth! and you—say on—
You curse me?
    Mildred.   As I dare approach that Heaven   105
Which has not bade a living thing despair,
Which needs no code to keep its grace from stain,
But bids the vilest worm that turns on it
Desist and be forgiven,—I—forgive not,
But bless you, Thorold, from my soul of souls!   110
                                   [*Falls on his neck.*

There! Do not think too much upon the past!
The cloud that's broke was all the same a cloud
While it stood up between my friend and you;
You hurt him 'neath its shadow: but is that
So past retrieve? I have his heart, you know;   115
I may dispose of it: I give it you!
It loves you as mine loves! Confirm me, Henry!
                                   [*Dies.*

93 *MS* struck my lover! Tres. No!| 94 *MS* him or had let   96 *MS* desisted—
96-103 *MS* ⟨why as .... at hand.⟩   98 *1843-65* it!   100 *1843-63* immov-
able! *1865* immovable *1868* immovable.   102 *1843-65* beneath!   104 *MS*
truth—   110 *MS* souls—   111 *MS* Past   113 *1843-65* you!
114 *MS* shadow,   115 *MS* {Macready's hand} | [Past] Remed[y]⟨iless⟩?
117 *MS* you even as mine—Confirm   s.d. *MS* ⟨*She Dies.*⟩

Tresham. I wish thee joy, Beloved! I am glad
In thy full gladness!
   Guendolen [*without*]. Mildred! Tresham!
            [*Entering with* AUSTIN.] Thorold,
I could desist no longer. Ah, she swoons!   120
That's well.
   Tresham. Oh, better far than that!
   Guendolen.   She's dead!
Let me unlock her arms!
   Tresham.   She threw them thus
About my neck, and blessed me, and then died:
You'll let them stay now, Guendolen!
   Austin.   Leave her
And look to him! What ails you, Thorold?
   Guendolen.   White   125
As she, and whiter! Austin! quick—this side!
   Austin. A froth is oozing through his clenched teeth;
Both lips, where they're not bitten through, are black:
Speak, dearest Thorold!
   Tresham.   Something does weigh down
My neck beside her weight: thanks: I should fall   130
But for you, Austin, I believe!—there, there,
'T will pass away soon!—ah,—I had forgotten:
I am dying.
   Guendolen. Thorold—Thorold—why was this?
   Tresham. I said, just as I drank the poison off,
The earth would be no longer earth to me,   135
The life out of all life was gone from me.

118 *MS* beloved—   119 *MS* gladness. . . . . Tresham! Thorold— (*enters with Austin.*)
121 *1843,1849*   Oh!   *MS*   that.   . . . .   dead.   122–4 *MS* {deleted}
123 *1843,1849* died.   125 *MS* {Macready's hand} ⟨And⟩ [Austin] look to him—
125–8 *MS* ⟨White . . . . black⟩   126 *1843,1849* Austin—   128 *1843–63*
black!   129–30 *MS* ⟨dearest Thorold— . . . . weight—⟩   130 *MS* thanks—I
believe   131 *MS* That I should fall but for you, Austin— {Macready's hand}
Th⟨ere⟩[anks]   132 *MS* ⟨'Twill pass away soon—⟩Ah— {Macready's hand} ⟨I had
forgotten—⟩ [dear friends!]   133–4 *MS* {deleted}   135 {Macready's hand}
Th⟨e⟩[is] earth w⟨ould⟩[ill] be   136 *MS* {Macready's hand} life ⟨was⟩ [is] gone
1843–65 me!

There are blind ways provided, the foredone
Heart-weary player in this pageant-world
Drops out by, letting the main masque defile
By the conspicuous portal: I am through—   140
Just through!
    Guendolen. Don't leave him, Austin! Death is close.
    Tresham. Already Mildred's face is peacefuller.
I see you, Austin—feel you: here's my hand,
Put yours in it—you, Guendolen, yours too!
You're lord and lady now—you're Treshams; name   145
And fame are yours: you hold our 'scutcheon up.
Austin, no blot on it! You see how blood
Must wash one blot away: the first blot came
And the first blood came. To the vain world's eye
All's gules again: no care to the vain world,   150
From whence the red was drawn!
    Austin.   No blot shall come!
   Tresham. I said that: yet it did come. Should it come,
Vengeance is God's, not man's. Remember me!   [*Dies.*
    Guendolen [*letting fall the pulseless arm*].
Ah, Thorold, we can but—remember you!

137–41 {the remainder of Thorold's speech is outlined in ink in *MS*, possibly for deletion}
137 *MS* provided—⟨the⟩ [which] foredone   138 *MS* Heart-weary player[s] in
139 *MS* Drop⟨s⟩ out   141 *MS* {deleted}   142 *MS,1843-63* peacefuller!
143 *MS* {Macready's hand} ⟨I see you,⟩ [Dear] Austin . . ⟨feel . . . . hand,⟩   144 *MS*
{Macready's hand} ⟨Put . . . . you⟩ Guendolen, ⟨yours too⟩ {illegible substitution}
145 *1843*[1] Tresham's name   146 *MS* up: 148–51 *MS* ⟨the first . . . . was
drawn!⟩   152 *MS* did come: *1863* did come!   153 *MS* Man's!   s.d. *MS*
{deleted} {added opposite in Macready's hand: 'Within a convents shade in stranger lands |
Penance & prayer shall ⟨waste⟩ [wear] my life away—'}   153 s.d. *MS pulseless hand*⟩
. . . . you! (*Curtain falls.*)

  137 *foredone*: exhausted, as (e.g.) in *A Midsummer Night's Dream*, v. i. 363.
  139 *masque*: masquerade, procession of actors.
  150 *gules*: red, as a colour in heraldry.
  153 *Vengeance is God's*: Rom. 12:19.
  s.d. *pulseless*: as in Shelley, *Hellas*, 142.

INTRODUCTION TO
COLOMBE'S BIRTHDAY

EXCITED by the production of *A Blot in the 'Scutcheon* in February 1843, Browning quickly decided to attempt 'another actable play'.[1] He began *Colombe's Birthday* soon afterwards. On 26 April Elizabeth Barrett told Miss Mitford that she had heard that 'M! Browning has two new tragedies, one of them near the press, viâ Belles [*sic*] & Pomegranates, & one near the stage, viâ M! Charles Kean—& for this last I am sorry'.[2] Three weeks later Browning told Domett that he had 'a desk full of scrawls at which I look, and work a little'. He went on: 'I want to publish a few more numbers of my "Bells"—and must also make up my mind to finish a play I wrote lately for Charles Kean, if he will have it. (Macready has used me vilely.)'[3] The following year, on 15 February, B. W. Procter asked about the progress of 'the coming Drama'.[4] On 10 March Browning told Christopher Dowson what had occurred, in a letter marked *'(Private.)*':

You may remember I told you my appointment with C. Kean *had* been for *that* morning (Monday)—and *then* stood over for the next Saturday (yesterday)—but that, having made an effort and ended work the evening I saw you, I meant to call on Kean the following morning:—I did so; but in consequence of my letter, received the day before, his arrangements were made for the week—so that till Saturday the business had to wait. Yesterday I read my play to him and his charming wife (who is to take the principal part)—and all went off *au mieux—but*—he wants to keep it till 'Easter next year'—and unpublished all the time!—His engagement at the Haymarket next May, is merely for twelve nights, he says:—he leaves London for Scotland to-morrow, or next day—and will be occupied for ten hours a day till he returns—my play will take him two months at least to study, he being a 'special slow-head, and after the Haymarket engagement nothing is to be done till this time next year.—Of all which notable pieces of information I was apprised for the first time *after* the play was read and approved of . . for, it certainly never entered into my mind that anybody, even an actor,

---

[1] Gosse, p. 69. According to Griffin and Minchin, 'Kean was anxious to perform in new parts, and . . . opened negotiations with Browning, to whom he was disposed to offer £500 for a suitable play. Within three months Browning had written, though not actually completed, *Colombe's Birthday*: for reasons unknown, the drama was not finished until March, 1844': p. 119. Browning mentioned £500 in a letter to Elizabeth Barrett in 1845: Kintner, i. 194.

[2] Raymond and Sullivan, ii. 212, 219.

[3] *Browning and Domett*, p. 55 (15 May).   [4] *Checklist*, 44: 67.

could need a couple of months to study a part, only, in a piece, which I could match with such another in less time by a good deal.

But, though I *could* do such a thing, I have a head,—that aches oftener now than of old,—to take care of; and, therefore, *will* do no such thing as let this new work lie stifled for a year and odd,—and work double-tides to bring out something as likely to be popular this present season—for something I *must* print, or risk the hold, such as it is, I have at present on *my* public: and, on consideration of the two other productions I have by me in a state of forwardness, neither seems nearly so proper for the requirements of the moment, as this play—and two or three hundred pounds[1] will pay me but indifferently for hasarding the good fortune which appears slowly but not mistakeably setting in upon me, just now. You will not wonder, therefore, that—tho' I was so far taken by surprise as to promise Kean a copy for Scotland and a fortnight's grace, to come to terms in, before I either published the play or accepted any other party's offer—I say, you will not wonder if I have determined to print it directly (acting on the best advice, I sent it to press yesterday) and merely put the right of *the acting* at his disposal—if he will purchase it with such a drawback as Macready would.: for I fear the only other alternative I shall allow—that of his getting up the part for *next* May, is quite beyond his power. The poorest Man of letters (if *really* of letters) I ever knew is of far higher talent than the best actor I ever expect to know: nor is there one spangle too many, one rouge-smutch too much, on their outside-man—for the *inward* . . can't study a speech in a month![2]

The fact that Browning sent his play 'to press' on the same day on which he had read it to Kean and his wife is a measure of his excitement and disappointment.[3] Within a few days he wrote to Procter to offer him the dedication of *Colombe's Birthday*. On the 21st Procter replied, in suitable terms, thanking Browning for his account of the play, and commenting: 'I am *quite* sure—& have *always* (& to every body) said that—if you would give yourself fair-play you would be sure to do great things—& you will do better than you *now* have done (whatever it may be).'[4] Procter was obviously afraid that Browning was over-excited, but assured him that he would back him 'against any of the Dramatists of the day'. About 26 March he wrote again, to thank Browning for an advance copy, and to tell him that he had read the play 'with very great pleasure'.[5] 'Colombe is a charming creature', he went on. 'The play . . . is *full* of interest & capital situations—The language excellent. You have done well—if I may say so— to lay aside all mystery language & speak direct.' After mild criticisms of two passages,[6] Procter concluded: 'And now let me wish you success in

[1] Cf. n. 1, p. 427 above.   [2] *Letters*, pp. 9–10.
[3] On the MS, see below.   [4] *Checklist*, 44:106.
[5] Ibid., 44:113.   [6] See our nn. to III. 231 and IV. 357.

this & other labours—& let me advise you not to worry yourself too much with them. You have an irritable brain, & one brain fever is more than enough to my thinking. One would not check the Muse when she is gracious—but one or two or three sittings will hurt no one—It is your week's—or month's—incessant labour that damages.'

In a brief unpublished letter written some time in April Browning told R. H. Horne that the 'causes' which might have postponed the publication of the play had 'suddenly ceased to operate', so that he was able to enclose a presentation copy.[1] *Colombe's Birthday* was advertised in the *Athenæum* for 20 April 1844, as 'Just published, price 1s.'[2]

While there is no specific source for the play it is of interest, as Griffin and Minchin point out, that Browning passed the principal places named in it—Ravestein, Cleves, and Juliers (Jülich)—in 1834.[3] If he was not already interested in the Thirty Years War—which seems unlikely, in view of Coleridge's translations from Schiller, *The Piccolomini* and *The Death of Wallenstein*[4]—he no doubt became interested then. Although its plot is unhistorical, *Colombe's Birthday* is set about 1610 and draws on the general historical situation at that time.

The little history that is relevant may be found in Schiller's *History of the Thirty Years' War*, a translation of which Coleridge mentions in the preface to the first edition of *The Piccolomini*.[5] There we read how on the death of Duke John William in 1609 'a doubtful and disputed succession arose in the territories of Juliers and Cleves'.[6] As Schiller points out, 'The dispute about the succession of Juliers was important to the whole German empire, and also attracted the attention of several European States':

The point was not merely, who was or was not to possess the Dutchy of Juliers. The real question was, which of the two religious parties in Germany, the Catholic or the Protestant, was to be strengthened by so important an accession;—for which *religion* this territory was to be lost or won. The question was, whether Austria was to be allowed to persevere in her usurpations, and to gratify her lust of dominion by another violent acquisition; or whether the liberties of Germany, and the equality of its power, were to be maintained against her encroachments. The succession of Juliers, therefore, was an event which

---

[1] *Checklist*, 44:118.　　　　　　　　　　　　　　　　　　　　[2] p. 346c.

[3] Griffin and Minchin, p. 62. As they point out, he travelled the same way in 1838, on a journey probably more relevant to this play.

[4] Cf. our note to II. 10.

[5] *The Complete Poetical Works of Samuel Taylor Coleridge*, ed. E. H. Coleridge (2 vols., 1912), ii. 598–9. The translation was published in 1799, and reprinted in Constable's *Miscellany* in 1828.

[6] *The Historical Works of Frederick Schiller*, translated by George Moir (2 vols., 1828), i. 92.

interested all those who were favourable to freedom, and hostile to Austria. The Evangelical Union, Holland, England, and particularly Henry IV. of France, took part in this discussion.[1]

It was a complicated situation, since 'Eight competitors laid claim to the succession of these countries, the indivisibility of which was guaranteed by solemn treaties; and the Emperor, who seemed inclined to take possession of the various lands as fiefs of the empire, might be considered as the ninth.'[2]

One need go no further to see how slight are the links between Browning's play and the events of history. There is no historical foundation for any of his characters, or for the plot which he devised. It is not enough to say, with Porter and Clarke, that 'Browning's supposition, on which the plot is based, that the Duke had concealed his child to shield her better and secure her reign surreptitiously, is conceivably historical, though not a matter of record.' It is pure fiction.

DeVane's claim, echoed by the Ohio editor, that Browning seems to have adapted 'The situation, in which the heroine chooses the less distinguished suitor, . . . from the *Mémoires* of the Marquis de Lassay', does not stand up to examination. The story to which he refers tells how a Duke of Lorraine fell in love with Mlle Marianne Pajot, a girl of comparatively humble birth. The Duke's sister begged the King and the Queen Mother to prevent the marriage, and this they managed to do, Marianne choosing to enter a convent. This story is told in the second of Browning's *Parleyings with certain People of Importance in their Day*, that with Daniel Bartoli, and is summarized in Mrs Orr's *Handbook*.[3] It seems to have no relevance to *Colombe's Birthday*, and is not mentioned by Mrs Orr in her section on the play.[4]

The Text, and the Production of 1853

The holograph now in the Pforzheimer Library is written in ink on thirty leaves of blue foolscap, folded to make sixty pages. The leaves are numbered in Browning's hand, while someone else has numbered the pages 1–59. The names of the compositors who worked for Bradbury and Evans, the firm which printed the *Bells and Pomegranates* for Moxon, are marked in the upper left-hand corner of the appropriate leaves: Ancott, Smith, Davidson, Hall, and Wood.

---

[1] *The Historical Works of Frederick Schiller*, i. 93.　　[2] Ibid., i. 92.
[3] Pp. 346–7.　　[4] Pp. 65 ff.

When he heard that Buxton Forman had bought this manuscript in 1877, Browning wrote to him about it:

I made it for the use of Charles Kean and his wife, to whom I read it. They would have acted the play—but in perhaps two or three years to come, and in the meantime I was to keep it unprinted—an arrangement which did not suit me—whereupon I withdrew it, and included it in my *Bells and Pomegranates*. It was never in the prompter's hands, I think. The excisions were my own, also the pencil-marks, which emphasize any word in a passage. When it came back from the printer, my father caused the MS. to be bound, and I have no notion how it passed out of his or my possession. It is the single poem in the series that I copied with my own hand, my sister being my amanuensis in those days. I think this bit of comment your due, as the purchaser.[1]

Browning's deletions are as follows (the opening and closing words of *1844* being given in brackets):

I. 160–86 (Then . . . themselves!)
IV. 50–6 (Enough! . . . course?)
IV. 77–86 (Yet . . . pay!)
IV. 101–3 (But . . . withdraw!)
V. 22–46 (Not . . . adventure!)
V. 109–16 (Like . . . scare.)
V. 205–7 (But how indebted . . . seek!)
V. 231–3 (What . . . circumstance?)

His underlinings (here italics) indicate emphases, contrasts, and key words. Those in the opening lines of Act I are typical:

Guibert.	That this should be her *birthday*; and the day
	We all invested her, twelve months ago
	As the late Duke's true heiress and our liege;
	And that *this* also must become the day . . .
	Oh, miserable lady!
1st Courtier.	Ay, indeed?
2nd Courtier.	Well, Guibert?
3rd Courtier.	But your *news*, my friend, your *news*!
	The *sooner*, friend, one learns Prince Berthold's pleasure,
	The better for us all: how *writes* the Prince?
	Give me—I'll read it for the common good—
Guibert.	In time, sir—but, *till* time comes, pardon me!

In Valence's soliloquy at the end of Act III the stage-direction 'with a burst' is added after 'me . . .' in l. 373.[2]

---

[1] *Letters*, pp. 179–80.
[2] Certain spellings of Browning's ('hasardous', 'provisos', 'choaks', and 'seneschal') are changed, no doubt to conform with the house style of Bradbury and Evans. The omission of

Another copy of the first edition, now in Brigham Young University, has the following note in Browning's hand: '(I made the alterations in this copy to suit some—I forget what—projected stage representation: not that of Miss Faucit, which was carried into effect long afterwards) RB. Feb. 10. '77.' Mr Michael Meredith comments that, since Kean had shown an interest in *Colombe's Birthday* before it was published, Browning may have hoped that 'he would reconsider the play *after* publication'.[1] 'I cannot in the least remember how I came to make those stage-directions', Browning wrote to Gosse in 1881, no doubt with reference to the same copy: '—possibly for some projected performance by Helen Faucit, to whom I read the play once'.[2] The letter quoted on p. 433 below confirms this conjecture. The next sentence in the letter of 1881—'Other matters at that time put such as these quite out of my head'—no doubt refers to his courtship of Elizabeth Barrett.

The Brigham Young copy indicates various cuts, and additional stage-directions. Browning counted the lines in each Act and noted the new length, estimating that Act I had been reduced from 368 lines to 277, II from 340 lines to 299, III from 358 lines to 294, IV from 381 lines to 289, and V from 380 lines to 311. Long speeches are generally shortened, while some of the more obvious poetical passages are sacrificed. The most remarkable cut is that of Valence's speech at IV. 209, which is to be omitted unless there is 'a *very* good Valence'.

An interesting feature of this copy is that it has markings to indicate how Browning visualized his play in the theatre. Entrances and exits are marked—many through an additional 'centre door'—and directions are given for movements and curtain-drops. Two small diagrams indicate the grouping of the actors at Colombe's first audience (II. 81 in the present edition) and her confrontation with Berthold (III. 162). In one or two other places markings have clearly been made with a view to the reprinting of the play.

Browning revised *Colombe's Birthday* with great care for the two-volume *Poems* of 1849. Lines are revised and omitted, while more than seventy new lines are added. In a letter quoted on p. 433, he stressed that these revisions 'are important to the sense'. The play was reprinted in subsequent collections without considerable changes, though there are a few

the word 'for' in v. 49 escaped attention: Browning inserted it in the Domett and Brigham Young copies.

[1] See his note on p. 72 of *Meeting the Brownings* (Armstrong Browning Library), the catalogue of an exhibition held in 1986 in Winfield, Kansas, and at Baylor University.
[2] *Letters*, p. 194. In 1846, according to Gosse, p. 73.

places where *1888* restores the reading of the Pforzheimer MS.[1] We have adopted the eight emendations in the Dykes Campbell copy of that edition, as well as those in the Brown University list, and have made a few necessary modifications in punctuation.

A brief account of the events surrounding the first production of *Colombe's Birthday*, which occurred in 1853 when Browning and his wife were in Italy, may be in place here. On 22 January Lady Martin ('or Helen Faucit as you knew her') wrote to Browning from London:

> Have you forgotten—it is very likely—the permission you gave me some years back to make use of your *Colombe's Birthday* for the stage? An opportunity of availing myself of your kindness is likely to present itself at the Haymarket, under the new lessee, Mr. Buckstone's Management, where I have accepted a short engagement in April next. The permission is of so old a date that I do not feel at liberty to act upon it unless renewed. May I therefore ask you to tell me frankly what your feeling is on the subject? If you still have no objection I confess I shall be delighted to have an opportunity of realizing my idea of Colombe who has always been a great pet with me ... Mr. Buckstone ... tells me it would be necessary to present the piece in three acts:—I hope you would not object to this.[2]

Browning replied:

> I shall be delighted if you can do anything for 'Colombe'—do what you think best with it, and for me—it will be pleasant to be in such hands—only, pray follow the corrections in the last edition—(Chapman and Hall will give you a copy)—as they are important to the sense. As for the condensation into three acts—I shall leave that, and all cuttings and the like, to your own judgment—and, come what will, I shall have to be grateful to you, as before. For the rest, you will play the part to heart's content, I *know*.[3]

On 5 March Browning remarked to Edward Chapman that, 'if there were to be any sort of success, it would help the poems to fetch up their leeway', or so he supposed, suggesting that he should 'advertise', and promising to give him 'something saleable, one of these days'.[4] The last comment, no doubt a reference to the poems to be published in *Men and Women*, helps to explain why Browning was less concerned about the production than was his wife.

---

[1] For example at I. 256; II. 285, and III. 181.

[2] Letter printed in *The Baylor Bulletin* (Baylor University Browning Interests, 2nd series), Waco, Tex., 1931, p. 9.

[3] *Life*, p. 185. First printed in Sir Theodore Martin, *Helena Faucit (Lady Martin)* (1900), pp. 237–8.

[4] *New Letters*, p. 59.

On 12 April she told Mrs Jameson that she was 'beginning to be anxious' about *Colombe's Birthday*:

I care much more about it than Robert does. He says that nobody will mistake it for *his* speculation, it's Mr. Buckstone's affair altogether. True; but I should like it to succeed, being Robert's play notwithstanding. But the play is subtle and refined for pits and galleries. I am nervous about it. On the other hand, those theatrical people ought to know; and what in the world made them select it if it is not likely to answer their purpose? By the way, a dreadful rumour reaches us of its having been '*prepared for the stage by the author.*' Don't believe a word of it. Robert just said 'yes' when they wrote to ask him, and not a line of communication has passed since. He has prepared nothing at all, suggested nothing, modified nothing. He referred them to his new edition; and that was the whole.[1]

'How odd the remembrance of play-going seems now', Browning wrote to Forster that same day: '—seven years since I was away—and for three or four years previous I had become strange to the benches, or boards, should one say?'[2]

It is evident that the manuscript of *Colombe's Birthday* submitted to the Lord Chamberlain on 11 April, with the result that the 'License [was] sent' the following day, has no textual authority.[3] The play was performed seven times at the Haymarket Theatre, beginning on Saturday the 16th.[4]

---

[1] *Letters of EBB* ii. 112–13.   [2] *New Letters*, p. 61.

[3] See the facsimile of the MS in James Hogg, *Robert Browning and the Victorian Theatre*, vol. ii (Salzburger Studien zur Anglistik, 4, 1977). The licence is initialled by William Bodham Donne.

[4] On 2 May EBB told George Barrett of the extreme anxiety with which she had rushed to see the first newspaper reviews: Landis, pp. 183–4. Two weeks later she told John Kenyon that she was satisfied, on the whole, with what she had heard of the play's reception: 'I never expected a theatrical success, properly and vulgarly so called; and the play has taken rank, . . in the right way, as a true poet's work: the defects of the acting drama seemed recognised as the qualities of the poem. It was impossible all that subtle tracery of thought and feeling should be painted out clear red and ochre with a house-painter's brush, and lose nothing of its effect . . . What I hope is, that the poetical appreciation of "Colombe" will give an impulse to the sale of the poems': *Letters of EBB* ii. 116. Cf. Raymond and Sullivan, iii. 386.

COLOMBE'S BIRTHDAY;

A PLAY

Ivy and violet, what do ye here
With blossom and shoot in the warm spring-weather,
Hiding the arms of Monchenci and Vere?—HANMER.

title *MS* Bells & Pomegranates. No. 6. Colombe's Birthday. A Play in Five Acts. By R.B.
1844 BELLS AND POMEGRANATES. Nᵒˑ VI.—COLOMBE'S BIRTHDAY. A Play, IN
FIVE ACTS. BY ROBERT BROWNING, Author of "Paracelsus." [epigraph has double
quotation marks] LONDON: EDWARD MOXON, DOVER STREET. MDCCCXLIV.

Epigraph: from 'Written after reading Horace Walpole's Account of Castle Hen-
ningham', in *Fra Cipolla, and Other Poems*, by Sir John Hanmer (1839), with slight differ-
ences in accidentals. Browning spent a week at Hanmer's seat in Flintshire in September
1842, and was delighted to find that his host knew Domett and had voted against Peel on
the Corn Laws: *Browning and Domett*, pp. 41-4, 57. He was presented with a copy of *Fra
Cipolla* and with Hanmer's *Sonnets*, each inscribed 'from his friend': Kelley and Coley, A
1131-2. In return he gave Hanmer a copy of *Sordello*, inscribed 'One did I meet whom
straight my heart did know': Kelley and Coley, C 563. Cf. the notes on 'The Flight of the
Duchess' in Vol. IV of this edition.

In the TLS for 12 December 1952 (p. 819) Harold F. Brooks pointed out an unexpected
connection between these lines and T. S. Eliot. 'Ivy and Violet are the names given to the
two imperceptive aunts in *The Family Reunion*. With Amy, Agatha, and the protagonist
Harry they are Monchenseys; Harry is Lord Monchensey. Browning and Mr. Eliot agree in
this form of the name, instead of the more usual Munchesey.' Brooks goes on to sketch
out 'resemblances, rather imprecise and general', between the two plays.

NO ONE LOVES AND HONOURS BARRY CORNWALL MORE THAN
DOES ROBERT BROWNING;
WHO, HAVING NOTHING BETTER THAN THIS PLAY TO
GIVE HIM IN PROOF OF IT,
MUST SAY SO.

LONDON: 1844.

dedication {not in *MS*} *1844,1849* Dedication. NO ONE *1844* THAN ROBERT .... *March*, 1844.
1849 THAN ROBERT BROWNING DOES;

Dedication: Barry Cornwall (Bryan Waller Procter, 1787–1874), a man with a gift for
friendship, was an early friend of Browning's. He was a member of the circle of Leigh Hunt
and Charles Lamb, and a knowledgeable enthusiast for Shakespeare and the drama of his
time. He wrote numerous Dramatic Scenes, which gave the title to his first volume (1819).
Mirandola: a Tragedy, was initially a great dramatic success, running for sixteen nights in
1821. He wrote a *Life of Edmund Kean* (1835), guaranteed (with T. L. Beddoes and T. F.
Kelsall) the expense of publishing Shelley's *Posthumous Poems*, and in 1839 addressed 'A
Familiar Epistle to Robert Browning'.

PERSONS.

COLOMBE OF RAVESTEIN, Duchess of Juliers and Cleves.
SABYNE, ADOLF, *her attendants.*
GUIBERT, GAUCELME, MAUFROY, CLUGNET, *courtiers.*
VALENCE, *advocate of Cleves.*
PRINCE BERTHOLD, *claimant of the Duchy.*
MELCHIOR, *his confidant.*

PLACE.—*The Palace at Juliers.*
TIME, 16—.

PLACE: see note on Juliers, in note on I. 14.

COLOMBE'S BIRTHDAY.

ACT I.

MORNING.

SCENE.—*A corridor leading to the Audience-chamber.*

GAUCELME, CLUGNET, MAUFROY *and other* COURTIERS, *round* GUI-
BERT, *who is silently reading a paper: as he drops it at the end—*

Guibert. That this should be her birthday; and the day
We all invested her, twelve months ago,
As the late Duke's true heiress and our liege;
And that this also must become the day . . .
Oh, miserable lady!
    1*st Courtier.*   Ay, indeed?   5
    2*nd Courtier.* Well, Guibert?
    3*rd Courtier.*   But your news, my friend, your news!
The sooner, friend, one learns Prince Berthold's pleasure,
The better for us all: how writes the Prince?
Give me! I'll read it for the common good.
    Guibert. In time, sir,—but till time comes, pardon me!   10
Our old Duke just disclosed his child's retreat,
Declared her true succession to his rule,
And died: this birthday was the day, last year,
We convoyed her from Castle Ravestein—

---

9 *MS-1865* me—

s.d. MORNING: cf. the divisions of *Pippa Passes.*

14 *Castle Ravestein*: Griffin and Minchin state (p. 62) that 'After leaving Rotterdam, on
his outward journey, 1834, Browning passed by the home of the heroine of his *Colombe's
Birthday* . . . , and then through "ancient famous happy Cleves", whence came Colombe's
lover, . . . Valence'; but Maynard queries this, with good reason, and points out that
Browning passed the area 'on his return from Italy in 1838 under more leisurely circum-
stances', concluding that 'the poetic reminiscences probably date from then': *Browning's
Youth*, p. 420 n. 246.

That sleeps out trustfully its extreme age   15
On the Meuse' quiet bank, where she lived queen
Over the water-buds,—to Juliers' court
With joy and bustle. Here again we stand;
Sir Gaucelme's buckle's constant to his cap:
To-day's much such another sunny day!   20
    Gaucelme. Come, Guibert, this outgrows a jest, I think!
You're hardly such a novice as to need
The lesson, you pretend.
    Guibert.   What lesson, sir?
That everybody, if he'd thrive at court,
Should, first and last of all, look to himself?   25
Why, no: and therefore with your good example,
(—Ho, Master Adolf!)—to myself I'll look.

                  Enter ADOLF.

    Guibert. The Prince's letter; why, of all men else,
Comes it to me?
    Adolf.   By virtue of your place,
Sir Guibert! 'T was the Prince's express charge,   30
His envoy told us, that the missive there
Should only reach our lady by the hand
Of whosoever held your place.
    Guibert.   Enough!   [ADOLF *retires*
Then, gentles, who'll accept a certain poor
Indifferently honourable place,   35
My friends, I make no doubt, have gnashed their teeth
At leisure minutes these half-dozen years,

16 *MS,1844* where queen she lived   18 *MS–1849* bustle: 21 *MS,1844* this
outgoes a   30 *MS* Princes   33 s.d. *MS,1844* †[*Exit* ADOLF.

    15 *extreme*: accented on the first syllable, as often in Browning. Cf. our note to *Pauline*,
908.
    17 *water-buds*: not in OED, but Shelley has 'water-blooms': 'The Sensitive Plant', iii. 42.
    19 *Sir Gaucelm's buckle's constant to his cap*: probably 'Sir Gaucelme's cap still retains its
buckle'.
    24 *if he'd thrive at court*: a commonplace. See *Outlandish Proverbs*, 795, in *The Works of
George Herbert*, ed. F. E. Hutchinson (1941).
    30 *express*: accented on the first syllable.
    34 *gentles*: gentlemen.
    35 *Indifferently honourable*: cf. *Hamlet*, III. i. 122.

To find me never in the mood to quit?
Who asks may have it, with my blessing, and—
This to present our lady. Who'll accept?   40
You,—you,—you? There it lies, and may, for me!
  Maufroy [*a youth, picking up the paper, reads aloud*].
"Prince Berthold, proved by titles following
"Undoubted Lord of Juliers, comes this day
"To claim his own, with licence from the Pope,
"The Emperor, the Kings of Spain and France" . . .   45
  Gaucelme. Sufficient "titles following," I judge!
Don't read another! Well,—"to claim his own"?
  Maufroy. "—And take possession of the Duchy held
"Since twelve months, to the true heir's prejudice,
"By" . . . Colombe, Juliers' mistress, so she thinks,   50
And Ravestein's mere lady, as we find.
Who wants the place and paper? Guibert's right.
I hope to climb a little in the world,—
I'd push my fortunes,—but, no more than he,
Could tell her on this happy day of days,   55
That, save the nosegay in her hand, perhaps,
There's nothing left to call her own. Sir Clugnet,
You famish for promotion; what say you?
  Clugnet [*an old man*]. To give this letter were a sort, I take
      it,
Of service: services ask recompense: 60
What kind of corner may be Ravestein?
  Guibert. The castle? Oh, you'd share her fortunes? Good!
Three walls stand upright, full as good as four,
With no such bad remainder of a roof.
  Clugnet. Oh,—but the town?
  Guibert.   Five houses, fifteen huts; 65
A church whereto was once a spire, 't is judged;
And half a dyke, except in time of thaw.

---

40 *MS-1865* This   *47 [reading of *MS*] *1844–89* own?"   51 *MS-1868* find!
52 *MS-1865* right!   57 *MS-1865* own!   60 *MS-1849* recompence:
65 *MS,1844* huts,   66 *MS,1844* judged

  51 *Ravestein's mere lady*: i.e. she is only lady of Ravestein. Cf. II. 280.

Clugnet. Still, there's some revenue?
Guibert.   Else Heaven forfend!
You hang a beacon out, should fogs increase;
So, when the Autumn floats of pine-wood steer   70
Safe 'mid the white confusion, thanks to you,
Their grateful raftsman flings a guilder in;
—That's if he mean to pass your way next time.
Clugnet. If not?
Guibert.   Hang guilders, then! He blesses you.
Clugnet. What man do you suppose me? Keep your paper!   75
And, let me say, it shows no handsome spirit
To dally with misfortune: keep your place!
Gaucelme. Some one must tell her.
Guibert.   Some one may: you may!
Gaucelme. Sir Guibert, 't is no trifle turns me sick
Of court-hypocrisy at years like mine,   80
But this goes near it. Where's there news at all?
Who'll have the face, for instance, to affirm
He never heard, e'en while we crowned the girl,
That Juliers' tenure was by Salic law;
That one, confessed her father's cousin's child,   85
And, she away, indisputable heir,
Against our choice protesting and the Duke's,
Claimed Juliers?—nor, as he preferred his claim,
That first this, then another potentate,
Inclined to its allowance?—I or you,   90
Or any one except the lady's self?
Oh, it had been the direst cruelty
To break the business to her! Things might change:

---

72 *MS,1844* The grateful   73 *MS- 1863* he means to   74 *MS-1868* then—he
MS-1849,1865,1868 you! *1863* you   76 *MS-1849* And let me say it shows *1863*
And, let me say it, shows   78 *1863* you may   85 *MS,1844* And one,

72 *guilder*: see note to 'The Pied Piper', l. 37, above.
81 *Where's there news at all?*: what is remarkable about that?
84 *Salic law*: the law which excluded females from succession.
86 *she away*: leaving her out of account.   88 *preferred*: presented.
93 *To break the business*: cf. 'to break the news'.

At all events, we'd see next masque at end,
Next mummery over first: and so the edge   95
Was taken off sharp tidings as they came,
Till here's the Prince upon us, and there's she
—Wreathing her hair, a song between her lips,
With just the faintest notion possible
That some such claimant earns a livelihood   100
About the world, by feigning grievances—
Few pay the story of, but grudge its price,
And fewer listen to, a second time.
Your method proves a failure; now try mine!
And, since this must be carried . . .

    Guibert [*snatching the paper from him*]. By your leave!   105
Your zeal transports you! 'T will not serve the Prince
So much as you expect, this course you'd take.
If she leaves quietly her palace,—well;
But if she died upon its threshold,—no:
He'd have the trouble of removing her.   110
Come, gentles, we're all—what the devil knows!
You, Gaucelme, won't lose character, beside:
You broke your father's heart superiorly
To gather his succession—never blush!
You're from my province, and, be comforted,   115
They tell of it with wonder to this day.
You can afford to let your talent sleep.
We'll take the very worst supposed, as true:
There, the old Duke knew, when he hid his child
Among the river-flowers at Ravestein,   120
With whom the right lay! Call the Prince our Duke!
There, she's no Duchess, she's no anything
More than a young maid with the bluest eyes:
And now, sirs, we'll not break this young maid's heart
Coolly as Gaucelme could and would! No haste!   125

---

104 *MS–1849* mine—   105 *1849* leave   107 *MS–1849* take;
110 *MS–1849* her   111 *MS,1844* knows: 117 *MS–1863* sleep!
118 (no equivalent in *MS,1844*)   120 (no equivalent in *MS,1844*)
121 *MS,1844* lay! Let the Prince be Duke!   125 *MS,1844* So coolly as he could

His talent's full-blown, ours but in the bud:
We'll not advance to his perfection yet—
Will we, Sir Maufroy? See, I've ruined Maufroy
For ever as a courtier!

    Gaucelme.   Here's a coil!
And, count us, will you? Count its residue,   130
This boasted convoy, this day last year's crowd!
A birthday, too, a gratulation day!
I'm dumb: bid that keep silence!

    Maufroy and others.   Eh, Sir Guibert?
He's right: that does say something: that's bare truth.
Ten—twelve, I make: a perilous dropping off!   135

    Guibert. Pooh—is it audience hour? The vestibule
Swarms too, I wager, with the common sort
That want our privilege of entry here.

    Gaucelme. Adolf!

              [*Re-enter* ADOLF.]

          Who's outside?

    Guibert.   Oh, your looks suffice!
Nobody waiting?

    Maufroy [*looking through the door-folds*]. Scarce our number!

    Guibert.   'Sdeath! 140
Nothing to beg for, to complain about?
It can't be! Ill news spreads, but not so fast
As thus to frighten all the world!

    Gaucelme.   The world
Lives out of doors, sir—not with you and me
By presence-chamber porches, state-room stairs,   145
Wherever warmth's perpetual: outside's free
To every wind from every compass-point,
And who may get nipped needs be weather-wise.

---

129 *MS-1849* coil—   132 *MS-1868* gratulation-day!   133 *MS-1863 that*
135 *MS-1863* dropping-off!   136 *MS-1849* audience-hour?   142 *MS* news
spread,   but   146 *MS,1844*   perpetual.   *147 {reading of *MS-*
1863,DC,BrU,*1889*} 1865–88 point

    129 *a coil*: trouble; a 'to-do'.
    142 *Ill news spreads*: proverbial: Tilley, N 147. Cf. *Samson Agonistes*, 1538.

The Prince comes and the lady's People go;
The snow-goose settles down, the swallows flee—   150
Why should they wait for winter-time? 'T is instinct.
Don't you feel somewhat chilly?
    Guibert.   That's their craft?   ·
And last year's crowders-round and criers-forth
That strewed the garlands, overarched the roads,
Lighted the bonfires, sang the loyal songs!   155
Well 't is my comfort, you could never call me
The People's Friend! The People keep their word—
I keep my place: don't doubt I'll entertain
The People when the Prince comes, and the People
Are talked of! Then, their speeches—no one tongue   160
Found respite, not a pen had holiday
—For they wrote, too, as well as spoke, these knaves!
Now see: we tax and tithe them, pill and poll,
They wince and fret enough, but pay they must
—We manage that,—so, pay with a good grace   165
They might as well, it costs so little more.
But when we've done with taxes, meet folk next
Outside the toll-booth and the rating-place,
In public—there they have us if they will,
We're at their mercy after that, you see!   170
For one tax not ten devils could extort—
Over and above necessity, a grace;
This prompt disbosoming of love, to wit—
Their vine-leaf wrappage of our tribute penny,

149 *MS,1844* and the People go; 'tis instinct: 151 (no equivalent in *MS,1844*) *1849-*
68 instinct;   155 *MS-1863* Lit up the *MS,1844* songs—   170 *MS-1849* see—
172 *MS* [Grace over and above necessity,] *1844* grace,   174 *MS-1849* vine-leaf-
wrappage *MS* tribute-pence, *1844-68* tribute-penny,

   157 *The People's Friend*: a 'People's Petition' was presented to parliament by T. Dun-
combe, the radical, on 2 May 1842. It was rejected. Cf. *Sordello*, iv. 298.

   163 *pill and poll*: ruin by extortions (literally, make bare of hair and skin): a common
phrase in the sixteenth and seventeenth centuries.

   173 *disbosoming*: OED has only this, and *The Ring and the Book*, iii. 614, as examples of
this form of the word.

   174 *wrappage*: the first example in OED is from Carlyle's essay on Richter (1827): Cen-
tenary ed., xxvi. 12.

And crowning attestation, all works well.   175
Yet this precisely do they thrust on us!
These cappings quick, these crook-and-cringings low,
Hand to the heart, and forehead to the knee,
With grin that shuts the eyes and opes the mouth—
So tender they their love; and, tender made,   180
Go home to curse us, the first doit we ask.
As if their souls were any longer theirs!
As if they had not given ample warrant
To who should clap a collar on their neck,
Rings in their nose, a goad to either flank,   185
And take them for the brute they boast themselves!
Stay—there's a bustle at the outer door—
And somebody entreating . . . that's my name!
Adolf,—I heard my name!

    Adolf.   'T was probably
The suitor.

    Guibert. Oh, there is one?

    Adolf.   With a suit   190
He'd fain enforce in person.

    Guibert.   The good heart
—And the great fool! Just ope the mid-door's fold!
Is that a lappet of his cloak, I see?

    Adolf. If it bear plenteous sign of travel . . . ay,

---

*175 (reading of *MS–1865*) *1868–89* crowding   *MS* A[nd] crowning   176 *MS,*
1844 us,—   177 *MS–1865* quick, and crook-   181 *MS–1849* curse you, the
first doit you ask;   *1863* (as *MS–1849* but with full stop after 'ask')   182 (no
equivalent in *MS,1844*)   *192 (reading of *1863–8*,DC,BrU,*1889*) *MS–1849* fold—
1888 fold   194 *MS–1863* plenteous signs of *MS* aye,

    175 *crowning*: 'crowding' (*1868–89*) is one of the 'vile misprints' to which Browning
drew attention in a letter. See v. 189 n. below.

    177 *crook-and-cringings*: cf. Jonson, *Sejanus*, I. 204: 'With sacrifice of knees, of crookes,
and cringe.'

    180 *tender made*: absolute. 'You are fond of that *absolute* construction', EBB noted on
Luria, I. i. 74, '—but I think that sometimes it makes the meaning a little doubtful': *New
Poems*, p. 160.

    181 *doit*: 'A small piece of money': Johnson.

    192 *the mid-door's fold*: one side of the folding door in the middle.

    193 *lappet*: 'A loose or overlapping part of a garment, forming a flap or fold': OED.

The very cloak my comrades tore!
  Guibert.   Why tore?   195
  Adolf. He seeks the Duchess' presence in that trim:
Since daybreak, was he posted hereabouts
Lest he should miss the moment.
  Guibert.   Where's he now?
  Adolf. Gone for a minute possibly, not more:
They have ado enough to thrust him back.   200
  Guibert. Ay—but my name, I caught?
  Adolf.   Oh, sir—he said
—What was it?—You had known him formerly,
And, he believed, would help him did you guess
He waited now; you promised him as much:
The old plea! 'Faith, he's back,—renews the charge! 205
[*Speaking at the door.*] So long as the man parleys, peace out-
  side—
Nor be too ready with your halberts, there!
  Gaucelme. My horse bespattered, as he blocked the path,
A thin sour man, not unlike somebody.
  Adolf. He holds a paper in his breast, whereon   210
He glances when his cheeks flush and his brow
At each repulse—
  Gaucelme. I noticed he'd a brow.
  Adolf. So glancing, he grows calmer, leans awhile
Over the balustrade, adjusts his dress,
And presently turns round, quiet again,   215
With some new pretext for admittance.—Back!
[*To* GUIBERT.]—Sir, he has seen you! Now cross halberts! Ha—
Pascal is prostrate—there lies Fabian too!
No passage! Whither would the madman press?
Close the doors quick on me!
  Guibert.   Too late! He's here. 220

195 *MS,1844* my comradc torc! 199 *MS-1863* morc, 202 *MS,1844*
—What said he?—You 206 *MS-1863* outside! *208 {reading of *MS-1868*}
1888,1889 path 218 *MS-1863* too— 220 *MS-1863* latc—hc's *1865* latc!
. hc's

196 *trim* : 'Dress; geer; ornaments. It is now a word of slight contempt': Johnson.
207 *halberts* : 'halberd' in Johnson, defined as 'A battle-axe fixed to a long pole.'

Enter, hastily and with discomposed dress, VALENCE.

Valence. Sir Guibert, will you help me?—me, that come
Charged by your townsmen, all who starve at Cleves,
To represent their heights and depths of woe
Before our Duchess and obtain relief!
Such errands barricade such doors, it seems: 225
But not a common hindrance drives me back
On all the sad yet hopeful faces, lit
With hope for the first time, which sent me forth.
Cleves, speak for me! Cleves' men and women, speak!
Who followed me—your strongest—many a mile   230
That I might go the fresher from their ranks,
—Who sit—your weakest—by the city gates,
To take me fuller of what news I bring
As I return—for I must needs return!
—Can I? 'T were hard, no listener for their wrongs,   235
To turn them back upon the old despair—
Harder, Sir Guibert, than imploring thus—
So, I do—any way you please—implore!
If you . . . but how should you remember Cleves?
Yet they of Cleves remember you so well!   240
Ay, comment on each trait of you they keep,
Your words and deeds caught up at second hand,—
Proud, I believe, at bottom of their hearts,
O' the very levity and recklessness
Which only prove that you forget their wrongs.   245
Cleves, the grand town, whose men and women starve,
Is Cleves forgotten? Then, remember me!
You promised me that you would help me once,
For other purpose: will you keep your word?
      Guibert. And who may you be, friend?
      Valence.   Valence of Cleves.   250

221 *MS-1868* —Me, that   228 *MS-1863* forth!   229 *MS-1863* speak—
232 *MS-1849* city-gates,   243 *MS* return   244 *MS-1868* Of the
245 *MS* That only   *MS,1844* prove yourself forget

   222 *Cleves* : 46 miles NW of Düsseldorf, 12 miles E of Nijmwegen, Cleves (Kleve in Ger-
man) lies on three small hills near the Dutch frontier, some two miles from the Rhine.
   235 *no listener for their wrongs* : absolute.

    Guibert. Valence of . . . not the advocate of Cleves,
I owed my whole estate to, three years back?
Ay, well may you keep silence! Why, my lords,
You've heard, I'm sure, how, Pentecost three years,
I was so nearly ousted of my land   255
By some knave's-pretext—(eh? when you refused me
Your ugly daughter, Clugnet!)—and you've heard
How I recovered it by miracle
—(When I refused her!) Here's the very friend,
—Valence of Cleves, all parties have to thank!   260
Nay, Valence, this procedure's vile in you!
I'm no more grateful than a courtier should,
But politic am I—I bear a brain,
Can cast about a little, might require
Your services a second time. I tried   265
To tempt you with advancement here to court
—"No!"—well, for curiosity at least
To view our life here—"No!"—our Duchess, then,—
A pretty woman's worth some pains to see,
Nor is she spoiled, I take it, if a crown   270
Complete the forehead pale and tresses pure . . .
    Valence. Our city trusted me its miseries,
And I am come.
    Guibert.   So much for taste! But "come,"—
So may you be, for anything I know,
To beg the Pope's cross, or Sir Clugnet's daughter,   275
And with an equal chance you get all three.
If it was ever worth your while to come,
Was not the proper way worth finding too?
    Valence. Straight to the palace-portal, sir, I came—
    Guibert. —And said?—

256 *1844,1849* knaves' pretext,— *1863-8* knaves'-pretext,—   257 *MS-1863* Clug-
net,)   259 *MS-1849* her)!   261 *MS-1863* you— *1865* you:
265 *MS-1863* time!   267 *MS,1844* —"No"—   268 *MS,1844* —"no"—
271 *MS-1863* Completes the   276 *MS-1868* three!

  254 *Pentecost*: Whit Sunday, the seventh Sunday after Easter.
  275 *the Pope's cross*: 'the badge of membership in the order of knighthood conferred by
the Pope': Porter and Clarke.

   Valence.   —That I had brought the miseries   280
Of a whole city to relieve.
    Guibert.   —Which saying
Won your admittance? You saw me, indeed,
And here, no doubt, you stand: as certainly,
My intervention, I shall not dispute,
Procures you audience; which, if I procure,—   285
That paper's closely written—by Saint Paul,
Here flock the Wrongs, follow the Remedies,
Chapter and verse, One, Two, A, B and C!
Perhaps you'd enter, make a reverence,
And launch these "miseries" from first to last?   290
   Valence. How should they let me pause or turn aside?
   Gaucelme [*to* VALENCE.]
My worthy sir, one question! You've come straight
From Cleves, you tell us: heard you any talk
At Cleves about our lady?
   Valence.   Much.
   Gaucelme.   And what?
   Valence. Her wish was to redress all wrongs she knew.   295
   Gaucelme. That, you believed?
   Valence.   You see me, sir!
   Gaucelme.   —Nor stopped
Upon the road from Cleves to Juliers here,
For any—rumours you might find afloat?
   Valence. I had my townsmen's wrongs to busy me.
   Gaucelme. This is the lady's birthday, do you know?   300
—Her day of pleasure?
   Valence.   —That the great, I know,
For pleasure born, should still be on the watch
To exclude pleasure when a duty offers:
Even as, for duty born, the lowly too

---

282 *MS* Won you admittance?   285 *MS,1844* audience; but, if so I do—
288 *MS–1863* C—   292 *MS–1865* question: you've   299 *MS* townsmens
301 *1849–65* pleasure?—I know that the great,   304 *1849–65* Even as, the lowly too,
for duty born,

   286 *Saint Paul*: the patron saint of preachers.

May ever snatch a pleasure if in reach: 305
Both will have plenty of their birthright, sir!
   Gaucelme [*aside to* GUIBERT].
Sir Guibert, here's your man! No scruples now—
You'll never find his like! Time presses hard.
I've seen your drift and Adolf's too, this while,
But you can't keep the hour of audience back   310
Much longer, and at noon the Prince arrives.
[*Pointing to* VALENCE.]
Entrust him with it—fool no chance away!
   Guibert. Him?
   Gaucelme.   —With the missive! What's the man to her?
   Guibert. No bad thought! Yet, 't is yours, who ever played
The tempting serpent: else 't were no bad thought!   315
I should—and do—mistrust it for your sake,
Or else . . .

     Enter an Official *who communicates with* ADOLF.

   Adolf.   The Duchess will receive the court.
   Guibert. Give us a moment, Adolf! Valence, friend,
I'll help you. We of the service, you're to mark,
Have special entry, while the herd . . . the folk   320
Outside, get access through our help alone;
—Well, it is so, was so, and I suppose
So ever will be: your natural lot is, therefore,
To wait your turn and opportunity,
And probably miss both. Now, I engage   325
To set you, here and in a minute's space,
Before the lady, with full leave to plead
Chapter and verse, and A, and B, and C,
To heart's content.
   Valence.   I grieve that I must ask,—
This being, yourself admit, the custom here,—   330

---

312 *MS–1863 him*   317 *MS–1865* Court! *1868* court!   319 *MS–1865* you:
1868 you!   320 *MS–1868* the folks   321 *MS–1849* alone *1863,1865* alone.
330 *MS,1844* From this yourself admit

To what the price of such a favour mounts?
    Guibert. Just so! You're not without a courtier's tact.
Little at court, as your quick instinct prompts,
Do such as we without a recompense.
    Valence. Yours is?—
    Guibert.   A trifle: here's a document   335
'T is some one's duty to present her Grace—
I say, not mine—these say, not theirs—such points
Have weight at court. Will you relieve us all
And take it? Just say, "I am bidden lay
"This paper at the Duchess' feet!"
    Valence.   No more?   340
I thank you, sir!
    Adolf.   Her Grace receives the court.
    Guibert [*aside*]. Now, *sursum corda*, quoth the mass-priest!
        Do—
Whoever's my kind saint, do let alone
These pushings to and fro, and pullings back;
Peaceably let me hang o' the devil's arm   345
The downward path, if you can't pluck me off
Completely! Let me live quite his, or yours!
    [*The* Courtiers *begin to range themselves, and move toward the door.*
After me, Valence! So, our famous Cleves
Lacks bread? Yet don't we gallants buy their lace?
And dear enough—it beggars me, I know,   350
To keep my very gloves fringed properly.
This, Valence, is our Great State Hall you cross;
Yon grey urn's veritable marcasite,
The Pope's gift: and those salvers testify
The Emperor. Presently you'll set your foot   355

---

331 *MS,1844* What will the price of such a favour {*MS* favor} be?   332 *MS– 1863*
tact!   334 *1844,1849* recompence   340 *MS–1865* feet."   341 *MS–*
1865 Court! *1868* court!   347 s.d. *MS– 1863 move towards the*   351 *MS–1865*
properly!

    342 *sursum corda* : lift up your hearts. From the Missal.

    351 *my very gloves* : even my gloves.

    353 *marcasite* : 'Pyrites, *esp.* the crystallized forms of iron pyrites used in the 18th c. for
ornaments': OED, which cites Jonson, *The Alchemist*, II. iii. 188.

. . . But you don't speak, friend Valence!
    Valence.   I shall speak.
    Gaucelme [*aside to* GUIBERT].
Guibert—it were no such ungraceful thing
If you and I, at first, seemed horror-struck
With the bad news. Look here, what you shall do.
Suppose you, first, clap hand to sword and cry   360
"Yield strangers our allegiance? First I'll perish
"Beside your Grace!"—and so give me the cue
To . . .
    Guibert. —Clap your hand to note-book and jot down
That to regale the Prince with? I conceive.
[*To* VALENCE.] Do, Valence, speak, or I shall half suspect   365
You're plotting to supplant us, me the first,
I' the lady's favour! Is 't the grand harangue
You mean to make, that thus engrosses you?
—Which of her virtues you'll apostrophize?
Or is 't the fashion you aspire to start,   370
Of that close-curled, not unbecoming hair?
Or what else ponder you?
    Valence.   My townsmen's wrongs.

---

358 *MS-1849* horrorstruck   *359 {reading of BrU,*1889*} *MS-1868* do! *1888* do
362 *MS-1849* Grace"!—   364 *MS-1865* conceive!   367 *MS* favor: *1844-65*
favour: 372 *MS-1865* wrongs!

ACT II.

NOON.

SCENE.—*The Presence-chamber.*

The DUCHESS *and* SABYNE.

The Duchess. Announce that I am ready for the court!
Sabyne. 'T is scarcely audience-hour, I think; your Grace
May best consult your own relief, no doubt,
And shun the crowd: but few can have arrived.
  The Duchess. Let those not yet arrived, then, keep away!   5
'T was me, this day last year at Ravestein,
You hurried. It has been full time, beside,
This half-hour. Do you hesitate?
  Sabyne.   Forgive me!
  The Duchess. Stay, Sabyne; let me hasten to make sure
Of one true thanker: here with you begins   10
My audience, claim you first its privilege!
It is my birth's event they celebrate:
You need not wish me more such happy days,
But—ask some favour! Have you none to ask?
Has Adolf none, then? this was far from least   15
Of much I waited for impatiently,
Assure yourself! It seemed so natural
Your gift, beside this bunch of river-bells,
Should be the power and leave of doing good
To you, and greater pleasure to myself.   20
You ask my leave to-day to marry Adolf?
The rest is my concern.
  Sabyne.   Your Grace is ever

4 *MS,1844* crowd; but if there's few arrived . . . *1849, 1863* arrived . . .   6 *1849, 1863*
me   14 *MS* favor!   17 *MS,1844* yourself! So natural it seemed,
19 *MS* leave to do you good! *1844* leave to do you good;   20 {no equivalent in
MS,1844} *1849* myself:

10 *thanker*: a rare word. OED cites Coleridge, *The Death of Wallenstein*, IV. ii. 113.
18 *river-bells*: not in OED.

Our lady of dear Ravestein,—but, for Adolf . . .
   The Duchess. "But"? You have not, sure, changed in your
     regard
And purpose towards him?
   Sabyne.   We change?
   The Duchess.   Well then? Well?   25
   Sabyne. How could we two be happy, and, most like,
Leave Juliers, when—when . . . but 't is audience-time!
   The Duchess. "When, if you left me, I were left indeed!"
Would you subjoin that?—Bid the court approach!
—Why should we play thus with each other, Sabyne?   30
Do I not know, if courtiers prove remiss,
If friends detain me, and get blame for it,
There is a cause? Of last year's fervid throng
Scarce one half comes now.
   Sabyne [*aside*].   One half? No, alas!
   The Duchess. So can the mere suspicion of a cloud   35
Over my fortunes, strike each loyal heart.
They've heard of this Prince Berthold; and, forsooth,
Some foolish arrogant pretence he makes,
May grow more foolish and more arrogant,
They please to apprehend! I thank their love.   40
Admit them!
   Sabyne [*aside*]. How much has she really learned?
   The Duchess. Surely, whoever's absent, Tristan waits?
—Or at least Romuald, whom my father raised
From nothing—come, he's faithful to me, come!
(Sabyne, I should but be the prouder—yes,   45
The fitter to comport myself aright)
Not Romuald? Xavier—what said he to that?
For Xavier hates a parasite, I know!   [SABYNE *goes out.*
  · *The Duchess.* Well, sunshine's everywhere, and summer
     too.

23 *MS,1844* My lady *1844* Ravenstein,—   25 *MS-1865* We   28 *MS-1849*
indeed"—   34 *MS* half come[s] now! *1844-63* now!   38 *MS-1863* Each
foolish   39 *MS,1844* More foolish and more arrogant may grow,   40 *MS-*
1863 love!   46 *MS-1863* And fitter   49 *MS* too! *1844,1849* too;

Next year 't is the old place again, perhaps—   50
The water-breeze again, the birds again.
—It cannot be! It is too late to be!
What part had I, or choice in all of it?
Hither they brought me; I had not to think
Nor care, concern myself with doing good   55
Or ill, my task was just—to live,—to live,
And, answering ends there was no need explain,
To render Juliers happy—so they said.
All could not have been falsehood: some was love,
And wonder and obedience. I did all   60
They looked for: why then cease to do it now?
Yet this is to be calmly set aside,
And—ere next birthday's dawn, for aught I know,
Things change, a claimant may arrive, and I . . .
It cannot nor it shall not be! His right?   65
Well then, he has the right, and I have not,
—But who bade all of you surround my life
And close its growth up with your ducal crown
Which, plucked off rudely, leaves me perishing?
I could have been like one of you,—loved, hoped,   70
Feared, lived and died like one of you—but you
Would take that life away and give me this,
And I will keep this! I will face you! Come!

Enter the Courtiers *and* VALENCE.

The Courtiers. Many such happy mornings to your Grace!
The Duchess [*aside, as they pay their devoir*].
The same words, the same faces,—the same love!   75
I have been overfearful. These are few;
But these, at least, stand firmly: these are mine.
As many come as may; and if no more,
'T is that these few suffice—they do suffice!

51 *MS* again, *1844,1849* again   59 *MS–1865* falsehood!   61 *MS–1849* for!
Why   66 *MS,1844* right, I have it not,   72 *MS* take my life . . . . me yours
73 *MS* keep yours! I will face you— *1844,1849* you—   75 s.d. *1844 their devoirs.*
76 *1844–65* over-fearful   77 *MS– 1863* mine!   78 *MS–1849* may,

What succour may not next year bring me? Plainly,   80
I feared too soon. [*To the* Courtiers.] I thank you, sirs: all
    thanks!
    Valence [*aside, as the* DUCHESS *passes from one group to another,*
    conversing].
'T is she—the vision this day last year brought,
When, for a golden moment at our Cleves,
She tarried in her progress hither. Cleves
Chose me to speak its welcome, and I spoke   85
—Not that she could have noted the recluse
—Ungainly, old before his time—who gazed.
Well, Heaven's gifts are not wasted, and that gaze
Kept, and shall keep me to the end, her own!
She was above it—but so would not sink   90
My gaze to earth! The People caught it, hers—
Thenceforward, mine; but thus entirely mine,
Who shall affirm, had she not raised my soul
Ere she retired and left me—them? She turns—
There's all her wondrous face at once! The ground   95
Reels and . . . [*suddenly occupying himself with his paper*]
        These wrongs of theirs I have to plead!
    The Duchess [*to the* Courtiers].
Nay, compliment enough! and kindness' self
Should pause before it wish me more such years.
'T was fortunate that thus, ere youth escaped,
I tasted life's pure pleasure—one such, pure,   100
Is worth a thousand, mixed—and youth's for pleasure:
Mine is received; let my age pay for it.
    Gaucelme. So, pay, and pleasure paid for, thinks your
    Grace,
Should never go together?
    Guibert.   How, Sir Gaucelme?
Hurry one's feast down unenjoyingly   105

•

80 *MS-1849* me!   81 *MS-1849* soon!   s.d. *MS-1868 the* Court.   85 *MS*
chose [me] to   97 s.d. *MS-1868 the* Court.   104 *MS* to-gether?

    101 *youth's for pleasure*: proverbial. Cf. Mark Akenside, 'Love. An Elegy', 90: 'Youth calls
for Pleasure, Pleasure calls for Love': *The Poetical Works* ('Edinburg' [*sic*], 1781), ii. 133.

At the snatched breathing-intervals of work?
As good you saved it till the dull day's-end
When, stiff and sleepy, appetite is gone.
Eat first, then work upon the strength of food!
   The Duchess. True: you enable me to risk my future,   110
By giving me a past beyond recall.
I lived, a girl, one happy leisure year:
Let me endeavour to be the Duchess now!
And so,—what news, Sir Guibert, spoke you of?
                [*As they advance a little, and* GUIBERT *speaks—*
—That gentleman?
   Valence [*aside*]. I feel her eyes on me.   115
   Guibert [*to* VALENCE]. The Duchess, sir, inclines to hear
    your suit.
Advance! He is from Cleves.
   Valence [*coming forward. Aside*]. Their wrongs—their
    wrongs!
   The Duchess. And you, sir, are from Cleves? How fresh in
    mind,
The hour or two I passed at queenly Cleves!
She entertained me bravely, but the best   120
Of her good pageant seemed its standers-by
With insuppressive joy on every face!
What says my ancient famous happy Cleves?
   Valence. Take the truth, lady—you are made for truth!
So think my friends: nor do they less deserve   125
The having you to take it, you shall think,
When you know all—nay, when you only know
How, on that day you recollect at Cleves,
When the poor acquiescing multitude
Who thrust themselves with all their woes apart   130

---

106 *MS* breathing intervals   108 *MS–1865* gone!   109 {no equivalent in
MS,1844} *1849, 1863* of it!   112 *MS,1844* A girl, one happy leisure year I lived:
113 *MS,1844* be Duchess now!   115 *MS–1865* me!   116 *MS–1863* suit!
120 *MS,1844* entertained us bravely,   125 *MS,1844* nor less do they
  122 *insuppressive*: as in *Julius Caesar*, II. i. 134.

Into unnoticed corners, that the few
Their means sufficed to muster trappings for,
Might fill the foreground, occupy your sight
With joyous faces fit to bear away
And boast of as a sample of all Cleves   135
—How, when to daylight these crept out once more,
Clutching, unconscious, each his empty rags
Whence the scant coin, which had not half bought bread,
That morn he shook forth, counted piece by piece,
And, well-advisedly, on perfumes spent them   140
To burn, or flowers to strew, before your path
—How, when the golden flood of music and bliss
Ebbed, as their moon retreated, and again
Left the sharp black-point rocks of misery bare
—Then I, their friend, had only to suggest   145
"Saw she the horror as she saw the pomp!"
And as one man they cried "He speaks the truth:
"Show her the horror! Take from our own mouths
"Our wrongs and show them, she will see them too!"
This they cried, lady! I have brought the wrongs.   150
    The Duchess. Wrongs? Cleves has wrongs—apparent now
        and thus!
I thank you! In that paper? Give it me!
    Valence. (There, Cleves!) In this! (What did I promise,
        Cleves?)
Our weavers, clothiers, spinners are reduced
Since . . . Oh, I crave your pardon! I forget   155
I buy the privilege of this approach,
And promptly would discharge my debt. I lay

---

*131 (reading of *MS-1849*) *1863–89* few,   137 *MS,1844* Clutching, inconscious,
each   140 *MS,1844* perfumes spent | 146 *MS,1844* pomp"—
147 *MS* "And   148 *MS,1844* horror—take   151 *MS,1844* wrongs—which
now and thus I know?   152 *MS-1865* you—in   155 *MS-1849* pardon—

131 *unnoticed corners*: cf. Shakespeare, *As You Like It*, II. iii. 42: 'And unregarded age in corners thrown'. See too *Sordello*, iii. 734–5.

137 *unconscious*: Johnson gives two meanings: 'Having no mental perception' and 'Unacquainted; unknowing.'

144 *black-point*: apparently a nonce-word.

This paper humbly at the Duchess' feet.

                              [*Presenting* GUIBERT'S *paper.*

    Guibert. Stay! for the present . . .

    The Duchess.   Stay, sir? I take aught

That teaches me their wrongs with greater pride   160

Than this your ducal circlet. Thank you, sir!

     [*The* DUCHESS *reads hastily; then, turning to the* Courtiers—

What have I done to you? Your deed or mine

Was it, this crowning me? I gave myself

No more a title to your homage, no,

Than church-flowers, born this season, wrote the words   165

In the saint's-book that sanctified them first.

For such a flower, you plucked me; well, you erred—

Well, 't was a weed; remove the eye-sore quick!

But should you not remember it has lain

Steeped in the candles' glory, palely shrined,   170

Nearer God's Mother than most earthly things?

—That if 't be faded 't is with prayer's sole breath—

That the one day it boasted was God's day?

Still, I do thank you! Had you used respect,

Here might I dwindle to my last white leaf,   175

Here lose life's latest freshness, which even yet

May yield some wandering insect rest and food:

So, fling me forth, and—all is best for all!

[*After a pause.*] Prince Berthold, who art Juliers' Duke it

    seems—

The King's choice, and the Emperor's, and the Pope's—   180

Be mine, too! Take this People! Tell not me

Of rescripts, precedents, authorities,

—But take them, from a heart that yearns to give!

Find out their love,—I could not; find their fear,—

158 *MS-1865 This*   159 *MS-1849* Stay—   165 *MS,1844* season gave the
167 *1863* me!   168 *MS* eyesore   174 *MS,1844* But I do thank you—had
1849 you—had   175 *MS,1844* to the last   176 *MS,1844* Till losing the poor
relic which even yet   177 *MS,1844* insect life and *1863* food.   180 *MS,1844*
The Pope's choice and the Emperor's, and the Kings'—

172 *with prayer's sole breath*: only with the breath of those who have been praying.
182 *rescripts*: Johnson defines 'rescript' as 'Edict of an emperour.'

I would not; find their like,—I never shall,   185
Among the flowers!   [*Taking off her coronet.*
                    Colombe of Ravestein
Thanks God she is no longer Duchess here!
    Valence [*advancing to* GUIBERT].
Sir Guibert, knight, they call you—this of mine
Is the first step I ever set at court.
You dared make me your instrument, I find;   190
For that, so sure as you and I are men,
We reckon to the utmost presently:
But as you are a courtier and I none,
Your knowledge may instruct me. I, already,
Have too far outraged, by my ignorance   195
Of courtier-ways, this lady, to proceed
A second step and risk addressing her:
—I am degraded—you, let me address!
Out of her presence, all is plain enough
What I shall do—but in her presence, too,   200
Surely there's something proper to be done.
[*To the others.*] You, gentles, tell me if I guess aright—
May I not strike this man to earth?
    The Courtiers [*as* GUIBERT *springs forward, withholding him*].
                    Let go!
—The clothiers' spokesman, Guibert? Grace a churl?
    The Duchess [*to* VALENCE]. Oh, be acquainted with your
                party, sir!   205
He's of the oldest lineage Juliers boasts;

---

185 *MS,1844* never will   186 *MS,1844* flowers.   197 *MS–1863* her
*198 (reading of *1849–68*) *MS,1844* you let *1888,1889* you (space) let   201 *MS–
1863* done!

189 *set*: took. Obsolete, as OED points out: 'Set', verb, 19d.
    192 *reckon*: settle accounts, no doubt by a duel.
        to the utmost: i.e. *à outrance.*
    195 *outraged*: stressed on the first syllable, as in Johnson.
    204 —*The clothiers' spokesman*: cf. 154 above.
        Grace: by seeming to treat him as an equal.
    205 *party*: 'An opponent, an antagonist. *Obs.*': OED, which has no example after the six-
teenth century.

A lion crests him for a cognizance;
"Scorning to waver"—that's his 'scutcheon's word;
His office with the new Duke—probably
The same in honour as with me; or more,   210
By so much as this gallant turn deserves.
He's now, I dare say, of a thousand times
The rank and influence that remain with her
Whose part you take! So, lest for taking it
You suffer . . .

    Valence.   I may strike him then to earth?   215
    Guibert [*falling on his knee*].
Great and dear lady, pardon me! Hear once!
Believe me and be merciful—be just!
I could not bring myself to give that paper
Without a keener pang than I dared meet
—And so felt Clugnet here, and Maufroy here   220
—No one dared meet it. Protestation's cheap,—
But, if to die for you did any good,
[*To* GAUCELME.] Would I not die, sir? Say your worst of me!
But it does no good, that's the mournful truth.
And since the hint of a resistance, even,   225
Would just precipitate, on you the first,
A speedier ruin—I shall not deny,
Saving myself indubitable pain,
I thought to give you pleasure (who might say?)
By showing that your only subject found   230
To carry the sad notice, was the man
Precisely ignorant of its contents;
A nameless, mere provincial advocate;
One whom 't was like you never saw before,
Never would see again. All has gone wrong;   235

---

*207 {reading of MS–1863,DC,BrU,1889} 1865,1868 cognisance 1888 cognizance
211 MS–1849 deserves; 1863,1865 deserves: 224 MS,1844 truth:
229 MS,1844 to get you pleasure, who might say?   230 MS,1844 In that your only
subject we could find

   207 *crests him*: serves as his crest. A 'cognizance' was 'A badge, by which any one is
known': Johnson.
   208 *his 'scutcheon's word*: his motto.

But I meant right, God knows, and you, I trust!

   The Duchess. A nameless advocate, this gentleman?

—(I pardon you, Sir Guibert!)

   Guibert [*rising, to* VALENCE]. Sir, and you?

   Valence. —Rejoice that you are lightened of a load.

Now, you have only me to reckon with.   240

   The Duchess. One I have never seen, much less obliged?

   Valence. Dare I speak, lady?

   The Duchess.   Dare you! Heard you not

I rule no longer?

   Valence.   Lady, if your rule

Were based alone on such a ground as these

                      [*Pointing to the* Courtiers.

Could furnish you,—abjure it! They have hidden   245

A source of true dominion from your sight.

   The Duchess. You hear them—no such source is left . . .

   Valence.   Hear Cleves!

Whose haggard craftsmen rose to starve this day,

Starve now, and will lie down at night to starve,

Sure of a like to-morrow—but as sure   250

Of a most unlike morrow-after-that,

Since end things must, end howsoe'er things may.

What curbs the brute-force instinct in its hour?

What makes—instead of rising, all as one,

And teaching fingers, so expert to wield   255

Their tool, the broadsword's play or carbine's trick,

—What makes that there's an easier help, they think,

For you, whose name so few of them can spell,

---

240 *MS-1865* with!   248 *MS,1844* rose this day to starve,   249 *MS,1844*
Are starving now, and will lie down at night   253 (no equivalent in *MS,1844*)
255-6 *MS* (so . . . . tool) *1844* †[so . . . . tool]†   258 *MS,1844* And you,

    251 *morrow-after-that*: apparently a nonce-word.

    252 *end things must*: proverbial. Cf. Tilley, E 120.

    254 *What makes*: what brings it about that? OED, 'Make', verb, 52, described as obsolete
or archaic.

    256 *carbine's trick*: Johnson defines 'carbine' as 'A small sort of fire-arm, shorter than a
fusil, . . . a kind of medium between the pistol and the musket, having its barrel two feet
and a half long.'

Whose face scarce one in every hundred saw,—
You simply have to understand their wrongs,   260
And wrongs will vanish—so, still trades are plied,
And swords lie rusting, and myself stand here?
There is a vision in the heart of each
Of justice, mercy, wisdom, tenderness
To wrong and pain, and knowledge of its cure: 265
And these embodied in a woman's form
That best transmits them, pure as first received,
From God above her, to mankind below.
Will you derive your rule from such a ground,
Or rather hold it by the suffrage, say,   270
Of this man—this—and this?
    The Duchess [*after a pause*]. You come from Cleves:
How many are at Cleves of such a mind?
    Valence [*from his paper*]. "We, all the manufacturers of
      Cleves—"
    The Duchess. Or stay, sir—lest I seem too covetous—
Are you my subject? such as you describe,   275
Am I to you, though to no other man?
    Valence [*from his paper*].
—"Valence, ordained your Advocate at Cleves"—
    The Duchess [*replacing the coronet*].
Then I remain Cleves' Duchess! Take you note,
While Cleves but yields one subject of this stamp,
I stand her lady till she waves me off!   280
For her sake, all the Prince claims I withhold;
Laugh at each menace; and, his power defying,
Return his missive with its due contempt!
                      [*Casting it away.*
    Guibert [*picking it up*].—Which to the Prince I will deliver,
      lady,

---

259 *MS,1844* one for every   260 *MS,1844* That you have simply to receive their
wrongs,   263–8 (no equivalent in *MS,1844*)   264 *1849, 1863* wisdom;
271 *MS,1844* Of this—and this—   *1863–8* Cleves.   281 *MS* withold,
282 *MS* menace,

    273 *manufacturers*: workmen, artificers.
    280 *stand*: stand firm as.

(Note it down, Gaucelme)—with your message too! 285
 The Duchess. I think the office is a subject's, sir!
—Either . . . . how style you him?—my special guarder
The Marshal's—for who knows but violence
May follow the delivery?—Or, perhaps,
My Chancellor's—for law may be to urge 290
On its receipt!—Or, even my Chamberlain's—
For I may violate established form!
[*To* VALENCE.] Sir,—for the half-hour till this service ends,
Will you become all these to me?
 Valence [falling on his knee]   My liege!
 The Duchess. Give me!
       [*The* Courtiers *present their badges of office.*
   [*Putting them by.*] Whatever was their virtue once, 295
They need new consecration.
    [*Raising* Valence.] Are you mine?
I will be Duchess yet!   [*She retires.*
 The Courtiers.   Our Duchess yet!
A glorious lady! Worthy love and dread!
I'll stand by her,—And I, whate'er betide!
 Guibert [to VALENCE]. Well done, well done, sir! I care not
  who knows, 300
You have done nobly and I envy you—
Tho' I am but unfairly used, I think:
For when one gets a place like this I hold,
One gets too the remark that its mere wages,
The pay and the preferment, make our prize. 305
Talk about zeal and faith apart from these,
We're laughed at—much would zeal and faith subsist
Without these also! Yet, let these be stopped,
Our wages discontinue,—then, indeed,
Our zeal and faith, (we hear on every side,) 310
Are not released—having been pledged away

---

285 *1844–68* †[Note . . . .   Gaucelme]†   289 *MS–1865*   delivery!
296 *MS,1844* There needs new   *MS–1863* consecration!   297 s.d. *MS,1844*
†[*Exit.*   309 {no equivalent in *MS,1844*}   310 *MS–1849* we . . . . side,

 287 *guarder*: as in *Sordello*, vi. 401.

I wonder, for what zeal and faith in turn?
Hard money purchased me my place! No, no—
I'm right, sir—but your wrong is better still,
If I had time and skill to argue it.   315
Therefore, I say, I'll serve you, how you please—
If you like,—fight you, as you seem to wish—
(The kinder of me that, in sober truth,
I never dreamed I did you any harm) . . .
    Gaucelme. —Or, kinder still, you'll introduce, no doubt,   320
His merits to the Prince who's just at hand,
And let no hint drop he's made Chancellor
And Chamberlain and Heaven knows what beside!
    Clugnet [*to* VALENCE].
You stare, young sir, and threaten! Let me say,
That at your age, when first I came to court,   325
I was not much above a gentleman;
While now . . .
    Valence.   —You are Head-Lackey? With your office
I have not yet been graced, sir!
    Other Courtiers [*to* CLUGNET]. Let him talk!
Fidelity, disinterestedness,
Excuse so much! Men claim my worship ever   330
Who staunchly and steadfastly . . .

                    Enter ADOLF.

Adolf.   The Prince arrives.
Courtiers. Ha? How?
Adolf.   He leaves his guard a stage behind
At Aix, and enters almost by himself.
    1*st Courtier.* The Prince! This foolish business puts all out.
    2*nd Courtier.* Let Gaucelme speak first!
    3*rd Courtier.*   Better I began   335

312 *MS-1865* wonder with what   313 *MS,1844* 'Twas money   326 *MS*
gentleman,   328 *1868* talk   330 *MS-1863* Men claimed my
331 *MS-1849* Who, stanch and   *MS-1863* arrives!   334 *MS-1865* out!

    331 *stanch* (*MS-1849*): Johnson's spelling.
    332 *a stage*: in Johnson's fourth sense: 'A place in which rest is taken on a journey; as
much of a journey as is performed without intermission.'

About the state of Juliers: should one say
All's prosperous and inviting him?
    4th Courtier.   —Or rather,
All's prostrate and imploring him?
    5th Courtier.   That's best.
Where's the Cleves' paper, by the way?
    4th Courtier [*to* VALENCE].   Sir—sir—
If you'll but lend that paper—trust it me,   340
I'll warrant . . .
    5th Courtier. Softly, sir—the Marshal's duty!
    Clugnet. Has not the Chamberlain a hearing first
By virtue of his patent?
    Gaucelme.   Patents?—Duties?
All that, my masters, must begin again!
One word composes the whole controversy: 345
We're simply now—the Prince's!
    The Others.   Ay—the Prince's!

             Enter SABYNE.

    Sabyne. Adolf! Bid . . . Oh, no time for ceremony!
Where's whom our lady calls her only subject?
She needs him. Who is here the Duchess's?
    Valence [*starting from his reverie*]
Most gratefully I follow to her feet.   350

---

*338 [reading of *MS–1868*,DC,BrU] *1888,1889* All s   *MS–1865* him! . . . . best! *1889*
best   340 *MS–1865* but give that   349 *MS–1865* him!   *MS*
Duchesses?   350 *MS–1865* feet!   s.d. *MS,1844* †[*Exit.*

  343 *patent* : 'A writ conferring some exclusive right or privilege': Johnson.

ACT III.

SCENE.—*The Vestibule.*

Enter PRINCE BERTHOLD *and* MELCHIOR.

Berthold. A thriving little burgh this Juliers looks.
[*Half-apart.*] Keep Juliers, and as good you kept Cologne:
Better try Aix, though!—
   Melchior.   Please 't your Highness speak?
   Berthold [*as before*]. Aix, Cologne, Frankfort,—Milan;—
   Rome!—
   Melchior. The Grave.
More weary seems your Highness, I remark,   5
Than sundry conquerors whose path I've watched
Through fire and blood to any prize they gain.
I could well wish you, for your proper sake,
Had met some shade of opposition here
—Found a blunt seneschal refuse unlock,   10
Or a scared usher lead your steps astray.
You must not look for next achievement's palm
So easily: this will hurt your conquering.
   Berthold. My next? Ay, as you say, my next and next!
Well, I am tired, that's truth, and moody too,   15

---

10 MS seneschal   13 MS-1849 So easy: this   MS-1865 conquering!

   3 *Aix*: in the words of the Ohio editor, this sequence constitutes a 'Political road map for becoming Holy Roman Emperor'. Aix was important for its associations with Charlemagne, as well as its geographical position: Cologne, 'the focal point of Rhenish culture', had been raised to an archdiocese by Charlemagne and was a city of great political importance: Frankfurt was the place where the Emperors had been crowned, from 1562. The crown of Italy would be conferred at Milan (here pronounced in the English way, with the stress on the first syllable).

   8 *proper*: own.

   10 *seneschal*: 'One who had in great houses the care of feasts or domestick ceremonies': Johnson.

This quiet entrance-morning: listen why!
Our little burgh, now, Juliers—'t is indeed
One link, however insignificant,
Of the great chain by which I reach my hope,
—A link I must secure; but otherwise,   20
You'd wonder I esteem it worth my grasp.
Just see what life is, with its shifts and turns!
It happens now—this very nook—to be
A place that once . . . not a long while since, neither—
When I lived an ambiguous hanger-on   25
Of foreign courts, and bore my claims about,
Discarded by one kinsman, and the other
A poor priest merely,—then, I say, this place
Shone my ambition's object; to be Duke—
Seemed then, what to be Emperor seems now.   30
My rights were far from judged as plain and sure
In those days as of late, I promise you:
And 't was my day-dream, Lady Colombe here
Might e'en compound the matter, pity me,
Be struck, say, with my chivalry and grace   35
(I was a boy!)—bestow her hand at length,
And make me Duke, in her right if not mine.
Here am I, Duke confessed, at Juliers now.
Hearken: if ever I be Emperor,
Remind me what I felt and said to-day!   40
    Melchior. All this consoles a bookish man like me.
—And so will weariness cling to you. Wrong,
Wrong! Had you sought the lady's court yourself,—
Faced the redoubtables composing it,
Flattered this, threatened that man, bribed the other,—   45
Pleaded by writ and word and deed, your cause,—

16 MS why.   21 *MS,1844,1863,1865* I esteemed it *1849* I esteem'd it
*24 (reading of *MS-1868*) *1888,1889* once . .   *MS-1863* but a short while
31 *MS,1844* from being judged apparent *1849-68* from being judged as plain
37 *MS* me [Duke] in   38 *MS-1863* now! *1865* now   40 *MS,1844* Will you
remind me this, I feel and say?   41 *MS-1863* me!   42 *MS-1865* you!
44 (no equivalent in *MS,1844*)   45 *MS,1844* that, and bribed

   44 *the redoubtables*: OED has no other example of the word as a noun.

Conquered a footing inch by painful inch,—
And, after long years' struggle, pounced at last
On her for prize,—the right life had been lived,
And justice done to divers faculties   50
Shut in that brow. Yourself were visible
As you stood victor, then; whom now—(your pardon!)
I am forced narrowly to search and see,
So are you hid by helps—this Pope, your uncle—
Your cousin, the other King! You are a mind,—   55
They, body: too much of mere legs-and-arms
Obstructs the mind so! Match these with their like:
Match mind with mind!
    Berthold.   And where's your mind to match?
They show me legs-and-arms to cope withal!
I'd subjugate this city—where's its mind?   60
                  [*The* Courtiers *enter slowly.*
    Melchior. Got out of sight when you came troops and all!
And in its stead, here greets you flesh-and-blood:
A smug œconomy of both, this first!
               [*As* CLUGNET *bows obsequiously.*
Well done, gout, all considered!—I may go?
    Berthold. Help me receive them!
    Melchior.   Oh, they just will say   65
What yesterday at Aix their fellows said—
At Treves, the day before! Sir Prince, my friend,
Why do you let your life slip thus?—Meantime,
I have my little Juliers to achieve—
The understanding this tough Platonist,   70

47 *MS,1844* Conquered yourself a footing inch by inch—   51 *MS,1844* Safe in that
brow: 52 *MS,1844* victor,—you, whom *1849,1863* then!   53 *MS,1844* Nar-
rowly am I forced to   54 *MS,1844* So by your uncle are you hid, this Pope,
58 *MS,1844* But, mind   *66 (reading of DC,BrU,1889) MS,1844* said, *1849-68*
said,— *1888* said   68 *1844,1849* Mean time,

  67 *Treves*: Trèves (Trier in German) ancient city on the right bank of the Moselle, about
69 miles SW of Coblenz.   69 *my little Juliers*: i.e. my little task.
  70 *this tough Platonist*: according to the *Biographie universelle*, Amelius, first a disciple of
Plato, became a disciple of Plotinus. Eusebius and others give an account of a passage in
which Amelius cites the opening of the Gospel of St John in confirmation of the teaching
of Plato on the divine nature.

Your holy uncle disinterred, Amelius:
Lend me a company of horse and foot,
To help me through his tractate—gain my Duchy!
    Berthold. And Empire, after that is gained, will be—?
    Melchior. To help me through your uncle's comment,
        Prince!   *[Goes.*
    Berthold. Ah? Well: he o'er-refines—the scholar's fault!   76
How do I let my life slip? Say, this life,
I lead now, differs from the common life
Of other men in mere degree, not kind,
Of joys and griefs,—still there is such degree—   80
Mere largeness in a life is something, sure,—
Enough to care about and struggle for,
In this world: for this world, the size of things;
The sort of things, for that to come, no doubt.
A great is better than a little aim: 85
And when I wooed Priscilla's rosy mouth
And failed so, under that grey convent-wall,
Was I more happy than I should be now
            [By this time, the Courtiers *are ranged before him.*
If failing of my Empire? Not a whit.
—Here comes the mind, it once had tasked me sore   90
To baffle, but for my advantages!
All's best as 't is: these scholars talk and talk.
                                [Seats himself.

    The Courtiers. Welcome our Prince to Juliers!—to his
        heritage!
Our dutifullest service proffer we!
    Clugnet. I, please your Highness, having exercised   95

71 *1849* uncle disinters, Amelius—   75 s.d. *MS,1844* †[*Exit.*   76 *MS–*
1865 Well!   *80 {reading of *1849–68*} *1888,1889* degree *MS,1844* and sorrows,—
such degree there is—   81 {no equivalent in *MS,1844*}   84 *MS–1865*
doubt!   87 *1844* convent wall,   89 *MS–1865* whit!   91 *MS,1844*
baffle, let advantages alone!   92 *MS–1863* and talk!   95 *MS,1844* please't
your   *MS* your Higness, having

    71 *Your holy uncle*: cf. v. 13. It may be suggested that Berthold is an illegitimate son of the
Pope.
    73 *tractate*: small book (here a pun).
    75 *comment*: commentary (an imaginary work).

The function of Grand Chamberlain at court,
With much acceptance, as men testify . . .
    Berthold. I cannot greatly thank you, gentlemen!
The Pope declares my claim to the Duchy founded
On strictest justice—you concede it, therefore,   100
I do not wonder: and the kings my friends
Protest they mean to see such claim enforced,—
You easily may offer to assist.
But there's a slight discretionary power
To serve me in the matter, you've had long,   105
Though late you use it. This is well to say—
But could you not have said it months ago?
I'm not denied my own Duke's truncheon, true—
'T is flung me—I stoop down, and from the ground
Pick it, with all you placid standers-by: 110
And now I have it, gems and mire at once,
Grace go with it to my soiled hands, you say!
    Guibert. (By Paul, the advocate our doughty friend
Cuts the best figure!)
    Gaucelme.   If our ignorance
May have offended, sure our loyalty . . .   115
    Berthold. Loyalty? Yours? Oh—of yourselves you speak!
I mean the Duchess all this time, I hope!
And since I have been forced repeat my claims
As if they never had been urged before,
As I began, so must I end, it seems.   120
The formal answer to the grave demand!
What says the lady?
    Courtiers [*one to another*].
      1*st Courtier.*   Marshal!
      2*nd Courtier.*   Orator!
    Guibert. A variation of our mistress' way!

100 *MS-1868* justice; if you   102 *MS-1868* Protesting they will see
103 *MS* assist us: *1844-68* assist us.   110 *MS* standers by—   117 *1849-68*
—*I* mean   119 *MS-1868* been made before,   120 *MS,1844* so probably I
end.   121 *MS-1849* demand—

108 *truncheon* : cf. *Pippa Passes*, II. 51 n.

Wipe off his boots' dust, Clugnet!—that, he waits!

  1st Courtier. Your place!

  2nd Courtier.   Just now it was your own!

  Guibert.   The devil's!   125

  Berthold [*to* GUIBERT]. Come forward, friend—you with

    the paper, there!

Is Juliers the first city I've obtained?

By this time, I may boast proficiency

In each decorum of the circumstance.

Give it me as she gave it—the petition,   130

Demand, you style it! What's required, in brief?

What title's reservation, appanage's

Allowance? I heard all at Treves, last week.

  Gaucelme [*to* GUIBERT]. "Give it him as she gave it"!

  Guibert.   And why not?

[*To* BERTHOLD.] The lady crushed your summons thus

    together,   135

And bade me, with the very greatest scorn

So fair a frame could hold, inform you . . .

  Courtiers.   Stop—

Idiot!

  Guibert. —Inform you she denied your claim,

Defied yourself! (I tread upon his heel,

The blustering advocate!)

  Berthold.   By heaven and earth!   140

Dare you jest, sir?

  Guibert.   Did they at Treves, last week?

  Berthold [*starting up*]. Why then, I look much bolder than I

    knew,

And you prove better actors than I thought:

---

124 *1849* Clugnet?   129 *MS–1865* circumstance!   130 *MS* petition . .
131 *MS–1865* (Demand . . . . it)—what's *1868* it—   132 *MS* apanage's
133 *MS–1865* week!   *134 {editors' emendation. All versions: it!"}
141 *MS,1844* Did he at

132–3 *appanage's / Allowance* : Johnson defines 'appanage' as 'Lands set apart by princes
for the maintenance of their younger children.'

139 *I tread upon his heel* : cf. *Hamlet*, v. i. 136–8: 'the toe of the peasant comes so near the
heel of the courtier he galls his kibe'.

Since, as I live, I took you as you entered
For just so many dearest friends of mine,   145
Fled from the sinking to the rising power
—The sneaking'st crew, in short, I e'er despised!
Whereas, I am alone here for the moment,
With every soldier left behind at Aix!
Silence? That means the worst? I thought as much!   150
What follows next then?
    Courtiers.   Gracious Prince, he raves!
    Guibert. He asked the truth and why not get the truth?
    Berthold. Am I a prisoner? Speak, will somebody?
—But why stand paltering with imbeciles?
Let me see her, or . . .
    Guibert.   Her, without her leave,   155
Shall no one see: she's Duchess yet!
    Courtiers [*footsteps without, as they are disputing*].
                      Good chance!
She's here—the Lady Colombe's self!
    Berthold.   'T is well!
[*Aside.*] Array a handful thus against my world?
Not ill done, truly! Were not this a mind
To match one's mind with? Colombe! Let us wait!   160
I failed so, under that grey convent wall!
She comes.
    Guibert. The Duchess! Strangers, range yourselves!
    [*As the* DUCHESS *enters in conversation with* VALENCE, BERTHOLD
        and the Courtiers *fall back a little.*
    The Duchess. Presagefully it beats, presagefully,
My heart: the right is Berthold's and not mine.
    Valence. Grant that he has the right, dare I mistrust   165
Your power to acquiesce so patiently
As you believe, in such a dream-like change

148 *MS,1844* moment! *1849* moment—   150 *MS-1863* worst—
152 *MS,1844* not have the   161 *MS-1865* convent-wall!   162 *MS-1865*
comes!   164 *MS-1865* mine!

  154 *paltering*: trifling.
  161 *I failed so*: cf. 87, above.
  163 *Presagefully*: OED has no other example of the adverb.

Of fortune—change abrupt, profound, complete?
   The Duchess. Ah, the first bitterness is over now!
Bitter I may have felt it to confront   170
The truth, and ascertain those natures' value
I had so counted on; that was a pang:
But I did bear it, and the worst is over.
Let the Prince take them!
   Valence.   And take Juliers too?
—Your people without crosses, wands and chains—   175
Only with hearts?
   The Duchess.   There I feel guilty, sir!
I cannot give up what I never had:
For I ruled these, not them—these stood between.
Shall I confess, sir? I have heard by stealth
Of Berthold from the first; more news and more: 180
Closer and closer swam the thundercloud,
But I was safely housed with these, I knew.
At times when to the casement I would turn,
At a bird's passage or a flower-trail's play,
I caught the storm's red glimpses on its edge—   185
Yet I was sure some one of all these friends
Would interpose: I followed the bird's flight
Or plucked the flower: some one would interpose!
   Valence. Not one thought on the People—and Cleves
     there!
   The Duchess. Now, sadly conscious my real sway was
     missed,   190
Its shadow goes without so much regret:
Else could I not again thus calmly bid you,
Answer Prince Berthold!
   Valence.   Then you acquiesce?
   The Duchess. Remember over whom it was I ruled!

---

173 *MS–1863* over: 178 *MS–1865* For these I ruled, not   181 *1844–65*
thunder-cloud, *1868* thunder cloud,   182 *MS–1868* knew!   186 *MS,1844*
of those about me   189 *1863* there   190 *MS– 1863* So, sadly

175 *crosses, wands and chains* : symbols of authority, ecclesiastical and civil.
184 *flower-trail* : not in OED.

Guibert [*stepping forward*]. Prince Berthold, yonder, craves
    an audience, lady!   195
The Duchess [*to* VALENCE]. I only have to turn, and I shall
    face
Prince Berthold! Oh, my very heart is sick!
It is the daughter of a line of Dukes
This scornful insolent adventurer
Will bid depart from my dead father's halls!   200
I shall not answer him—dispute with him—
But, as he bids, depart! Prevent it, sir!
Sir—but a mere day's respite! Urge for me
—What I shall call to mind I should have urged
When time's gone by: 't will all be mine, you urge!   205
A day—an hour—that I myself may lay
My rule down! 'T is too sudden—must not be!
The world's to hear of it! Once done—for ever!
How will it read, sir? How be sung about?
Prevent it!
    Berthold [*approaching*]. Your frank indignation, lady,   210
Cannot escape me. Overbold I seem;
But somewhat should be pardoned my surprise
At this reception,—this defiance, rather.
And if, for their and your sake, I rejoice
Your virtues could inspire a trusty few   215
To make such gallant stand in your behalf,
I cannot but be sorry, for my own,
Your friends should force me to retrace my steps:
Since I no longer am permitted speak
After the pleasant peaceful course prescribed   220
No less by courtesy than relationship—
Which I remember, if you once forgot.
But never must attack pass unrepelled.

196 MS I have to only turn   203 MS,1844 a day's sole respite!   211 MS-
1865 me!   213 {no equivalent in MS,1844}   214 MS and [your] sakes, I
1844-68 your sakes, I   218 {no equivalent in MS,1844} 1849-68 steps,
220 {no equivalent in MS,1844}   221 MS,1844 less of courtesy
222 MS,1844 —If you forgot once, I remember now! 1849-65 Which, if you once forgot, I
still remember: 223 MS,1844 But, unrepelled, attack must never pass.

Suffer that, through you, I demand of these,
Who controverts my claim to Juliers?
    The Duchess.   —Me   225
You say, you do not speak to—
    Berthold.   Of your subjects
I ask, then: whom do you accredit? Where
Stand those should answer?
    Valence [*advancing*].   The lady is alone.
    Berthold. Alone, and thus? So weak and yet so bold?
    Valence. I said she was alone—
    Berthold.   And weak, I said.   230
    Valence. When is man strong until he feels alone?
It was some lonely strength at first, be sure,
Created organs, such as those you seek,
By which to give its varied purpose shape:
And, naming the selected ministrants,   235
Took sword, and shield, and sceptre,—each, a man!
That strength performed its work and passed its way:
You see our lady: there, the old shapes stand!
—A Marshal, Chamberlain, and Chancellor—
"Be helped their way, into their death put life   240
"And find advantage!"—so you counsel us.
But let strength feel alone, seek help itself,—
And, as the inland-hatched sea-creature hunts
The sea's breast out,—as, littered 'mid the waves
The desert-brute makes for the desert's joy,   245
So turns our lady to her true resource,
Passing o'er hollow fictions, worn-out types,

---

224 *MS,1844* Suffer, through you, your subjects I demand,   228 *MS–1868* alone!
240 *MS,1844* Be   241 *MS,1844* advantage,— .... us!   246–7 (no equivalent
in *MS,1844*)

    231 *When is man strong*: Elizabeth Barrett quoted this line (from memory) in a letter to
Browning, calling it '[his] own great line': Kintner, i. 263. Procter wondered whether the
speech might not be 'too long, considering the predicament of the speaker?' 'It begins well',
he continued, '& with a truth that I do not remember to have seen in verse before': *Check-
list*, 44:113.
    236 *Took sword, and shield, and sceptre,—each, a man!*: cf. II. 287 ff.
    243 *inland-hatched*: a nonce-word.
    247 *types*: symbols.

—And I am first her instinct fastens on.
And prompt I say, as clear as heart can speak,
The People will not have you; nor shall have!   250
It is not merely I shall go bring Cleves
And fight you to the last,—though that does much,
And men and children,—ay, and women too,
Fighting for home, are rather to be feared
Than mercenaries fighting for their pay—   255
But, say you beat us, since such things have been,
And, where this Juliers laughed, you set your foot
Upon a steaming bloody plash—what then?
Stand you the more our lord that there you stand?
Lord it o'er troops whose force you concentrate,   260
A pillared flame whereto all ardours tend—
Lord it 'mid priests whose schemes you amplify,
A cloud of smoke 'neath which all shadows brood—
But never, in this gentle spot of earth,
Can you become our Colombe, our play-queen,   265
For whom, to furnish lilies for her hair,
We'd pour our veins forth to enrich the soil.
—Our conqueror? Yes!—Our despot? Yes!—Our Duke?
Know yourself, know us!
    Berthold [*who has been in thought*].
                    Know your lady, also!
[*Very deferentially.*]—To whom I needs must exculpate myself   270
For having made a rash demand, at least.
Wherefore to you, sir, who appear to be
Her chief adviser, I submit my claims,   [*Giving papers.*
But, this step taken, take no further step,

248 *MS–1863* —So, I   *MS,1844* on; *1849–65* on!   249 *MS–1849* say so clear
258 *1849* a streaming bloody   259 *MS,1844* Lord as there   261 *MS* ardors
262 *MS,1844* it 'mongst priests   266 *MS,1844* Whom we, to   267 *MS,1844*
Would pour   *MS–1868* soil!   271 *MS–1865* From having   273 *MS* The
chief-adviser, *1844* The chief

   258 *plash* : as in *A Blot*, iii. ii. 37, and 'Childe Roland', 131.
   260 *you concentrate* : in yourself.
   261 *A pillared flame* : see Exod. 13:21–2, Numb. 14:14.
      ardours : ardent spirits, in addition to the literal sense. Cf. *Paradise Lost*, v. 249.
   265 *our play-queen* : see I. 84 ff.

Until the Duchess shall pronounce their worth.   275
Here be our meeting-place; at night, its time:
Till when I humbly take the lady's leave!
    [*He withdraws. As the* DUCHESS *turns to* VALENCE, *the* Courtiers
      interchange glances and come forward a little.
    1*st Courtier.* So, this was their device!
    2*nd Courtier.*   No bad device!
    3*rd Courtier.* You'd say they love each other, Guibert's
      friend
From Cleves, and she, the Duchess!
    4*th Courtier.*   .   —And moreover,   280
That all Prince Berthold comes for, is to help
Their loves!
    5*th Courtier.* Pray, Guibert, what is next to do?
    Guibert [*advancing*]. I laid my office at the Duchess' foot—
    Others. And I—and I—and I!
    The Duchess.   I took them, sirs.
    Guibert [*apart to* VALENCE]. And now, sir, I am simple
      knight again—   285
Guibert, of the great ancient house, as yet
That never bore affront; whate'er your birth,—
As things stand now, I recognize yourself
(If you'll accept experience of some date)
As like to be the leading man o' the time,   290
Therefore as much above me now, as I
Seemed above you this morning. Then, I offered
To fight you: will you be as generous
And now fight me?
    Valence.   Ask when my life is mine!
    Guibert. ('T is hers now!)
    Clugnet [*apart to* VALENCE, *as* GUIBERT *turns from him*].
               You, sir, have insulted me   295

276 *MS,1844* placc,   277 s.d. *MS,1844* †[*Exit.*   279 *MS,1844* They love
each other, Guibert's friend and she!   280-1 {no equivalent in *MS,1844*}
282 *MS,1844* 4*th Court.* Plainly! 5*th Court.* Pray,   283 *MS,1844* I lay . . . . foot!
284 *MS-1865* sirs!   285 *MS,1844* †[*To* VALENCE.]† . . . . sir, simple knight again am
I—   291 *MS,1844* And so as   295 s.d. *MS,1844* †[*Advancing to* VALENCE.]†
You,

Grossly,—will grant me, too, the selfsame favour
You've granted him, just now, I make no question?
    Valence. I promise you, as him, sir.
    Clugnet.   Do you so?
Handsomely said! I hold you to it, sir.
You'll get me reinstated in my office   300
As you will Guibert!
    The Duchess.   I would be alone!
               [*They begin to retire slowly; as* VALENCE *is about to follow*—
Alone, sir—only with my heart: you stay!
    Gaucelme. You hear that? Ah, light breaks upon me!
      Cleves—
It was at Cleves some man harangued us all—
With great effect,—so those who listened said,   305
My thoughts being busy elsewhere: was this he?
Guibert,—your strange, disinterested man!
Your uncorrupted, if uncourtly friend!
The modest worth you mean to patronize!
He cares about no Duchesses, not he—   -   310
His sole concern is with the wrongs of Cleves!
What, Guibert? What, it breaks on you at last?
    Guibert. Would this hall's floor were a mine's roof! I'd
      back
And in her very face . . .
    Gaucelme.   Apply the match
That fired the train,—and where would you be, pray?   315
    Guibert. With him!
    Gaucelme.   Stand, rather, safe outside with me!
The mine's charged: shall I furnish you the match
And place you properly? To the antechamber!
    Guibert. Can you?
    Gaucelme.   Try me! Your friend's in fortune!

---

296 *MS* favor   298 *MS–1865* sir!   299 *MS–1865* sir!   302 *1863* stay
303–12 {no equivalent in *MS,1844*}   311 *1849–65* sole contest is
313 *MS,1844* roof!–I'll back   315 *MS,1844* That fires the . . . . where will you
318 *1844,1849* ante-chamber

315 *the train* : see above, *King Victor*, II. 5 n.

Guibert.   Quick—

To the antechamber! He is pale with bliss!   320

Gaucelme. No wonder! Mark her eyes!

Guibert.   To the antechamber!

                                  [*The* Courtiers *retire.*

The Duchess. Sir, could you know all you have done for
    me

You were content! You spoke, and I am saved.

Valence. Be not too sanguine, lady! Ere you dream,

That transient flush of generosity   325

Fades off, perchance. The man, beside, is gone,—

Him we might bend; but see, the papers here—

Inalterably his requirement stays,

And cold hard words have we to deal with now.

In that large eye there seemed a latent pride,   330

To self-denial not incompetent,

But very like to hold itself dispensed

From such a grace: however, let us hope!

He is a noble spirit in noble form.

I wish he less had bent that brow to smile   335

As with the fancy how he could subject

Himself upon occasion to—himself!

From rudeness, violence, you rest secure;

But do not think your Duchy rescued yet!

   The Duchess. You,—who have opened a new world to me,   340

Will never take the faded language up

Of that I leave? My Duchy—keeping it,

Or losing it—is that my sole world now?

   Valence. Ill have I spoken if you thence despise

Juliers; although the lowest, on true grounds,   345

Be worth more than the highest rule, on false:

---

320 *1844,1849* ante-chamber   321 *1844,1849* ante-chamber   s.d. *MS,1844*
†[*Exeunt* Courtiers.   323 *MS–1868* saved!   324 *MS,1844* Ere now, even,
326 *MS–1868* perchance!   *MS,1844* man and mood are gone—   327 [no equiva-
lent in *MS,1844*] *1849, 1863* Whom we   330 *MS,1844* there was a   334 *MS–
1849* form!

   331 *incompetent* : incapable.

Aspire to rule, on the true grounds!
   The Duchess.   Nay, hear—
False, I will never—rash, I would not be!
This is indeed my birthday—soul and body,
Its hours have done on me the work of years.   350
You hold the requisition: ponder it!
If I have right, my duty's plain: if he—
Say so, nor ever change a tone of voice!
At night you meet the Prince; meet me at eve!
Till when, farewell! This discomposes you?   355
Believe in your own nature, and its force
Of renovating mine! I take my stand
Only as under me the earth is firm:
So, prove the first step stable, all will prove.
That first, I choose: [*Laying her hand on his.*]—the next to take,
    choose you!   [*She withdraws.*
    Valence [*after a pause*]. What drew down this on me?—on
    me, dead once,   361
She thus bids live,—since all I hitherto
Thought dead in me, youth's ardours and emprise,
Burst into life before her, as she bids
Who needs them. Whither will this reach, where end?   365
Her hand's print burns on mine . . . Yet she's above—
So very far above me! All's too plain:
I served her when the others sank away,
And she rewards me as such souls reward—
The changed voice, the suffusion of the cheek,   370
The eye's acceptance, the expressive hand,
—Reward, that's little, in her generous thought,
Though all to me . . .
              I cannot so disclaim

347 *MS,1844* to that, on   348 *MS* False will I never   354 *MS,1844* night the
Prince you meet—meet *1849* eve; *1863,1865* eve: 357 *MS-1865* mine.
359 *MS-1849* will be! *1863,1865* prove!   360 s.d. *MS,1844* †[*Exit.*   361 *MS-*
1849 me! On   365 *MS-1865* them!   367 *MS* to[o]   370-1 {no
equivalent in *MS,1844*}   372 *MS,1844* little, that is nought to her,   373 *MS*
me . . . [(with a burst)]

   363 *emprise* : enterprising courage.

Heaven's gift, nor call it other than it is!
She loves me!
[*Looking at the* Prince's *papers*.]—Which love, these, perchance,
    forbid.   375
Can I decide against myself—pronounce
She is the Duchess and no mate for me?
—Cleves, help me! Teach me,—every haggard face,—
To sorrow and endure! I will do right
Whatever be the issue. Help me, Cleves!   380

---

375 *MS,1844* these forbid, perchance! *1849* forbid!   380 s.d. *MS,1844* †[*Exit.*

  375 *She loves me!*: Alma Murray (Mrs Forman), who played Colombe in the Browning
Society production of the play on 19 November 1885, disagreed with Furnivall's view that
'Colombe had at the beginning fallen in love with Valence'. Browning replied to an enquiry
from Furnivall on 1 November 1885: 'Mrs Forman is right . . . Colombe, in the 3d Act at
the close, "does not mean that she loves Valence"—is not even aware that the seeds of what
may grow to Love are already implanted in her by the devotion of Valence—and only
expresses, no more warmly than the occasion requires, her appreciation of his conduct and
thorough trust in what he shall advise': *Trumpeter*, p. 119.

ACT IV.

EVENING.

SCENE.—*An Antechamber.*

Enter the Courtiers.

Maufroy. Now, then, that we may speak—how spring this
  mine?
Gaucelme. Is Guibert ready for its match? He cools!
Not so friend Valence with the Duchess there!
"Stay, Valence! Are not you my better self?"
And her cheek mantled—
  Guibert.   Well, she loves him, sir: 5
And more,—since you will have it I grow cool,—
She's right: he's worth it.
  Gaucelme.   For his deeds to-day?
Say so!
  Guibert. What should I say beside?
  Gaucelme.   Not this—
For friendship's sake leave this for me to say—
That we're the dupes of an egregious cheat!   10
This plain unpractised suitor, who found way
To the Duchess through the merest die's turn-up
A year ago, had seen her and been seen,
Loved and been loved.
  Guibert.   Impossible!
  Gaucelme.   —Nor say,
How sly and exquisite a trick, moreover,   15
Was this which—taking not their stand on facts
Boldly, for that had been endurable,

1844,1849 Ante-chamber.   4 *MS–1849* Valence—   12 *MS* turn up—
16 *MS,1844* not his stand

  5 *mantled*: blushed.
  12 *die's turn-up*: fall of the dice.

But worming on their way by craft, they choose
Resort to, rather,—and which you and we,
Sheep-like, assist them in the playing-off!   20
The Duchess thus parades him as preferred,
Not on the honest ground of preference,
Seeing first, liking more, and there an end—
But as we all had started equally,
And at the close of a fair race he proved   25
The only valiant, sage and loyal man.
Herself, too, with the pretty fits and starts,—
The careless, winning, candid ignorance
Of what the Prince might challenge or forego—
She had a hero in reserve! What risk   30
Ran she? This deferential easy Prince
Who brings his claims for her to ratify
—He's just her puppet for the nonce! You'll see,—
Valence pronounces, as is equitable,
Against him: off goes the confederate: 35
As equitably, Valence takes her hand!
    The Chancellor. You run too fast: her hand, no subject
      takes.
Do not our archives hold her father's will?
That will provides against such accident,
And gives next heir, Prince Berthold, the reversion   40
Of Juliers, which she forfeits, wedding so.
    Gaucelme. I know that, well as you,—but does the Prince?
Knows Berthold, think you, that this plan, he helps,
For Valence's ennoblement,—would end,
If crowned with the success which seems its due,   45
In making him the very thing he plays,
The actual Duke of Juliers? All agree •

18 *MS,1844* worming in his way .... he chose *1849* worming in their   20 *MS,1844*
assist him in   *MS–1868* playing off!   21 *MS,1844* The fruit is, she prefers him to
ourselves,   22 *MS,1844* the simple ground   23 *MS,1844* First seeing ....
and so an   26 *MS* man[!]   27 *MS–1849* And she, too,   28 *MS,1844*
And careless,   32 *MS,1844* That brings   *MS* his claim for   37 *MS–1849*
takes!   39 *MS,1844* Against such accident that will provides,   {*MS* has 'that'
altered from 'the'}   42–8 {no equivalent in *MS,1844*}

That Colombe's title waived or set aside,
He is next heir.

    The Chancellor. Incontrovertibly.

    Gaucelme. Guibert, your match, now, to the train!

    Guibert.   Enough!   50
I'm with you: selfishness is best again.
I thought of turning honest—what a dream!
Let's wake now!

    Gaucelme.   Selfish, friend, you never were:
'T was but a series of revenges taken
On your unselfishness for prospering ill.   55
But now that you're grown wiser, what's our course?

    Guibert. —Wait, I suppose, till Valence weds our lady,
And then, if we must needs revenge ourselves,
Apprise the prince.

    Gaucelme.   —The Prince, ere then dismissed
With thanks for playing his mock part so well?   60
Tell the Prince now, sir! Ay, this very night,
Ere he accepts his dole and goes his way,
Explain how such a marriage makes him Duke,
Then trust his gratitude for the surprise!

    Guibert. —Our lady wedding Valence all the same   65
As if the penalty were undisclosed?
Good! If she loves, she'll not disown her love,
Throw Valence up. I wonder you see that.

    Gaucelme. The shame of it—the suddenness and shame!
Within her, the inclining heart—without,   70
A terrible array of witnesses—
And Valence by, to keep her to her word,
With Berthold's indignation or disgust!

49 *MS,1844* heir? Incontrovertibly!   51 *MS–1865* again!   55 *MS,1844*
Upon unselfishness that prospered ill.   58–9 *MS,1844* And then apprise the
Prince— *Gau.* —Ere then retired?   60 (no equivalent in *MS,1844*)
62a,b *MS,1844* Tell what has been, declare what's like to be, | And really makes him all he
feigned himself;   63 (no equivalent in *MS,1844*)   65–6 (no equivalent in
MS,1844)   66 *1849–65* undisclosed!   67 *MS,1844* Good! I am sure she'll
68 *MS–1849* up—....that!   70–1 (no equivalent in *MS,1844*)   72 *MS,1844*
With Valence there, to *1849* With Valence   73 *MS,1844* And Berthold's own
reproaches or disgust— *1849* And Berthold's....disgust—

We'll try it!—Not that we can venture much.
Her confidence we've lost for ever: Berthold's   75
Is all to gain.
    Guibert.   To-night, then, venture we!
Yet—if lost confidence might be renewed?
    Gaucelme. Never in noble natures! With the base ones,—
Twist off the crab's claw, wait a smarting-while,
And something grows and grows and gets to be   80
A mimic of the lost joint, just so like
As keeps in mind it never, never will
Replace its predecessor! Crabs do that:
But lop the lion's foot—and . . .
    Guibert.   To the prince!
    Gaucelme [*aside*]. And come what will to the lion's foot, I
       pay you,   85
My cat's-paw, as I long have yearned to pay.
[*Aloud.*] Footsteps! Himself! 'T is Valence breaks on us,
Exulting that their scheme succeeds. We'll hence—
And perfect ours! Consult the archives, first—
Then, fortified with knowledge, seek the Hall!   90
    Clugnet [*to* GAUCELME *as they retire*].
You have not smiled so since your father died!

        As they retire, enter VALENCE *with papers.*

    Valence. So must it be! I have examined these
With scarce a palpitating heart—so calm,
Keeping her image almost wholly off,
Setting upon myself determined watch,   95
Repelling to the uttermost his claims:
And the result is—all men would pronounce
And not I, only, the result to be—

74 *MS,1844* much! *1849* much: 75 *MS,1844* ever—his *1849* ever— *1863,1865*
ever.—   76 *MS,1844* Must be to gain! *1849–65* gain!   77 *MS,1844* Yet—may
a lost love never be renewed?   78 *MS* natures: [with the] base *1844* natures:
81 *MS,1844* the joint, and just   86 *MS–1868* pay!   87 *MS–1849* Footsteps
.. ....us!   88 *MS,1844* Waits her to boast their scheme succeeds! *1849* succeeds!
89–90 *MS,1844* ours! To the Archives, and the Hall!   91 s.d. *MS,1844* †[*Exeunt Court-
iers*.| *Enter*   96 *MS–1868* claims,   98 *MS* be

Berthold is heir; she has no shade of right
To the distinction which divided us,   100
But, suffered to rule first, I know not why,
Her rule connived at by those Kings and Popes,
To serve some devil's-purpose,—now 't is gained,
Whate'er it was, the rule expires as well.
—Valence, this rapture . . . selfish can it be?   105
Eject it from your heart, her home!—It stays!
Ah, the brave world that opens on us both!
—Do my poor townsmen so esteem it? Cleves,—
I need not your pale faces! This, reward
For service done to you? Too horrible!   110
I never served you: 't was myself I served—
Nay, served not—rather saved from punishment
Which, had I failed you then, would plague me now.
My life continues yours, and your life, mine.
But if, to take God's gift, I swerve no step—   115
Cleves! If I breathe no prayer for it—if she,

                                                    [*Footsteps without.*

Colombe, that comes now, freely gives herself—
Will Cleves require, that, turning thus to her,
I . . .

                         Enter PRINCE BERTHOLD.

    Pardon, sir! I did not look for you
Till night, i' the Hall; nor have as yet declared   120
My judgment to the lady.
    Berthold.   So I hoped.
    Valence. And yet I scarcely know why that should check
The frank disclosure of it first to you—

101-2 *MS,1844* But, suffered rule first by these Kings and Popes   103 *1844* gain'd,
104 *MS,1844* To serve some devil's-purpose must withdraw!   107 *MS,1844* opens
to us   110 *MS,1844* to them? Too   111 *MS,1844* served them—'twas
MS-1865 served!   113 *MS-1868* now!   116 *MS,1844* Cleves,—if no prayer I
breathe for   *1849-63* if   117 *MS* [Colombe,] that   119 *MS-1865* sir—
MS,1844 I had not looked for   120 *1849-68* in the   121 *MS* Lady[!]
1844,1849 Lady!   122 *MS,1844* I scarce know wherefore that prevents
123 *MS,1844* Disclosing it to you—disclosing even

What her right seems, and what, in consequence,
She will decide on.
  Berthold.   That I need not ask.   125
  Valence. You need not: I have proved the lady's mind:
And, justice being to do, dare act for her.
  Berthold. Doubtless she has a very noble mind.
  Valence. Oh, never fear but she'll in each conjuncture
Bear herself bravely! She no whit depends   130
On circumstance; as she adorns a throne,
She had adorned . . .
  Berthold.   A cottage—in what book
Have I read that, of every queen that lived?
A throne! You have not been instructed, sure,
To forestall my request?
  Valence.   'T is granted, sir!   135
My heart instructs me. I have scrutinized
Your claims . . .
  Berthold. Ah—claims, you mean, at first preferred?
I come, before the hour appointed me,
To pray you let those claims at present rest,
In favour of a new and stronger one.   140
  Valence. You shall not need a stronger: on the part
O' the lady, all you offer I accept,
Since one clear right suffices: yours is clear.
Propose!
  Berthold. I offer her my hand.
  Valence.   Your hand?
  Berthold. A Duke's, yourself say; and, at no far time, 145
Something here whispers me—an Emperor's.
The lady's mind is noble: which induced
This seizure of occasion ere my claims

---

124 {no equivalent in *MS,1844*} 125 *MS,1844* What she determines—That *1849-*
68 on—   128 *MS-1849* mind! 130 *MS-1849* bravely; she *1863,1865* she
132 *MS* a hovel—in *1844* A hovel—in 134 *MS-1863* throne?   135
1863,1865 forestal *MS-1865* sir— 137 *MS,1844* mean, I first *MS-1865*
preferred! 138 *MS,1844* Before our late appointment, sir, I come, 139 *MS*
you leave those 140 *MS* favor 142 *MS,1844* Of the 143 *MS,1844*
clear: 145 *MS,1844* say, 146 *MS-1868* me—the Emperor's.

Were—settled, let us amicably say!
   Valence. Your hand!
   Berthold.   (He will fall down and kiss it next!)   150
Sir, this astonishment's too flattering,
Nor must you hold your mistress' worth so cheap.
Enhance it, rather,—urge that blood is blood—
The daughter of the Burgraves, Landgraves, Markgraves,
Remains their daughter! I shall scarce gainsay.   155
Elsewhere or here, the lady needs must rule:
Like the imperial crown's great chrysoprase,
They talk of—somewhat out of keeping there,
And yet no jewel for a meaner cap.
   Valence. You wed the Duchess?
   . *Berthold.*   Cry you mercy, friend!   160
Will the match also influence fortunes here?
A natural solicitude enough.
Be certain, no bad chance it proves for you!
However high you take your present stand,
There's prospect of a higher still remove—   165
For Juliers will not be my resting-place,
And, when I have to choose a substitute
To rule the little burgh, I'll think of you
Who need not give your mates a character.
And yet I doubt your fitness to supplant   170

152 *MS-1849* cheap!   154 *MS* Margraves,   155 *MS,1844* daughter— *1849-65* daughter;   *MS-1865* gainsay!   158 *MS,1844* They tell me—somewhat 159 *MS-1849* cap!   161 *MS,1844* The match will influence many fortunes *1849-65* match influence many fortunes   162 *MS,1844* natural enough solicitude! *1849-65* enough!   168 (no equivalent in *MS,1844*) *1849-68* you.   169 *MS-1868* You need   *MS-1865* character!

   154 *Burgraves*: OED defines 'Burgrave' as 'The governor of a town or castle; later, a noble ruling by hereditary right a town or castle, with the adjacent domain': 'Landgrave' as 'a count having jurisdiction over a territory, and having under him several inferior counts': and 'Margrave' as 'the hereditary title of the princes of certain states of the Holy Roman Empire'.
   157 *chrysoprase*: 'The ancient name of a golden-green precious stone, now generally believed to have been a variety of the beryl, or to have included that among other stones of similar appearance. It was one of the stones to which in the Middle Ages was attributed the faculty of shining in the dark': OED.
   165 *remove*: 'A step in the scale of gradation' (Johnson): here, in the career of Valence.
   169 *Who need not give your mates a character*: i.e. I see through them, without your help.

The grey smooth Chamberlain: he'd hesitate
A doubt his lady could demean herself
So low as to accept me. Courage, sir!
I like your method better: feeling's play
Is franker much, and flatters me beside.   175
    Valence. I am to say, you love her?
    Berthold.   Say that too!
Love has no great concernment, thinks the world,
With a Duke's marriage. How go precedents
In Juliers' story—how use Juliers' Dukes?
I see you have them here in goodly row;   180
Yon must be Luitpold—ay, a stalwart sire!
Say, I have been arrested suddenly
In my ambition's course, its rocky course,
By this sweet flower: I fain would gather it
And then proceed: so say and speedily   185
—(Nor stand there like Duke Luitpold's brazen self!)
Enough, sir: you possess my mind, I think.
This is my claim, the others being withdrawn,
And to this be it that, i' the Hall to-night,
Your lady's answer comes; till when, farewell!   190
                                     [*He retires.*

    Valence [*after a pause*]. The heavens and earth stay as they
      were; my heart
Beats as it beat: the truth remains the truth.
What falls away, then, if not faith in her?
Was it my faith, that she could estimate
Love's value, and, such faith still guiding me,   195
Dare I now test her? Or grew faith so strong
Solely because no power of test was mine?

171 *MS,1844* The grew smooth   *MS* he'd volunteer   174 *MS* {?} ⟨rather⟩ [bet-
ter]   180 {no equivalent in *MS,1844*}   181 *MS,1844* (Yon . . . . sire!) {in *MS*
this line is squeezed in between ll. 180 and 182} *1849* sire!)   183 *MS,1844* course . .
say, rocky   186 *MS* {this line is squeezed in between ll. 185 and 187}   188-
9 *MS,1844* To this claim, be it in the Hall at night   189 *1849-68* in the
190 s.d. *MS,1844* †[*Exit.*   192 *MS-1865* truth!   193 *MS,1844* away, if not
my faith   196 *MS,1844* Dare I to test her now,—or had I faith

    171-2 *he'd hesitate* / *A doubt* : cf. Pope, *Epistle to Dr. Arbuthnot*, 204.
    179 *how use* : what is the custom of the Dukes of Juliers?

Enter the DUCHESS.

The Duchess. My fate, sir! Ah, you turn away. All's over.
But you are sorry for me? Be not so!
What I might have become, and never was,   200
Regret with me! What I have merely been,
Rejoice I am no longer! What I seem
Beginning now, in my new state, to be,
Hope that I am!—for, once my rights proved void,
This heavy roof seems easy to exchange   205
For the blue sky outside—my lot henceforth.
          Valence. And what a lot is Berthold's!
          The Duchess.   How of him?
          Valence. He gathers earth's whole good into his arms;
Standing, as man now, stately, strong and wise,
Marching to fortune, not surprised by her: 210
One great aim, like a guiding-star, above—
Which tasks strength, wisdom, stateliness, to lift
His manhood to the height that takes the prize;
A prize not near—lest overlooking earth
He rashly spring to seize it—nor remote,   215
So that he rest upon his path content:
But day by day, while shimmering grows shine,
And the faint circlet prophesies the orb,
He sees so much as, just evolving these,
The stateliness, the wisdom and the strength,   220

198 *MS-1849* away—all's over! *1863,1865* away: all's over!   199 *MS-1849* me—be
1863,1865 be   201 *MS- 1863* me;   202 *MS,1844* longer; what I now *1849,
1863* longer; what *1865* longer! what   203 *MS,1844* Begin, a simple woman now,
to   204 *MS,1844* am,—for, now my rights are void, *1849,1863* am,
206 *MS-1863* henceforth!   208 {no equivalent in *MS,1844*}   209 *MS,1844*
He stands, a man now;   *210 {reading of *1849* ; no equivalent in *MS,1844*} *1863-89*
her.   211 *MS,1844* star, before—   212 *MS,1844* to follow,
212a *MS,1844* As, not its substance, but its shine he tracks,   213-18 {no equivalent
in *MS,1844*}   216 *1849* he rests upon   219 *MS,1844* Nor dreams of more
than, just   220 {no equivalent in *MS,1844*}

          209 *Standing, as man now*: in a note in the annotated copy, now in the Carl H. Pforz-
heimer Library, Browning wrote that 'unless a *very* good Valence' was found this speech
was to be left out. Cf. Gosse, p. 70. Gosse gives the text which may be reconstructed from
our textual footnotes. Cf. Introduction, pp. 430 ff. above.
          219 *evolving*: developing (transitive).

To due completion, will suffice this life,
And lead him at his grandest to the grave.
After this star, out of a night he springs;
A beggar's cradle for the throne of thrones
He quits; so, mounting, feels each step he mounts,   225
Nor, as from each to each exultingly
He passes, overleaps one grade of joy.
This, for his own good:—with the world, each gift
Of God and man,—reality, tradition,
Fancy and fact—so well environ him,   230
That as a mystic panoply they serve—
Of force, untenanted, to awe mankind,
And work his purpose out with half the world,
While he, their master, dexterously slipt
From such encumbrance, is meantime employed   235
With his own prowess on the other half.
Thus shall he prosper, every day's success
Adding, to what is he, a solid strength—
An aëry might to what encircles him,
Till at the last, so life's routine lends help,   240
That as the Emperor only breathes and moves,
His shadow shall be watched, his step or stalk
Become a comfort or a portent, how
He trails his ermine take significance,—
Till even his power shall cease to be most power,   245

---

221 *MS,1844* To fulness, {*MS* fullness,} will suffice him to life's end.   222 [no
equivalent in *MS,1844*]   225 *MS–1849* quits,   236 *MS* ⟨In⟩ [Of] his *1844* In
his   *MS,1844* prowess with the   237 *MS,1844* So shall he go on, every
239 *MS,1844* An airy might   240 *MS,1844* routine shall grow,   241 *MS*
Emperor [only] breathes   243 *MS–1849* portent;   245 *MS,1844* cease his
power to be,

   223 *After*: in pursuit of.
   224 *the throne of thrones*: that of the Holy Roman Emperor.
   227 *grade*: step, rung.
   231 *panoply*: 'Complete armour': Johnson.
   239 *aëry*: 'Aerial; hence etherial, spiritual, incorporeal, unsubstantial, visionary': OED,
which notes that it is 'a favourite word with Milton'.
   241 *only*: merely, even.
   244 *significance*: cf. 'How It Strikes A Contemporary', 9.

And men shall dread his weakness more, nor dare
Peril their earth its bravest, first and best,
Its typified invincibility.
Thus shall he go on, greatening, till he ends—
The man of men, the spirit of all flesh,   250
The fiery centre of an earthly world!
    The Duchess. Some such a fortune I had dreamed should
        rise
Out of my own—that is, above my power
Seemed other, greater potencies to stretch—
    Valence. For you?
    The Duchess.   It was not I moved there, I think: 255
But one I could,—though constantly beside,
And aye approaching,—still keep distant from,
And so adore. 'T was a man moved there.
    Valence.   Who?
    The Duchess. I felt the spirit, never saw the face.
    Valence. See it! 'T is Berthold's! He enables you   260
To realize your vision.
    The Duchess.   Berthold?
    Valence.   Duke—
Emperor to be: he proffers you his hand.
    The Duchess. Generous and princely!
    Valence.   He is all of this.
    The Duchess. Thanks, Berthold, for my father's sake! No
        hand
Degrades me.
    Valence.   You accept the proffered hand?   265

246 *MS,1844* And most his weakness men shall fear, nor vanquish   247 {no equiva-
lent in *MS,1844*}   248 *MS,1844* Their typified   249 *MS,1844* So shall he go
on, so at last shall end, *1849* So shall   251 *MS–1865* an earthy world!
258 *MS,1844* A man 'twas moved there! *1849–65* there!   259 *MS–1849* face!
260 *MS* 'tis Berthold! He   261 *MS–1849* vision!   264 *MS–1849* sake—no
1863,1865 no   265 *MS–1868* me!

   246–7 *nor dare/Peril their earth* : the revision of *1849* renders this obscure. The meaning is
probably that men will not dare to endanger the Emperor, who embodies the invincibility
of their world.
   251 *The fiery centre* : cf. *Sordello*, ii. 805.
   253 *above my power* : cf. *Sordello*, iii. 316 ff. and vi. 41.

The Duchess. That he should love me!

Valence.   "Loved" I did not say.
Had that been—love might so incline the Prince
To the world's good, the world that's at his foot,—
I do not know, this moment, I should dare
Desire that you refused the world—and Cleves—   270
The sacrifice he asks.

The Duchess.   Not love me, sir?

Valence. He scarce affirmed it.

The Duchess.   May not deeds affirm?

Valence. What does he? . . . Yes, yes, very much he does!
All the shame saved, he thinks, and sorrow saved—
Immitigable sorrow, so he thinks,—   275
Sorrow that's deeper than we dream, perchance.

The Duchess. Is not this love?

Valence.   So very much he does!
For look, you can descend now gracefully:
All doubts are banished, that the world might have,
Or worst, the doubts yourself, in after-time,   280
May call up of your heart's sincereness now.
To such, reply, "I could have kept my rule—
"Increased it to the utmost of my dreams—
"Yet I abjured it." This, he does for you:
It is munificently much.

The Duchess.   Still "much"!   285
But why is it not love, sir? Answer me!

Valence. Because not one of Berthold's words and looks
Had gone with love's presentment of a flower
To the beloved: because bold confidence,
Open superiority, free pride—   290

266 *MS–1868* say!   267 *MS,1844* been—so might love incline   270 *MS,1844*
Give counsel you refuse the   271 *1844,1849* asks!   272 *MS,1844* deeds say
more?   276 *MS–1868*   perchance!   281 *MS–1849*   now:
282 *MS,1844* reply, "My rule I could have kept—   284 *MS,1844* "Yet abjured all!"
This, Berthold does *MS* you!   *285 (reading of *MS,1844*) 1849–89 "much!" *MS–
1865* munificently much!

275 *Immitigable*: incapable of being relieved.
288 *Had gone with*: would fittingly have accompanied.
    presentment: presentation.

Love owns not, yet were all that Berthold owned:
Because where reason, even, finds no flaw,
Unerringly a lover's instinct may.
    The Duchess. You reason, then, and doubt?
    Valence.   I love, and know.
    The Duchess. You love? How strange! I never cast a thought   295
On that. Just see our selfishness! You seemed
So much my own . . . I had no ground—and yet,
I never dreamed another might divide
My power with you, much less exceed it.
    Valence.   Lady,
I am yours wholly.
    The Duchess.   Oh, no, no, not mine!   300
'T is not the same now, never more can be.
—Your first love, doubtless. Well, what's gone from me?
What have I lost in you?
    Valence.   My heart replies—
No loss there! So, to Berthold back again:
This offer of his hand, he bids me make—   305
Its obvious magnitude is well to weigh.
    The Duchess. She's . . . yes, she must be very fair for you!
    Valence. I am a simple advocate of Cleves.
    The Duchess. You! With the heart and brain that so helped
        me,
I fancied them exclusively my own,   310
Yet find are subject to a stronger sway!
She must be . . . tell me, is she very fair?
    Valence. Most fair, beyond conception or belief.
    The Duchess. Black eyes?—no matter! Colombe, the world
        leads

---

291 *MS,1844* not, and were   293 *MS* ⟨A lover's instinct may, unerringly.⟩ {altered
to read as *1844–89*}   296 *MS–1849* selfishness—you *1863,1865* you
299 *MS–1849* it!   *300 {reading of *1863–68,*DC,BrU,*1889*} *MS–1849* wholly! *1888*
wholly   301 *MS–1865* be!   302 *MS–1865* doubtless!   304 *MS,1844*
So of Berthold's proposition,—   *1849–65* again!   305 {no equivalent in *MS,1844*}
306 *MS* weigh— *1844,1849* weigh!   309 *MS* You?   310 *MS,1844* fancied
both exclusively   *311 {reading of all other versions} *1888* sway   313 *MS–*
1865 belief!   314 *MS* ⟨Colombe—

Its life without you, whom your friends professed   315
The only woman: see how true they spoke!
One lived this while, who never saw your face,
Nor heard your voice—unless . . . Is she from Cleves?
   Valence. Cleves knows her well.
   The Duchess.   Ah—just a fancy, now!
When you poured forth the wrongs of Cleves,—I said,   320
—Thought, that is, afterward . . .
   Valence.   You thought of me?
   The Duchess. Of whom else? Only such great cause, I
     thought,
For such effect: see what true love can do!
Cleves is his love. I almost fear to ask
. . . And will not. This is idling: to our work!   325
Admit before the Prince, without reserve,
My claims misgrounded; then may follow better
. . . When you poured out Cleves' wrongs impetuously,
Was she in your mind?
   Valence.   All done was done for her
—To humble me!
   The Duchess.   She will be proud at least.   330
   Valence. She?
   The Duchess. When you tell her.
   Valence.   That will never be.
   The Duchess. How—are there sweeter things you hope to
     tell?
No, sir! You counselled me,—I counsel you
In the one point I—any woman—can.
Your worth, the first thing; let her own come next—   335
Say what you did through her, and she through you—
The praises of her beauty afterward!
Will you?
   Valence. I dare not.

<hr>

316 *MS,1844* The single woman— .... they were!   319 *MS-1865* well!
322 *MS-1849* Of what else?   *MS,1844* such a cause,   324 *MS-1865* love!
325 *MS-1849* . . . Nor will not!   330 *MS-1865* least!   331 *MS-1849* her!
.... be!   334 *MS-1865* can!   338 *MS-1849* I dare not!

The Duchess.   Dare not?
Valence.   She I love
Suspects not such a love in me.
   The Duchess.   You jest.
   Valence. The lady is above me and away.   340
Not only the brave form, and the bright mind,
And the great heart, combine to press me low—
But all the world calls rank divides us.
   The Duchess.   Rank!
Now grant me patience! Here's a man declares
Oracularly in another's case—   345
Sees the true value and the false, for them—
Nay, bids them see it, and they straight do see.
You called my court's love worthless—so it turned:
I threw away as dross my heap of wealth,
And here you stickle for a piece or two!   350
First—has she seen you?
   Valence.   Yes.
   The Duchess.   .   She loves you, then.
   Valence. One flash of hope burst; then succeeded night:
And all's at darkest now. Impossible!
   The Duchess. We'll try: you are—so to speak—my subject
     yet?
   Valence. As ever—to the death.
   The Duchess.   Obey me, then!   355
   Valence. I must.
   The Duchess.   Approach her, and . . . no! first of all
Get more assurance. "My instructress," say,
"Was great, descended from a line of kings,
"And even fair"—(wait why I say this folly)—

---

339 *MS–1865*   jest!   340 *MS–1865*   away!   343 *MS–1868*   Rank?
347 *MS–1865* see!   348 *MS* it grew: 351 *MS–1849* Yes!   *MS* then!
354 *MS,1844* are—somehow—my   355 *MS–1865* death!   356 *MS–1849*
must!   *MS–1863* No! First   357 *MS–1849* assurance;   *MS,1844* my instruct-
ress, say,_____   358 *MS,1844* Was   359 *MS,1844* fair—

  340 *above me and away*: cf. 'far and away'.

  357 *Get more assurance*: Procter objected to the word 'Get': *Checklist*, 44:113. Browning
paid no attention.

"She said, of all men, none for eloquence,   360
"Courage, and (what cast even these to shade)
"The heart they sprung from,—none deserved like him
"Who saved her at her need: if she said this,
"What should not one I love, say?"
    Valence.   Heaven—this hope—
Oh, lady, you are filling me with fire!   365
    The Duchess. Say this!—nor think I bid you cast aside
One touch of all the awe and reverence;
Nay, make her proud for once to heart's content
That all this wealth of heart and soul's her own!
Think you are all of this,—and, thinking it,   370
. . . (Obey!)
    Valence. I cannot choose.
    The Duchess.   Then, kneel to her!
                    [VALENCE *sinks on his knee.*
I dream!
    Valence. Have mercy! Yours, unto the death,—
I have obeyed. Despise, and let me die!
    The Duchess. Alas, sir, is it to be ever thus?
Even with you as with the world? I know   375
This morning's service was no vulgar deed
Whose motive, once it dares avow itself,
Explains all done and infinitely more,
So, takes the shelter of a nobler cause.
Your service named its true source,—loyalty!   380
The rest's unsaid again. The Duchess bids you,
Rise, sir! The Prince's words were in debate.
    Valence. [*rising*]. Rise? Truth, as ever, lady, comes from
        you!
I should rise—I who spoke for Cleves, can speak
For Man—yet tremble now, who stood firm then.   385

360 *MS,1844* She   361 *MS,1844* what . . . . shade, *MS* and [what] cast even those to
364 *MS,1844* say?   367 *MS-1849* all that awe   *MS-1863* reverence!
369 *1865* own: 371 *MS-1849* choose!   *1865* her *1868* her—   373 *MS*
obeyed!   *1844-65* die.   379 *MS,1844* a meaner cause,   379a *MS,1844*
Whence rising, its effects may amply show.   383 *MS-1849* Rise!   384 *MS-*
1849 I that spoke   385 *MS-1849* now, that stood   *MS-1868* then!

I laughed—for 't was past tears—that Cleves should starve
With all hearts beating loud the infamy,
And no tongue daring trust as much to air:
Yet here, where all hearts speak, shall I be mute?
Oh, lady, for your own sake look on me!   390
On all I am, and have, and do—heart, brain,
Body and soul,—this Valence and his gifts!
I was proud once: I saw you, and they sank,
So that each, magnified a thousand times,
Were nothing to you—but such nothingness,   395
Would a crown gild it, or a sceptre prop,
A treasure speed, a laurel-wreath enhance?
What is my own desert? But should your love
Have . . . there's no language helps here . . . singled me,—
Then—oh, that wild word "then"!—be just to love,   400
In generosity its attribute!
Love, since you pleased to love! All's cleared—a stage
For trial of the question kept so long:
Judge you—Is love or vanity the best?
You, solve it for the world's sake—you, speak first   405
What all will shout one day—you, vindicate
Our earth and be its angel! All is said.
Lady, I offer nothing—I am yours:
But, for the cause' sake, look on me and him,
And speak!
    The Duchess. I have received the Prince's message: 410
Say, I prepare my answer!
    Valence.   Take me, Cleves!
                                          [*He withdraws.*

387 *MS* loud 'twas infamy,   388 *MS,1844* air— *1849,1863* air!
392 *MS,1844* gifts—   395 *1863* nothingness.   396 *MS,1844* What would a
crown gild, or   398 *MS* Oh what is my desert?   *400 (reading of *MS,1844*)
1849-89 "then!"   402 *MS,1844* Love, as you pleased love! All is cleared—
403 *MS-1849* long   404 *MS-1849* For you—   405 *MS,1844* you, say first
407 *MS* said—   408 *MS-1863* yours,   411 s.d. *MS,1844* †[*Exit.*

    391-2 *heart, brain, / Body and soul*: cf. 'In a Gondola', 12.
    397 *speed*: make it succeed.

The Duchess. Mournful—that nothing's what it calls itself!
Devotion, zeal, faith, loyalty—mere love!
And, love in question, what may Berthold's be?
I did ill to mistrust the world so soon: 415
Already was this Berthold at my side.
The valley-level has its hawks no doubt:
May not the rock-top have its eagles, too?
Yet Valence . . . let me see his rival then!

ACT V.

NIGHT.

SCENE.—*The Hall.*

Enter BERTHOLD *and* MELCHIOR.

Melchior. And here you wait the matter's issue?
Berthold.   Here.
Melchior. I don't regret I shut Amelius, then.
But tell me, on this grand disclosure,—how
Behaved our spokesman with the forehead?
  Berthold.   Oh,
Turned out no better than the foreheadless—   5
Was dazzled not so very soon, that's all!
For my part, this is scarce the hasty showy
Chivalrous measure you give me credit of.
Perhaps I had a fancy,—but 't is gone.
—Let her commence the unfriended innocent   10
And carry wrongs about from court to court?
No, truly! The least shake of fortune's sand,
—My uncle-Pope chokes in a coughing fit,
King-cousin takes a fancy to blue eyes,—
And wondrously her claims would brighten up;   15
Forth comes a new gloss on the ancient law,
O'er-looked provisoes, o'er-past premises,

---

2 *MS–1849* then!　　　　4 *MS,1844* Oh,—he　　　8 *MS–1849* of!　　　9 {no
equivalent in *MS,1844*} *1849* had the fancy,—　　　10 *MS,1844* commence unfriended
13 *MS,1844* uncle chokes {*MS* choaks} in his next coughing-fit,　　　14 *MS,1844* King
Philip takes　　　15 *MS–1865* up!　　　16 *MS* Forthcomes　　　17 *MS–1868*
provisoes, {*MS* provisos,} past o'er premises,

  2 *Amelius*: see III. 70–1.　　　4 *our spokesman with the forehead*: Valence: cf. I. 212.
  5 *the foreheadless*: the less thoughtful or intelligent. OED's 'destitute of confidence' is
unconvincing.
  8 *Chivalrous*: stressed on the second syllable: cf. *King Victor*, I. 27 n.
  10 *commence*: begin to play the role of.
  13–14 *My uncle-Pope . . . King-cousin*: cf. III. 54–5.
  17 *premises*: antecedent propositions.

Follow in plenty. No: 't is the safe step.
The hour beneath the convent-wall is lost.
Juliers and she, once mine, are ever mine. 20
    Melchior. Which is to say, you, losing heart already,
Elude the adventure.
    Berthold.   Not so—or, if so—
Why not confess at once that I advise
None of our kingly craft and guild just now
To lay, one moment, down their privilege 25
With the notion they can any time at pleasure
Retake it: that may turn out hazardous.
We seem, in Europe, pretty well at end
O' the night, with our great masque: those favoured few
Who keep the chamber's top, and honour's chance 30
Of the early evening, may retain their place
And figure as they list till out of breath.
But it is growing late: and I observe
A dim grim kind of tipstaves at the doorway
Not only bar new-comers entering now, 35
But caution those who left, for any cause,
And would return, that morning draws too near;
The ball must die off, shut itself up. We—
I think, may dance lights out and sunshine in,
And sleep off headache on our frippery: 40
But friend the other, who cunningly stole out,
And, after breathing the fresh air outside,
Means to re-enter with a new costume,
Will be advised go back to bed, I fear.

18 *MS* the safer step— *1844-68* the safer step.   19 (no equivalent in *MS,1844*)
22 *MS-1865* adventure!   27 *MS-1849* it— *1863* it?   *MS* hasardous! *1844-65*
hazardous!   37 *MS* near   41 *MS* who [cunningly] stole   42 (no
equivalent in *MS,1844*)   43 *MS,1844* And thinks re-enter with a fresh costume,

    19 *The hour beneath the convent-wall is lost*: cf. III. 87: the chance of real love, which
Berthold failed to grasp.
    24 *our kingly craft and guild*: my fellow monarchs.
    29 *our great masque*: masquerade. Cf. *A Blot in the 'Scutcheon*, III. ii. 139.
    30 *the chamber's top*: the place of honour.
    34 *tipstaves*: legal officers.
    40 *frippery*: 'Old clothes; cast dresses; tattered rags': Johnson.

I stick to privilege, on second thoughts.   45
   Melchior. Yes—you evade the adventure: and, beside,
Give yourself out for colder than you are.
King Philip, only, notes the lady's eyes?
Don't they come in for somewhat of the motive
With you too?
   Berthold.   Yes—no: I am past that now.   50
Gone 't is: I cannot shut my soul to fact.
Of course, I might by forethought and contrivance
Reason myself into a rapture. Gone:
And something better come instead, no doubt.
   Melchior. So be it! Yet, all the same, proceed my way,   55
Though to your ends; so shall you prosper best!
The lady,—to be won for selfish ends,—
Will be won easier my unselfish . . . call it,
Romantic way.
   Berthold.   Won easier?
   Melchior.   Will not she?
   Berthold. There I profess humility without bound: 60
Ill cannot speed—not I—the Emperor.
   Melchior. And I should think the Emperor best waived,
From your description of her mood and way.
You could look, if it pleased you, into hearts;
But are too indolent and fond of watching   65
Your own—you know that, for you study it.
   Berthold. Had you but seen the orator her friend,
So bold and voluble an hour before,
Abashed to earth at aspect of the change!

45 *MS–1863* thoughts!   46 *MS–1865* adventure!—   47 *MS* are—
49 *1844* in somewhat   50 *MS–1863* now!   51 *MS–1865* my eyes to
53 *MS* rapture—   *MS–1865* Gone!   54 *MS–1849* better's come
55 *MS,1844* Yet, proceed my way, the same,   56 *MS–1865* your ends; so . . . . best.
59 *MS* way!   60 *MS–1863* bound!   61 *MS–1863* Emperor!   63 *MS–
1863* way!   64 *MS* hearts   . 66 *MS–1849* it!   68 (no equivalent in
MS,1844)

   48 *King Philip*: see textual n. to 14 above.
   61 *Ill cannot speed*: evil cannot prosper. The words have a proverbial ring: cf. *3 Henry VI*,
II. ii. 46: 'things ill got had ever bad success'.
   69 *aspect*: sight of.

Make her an Empress? Ah, that changed the case!　　　70
Oh, I read hearts! 'T is for my own behoof,
I court her with my true worth: wait the event!
I learned my final lesson on that head
When years ago,—my first and last essay—
Before the priest my uncle could by help　　　75
Of his superior, raise me from the dirt—
Priscilla left me for a Brabant lord
Whose cheek was like the topaz on his thumb.
I am past illusion on that score.
　　Melchior.　　　　　　　　Here comes
The lady—
　　Berthold. —And there you go. But do not! Give me　80
Another chance to please you! Hear me plead!
　　Melchior. You'll keep, then, to the lover, to the man?

　　　Enter the Duchess—*followed by* Adolf *and* Sabyne *and, after an
interval, by the* Courtiers.

　　Berthold. Good auspice to our meeting!
　　The Duchess.　　　　　　May it prove!
—And you, sir, will be Emperor one day?
　　Berthold. (Ay, that's the point!) I may be Emperor.　85
　　The Duchess. 'T is not for my sake only, I am proud
Of this you offer: I am prouder far
That from the highest state should duly spring
The highest, since most generous, of deeds.
　　Berthold. (Generous—still that!) You underrate yourself.　90
You are, what I, to be complete, must gain—

---

70 {no equivalent in *MS,1844*}　　　71 *MS* hearts, friend! For *1844-65* hearts! And for
72 *MS-1865* worth: see the　　　74 *MS-1865* essay!　　　75-6 {squeezed in in *MS*}
75 *MS-1865* Before my uncle could obtain the ear　　　76 *MS-1865* superior, help me
77 *MS-1865* Brabant Duke　　　79 *MS* score!　　　80 *MS-1865* go!
81 *MS-1865* you.　　　82 *MS,1844* the gallant, to　　　85 *MS,1844* point.)
90 *MS* yourself! *1865* yourself:　　　91 *MS-1868* must have—

　72 *the event!*: the outcome. Cf. 'Artemis Prologizes', 121.
　75 *the priest my uncle*: cf. 13 above.
　77 *Priscilla*: the girl at the convent-wall: III. 86-7, and 19 above.
　　Brabant: coming from the southern part of the province of Brabant, which was under
Spanish rule at the time of the action of the play.

Find now, and may not find, another time.
While I career on all the world for stage,
There needs at home my representative.
　　The Duchess. —Such, rather, would some warrior-woman
　　　　be—　　　　　　　　　　　　　　　　　　　　　　　　　95
One dowered with lands and gold, or rich in friends—
One like yourself.
　　Berthold.　　　　Lady, I am myself,
And have all these: I want what's not myself,
Nor has all these. Why give one hand two swords?
Here's one already: be a friend's next gift　　　　　　100
A silk glove, if you will—I have a sword.
　　The Duchess. You love me, then?
　　Berthold.　　　　　　　　　　Your lineage I revere,
Honour your virtue, in your truth believe,
Do homage to your intellect, and bow
Before your peerless beauty.
　　The Duchess.　　　　　　But, for love—　　　　105
　　Berthold. A further love I do not understand.
Our best course is to say these hideous truths,
And see them, once said, grow endurable:
Like waters shuddering from their central bed,
Black with the midnight bowels of the earth,　　　　110
That, once up-spouted by an earthquake's throe,
A portent and a terror—soon subside,
Freshen apace, take gold and rainbow hues
In sunshine, sleep in shadow, and at last
Grow common to the earth as hills or trees—　　　　115
Accepted by all things they came to scare.
　　The Duchess. You cannot love, then?

---

97 *MS–1865* yourself!　　　101 *MS–1865* sword!　　　104 *MS,1844* to intelligence, and　　　105 *MS,1844* Before a peerless　　　107 *MS* One's best　　　108 *MS–1849* endurable.　　　114 *MS,1844* Under the sun and in the air,—at last 115 *MS* hills and trees— (between ll. 116 and 117 in *MS* two lines have been deleted: (High souls insist on Truth—the rest, on Truths | Only that have been so insisted on.))

　　93 *all the world for stage*: cf. *As You Like It*, II. vii. 139.
　　109 *Like waters shuddering*: cf. the earthquake described in *Sordello*, iii. 84 ff.
　　111 *up-spouted*: as in Cowper, 'On the Queen's Visit to London', 19.

Berthold.   —Charlemagne, perhaps!
Are you not over-curious in love-lore?
     The Duchess. I have become so, very recently.
It seems, then, I shall best deserve esteem,   120
Respect, and all your candour promises,
By putting on a calculating mood—
Asking the terms of my becoming yours?
     Berthold. Let me not do myself injustice, neither.
Because I will not condescend to fictions   125
That promise what my soul can ne'er acquit,
It does not follow that my guarded phrase
May not include far more of what you seek,
Than wide profession of less scrupulous men.
You will be Empress, once for all: with me   130
The Pope disputes supremacy—you stand,
And none gainsays, the earth's first woman.
     The Duchess.   That—
Or simple Lady of Ravestein again?
     Berthold. The matter's not in my arbitrament:
Now I have made my claims—which I regret—   135
Cede one, cede all.
     The Duchess.   This claim then, you enforce?
     Berthold. The world looks on.
     The Duchess.   And when must I decide?
     Berthold. When, lady? Have I said thus much so promptly
For nothing?—Poured out, with such pains, at once
What I might else have suffered to ooze forth   140
Droplet by droplet in a lifetime long—
For aught less than as prompt an answer, too?
All's fairly told now: who can teach you more?
     The Duchess. I do not see him.
     Berthold.   I shall ne'er deceive.

119 *MS* recently!   124 *MS–1865* neither! *1868* neither   129 *MS–1865* wide
professions of   132 *MS–1865* woman!   134 *MS– 1863* my arbitrement!
1865 my arbitrement: 136 *MS–1863* all!   138 *MS–1849* "When," *MS,1844*
much at first   141 *MS* life-time-long *1844,1849* life-time   144 *MS,1844*
him!.... deceive!

126 *acquit*: perform, make good.

This offer should be made befittingly   145
Did time allow the better setting forth
The good of it, with what is not so good,
Advantage, and disparagement as well:
But as it is, the sum of both must serve.
I am already weary of this place;   150
My thoughts are next stage on to Rome. Decide!
The Empire—or,—not even Juliers now!
Hail to the Empress—farewell to the Duchess!
    [*The* Courtiers, *who have been drawing nearer and nearer, interpose.*
    Gaucelme. —"Farewell," Prince? when we break in at our
      risk—
    Clugnet. Almost upon court-licence trespassing—   155
    Gaucelme. —To point out how your claims are valid yet!
You know not, by the Duke her father's will,
The lady, if she weds beneath her rank,
Forfeits her Duchy in the next heir's favour—
So 't is expressly stipulate. And if   160
It can be shown 't is her intent to wed
A subject, then yourself, next heir, by right
Succeed to Juliers.
    Berthold.   What insanity?—
    Guibert. Sir, there's one Valence, the pale fiery man
You saw and heard this morning—thought, no doubt,   165
Was of considerable standing here:
I put it to your penetration, Prince,
If aught save love, the truest love for her
Could make him serve the lady as he did!
He's simply a poor advocate of Cleves   170
—Creeps here with difficulty, finds a place

145 *MS,1844* offer had been made more leisurely *1849* offer had been made
146 *MS–1849* Would time   *MS,1844* setting off   147 (no equivalent in
MS,1844)   151 *MS,1844* Rome. Now either,   152 (no equivalent in
MS,1844)   153 *MS,1844* the Lady!   s.d. *MS drawing near and*   154 *MS–
1865 Courtiers.* ... "Farewell,"   155 *MS–1849* (Almost .... trespassing)   *MS*
Court-license   156 *MS–1865 Courtiers.* To   159 *MS* favor—
161 *MS* her intend to   162–3 *MS,1844* yourself ... *Berth.* What insolence? ...
169 *MS,1844* Had made him

With danger, gets in by a miracle,
And for the first time meets the lady's face—
So runs the story: is that credible?
For, first—no sooner in, than he's apprised   175
Fortunes have changed; you are all-powerful here,
The lady as powerless: he stands fast by her!
    The Duchess [*aside*]. And do such deeds spring up from
      love alone?
    Guibert. But here occurs the question, does the lady
Love him again? I say, how else can she?   180
Can she forget how he stood singly forth
In her defence, dared outrage all of us,
Insult yourself—for what, save love's reward?
    The Duchess [*aside*]. And is love then the sole reward of
      love?
    Guibert. But, love him as she may and must—you ask,   185
Means she to wed him? "Yes," both natures answer!
Both, in their pride, point out the sole result;
Nought less would he accept nor she propose.
For each conjuncture was she great enough
—Will be, for this.
    Clugnet.   Though, now that this is known,   190
Policy, doubtless, urges she deny . . .
    The Duchess. —What, sir, and wherefore?—since I am not
      sure
That all is any other than you say!
You take this Valence, hold him close to me,   .
Him with his actions: can I choose but look?   195
I am not sure, love trulier shows itself
Than in this man, you hate and would degrade,

---

177 *MS* power-less—   178 *1844,1849* (And   *MS–1849* alone?)   184 *MS–*
1849 (And . . . . love?)   186 *MS* Ventures she wed   188 *MS–1863* propose!
*189 {reading of *MS–1863*} *1865–89* each conjecture was   190 *MS–1863* this!
193 *MS* is [any] other   *MS–1863* say?   195 *MS,1844* his action . . can

   189 *conjecture* (*1865–89*): one of two 'vile misprints' in this play which Browning noticed
in *1868*: cf. 1. 175 n. above. As John Maynard has pointed out, *Browning and his Circle* (Fall
1974), p. 87, the Ohio editor retains this error, though not that at 1. 175.

Yet, with your worst abatement, show me thus.
Nor am I—(thus made look within myself,
Ere I had dared)—now that the look is dared—   200
Sure that I do not love him!
   Guibert.   Hear you, Prince?
  Berthold. And what, sirs, please you, may this prattle mean
Unless to prove with what alacrity
You give your lady's secrets to the world?
How much indebted, for discovering   205
That quality, you make me, will be found
When there's a keeper for my own to seek.
   Courtiers. "Our lady"?
  Berthold.   —She assuredly remains.
  The Duchess. Ah, prince—and you too can be generous?
You could renounce your power, if this were so,   210
And let me, as these phrase it, wed my love
Yet keep my Duchy? You perhaps exceed
Him, even, in disinterestedness!
  Berthold. How, lady, should all this affect my purpose?
Your will and choice are still as ever, free.   215
Say, you have known a worthier than myself
In mind and heart, of happier form and face—
Others must have their birthright: I have gifts,
To balance theirs, not blot them out of sight.
Against a hundred alien qualities,   220

---

198 *MS* thus! *1849* thus: 200 *MS is*   202 *MS–1849* mean?   204 *MS*
give [your lady's] secrets   *MS–1849* world—   205 *MS,1844* —But how indebted,
207 *MS–1865* When next a keeper for my own's to seek!   *208 (editors' emenda-
tion) *MS,1844* Our Lady? *1849–89* "Our lady?"   211 *MS,1844* these argue, wed
212 *MS,1844* And keep   215 *MS–1865* free!   217 *MS* face
*218 (reading of *MS–1868*) *1888,1889* gifts.   *MS–1849* birthright!   219 *MS–*
1849 sight!   220 *MS* Against the hundred other qualities, *1844–65* other qualities,

    201 *Sure that I do not love him!*: Browning answered a query from Furnivall about this pas-
sage in the letter already quoted with reference to I. 375: 'She [Mrs Forman, Alma Murray]
is equally right in her reading of what is meant in the 5th Act when the Duchess is made to
listen to—and definitely pronounce upon—that conduct [of Valence],—forced upon her as
the task is by the officiousness and malice of the courtiers: they desire to show that she has
put herself in a necessity of returning his love with her own,—though she will be mad to
do so,—and her answer is that she sees the urgency of their argument, accepts the situation,
and does so really return it': *Trumpeter*, p. 119.

I lay the prize I offer. I am nothing:
Wed you the Empire?
    The Duchess.   And my heart away?
    Berthold. When have I made pretension to your heart?
I give none. I shall keep your honour safe;
With mine I trust you, as the sculptor trusts   225
Yon marble woman with the marble rose,
Loose on her hand, she never will let fall,
In graceful, slight, silent security.
You will be proud of my world-wide career,
And I content in you the fair and good.   230
What were the use of planting a few seeds
The thankless climate never would mature—
Affections all repelled by circumstance?
Enough: to these no credit I attach,—
To what you own, find nothing to object.   235
Write simply on my requisition's face
What shall content my friends—that you admit,
As Colombe of Ravestein, the claims therein,
Or never need admit them, as my wife—
And either way, all's ended!
    The Duchess.   Let all end!   240
    Berthold. The requisition!
    Guibert.   —Valence holds, of course!
    Berthold. Desire his presence!   [ADOLF *goes out.*
    Courtiers [*to each other*].   Out it all comes yet;
He'll have his word against the bargain yet;
He's not the man to tamely acquiesce.
One passionate appeal—upbraiding even,   245
May turn the tide again. Despair not yet!
                     [*They retire a little.*

223 *MS* Where have   *1865* made pretensions to   224a *MS* ⟨Safe will you keep
mine—both our characters⟩   225 *MS* ⟨Assure that: safely⟩ [With mine I trust you—]
as   232 *MS* the [thankless] climate   240 *MS–1865* ended.   241 *MS–
1865* Requisition! *Courtiers.* —Valence   242 s.d. *MS,1844* †[*Exit* ADOLF.   *MS*
⟨Out   *MS–1863* yet!   243 *MS–1863* bargain still! *1865* bargain still:
244 *MS–1863* acquiesce!   246 *MS–1865* Might turn   *MS–1863* again!

    235 *own* : admit.

Berthold [*to* MELCHIOR]. The Empire has its old success,
    my friend!
Melchior. You've had your way: before the spokesman
    speaks,
Let me, but this once, work a problem out,
And ever more be dumb! The Empire wins?   250
To better purpose have I read my books!

                    Enter VALENCE.

Melchior [*to the* Courtiers].
Apart, my masters!
        [*To* VALENCE.] Sir, one word with you!
I am a poor dependant of the Prince's—
Pitched on to speak, as of slight consequence.
You are no higher, I find: in other words,   255
We two, as probably the wisest here,
Need not hold diplomatic talk like fools.
Suppose I speak, divesting the plain fact
Of all their tortuous phrases, fit for them?
Do you reply so, and what trouble saved!   260
The Prince, then—an embroiled strange heap of news
This moment reaches him—if true or false,
All dignity forbids he should inquire
In person, or by worthier deputy;
Yet somehow must inquire, lest slander come: 265
And so, 't is I am pitched on. You have heard
His offer to your lady?
    Valence.   Yes.
    Melchior.   —Conceive
Her joy thereat?
    Valence.   I cannot.
    Melchior.   No one can.

248 *MS-1865* spokesman comes,   250 *1863,1865* dumb   251 *1844-63* pur-
pose I have read   253 *MS-1865* poor dependent of   *MS* the Prince— *1844* the
Princes'—   254 *MS-1849* consequence: *1863,1865* consequence;   257 *MS-
1849* fools: 258 *MS,1844* So, I shall speak   259 *MS-1849* them—
260 *MS-1849* trouble's saved!   263 *MS-1849* should enquire   265 *MS-
1849* must enquire, lest   267 *MS,1844* Yes!   268 *MS,1844* Cannot! . . . .
can! *1849-68* can:

All draws to a conclusion, therefore.
    Valence [*aside*].   So!
No after-judgment—no first thought revised—   270
Her first and last decision!—me, she leaves,
Takes him; a simple heart is flung aside,
The ermine o'er a heartless breast embraced.
Oh Heaven, this mockery has been played too oft!
Once, to surprise the angels—twice, that fiends   275
Recording, might be proud they chose not so—
Thrice, many thousand times, to teach the world
All men should pause, misdoubt their strength, since men
Can have such chance yet fail so signally,
—But ever, ever this farewell to Heaven,   280
Welcome to earth—this taking death for life—
This spurning love and kneeling to the world—
Oh Heaven, it is too often and too old!
    Melchior. Well, on this point, what but an absurd rumour
Arises—these, its source—its subject, you!   285
Your faith and loyalty misconstruing,
They say, your service claims the lady's hand!
Of course, nor Prince nor lady can respond:
Yet something must be said: for, were it true
You made such claim, the Prince would . . .
    Valence.   Well, sir,—would? 290
    Melchior. —Not only probably withdraw his suit,
But, very like, the lady might be forced
Accept your own. Oh, there are reasons why!
But you'll excuse at present all save one,—
I think so. What we want is, your own witness,   295
For, or against—her good, or yours: decide!
    Valence [*aside*]. Be it her good if she accounts it so!
[*After a contest.*] For what am I but hers, to choose as she?
Who knows how far, beside, the light from her

273 *MS-1865* embraced!   276 *MS,1844* Might record, hug themselves they chose
not so—   279 *MS,1844* Could have the chance *1849-65* Could have
283 *MS* old!)   287 *MS,1844* The lady's hand your service claims, they say!
293 *1844* why,   294 *MS-1863* save this,—

May reach, and dwell with, what she looks upon?   300
    Melchior [*to the* Prince]. Now to him, you!
    Berthold [*to* VALENCE]. My friend acquaints you, sir,
The noise runs . . .
    Valence.   —Prince, how fortunate are you,
Wedding her as you will, in spite of noise,
To show belief in love! Let her but love you,
All else you disregard! What else can be?   305
You know how love is incompatible
With falsehood—purifies, assimilates
All other passions to itself.
    Melchior.   Ay, sir:
But softly! Where, in the object we select,
Such love is, perchance, wanting?
    Valence.   Then indeed,   310
What is it you can take?
    Melchior.   Nay, ask the world!
Youth, beauty, virtue, an illustrious name,
An influence o'er mankind.
    Valence.   When man perceives . . .
—Ah, I can only speak as for myself!
    The Duchess. Speak for yourself!
    Valence.   May I?—no, I have spoken,   315
And time's gone by. Had I seen such an one,
As I loved her—weighing thoroughly that word—
So should my task be to evolve her love:
If for myself!—if for another—well.
    Berthold. Heroic truly! And your sole reward,—   320
The secret pride in yielding up love's right?
    Valence. Who thought upon reward? And yet how much
Comes after—oh, what amplest recompense!
Is the knowledge of her, nought? the memory, nought?

303 *MS-1865* of it,   308 *MS* itself!   313 *MS,1844* o'er the world! When
1849 mankind!   315 *1863,1865* yourself.   *MS* I?—ah, I   316 *MS-1865*
by!   319 *MS-1849* well!   321 *MS-1865* up your own?   323 *MS-*
1863 —Oh *1844,1849* recompence!

    302 *The noise runs*: it is rumoured. Cf. *Troilus and Cressida*, I. ii. 12.
    318 *evolve*: develop (transitive: cf. IV. 219).

—Lady, should such an one have looked on you, 325
Ne'er wrong yourself so far as quote the world
And say, love can go unrequited here!
You will have blessed him to his whole life's end—
Low passions hindered, baser cares kept back,
All goodness cherished where you dwelt—and dwell. 330
What would he have? He holds you—you, both form
And mind, in his,—where self-love makes such room
For love of you, he would not serve you now
The vulgar way,—repulse your enemies,
Win you new realms, or best, to save the old 335
Die blissfully—that's past so long ago!
He wishes you no need, thought, care of him—
Your good, by any means, himself unseen,
Away, forgotten!—He gives that life's task up,
As it were . . . but this charge which I return— 340
                          [*Offers the requisition, which she takes.*
Wishing your good.
    The Duchess [*having subscribed it*]. And opportunely, sir—
Since at a birthday's close, like this of mine,
Good wishes gentle deeds reciprocate.
Most on a wedding-day, as mine is too,
Should gifts be thought of: yours comes first by right. 345
Ask of me!
    Berthold. He shall have whate'er he asks,
For your sake and his own.
    Valence [*aside*].   If I should ask—
The withered bunch of flowers she wears—perhaps,
One last touch of her hand, I never more
Shall see!
              [*After a pause, presenting his paper to the* Prince.

330 *MS* dwell!   331 *MS* have—he has you— *1844* He has you—   *MS,1844* you, the
form,   332 *MS,1844* And you, the mind, where self-love made such
335 *MS-1865* best, in saving you *1868* best, in saving old   339 *MS* forgotten,—gives
1844 forgotten,—he   340 *1865* {'b' of 'but' turned}   341 *MS-1865* good!
s.d. *The D.* {*Who has subscribed*   344 *MS-1868* wedding day,   345 *MS,1844*
gifts go forward: yours   347 *MS,1844* For his sake and for yours!   *1849,1863*
own!   349-50 *MS,1844* One last touch of . . .   {s.d. as *1888*} Redress

Cleves' Prince, redress the wrongs of Cleves!   350
Berthold. I will, sir!
   The Duchess [*as* VALENCE *prepares to retire*]. —Nay, do out
     your duty, first!
You bore this paper; I have registered
My answer to it: read it and have done!

                                 [VALENCE *reads it*

I take him—give up Juliers and the world.
This is my Birthday.
   Melchior.   Berthold, my one hero   355
Of the world she gives up, one friend worth my books,
Sole man I think it pays the pains to watch,—
Speak, for I know you through your Popes and Kings!
   Berthold [*after a pause*]. Lady, well rewarded! Sir, as well
     deserved!
I could not imitate—I hardly envy—   360
I do admire you. All is for the best.
Too costly a flower were this, I see it now,
To pluck and set upon my barren helm
To wither—any garish plume will do.
I'll not insult you and refuse your Duchy—   365
You can so well afford to yield it me,
And I were left, without it, sadly lorn.
As it is—for me—if that will flatter you,
A somewhat wearier life seems to remain
Than I thought possible where . . . 'faith, their life   370
Begins already! They're too occupied
To listen: and few words content me best.
[*Abruptly to the* Courtiers.] I am your Duke, though! Who
     obey me here?
   The Duchess. Adolf and Sabyne follow us—
   Guibert [*starting from the* Courtiers].   —And I?

---

351 *1863-8* sir.   354 *MS-1863* world!   355 *MS-1849* Birth-day.
357 *MS* it worth my pains   359 *MS* well guerdoned! Sir   361 *MS-1865*
you! . . . . best!   362 *MS-1865* were you, I   363 *MS,1844* and put upon
364 *MS-1865* do!   365 *MS,1844* your rule—   367 *MS-1865* sadly off! *1868*
sadly off.   371 *MS-1863* already—they're *1865* already! they're   372 *MS-*
1865 best!   374 *MS* {no s.d.]

Do I not follow them, if I may n't you?   375
Shall not I get some little duties up
At Ravestein and emulate the rest?
God save you, Gaucelme! 'T is my Birthday, too!
  Berthold. You happy handful that remain with me
... That is, with Dietrich the black Barnabite   380
I shall leave over you—will earn your wages
Or Dietrich has forgot to ply his trade!
Meantime,—go copy me the precedents
Of every installation, proper styles
And pedigrees of all your Juliers' Dukes—   385
While I prepare to plod on my old way,
And somewhat wearily, I must confess!
  The Duchess [*with a light joyous laugh as she turns from them*].
Come, Valence, to our friends, God's earth...
  Valence [*as she falls into his arms*]. —And thee!

---

375 *MS,1844* may'nt   378 *MS–1849* Birth-day,   *380 (reading of *MS-1868*)
1888,1889 .. That *MS* with Diedrick the   382 *MS* Or Diedrick has
384 *MS* proper style,   385 *MS* And pedigree of   386 *MS-1865* to go on
388 *MS-1849* earth—   s.d. *MS,1844 Curtain falls.*

  380 *the black Barnabite*: an order of regular clerks of St Paul, so called because the church
of St Barnabas, in Milan, was given them to preach in. The symbol of St Barnabas is a rake.

At the end of *MS* Browning wrote 'L.D.I.E.', for 'Laus Deo in excelsis', Praise be to God in
the highest.

APPENDIX A

'The Pied Piper of Hamelin'
by Robert Browning sen.

BROWNING's father wrote more than one version of a poem about the Pied Piper. One survives in a holograph manuscript which is unavailable at the moment, but we have three transcriptions of different versions of the story, one made by C. Elkin Mathews about 1882[1] (entitled 'Hamelin', this is now at Northwestern University, and is probably a copy of the holograph), and two made by the biographer W. Hall Griffin, which are now in the Alexander Turnbull Library in New Zealand. The New Zealand transcriptions are preceded by the following note by Hall Griffin:

The original M.S. was forwarded to me by *Miss K Lemann of Home Lodge, Bathampton. Bath* —this address indeed appears stamped on the fools-cap paper on which the verses are written. The mother of Miss Lemann was Miss Earles for whom & her sister (Mᵣˢ Cole & Mᵣˢ   ) this "Piper" was written: & for whom many *sketches* were made

The versions transcribed by Hall Griffin are entitled "The Pied Piper of Hamelin". As mentioned above (pp. 262-3), the first is a 66-line fragment, which ends with a note, dated 2 March 1843, explaining that Browning's father 'stopped short' when he heard that his son 'had written on this subject'. Since *Dramatic Lyrics* appeared in the last week of November 1842, Browning presumably showed his father the manuscript of his poem earlier that year, and probably soon after he had written it. Mr Earles, who lived at Hackney, was a colleague of Browning's father at the Bank (Maynard, p. 429 n. 11): R. B. sen. is said to have shown him a copy of *Sordello* with the comment that he himself could make nothing of it.[2]

---

[1] This was published in *The Bookman* for 4 May 1912, by W. R. Nicoll. His version is not altogether accurate: the third source, for example, appears in his transcription as 'Kirk historians'. Griffin and Minchin give the first twenty lines of the completed New Zealand version on p. 21 of their *Life*.

[2] Maynard, p. 38.

The transcription by Elkin Mathews has this note at the end:

This transcript was made by me about 1882 from the original MSS of the elder Browning who gave them to his friend the late Baroness Von Muller who kindly lent them to me {and *del.*} she also presented the 'Crescentius' MS to me

Those who wish to pursue the entertaining matter of the Baroness (or Mrs) von Müller may do so by turning to *Robert Browning: A Portrait*, by Betty Miller (1952), and subsequent biographies.

We must believe the father's statement that he did not know that his son 'had written on this subject', and can only suppose that the topic had been mentioned in conversation, perhaps as a suitable subject for Willie Macready to illustrate.[1]

The question of priority as between the two versions by R.B. sen. is not important;[2] but something should be said about the differences between the two men's narratives and the question of the sources on which they drew. Of the five features common to the son's poem and the account in Verstegan's *Restitution of Decayed Intelligence*, four are absent from the father's versions. Since the tradition that the missing children had gone to Transylvania is mentioned in several of the prose narratives (including that in Collier's *Dictionary*), there is no reason to believe that R.B. sen. knew (or used) Verstegan. But what are we to make of the 'German authors who have written upon this subject' named in the unfinished version as '*Schochius—Erithius* / And *Kirkmaleus*' (the last being almost certainly a mistranscription)?

It seems likely that Browning sen. looked at one of the three works, at least: *Martini Schoockii Fabula Hamelensis, sive Disquisitio Historica, qua ostenditur fabulis accenseri debere, quod refertur de infausto Exitu puerorum Hamelensium, qui inciderit in annum à Christo nato MCCLXXXII* (a misprint for MCCLXXXIV). This painstaking work was published in Latin in Groningen in 1659. The first of its two parts recommends a critical approach to what profess to be historical narrations, while the second is accurately entitled 'Destructio Fabulæ Hamelensis'. The author (who follows most writers in giving 26 June 1284 as the date of the supposed

---

[1] The unavailable holograph has this note on the fly-leaf: 'This poem, . . . was written by the father of Robert Browning . . . Mr. Browning, some two years before his death, told Mr. T. J. Wise (who showed him this MS. on behalf of its then owner) that his father wrote the poem while he, R.B., was in Germany. That upon his (R.B.'s) return to England Mr. Browning Senr. showed this very MS. to his son—who afterwards composed his own work upon the same subject . . .' We prefer the account given by Browning's father.

[2] It will be noticed that the fragmentary version now in New Zealand is closer to the Northwestern text than is the completed New Zealand version.

events) quotes from Wierius, *De Præstigiis Dæmonum*, and from an 'extraordinary book'[1] by Samuel Erich or Erichius. This is probably the 'Erithius' of the transcribers. Schoockius has no difficulty in demonstrating the implausibility of Erichius as a historical source: he mentions, for example, that nothing about the Pied Piper is to be found in writers of the time when the events are supposed to have taken place, or in those of the next two centuries. He quotes enough from Erichius to make it unlikely that Browning's father had any need to seek out this scarce book.

The identity of the third work must remain uncertain at the moment. It may have been by the celebrated Athanasius Kircherus, mentioned by Schoockius on pp. 141 ff. of his *Fabula Hamelensis*, or even *Historia Hamelensis; sive Dissertatio de Inauspicato Liberorum Hamelensium Egressu*, a thesis defended under the chairmanship of Theodorus Kirchmaierus by Nicolaus Nieremberger and printed in Wittenberg in 1671. But the references are playful: it is unlikely that Browning's father did much more than glance at either work, and there is no reason to suppose that his son read either.

We print below, on facing pages, (left) the text of the version transcribed by Elkin Mathews (*NW*) and (right) that of the complete version transcribed by Hall Griffin (*NZ*), with at the foot of pp. 523 and 525 substantive variants in the unfinished version transcribed by the latter. We hope to give details of the holograph manuscript in a later volume of this edition, as soon as it becomes available.

---

[1] *Exodus Hamelensis, Das ist der Hammelischen Kinder Ausgang* (Hanover 1655).

Hamelin

There is at a moderate distance from Hanover
  On the *Weser*, a river of singular fame,
A town which the French & the rats often ran over,
    But though report varies,
    Yet sage Antiquaries   5
Are all in one story concerning its name,—
Which is Hamelin—(But you had better perhaps
Turn over our Atlas & look at the maps)
    This place without flattery
    Seem'd one vast rattery—   10
Where the rats came from no mortal could say
    For one put to flight
    There were ten the next night
And for 10 over night, there were 20 next day:
With double the number before the next morning   15
Indeed the inhabitants gave the Mayor warning
That unless these intruders were driven away
    The rats and taxation
    Would bring on starvation—
And if so—then this was their firm declaration   20
        That they would'nt stay!
The rats however laughed at that
Down they came trooping—pit-a-pat—
And all the town seem'd—Rat, rat, rat!
    This made the magistrates determine   ·   25
    To lay their heads together
        And reckon whether
They could not 'oust' these vermin—
Traps, poison, Terriers, Cats and Ferrets
Each discuss'd their several merits,   30
Not one of which, nor all together,
Weigh'd with the Aldermen, one feather:—
    Since every man
    Pursued his plan;
To which if no one else agreed,   35
No plan of theirs should e'er succeed:

The Pied Piper of Hamelin

There is at a moderate distance from *Hanover*—
  A town on the *Weser* of singular fame:
A place which the French & the rats often ran over—
    But though my tale varies
    Yet sage antiquaries   5
Are all in one story concerning its name—
  'Tis *Hammelin* (but you had better perhaps
  Turn over your atlas & look at the maps)—
    Which, without flattery
    Seem'd one vast rattery—   10
Where the rats came from no mortal could say—
    But for one put to flight
    There were ten the next night;—
And for ten over night, there were twenty next day:—
With double the number perhaps the next morning—   15
In vain did the lodgers & tenants give warning—
And declared that unless they were driven away—
    The rats & taxation
    Would bring on starvation—
And they wouldn't stay to be famish'd—not they!   20
Determin'd to remain in Power
Fresh rats kept coming every hour—
Down they came trooping—pit a pat—
Nothing was seen but Rat,—Rat,—Rat—
Which made the magistrates determine   25
    To lay their civic heads together
    And in a little time see whether
They could not rid the town of vermin—
Traps, Poison, terriers, cats & ferrets
Had these discuss'd, their several merits—   30
Not one of which, nor all together
Weighed with the mayor & aldermen—one feather!

2 On the Weser, of singular fame,   3 A town which   4 though report varies
7 It is *Hamelin*   9 The place, without   15 Number before   16-
17 Indeed the Inhabitants gave the Mayor warning | Unless these intruders were driven
away   20-2 —And they wouldn't stay— | The rats however laughed at that
24 And all the town seem'd Rat—Rat—Rat!   25 This made   28 not oust
these Vermin—   32 with the aldermen one

Nor could they for a moment bear it
That other men should have the merit
    Of clearing Hamelin from rats—
The Market rose:—and Cats were done   40
At half—3 quarters—7 eights—one!
The House were *Bulls* for the account:
    And several Jobbers that had *Bear*'d
    Were on the settling day declared,
Ducks to a large amount!   45
    Still, cats were on the rise:—
But, notwithstanding this control,
The rats contriv'd to 'head the poll'
    In vast majorities!—
[Now,—should the slightest hesitation   50
    Come across the readers mind
Because the proofs of this narration
    Are very difficult to find:
        Here are *Schochius*
          Erithius—   54a
And Kirk mœteus lying by us: 55
    It were absurd
    To doubt the word
Of men so famous learn'd and pious.—
So let us—once for all be just
And take this narrative, on trust]   60
The Mayor & Aldermen in council sat,
Striving—contriving—pondering—scheming
Rating—debating—musing—dreaming—
Abusive words, and contests rising—
Surprizing schemes of their advising   65
Outdone by schemes still more surprising—
    —And all about a rat!
Amidst this terrible uproar
The porter stationed at the door
Announc'd a stranger calling there,   70

59–60 *om.*)

    42–5 *Bulls* . . . *Bear'd* . . . *Ducks*: Stock Exchange jargon. A 'bull' buys in anticipation of
rising prices. A 'bear' sells in anticipation of falling prices. 'Ducks' are defaulters.
    54–5 See above, pp. 520–1.

For every man
    Had got his plan
To which, if no one else agreed—   35
No plan of theirs should e'er succeed—
Among them all, not one could bear it
That every {any} other had the merit
        Of clearing *Hammelin* from rats—
And when their schemes had been rejected   40
Out came—what all the world expected—
        That each possessed—a colony of cats!—

Amidst this terrible uproar
The Porter station'd at the door
Mention'd a stranger calling there—   45
    Breathless—with something to declare
Of vast importance to the may'r—
        —"About these Rats?"
"It is," replied the porter:—"That's"—
"The very thing!" the court declare: 50
        This news, of course
        Came with electric force:—
All discord in a moment vanish'd—
Black looks & angry words were banish'd—
        A smile arose on ev'ry face—   55
            Hope took the place
            Of Discord & Despair—
            Whilst Mr May'r—
            Cried from the chair—
        "Walk in—if that's the case"—   60
"Well Sir—and what are your pretensions?"
        This language was addres't—
Just in the tone which those repeat
When apprehensive of some cheat—
They strive to scan the knave's intentions—   65
Not without some unpleasant feeling
About the man with whom they're dealing—

34 Proposed his plan   37 Nor could they for a moment bear it—   38 any
other had   39a And—what a start in price of cats!   {*NZ* 40–283 *om.*; instead
as *NW* 40–67 except: 43 jobbers who had   52 And tho'   54–54a Yet there
are *Schochius—Erithius*   55 And *Kirkmaleus*   56 And 'twere   57–8 Of
men so well known, learn'd & pious | To doubt the word

With something urgent to declare
Of vast importance to the Mayor:
"About the rats?"
"It is"—replied the porter: "Thats'
"The very thing!" the court declare—   75
    This news of course,
    Came with electric force;
All discord in a moment vanish'd—
Scarcely a whisper now was heard,
"Hush! & shake hands!" were ev'ry word—   80
The Mayor put on a serious face:—
And cried—"Walk in; if thats the case"—
"Well, Sir? & what are your pretensions?"
    This was addressed
Just in the tone which folks repeat   85
    When of some cheat
    They're under apprehensions;
With rather an unpleasant feeling
About the man with whom they're dealing;
    (But let that rest)   90
Indeed, the fellow talk'd to so
Seem'd of the lowest of the low—
Let your fancy now describe
A vagrant of the gypsy tribe:
Tall gaunt and meagre:—in a dress   95
Which spoke the depth of wretchedness
Patches—Black, Yellow, Red & Blue,—
Rags of ev'ry shape and hue
His hungry look—his piercing eye
Close lip bent brow & stooping gait   100
Seem'd all conjecture to defy
About his state.—
Yet—there was in his face
Something about (above) the commonplace:
Something which gave one a surmise   105
Of greatness in disguise:—
The wandering jew,
For aught they knew:
      Whilst, others fancy

But let that rest,—
Indeed—the fellow talk'd to, so,
Seem'd to be lowest of the low—   70
Tall—gaunt & meagre:—in a dress
   Singular in shape & hue—
   All patches red-white—black & blue:—
Which spoke the depth of wretchedness—
   His hungry look—his piercing eye—   75
   Close lip—brow bent—& stooping gait—
Seem'd all conjecture to defy—
     About his state—
   Yet there was in his face
Something above the common place:—   80
Something that gave one a surmise
   Of greatness in disguise—
The wandering Jew
For ought they knew,
     Whilst others fancy   85
   Brought to light
   Some conjuring sprite,
Burnt, ages since, for necromancy.

The May'r display'd a world of tact
Canvassing the vagrant act:—   90
He could do that,—I could do this—
And, were there any thing amiss
Aye, that he would:—& this confes't
He left the world to guess the rest.

Rubbing his chin, at last, out came—   95
"I say—you, mister—what's your name—
    "Pray—who are you?
"And what is it you want to do?"
Wrath kindled in the Vagrant's eye—
He paused:—then made him this reply—   100
"Who am I?—when I tell my name—
"You'll know, 'tis on the rolls of fame—
    "What is it that I want to do?—
    "I ask you if you ever knew

'Twas *Nostradamus*   110
   Once so famous
For catching rats and necromancy—
The Mayor display'd a world of tact
When canvassing the vagrant act:—
Rubbing his chin, at last, out came—   115
  "I say—You—Mister whats your name—
   "Pray—who are you?
    Why is it, thus
    You come to us—
  And what is it you want to do?   120
Wrath sparkled in the vagrant's eye:—
He paus'd—then made him this reply:—
"Who *am* I?—then, you never knew
"Or heard of the Pied Piper?—whew!
Their hands & eyes—were all surprize—   125
"*You* —the pied Piper!" each one cries:
"And from this nuisance if set free
   Are we to be
"Indebted to the Devil & thee?—
"No—let us twenty fold endure,   130
"Than have recourse to such a cure"—
   But from without
   Was heard a shout—
"Mind Aldermen what you're about!"
  This was interrupted by   135
"Pray, whats all that to you & I?
   "We're ruin'd if these rats remain—
  "And, wheres the harm
  "Of any charm
"That gives the Devil his rats again?   140

The council act on this advice:
  All is agreed except the price
They then call in & ask the man—
Can you, my friend—no doubt you can—
Drive all these rats from Hamelin?—come   145
We'll not dispute about the sum:

110 *Nostradamus*: the Latinized name of Michel de Notre-Dame (1503–66), the French physician and astrologer, author of a book of prophecies in rhymed quatrains.

"Of the Pied Piper?—(Here surprize   105
Star'd broad from all their Civic eyes)
"You the pied Piper?—and shall we
"Indebted to the Devil & thee—
        "Be from this mischief free?
"No!—Let us ten times more endure—   110
"Ere we submit to such a cure—"
        (Here from without
            Was heard a shout—
"Mind my good Sirs, what you're about!—"
        These were interrupted by   115
            "What is that, to you & I?—
"We're ruin'd if these rats remain
        "And where's the harm
            "Of any charm
"Tho' Lucifer himself should come   120
"With Horns & Hoofs & carry home
            "His rats again?").
Acting upon this advice
The matter settled in a trice—
        "Come, fellow, come,—   125
        Just name the Sum—"
            He would have said—
            But half afraid—
Impress'd with supernatural dread—
            Meek & demure   130
            As Simon Pure—
He blush'd & bow'd his head—
            And half afraid—
Ask'd "how his honour would be paid?"

"My usual fee!—my usual fee!"   135
"And what, Sir, may this bonus be?"—
"Five hundred pounds! I'll take no more—
"This granted, I shall soon restore—
        "By my ability—
    Hamelin to its tranquility—   140
        "And never more
"Shall Rat or any thing destroy

Just tell us what you would be paid—
Short bargains are the best, 'tis said—
    "Five Hundred Pounds—I ask no more:
    (said he)—"this granted, I restore—   150
    "To the best of my ability
    Hamelin to its tranquility"—

Ashamed and trembling at the deed
The common councilmen agreed:—
And this the mob outside 'encore'   155
Sixteen times louder than before
[Where were the consciences? you cry—
Whats that to you—was their reply
    Let him but fray—the rats away,
We'll rub that score off by & by.]   160
The piper struck up—"Toot—toot—toot!"
Upon his more than magic flute:—
Yes—I'm in tune he cried, and now
    (Making the citizens a bow)
Just for a moment follow me—   165
And you shall see what you shall see!"

    And—what a sight they saw!—
Lur'd by the magic notes,—a throng
Of rats came scampering along—
In companies some millions strong   170
Quitted the town.—The roads were lin'd,
Nor was one straggler left behind:
When they came to the *Weser*'s bank:
    Then with a general scream,
      Plung'd headlong in the stream,   175
      And sank!
The business was compleatly done:—
The rats had vanish'd ev'ry one!
Yet as they saunter'd round the place
There was on every townsman's face   180
    —a blank!—

159 *fray*: scarc.
162 *more than magic flute*: a reference to Mozart's opera, *Die Zauberflöte.*

"The happiness you'll then enjoy"—
Asham'd & trembling at the deed—
The common council cried—"agreed"—   145
And this—the mob outside encore—
      Ten times louder than before.—

"Where were their conscience(s)?" you cry.—
"What's that to you?" is their reply
      "Let him but fray   150
      "The rats away
"We'll settle with him by'nd bye!"—

The Piper then plaid—toot-toot-toot!
Upon his more than magic flute
"Yes—I'm in time (he cried) and now",   155
      Making the Citizens a bow
"Just for a moment follow me,—
"And you shall see—what you shall see!"
Lur'd by the music & the song
The rats came scampering along   160
In companies some millions strong
      And left the town—
      All of one mind
      The roads were lin'd—
Nor was one straggler left behind—   165
Till they came to the Weser's bank
      Then with a general scream
      All plunged into the stream
            And sank!—
The business was completely done: 170
The rats had vanish'd—every one!
Yet there was not a townsman's face
      About the place
But what seem'd blank
Now they had Lucifer to thank!   175
      And the same crowd
      That roar'd aloud
To have infernal means employ'd:—

For a few moments recollection
Brought powerfully, this reflexion
    They now had Lucifer to thank!
The very crowd—that roar'd aloud   185
    To have infernal means employ'd:
Rack'd with despair—now ask the May'r
    How he could dare
Employ the devil in this affair?
Oh how much better had it been,   190
    Even to let the rats remain—
Indeed their feelings were so keen,
    They almost wish'd them back again
But mind(?) the rats were all decoy'd
    Into the Weser & destroy'd   195
The May'r quite frighten'd by the crew,
Ask'd of the Bishop what to do?
    The Bishop groan'd:—
And told him—"rather Sir, than I
Would have a finger in the pie   200
    I would myself be drown'd:—
Didn't I warn you all—"Not you!"
Exclaimed the Aldermen—"tis true
    "You said the end would justify
    "The means: and gave us leave to try: 205
"And if successful, then defy
    "His works—& him—& his queer clothing
Then said the Bishop—Give him nothing!"
    All this while the piper stood
    'Rapt in a melancholy mood,   210
    Outside the door:
    The scorn of all the neighbourhood,
    And hooted at by rich & poor—
Twas then a Beadle from the corporation
Gave him most civilly an intimation   215
The Mayor & Aldermen thought fit
    "That he should quit
"Could he do better than submit?"
"No"—said the Piper—"stop a bit!"—

Now ask the may'r
  How he would dare   180
Employ the devil in this affair—
Why not have let the rats remain?
Wish'd they could all come back again.
Tho' all complain'd—yet none confess'd—
Each threw the odium on the rest—   185
But mind—the rats were all destroy'd!
   The may'r quite frightened by the crew
   Ask'd of the Bishop—what to do?—
   The Bishop scowl'd & frown'd:—
And told him—"rather, Sir, than I   190
   "Would have a finger in the pie—
   "I'd lose ten thousand Pound!—
"Did n't I warn you all?"—"not you!"—
   Exclaim'd the Aldermen—'tis true
   "You said the end might justify   195
   "The means, & gave us leave to try—
   "And if successful, then defy
   "His works & him & his queer clothing—"
Then said the Bishop—"Pay him nothing!"

All this while the Piper stood   200
Quite in a melancholy mood
      Outside the door:—
The scorn of all the neighbourhood
      And hooted at by rich & poor—
'Twas then a beadle from the corporation   205
      Gave him an intimation—
         They thought it fit
         That he should quit—
Could he do better than submit?—
"No"—said the Piper—"stop a bit—   210
"Go back & ask them if they dare
"Bilk me of my legal fare?
"Give me my wages; I depart—
"And leave the town with all my heart
         "But till you pay—   215
         "Here shall I stay"—

"Go back and ask them if they dare 220
Bilk me of any (? my) legal fare?
Give me my wages:—I depart
And leave the town with all my heart
But till the promis'd sum you pay
   Here will I stay—" 225
"Nay," quoth the Beadle, gently—"nay!"
No—(cried the people)—go away
   And if you fail,
Here are the stocks and there's the jail:
  Know then that we're 230
  Extremely & bitterly severe
  On every vagabond found here.—
Well then if you will have it so
Said the Pied Piper I must go—
   But let me play, 235
By way of letting people see
Since you have kept your word with me
How very grateful I can be:
  One little tune—then haste away"—

We've heard in olden time of one 240
That turn'd beholders into stone:—
And could the story be believed
What wonders music has achieved:—
   'Twas with the piper so—
Scarcely had he play'd when lo! 245
  Every bosom felt a thrill—
  Mayor and Aldermen stood still—
  Travellers on Horse & Foot
  Stood as if they'd taken root
   All bow'd to music's power— 250
And Magic seem'd to rule the hour.—
Heads and hearts allow the sway
Old and Young the spell obey—
   Its influence held them dumb—
Fain would they struggle—fain they'd fly— 255
But 'tis in vain they strive and try,
  All to its power succumb

"No"—cried the people—"go away!
 And if you fail—
"Here are the stocks & there's the jail—
  "And know that we're   220
   "Extreme severe
"On every vagabond found here"—
"Well then, if it must be so"—
 Said the piper—"I must go—
 But, only let me play   225
One little tune before I go away!

We've heard in olden time of one
That turn'd beholders into stone:—
And, could the story be believed,
What wonders music has achieved—   230
 'Twas with the piper so—
Scarce had he plaid a note—when lo!
  Every bosom felt a thrill
  May'r & aldermen stood still,
  Travellers on horse or foot   235
  Stood as if they'd taken root—
   Bowing before music's Power,
   Magic seem'd to rule the hour:
   Heads & hearts the spell obey—
   Old & young allow the sway— 240
    And to its spell succumb.
  Fain would they struggle—fain they'd fly—
  In vain they strive—in vain they try—
  Whilst magic influence held them dumb!
The minstrel from beneath his coat   245
  Another reed pipe drew:—
There was a cheerful lively note
  Heard every street & alley through—
   Whilst his stern brow
Scowl'd with the blackest hatred now— 250
From side to side his fierce eye roll'd—
His look was dreadful to behold—
He stampt his foot—Tho' not a word
Was said—twas plain his victims heard

The minstrel from beneath his coat
        Another reedpipe drew:—
Then was a cheerful lively note   260
Heard every street and alley through.—
Whilst the strange mendicant's stern brow
Scowl'd with the blackest hatred now:
From side to side his dark eye roll'd
His look was dreadful to behold—   265
    He stamp't his foot! tho' not a word
Was spoken—Yet his victims heard.—
The loveliest children in the place,
Laughing—smiling—full of play
Dancing to the lively measure,   270
Following the sound with pleasure
        As the piper led the way
But of a sudden—one might trace
A change in every dancers face—
        Grinning ghastly—staring wild   275
        An awful spectre every child
            In that vast crowd—
        Raving—shrieking—groaning, till
        The dance was stopt at *Coppleburg* hill—
When lo!—a cavern opened wide   280
        By magic malice reft—
The whole procession went inside—
        —Not one was left!
The spell was now compleat! Then clos'd the cave
Over them all—a sad untimely grave!—   285
    The corporation, unprepar'd
    For this, at one another star'd:
    And many a scheme was tried in vain
    To get the children back again.—
        At length, pursuant   290
To some grand scheme of their recorder
        They by an edict gave an order
That children never should play truant,
    Nor organ ever should be playing:—
And all Italian boys found straying   295
    With hurdy-gurdy, pipe, or mouse—

And who were these?—an infant race— 255
The loveliest children in the place—
Maries & Kates, in children's dresses—
Sarahs, & Susans—Essies—Bessies!
 Full of smiles & full of play
 Dancing to the lively measure:— 260
 All these follow'd him with pleasure—
  But with a tinge of mirth—
 Different from what's seen on earth—
  Smiling ghastly—staring wild—
  Leaping madly—roaring loud— 265
  Each a monster—not a child—
  Such was that fantastic crowd—
Tho' parents no complaints preferr'd—
Not one of all breath'd out a word:—
  —They made essay— 270
But power infernal stopt the way—

 The Piper turned from time to time—
 As if he gloried in the crime—
 The children followed him until—
Their race was stoppt by Coppleburg hill— 275
 When lo! a cavern open'd wide
 By magic power reft
 All the procession went inside—
  —Not one was left!
 Then was the spell remov'd— 280
Parents their kindred sought in vain—
But never could they find again—
  The children that they loved!

The new police were told to seize on,
As rogues found guilty of high treason,
   And lodge[?] them in the station House.—
Moreover:—any of the throng   .   300
That dar'd to hum, or sing a song,
   Were sure to rue it—
And all were seizd, who right or wrong,
   Were listening to it—
And not content   305
With this, they rais'd a monument,
    Not quite so tall
    As that which Pope was pleas'd to call
"London's tall bully"; but so high
That ev'ry traveller passing by   310
   Might read thereon, engrav'd in stone,
In Latin (true monastic jargon)
     The story we have just completed
     Shewing how vilely they'd been treated,
   —But! not a word about their bargain—   315

Well! after several summers past
    And all enquiry at a stand
A traveller from some distant land
    Waited upon the May'r,
   Having something to declare   320
   That probably would make him stare.—
Most certainly he star'd:—and "well,
   Said he, "& what have you to tell?"—
Why all the children that you know
   About a century ago—   325
   Were swallow'd up, you think, & still
   Lie buried under Coppleburg Hill
     Are found at last:
Rid of all their travelling mania,
Safe and sound in Transylvania: 330
     How got they there?
Railroads and steam were not invented,
The world with horses were contented

---

309 *"London's tall bully"*: see Pope, *Epistle to Bathurst*, 339–40.

Moving about was rather tardy
Neither *Montgolfier* nor *Lunardi*   335
   Having yet travelled through the air
The fact is, he had read by chance
Something about the "Pipers dance"
And having blunder'd on a race
Whose origin he could not trace,   340
To this conclusion wisely came
"They certainly must be the same".—
Where it is useless to dispute
It shews our wisdom to be mute
So what became of that wild rout   345
Seems settled now beyond a doubt.

335 *Montgolfier nor Lunardi* : the Montgolfier brothers and Vincenzo Lunardi were pioneer balloonists, in 1783-4.

APPENDIX B

Lines to Helen Faucit[1]

There's a sisterhood in words—
Still along with 'flowers' go 'birds.'
Is it but three weeks to-day
Since they played a luckless play,
And 'the Treshams,' like a band
Of full-fledged nestlings, left my hand
To flutter forth, the wide world over?
Just three weeks! yet see—each rover
Here, with more or less unsteady
Winglets, nearly reached already,
In the Past, so dim, so dim,
A place where Lucy, Strafford, Pym,
My elder brood of early years,
Wait peacefully their new compeers.
Then, good voyage! shall it grieve me
Vastly, that such ingrates leave me?
Why, this March, this very morning
Hatched my latest brood, take warning,
Each one worth you put together!
April sees them full in feather—
And how we'll welcome May's glad weather!

Helen Faucit, you have twice
Proved my Bird of Paradise!
He, who would my wits inveigle
Into boasting him my eagle,

---

[1] Text from *On Some Of Shakespeare's Female Characters*, by Helena Faucit, Lady Martin (5th ed., 1893 [1st ed., 1885]), p. 396. 'I played Mildred Tresham, as I had formerly played Lucy Percy, Countess of Carlisle, in Mr Browning's *Strafford*. With his wonted generosity Mr Browning spoke of what I had done for his heroines in the following lines, written in my album soon after the production of *The Blot on the Scutcheon*. On the opposite page were some verses, in which flowers played a prominent part. This circumstance, and the particulars above given, will explain allusions in the lines, which might otherwise be obscure': p. 395. The lines were accompanied by a brief complimentary letter.

Turns out very like a Raven:
Fly off, Blacky, to your haven!
But *you*, softest dove, must never
Leave me, as he does, for ever—
I will strain my eyes to blindness,
Ere lose sight of you and kindness.
'Genius' is a common story!
Few guess that the spirit's glory,
They hail nightly, is the sweetest,
Fairest, gentlest, and completest
Shakespeare's-Lady's, ever poet
Longed for! Few guess this: *I* know it.[1]

HATCHAM, SURREY, *March* 4, '43.

---

[1] Lines 17 ff. may refer to *Colombe's Birthday*: 24 ff. no doubt refer to Macready.

Printed in the United States
2086